# C and Unix Programming

# C and Unix Programming:

## A Comprehensive Guide Incorporating the ANSI and POSIX Standards

**By N. S. Kutti, Ph.D.**

LIGHTSPEED BOOKS

**Mt. Pleasant, S. C.**

Publishers Cataloging-in-Publication Data
(Provided by Quality Books, Inc.)

Kutti, N. S.

C and Unix programming: a comprehensive guide incorporating the ANSI and POSIX standards / N.S. Kutti. -- 1st ed.

p. cm.

LCCN: 00-111817

ISBN: 1-929175-40-X (HC)

ISBN: 1-929175-26-4 (PA)

1. C (Computer program language) 2. Computer programming. 3. UNIX (Computer file) I. Title

QA76.73.C15K88 2001 005.13'3

QBI00-1080

This book is printed on archival-quality paper which meets the guidelines for performance and durability of the Committee on Production Guidelines for Book Longevity for the Council on Library Resources.

Lightspeed Books
an imprint of The Côté Literary Group
P.O. Box 1898
Mt. Pleasant SC 29465-1898 USA
(843) 881-6080
http://www.lightspeedbooks.com

To
my wife, Padma

my daughter, Uma Maheswari
and
my son, Mani Vannan

# Contents

**Preface** .......... **xvii**

**Chapter 1: Introduction** .......... **1**
1.1 Background .......... 1
1.2 General Features of C-Language .......... 2
1.3 Supporting Processing Environment .......... 16
1.4 C-Program Model .......... 18
1.5 Summary .......... 20
Exercises .......... 21

**Chapter 2: Starting with C-Programming** .......... **25**
2.1 Introduction .......... 25
2.2 Language Conventions .......... 26
2.3 Statements in C programs .......... 32
2.4 Conventions Used in Preparing C-source Texts .......... 34
2.5 Learn To Declare Main Function .......... 34
2.6 Include Header Files .......... 35
2.7 Commenting in C-Programs .......... 36
2.8 First C-Program Using the printf Function .......... 37
2.9 Declaring the Data Objects .......... 43
2.10 Input/Output Conventions .......... 48
2.11 C-Program Using Stream I/O Functions .......... 49
2.12 Diagnostic Aid (Use of assert Macro) .......... 51
2.13 C-Virtual Machine for Statement Execution .......... 53
2.14 Summary .......... 55
Exercises .......... 56

**Chapter 3: Meaning of Variables and Expressions ..................................... 59**
3.1 Introduction ..................................... 59
3.2 Meaning of Variable ..................................... 63
3.3 Temporal Aspects of Variables ..................................... 65
3.4 Meaning of Declarations ..................................... 67
3.5 Types of Variables in ANSI-C ..................................... 67
3.6 The const Variables ..................................... 70
3.7 Significance of Volatile Qualifier ..................................... 71
3.8 Meaning and Evaluation of Expressions ..................................... 73
3.9 Types of Operators ..................................... 78
3.10 Types of Expressions ..................................... 80
3.11 Summary ..................................... 94
Exercises ..................................... 95

**Chapter 4: Meaning and Definition of C-Functions ..................................... 97**
4.1 Introduction ..................................... 97
4.2 Function Definition ..................................... 98
4.3 Meaning of a Function ..................................... 99
4.4 Compiler's View on Function Definition ..................................... 103
4.5 Function Interface Conventions ..................................... 108
4.6 Meaning of Call by Value or by Reference ..................................... 109
4.7 Summary ..................................... 113
Exercises ..................................... 114

**Chapter 5: Storage Classes, Scope and Initialization of Variables ....... 117**
5.1 Introduction ..................................... 117
5.2 The Meaning of Scope of a Variable ..................................... 118
5.3 What Is a Storage Class? ..................................... 120
5.4 Storage Classes ..................................... 120
5.5 Storage Environment Around a Function ..................................... 126
5.6 Initializing Variables ..................................... 130
5.7 Typedef ..................................... 131
5.8 Dynamic Storage Type ..................................... 132
5.9 Summary ..................................... 132
Exercises ..................................... 133

**Chapter 6: Statements in C ........ 135**
6.1 Introduction ........ 135
6.2 Simple Expression Statements ........ 138
6.3 Control Statements ........ 141
6.4. Compound or Block Statements ........ 149
6.5 Miscellaneous Statements ........ 151
6.6 Summary ........ 151
Exercises ........ 152

**Chapter 7: The Macro Preprocessor ........ 155**
7.1 Introduction ........ 155
7.2 Description of Macro Commands ........ 156
7.3 The define Macro ........ 157
7.4 Include Macro ........ 166
7.5 Conditional Macros ........ 170
7.6 Macros for Debugging ........ 171
7.7 Miscellaneous Macros ........ 173
7.8 Predefined Macro Names ........ 174
7.9 The # and ## Preprocessor Operators ........ 175
7.10 Summary ........ 176
Exercises ........ 177

**Chapter 8: Integer and Real Variables ........ 179**
8.1 Introduction ........ 179
8.2 Integer Types ........ 180
8.3 Real Type ........ 190
8.4 Integer and Real Arrays ........ 193
8.5 Declaration of a Buffer (Byte Array) ........ 198
8.6 Summary ........ 198
Exercises ........ 199

**Chapter 9: Operations on Integer and Real Variables .......................... 201**
9.1 Introduction .......................... 201
9.2 Increment and Decrement Operations .......................... 202
9.3 Arithmetic Operations .......................... 204
9.4 Bitwise Logical Operations on Integers .......................... 204
9.5 Assignment Operation .......................... 208
9.6 Input and Output Operations .......................... 209
9.7 The sizeof Operation .......................... 221
9.8 The Cast Operation .......................... 223
9.9 Scientific Operations on Real Types .......................... 223
9.10 Summary .......................... 225
Exercises .......................... 226

**Chapter 10: Character and String Variables .......................... 227**
10.1 Introduction .......................... 227
10.2 Character Value and Character Set .......................... 228
10.3 Character Variable .......................... 229
10.4 String Values .......................... 232
10.5 String Variables .......................... 233
10.6 Summary .......................... 237
Exercises .......................... 238

**Chapter 11: Operations on Character Variables .......................... 241**
11.1 Introduction .......................... 241
11.2 Expressions and Assignment Operations .......................... 242
11.3 Character I/O .......................... 245
11.4 Character Testing and Manipulation .......................... 250
11.5 Summary .......................... 257
Exercises .......................... 258

**Chapter 12: Pointers and Array References ........ 259**
12.1 Introduction ........ 259
12.2 Pointer Variable ........ 260
12.3 Address Constants ........ 260
12.4 Declaring Pointers ........ 263
12.5 Operations on Pointers ........ 269
12.6 Pointer Mechanism for Dynamic Data Structures ........ 276
12.7 Summary ........ 276
Exercises ........ 277

**Chapter 13: Advanced Concepts of C-Functions ........ 279**
13.1 Introduction ........ 279
13.2 Declaring Pointers to Functions ........ 279
13.3 Recursion ........ 285
13.4 Functions with Variable Number of Arguments ........ 286
13.5 Summary ........ 289
Exercises ........ 290

**Chapter 14: Operations on String Variables ........ 291**
14.1 Introduction ........ 291
14.2 The Header File, string.h ........ 292
14.3 String Operations ........ 296
14.4 Operations on Memory Regions (or Memory Buffers) ........ 314
14.5 String Utility Function for Decoding System Errors ........ 317
14.6 String Conversion Operations ........ 318
14.7 String Composition and Decomposition ........ 321
14.8 Summary ........ 322
Exercises ........ 323

**Chapter 15: Composite Data Structures and Unions ............................ 325**
15.1 Introduction ............................................................ 325
15.2 Structure Declaration in C ............................................. 328
15.3 Pointer to a Structure ................................................. 334
15.4 Accessing Elements of a Structure ..................................... 335
15.5 Union ................................................................... 344
15.6 Summary ................................................................. 346
Exercises ................................................................... 347

**Chapter 16: Storage Management and Dynamic Data Structure ........ 349**
16.1 Introduction ............................................................ 349
16.2 Dynamic Storage Management ............................................ 350
16.3 Meaning of Dynamic Data Structures ..................................... 353
16.4 Dynamic Arrays .......................................................... 354
16.5 Linked Data Structures .................................................. 357
16.6 Summary ................................................................. 372
Exercises ................................................................... 373

**Chapter 17: ANSI-C File System ............................................ 375**
17.1 Introduction ............................................................ 375
17.2 Overview of ANSI-C File System ......................................... 377
17.3 Concept of Stream I/O ................................................... 380
17.4 Use of stdio.h in Stream I/O ............................................ 382
17.5 The stdio Streams ....................................................... 383
17.6 Descriptions of Stream I/O Control Functions ........................... 383
17.7 Stream Functions for Character I/O ..................................... 395
17.8 String and Line I/O Operations .......................................... 403
17.9 Binary I/O in Streams ................................................... 405
17.10 Formatted I/O .......................................................... 412
17.11 Summary ................................................................ 420
Exercises ................................................................... 421

**Chapter 18: Signal and Time Management .... 423**
18.1 Introduction .... 423
18.2 Signal Management .... 423
18.3 Time Management in Standard C .... 430
18.4 Summary .... 438
Exercises .... 439

**Chapter 19: Standard Unix-Kernal Interface .... 441**
19.1 Introduction .... 441
19.2 The Meaning of Operating System Kernel .... 442
19.3 Unix Kernel .... 443
19.4 Error Handling with System Calls .... 448
19.5 What Is Systems Programming? .... 449
19.6 C as a System Programming Language .... 450
19.7 Why Standard for Operating System Interface? .... 450
19.8 What Is POSIX Standard? .... 452
19.9 System Identification .... 453
19.10 Summary .... 454
Exercises .... 455

**Chapter 20: Project Management Using System Calls .... 457**
20.1 Introduction .... 457
20.2 Process Concept .... 458
20.3 Process Model in Unix .... 458
20.4 Description of Process Management System Calls .... 472
20.5 Signaling System Calls .... 483
20.6 Summary .... 512
Exercises .... 513

**Chapter 21: Unix File I/O ........ 515**
21.1 Introduction ........ 515
21.2 Concept of Direct (or Basic) I/O ........ 516
21.3 How Is a File Maintained in Unix? ........ 517
21.4 File Protection and File Creation Mask ........ 520
21.5 Directories ........ 523
21.6 System Calls for Regular Files ........ 530
21.7 Inode-Related System Calls ........ 541
21.8 FIFO (Named Pipe) File ........ 548
21.9 Device Files ........ 551
21.10 Configuration Information of File System ........ 553
21.11 The sync System Call ........ 554
21.12 Summary ........ 554
Exercises ........ 556

**Chapter 22: Program Call Interface ........ 559**
22.1 Introduction ........ 559
22.2 The execve Function ........ 560
22.3 Derived exec** Functions ........ 561
22.4 Argument Retrieval and Processing by a Called Program ........ 568
22.5 Unix Command Programs ........ 572
22.6 How shell Executes Command Programs ........ 572
22.7 Environment Around a Command Process ........ 574
22.8 Structure of a shell Command ........ 577
22.9 Summary ........ 588
Exercises ........ 589

**Chapter 23: Programming with Threads ........ 591**
23.1 Introduction ........ 591
23.2 Meaning of Concurrent Programming ........ 592
23.3 Concept of Thread ........ 592
23.4 The pthread.h Header ........ 594
23.5 Thread Creation and Termination ........ 594
23.6 Synchronization Mechanisms for Thread Concurrency ........ 601
23.7 Miscellaneous Functions ........ 610
23.8 Summary ........ 611
Exercises ........ 612

**Appendix A: Glossary** ........ **615**
A.1 Keywords in C ........ 615
A.2 Types of Operators in C ........ 616

**Appendix B: Character Sets** ........ **619**
B.1 ASCII Character Set ........ 619
B.2 EBCDIC Character Set ........ 621

**Appendix C: ANSI-C Standard Libraries and Their Header Files** ........ **627**
C.1 Standard Headers ........ 627
C.2 Definitions in the Standard Header Files ........ 627

**Appendix D: Implementation Limits in ANSI-C: Header Files** ........ **635**
D.1 limits.h (Limits of integral types) ........ 635
D.2 float.h (Limits of real values) ........ 636

**Appendix E: POSIX Unix Interface: Standard Calls and Related Headers** ........ **637**
E.1 POSIX.1 Standard Headers ........ 637
E.2 Definitions in the Standard Headers ........ 637

**Appendix F: Bibliography** ........ **649**

**Index** ........ **651**

# Preface

The popularity of ***C*** is mainly due to its versatile nature. First, it has a set of rich data types to teach algorithms; then its Unix interface makes it suitable for teaching operating systems. After experiencing the wide use of ***C*** in industries, researchers were tempted to improve the same language with advanced data types for object-oriented programming and real-time programming. The results are C++ in the 1980s and ***Java*** in the late 1990s. In the past ten years C++ has taken the position of the second language in the computer curriculum. Now its rival, ***Java***, is jockeying for the same position. Even though C++ and ***Java*** have come as better versions of ***C*** both languages, due to their complex data types, will take a long time to become first in the curriculum. Both languages are, in fact, based on the ***C-Syntax*** and, hence, it may become easy to learn them after becoming familiar with ***C***. This clearly indicates that ***C*** will still maintain its status as the first language in computer science as well as in other related disciplines such as engineering for many more years.

This book is written chiefly for Computer Science and Engineering students who learn ***C*** as their first language, as well as students in general as programmers with strong programming backgrounds. A significant feature of this book is that it introduces the principles of ***C*** programming with ***ANSI*** standard as well as principles of Unix-like system programming with ***POSIX*** standard. It introduces the basic concepts of programming with ***C*** (originally designed by ***Kernighan*** and ***Ritchie***) and the extended concepts of ANSI-C. It discusses the characteristics and built-in concepts of ***C*** using ***C-Virtual Machine*** concept and highlights their importance to application as well as system programming. ***Section 1*** of this book has ***ANSI*** features of ***C***. ***Section 2*** introduces more powerful features of ***C***-related to Unix-like System Programming as specified by the ***POSIX*** standard.

Unlike other languages, ***C*** expects users to have a clear understanding of the built-in concepts. First, the structure of variables (including pointers and other abstract data structures), the structures of different kinds of expressions (including rvalue and lvalue expressions) and their semantics are explored for their correct use in C-Statements. Second, the extended operations such as character and string manipulations, ***ANSI-stream I/O***, ***Unix I/O***, etc. via easily adaptable library facility are thoroughly explored. The highlight of this book is the ***C-Virtual Machine*** concept used in exploring some of the programming concepts in C.

***Chapter 1*** gives a concise summary of the various features of ***C*** and also presents the modular organization of C-programs. ***Chapter 2*** illustrates some simple C-programs and the steps involved in their execution. ***Chapter 3*** is useful to understand the concepts of variables and expressions, while ***Chapter 4*** introduces the functions and their definitions. ***Chapter 5*** explains the storage classes maintained by the ***C-Virtual Machine*** and then allocation to the declared variables. ***Chapters 6*** and *7* explain the statement structures and macro facility available in C. ***Chapters 8-11*** deal with simple variables (integer, real, and character type) and the various operations involving them. ***Chapter 12*** explains the pointer variables and pointer manipulation with examples.

The description of ***C-Functions*** is carefully divided into logical sections. ***Chapter 1*** gives the peripheral details of functional organization of C-programs. ***Chapter 4*** introduces C-functions and explains how to declare them in C-programs. ***Chapter 5*** explains the effect of functions on the scope of variables and ***Chapter 13*** explains some advanced concepts, such as pointer to functions, recursive function calls and functions with variable arguments.

***Chapter 14*** builds upon the knowledge of pointer variable introduced earlier and explains the operations on string variables. Composite data structures (i.e. structures and unions similar to Pascal's variant records) are introduced in ***Chapter 15***. ***Chapter 16*** explains the power of C-pointers, structures and dynamic storage management.

Another important feature of this book is that it maintains a clear distinction between the two I/O facilities, ***ANSI-I/O*** and ***Unix-I/O***, explaining with necessary details, how to understand the working concept of both. ***Chapter 17*** deals comprehensively with ***ANSI-I/O***.

***Chapters 18-22*** introduce the ***Unix-like interface*** as specified by the ***POSIX*** standard in a simple manner on top of the basic operating system concepts such as ***system call***, ***Unix process***, ***Unix file***, ***Unix-shell interface***, etc. Although this book does not cover all aspects of system programming, readers can use the basic concepts learned through this book to build further knowledge in the area. Finally, ***Chapter 23*** introduces threads in ***C***.

**Materials for use by instructors can be found on the following website: www.nskutti.com.**

Suggestions for further improvement of this text are always welcome.

N. S. Kutti

# 1

# Introduction

**Chapter contents:**

*This chapter describes all the major features of C-language. It outlines the structure of C-programs and shows what simple and multiple module C-programs look like. It concludes with a description of the program model supported by C-language (C-Virtual Machine).*

**Organization:**

*1.1 Background*
*1.2 General Features of C-Language*
*1.3 Supporting Processing Environment*
*1.4 C-Program Model*
*1.5 Summary*
*Exercises*

## 1.1 Background

The C-language was developed at AT&T's Bell Laboratory by Dennis Ritchie in 1972. It was mainly designed to implement a portable operating system, i.e. Unix. It was also used to write compilers, assemblers, text editors, and other software tools. Although C was originally used to implement system software, its use has been extended to implement commercial applications such as database packages. Moreover, its machine language like features and versatile data types have made it a popular language for industrial applications such as real-time and network programming, as well as for scientific and engineering applications. In fact, C has already taken the place of BASIC, FORTRAN, Pascal and PL/1, languages that have been used in the past for scientific and engineering programming. With the changing Information Systems technology, C has been used to make CASE-based tools and commercial database packages. The fast growing popularity of C mandated the need for refining its features so that programs could be ported to different supporting environment. In 1989 the American National Standard Institute (ANSI) introduced the necessary features for portability. The language then became known as ANSI-C. In the following year the International Standards Organization (ISO) adopted the recommendations made by ANSI. Since then, ANSI-C is also called Standard C. With the introduction of the ANSI standard, popular commercial languages such as COBOL have lost their significance in the IT industry. The standard C has now been best known as a fundamental implementation tool for most of the software engineering tools.

The popularity of C has indirectly influenced the emergence of an object-oriented version called C++. In turn, the popularity of both C and C++ and a demand for a programming tool for embedded real-time applications further influenced the development of a new language. It was called Java, and it is a refined version of C++. Even though C++ and Java have become as popular as C, they cannot be introduced as the first language in the computing curriculum because of their object-oriented nature. Since C forms the base for both C++ and Java, C is obviously the best choice as the prerequisite for learning C++ and Java.

## 1.2 General Features of C-Language

C started as a small language. It had a simple syntax, few keywords, and lacked built-in functions. However, C, as originally defined by Kernighan and Ritchie (referred as K&R C) has a number of features which makes it such a powerful language. By incorporating new features recommended by the American National Standards Institute (ANSI), the C language has become more efficient, particularly from the portability aspect of application programs. Before getting into actual programming, it is first worth looking at the significant features of C.

### 1.2.1 Modularity

Dividing the whole program into manageable modules makes the task of program development and testing less tedious. A program can be divided into virtually independent subtasks called functional modules. Program development can start by coding and testing an initial module (or main functional module) and proceed by adding and testing further functional modules one-by-one.

A C-program displays both aspects of modularity, i.e. a program can be divided into individual modules which can be compiled separately, and each module hides the locally declared objects or data elements. In general, a C-program consists of a main module (i.e. main function) and one or more modules (i.e. subordinate functions) as shown in ***Fig 1.1***. *Every module in C is called a function.*

### The Structure of C-Function

The basic structure of a C-function is the description of a function name and its parameters (or function head description) followed by the functional block. The functional block starts with an opening brace (i.e. the character '{') and ends with a closing brace (i.e. '}'). Within these block boundaries a set of data declarations followed by a sequence of statements are coded. Within a functional block a group of statements may be optionally enclosed in a pair of braces to form a *nested* block. A function by definition has to return some value via a ***return*** statement. ***Example 1.1*** shows a function called ***zero*** to return the integer zero.

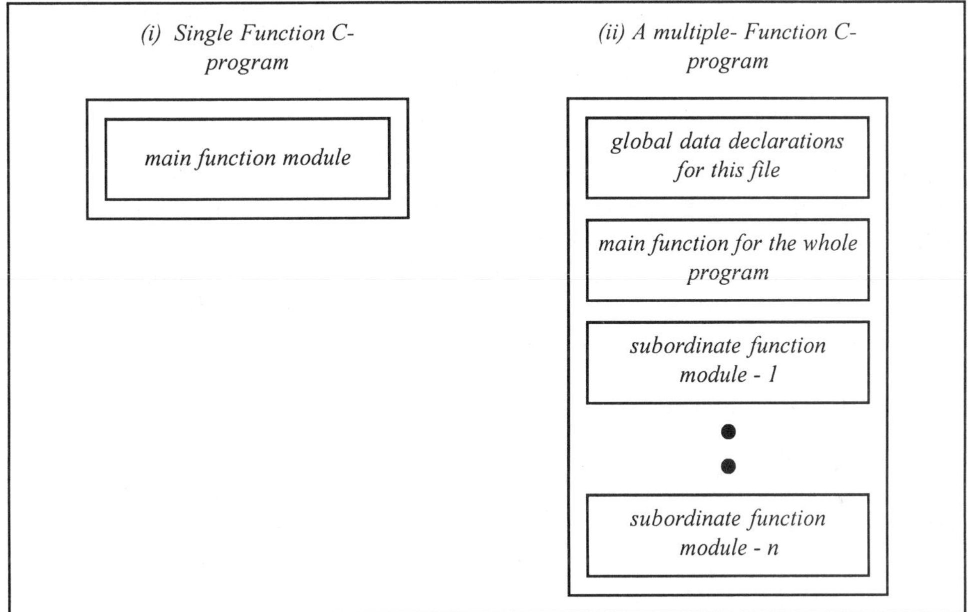


*Fig. 1.1 Modular structure of a C-program*

**The syntax diagram for C-function (or module):**

> ***Remark:*** *A block is identified as a group of statements including data declarations enclosed by an opening and a closing brace. A null block is one which contains no statement within the braces.*

**Example 1.1:** Show a subordinate C-Function called ***zero*** that returns always an integer zero.

```
int zero(void)
{
   return(0);
}
```

The first line, *int zero(void)* is the *function head* denoting the name of the function and the type of value that it can return. In this example, the function returns the value, 0 and hence there is no need for any local data declaration.

A subordinate function like this cannot stand alone as a C-program. A ***main*** function is necessary to hold associated subordinate functions in a C-program. The subordinate functions are in fact the building blocks of a modular program.

### The Structure of C-main function

The main function is distinguished from other functions by the first statement. The first statement in a main function is always named using the keyword ***main*** whereas the first statement in a subordinate function is a user-defined function name like ***zero*** in the previous example.

### The syntax diagram for C-main function:

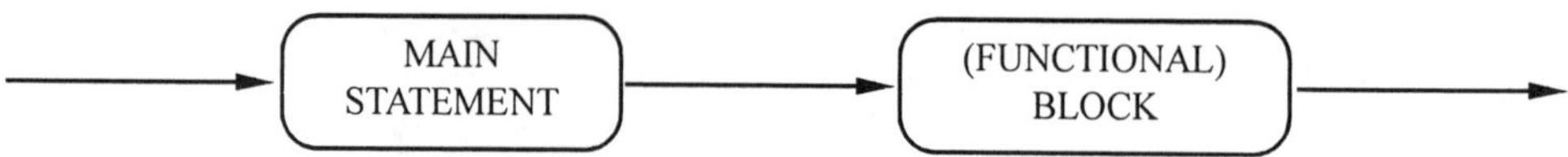


**Example 1.2:** Show the structure of a C-main function.

```
void main(void)
{
  int K;
     K = 100;
     return;
}
```

The structure of a main function is similar to any subordinate function except that the name is always main. The ***main*** is itself a key word representing the main holder of the program. The above main function can itself be a complete program and it can be compiled and run without any problem. Note that the last statement is return which indicates that the main function (or the program) returns the execution control to its caller.

### The Structure of C-program

As mentioned before, a C-program is made up of C-functions, and there must be a ***main*** function to hold all other subordinate functions in that program. Actually the main function is the essential body of the program without which a C-program does not exist. Another essential characteristic of a C-program is that the execution starts only in the first statement of the main function. Since the execution of a C-program always starts at the main function, every program must have a main function. This also implies that a program cannot have more than one main function. This is explained in ***Fig 1.2***.

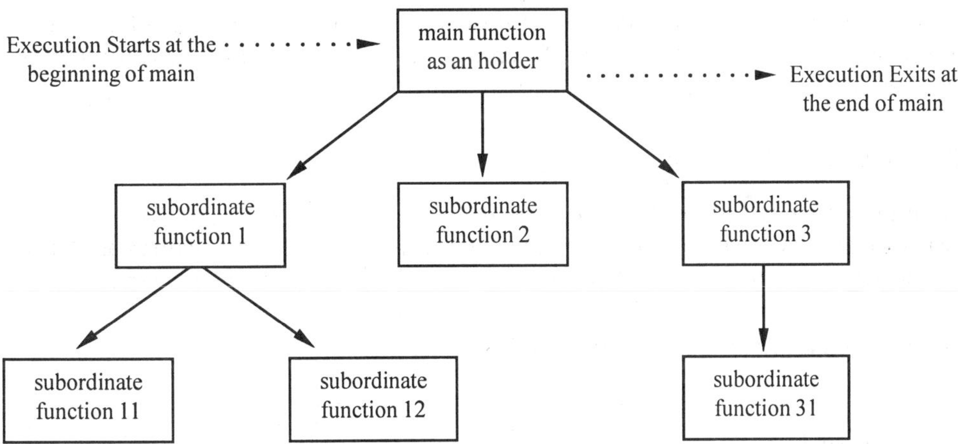


*Fig 1.2 Role of main function in a C-program*

**The syntax diagram for a C-program:**

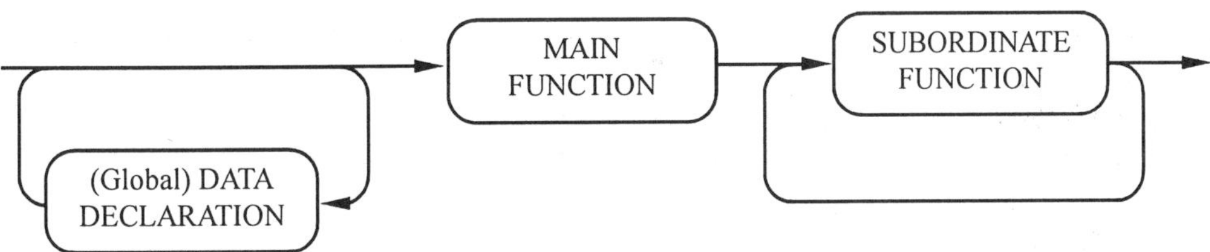


From the above syntax diagram it can be shown that a C-program can be of either a single module or multiple modules, depending upon the size and complexity of the algorithm that is coded in. If a program happens to be a single module, then that module should obviously be the main function of that program.

**Example 1.3:** Show a single module C-program.

```
void main(void)
{
  int I, J, K;
     I = 100;
     J = I + 200;
     K = J+300;
     return;
}
```

A single module C-program can have only main function as illustrated in the above example. Note that the integer variables (I, J, and K) are used exclusively by the main function and hence they are declared as local variables. The text in this program is simply a set of assignment statements. Though the program looks incomplete without I/O (Input/Output) statements, it can be compiled and run without any problem. We will explore other features of C through more concrete examples in the next chapter.

A multiple module C-program can have one or more subordinate functions in addition to a main function. The global data declarations become meaningful in this case because of cooperative task performed on the same data structures by all functions. This is shown in ***Example 1.4***.

**Example 1.4:** Show a multiple module (or multiple function) C-program.

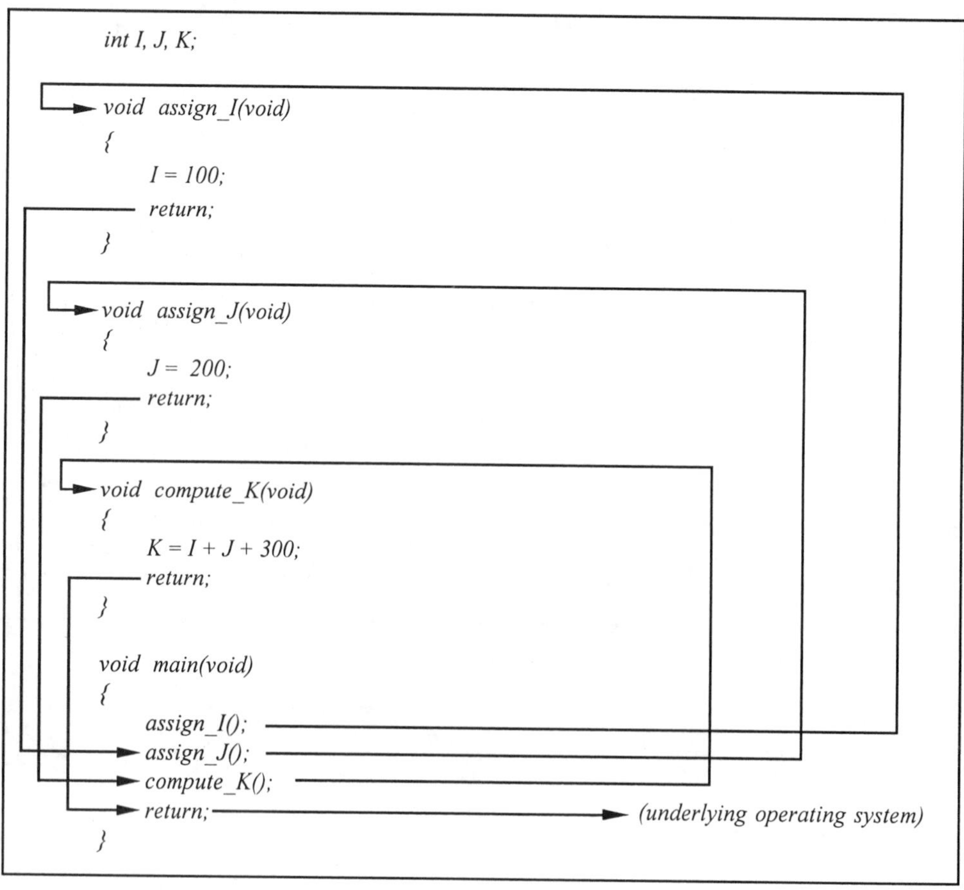

In the above example, each function upon a call updates a global variable and returns the execution control back to the caller (in this case ***main***). I, J and K are declared as global variables and hence they become sharable among the functions that follow their declarations in the program.

In a multiple module program, the position of the ***main*** module is immaterial and, in general, the modules of a program can be positioned in any order. Some compilers will resolve the references appropriately. However most of the implementations may require strictly the function definitions before they are referenced in a C-program.

In C, since the main function of every C-program always starts with the ***main ()*** statement, *a C-program is identified by its file name*. Program identification is essential to maintain a C-program in a system. We will discuss more about naming the program files, program compilation, and execution in the next chapter.

## Why is main treated as a function?

When a user tells the host operating system to execute a C-program, it transfers the control to the starting point of this program (i.e. the first statement of ***main***) through a function-like call. In this respect a C-program is structured as a function rather than a program module. Moreover, the host operating system may need to convey user-supplied arguments to their C-programs. In this situation, the main module that represents basically a C-program must be structured as a function to receive arguments. (The argument passing to C-programs is discussed in ***Chapter 22***.) Every C-program (via ***main***) ought to return the control back to the host operating system at the end of its execution. It is appropriate for the main to return a value to the caller (i.e. the host operating system) at the end of program execution to indicate the return is normal or due to some abnormal condition. This is shown in ***Fig. 1.3***. We will limit our discussion here only to the overview of C-program structure. We will see more details about C-programs and C-functions in subsequent chapters.

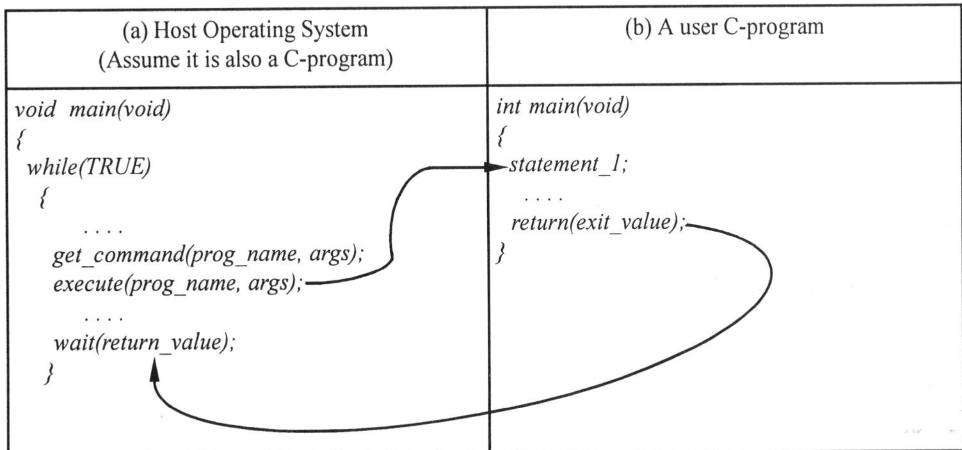


*Fig 1.3 Program call from the operating system*

We notice that the main returns its control similar to a subordinate function using a ***return*** statement. There is one difference. Every subordinate function must have at least one return statement to return a value required by the caller, whereas in the main function the **return** statement is an optional statement. Even without a ***return*** statement a ***main*** function will automatically return the control back to the host operating system after executing its last statement. We will also see that a ***main*** can use an ***exit*** statement with the same effect as a ***return*** statement.

## Advantage of Modular Organization

The modular structure helps a C-programmer to code and compile functions separately, and then link these new modules along with previously tested modules for further testing. In this manner, C-programmers can develop very large programs in a step-by-step manner. Another advantage of the modular structure is that the functions developed for one program can be used by other programs without any modification (i.e. recompiling may not be necessary). This concept of sharing can even be extended to programs of several users if the reusable functions are kept in a global library. This could save the programmers considerable coding time, particularly when developing large programs. This modular programming concept also helps the C-related application libraries to grow due to the contribution of useful utilities from the common C-programming community. Effectively this feature of C gives support for programming-in-the-large.

***Information Hiding*** is another feature that is achieved in this manner. A module means a self-contained section of code with a set of local data elements. What is more important in the design of a module is to be able to make its service available through a simple call statement. Modules can hide the details of their codes and data declarations from the calling modules without degrading their roles.

## 1.2.2 Structured Programming

First, the functional organization of a C-program provides a good structure. Second, the layout of each function with its block structure makes the code sequences quite distinct and automatically indented. Moreover the block structure limits the scope of variables within the boundary of a block in which variables are declared. Third, C provides a rich set of control statements which include the following categories:

- *conditional control statements (e.g. if_else).*
- *selective control statement (e.g. switch).*
- *iterative statements (e.g. for loop, while, do_while, etc.).*
- *unconditional jump statement (e.g. goto).*

These control statements (without the use of unconditional) enable the implementation of algorithms with a neat control flow. Within these control statements a control phrase may be followed by a block to accommodate its own local declarations and a sequence of statements. For example, in an ***if_else*** statement after the ***'if'*** clause a block may follow and after the ***'else'*** clause another block may follow. ***Fig. 1.4*** shows an overview of block structure in a C-program.

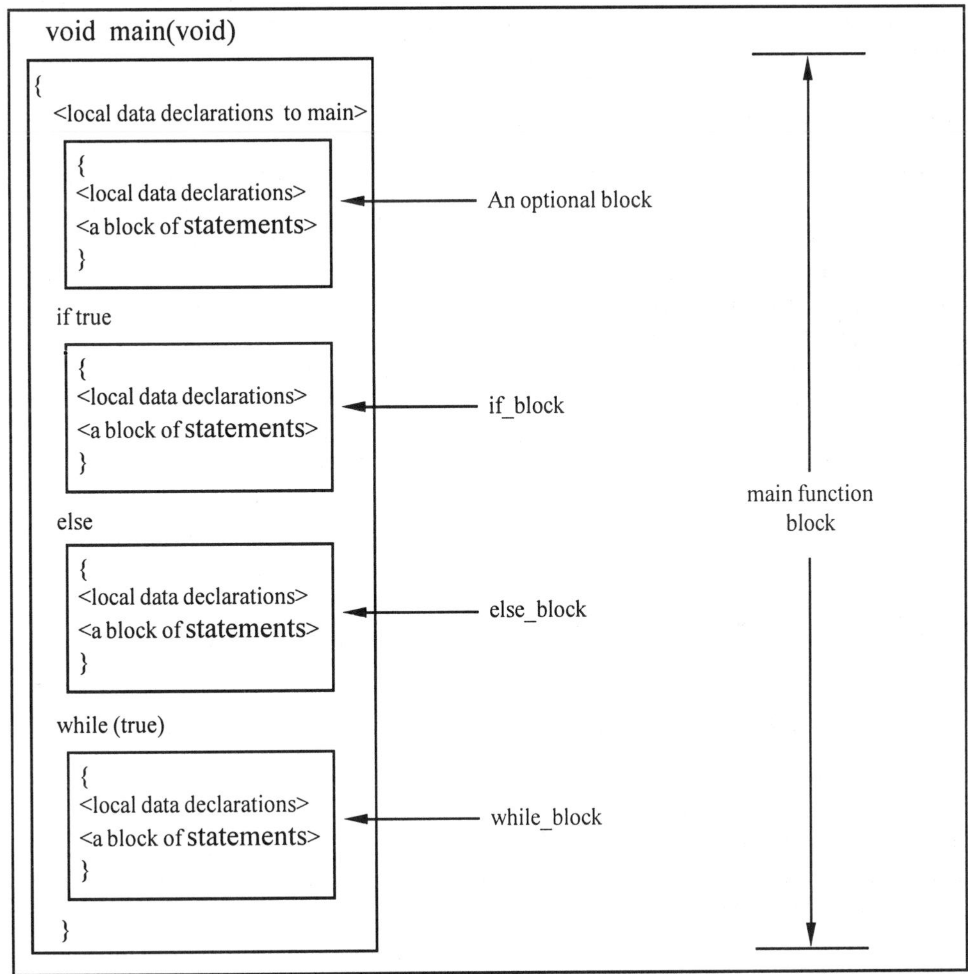


*Fig. 1.4 Block structure within C-functions*

### 1.2.3 Macro Facility

Usually assembly languages (called macro assemblers) provide a macro facility in order to help the coding at machine level. Basically, the macro facility is a text substitution technique by which a large piece of text can be represented by a symbolic string (called a macro name or simply a macro) which is then used in the source programs. One such situation in which the macro facility could be used would be when a group of statements are repeated often in a program. This original text can be represented by a macro name which can then be used in the source program wherever this repeated text occurs. In this way, programmers can shorten their coding time considerably. The macro facility can also be used to improve the readability of a program.

For instance a specific constant can be expressed symbolically to make the coding more meaningful or readable. Let us take a specific case where the constant ***3.14*** is to be used as the value of ***pi***. This can be defined as a macro under the name ***"PI"***, and then this symbol can be used wherever it is needed in the program coding as shown in ***Example 1.5.***

**Example 1.5:** Show the use of macro facility in a C-program.

```
#define PI 3.14
void main(void)
{
float radius, area;
     radius = 2.0;
     area = PI * radius *radius;
     return;
}
```

C provides a powerful macro facility not only for ***text substitution*** (using the ***#define*** statement), but also for ***text inclusion*** (using the ***#include*** statement) and ***text selection*** (using the ***#if_else*** clause) during the compilation process. This is a useful feature to improve the readability and the flexibility of a C-program.

### 1.2.4 Rich Data Structures and Operations

The basic data types available in the standard C are chiefly able to support system programming as well as scientific and engineering applications. The simple data types include ***int***, ***float***, and ***char***. C enhances the properties of some data types in a comprehensive manner. For example, we can declare either ***signed*** or ***unsigned integer*** variables; in either case, ***short***, ***normal*** and ***long*** range integer variables can be declared. In the ***real*** type, ***normal (i.e. float type)*** as well as ***double*** precision ***(i.e. double type)*** variables can be declared. One may wonder why so many types are provided by C. The reason is that scientific and engineering applications normally handle data of higher range and precision while short types are made available so that programs can use storage in an optimum manner.

The structured types include ***strings*** (i.e. ***character arrays***), ***integer*** and ***real arrays***, ***structure***, ***union***, and ***pointer***. Pointer is a very powerful mechanism to manipulate variables of array types, structures, and unions in a more efficient manner.

### Rich Operations

The standard operations (i.e. addition, subtraction, multiplication, division, logical comparisons) on the simple types (i.e. integer, real, and even character) are available in C. The logical comparisons, useful in controlling the flow of execution within a C-function, include ***greater than***, ***greater than or equal***, ***less than***, ***less than or equal***, ***equal*** and ***not equal***. More significantly, C provides a set of ***bitwise*** logical operations that are essential for systems programming as well as in some scientific and engineering applications. They include logical ANDing, ORing, Exclusive ORing and Negation. C is accompanied by a macro library for character processing and a string library to support string operations.

## 1.2.5 Rich Library of Functions

To enhance the operations on the data structures, C is supported by a set of standard library functions. Operations on character and string variables are performed with the help of macros and library functions. In addition to the libraries for character and string manipulations, libraries are available to support double precision mathematical functions, standard utility functions (such as conversion from one notation to another), stream-oriented I/O (i.e. character I/O, string or line I/O, and binary I/O) functions, etc. All these libraries are maintained as run-time (i.e. already compiled) modules, and a user program has simply to include the appropriate prototype or header files before using functions from the desired modules. The following header files are frequently used in a C-program:

***stdio.h*** defines constants and macro functions for stream-oriented standard I/O.
***ctype.h*** contains character testing and manipulation macro functions.
***string.h*** defines string manipulation functions.
***stdlib.h*** defines commonly used utility functions.
***math.h*** defines mathematical functions.

**Example 1.6:** Show the use of ***stdio.h*** header file in a C-program.

```
#include stdio.h
void main(void)
{
  puts("Hello World");
  return;
}
```

In this example, the ***puts*** function is a standard output function for displaying strings and is defined in the ***stdio.h*** header file. By including this header file the compiler will be able to resolve the call to ***puts*** function without any problem.

### 1.2.6 Various Notations for Constants

C allows decimal, octal or hexadecimal notation for expressing a constant value in an expression. Signed and unsigned integer constants, as well as floating point constants (which represent some permanent data in scientific, engineering and commercial applications), are normally expressed using decimal notation, whereas unsigned constants particularly in system programming can be conveniently expressed using either octal or hexadecimal notation. The following examples show how numbers are expressed in different notations.

*decimal constant:* *53 (no leading zero)*
*octal constant:* *065 (a leading zero indicates that it is octal)*
*hexadecimal constant:* *0x41 (zero followed by 'x' signifies that the following digits are hexadecimal).*

Real constants can be expressed either in a natural way, i.e. fixed-point notation (e.g. 278.67) or by using exponential or floating-point notation (e.g. +2.7867E+02). A character constant in a C-program is expressed within a pair of single quotes (e.g. 'A'). Alternatively, a character constant may be expressed in ordinal form also. For example, the ordinal value of the (ASCII) character 'A' is 65 in decimal, 0101 in octal and 0x41 in hexadecimal. The convention to express a string constant in a C-function is to enclose a string of characters within a pair of double quotes. For example, "A TEXT" is a string constant.

### 1.2.7 Conciseness

C allows notational symbols to express operations in concise form. This feature makes the statements smaller, and in turn C-programs become smarter. For example a simple increment on a variable like

*A = A + 1*

can be written as

*A++;*

similarly,

*A = A - 1;*

can be written as

*A—;*

A sequence of assignment expressions like

*A = 0;*
*B = 0;*
*C = 0;*

can be written in the form of a multiple assignment

*A = B = C = 0;.*

Another unique operation in C is the assignment operator. Using this operator type, the accumulation expression

*A = A + 100;*

can be written as

*A += 100;*

The operators for ***logical*** or ***relational*** comparison and ***bitwise*** logical operations are also given concise notation as shown in ***Table 1.1***.

*Table 1.1 Concise notations used in C*

| Operation | Concise Notation | Operation | Concise Notation |
|---|---|---|---|
| (a) Comparison operation for signed values | | (d) Assignment Operators | |
| greater | > | Add and assign | += |
| greater or equal | >= | Subtract and assign | -= |
| Lesser | < | Multiply and assign | *= |
| lesser or equal | <= | Divide and assign | /= |
| equal to | == | Modulo divide and assign | %= |
| not equal | != | Shift Right and assign | >>= |
| (b) Comparison operations for unsigned integers | | Shift Left and assign | <<= |
| AND test | && | (e) Increment/Decrement | |
| OR test | \|\| | Increment | ++ |
| NOT test | ! | Decrement | -- |
| (c) Bitwise operations for unsigned integers | | | |
| Bitwise AND | & | | |
| Bitwise OR | \| | | |
| Bitwise eXclusive OR | ^ (up arrow) | | |
| Bitwise Negotiation (1's complement) | ~ (tilde) | | |
| Left shift by one bit | << | | |
| Right shift one bit | >> | | |

*Note:*

*These concise expressions also enable the compiled machine codes to be concise and more efficient. Taking the previous example, the normal expression A = A + B would be compiled into four machine instructions,*

***Load A into register_1***
***Load B into register_2***
***Add both and leave sum in register_3***
***Store register_3 into A***

*and the concise expression A += B would now be compiled into three machine instructions*

***Load A into register***
***Add B to register***
***Store register into A***

*The first case requires 4 machine operations whereas the second case requires only 3 operations.*

### 1.2.8 Machine Language Features

A major difference between C and other high-level languages is that C allows programmers to work more closely with the underlying machine features. For example, memory locations can be either directly or indirectly addressed using some special C- features. Pointer variable is such a feature in C that can behave like a hardware index register and can even be used to traverse along the bytes of main memory. Pointers can also be used to address the input/output ports directly. C also allows programs to interpret a character variable as a pure byte and an unsigned integer variable as a memory word.

More interestingly C allows bitwise logical operations. That is, the bits of two bytes (or two words) can be ***ANDed***, ***ORed*** or ***eXclusively ORed*** just as in machine language programming. All these machine language features make C suitable for system programming.

### 1.2.9 Various Storage Classes

C maintains three types of storage: permanent memory, stack memory, and register memory, and allows us to declare variables using these storage classes. We can declare some variables as permanent and global, some as permanent and local, some as temporary and local (or auto) and some as register type. Global variables are normally sharable by all functions in a C-program, and hence, they are created in permanent storage. Certain variables are private to a functional module and these can be declared as either permanent or temporary variables. The temporary and local variables are normally created in the ***run-time stack*** (i.e. a stack memory allocated to a program during execution and sharable by its functions). Some temporary variables can be created using ***registers*** to speed up the processing with the assumption that the read and write operations on registers are faster than those operations on memory locations. The significance of this facility (i.e. declaring variables under various storage class) is that it allows improvement in the efficiency of programs in terms of speed of execution, optimizing the use of main memory, etc. For example, when we write some real-time programs, we can create some frequently used variables under class, so that the execution of those programs will be faster. In a different situation, suppose we want to run a program in a system with a limited main memory. Then we may adopt a policy of declaring variables such that only the essential variables are declared under global class (i.e. in permanent memory) and the remaining ones are declared under auto class (i.e. in stack or register).

### 1.2.10 Portability and Efficiency due to ANSI Standard

Although the original C by Kernighan and Ritchie (K&R C) possesses a rich set of features, it displays some weaknesses in the basic syntax. On the other hand, the clone versions of C have introduced new features that belong to other languages. The lack of standard in the overall language specification not only makes program development much harder, but also produces programs that are not easily portable. A general feeling developed among users as well as C-vendors that a standard must be adopted before too many versions of C confused the programming community. Hence, the American National Standards Institute (ANSI) formed a committee called X3J11 in 1983 to propose an international standard for the C language. In general, the new standard that was approved in December 1989 improves C with the following factors.

**Efficiency:**

- *C-programs with clear code and complete specification of declarations so that compiler would be able to check code thoroughly.*
- *Extension to existing basic data types and improvement in handling of abstract data structures (i.e. struct and union) make compiler produce more reliable object code.*

**Portability:**

- *Defining the limits on the ranges of data structures improves the portability;*
- *Defining a standard set of library functions make programs portable;*
- *Defining the ANSI-C file system that is completely independent of supporting operating system makes the programs highly portable;*
- *Detaching the Unix specific interface makes programs portable to any system;*
- *Although normal (K&R) C-programs are apparently portable, ANSI-C avoids any patching due to minor variations that are found in the current C-compilers.*

### 1.2.11 Standard Operating System Interface

In addition to supporting portability of applications at source level, C is allowed to continue to provide an operating system interface (as with the Unix interface in K&R C) as an option. Such optional feature with POSIX standard ( i.e. IEEE Std 1001.1 for Portable System Interface for Computer Environments) is called as Unix-like Application Program Interface (API) that extends the ANSI-C facility to provide a richer C-programming environment under any operating system. This extended ANSI-C can be used for developing application as well as system programs.

This ***standard Unix-like interface*** has, in general, functions to manage the operating system resources such as ***processes, files***, ***I/O devices***, etc. and allow C-programs to access those resources directly. Hence, the Extended ANSI-C cannot be treated as a simple application language (like Basic, FORTRAN or Pascal), but it represents a ***powerful virtual machine***. This virtual machine is not only capable of executing C-Statements, but also providing virtual instructions to access the resources of the supporting operating system as shown in ***Fig. 1.5***.

> ***Note 1:*** *At this point we can raise the question, what is system programming? A quick answer is that programs that provide services of an operating system can be considered as system programs, and the process of making all those programs is called system programming. For example, a command line interpreter, high-level I/O functions (e.g. stream I/O functions in C), language compilers, loaders and even the operating systems are all the outcome of system programming. Those who had experience with Unix can realize that Bourne-shell, csh or any other shell is purely a C-program to provide kernel's services at user level interactively. Unix users can even emulate other operating systems by implementing their interactive languages in C.*
> ***Note 2:*** *The term kernel represents the inner facilities of an operating system, and these facilities are available in the form of callable functions most commonly referred to as system calls. It is a virtual machine with its system call functions as virtual machine instructions.*

## 1.3 Supporting Processing Environment

The standard also specifies two environments under which a C-program can be run. The first one is called host operating system or simply ***hosted environment***. A C-program under this environment gets full support of library functions, macros, headers, typedefs etc. This environment is used to develop portable programs mostly for data processing applications. The second one is freestanding environment in which a C-program can get only a minimal set of software resources such as macros and restricted level of library functions. Microprocessor controllers are typical processing platforms to support this kind of environment. It should be noted that a C-program developed under hosted environment may not be executed in a freestanding environment. But a C-program developed under a freestanding environment may be ported to an hosted environment.

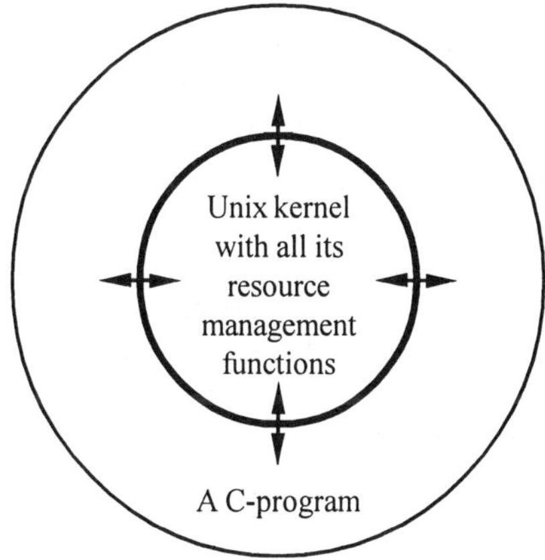


(a) C Virtual Machine

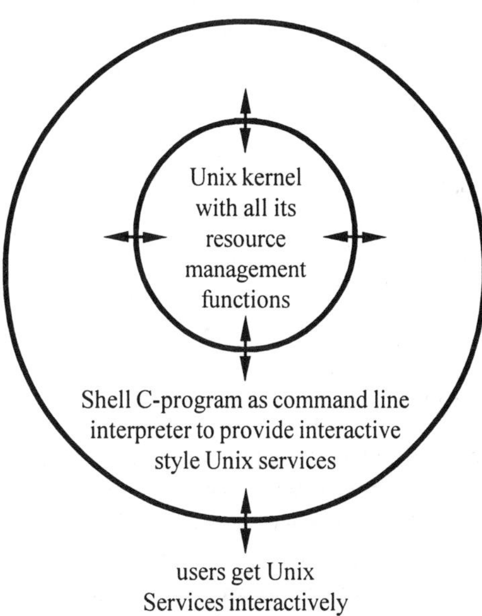


(b) Shell-Interpretive Virtual Machine

*Fig. 1.5 A simple view of C virtual machine*

Before we start writing any C-program, we ought to understand the environment that exists during the execution of a C-program. A C-program is basically meant to process on a set of data structures that is declared in its body. The execution environment that carries all operations on the declared data structures, consists of hardware resources such as CPU, main memory, a terminal and disk, and software resources such as C-related libraries and operating system functions as shown in ***Fig. 1.6***.

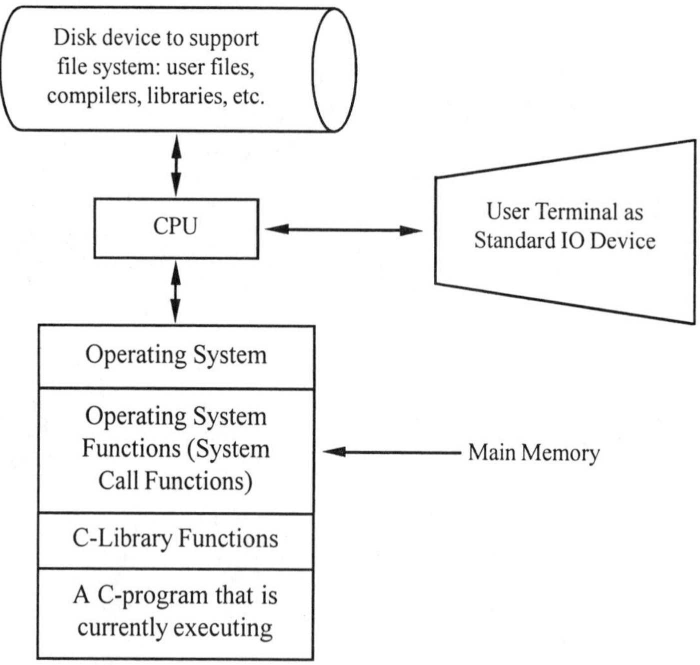


*Fig. 1.6 Hardware and software resources around a C-program*

## 1.4 C-Program Model

A C-program is not only processing on the locally declared data structures, it might also have to interact with the terminal device for inputting data and displaying the results of its progress during execution. In addition, the programs may also need some disk files for reading and writing large data sets. When a program starts its execution, it is given with three standard streams automatically kept open to communicate with the terminal device file by C-Virtual Machine. The programs can also open streams to communicate with the disk files. A typical C-program Model with an essential set of streams is shown in ***Fig. 1.7***.

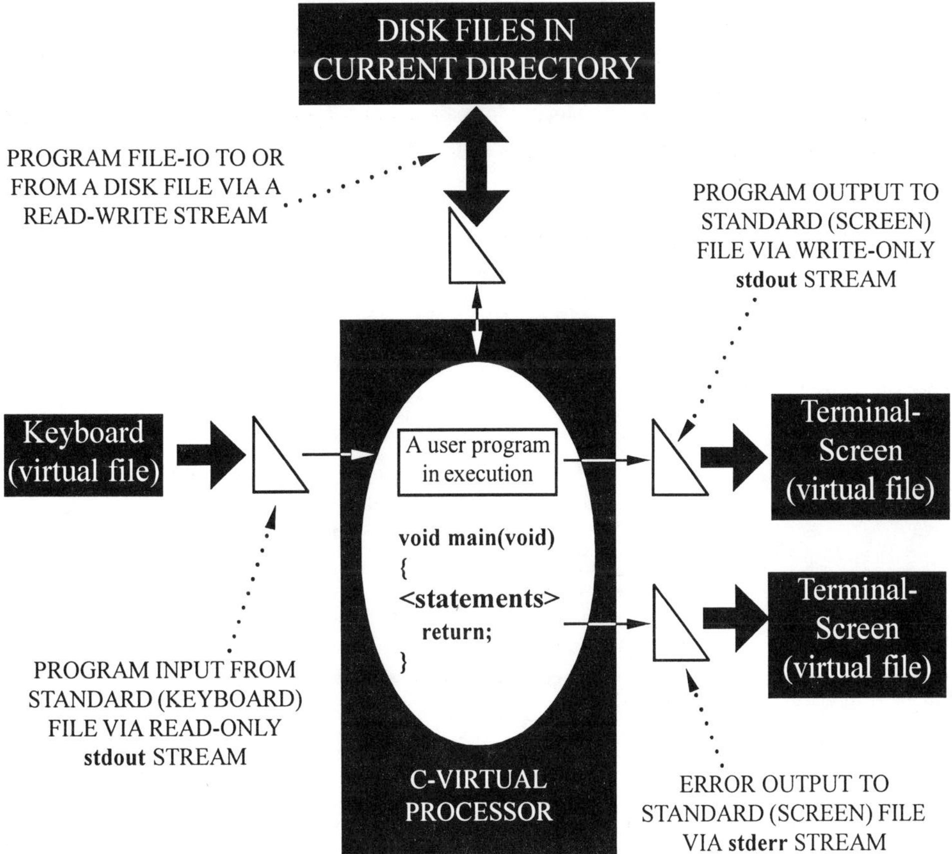


*Fig 1.7 C-program model supported by C-virtual processor*

> ***Note:*** *A stream is basically a low speed data channel to communicate at character or byte level. Usually streams use buffering to control the data flow according to an application. This buffering is similar to a dam to control the water flow. Hence a dam-like symbol is used to denote a stream.*
>
> *The keyboard and screen are treated exactly same as a disk file except that they are virtual in nature. A key board supplies characters as if they are read from a disk file. It is acting as a read-only file with infinite length. Similarly, a program can write characters to terminal screen (i.e. a virtual file) that acts as a write-only file with infinite length.*

## 1.5 Summary

This chapter presented an overview of C-language and its features. Although most of the features are common to many other languages, some special features such as macro facility, operations at bit, byte, and pointer level, and ANSI-standard make C a powerful application programming language. This chapter also explained the general structure of a C-program and presented the program model supported by the C-Virtual Processor.

## Exercises

1.1 Select the best answer for each of the following questions:

(i) Modular design makes ....

(a) a program more beautiful;
(b) a program debugging easy;
(c) a program development and maintenance more convenient;
(d) a program more concise;

(ii) Which of the following assertions are true?

(a) C is a structured language;
(b) C is a modular language;
(c) C is neither structured nor modular language;
(d) C is a machine-level language;

(iii) A block in C is identified by a section of code within:

(a) a pair of parenthesis;
(b) a pair of rectangular brackets;
(c) a pair of curly braces;
(d) a pair of single quotes;
(e) a pair of double quotes;

1.2 How is a function identified in a C-program?

1.3 Identify the incorrect modules and their organizations in the following C-programs and state your reasons:

Program A
```
program A
{
   ......
}
```

Program B
```
void main
{
   ......
}
```

Program C
```
void main ()
{
   ......
}
```

Program D
```
void main(void)
{
   ......
}

void fun1(void)
{
   ......
}
```

Program E
```
void main(void)
{
   ......
}

void fun1(void)
{
   ......
}

void main(void)
{
   ......
}
```

1.4 The purpose of main function in a C-program is:
- (a) to declare all global variables;
- (b) to call all subordinate functions;
- (c) to set all variables to zero;
- (d) to initialize variables, open/close files and maintain the overall control structure;

1.5 A C-program starts its execution:
- (a) at any statement of any function;
- (b) at the first statement of any function;
- (c) at the first statement of its main function;
- (d) at the last statement of its main function;
- (e) at any statement of its main function;

1.6 A C-program ends its execution:
- (a) at any statement of any function;
- (b) at the last statement of any function;
- (c) at the last statement of its main function;
- (d) at a return statement of its main function;
- (e) at a return statement of its main function;

1.7 Match the following:

| | |
|---|---|
| (a) Logical operation | (1) Header files |
| (b) Global variables | (2) less than or equal to (i.e. <= operator) |
| (c) Rich Library facility | (3) portable programs |
| (d) Modular form of a program | (4) Multi-function C-program |
| (e) bitwise logical operations | (5) C-functions can be compiled separately |
| (f) Macro facility | (6) C has machine level language facility |
| (g) ANSI-C | (7) Reusable functions |

1.8 Where does the control return after executing a return statement in a main?

1.9 What is the effect when there is no return statement in a main?

1.10 Distinguish the hosted environment from freestanding environment with respect to facilities available.

1.11 Can a C-program developed in a freestanding environment be ported to other environment? Why or why not?

1.12 Show main functions for both environments.

1.13 What are the different number notations used in C-programs? Give some examples.

1.14 Why should there be a main function in a C-program? Give at least one reason.

1.15 What is the meaning of the following concise notations?

(a) a += 10;
(b) a -= 10;
(c) a *= 10;
(d) a /= 10;
(e) a++;
(f) a—;

# 2

# Starting with C-Programming

***Chapter contents:***
*After covering an overview of C-language features through Chapter 1, this chapter exposes readers to real C-programming. It includes the naming conventions of C-source files and the conventions followed to compile and run C-programs, presented like a tutorial introducing the basics of writing simple C-programs and increasing the readers familiarity with C-statements used for IO. After reading this chapter, readers should be able to get the general picture of C programs.*

***Organization:***

*2.1 Introduction*
*2.2 Language Conventions*
*2.3 Statements in C-Programs*
*2.4 Conventions Used in Preparing C-source Texts*
*2.5 Learn To Declare Main Function*
*2.6 Include Header Files*
*2.7 Commenting in C-Programs*
*2.8 First C-Program Using the printf Function*
*2.9 Declaring the Data Objects*
*2.10 Input/Output Conventions*
*2.11 C-Program Using Stream I/O Functions*
*2.12 Diagnostic Aid (Use of assert Macro)*
*2.13 C-Virtual Machine for Statement Execution*
*2.14 Summary*
*Exercises*


## 2.1 Introduction

This chapter introduces general C-programming conventions and initiates the reader into the writing of simple C-programs with minimal knowledge of C. The general conventions in practicing C-language are parallel other languages and, hence, grasping these concepts will be less tedious with some programming background. Learning C starts with displaying strings on the standard output stream (i.e. terminal screen). The first examples are designed to introduce the basics of a C-programming with the help of the most commonly used output functions such as ***printf*** and ***puts***. Further examples with simple integer and real declarations are used to convince the readers that the C-programs are quite similar to other procedural language programs.

## 2.2 Language Conventions

### 2.2.1 C-Translation Process

A C-language text, whether it exists on a paper or in a disk file, is called a ***source program*** (or source code). A translator (or compiler), which is also a program, reads a source program and produces an equivalent machine language program that can be executed in a target machine. Such a target code that is ready for loading and execution is called absolutely or actually executable output code. We can also call this code the fully compiled object code. On the other hand, semicompiled object codes result when a multiple functions program is translated. In a multiple functions program, one function may reference other functions or even variables defined in other functions and, unless all the functions are compiled, these cross-references cannot be resolved. Hence, the translator compiles each function to produce a semicompiled (i.e. unresolved) object code first, and then combines (or links) all these semicompiled codes to form a single executable output file.

In summary, the complete translation of a C-source has three distinct phases: preprocessing, compiling and linking.

The preprocessing resolves all macro names that are used in a source program into original C-text. The compilation process converts the expanded text into semicompiled object code, which include unresolved function and/or variable references, and the linking process occurs after resolving all cross references to produce actual output (machine) code. A schematic diagram showing the roles of these three phases in a C-translation process is given in ***Fig. 2.1***.

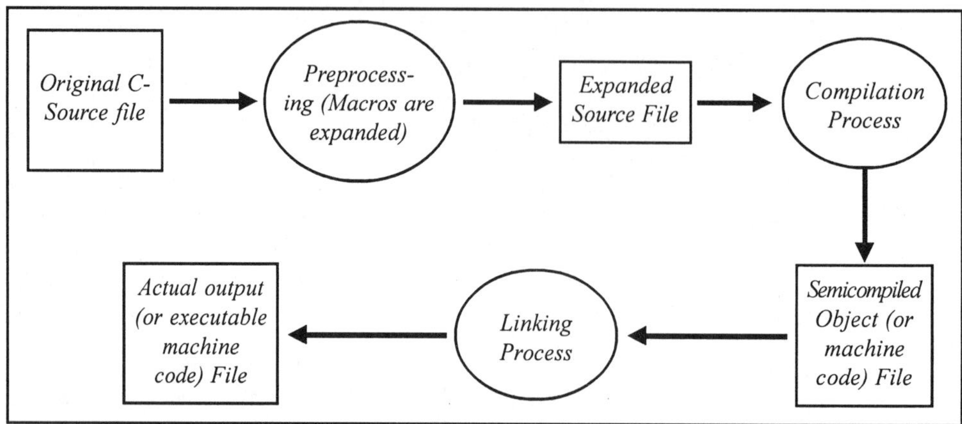


*Fig. 2.1 Processes involved during C-translation*

### 2.2.2 Naming the Files

The C-compilers expect their source files to have names with the "*.c*" extension showing that they are C-texts. (Note that the character '*c*' should be in lower case.) Other restrictions on the file names, in general, depend upon the file system of the supporting operating system. In the Unix File System, file names are case-sensitive, numerical characters, such as the underscore and period can be freely used. Even the file names can start with one of these characters. The restriction on the size of the file names depends upon the Unix implementation. For example, Unix System V recognizes names to a maximum of 14 characters. The following shows some file names under the Unix conventions:

***factorial.c PROJECT2.c 9temp.c 9_temp.c***
***RANDOM.c x123.c 999.c _temp.c***
***TemP.c p2c.c 9.9.9.c temp_1.c***

Naming the semicompiled output files is completely controlled by the compiler. The semicompiled files are created by modifying the source file names from the "*.c*" extension to the "*.o*" extension. For example, if a user requests the compiler to semicompile a C-file called "***Random.c***," the output file will be created as "***Random.o***." When the executable object files are created as the result of a linking phase, the compiler gives a default name, "***a.out***," which means the actual output. It is also possible to create executable files under user-specified names by appropriately informing the compiler via the user commands that invoke the C-compilation. This is explained in the next section.

### 2.2.3 Compiler Command

The command for compiling C-sources includes many options, such as compile and produce executable output, compile and produce semicompiled code only, apply only preprocessing on the given source, and produce the executable files under the user specified names. More details about the available options can be found in the Unix Manual under the *cc*-entry. The format of C-command is

*cc [option 1] [option 2] . . . [option N] source_files*

The keyword "*cc*" in the above format stands for the execution of the *C*-Compiler. The keyword can be followed by one or more options indicating the preferred modes of compilation on sources which are supplied as the last parameter of the command line. An optional flag is identified by a hyphen, followed by a single alphabetical character or a string indicating the name of option. The use of some of the options in C-commands is explained in the following sections.

### Case 1: Command to produce executable file

The logical structure of a C-program (or program module) consists of a set of global data declarations followed by a set of functional modules. In general, a C-program can be prepared either in a single or multiple file modules. Each file module of a program might contain a related set of functional modules preceded by their global data declarations as shown in ***Fig 2.2***. Also, refer to the syntax diagrams for the definition of a C-Program organization. Each file module can be compiled separately in the program development process. Finally, we have to submit all the file modules of a program to C-compiler to get the executable binary program as explained in the following section.

### The Syntax diagram for file module:

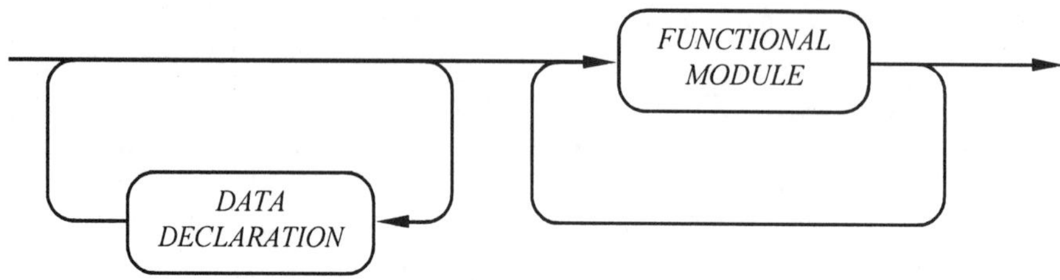


### The Syntax diagram for a C-program:

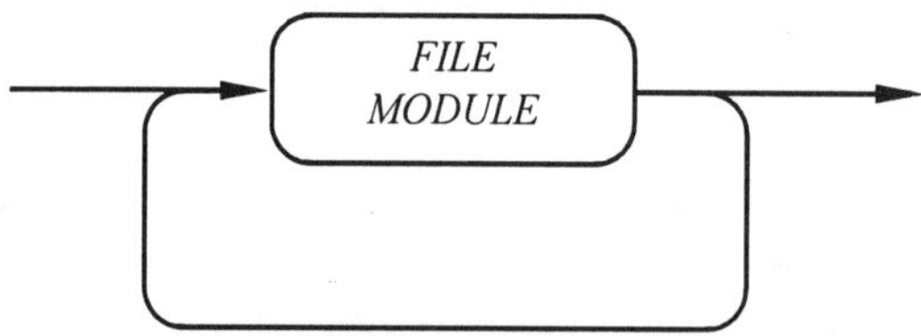


Once we have prepared a C-source program text, either in a single file or multiple files, we can issue a simple compilation command with the source files as the only command argument (i.e. *cc*-command without any optional flags) to directly produce the executable code. For example, let us assume that our source program is prepared in a single file called Prog1.c and we can then issue a simple command after the Unix Shell prompt ( i.e. '%'), such as:

*% cc Prog1.c*

This will perform all three functions: preprocessing, compiling and linking. If no error occurs during these functions, we can assume that the compiler will create the executable object code under the default name, "***a.out.***" This is shown in ***Fig. 2.3***.

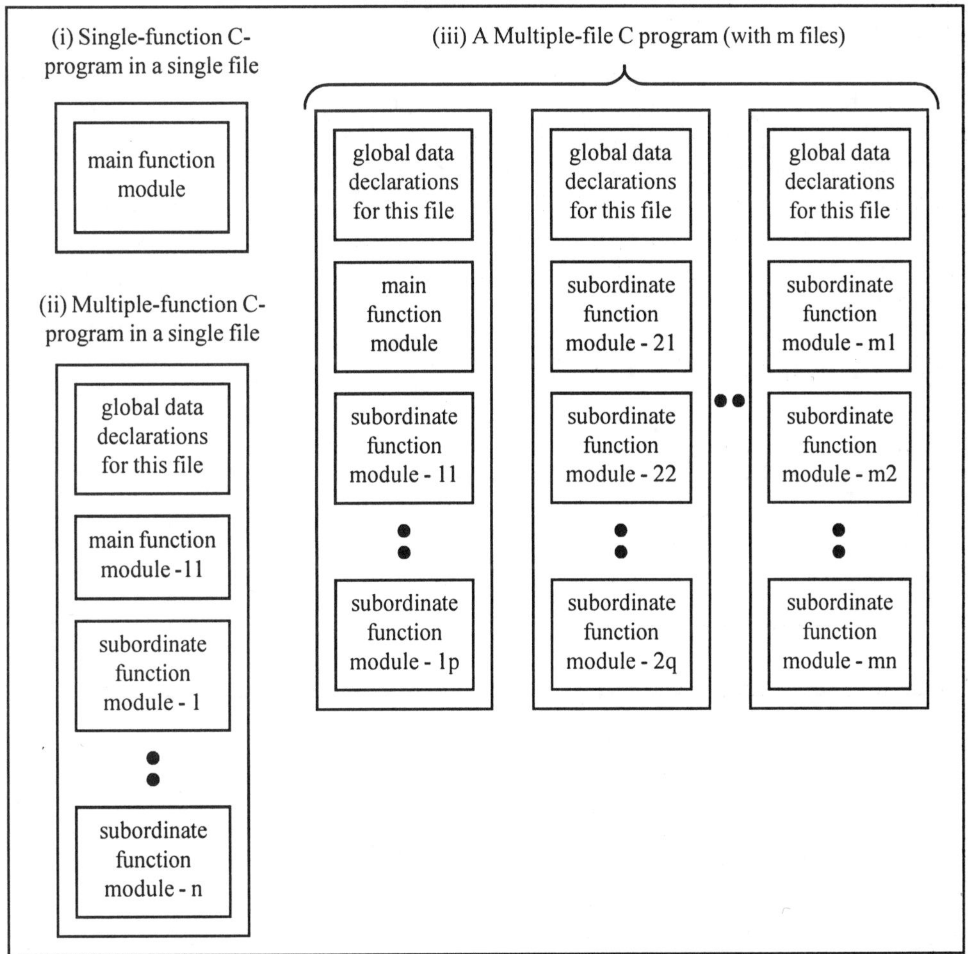


*Fig. 2.2 Organizational structure of C-program*

If a C-program exists in multiple files, say *main.c, funct1.c, funct2.c* and *funct3.c,* then the translation process may be carried on all files at once for the ***cc***-command shown below:

*% cc main.c funct1.c funct2.c funct3.c*

The above command will complete preprocessing and compiling on the supplied files and then link all the compiled files to form a single executable object file under the default name, "***a.out***" as shown in ***Fig. 2.4***.

In the schematic diagram, we notice that the output of the compilation process will produce semicompiled files with an extension ".o," which are then linked to form the "***a.out***" file.

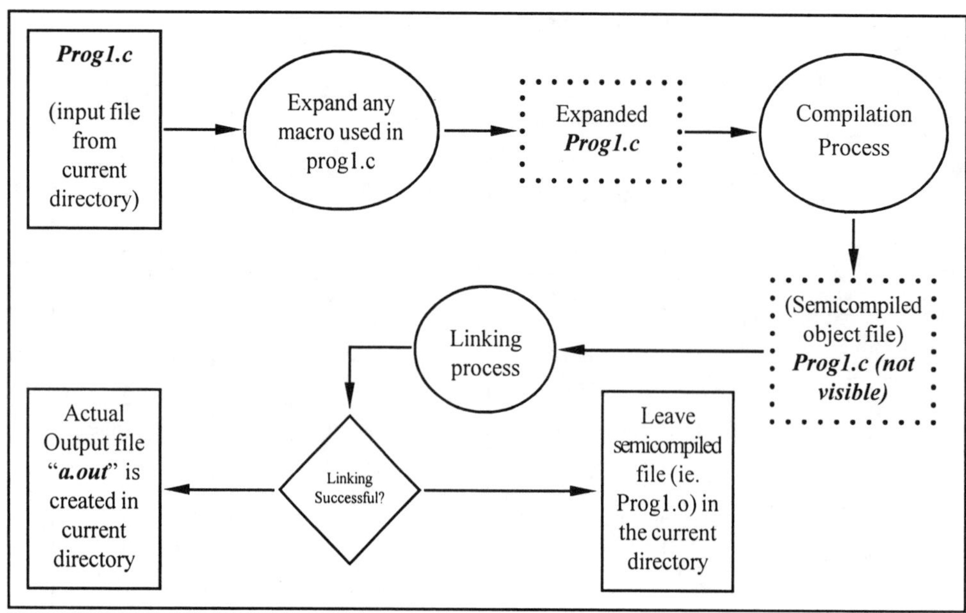


*Fig. 2.3 Translation process for the command "cc Prog1.c"*

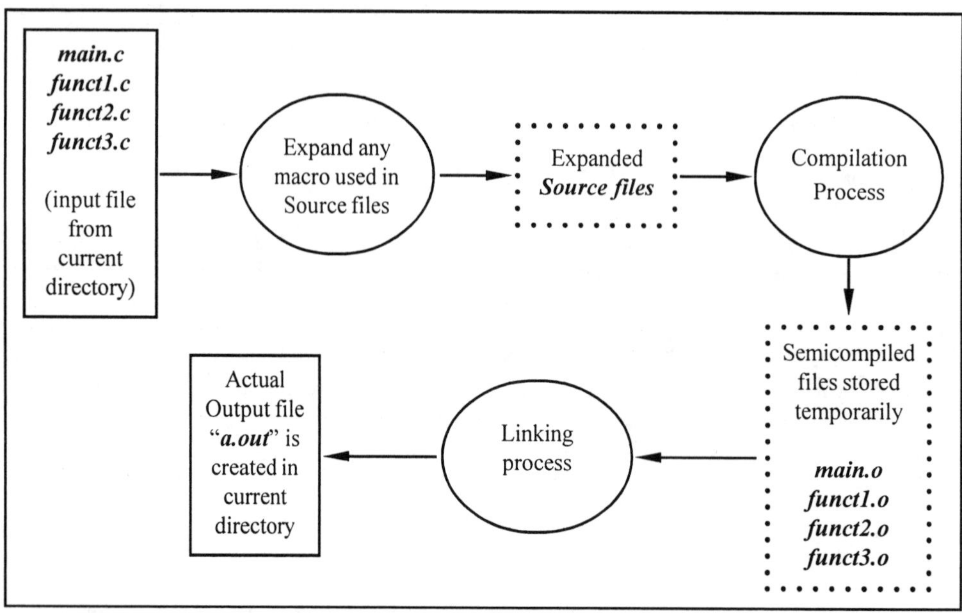


*Fig. 2.4 Translation process for the command "cc main.c funct1.c funct2.c funct3.c"*

### Case 2: Command to Redirect output to a named file

One of the options allows the users to output the executable file under a specific name. To make this option available, a cc-command with "*-o*" flag can be used. For example, the command

*% cc -o myout1 Prog1.c*

will produce the output file under the user specified name "***myout1***" instead of "***a.out.***" Similarly, the command

*% cc -o myout2 main.c funct1.c funct2.c funct3.c*

will produce the output file under the name "***myout2***". The character '***o***' in the flag signifies that the ***output*** is to be named using the user-supplied identifier.

### Case 3: Incremental Compilation Process

Let us assume that a user develops program modules in separate files and likes to test them one by one. In this case, the user can compile modules separately, and then link all the compiled modules to get a single executable file. To compile a source file without activating the linking phase, the ***compilation-only*** option using the"***-c***" flag can be used in a ***cc***-command. The following example shows a sequence of compiler commands used to compile the functions of a program separately and finally link them to produce an executable object file.

| | |
|---|---|
| *% cc -c main.c* | *produces the semicompiled output, "main.o";* |
| *% cc -c funct1.c* | *produces the semicompiled output, "funct1.o";* |
| *% cc -c funct2.c* | *produces the semicompiled output, "funct2.o";* |
| *% cc -c funct3.c* | *produces the semicompiled output, "funct3.o";* |
| *% cc -o myout2* | *main.o funct1.o funct2.o funct3.o links the semicompiled files to produce "**myout2**" as the executable file.* |

> ***Remark:*** *The same cc-command, when supplied with the ".o" files, activates the link editor to perform the linking process*

There are many options provided to control the compilation process. ***Table 2.1*** gives a summary of options that can be used by a C-language beginner.

### 2.2.4 To Execute an Object File

The actual output file (i.e. ***a.out*** or named output file), produced as a result of the translation process is simply used as the command input to invoke its execution. For example, if the created binary file exists as "***a.out***", then the command

*% a.out*

will start the execution at the ***main*** function of a.out. On the other hand if the created output file is, say ***myout2***, then the command

*% myout2*

will start execution of *myout2* at its ***main*** function.

*Table 2.1 Some useful C-compiler options*

| *Compiler options* | *Function performed by the compiler* |
|---|---|
| -c | Suppresses the loading phase of the compilation |
| -C | Prevents the macro preprocessor from suppressing comments |
| -E | Runs only the macro preprocessor on the named C-programs and sends the output to the standard output file or terminal screen |
| -g | Causes the compiler to produce an additional symbol table infor mation for the debugger, "***dbx***" |
| -o | Specifies the name of the executable output file |
| -O | Invokes the object code optimizer |
| -S | Compiles the specified C-programs and puts into the assembly language |
| -w | Suppresses warning diagnostics. |

## 2.3 Statements in C Programs

This section briefly introduces various statement types available in C for the purpose of understanding the programming examples in the initial chapters. A detailed study of C-statements is presented in ***Chapter 6***.

C functions can be constructed using ***simple***, ***block***, ***conditional*** and ***null*** statements. In general, a statement in C is terminated by a *semicolon*. For example,

| | |
|---|---|
| *;* | is a null statement, |
| *b = 10;* | is a simple assignment statement, |
| *a = b + 20;* | is a simple statement with arithmetic and assignment operations. |

A *block statement* is enclosed by a pair of braces. Within a block, variables can be declared as local data objects. These variables will exist only within the block in which they are declared. For example,

```
{ /* this block statement calculates the area of a circle */
float area; /* "area" declared a real variable, but should be used within the braces */
float radius; /* "r" is declared a real variable, but should be used within the braces */
   radius = 10;
   area = 3.14 * radius * radius;
   . . .
}
```

is a block of statements, or simply a block statement. Note that a block statement is terminated by a closing brace, but not a semicolon. A semicolon is necessary to terminate only a normal or simple statement.

Conditional statements in C are *if_else, switch, for_loop, while_loop* and *do_while_loop* statements, and their structures are shown below:

***(a) simple if statement:***

```
if(expression)
  statement_1;
```

***(b) if_else statement:***

```
if(expression)
  statement_1;
else
  statement_2;
```

***(c) switch statement:***

```
switch(integer expression)
  {
   case value_1:  statement_1;
     . .
   case value_n:  statement_n;
     . . .
  }
```

***(d) for_loop statement:***

```
for(set and test expressions for loop counter)
  statement;
```

***(e) while_loop statement:***

*while(expression)*
*statement;*

***(f) do_while_loop statement:***

*do*
*statement;*
*while(expression);*

## 2.4 Conventions Used in Preparing C-source Texts

Like other languages, there are several coding conventions with which a C-Programmer must become familiar. Some conventions are required by the compiler and others may be required for program maintenance. First, we will start writing C-Programs through which we will become familiar with the necessary conventions one by one. The following is a list of conventions used in C-Programs:

1. *Declaring main function,*
2. *Including header files,*
3. *Embedding comments,*
4. *Input/Output Convention,*
5. *Diagnostic Aid (Use of assert macro to catch fatal errors).*

## 2.5 Learn To Declare Main Function

As discussed in ***Chapter 1***, a ***C-program*** in a *hosted environment* is called for execution by the underlying operating system and, after execution, the called C-Program returns the control back to the system. During this call, the C-program must always start its execution at the beginning of its ***main*** function, returning the control by executing an exit call or falling through the end of the functional block. In either case of exiting, the ***main*** can return a value to the calling system. The ***main*** function also has the capability to receive some arguments from the calling system. Hence, the ***main*** function declaration similar to any other C-function should indicate both the type of the returned value and the formal arguments expected in a call.

> ***Remark:***
> *An exit is more appropriate to return a control to an operating system, whereas a return may be more appropriate in a freestanding environment. However, one can use either statement in any environment. The compiler will resolve the return control properly.*

Since the interface between the calling system and the called programs is implementation dependent and not specified by the standard, a programmer is free to choose one of the following conventions to declare a ***main*** function:

```
int main(void)
{<Local Data Declarations>
  <Main's statements>
  exit(exit_status); /* return (exit_status); */
}
```

*This declaration is more appropriate when the function uses an exit statement and no formal parameters are expected. (The exit_status can be EXIT_SUCCESS or EXIT_FAILURE as defined in stdlib.h)*

```
int main(int argc, char argv[][])
{ <Local Data Declarations>
  <Main's statements>
  exit(exit_status); /* return (exit_status); */
}
```

*One may use this declaration when the program expects the arguments that are supplied along with the command that invokes the execution of a C-Program.*

```
void main(void)
{
  <Local Data Declarations>
  <Main's statements>
}
```

*This is the simplest declaration that may be used when our programs exit implicitly and don't expect any command line argument.*

## 2.6 Include Header Files

This convention makes the programmer's job easy. The supporting system maintains a set of the most commonly used macros and function definitions that can be used by C-programs in separate files called ***header files***. Each ***header file*** maintains a set of macro definitions that are useful for a particular application. An application program can choose the appropriate header file and include in its text to make the coding task easier. For example, "***stdio.h***" ( ***st***an***d***ard ***i***nput/***o***utput ***h***eader file) in which some useful macro constants such as ***NULL*** and ***EOF***, and macros for character I/O like ***getc***, ***putc***, ***getchar*** and ***putchar*** and prototype definitions for formatted IO functions (***printf***, ***scanf***) as well as for string IO functions (***puts***, ***gets***, etc.) are defined. Whenever we want to use a macro or a function prototype defined in this file, it is necessary to include this file in our C-program using the "***#include***" macro statement. For example, the NULL can be used to clear a character variable as shown below.

```
#include <stdio.h>
void main(void)
{ char ch;
   . . .
   ch = NULL;   /* NULL is defined in the stdio.h header file */
   . . .
}
```

## 2.7 Commenting in C-Programs

Comment text is quite useful for documenting a program text. These texts can be introduced within a program text using special character sequences as delimiters. A "/*" sequence signifies the start of a comment, and "*/" signifies the end of a comment. For example,

```
/* This is comment text */
```

is a comment. Comment texts can be inserted anywhere in a C-program. During compilation, these texts are treated as ***white spaces*** (a computing term for characters that have no effect) and hence, ignored. C-compilers may not allow comment texts nested within comments. For example, we will embed comments in the previous example and see the difference now.

```
#include <stdio.h>                /* This is equivalent to including the entire text of stdio.h
                                  file in our program at this place */
void main(void) /* Program with main function only */
{ char ch; /* "ch" is a character variable */
   . . .
  ch = NULL; /* initialize "ch" with NULL value that is defined in the stdio.h file */
   . . .
} /* End of main function and program */
```

If a comment line causes any trouble, it can take a considerable amount of the programmer's time to find those errors. In general, one would not normally suspect a comment statement.

While developing programs, one can follow some general commenting procedures that are given below:

- *Include the heading information for each function of a C-program; this information may include such details as the programmer name, date on which this function was tested, the references to other functions, brief details of input, parameters and the type of operation performed by the function, etc.;*
- *Include documentation at the beginning of a block statement;*
- *While declaring variables in a program, if the variable names are not self explanatory, append comments to explain their significance in the program;*
- *Include comments to indicate the end of a control statement or a block statement so that the matching of the braces can be seen clearly.*

The following examples show the different placements of comment texts in a statement:

```
/* This is a comment line in C-program */
a = 0;   /* A comment may follow a statement construct */
/* A comment may precede a statement construct */ x = NULL;
printf("Hello") /* A comment can be embedded */ ;
```

We will see the use of the above conventions in the actual C-Programs introduced in the following sections.

## 2.8 First C-Program Using the printf Function

***Printf*** is a function which outputs data, by default, to the ***stdout*** stream (i.e. terminal screen file). It is normally used to print the data in a formatted manner. For example, an integer which is stored in memory as binary data can be printed in a more readable integer form. Similarly, *real*, *character* and *string* type data can be printed in their readable formats. In addition to its formatting characteristic, ***printf*** can introduce message items along with the formatted data. To begin with, we shall use ***printf*** to print some messages in our first programs. Remember to include the stdio.h and introduce comments.

### Example 2.1

A single module C-program called prog1.c is written to print the message "This is my first C-program" on stdout (i.e. screen) file.

### Prog1.c (Version 1)

**Step 1:** Create the following code in a disk file called prog1.c

```
/*****************************************************************/
/* Program's name: prog1.c (Version 1)                           */
/* Programmer's name: nsk                                        */
/* Task performed by the program: To print a greeting message on the screen   */
/*****************************************************************/
 #include <stdio.h>        /* printf definition is included via stdio.h header file */
 void main (void)                 /* main does not return any value, so it is of void type */
 {
  printf("This is my first C-program");/* print the message via stdout to screen */
 }
```

**Step 2:** Compile prog1.c
  % cc prog1.c
**Step 3:** Run prog1.c
  % a.out
Outout will be:
*This is my first C-program % (Cursor position)*

*Remark: Assume that the prompt of the supporting host system is indicated by %.*

From the above program, we observe the following:

- *prog1.c contains only the main module which always starts with the reserved function name "**main**".*
- *The program text (i.e. program code) in the above main block consists of a single statement that calls the **printf** function with a string constant as the only argument.*
- *A string constant (i.e. a string value) is represented in C as a string of characters within a pair of double quotes.*
- *A C-statement ends with a semicolon.*
- *After printing the message, the cursor is positioned after the last printed character.*

### Prog1.c (Version 2)

We noticed that the output of prog1.c leaves the cursor on the screen at the end of the printed line. To bring the cursor to the beginning of a new line, a new line character may be output after printing the message. This is shown below:

**Step 1:** Edit prog1.c

```
/* ************************************************************/
/* Program's name: prog1.c (Version 2)                        */
/* Programmer's name: nsk                                     */
/* Task performed by the program: To print a message on the screen  */
/*************************************************************/
#include <stdio.h>        /* printf definition is included via stdio.h header file */
void main (void)
{
 printf("This is my first C-program");
 printf("\n");
}
```

**Step 2:** Compile prog1.c
  *% cc prog1.c*
**Step 3:** Run prog1.c
  *% a.out*
Now the output on the screen will be
  *This is my first C-program*
  % (Cursor position)

## Prog1.c (Version 3)

Alternatively, a new line character may be sent as the last character of the message argument as shown below:

**Step 1:** Edit prog1.c

```
/*****************************************************************/
/* Program's name: prog1.c (Version 1)                              */
/* Programmer's name: nsk                                           */
/* Task performed by the program: To print a message on the screen  */
/*****************************************************************/
#include <stdio.h>
void main (void)          /* printf definition is included via stdio.h header file */
{
 printf("This is my first C-program \n");
}
```

**Step 2:** Compile prog1.c
  *% cc prog1.c*
**Step 3:** Run prog1.c
  *% a.out*

Obviously, this version saves one printf statement, but performs the same as in the previous version. The following notes are made with respect to Example 1.

- *A new line character also belongs to a character set (either 7-bit ASCII or 8-bit EBCDIC set), but it is non-printable. Note that as well as the new line character, there are many other non-printable characters in a chosen character set. In order to express non-print able characters in a program text, C allows a unique symbol of two* *characters of which the first character is '\' (backslash) acting as escape and the next character is a meaningful single character mnemonic. For the new line character, 'n' stands for new line and '\n' means a new line character. This notation is also called an escape sequence.*

- *Since the backslash character is used as an escape symbol for representing non-printable characters, double backslash is used to represent a backslash character itself.*
- *To become familiar with other non-printable characters in C, use Table 2.1.*

### Example 2.2

The ***prog1.c*** is modified now to print a message on the screen in two separate lines, and will be called ***prog2.c***.

### Prog2.c (Version 1)

**Step 1:** Create ***prog2.c*** as a separate disk file with the help of an editor.

```
/*****************************************************************/
/* Program's name: prog2.c (Version 1)                           */
/* Programmer's name: nsk                                        */
/* Task performed by the program: To print a message on the screen */
/*****************************************************************/
#include <stdio.h>          /* printf definition is included via stdio.h header file */
void main (void)
{
    printf("\n");
    printf("I am a C-language Beginner ");
    printf("\n");
    printf("This is my second C-program");
    printf("\n");
}
```

**Step 2:** Compile ***prog2.c***

```
% cc prog2.c
```

**Step 3:** Run ***prog2.c***

```
% a.out
```

Now the output on the screen will be

*I am a C-language Beginner*
*This is my second C-program*
% (Cursor position)

## Prog2.c (Version 2)

**Step 1:** Edit ***prog2.c*** to include new line control along with the output strings.

```
/*****************************************************************/
/* Program's name: prog2.c (Version 2)                            */
/* Programmer's name: nsk                                         */
/* Task performed by the program: To print a message on the screen */
/*****************************************************************/

#include <stdio.h>        /* printf definition is included via stdio.h header file */
void main (void)
{
  printf("\nI am a C-language Beginner ");
  printf("\nThis is my second C-program\n");
}
```

**Step 2:** Compile ***prog2.c***

```
% cc prog2.c
```

**Step 3:** Run ***prog2.c***

```
% a.out
```

Now the output on the screen will be

*I am a C-language Beginner*
*This is my second C-program*
*%* (Cursor position)

## Prog2.c (Version 3)

Both versions of prog2.c produce the same output except that the text of version 1 is bigger than that of version 2. When this program is run, the message will appear on the screen in two separate lines. The above program outputs new line characters in the beginning of each output message to make sure that the lines will start from the left boundary of the screen. The above example can be modified to include some tab spacing before each output. This is shown below:

**Step 1:** Edit ***prog2.c***

```
/*****************************************************************/
/* Program's name: prog2.c (Version 3)                            */
/* Programmer's name: nsk                                         */
/* Task performed by the program: To print a message on the screen */
/*****************************************************************/
```

```
#include <stdio.h>
void main (void)
{
   printf("\n\tI am a C-language Beginner ");
   printf("\n\tThis is my second C-program\n");
}
```

**Step 2:** Compile ***prog2.c***
  *% cc prog2.c*
**Step 3:** Run *prog2.c*
  *% a.out*

Now the output (with tab space) on the screen will be
  *<tab_space> I am a C-language Beginner*
  *<tab_space> This is my second C-program*
  *%* (Cursor position)

## Prog2.c (Version 4)

Version 4 of this program will print those lines within double quotes. Note that the double-quote character is represented by **\"** .

**Step 1:** Edit ***prog2.c***

```
/****************************************************************/
/* Program's name: prog2.c (Version 4)                          */
/* Programmer's name: nsk                                       */
/* Task performed by the program: To print a message on the screen */
/****************************************************************/

#include <stdio.h>
void main (void)
{
   printf("\n\t\"I am a C-language Beginner ");
   printf("\n\tThis is my second C-program\"\n");
}
```

**Step 2:** Compile ***prog2.c***
  *% cc prog2.c*
**Step 3:** Run ***prog2.c***
  *% a.out*

Now the output on the screen will appear as shown below:

*<tab_space> "I am a C-language Beginner*
*<tab_space> This is my second C-program"*
*%* (Cursor position)

## 2.9 Declaring the Data Objects

Data objects include variables, constants and even fuctions. We will discuss more on the data objects in ***Chapter 3***. Some general rules in declaring variables are given as follow:

- *Variables can be declared under* **C-supplied type_specifiers,** *such as* **int** *for declaring integer variables,* ***float*** *for declaring real variables,* **char** *for declaring character and string variables, etc.;*
- *Variables can be declared outside a function, but within a program file, inside a function block or within a block statement;*
- *Variables cannot be redeclared within a block statement, function block or program file;*
- *Variables or functions can be declared in an external file. In that case, those objects can be referenced using external declaration;*
- *Compiler strictly requires that all objects (i.e. constants, variables and functions) are declared before they are referenced.*
- A detailed discussion on the scope of variable declarations is presented in ***Chapter 5***.

### 2.9.1 Naming the Data Objects

The names within a program text are merely the user defined symbols (or identifiers) to denote the created data objects, such as *constants*, *variables* and *functions*. Similar to other programming languages, C also has some restrictions in naming the program objects. When declaring such objects, the programmers should follow the rules given below:

- *Any alphanumeric character (including underscore ) can be used to form an identifier (e.g. item, a, b, first_item);*
- *An identifier always starts with an alphabetic character or underscore (e.g. total, TRUE, First_item, _flag);*
  ***Note:*** *It is best not to use an underscore as a starting character in a user-defined identifier.*
- *Upper and lower cases are significant (e.g. total and Total represent two different objects);*
- *Identifiers must be defined before they are used;*

- *Identifiers can be of any length,* ***only the first 6 characters will be significant for the variables with external linkage (i.e. global variables and functions),*** *and* ***the first 31 characters will be significant for the identifiers with internal linkage*** *(i.e. identifiers that have file scope include static global variables and functions). However, in most of the standard compilers, the first 31 characters may be significant for all types of identifiers.*

**Syntax diagram for Identifier:**

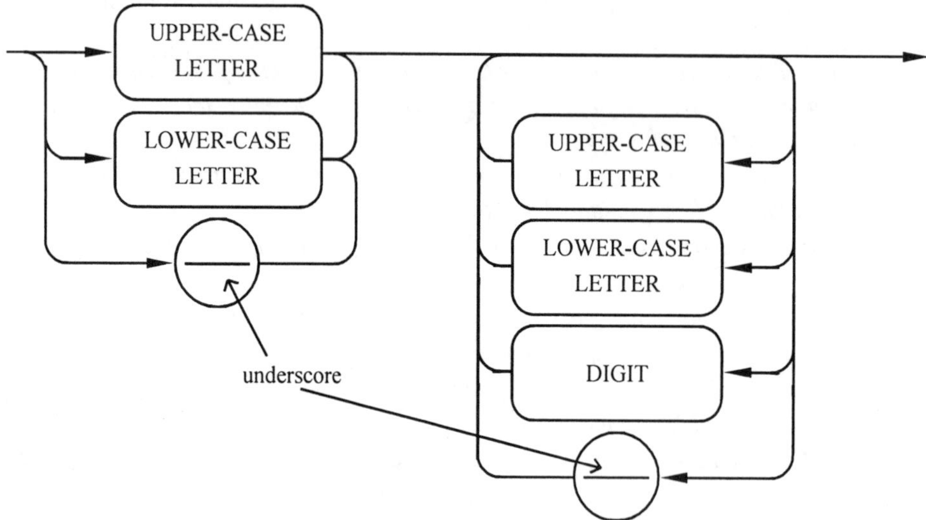


### 2.9.2 Avoid Declaring C-Defined Symbols (or Keywords)

C reserves the names of data types, statement indicators, names of some functions, etc. as its own symbols, and hence, these reserved names must never be implemented by users for naming their objects. For example, ***main***, ***define***, ***int***, ***unsigned***, ***register***, ***auto***, ***long***, ***short***, ***float***, ***double***, ***if***, ***else***, ***while***, ***switch*** and many other symbols are key symbols in C. ***Appendix A*** lists all key symbols in ANSI-C.

### 2.9.3 Declaration of Simple Variables

We will show now how simple data objects (or variables) of ***int*** (integer), ***float*** (real) and ***char*** (character) types can be declared in a C-Program. While declaring variables, the following thumb rules may be used: when there is only one main function, all variables can be declared as local to main; when a C-Program has subordinate functions, declare all sharable variables as global, and private variables as local, to their respective functions. The examples show these features.

## Example 2.3:

Write a program to declare some simple variables, assign them with some values and print their values using the ***printf*** function.

**Step 1:** Prepare ***prog3.c***

```
/****************************************************************/
/* Program's name: prog3.c                                      */
/* Programmer's name: nsk                                       */
/* Task performed by the program: To declare some simple variables as local  */
/****************************************************************/

#include <stdio.h>
void main (void)
{ int  k;  /* Declare k as an integer variable */
  float a;  /* Declare ch as a real variable */
  char ch;   /* Declare ch as a character variable */

   k = 100;          /* Assign the integer value 100 to the integer variable k */
   a = 0.999;  /* Assign the real value 0.999 to the float variable a */
   ch = 'A';  /* Assign the character value 'A' to the character variable ch; Note that single
quotes are used to express a character constant*/
   printf(" %d \t %f \t %c \n", k, a, ch); /* print k using integer (%d) format, a using floating
point (%f) format and ch using character (%c) format */
  }
```

**Step 2:** Compile ***prog3.c***

```
% cc prog3.c
```

**Step 3:** Run ***prog3.c***

```
% a.out
```

Now the output on the screen will appear as shown below:

```
100   0.999000  A
% (Cursor position)
```

Since there is no other function to share the variables, all variables are declared as local to main. Note that the printf is really a formatted output function. The format of the values are described in the string constant argument of the printf function.

## Example 2.4:

Given the annual salaries of four persons in a family as $20,000, $28,000, $40,000 and $60,000, calculate the total income of that family.

Before we start coding, we have to select the appropriate data type to deal with our application data. In this problem, the data supplied (i.e. the salaries) is of discrete nature, and the result (i.e. total) can also be represented in discrete type without losing any accuracy. Hence, integer type is quite sufficient.

**Step 1:** Edit ***prog4.c***

```
/*****************************************************************/
/* Program's name: prog4.c                                        */
/* Programmer's name: nsk                                         */
/* Task performed by the program: To print total income of a family */
/*****************************************************************/

#include <stdio.h>
void main (void)
{ int total; /* Declare total as an integer variable local to main to hold total income */
  total = (20000+28000+40000+60000);
  printf(" Total Income is $ %d \n ", total); /* print total in discrete form */
}
```

**Step 2:** Compile ***prog4.c***

```
% cc prog4.c
```

**Step 3:** Run ***prog4.c***

```
% a.out
```

Now the output on the screen will appear as shown below:

*Total Income is $148,000*

% (Cursor position)

In the above program, there is only one function (i.e. main) and hence, the variable *total* is declared as local variable to main. Also note that the printf statement is used to print the result in a formatted manner (i.e. a string constant followed by integer-formatted *total*).

## Example 2.5:

Given the weights of four persons in a family as 50kg, 55kg, 60kg and 65kg, calculate the average weight of that family.

In this problem, the computations for finding out an average require some addition and division and the result may end up with some fraction. Hence, the variables involved with this computation need to be of float type.

**Step 1:** Edit ***prog5.c***

```
/*****************************************************************/
/* Program's name: prog5.c                                       */
/* Programmer's name: nsk                                        */
/* Task performed by the program: To print average weight of a family */
/*****************************************************************/

#include <stdio.h>
void main (void)
{ float average; /* Declare average as a real variable local to main to hold average
            weight */
   average = (52.0+55.0+60.0+65.0) /4.0;
   printf(" %f KG \n ", average); /* average is printed in floating form */
}
```

**Step 2:** Compile **prog5.c**

```
% cc prog5.c
```

**Step 3:** Run ***prog5.c***

```
% a.out
```

Now the output on the screen will appear as shown below:

*57.500000 KG*
% (Cursor position)

Since there is only one function (i.e. main), the variable *average* is declared as local to main. Also note that the printf statement is used to print the result in a formatted manner (i.e. a string constant followed by floating point-formatted *average*).

## Example 2.6:

Write a program to calculate the salary of an employee using the hourly rate and number of hours worked in a week. Assume that the hourly rate is $10 and working hours per week are 40. Assume a program file has main and one subordinate function called *func_x* to compute the weekly salary.

In this problem, the data supplied is discrete and the computation required to calculate the weekly salary requires only multiplication. Hence, the result in this case will also be of discrete type. However, the number of hours and the hourly rate can fall into real values. In order to cope with this situation, it is better to declare the variables as float type.

**prog6.c (Version 1):**

```
/**************************************************************/
/* Program's name: prog6.c (Version 1)                        */
/* Programmer's name: nsk                                     */
/* Task performed by the program: To calculate weekly salary  */
/**************************************************************/

/* Global variables can be shared by all functions in this file * /
float hourly_rate; /*   "hourly_rate" is declared as global variable for this file   */
float hours;       /* "hours" is declared as global variable for this file   */
void main (void)
{ float week_salary; /* "week_salary " is declared as local variable for main   */

     hourly_rate = 10.00; /* These statements can use global variables   */
     hours = 40.0;
     week_salary=func_x();      /* func_x is called to calculate weekly salary*/
     printf(" %f \n ", week_salary); /*   total is printed in floating form   */
}

float  func_x(void)
{ float temp;     /* temp is used only here and hence declare it as local variable */
      temp = hourly_rate*hours;    /* as a local variable for this function   */
      return(temp);
}
```

The above program is implemented with two functions, ***main*** and ***func_x***. The variables ***hourly_rate*** and ***hours*** are shared by both functions and are declared as ***global variables***. On the other hand, ***week_salary*** is used only in ***main*** while ***temp*** is used only in ***func_x***. Hence, they are declared as local variables in their respective functions.

## 2.10 Input/Output Conventions

ANSI-I/O includes higher level input/output functions which cause all files (either a disk file or a terminal device) to uniformly behave like character-oriented files. It is called ***character stream I/O*** or simply ***stream I/O***. We will study more about this I/O in ***Chapter 17***.

> ***Note:***
> ***Unix-like I/O***: *The functions of this type are provided by the Unix or any underlying kernel to comply with the POSIX standard and can be called from a C-program. These functions are called I/O system calls. This system call I/O (direct I/O) is suitable for systems programming and not supported by ANSI standard.*

In stream I/O, the terminal is treated as two separate character files. The keyboard is opened as ***stdin*** stream and screen as ***stdout*** stream. A C-program cannot distinguish between a disk-file that is open as a read-only stream and the open ***stdin*** stream. The only difference is that the reference addresses obtained during opening of these streams are different. By convention, every stream must be open before it can be used. Since the terminal keyboard and screen are essential devices (or device files) to provide users an interface with their running C-programs, these two files are automatically kept open as standard input and standard output streams by the system. The system supplies the symbolic names (reference addresses also called ***file/stream pointers***) for these open-streams as "***stdin***" and "***stdout***" respectively. Thus, a C-program can readily use these symbolic addresses to perform character I/O operations on the terminal.

Hereafter, "***stdin***" means the already open keyboard character file and "***stdout***" means the open screen character file. Some general I/O conventions are:

- *The stream I/O functions are sufficient to any application program;*
- *When a program uses a **stream I/O** function, always include the **stdio.h** file;*
- *(This file has the basic macro functions for stream I/O.);*
- *Always use the **stream I/O** functions such as **getchar** [or getc(**stdin**)] for inputting characters from the keyboard and **putchar** [or putc(**stdout**)] for outputting characters to the screen;*
- *Use **scanf** to input formatted data from the keyboard file and **printf** to output the formatted data to the screen file.*

## 2.11 C-Program Using Stream I/O Functions

### 2.11.1 Use of Puts

In our first programming exercise, we used ***printf*** function to print a message on the screen. Actually, the ***printf*** function is a formatted output statement intended to print a list of values along with declarative messages on the screen. We took the option of only printing messages for the sake of starting our C-programming. A more appropriate function to display messages on the screen (via ***stdout*** stream) is the line-oriented output function called ***puts(string_argument)***. This function prints the given string argument (or string constant) supplied within the parenthesis as a line (i.e. terminating the supplied string with a new line character). For example,

*puts("Hello"); will print Hello on the screen and move the cursor to new line.*
*puts(""); will print a NULL string (i.e. simply move the cursor to new line.)*

**Example 2.7:**

Write a program to print the messages of Version 4 of ***prog2.c*** using the ***puts*** function.

**Step 1:** Create ***prog7.c***

```
/*****************************************************************/
/* Program's name: prog7.c                                       */
/* Programmer's name: nsk                                        */
/* Task performed by the program: To output a message using puts function */
/*****************************************************************/
#include <stdio.h>        /* stdio.h contains the prototype definition of puts */
void main (void)
{
   puts(""); /* Simply move the cursor to new line */
   puts("\t\"I am a C-language Beginner ");
   puts("\tThis is my second C-program\"");
   puts(""); /* Simply move the cursor to new line */
}
```

**Step 2:** Compile ***prog7.c***

```
% cc pro7.c
```

**Step 3:** Run ***prog7.c***

```
% a.out
```

Now the output on the screen will appear as shown below:

```
<tab_space>"I am a C-language Beginner
<tab_space>This is my second C-program"

% (Cursor position)
```

## 2.11.2 Character Stream I/O

Now we will see the use of the basic stream macro functions i.e. ***getchar*** and ***putchar*** in C-programs. Since these macros are defined in the ***stdio.h*** file, we have to include this file before they are used in a program. The following example shows the use of these macros:

**Example 2.8:**

Write a program called ***Prog8.c*** to read characters from the keyboard file (via ***stdin*** stream) until a new line character is input and write them to ***stdout*** stream for displaying on the screen.

**Step 1:** Prepare ***prog8.c***

```
#include <stdio.h>
void main (void)
{
 char  ch;  /* Declare a character variable to act as a character buffer */
 char  nl;  /* declare another variable to hold the new line character */
    nl = '\n'; /* new line character value is assigned to nl */
     do  /* do-while loop statement  */
    {
           ch = getchar;  /* get a character from the stdin stream */
    putchar(ch);    /* output that character to the stdout stream  */
     }while(ch != nl); /* if character is NOT EQUAL to new line, repeat the loop */
}
```

**Step 2:** Compile ***prog8.c***

*% cc prog8.c*

**Step 3:** Run ***prog8.c***

*% a.out*

Now the program is waiting for characters from the keyboard; when we input the following text with the new line as the last character,

*This is the first character I/O program<new line>*

the output on the screen will be

*This is the first character I/O program*

% (Cursor position)

## 2.12 Diagnostic Aid (Use of assert Macro)

When we start developing C-Code, an intermediate check can be performed by inserting the ***assert*** macro defined in the ***assert.h*** header file. This function takes a comparison expression and outputs a diagnostic message, depending upon the result of the comparison test. This test is applied in places where some conditions are expected for the progress of the program. These conditions (pre-condition and/or post-condition) can be tested only during execution. For instance, the statements that are used to allocate storage to a variable object can be checked using the ***assert*** macro. Before calling the ***assert*** macro, the header file ***assert.h*** must be included in the beginning of our text.

## Example 2.9:

Usually C compilers initialize the declared variables. To ensure the validity of such assumptions during our program development, we may use an assert statement. Let us assume that we want to input exactly 10 characters and print them on the screen. We will show the use of the assert macro to verify whether we need to initialize the controlling counter explicitly.

**Step 1:** Create ***prog9.c***

```
/*****************************************************************/
/* Program's name: prog9.c                                       */
/* Programmer's name: nsk                                        */
/* Task performed by the program: Use of assert macroas debugging aid */
/*****************************************************************/
#include <stdio.h>        /* stdio.h contains the macro definition of getchar  */
#include <assert.h>       /* assert.h contains the macro definition of assert  */
void main (void)
{ char ch;
  int i;            /*  i is used to count number of characters input      */
   assert(i == 0);/* if i is not zero, precondition is false and program is aborted */
   while (i < 10)
      {
        getchar(ch);
        putchar(ch);
        i++;              /*  it is equivalent to i = i + 1;       */
      }
 }
```

**Step 2:** Compile ***prog9.c***

```
% cc prog9.c
```

**Step 3:** Run ***prog9.c***

```
% a.out
```

*When this implementation does not initialize variables, then the output* on the screen will appear as shown below:

```
Assertion fails: i == 0, prog9.c, line 10
% (Cursor position)
```

Once the conditions are confirmed true, as expected according to our program design, the assert statements are no longer required and, hence, they can be removed. On the other hand, it is better to leave them in the embedded state so that those assert statements may be useful future maintenance. In order to ignore the effect of assert statements, ANSI-C provides a *switch* called ***NDEBUG*** which is defined in the ***assert.h***. To switch the assert statements, simply include

*#define NDEBUG*

before

*#include <stdio.h>*

## 2.13 C-Virtual Machine for Statement Execution

From the examples shown before, we have summarized several features of C-Language. A high-level language is the concept of a virtual machine developed to simplify the programming task. Understanding the language at the conceptual level is vital to know the nature of the language and then appreciate the flexibility property provided by C.

C-virtual machine, an abstract view of a C-programs' execution environment, extends the machine operations from those on the actual CPU (Central Processing Unit) to the operations at C-Statements. The extended machine is emulated from the semantic description of the C-Language.

When CPU executes a C-program, it produces the view of a C-Processor which starts execution at the first statement of the main function and proceeds by fetching and executing statements one by one until the last statement. By combining this concept with the concept of physical environment around a running C-program, as shown in ***Fig 1.6***, C-Virtual Machine architecture has been derived, as shown in ***Fig. 2.5***. This virtual machine has a memory called ***C-memory*** to store a C-program and a virtual processor called ***C-Processor*** to execute C-statements. The ***C-processor*** consists of the following components:

- *a **statement buffer** to hold a current statement that is being executed;*
- *a **statement execution unit** to process the fetched statement;*
- *a **function call processor** to execute the referred functions in the fetched statement;*

The function call processor basically represents a set of virtual resources (e.g. floating point emulator, window manager, owner's directory, opened files or devices) that are under the disposal of the current user and their associated accessing functions. For example, the maths library provides functions in double precision mode which may not be directly supported by the underlying hardware. The standard I/O library functions provide operations for reading and writing streams of characters with respect to a currently opened file or device, etc. The power of this function call processor can be improved by adding a new set of functions and/or modifying the existing ones. For example, a set of arithmetic functions based on Binary-Coded-Decimal mode can be added to support commercial processing. In general, the C-Processor can virtually grow to any extent.

A more detailed version of this virtual machine concept is presented in ***Chapter 3*** to explain the full semantics of ***C-Variables*** and ***C-Expressions***.

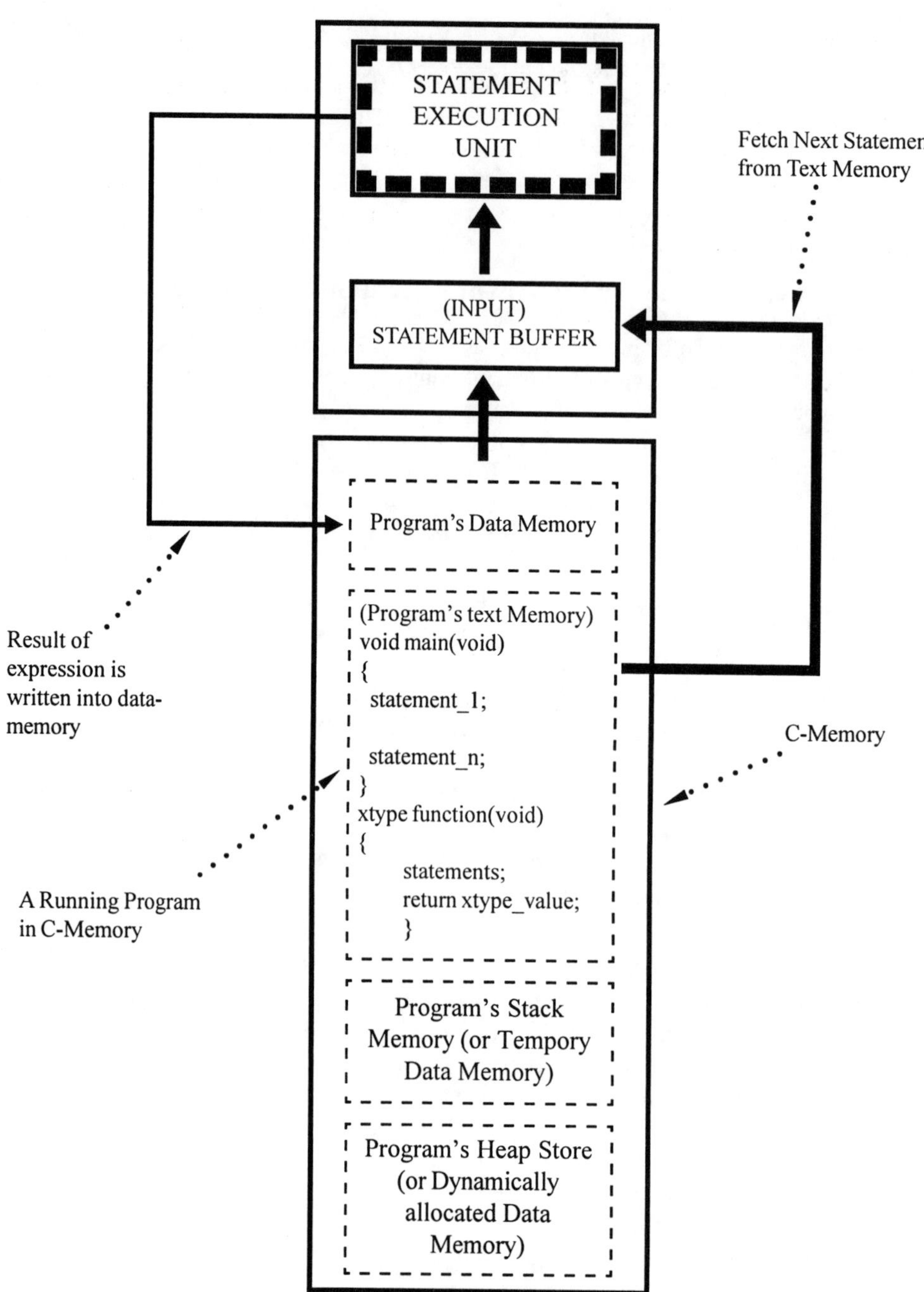


Fig. 2.5 An overview of C-virtual machine at statement level

## 2.14 Summary

This chapter introduced some of the basic C-programming conventions required to prepare, compile and execute a program. These conventions include how to write comment texts, naming the variables, declaring variables, inclusion of stdio.h for character stream I/O, etc. The readers were guided on what a C-program is and how it looks with the help of simple programming examples. Some significant concepts that are exposed to the readers through these programming examples are as follows:

- ***printf*** *provides fomatting feature that can be used to print a string constant and values of variables;*
- *although* ***printf*** *is useful for outputting a string,* ***puts*** *is a more appropriate function for outputting a string;*
- ***getchar*** *and* ***putchar*** *are appropriate functions for character I/O with respect to terminal files;*
- *if a program needs an item from an external file, then include that file using the include macro. To use* ***printf, puts, gets, getchar*** *and* ***putchar and other standard*** *I/O definitions a program should include* ***stddio.h****.*

## Exercises

2.1 Given a compiler command

*cc account*

select the appropriate answer:

(a) after compiling account.o will be created as binary file;
(b) after compiling a.out file will be created as binary file;
(c) compiler will complain that the given file is not a C- source file;
(d) compiler will change the name of the file in our directory from account to account.c and then compile to produce a.out.

2.2 What will the output files for the following compilation commands be?

(a) A simple command:
```
cc temp.c
```
(b) Another simple command:
```
cc -o exer1 exer1.c
```
(c) A sequence of commands:
```
cc -c dbmain.c
cc -c dbinit.c
cc -c dbupdate.c
cc -c dbshow.c
cc -o dbase dbmain.o dbinit.o dbupdate.o dbshow.c
```

2.3 What is the advantage of the incremental compilation facility?

2.4 Identify legal source file names for the C-compiler:

| | | | |
|---|---|---|---|
| assn.C | ccc.c | 1st_func.c | no_of_items |
| display.c | init..c | ..c | _xxx.c |
| $print.c | main.c | -input.c | get_line.c |
| c.c | c.c.c | c..c.c | temp__1.c |

2.5 Identify legal user-defined variable names from the following:

| | | | |
|---|---|---|---|
| Price | grand-total | 1st_item | no_of_items |
| student_name | student_id | $AUS | #item |
| EmPlOyEe | status/flag | main | cc |
| printf | a.out | Tab | CR&LF |
| _2nd_item | pascal | vi | @value |

2.6 Give ten keywords used by C.

2.7 Assume that a program file contains two functions, ***main*** and f1 and the code for ***main*** appears first. When the compiler finds that ***main*** has references to f1, will it complain? Explain.

2.8 How are the comments introduced in C?

2.9 Correct the errors due to comment texts in the following C-program:

```
 /* Program Name:   xxx.c * /
 //*  Programmers Name: nsk  **/
 /* Date: Jan 1991       /*
void main(void)  // start of main function
{
. . .
} /* end of main /
```

2.10 What will happen if we compile the following program? ***Hint***: some thing went wrong with comment.

```
void main(void )
{
. . .
func1; /* function call */
. . .
} /* end of main /
void func1(void)
{
. . .
} / end of func1 */
```

2.11 Write a program to print the following message: "A backslash in C-text is represented by the symbol '\\' ".

2.12 Write a C-program to output Table 2.1. (Ignore the vertical lines.)

2.13 Would you prefer ***printf*** or ***puts*** in outputting a message? Why?

2.14 Print the results starting from 1 multiplied by 10 to 10 multiplied by 10.

2.15 Write a program to find out the average of a list of real numbers, i.e. {10.0,20.0, 30.0,40.0, 50.0, 60.0, 70.0, 80.0, 90.0, 100.0}, and print both the list and the average on the screen.

2.16 Write a program to input characters (using ***getchar*** ) from the keyboard until a new line is input and print the number of occurrences of the character 'a'.

2.17 After observing the working principle of ***getchar*** in the previous exercise, does ***getchar*** read every character interactively or in a batch mode? Can you give your comments on the behavior of ***getchar***?

2.18 Write a program to input a character from the keyboard file and output its equivalent decimal, octal and hexadecimal equivalents.

2.19 Write a C-program to print the following memorandom-heading:

| C_Corporation | |
|---|---|
| MEMORANDUM | Date: |
| To: | From: |
| Subject: | |

# 3

# Meaning of Variables and Expressions

**Chapter contents:**

*This chapter introduces the basic variables and expressions that are used to construct C-statements. Readers will be able to understand why C became systemès programming language after studying the type and structure of variables in this chapter. They will also have a good grounding in constructing powerful C-expressions.*

**Organization:**

*3.1 Introduction*
*3.2 Meaning of Variable*
*3.3 Temporal Aspects of Variables*
*3.4 Meaning of Declarations*
*3.5 Types of Variables in ANSI-C*
*3.6 The const Variables*
*3.7 Significance of Volatile Qualifier*
*3.8 Meaning and Evaluation of Expressions*
*3.9 Types of Operators*
*3.10 Types of Expressions*
*3.11 Summary*
*Exercises*

## 3.1 Introduction

This chapter is devoted to introducing the concepts of variables and the various types of expressions, the basic building blocks of C-statements. By understanding both the structure and semantics of a C-variable, a C-programmer can actually capture the meaning of some key terms, such as ***value parameter***, ***reference parameter***, ***variable parameter***, ***lvalue*** and ***rvalue***.

In C, the treatment of expressions is somewhat different from other languages. For example, an assignment is treated like an expression rather than a statement. The meaning of expressions, including the new comma and ternary operator expressions, are explored with the help of the C-virtual machine concept. This chapter also introduces function declaration.

## Role of Variables

Before defining C-Variables, we must understand the role played by them. It is interesting to map this role from the expressions supported by C. Using a simple example to understand the architecture of the C-Virtual Machine, we can explore the role played by variables to support programming in such C-Machine architecture.

**Example 3.1:** Consider a simple program for adding two integers. The program is shown with only one expression statement to add as shown below:

```
void main(void)
{
   100 + 200;
}
```

This program looks surprisingly like a calculator program. In fact, it is an error-free C-program that can be compiled and run. By recalling the C-Virtual machine model (as shown in Fig 1.4 in ***Chapter 1***), in which a C-program is executed statement by statement by a C-processor, we can show how that C-Processor executes an expression. We may assume that the C-Processor has an *expression evaluator* and two registers (one for keeping an operand and another for accumulating the intermediate result). The register that accumulates the intermediate result is simply called the *accumulator* and the other register may be called the *operand buffer*. The C-Processor also has a statement buffer to hold the current statement until it is completed. ***Fig 3.1*** shows how the statement expression in the above example is executed.

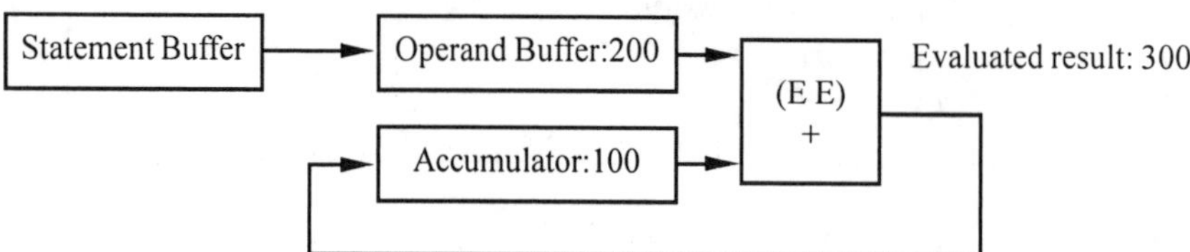


*Fig 3.1 A simple execution model of C-statement*

The only statement in the above program is an expression of adding two constants. During execution of this expression, two integer values are loaded in the registers. Register values are then added with the help of the Expression Evaluation (EE) Unit and, finally, the result of the evaluation (i.e., 300) is stored in the accumulator. The execution model is almost similar to a calculator. Since the internal registers do not have an address, a user program cannot directly access their contents. At the end of the statement, if the result of an expression is not saved in an addressable location, it is simply left in the accumulator. The result cannot be used further in the next statement or remaining program segment. We will see later how the accumulator value can be accessed by the programs.

**Example 3.2:** The following program has three statement expressions, and the execution of those statements are shown in ***Fig 3.2***.

```
void main(void)
{
   100 + 200;
   300 - 200;
   100 * 40;
}
```

The execution of this program starts with the first statement expression (***Fig. 3.2a***). Without saving the result of first statement, the processor goes to the second statement (***Fig. 3.2b***).

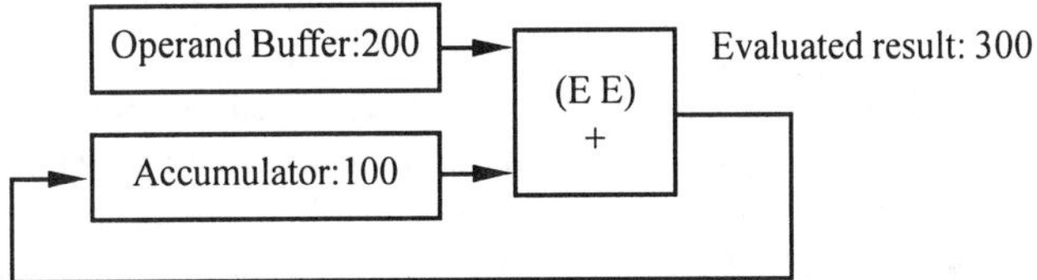


(a) During the execution of the first statement

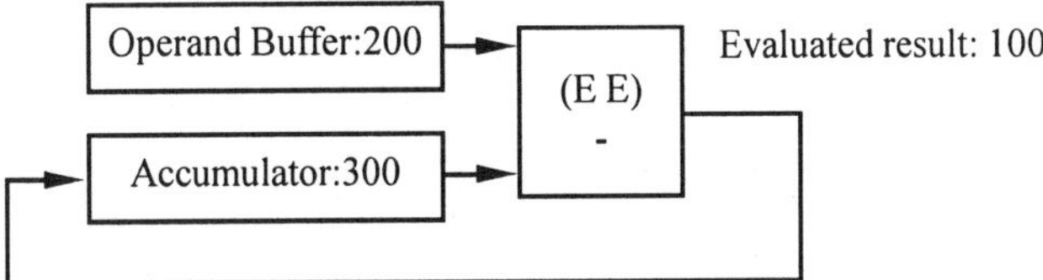


(b) During the execution of the second statement

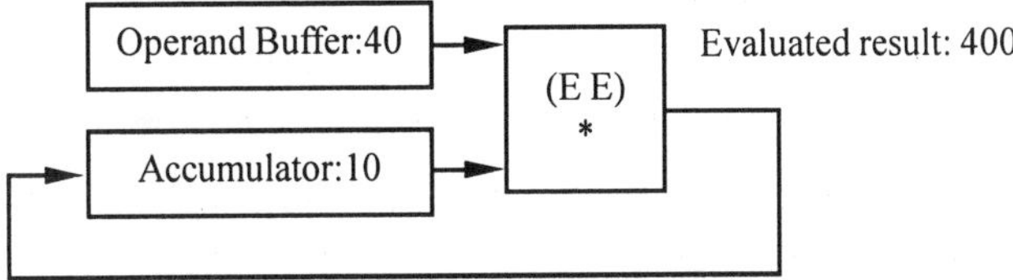


(c) During the execution of the third statement

*Fig 3.2 Execution of the program in Example 3.2*

At the end of each statement the accumulator has the evaluated result, and the accumulator will be cleared at the beginning of the next statement. That is, the result of one statement is not carried automatically over to next statement. If the user program wants to use the result of an expression before the end of the statement in which it was computed , it should be saved in an addressable memory element. That is where the role of a variable becomes significant. The following example shows the role of a variable in saving the accumulator value.

**Example 3.3:** Modify the C-program shown in Example 3.1 so that a memory can be used to store the intermediate results for further use.

```
void main(void)
{
  int K;
      K = 100;
      K = K + 200;
}
```

In this C-program, the variable ***K*** is declared as an integer variable to save the intermediate results in each statement. In the first C-statement, the immediate value 100 is loaded into the internal accumulator and from there, it is assigned to ***K***. In the second C-statement, the immediate value 200 is loaded into the internal accumulator, then added with the value held in ***K*** (i.e., 100), leaving the sum in the accumulator. Finally, the accumulated value is assigned to ***K***. Since ***K*** is declared by the user, the programmer can access its value any time within this program. The value assigned to ***K*** can also be displayed or printed without any problem.

The example below demonstrates the role of variables as the intermediate storage until the end of the remaining function or program segment.

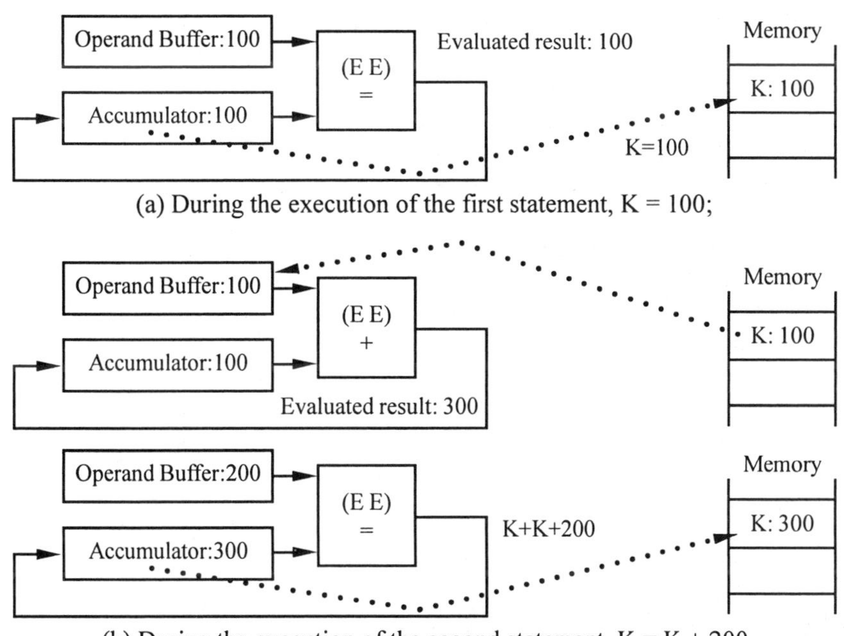


(a) During the execution of the first statement, K = 100;

(b) During the execution of the second statement, K = K + 200

*Fig 3.3 Execution of the program in Example 3.3*

## 3.2 Meaning of Variable

A variable is an instance (or an object) of a type of data structure, and each created variable is assigned with memory of sufficient size to store its value. The variable name or identifier is also associated with an object to reference the currently stored value. A variable is created by formally declaring an identifier to belong to a selected type of data structure. The declaration format of a variable is shown in the following syntax diagram.

**Syntax diagram for variable declaration:**

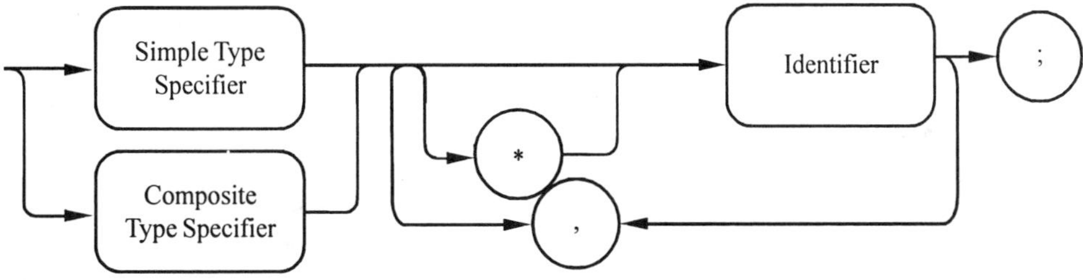

We will explore all these types in the next section. To show some declarations using the above diagram, we will use simple type, ***int***, which was introduced in the last chapter.

```
int K;        /* Declare an integer variable whose identifier is K */
int L, M, N;  /* L, M and N are declared in a single declaration */
int *PTR;     /* PTR is declared as a pointer variable of integer type*/
```

The identifier of a declared variable is a symbol consisting of alphanumeric characters normally chosen by programmers. As mentioned in ***Chapter 2***, an identifier starts with an ***alphabetic*** character (or ***underscore***), and its first ***8 characters***, at least, are significant in the standard C-compilers.

A variable is analogous to a frame that holds a picture. Here, the picture represents the value of a variable. A general characteristic of a variable is that its value may be changing during the course of program execution, similar to changing the pictures in a frame. Creating a variable is similar to making a frame, and assigning a value to a variable is similar to attaching a new picture in a frame. The terms "attaching" and "assigning" are quite similar. The frame size denotes how much memory is required to hold a value, and this size varies from one type of variable to another. For example, the frame size for holding a character value is one byte. When we construct a frame, we normally put in a "null" picture, or some dummy picture to fill it. Alternatively, we may intend to attach a specific picture to a new frame. Similarly, when a C-compiler processes variable declarations, it creates variables with either a default value (i.e., ***NULL*** value), a garbage value, or a specified value, depending upon the nature of declaration.

The ***framed-picture*** now represents our variable. The name of a variable may represent either the picture currently attached to its frame (i.e., current value) or the frame itself depending upon the context. The context refers to whether a variable is used in an ***lvalue expression*** or ***rvalue expression***. This is called semantics of variable names. It is essential to know how the compiler interprets this name in an expression in order to understand the meanings of ***lvalue*** and ***rvalue***. For example, in an assignment expression, the compiler interprets a variable name in the right hand side of an assignment operator as a value parameter or picture, and in the left hand side, as the reference parameter or frame itself. This is further explained later in this chapter.

Another characteristic of a variable is that it needs memory to exist, similar to a place or location on the wall to hang a created frame. During declaration, the compiler allocates memory locations to keep the created variables (or frames). Once created, its identifier represents some value that is currently stored in the allocated memory location. The location address is normally transparent and not important for manipulating the value of a simple integer variable. However, an address value of the allocated storage word can be derived from the declared name (i.e., variable name) by prefixing the symbol '***&***'. For example, if ***K*** is declared as an integer variable, then ***&K*** is the address of its storage location. Meaning, ***K*** refers to the frame that holds the current value in the location whose address is ***&K***. The symbol ***&K*** represents an address constant, and cannot be used as a variable name for assigning a new address value. The structure of a variable is shown in ***Fig. 3.4***.

**Declare a variable K:**

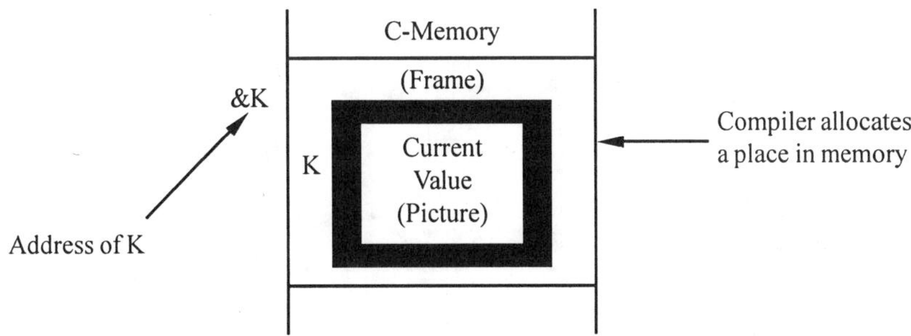


*Fig 3.4 Variable structure*

> ***Remark:*** *When we refer to the current value of a variable (not only in C, but also in any other programming language), we can use its name. In the above example, when K is assigned with a value, then it represents the currently assigned value when used in any expression except on the left hand side of an assignment operator. We should say that "K is this value or holds this value," but it is wrong to say that "K contains the current value." In fact, &K contains the current value.*

## 3.3 Temporal Aspects of Variables

With ANSI-C compiler, we are allowed to declare variables with temporal characteristics in order to improve the efficiency of data structures. According to temporal characteristics, C-Variables can be classified into three types: ***synchronous variables***, ***asynchronous variables*** and ***constant variables***.

A synchronous variable can only change its associated value through assignments at the specified or synchronous points in the programs. In-between two assignments, the value of a variable never changes and, hence, the consistency of the value is maintained in any reference to that variable in that interval. An asynchronous variable is one which represents a resource owned by the system, changing its value depending upon the state of that resource. Programs cannot assume that its value can be the same as in last reference. On the other hand, a constant variable is one whose value can only be read, but not rewritten, after initialization. They are also called read-only variables.

In order to associate a temporal characteristic with a variable, the declaration format expects an appropriate qualifier along with the type specifier. An ***asynchronous*** variable can be declared by associating the ***volatile*** qualifier; a ***constant*** variable can be declared by associating the ***const*** qualifier; and a ***synchronous*** or a normal variable can be declared by not associating with any of these two qualifiers. ***Figures 3.5*** and ***3.6*** show the memory maps for asynchronous and constant variables, respectively. This concept is further discussed in the following section.

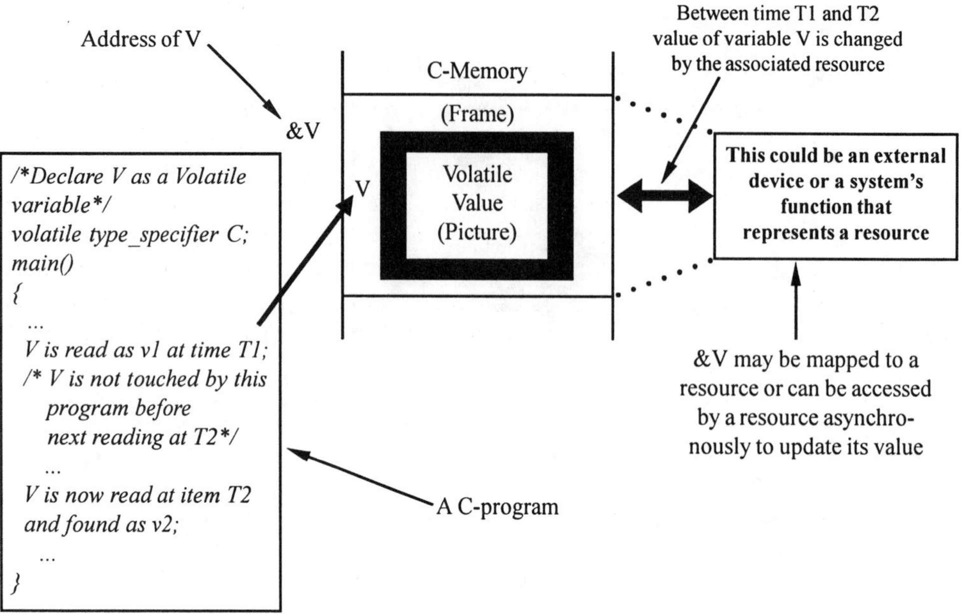


*Fig 3.5 Structure of asynchronous (or volatile) variable*

> ***Remark:*** *This temporal characteristic is different from the scope of a variable, which will be explained in a later chapter.*

## Declare K as a Constant Variable: *const type_specifier K*

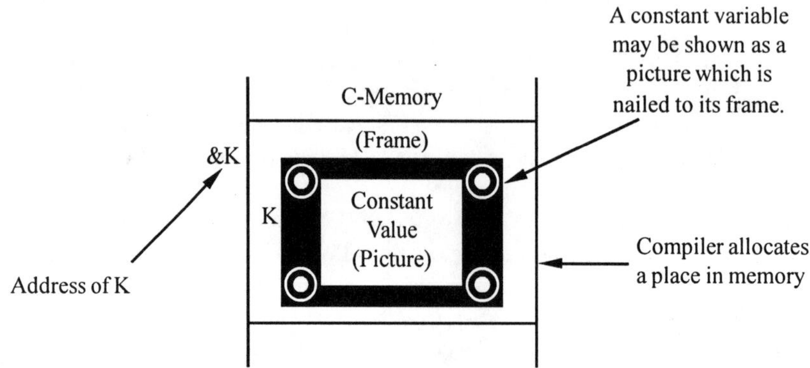


*Fig 3.6 Structure of constant variable*

## 3.4 Meaning of Declarations

According to a compiler, a variable must be declared before it is used in the program statements. The term declaration is used more generally to mean either a variable is created to exist in memory or it would eventually come into existence. The former is properly called a definition of a variable, while the latter is referred to as a declaration. Defining a variable is merely creating a variable of specified type in the memory. On the other hand, declaring a variable is simply re-declaring the already defined variable. During the compilation process, a compiler checks whether the variables that are used in a program are declared or not. It expects the definitions of all declared variables during the final pass in which the actual binary code is produced. The reader should note that the terms "definition" and "declaration" are used interchangeably, although there is a difference between them.

> ***Remark:*** *In general, a variable or function definition may mean that the compiler allocates memory for the object to exist in the program address space. On the other hand, a declaration may mean a reference to an already created object.*

## 3.5 Types of Variables in ANSI-C

The data types in ANSI-C can be broadly grouped into ***simple*** and ***abstract*** as listed below:

**(i) Simple Types**

(a) ***int*** denotes ***integer type specifier***:

e.g.

*int i; /* i is an integer variable; signed by default */*

(See ***Chapter 8*** for more details on various types of integer declarations.)

(b) ***float*** denotes ***real type specifier***:

e.g.

*float f; /* f is a real variable */*

(See ***Chapter 8*** for more details on real declarations.)

(c) ***double*** denotes ***double precision real type specifier***:

e.g.

*double d; /* d is also a real variable, but with more precision */*

(See ***Chapter 8*** for more details on real declarations.)

(d) ***char*** denotes ***character type specifier***:

e.g.

*char ch; /* ch is a character variable */*

(See ***Chapter 10*** for more details on character declarations.)

**Syntax of Simple Type Specifier:**

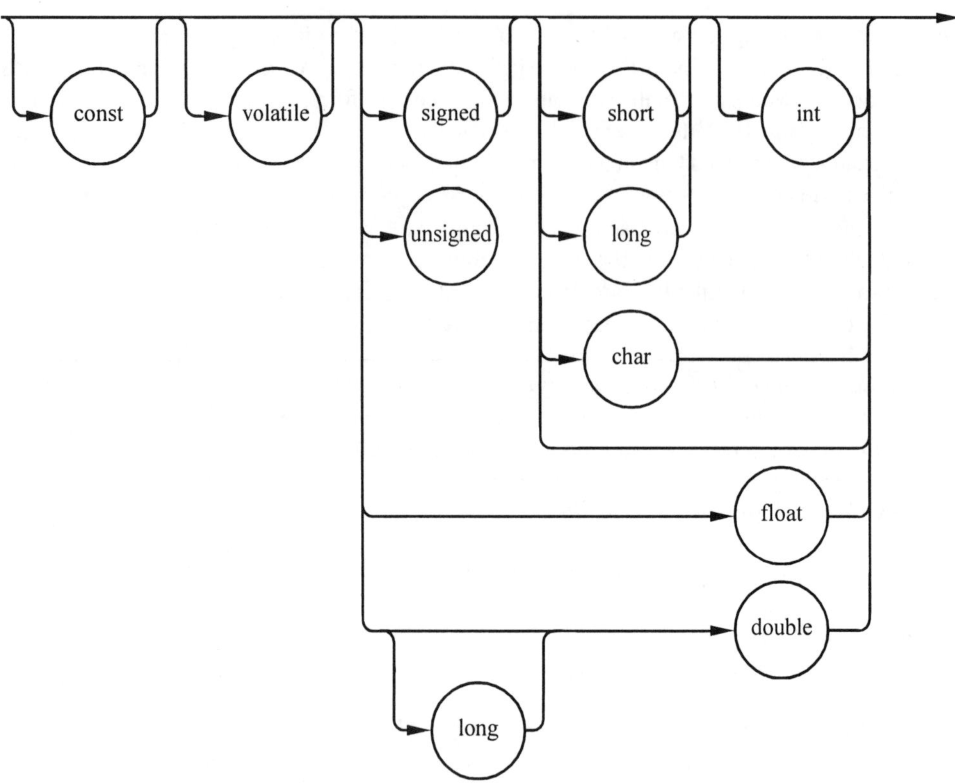


**(ii) Abstract (or Composite Data) Type:**

(a) ***struct {}*** denotes ***structure type specifier***.

e.g.

```
struct
    {
      int    i;
      float f;
      char  ch;
    } str;   /* str is defined as a structure variable   */
```

(See ***Chapter 15*** for more details on struct declarations.)

(b) ***union*** denotes ***union type specifier***.

e.g.

```
union
   {
      int     i;
      float f;
   } u;    /* u is a union variable    */
```

(See ***Chapter 15*** for more details on union declarations.)

(c) ***enum*** denotes ***enumeration type specifier***.

e.g.

*enum    day   {Monday, Tuesday, . . . , Sunday};*

where ***day*** is an enumerated variable that can take values from Monday to Sunday.

(See ***Chapter 15*** for more details on enum declarations.)

(d) ***void*** denotes ***Empty type specifier***. This type of variable maintains an empty set of values.

*e.g.*

```
void funct(void) /* function neither receives a parameter nor returns a value*/
   {
      function text;
   }
```

(See next chapter for more details on function with ***void*** declarations.)

(e) ***type_specifier **** denotes ***address or pointer type specifier***:

e.g.

```
char      *pch;    /* pch is address variable of char type                    */
int       *pi;     /* pi is address variable of int type                      */
float     *pf;     /* pf is address variable of real type                     */
double    *pd;     /* pd is address variable of double precisionreal type */
void      *p;      /* p is address variable of generic type                   */
```

Note that a pointer variable is capable of holding the address of a created data object. It is similar to hardware index registers provided in a CPU to hold memory addresses. (See ***Chapter 12*** for more details on pointer declarations.)

**Syntax of Composite Type Specifier:**

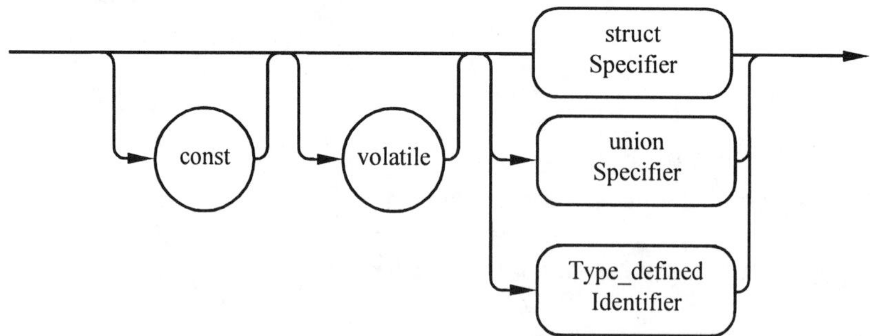


In addition to these types, ANSI C provides a set of ***qualifiers*** to refine the characteristics of objects being declared. The qualifiers that can be placed before to the int types are listed below:

- ***signed***
- ***unsigned***
- ***short***
- ***long***
- ***const***
- ***volatile***

The first four of these qualifiers are, in general, used with the ***integer*** type declarations. The significance of these qualifiers is explained in ***Chapter 8***. The ***const*** and ***volatile*** qualifiers can be used with any of the basic type specifiers to declare ***read-only*** type of variables and asynchronous variables, respectively. The following sections explain the significance of these two qualifiers.

## 3.6 The const Variables

In ***K&R C***, a symbolic literal or a constant can be declared using the define macro facility. Such symbolic constants make programs more readable. These constants become part of machine instructions after compilation. In the same manner, PASCAL provides a ***const*** declaration type to declare symbolic literals. The ***const*** construct in ANSI-C is quite different. ANSI-C provides the ***const*** declaration to qualify the created variables as ***read-only*** objects. Also, it allows proper typing of ***const*** objects.

The ***const*** qualifier is used along with any basic type declaration in the following format:

***const <type_specifier> <identifier list with initialization>***

**Examples:**

(a) ***const*** int TRUE = 1, FALSE = 0; /* TRUE and FALSE are created as read-only integer objects */

(b) ***const*** float PI= 3.14; /* PI is created as read-only real object */

(c) ***const*** double PI= 3.14; /* PI is created as read-only double object */

(d) ***const*** char NEWLINE='\n'; /* NEWLINE is created as read-only character object */

### 3.6.1 Significance of Read-Only Data Representation

Certain applications require a data declaration facility to create data objects of read-only type using the ***const*** qualifier. For example, an assembler program maintains the machine instruction table as reference data while assembling symbolic instructions. If this table is corrupted by one of the functions of the program, then the assembled output may have incorrect binary code. Since this table is used purely for references, a programmer would normally think that this is a read-only table (although it was not declared so) and, hence, would not suspect any occurrence of overwritten data in this table. This would lead to a costly debugging process. Similarly, compiler programs maintain the keyword tables and instruction tables that are purely used as reference information during the compilation processes. For such programs, it may be necessary to maintain these tables as read-only objects. If any function tries to overwrite a read-only table (or read-only data object), the compiler can easily trap such situations. The ***const*** qualifier is often useful to declare variables as read-only data objects.

Read-only data is also useful in guarding variables that are passed as parameters to functions. When a function needs only value parameters, pass them as read-only parameters so that the function is prohibited from rewriting to those variables. In fact, this facility helps programmers to implement their functions with proper behavior in an imported environment.

## 3.7 Significance of Volatile Qualifier

Basically, programs are written to process application data. To hold this data, a program declares some variables. As discussed before, the modifiable type of variables can be classified as synchronous and asynchronous. The synchronous variables are explicitly assigned before applied to any expression evaluation. For example, a program may be written to sum up to 10, as shown below:

```
void main(void)
{
   int    i, sum;        /* declare i and sum as integer variables */
   int  TEN = 10;        /*TEN is a synchronous variable and it holds the assigned value, 10,
                           until next explicit assignment */
    sum = 0;             /* sum, too, is a synchronous variable */
    while(i <= TEN)      /* the following block of statements until i is less than or equal to 10 */
      {
        sum = sum + 1;
        i = i + 1;
      }
}
```

Since *TEN* is a synchronous variable, its value can be changed only by an explicit assignment expression. Similarly, *i* and *sum* are also synchronous variables and are explicitly assigned with new values at specific places in the program. In the above program, after the initial assignment, the value of *TEN* is 10 and maintains the same value until the next assignment with a different value. Since there is no further assignment to *TEN*, its value will be 10 until the end of the program execution. When an optimizing compiler translates this program, it detects that *TEN* is not assigned anywhere in the scope of the while-loop and decides to keep the *TEN* value in a CPU-register for comparing with the changing *i* value at the beginning of every iteration. The while-loop will perform correctly whether *i* is compared with the *TEN* value directly from the memory location, &TEN, or the copied-value in a register. However, the compiler assumes register operation is faster than memory operation.

On the other hand, a variable may represent a dynamic data object, in which case it is subjected to change implicitly with respect to time. We already mentioned that such a variable is called ***asynchronous*** or ***volatile***. Unless this property is not known to a compiler, the optimized machine code produced by that compiler would create a different result. For example, let us write a program which declares an asynchronous variable and uses the same in controlling, as shown below:

```
void main(void)
{
   TIMER   time; /* Declare time as a timer */
    time = 0;     /* Reset the time variable */
    while(time <= 10)
     {
      printf( " %d \n", time);
     }
}
```

In this case, the compiler detects from the written code that the ***time*** variable is not altered within the scope of the while-loop and, hence, decides to keep the time value in a register simply to improve the speed of comparison operation. On the one hand, the programmer assumed that the loop will use the current value of the ***time*** variable, which is, in fact, updated by the associated timer resource. On the other hand, since the declaration of time does not show that it is an asynchronous or volatile variable, the compiler translates it as if the value of ***time*** is not going to change in the loop. The result is an infinite while-loop.

To avoid this undesirable effect, the ***volatile*** qualifier is introduced by ANSI-C. Programs should declare asynchronous variables with this qualifier to prompt the compiler for correct translation. The compiler would make the translated code to use the time value directly from the memory location for every comparison in the while-loop. The ***volatile*** qualifier assures that the comparison uses the current time value. (See the example below.)

```
void main(void)
 {
   volatile TIMER time;
     time = 0;    /* clear the time variable */
     while(time <= 10)
      {
       printf( " %d \n", time);
      }
 }
```

## 3.8 Meaning and Evaluation of Expressions

Most of the calculations in a statement involve evaluation of expressions or subexpressions in a predefined order. An expression represents the evaluated value of a meaningful combination of data objects and operators. Data objects, in general, comprise constants, variables or functions. Expression evaluation is done in two steps. In the first step, the compiler translates the given expressions into a sequence of steps in the machine language form using a set of rules. In the second step, the translated code is executed during run time to produce the value of the given expression. The translating rules, such as ***left to right*** or ***right to left*** and ***operator precedence***, order the evaluation steps so the resulting value of an expression is always consistent.

Since the evaluation of an expression progresses step by step, starting from a subexpression in a recursive manner, the evaluated value of each step must be kept in temporary storage called an accumulator, which can then be used as one of the values of the next subexpression. Once the evaluation is completed, the final value of the given expression is always left in the accumulator. This final value can be printed or used indirectly to control the statement flow. This concept is followed in every C-expression evaluation. For the purpose of binary branching in a statement, the nature of the accumulated value after every subexpression must be automatically reflected by a simple boolean value (1 for any positive or negative value; 0 for zero accumulated value) in a separate status register. This concept explains that testing the status register for 0 or 1 is easier than a signed value in the accumulator.

Since C provides a rich set of expressions, a C-programmer must understand the meaning of each expression clearly. For this purpose, the concept of virtual C-machine architecture, with an expression evaluator based on the above concepts, has been derived, as shown in ***Fig. 3.4***. We will later discover the effective use of this virtual machine in understanding some of the unique features of C-expressions. The diagram in ***Fig. 3.7*** is the expanded version of the *C-Virtual Machine* shown in ***Fig. 1.7*** of ***Chapter 1*** and ***Fig 2.5*** of ***Chapter 2***.

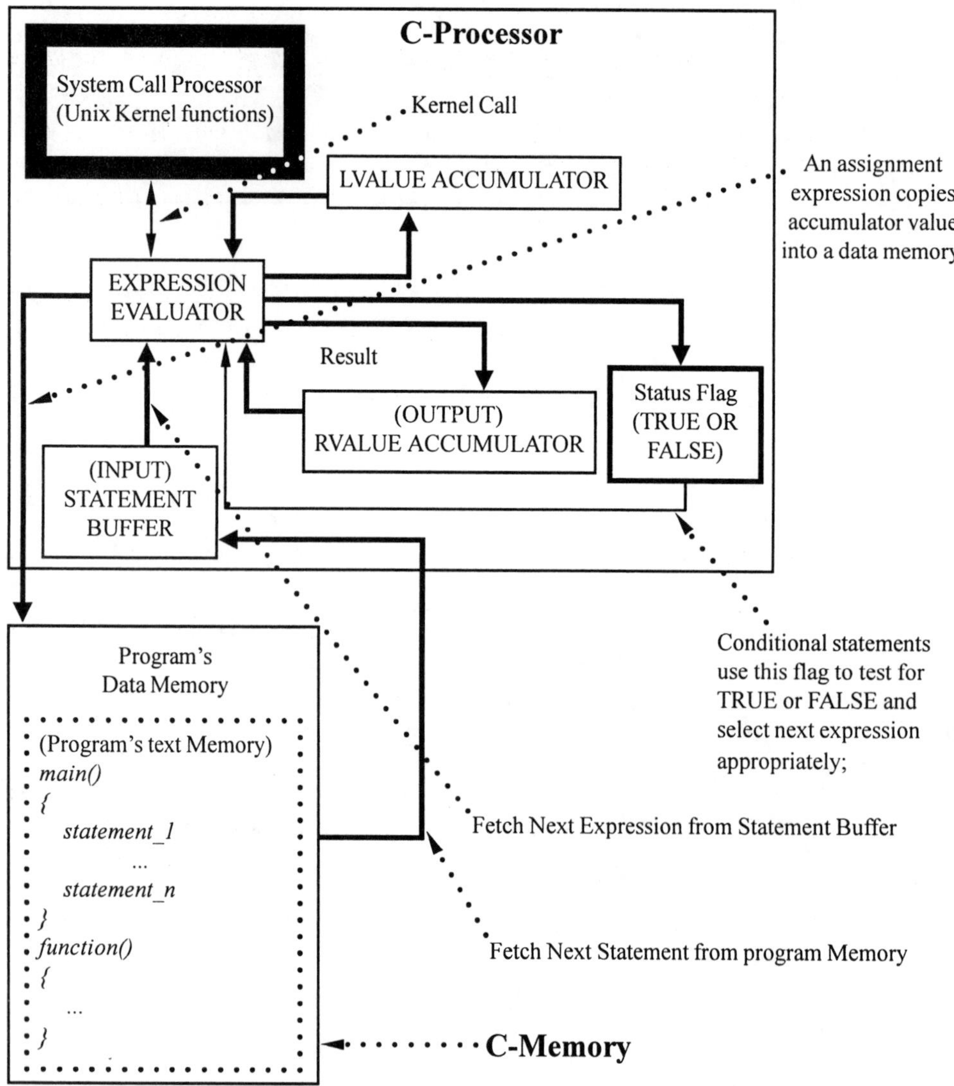


*Fig. 3.7 Expression evaluation unit of the C-virtual machine*

This virtual machine has a memory, ***C-memory***, to store a C-program and a virtual processor, ***C-Processor***, to execute C-statements. The C-processor consists of the following components:

- *an **expression evaluator** to process the expressions of a statement in a sequential manner;*
- *a set of **functional processors** to execute functions from the included libraries;*
- *an **input buffer** to hold a current statement that is being executed;*
- *an **rvalue accumulator** to accumulate the value of the expressions that occur in the **Right Hand Side** of an assignment statement;*
- *an **lvalue accumulator** to accumulate the value of expressions that occur in the **Left Side** of an assignment statement;*
- *a **status flag** to indicate the Boolean status (i.e., **TRUE** or **FALSE**) of the current value in the **rvalue accumulator**.*

The details of the C-processor (or C virtual machine) are transparent to a C-programmer. As mentioned before, an expression is a combination of subexpressions (or simply other expressions) with the use of operators. In the process of evaluating such compound expressions, the accumulator is used to hold the updated result of the previous subexpression at every stage. For example,

5 + 8;

is a simple binary expression statement. In this case, if we proceed from left to right:

- *5 is a subexpression, say E1, whose value is evaluated as 5 and stored in the rvalue accumulator; then*
- *accumulator (E1)+ 8 is the next expression whose value is evaluated as 13 and stored in the accumulator.*

Then the end of the statement indicates that the accumulators must be cleared and the next statement from the program text memory is to be fetched. This is shown in ***Fig. 3.8***.

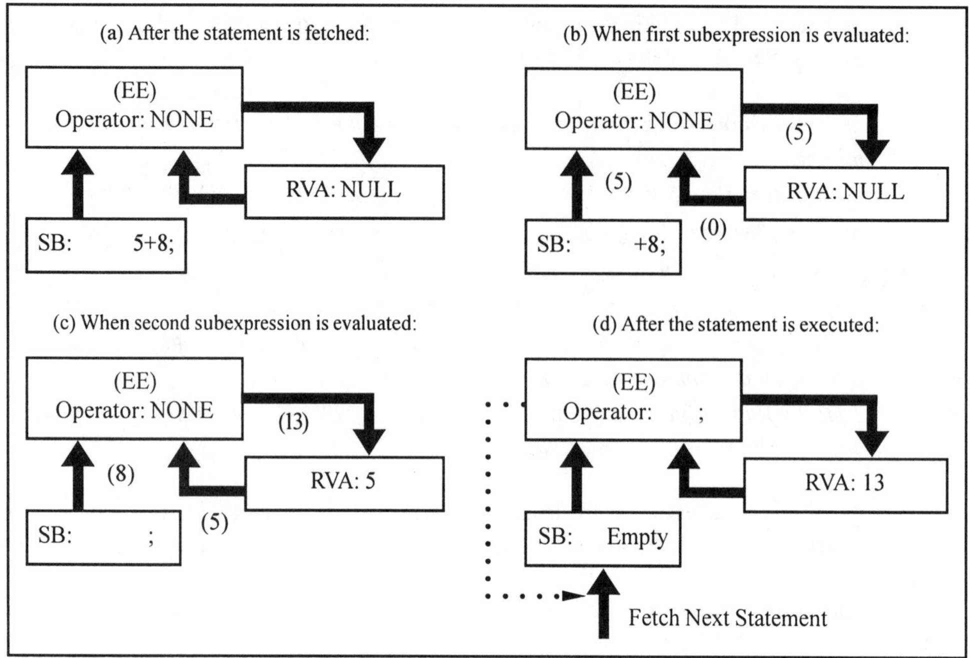


SB: Statement Buffer, EE: Expression Evaluator, RVA: RValue Accumulator.

*Fig. 3.8 Execution of expression statement in CVM*

Since the statement is finished with the evaluation of this expression, the accumulator is reallocated for the next statement. At the start of next statement, the accumulator contents will be NULL. Of course, after processing the statement, we didn't save (or use) the result, and effectively the statement execution is quite meaningless. Hence, to save or use the accumulated result, the assignment expression, or a functional expression, comes into picture. The following expressions are more meaningful:

```
K = ( 5 + 8);
printf("%d ", 5+8);
```

In the assignment statement shown above, the accumulated right hand side value (also called rvalue) in the rvalue accumulator is assigned to K. In the next statement, the ***printf()*** function receives the accumulator value (i.e., 5+8) as one of its arguments. ***Fig. 3.9*** shows evaluation of the first assignment expression in the virtual machine. We will discuss the types of objects, operators and expressions in the following sections.

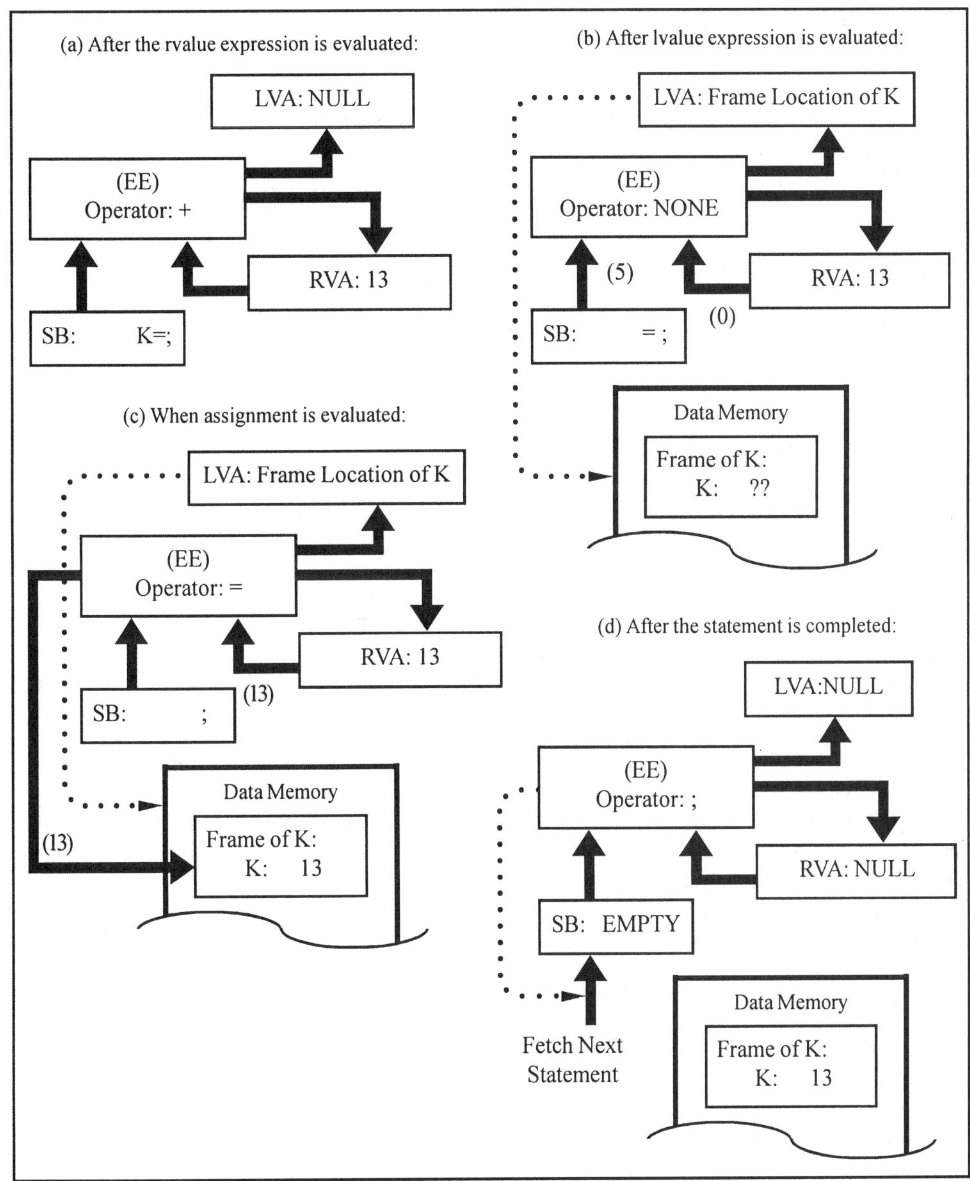


*Fig. 3.9 Evaluation of assignment expression (k=5+8)*

## 3.9 Types of Operators

C provides a rich set of operators, broadly classified into ***unary***, ***binary***, ***ternary*** and other special types, such as comma type operators. A ***unary*** operator requires *one operand*, a ***binary*** operator requires *two operands* and a ***ternary*** operator requires *three operands,* as shown below:

1. ***Unary operators:*** A unary operator is meant to manipulate the value of a given operand. Such manipulations include negation of an integer, negation of a boolean value, incrementing or decrementing the numerical operands, converting one type of numerical operand into another type of numerical operand, etc. The unary operators in C are:

| Unary operator | Description |
|---|---|
| + | Unary Plus |
| - | Unary Minus: Negation operator used to invert a given numerical value |
| & | Address expression operator |
| * | Indirection operator used normally with a pointer variable |
| ~ | Bitwise negation used normally with a unsigned integer variable |
| ! | NOT operator, used normally with a discrete variable for testing |
| cast | To convert one type of numeric value to another type |
| sizeof | To find out the memory size of a variable or type |
| ++ and -- | Increment and decrement operators used to move the pointers along an array of data or to maintain counters |

**Examples:**

```
int  x = -100;               /* the given value (i.e., 100) is negated and then assigned */

int  x = +200;               /* unary plus does not alter the value of the expression */

int  *pi = &K;               /* address of the variable K is assigned */

unsigned m = ~0xffff;        /* complement of the given binary pattern, assigned to m */

int  flag = 0;               /* flag is set to false */
if (!flag) { statements; }   /* if-statement tests whether the flag is true */

float  f;
int K = (int)f;              /* convert float value into integer type value before assigning */
```

```
sizeof f;            /* returns the memory size of float variable   */

sizeof(double);      /* returns the size of memory allocated to double type */
++ptr;               /* pointer value is incremented by one */
—ctr;                /* counter value is decremented by one */
```

2. ***Binary operators:*** Binary operators are the basic mechanisms to build expressions and statements in a program. These operators are explained in Sections 3.10.5 to 3.10.7 under various types of logical expressions.

| | | |
|---|---|---|
| + - | additive operators | e.g. x + y , a - b |
| * / % | multiplicative operators | e.g. x * y , a / b, m % n |
| & \| ^ | bit-wise operators | e.g. x & y , a \| b , m ^ n |
| && \|\| | logical operators | e.g. x && y , a \|\| b |
| == != | equality operators | e.g. x == y , a != b |
| < > <= >= | relational operators | e.g. x > y , a < b, m >= n, p <= q |
| >> << | bit-shift operators | e.g. x >> nbits , a << mbits |
| = | assignment operator | e.g. x = y |
| =+ =- =* =/ | composite arithmetic operators | e.g. x =+ y |

3. ***Ternary operator:*** The ternary operator is useful to select one of target expressions based on the true or false value of a a given test expression. It is similar to an if-statement except for its cryptic form. A detailed explanation is given in ***Section 3.10.8***.

*operand_1 ? operand_2 : operand_3;*

```
x>y?   printf("%d", x) : printf("%d",y) ;  /* if x is larger than y, print x else print y  */
```

4. ***Comma ( , ) operator:*** The comma operator helps to construct a statement with a sequence or a block of expressions. A more detailed explanation is given in ***Section 3.10.9***.

e.g. *a = 10, b = 20, c = a*b;*

The first two types are similar to operators available in other programming languages. However, some operators are unique to C. For example, binary operators like bit-wise, composite arithmetic operators, etc.; unary operators like cast, sizeof, increment, decrement, etc.; as well as the ternary operator and comma operator. A summary of operators that are used in expressions are shown in ***Table A.2*** in Appendix A.

## 3.10 Types of Expressions

In general, an expression in C can belong to any one of the following:

1. *simple expression.*
2. *arithmetic expression.*
3. *assignment expression.*
4. *multiple assignment expression.*
5. *equality and relational expression.*
6. *bit-wise operation expression*
7. *logical comparison expression*
8. *ternary expression.*
9. *comma expression.*
10. *sizeof expression.*
11. *cast expression.*
12. *mixed expression.*
13. *void expression.*

The syntax of these expressions are explained in ***Chapter 6***.

### 3.10.1 Simple Expression

A simple expression is one which contains a single object with an operator. The following examples show the meaning of a simple expression.

```
i++ ;                  /* variable i with an incremental operator   */
i— ;                   /* variable i with a decremental operator    */
puts("a_string") ;     /* a string constant with functional operator */
```

### 3.10.2 Arithmetic Expression

An arithmetic expression provides for arithmetic processing of the values of variable and constant parameters. This type of expression usually consists of integer or real values linked by allowed operators. Since the semantics of unary and binary operators are quite distinct and, moreover, as each operator in each type has a distinct meaning, evaluation of an arithmetic expression requires careful interpretation. For this reason, the operators are given certain priority (called precedence) levels which in turn dictate the order of the evaluation process to maintain consistency.

## Operator Precedence and Associativity Rules

Expressions with multiple operations can sometimes lead to more than one interpretation and, hence, different results might be obtained for the same expression. For example,

10+10/5

could be interpreted as either

(10+10)/5 which results to 4,

or 10+(10/5) which results to 12.

These two interpretations result in different values. Similarly, another expression with the division and the multiplication operator,

100/10*5

could also be interpreted as either

(100/10)*5 resulting to 50,

or (100/(10*5) resulting to 2.

If the structure of an expression is not clearly defined, compilers, not knowing the intention of the programmer can produce the machine code (that operates) in an unexpected manner. This will lead to unpredictable results during program execution. One way to resolve this crisis is to explicitly add parenthesis wherever an ambiguous interpretation might result. If the expression 10 + 10/5 is written as (10 + 10)/5, then the compiler understands the significance of parenthesis and it evaluates the subexpression inside the parenthesis first, as the programmer expected. On the other hand, compilers may implicitly adopt two rules: operator precedence and associativity.

The operator precedence rule helps to resolve situations in which an expression contains different types of operators, whereas the associativity rule is applied when more than one operator of the same level of precedence appears in an expression. In general, C-compilers maintain a table (with all allowed operators) describing these two rules (as shown in ***Table 3.1***) in order to resolve ambiguities in expressions.

*Table 3.1 Precedence and associativity rule for base or arithmetic operators*

| | precedence | associativity |
|---|---|---|
| high | () i.e., parenthesis and [ ] i.e., brackets | left to right |
| ↑ | * / % | left to right |
| low | + - | left to right |

Considering the example, 10+10/5, the compiler will evaluate 10/5 first and then the addition operation. (Note that the division operator has higher precedence than the addition operator.) Similarly, the expression *i+j*(k-p)/100* will be evaluated as follows:

| | | | |
|---|---|---|---|
| step 1: | (k-p) | as e1 | parenthesis has the highest precedence; |
| step 2: | j*e1 | as e2 | ' * ' has the next highest precedence; |
| step 3: | e2/100 | as e3 | / has same precedence as *; but left to right specifies * can be evaluated first. |
| step 4: | i+e3 | as e4 | i.e., the final value; '+' has the lowest precedence of the operators in this expression |

> ***Note:*** *A complete table of precedence and associativity for all operators is shown in Appendix A.*

### 3.10.3 The Assignment Expression

The assignment operation is commonly applied to simple objects of character, integer (signed and unsigned), float (i.e., real) and pointer types. The assignment operator in C is '='. The purpose of an assignment is to catch the evaluated value of an expression on the right side of '=' in the variable, or the effective reference value of an expression, specified on the left side. The expression on the right side of the operator is called an *rvalue* expression (or simply *rvalue*) and the expression on the left side is called an *lvalue* expression (or simply *lvalue*). The format of the assignment expression and its meaning is shown in ***Fig. 3.10***.

Most calculations involve evaluation of expressions and, as we have already mentioned, the evaluated results are normally available in an internal accumulator. Such intermediate results are available only during the evaluation/processing of the statements in which expressions occur. Simply, the evaluated result (from the internal accumulator) is assigned to a variable or lvalue in an assignment operation. We may also state that the value of an assignment expression is simply its rvalue (or the current value of the accumulator).

> ***Remark:***
> *From the basic definition of assignment, an lvalue expression should yield a result or reference value which is capable of holding a value that results from an rvalue expression.*

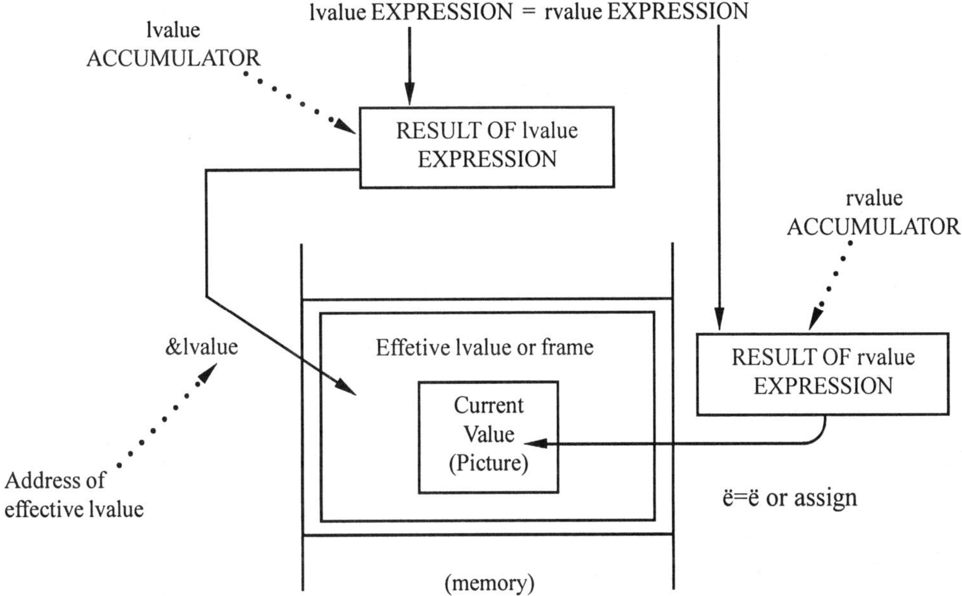


*Fig. 3.10 Evaluation of assignment expression*

## The Meaning of rvalue and lvalue

An expression in the right side of an assignment operator can be an arithmetic, logical, comparison, assignment or any other legal expression, always yielding an ***rvalue*** (or data) that corresponds to a picture of a variable. An ***lvalue*** (i.e., left side expression of assignment operator) is evaluated as reference to an object of variable type. It is equivalent to a frame of a variable which can be attached (or assigned) with a picture (or rvalue). (Recall our framed-picture interpretation of a variable object described in the beginning of this chapter.) This type of memory addressing is also called ***frame addressable***.

**Example 3.4:** Let us consider a simple assignment expression as shown below:

int X = 0 where X is a variable of integer type.

The effective value of the ***lvalue*** expression (in this case, it is simply X) represents the frame of the variable X to which the effective value of the ***rvalue*** expression (i.e., the value 0) is assigned.

**Example 3.5**: Let us consider another assignment expression where the variable X occurs in both the ***lvalue*** and ***rvalue*** expressions as shown below:

X = X + 1

As in the previous case, the ***lvalue*** expression contains only one ***lvalue*** parameter, i.e., X, while its effective value is the frame of X. The ***rvalue*** expression contains one variable parameter (i.e., X) and one constant parameter (i.e., the value 1). The effective value of this expression is calculated by adding 1 to the value of X. In this case, X is treated as a value parameter (i.e., reference to its picture).

### Syntax of lvalue:

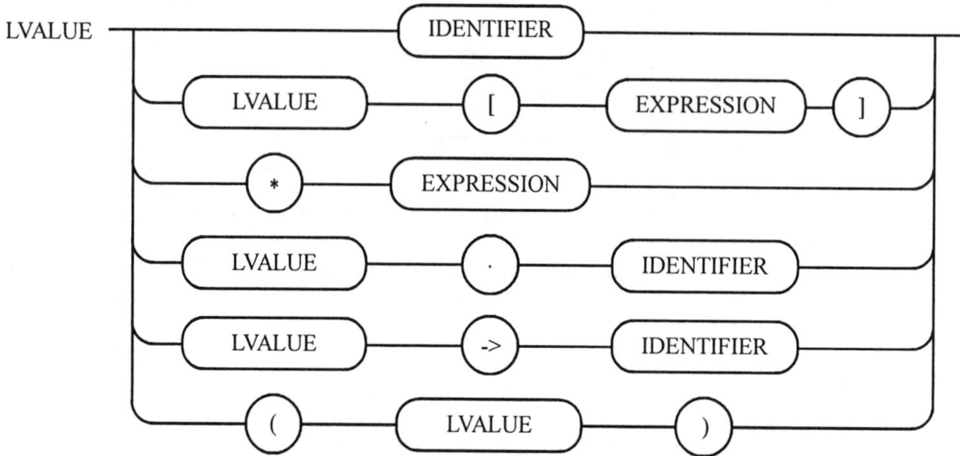


In the previous examples, we encountered *lvalue* expressions containing only a variable. We will now encounter an *lvalue* expression containing arithmetic and some complex expressions.

**Example 3.6:** A typical *lvalue* expression with indirect reference operators could exist when we refer a variable with the help of address references. (To understand more about these *lvalue* expressions, turn to the chapter on pointers, ***Chapter 12***). In this example, let us consider a simple assignment expression with an integer variable, K, as shown below:

```
K = 2 + 8/4;
```

Since the address of K is &K, we can show an expression which is equivalent to the above as

```
*&K = 2 + 8/4;
```

The *lvalue* expression, *&K, is evaluated as K, having a frame to which the value of the *rvalue* expression is assigned. This is shown in ***Fig. 3.11***.

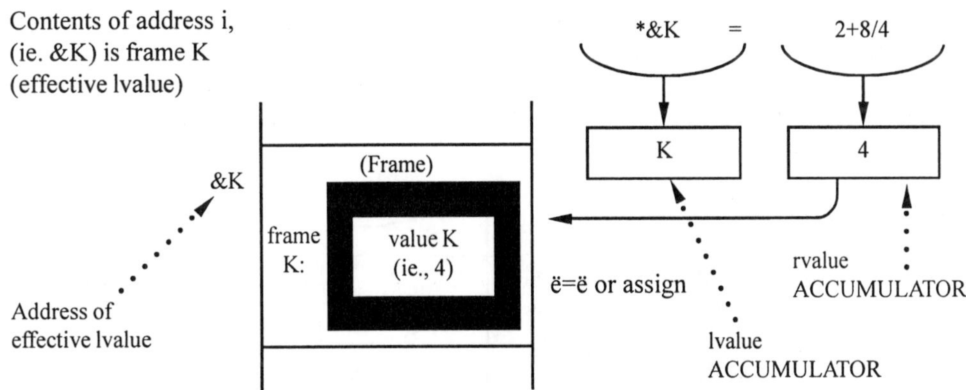


*Fig. 3.11 Evaluation of indirect type lvalue-expression*

> ***Remark:*** *An asterisk before an address variable denotes indirect reference. That is, the expression, *&K, is interpreted as "the contents of the address &K".*

**Example 3.7:** Let us consider a third example where both the lvalue and rvalue expressions contain arithmetic. This is shown in ***Fig. 3.12***.

```
int     I, J;              /* declare I and J as adjacent integers  */
*(&I + 1) = 2 + 8/2;       /* assign the evaluated rvalue to J indirectly  */
```

In our example, we can assume that the variables I and J occupy adjacent memory locations as shown in Figure 3.9. Hence, their memory addresses are &I and &J (or &I and &I+1), respectively. Now, in the lvalue expression (i.e., *(&I+1) ), &I is the address of I and &I+1 is the address of the next location, which is same as the address of J (i.e., &J). This partially evaluated expression results to *(&J). Effectively, further evaluation of the lvalue expresision has led to the variable parameter J, which is really a legal lvalue (i.e., a frame or an assignable entity). Now the derived lvalue expression is I2 and the equivalent arithmetic expression is I2 = 2+8/4 which is quite legal.

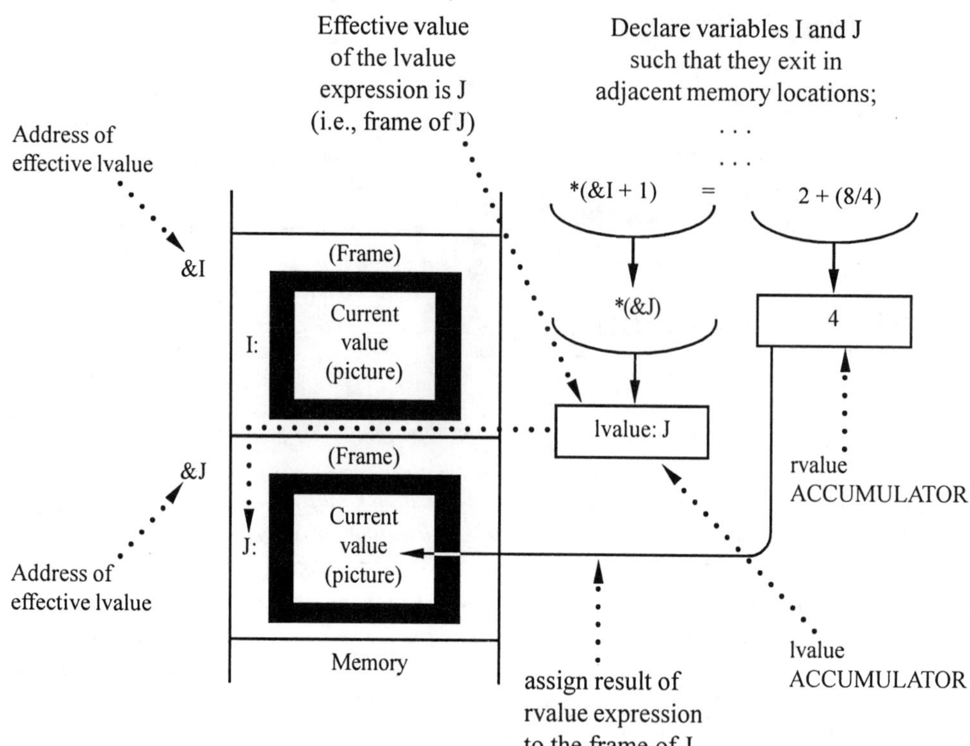


*Fig. 3.12 Evaluation of arithmetic type lvalue-expression*

**Example 3.8:** Let us show some illegal lvalue expressions.

```
int    i = 10;        /*  declare i as an integer with the initial value, 10  */
       100 = i;       /*  Case 1  */
       i + 1 = 100;   /*  Case 2  */
```

In Case 1, lvalue expression yields a value parameter (i.e., 100, which is not a frame) and, hence, it cannot be assigned with an rvalue. In Case 2, the lvalue expression (i.e., *i*+1) is evaluated as 11, which is also a value parameter (simply a picture, but not a frame). In both cases, the lvalues are illegal and cannot hold values.

From the above examples, we conclude that

- *Both **lvalue** and **rvalue** expressions may contain both variable and constant parameters; **rvalue** expression results to an rvalue which is simply a value parameter. However, an **lvalue** expression results to a value that should yield an **lvalue** (i.e., a reference parameter).*
- *The compiler interprets the effective value of an **lvalue** expression as a frame and the effective value of an **rvalue** expression as a picture.*

### 3.10.4 Multiple Assignment Expression

A multiple assignment expression is one which consists of multiple expressions that are separated by assignment operators. A multiple assignment expression is evaluated from right to left. When we write an expression, I = 0, the effective value of the rvalue expression is accumulated first and then assigned to the frame I. The rvalue accumulator still retains its value as the effective value of the assignment and it can be further used to assign to another lvalue and so on. ***Figure 3.13*** shows the evaluation of a multiple assignment expression to initialize variables I and J. Since the value of the expression, J = I = 0, is still available in the rvalue accumulator, this expression can be extended to assign further variables. Note that at the end of statement (i.e., once the statement delimiter ';' is encountered), the contents of both lvalue and rvalue accumulators will be lost and the accumulators will be emptied, leaving them ready to accumulate the values of the expressions in the next statement.

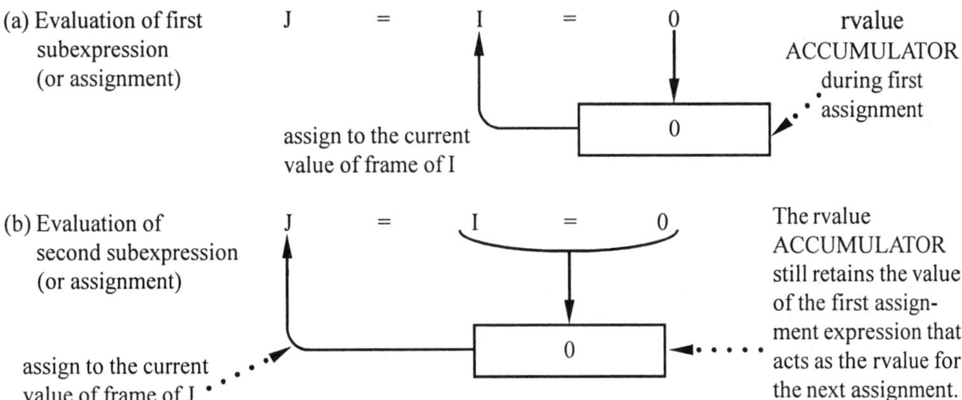


*Fig. 3.13 Evaluation of multiple assignment expression*

### 3.10.5 Equality and Relational Expression

An equality or a relational expression is also a binary operation, but the evaluated result is always interpreted as either TRUE (i.e., a non-zero value) or FALSE (i.e., a zero value). For example, the expression

A == B

is testing for equality of two operands (i.e., A and B). It is evaluated by performing

A - B

and testing this result for non-zero or zero condition (See **Fig. 3.14**). That is, if A - B is zero, then a true value (i.e., 1) will be stored in the **Expression Status Flag**; otherwise, a false value (i.e., 0) will be stored. (Recall the C-virtual machine shown in **Fig. 3.7**.) Then, this boolean result stored in this condition flag is used for directing the further execution of a control statement in which this conditional expression occurs.

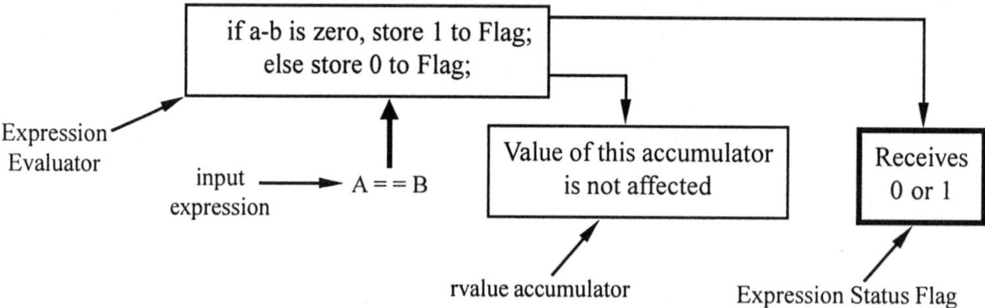


*Fig. 3.14 Evaluation of equality expression (recall C-machine from Figure 1.4)*

In the case of greater and lesser relational expressions like

case 1: A > B and
case 2: A<B

the evaluation is performed in a similar fashion. That is, after performing

A - B

the conditional result is stored in the ***Expression Status Flag*** for further use. When the subtracted result is positive, a value equivalent to true (i.e., 1) is stored in the ***Flag*** for case 1. In case 2, a negative result would cause a true value in the ***Flag***. Note that the contents of the accumulators will not be affected by these conditional expression evaluations.

### 3.10.6 Bitwise Logical Expressions

All bitwise operations come under this category. The bitwise ANDing, ORing, Exclusive ORing and shifting are binary operations, but the complement operation is unary.

**Examples:**

(i) A & B /* corresponding bits of A and B are ANDed and the result is saved in the rvalue accumulator */

(ii) A | B /* corresponding bits of A and B are ORed and the result is saved in the rvalue accumulator */

(ii) A ^ B /* corresponding bits of A and B are EXCLUSIVE-ORed and the result is saved in the rvalue accumulator */

(iii) A >>8 /* bits in A are SHIFTed to right 8 times and the result is saved in the rvalue accumulator */

(iv) A <<8 /* bits in A are SHIFTed to left 8 times and the result is saved in the rvalue accumulator */

(v) ~A /* bits of A are COMPLEMENTed and the result is saved in the rvalue accumulator */

### 3.10.7 Logical Comparison Expressions

The bitwise operations in this category are used to test the sets. That is, one can find out whether any one of the given sets is nonempty or all are non-empty sets.

**Examples:**

(i) A && B /* tests whether both A and B sets are non-empty */

(ii) A || B /* tests whether one of the given sets, A or B, is non-empty */

> ***Note:*** *The C-compiler does not provide macro definitions (i.e., TRUE and FALSE) for the true and false status of a result. Hence, C-coding should never use these symbols in their comparison expressions.*

### 3.10.8 Ternary Expression

A ternary expression is useful to test a given condition (or expression) and then select one of the two given values (or target expressions) as the effective value of this expression. The format is shown below:

***<test_expn> ? <target_expn_1> : <target_expn_2>***

The value of the test_expn is tested for true (any non-zero value) or false (zero value). If true, target_expn_1 will be evaluated. Otherwise, target_expn_2 will be evaluated (see ***Fig. 3.12***).

**Examples:**

(i) (A < B) ? printf("A smaller than B") : printf("A greater or equal to B")
(ii) (A = B) ? printf("A is not zero") : printf("A is zero")
(iii) (A == B) ? printf("A and B same") : printf("A is not same as B")

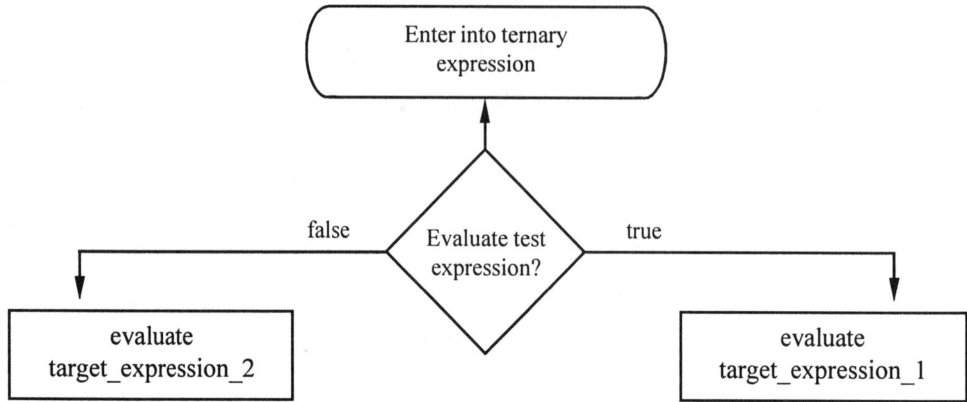


*Fig. 3.12 Meaning of ternary expression*

### 3.10.9 Comma Expression

Similar to the multiple assignment case, a comma expression is a multiple expression type. Here, expressions are delimited by the comma operator. The format of this expression is

*expression_1, expression_2, expression_3, . . . expression_n*

A ***comma*** expression is evaluated from left to right, and the value of the comma expression is the value of the last (i.e., the right_most) expression. Usually, a ***comma*** expression is used to put together a set of related expressions in a proper sequence. For example, finding the area of a circle can be accommodated in a comma expression as shown below:

*pi = 3.14, Radius = 10, Area = pi*power(Radius,2);*

The evaluation starts from the leftmost expression and ends with the rightmost. After each expression evaluation, the result in the rvalue accumulator is cleared. At the end of the above comma statement, the ***rvalue*** accumulator will have the value of area, or the value of the last comma expression in that statement.

> ***Remark:*** *In the above case, the rvalue accumulator contains the value of the comma expression, the statement can be extended either by assigning the contents of the accumulator to a variable or by comparing and branching according to a condition. Examples:*
>
> *(a) A = (pi = 3.14, radius = 10, area = pi*power(radius,2) );*
> *(b) A1 = A2 = (pi = 3.14, radius = 10, area = pi*power(radius,2) );*
> *(c) if (pi = 3.14, radius = 10, area = pi*power(radius,2) ) == 0.0)*
> *{. . .}*

> ***Note:*** *C does not provide an exponential operator; instead, the power() function is made available in the run-time library. It requires two operands as shown above.*

### 3.10.10 Sizeof Expression

The ***sizeof*** expression is used to get the amount of memory (in bytes) occupied by a declared object or the memory size required by a type of data structure. The formats for both cases are shown below:

**Format 1: sizeof** <expression>

***sizeof*** a (or) ***sizeof (a)*** will return the number of bytes required for storing the object a;
***sizeof*** 10000000 will return the number of bytes required for storing the constant object 10000000.

**Format 2: sizeof** (type_specifier_key word)

***sizeof(int)*** will return the number of bytes required for an integer type object;
***sizeof(float)*** will return the number of bytes required for a floating point type object.

### 3.10.11 Cast Expression

In general, C allows the mixing of various types of objects in an expression. The evaluation process of such expressions automatically takes care of converting ***all subtypes*** to an appropriate ***super type*** so that the result of the *rvalue* expression will be in a common ***super type***. Sometimes, we may like to force the evaluation to maintain a required type, rather than have a compiler selected super type. In such situations, the cast expression is quite useful. It forces a given object to the specified type. The format of the cast operation is shown below:

*(type_specifier_keyword) data_object*

```
int    k;
float x, y;
x = 10.0;
y = 20.0;
k = (int)x * (int)y      /* will convert the real values of x and y into integer type before
                          multiplication. */
```

### 3.10.12 Mixed Expression

When we mix different types of objects in an arithmetic expression, the compiler chooses a common super type to which objects are converted before evaluation is done. For example, consider the following mixed expression:

```
int  i=10;
float    f=20.0;
i = i+f;
```

In this expression, both integer and real values take part. Since ***float*** has a higher range and higher precision than ***int*** it is considered as the super type. Hence *i* is converted to a float type (i.e., integer 10 is converted into real 10.0) and then added with the value of *f*. The resulting real value is converted to an integer before it is assigned to the integer variable. In other words, the compiler treats the above expression implicitly as

```
i = (int) ((float)i+f);
```

In order to maintain the consistency of automatic conversion, a C-compiler follows a set of conventions as explained below:

(a) In general, the physical processor, or Central Processing Unit (i.e., CPU), of a computer system normally supports integer operations at integer or word level. If an arithmetic expression contains only ***signed char*** and ***short integer*** types, then all these values are promoted to ***int*** or ***signed int***. Similarly, all ***unsigned char*** and ***unsigned short*** types are promoted to ***unsigned int***. In other words, the minimum or standard machine executable type is normally integer. Smaller sized types are promoted to this type before arithmetic processing is carried out.

(b) When different types are mixed, the promotion from lower to a common super type is carried with the help of the type hierarchy as shown in ***Table 3.2***.

*Table 3.2 Type conversion precedence*

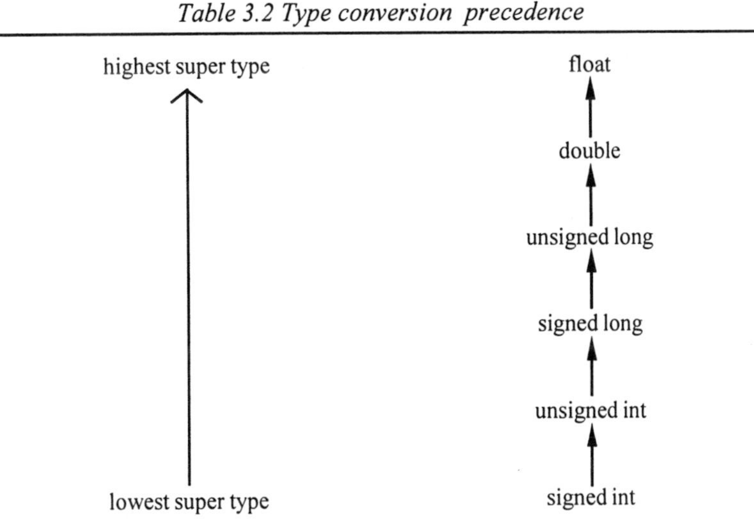


**Examples:**

| **Mixed Expression** | | **Evaluated type** |
|---|---|---|
| expression(char only) | → | expression(int) |
| expression(unsigned char only) | → | expression(unsigned int) |
| expression(short only) | → | expression(int) |
| expression(unsigned short only) | → | expression(unsigned int) |
| expression(short, int) | → | expression(int) |
| expression(short, int, long) | → | expression(long) |
| expression(int, long, float) | → | expression(float) |
| expression(int, long, float, double) | → | expression(double) |
| expression(float, double, long double) | → | expression(long double) |

### 3.10.13 Void Expression

An expression can be cast to ***void*** type to ignore the value of that expression. For example, a special situation may happen as shown below:

```
Current_char = (x>0? getchar()  :  (void)(0));
```

The value of Current_char should change only when the condition variable is positive, or it should retain its old value. The second target expression in the above ternary expression evaluates to ***no value***.

## 3.11 Summary

In this chapter, we discussed about the two very important concepts used to build programs in C-language, i.e., C-variable and C-expression. Our discussion using C-Virtual Machine concept revealed the following features of C-language:

1. *C-variables are distinct from other language variables in that they are associated with memory addresses. When the name of a variable represents its data value, the same name prefixed with "&" represents its address in the memory.*
2. *The above characteristic allows C-language to provide pointer variables, using which value parameters of variables can be accessed indirectly, similar to machine language programming.*
3. *C provides standard data types such as* ***int, float, char*** *and* ***struct****; in addition, it provides* ***union, void*** *and* ***pointer*** *types to improve programming efficiency.*
4. *Expression handling in C is quite unique in that* ***assignment*** *operator is treated as any other* ***arithmetic*** *operator. A* ***comma*** *operator,* ***ternary*** *operator,* ***sizeof*** *operator and* ***cast*** *operator are introduced. As a result, multiple assignment expression and multiple mixed expressions are made possible.*

## Exercises

3.1 If x is a simple variable, then where is it stored in the memory?

3.2 If x is a variable, then what is represented by the name, x? What is the reference value of x?

3.3 Assume that we have declared two simple variables of the same type, say x and y. In what respect do they differ from each other?

3.4 Let i and j be two simple variables of same type declared consecutively. Show their memory maps.

3.5 In what respect a C-variable is different from Pascal or any other language variable? Explain with examples.

3.6 Identify the type of value parameter associated with the following variables:

(a) int I, *PI;
(b) float F, *PF;
(c) char C, *PC;

3.7 Identify illegal expressions:

(a) x = 10
(b) x = *&x + 1
(c) 1000 = x
(d) *1000 = x
(e) *&x*2 = x +y

where x and y are integer variables.

3.8 Evaluate the following expressions using C-Virtual Machine:

(a) j = i =0;
(b) j += j = 1;
(c) k = 10 + (j *= j = 2);

3.9 What will be the value left in the ***rvalue Accumulator*** at end of each of the following expressions? Also show the value of ***Expression Status Flag*** progressively.

```
i =-1;
J = +1;
i? 100 : -100;
(i&j) ? j-i : 0;
```

3.10 Evaluate the following expressions. Show the results in the rvalue Accumulator and Status Flag progressively.

(a) a = 10, b = 20, c = a*b
(b) x = (a = 10, b = 20, c = a*b)

3.11 Evaluate the following conditional expressions and show the values in the ravalue Accumulator and Status Flag:

```
x = -10;
y = +10;
```

(a) x < y
(b) x - y > 0
(c) x == y
(d) x < 0 && y> 0

3.12 Consider the following expressions:

(a) sizeof k + 3
(b) 3 + sizeof k

where k is an integer.

Evaluate why both are same.

3.13 Are the following conversions valid?

```
int i; float x; short s; long l = 100;
i = (float) 10;
x = (float)10.0;
s = (int) 200;
i = (short)200;
x = (float)l;
i = (int)l;
s = (short)s
```

# 4

# Meaning and Definition of C-Functions

**Chapter contents:**

*This chapter explains the meaning of C-function and conventions for parameter passing. Function definition explores some characteristics of C-functions that are comparable to normal variables.*

**Organization:**


*4.1 Introduction*
*4.2 Function Definition*
*4.3 Meaning of a Function*
*4.4 Compiler's View on Function Definition*
*4.5 Function Interface Conventions*
*4.6 Meaning of Call by Value or by Reference*
*4.7 Summary*
*Exercises*


## 4.1 Introduction

In ***Chapter 1***, we surveyed the modular organization of C-programs. Modularity using functions not only helps to construct a large program in an incremental fashion, but also allows us to use a large range of library functions that are already tested and made available with a C-compiler. This characteristic of C-language makes the programming task more productive and effective. Apart from the programming structure, functions help to construct abstract operations that are not available in basic C. In other words, the usage of functions in expressions augments the scope of C to wide range of applications.

This chapter is devoted to using the standards that have been introduced by ANSI in declaring and structuring C-functions. We will also study how these standards improve the portability and reliability of C-programs. With the ANSI standard specifications, it is now possible for a C-compiler to check the type consistency of the actual arguments being passed and the type of the returned value.

## 4.2 Function Definition

A function in C is a subprogram module that receives a set of arguments and returns a value to its calling function. A function acts as a typed variable, and it can be used in any expression similar to other variables. The function definition during declaration specifies such information as function name and the type of value that is returned by this name, plus the quantity and types of arguments expected. In fact, this information is necessary for a calling function to set up a function call correctly.

A function definition in ANSI-C starts with a function's header description in the first line. This header description contains a type specifier followed by the function name with all formal parameters specified within parenthesis. These must match the actual arguments of a functional call to this function. A function definition is completed by a function block, which accommodates some local data declarations and a required program text (i.e., statements). The definition of a function in ANSI-C is as follows:

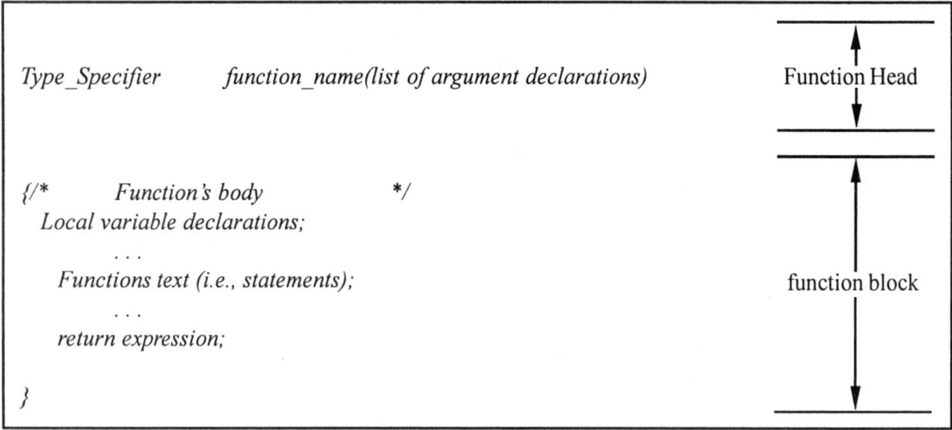


*Function definition in text form*

**The syntax diagram for C-function (or functional module)**

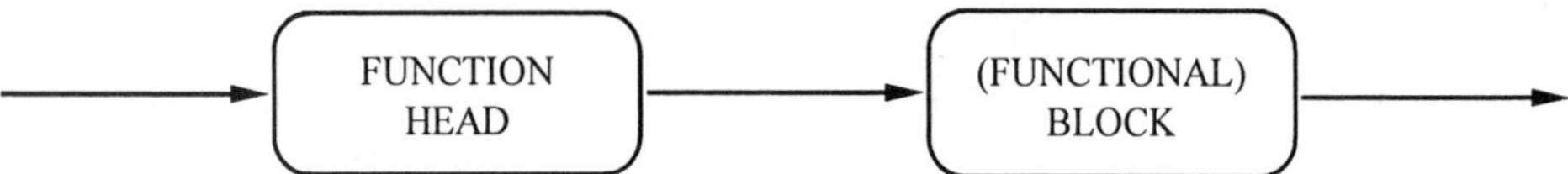

**The syntax diagram for FUNCTION HEAD**

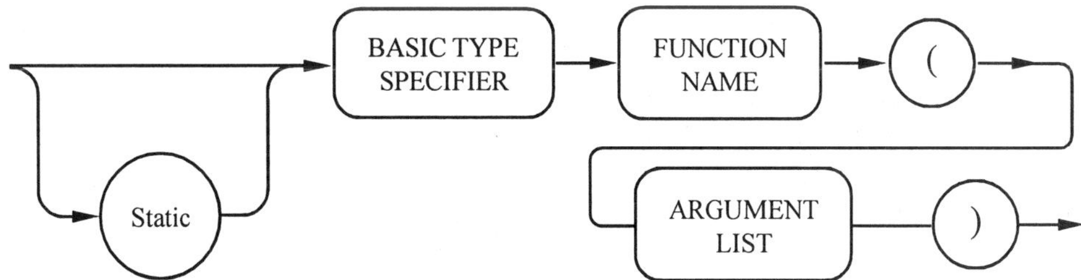


**The syntax diagram for function block**

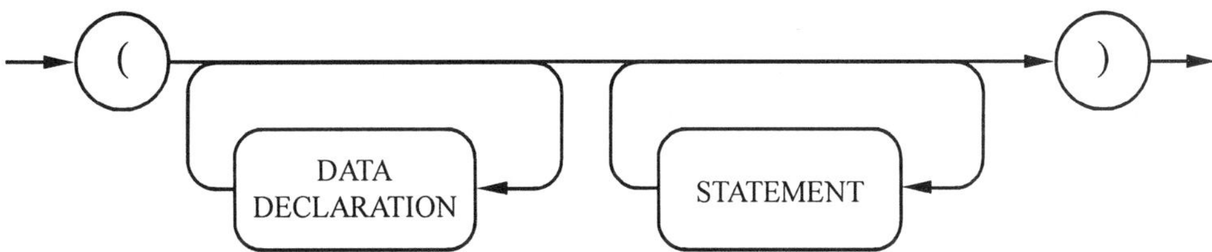


### 4.2.1 Function Names

The names of the subordinate functions of a program can be any user_created alphanumeric symbol similar to a variable name. However, users should avoid the names of functions that are defined in the systems and C libraries. The system, in general, uses a convention to name its functions with a starting underscore. Hence, it is advised not to use the same convention to name the user defined functions.

***Remark:*** *The name "main" is reserved for the main function of any C-program, and it is used by the loader to identify the start of a C-program after loading in the main memory.*

## 4.3 Meaning of a Function

### 4.3.1 Function as a Variable

A function also acts as a variable to hold a data object during expression evaluation, similar to other variables like character, integer, float, etc. This implies that the function definitions follow similar rules to other variable declarations. For example, the following integer variable declaration and integer function declaration show a close similarity:

```
int   i;               /* i is declared as a variable of integer type */
            AND
int   ifunc(void)      /* ifunc is declared as a function variable of integer type  */
{                      /* function body  */
        . . .
}
```

By recalling our discussion on variables in the last chapter, we understand that a declared variable is allocated an appropriate space in the memory, the variable name itself represents its value and the name preceded by **&** is the address of the allocated memory location where the value is stored. In the above integer declaration, ***i*** is the integer variable representing the value parameter and ***&i*** represents the address of memory where ***i*** is stored. A declared function variable is a somewhat different category, comprised of the function definition and a variable parameter. The function definition or code is required to compute a value and the variable parameter is required to hold the computed value until it is effectively returned to the caller. Hence, for each function definition there are two associated storage spaces involved. One is allocated for storing the definition and the other for storing the computed value. During compilation, the function definition is allocated a sufficient space from the C-memory, as shown in ***Fig 4.1***. How the compiler allocates space for the associated variable parameter depends entirely on the implementation. The storage for the associated variable parameter may be allocated along with the function call environment, or dynamically using the stack, register or some temporary memory by the system at run time.

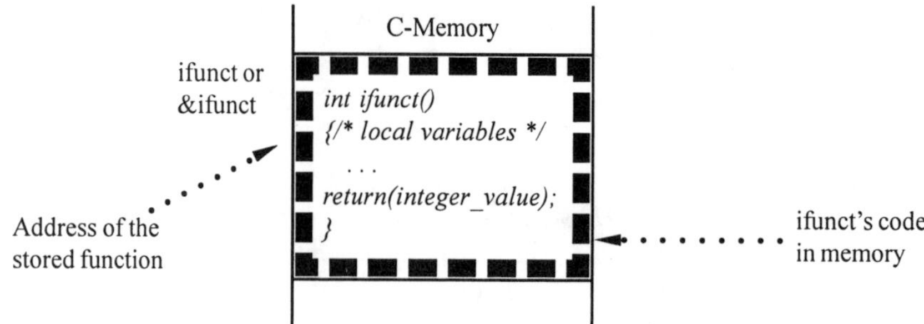


*Fig 4.1 Memory map for C-function definition:* ***int ifunct();***

The function name, alone or preceded by **&**, represents the address of the start of the function definition. The function name along with the reference operator (i.e., parenthesis) represents the value parameter, and this value parameter preceded by **&** represents the address of this function variable. In the example shown in ***Fig. 4.1*** and ***Fig. 4.2***, ***ifunct*** represents the address of the function definition and it is a constant pointer that cannot be altered. ***ifunct()*** represents the function's value parameter indicating the current value, and ***&(ifunct())*** represents the address of that function variable in the memory. This address also belongs to constant type, but depending upon the implementation, this address may change from one function call to another.

> ***Remark:***
> *The address of a function definition (e.g. ifunct in the above example) can be stored in a pointer variable, which can then be used as a carrier to move the function around a program's modules. However, the convention of creating a function pointer is bit odd, and is explained in* ***Chapter 13***.

### 4.3.2 Function as a Read-Only Variable

Although a function can be declared as a normal variable, it should be interpreted as a ***read-only*** variable. It can be used only as an ***rvalue*** in an expression, but cannot be assigned. For example:

```
int      i;
int    ifunct(void)   /*     ifunct is returning an integer value.    */
    {
         . . .
       return (an_integer_value);
    }

void  main(void)
{
       . . .
    i = ifunct();   /* This is LEGAL.  */
       . . .
    ifunct() = i;  /* ERROR, compiler may not allow this. */
       . . .
}
```

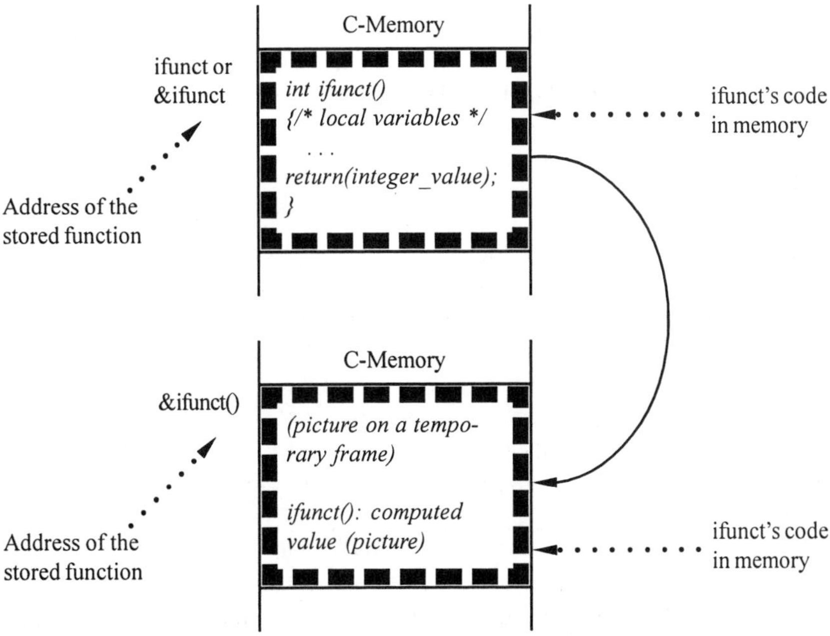


*Fig 4.2 Memory map for a function reference:* ***int ifunct();***

> *Note: Although a function variable is regarded as a read-only object, using an indirect mean, it may be possible to assign a value. The following explanation is purely a hypothetical one. From the previous example, ifunct() is the variable parameter and, hence, we can state that &ifunct() is the address of the location where the value ifunct() is stored. In that case, using the indirect operator, *, we can write an expression like*
>
> **&ifunct() = i;*
>
> *The meaning of this expression is to write the value, i, in the location pointed by the address, &ifunct(). Even if this is allowed by a compiler, it will be very difficult to predict the effect on the value, ifunct(). Since the location and type of memory allocated to a function variable is unknown, whether the assigned value is reusable also remains unknown. It is advised not to try an experiment like this even though it may be allowed.*

### 4.3.3 Function as a Dynamic Variable

Unlike a normal variable whose value will be permanent until reassigned, a function variable need not hold the same value in any two consecutive calls. When a reference is made to a function, i.e., a function call is made, the called function computes its value ***dynamically*** and supplies it as its ***rvalue***. Since we don't know the type of memory allocated to a function variable, it will be difficult to say whether the computed value would exist permanently in the allocated location. Assuming that an implementation uses a stack for exchanging the parameters, then between two consecutive calls to the same function, the stack might have been reallocated to some other calls while the original contents might have been lost. Hence, the following assumption may be justified without affecting the concept of function usage in our programs.

> ***Remark:***
>
> *1. A function variable dynamically computes the data (i.e., a new picture is created dynamically) of the specified type that it represents and returns it (picture only) at the time of reference without storing it permanently. Since there is no frame to hold the computed value, it should be caught immediately. Though it is a dynamic type, it is still considered as a synchronous type variable.*
>
> *2. Defining a function is akin to declaring a variable of abstract type. In fact, function definitions suggest the creation of dynamic objects in some respects. For example, let us define a simple integer variable called k and an integer function returning a random number called rand() in our program. When we use these variables in an expression, they behave quite differently. The variable k represents simply as a static rvalue, whereas the variable rand() computes as a rvalue computed dynamically. In general, a function definition is equivalent to a data declaration of abstract (object) type.*

## 4.4 Compiler's View on Function Definition

As explained in ***Chapter 1***, a C-program may be developed in a single file or in multiple files. In general, the compiler applies the following conventions in the case of function declarations and their usage in C-expressions.

### 4.4.1 Convention 1 (Functions must be typed)

In ***ANSI-C*** every function must be typed. The type space includes all data types available in K&R C and, in addition, includes a special type called the ***void*** type, meaning no object or an empty set of values. If a function does not return any value, then it must be typed as ***void***. This helps the compiler to check the correct usage of functional references in the expressions.

When a function is defined with a type other than ***void***, it should return a value of the specified type. Hence, there must be a return statement with an ***rvalue*** expression wherever the function exits. For a void function, a function may exit without a return statement or its exit may use a simple return statement without any expression. ***Chapter 6*** explains more about the return statement.

The compiler, in general, checks for compatibility of function type with the types of other variables in an expression. However, the compilers don't expect type compatibility in expressions that consists of only simple variables (of ***char***, ***int and float*** type). In other words, compilers allow mixed expressions of these types. On the other hand, the compilers apply type checking very strictly on expressions mixing normal variables with pointer (or address) variables, mixing pointer variables of different types, or mixing normal variables with value parameters of ***void*** type because these mixes cause data conflict during processing. The following example shows just one case of the data conflicts.

**Example 4.1:** Use of void function in an expression.

```
void func(void) /* func neither carries any argument nor returns any value */
{
     . . .
     /* No return statement  */
}
void  main(void)
{ int K;
     . . .
   K = K + func(); /* It is illegal to use a function that returns void */
     . . .      /*   Compiler would indicate an error       */
}
```

In this example, the compiler interprets the function definition, ***func***, as returning a ***void*** value (i.e., no value). When the compilation reaches the function call statement in the ***main*** module, it finds an error due to illegal use of void function in the assignment expression.

> ***Remarks:***
> 1. *Although main is also a C-function, it is not typed. It is the starting function of a program, acting only as a caller, but cannot be called a normal function. For this reason, the return statement is never used in the main function.* ***(This is contradictory to what we stated before: that main is also a function which has parenthesis to receive parameters and can be called by other functions in special situations. We will return to this concept in Chapter 21. We will assume, in the meantime, that main is simply a calling function.)***
> 2. *A function can be defined as belonging to any simple data type* ***(i.e., char, int, float,, long, double, void, etc.)****, **a composite type (i.e., struct, union) or an abstract type (i.e., pointer to an array).***
> 3. *A return statement is normally used to return a value, but is also simply used to simply return from any place in a function.*

> ***Note:***
> 1. *In K&R C, the function construct is loosely defined. That is, a function need not be typed if it either returns an integer or no value. Hence, the compiler may not be able to detect such errors as*
>
>     - *a function returns a value which is not used;*
>     - *a function does not return any value, but is used in an expression;*
>     - *a function returns a value, but is used in an expression of incompatible or nonconvertible type.*
>
> *In order to remove these inconsistencies, ANSI imposes a standard which specifies that the function name in every function declaration except main must be typed explicitly to show what type of value it returns.*
>
> 2. *Since most of the compilers at present accept both K&R C and ANSI-C, a function header without a type specifier would be treated as belonging to integer type by default. If a function does not return any value, then the function is assumed returning void, i.e., no value.*

### 4.4.2 Convention 2 (Declare argument types)

Another fault with K&R C is that there is no way a C-compiler can check the validity of parameters that are passed in a function call. A normal C-compiler simply ignores testing whether the number of passed (or actual) arguments and their types are matched with those of the formal argument list in a function declaration. An error in argument passing could result in abnormal termination of program execution. Hence, every function definition must declare the formal parameters with their types in a predetermined order.

When a function does not expect any parameter, it must be indicated as ***void*** in the definition. The following examples explain a difference between function declaration in K&R C and function declaration in ANSI C with these features.

**Example 4.2:** Let us write a function to output a prompt. Since this function is simply an output function, obviously there is no need for it to return a value. We will show the code in ANSI- C and K&R C.

| ANSI-C code | K&R C code |
|---|---|
| ***void*** *prompt(**void**)*<br>{ {<br>/* prompt in a new line */<br>printf(" \n");<br>printf("$ ");<br>} | *prompt()*<br><br>/* prompt in a new line */<br>printf(" \n");<br>printf("$ ");<br>} |

**Example 4.3:** Let us write a function that requires no parameter, but returns a number of characters, including the new line character read from **stdin** stream. We will show the code in ANSI-C and K&R C.

| ANSI-C code | K&R C code |
|---|---|
| ***int*** *count_input(**void**)*<br>{ int counter;<br>counter = 0;<br>while(getchar() != '\n')<br>counter++;<br>return(counter+1);<br>} | *count_input()*<br>{ int counter;<br>counter = 0;<br>while(getchar() != '\n')<br>counter++;<br>return(counter+1);<br>} |

### 4.4.3 Convention 3 (Supply prototype definitions when functions are defined out of the scope of their references)

In general, function declarations in a file can be organized in any order, although some compilers may expect that a function must be defined before it is referenced. Let us discuss this issue as a general case.

As explained in ***Chapter 2***, a C-compiler has two distinct passes. In the first pass, the compiler, after checking the syntax of a given source program, produces a semi-compiled output. In the second pass, it links the semi-compiled program files to other referenced functions to form a single binary file that can be loaded and executed. Hence, compilers allow us to either compile a program step by step by carrying out these two phases using separate commands, or to complete both phases by a single command.

As far as functions are concerned, the compiler checks in its first pass whether the referred functions in function call statements are defined for their types in the same file. This pass does not check whether the referred functions are supplied at that time. What a compiler expects is either the presence of the actual function declaration in the same file (whether the declaration occurs before or after its call) or the presence of a referential declaration, called ***prototype definition***, showing that it has been declared in some other file. (Note that the referential declarations using the ***extern*** class will be discussed in ***Chapter 5***.) In the second pass only, the compiler checks whether all referred functions are supplied. If a function is not found in the supplied files, then the compiler looks into C-library to satisfy the function call.

> ***Remark:*** *The compiler checks for the compatibility of both the type of value returned and the actual arguments passed by a function call against formal specification in its definition. When a function is declared in another file or later in the same file, a prototype definition must be included prior to a call to that function.*

#### 4.4.3.1 Meaning of Prototype Definition

When a function is defined outside a program file or after the function reference in the same file, a formal declaration of the real function can be specified before any reference is made to it. This specification, called prototype definition, is merely the header description of a function definition showing the returned type and parameter types and their order. The compiler does not allocate any memory for prototype definitions.

## Example 4.4:

Let us write a program with a function to return a sum of two integer arguments. Assume that our compiler expects function definition before function reference.

```
#include <stdio.h>
int   sum(int a, int   b); /* Prototype definition of the function   */
      (or)
int   sum(int , int  );       /* Showing that it returns an integer   */
        /* and requires two integer arguments   */
void main(void)
{
  int   i, j, result;
  i = 100, j =200;
  result = sum(i, j);  /* Function reference   */
  printf("SUM of i and j: %d \n", result);
}

int sum(int  a, int  b)   /* Actual definition of the sum function   */
{
    return(a+b);
}
```

The prototype definition of ***sum*** in the above coding clearly shows what types of parameters are expected and what type of value returned. Since ANSI-C checks both the type of actual argument with the expected parameter type and compatibility of the returned value in an expression, it can detect the presence of any error in the calling statement by referring to its corresponding prototype definition.

### 4.4.4 Convention 4 (Include appropriate prototype definition files when library functions are used.)

C comes with many libraries in semi-compiled form, each accompanied with a prototype definition file. For example, string function library comes with its prototype definition file called ***string.h***. Programmers should include this header file when any function from this library is used in their programs. For example, the following program includes the prototype definitions stored in ***string.h*** so that the compiler can check the function calls made to some of the library functions. The following program calls the ***strlen*** function to calculate the length of *str1* and ***strcmp*** to compare the strings, *str2* and *str3*.

```
#include <stdio.h>
#include <string.h>
char str1[] = "This is a string whose size is not known."
char str2[] = "CAT"
char str3[] = "DOG"
void main(void)
{
  int L;
   L = strlen(str1); /* string function strlen returns length of str1 */
   printf("Length of str1 = %d \n", L);
   if(strcmp(str2, str3) == 0) /* strcmp compares two strings */
     printf("str2 and str3 are not same. \n");
}
```

## 4.5 Function Interface Conventions

The concept of this multi-module structure can be found in many languages, such as Fortran and COBOL. In Fortran, subprogram modules are classified into subroutines and functions, according to the manner in which both calling and called modules exchange arguments. A Fortran subroutine normally communicates with its calling program entirely using an argument passing mechanism; both the input and returned values are through a set of arguments passed via a subroutine call. On the other hand, a Fortran-function may receive input values through the arguments along with a call, similar to a subroutine, but it always returns the evaluated result via its name. In summary, a function can return only one value, whereas a subroutine can return more than one value. This distinction is maintained in Fortran by the provision of separate definitions for these modules. (A function definition in Fortran starts with the keyword "***function***" followed by a function name, whereas a subroutine starts with "***subroutine***" followed by a subroutine name.) C is implemented using the same concept (i.e., provision for making subroutines and functions) in a somewhat simplified manner. In C, a program module can be used as a subroutine or a function. This subprogram module is always called a function. (Note that the name "***subroutine***" is never used in a ***C context***. The difference between a function and a subroutine is explained below as side information.) That is, a C-function can act either as a true function or a subroutine, depending upon the mode of returning values. There is no separate definition facility to distinguish these two categories in C. For example, a ***void*** function is a function emulating a subroutine definition.

> ***Remark:*** *According to the original definition, a function performs a task by receiving input values via passed arguments and always returns a value via its name parameter. A function call expression can use arguments to pass values to a called function, but not the other way. On the other hand, a subroutine call uses arguments in both directions. In C, the function definition is modified such that a function call can be used to return value either via the name of a called function, via arguments or both.*

When we design our C-programs using functional modules, we need to provide communication among the modules so that they can receive and send parameters. Knowing that every C-function can return a type of result through its name parameter, we now have to study the conventions while passing arguments to a function.

The argument list following the name of a function simply contains a list of parameters (i.e., constants, identifiers representing value parameters, and identifiers representing addresses) delimited by commas. The argument passing interface between a calling function and a called function can vary depending upon:

1. *whether a function requires any input argument or is expected to return any result;*
2. *whether an argument that is to be passed is an* ***rvalue*** *(i.e., a value parameter) or* ***lvalue*** *(i.e., reference or address parameter);*
3. *whether an argument is of simple, array or composite type.*

We will now discuss all the interfaces that can be implemented with C-functions.

## 4.6 Meaning of Call by Value or by Reference

In C, arguments that are passed to a function are always value parameters. These parameters may represent either data values or references to variables (i.e., address values), depending upon how a passed argument is going to be used in a called function. In our above discussion, a caller passes a set of values as input to a function and receives a result value via the name parameter of the called function. In other words, a caller simply passes the ***rvalues*** to a function and the called function returns an ***rvalue*** via its name parameter. On the other hand, when a function is expected to return a value via an argument, then the caller has to pass an appropriate argument (i.e., reference to a variable or address of an object) that can be used to form the ***lvalue*** of the target variable. Then, the called function can actually assign a value to the target variable using the passed reference parameter. Hence, the following can be asserted:

1. *a function call with all arguments as data values is termed* ***call by value (See examples in Case 3.);***
2. *a function call with all arguments as reference (or address) values is termed* ***call by reference;***
3. *a function call with both type of arguments is termed* ***call by value and reference****.*

Now we will show the conventions that should be followed by programmers in dealing with the above mentioned *function call types.*

### Convention 1: A function receives value parameters of simple variables

In this case, the functions receive the data values from the callers. The use of these parameters will not affect the corresponding variables defined in the callers.

## Example 4.5:

We will define a function that receives two real values and returns the bigger one. Call this function as .

```
#include <stdio.h>
float big(float  r1, float  r2)
{
  if(r1 > r2)
    return r1;
  else
    return r2;
} /* End of big block*/

void  main(void)  /* main as a caller function   */
{
float  v1 = ???, v2 = ???, big_val;
    . . .
   big_val = big( v1, v2);  /* caller sends simply values  */
   printf("larger value: %f ", big_val);
    . . .
} /* End of main block*/
```

## Convention 2: A function receives value parameters of simple variables and a reference parameter to receive the computed result

In this case, the functions receive the data values from the callers The use of these parameters will not affect the corresponding variables defined in the callers.

## Example 4.6:

We will now define the ***big*** to receive and send values by parameters. Since the result must be sent via a third parameter, its address is expected by this function. The pointer declaration, introduced here, is further explained introduced in ***Chapter 12***.

```
#include <stdio.h>
void  big(float  r1, float  r2,  float  *r3)  /* r3 is reference or address parameter */
{
  if(r1 > r2)
    *r3 = r1; /*  indirectly assign r1 to target variable using pointer variable, r3;  */
else
    *r3 = r2; /*  indirectly assign r2 to target variable using pointer variable, r3;  */
} /* End of big block*/
```

```
void main(void) /* main as a caller function */
{
float v1 = ???, v2 = ???, big_val;
 . . .
 big( v1, v2, &big_val); /* caller sends v1 and v2 as input values and address of big_value i.e.,
&big_val to recieve big value */
 printf("larger value: %f ", big_val);
 . . .
} /* End of main block*/
```

## Convention 3: A function receives value parameters indirectly via reference parameters

When functions process values of abstract data type, like arrays and strings, it is difficult to send the values of all elements in a simple manner. To process the values of an aggregate, the functions can receive the starting address of that aggregate to indirectly access the values. This allows functions to access the elements of aggregates for both reading and writing. We have tackled the problem of passing aggregates as input parameters to a function, but if functions are not implemented correctly, these input parameters may be corrupted accidentally. If we want to preserve the original values of such passed parameters, the **const** qualifier must be applied to them in the function definition.

## Example 4.7:

The ***strlen*** function is a typical example of this case. This function receives the address or name of a string and returns the length via its name. This function is supposed to read the string until the end of string marker for counting the characters. It is not supposed to alter any value in the string.

```
#include <stdio.h>
unsigned strlen(const char *ps) /* pointer argument to carry address of a string*/
{
 unsigned length;
/* Move the pointer, ps, through the string to which it is pointing and read
   indirectly for the end of string and count at the same time number of characters*/
 . . .
 return(length);
} /* End of strlen block*/

char s[] = "This is main's private string"; /*    Declare a character string and
                                                  initialize with a string constant */
```

```
void main(void) /* main as a caller function */
{
 unsigned s_len;
  s_len = strlen(&s[0]); /* starting address of the string, i.e., address of the first
                            element, passed as reference parameter */
  printf("The length of string s : %d", s_len);
} /* End of main block */
```

In the above coding, ***const*** qualifier in the function definition allows only to read the values pointed by the pointer variable and, thus, protects the passed parameter from being corrupted.

> ***Remark:*** *In general, the value of a simple variable can be passed to a function. There is no provision to pass an array of values as a single value parameter to another function. The only way it can be done is by passing the address of an array. This is equivalent to passing the lvalue expression of an array. In such situation, the* **const** *qualifier is quite useful to protect the passed parameters.*

## Further Examples:

(a) The string comparison function simply reads and compares the character values of two strings. Hence, it requires two read-only strings as input arguments, shown in the following prototype definition as constant type of input parameters:

```
int   strcmp(const char s1[], const char s2[]);
```

(b) A function sums the elements of an integer array and returns the result to a calling function. Since the function simply reads the values of an array, it is sufficient to pass an array to this function for read-only purpose. The prototype definition is shown below:

```
int    array_total(const int arr[], int arr_size);
```

(c) A function simply reads corresponding elements of two integer arrays and stores that value in a third array. In this case, the first two arrays must be passed as read-only parameters and the third array as reference parameter. The prototype definition is shown below:

```
void add_arrays(const int arr1[] , const int arr2[] , int arr3[], int arr_size);
```

## 4.7 Summary

This chapter explained the meaning of a function using the picture-frame memory model and extended the concept of variable to the function definition. This model also helps to clearly distinguish the meanings of different symbolic notations used to refer to concepts around a function, such as function definition (or simply a function), function call or function value, function address and address of function value. In ***Example 4.4***, the name, ***sum***, refers to function itself (or function definition), &sum refers to function address, ***sum()*** refers to function value and ***&sum()*** refers to address of function value in the memory. Since we can use ***sum()*** in any expression, we may call it a function variable. These symbolic conventions may be as standard notations in books that explain the language concepts. The ANSI conventions to be followed in the function definitions and their significance during compilation were summarized. In particular, the significance of the ***void*** type and the ***const*** qualifier in the function definitions have been discussed. The parameter passing modes, ***call by value*** and ***call by reference***, have also been discussed.

## Exercises

4.1 What is the difference between a subroutine call and a function call?

4.2 What is the difference between a function and a normal variable?

4.3 Show the memory map for the following function definitions:

(a)
```
int sum(int A, int B)
{int temp;
    temp = A + B;
    return(temp);
}
```

(b)
```
void prompt(void)
{
  printf("\n $");
}
```

4.4 What is a prototype definition? When will you use a prototype definition in a C-program?

4.5 What is the role of the ***void*** type in a function definition?

4.6 Can the compiler check whether a function returns an expected value or not?

4.7 Which of the following are true with respect to ANSI-C? Give your explanation, if necessary.

(a) functions should be defined in the same file before they are referenced;
(b) a function's name always starts with a upper case letter;
(c) a function must always be typed;
(d) formal arguments need to be declared with their types;
(e) a function returns a character value by default;
(f) a function returns a void value by default;
(g) a function returns an address value by default;
(h) a function always uses return statement to return its control to its caller;
(i) a function uses return statement to terminate prematurely or to return some value back to its caller;
(j) a function can return more than one value;
(k) a function cannot return an address value.

4.8 Define the meaning of *call by value* and *call by reference*. Give some examples.

4.9 Can a function receive an array or a string variable? How? Explain.

4.10 Make corrections in the following function with ANSI-conventions:

```
read_ch()
   {int  ch;
      ch =getchar();  /* get character from stdin stream (keyboard) */
      return(ch);
   }
```

# 5

# Storage Classes, Scope and Initialization of Variables

**Chapter contents:**

*This chapter explains how the variables declared at different places in a program have the scope of their usage. It also explains how these scope rules are used in constructing modular C-programs.*

**Organization:**


*5.1 Introduction*
*5.2 The Meaning of Scope of a Variable*
*5.3 What Is a Storage Class?*
*5.4 Storage Classes*
*5.5 Storage Environment Around a Function*
*5.6 Initializing Variables*
*5.7 Typedef*
*5.8 Dynamic Storage Type*
*5.9 Summary*
*Exercises*


## 5.1 Introduction

In some languages, the concept of programming is simplified. For example, in a BASIC program, all variables declared are treated as permanent and global. When we deal with C, the programming concepts extend to:

1. *maintaining a program in more than one source file module, and allowing compilation separately before linking into a single binary module;*
2. *structuring a program using multiple functional modules;*
3. *structuring a module using blocks;*
4. *exploiting high speed memory, i.e., registers for frequently used variables;*
5. *organizing variables according to their temporal scope;*
6. *the usage of dynamic storage for maintaining abstract data structures.*

After introducing the general organization of C-programs in ***Chapter 1*** and function declarations in ***Chapter 4***, this chapter explains how the three level hierarchical structure (file, function and statement block, as mentioned above) of a C-program distinguishes the scope of variables declared at different levels. In addition, this chapter explains how C-machine allocates and manages storage classes (or simply different types of spaces) for variables with different scopes to achieve cost and time efficiency and takes us to the next step in exploring further characteristics of C-functions.

## 5.2 The Meaning of Scope of a Variable

As we have discussed in ***Chapter 1*** the structure of a C-program should contain a main function and, optionally, one or more supporting functions. In general, a C-program is modular as well as structured. This ability of C-language is enhanced by the possibility that the declaration of a variable can occur freely anywhere in a program. The location of a declaration can be within one of the program's three boundaries, such as block statement, functional module and file module.

A boundary defines a program space in which local data declarations and the related statements can be put together as a block. In general, it limits the availability of a declared local variable to the statements within that block. Hence, we may state that the program space (or part of a program) within which a variable can be accessed is called the ***spatial scope of a variable***. For example, a variable declared at the beginning of a function block will be available to the remaining section of that functional block, but not outside its function boundary. In general, a variable declared at the start of a boundary has the scope of that boundary. If a variable is declared outside a function, its spatial scope (or physical accessibility) is extended to those functions that follow this declaration in a file. However, We cannot call this global because the functions that occur before this variable declaration cannot access the variable. When variables are declared at the beginning of a file, the spatial scope of these variables is extended to all functions in that file. These are, in fact, global variables in that file. When all functions of a program exist in a single file, then the global variables of this file are global variables of the whole program. This is shown in ***Fig. 5.1***.

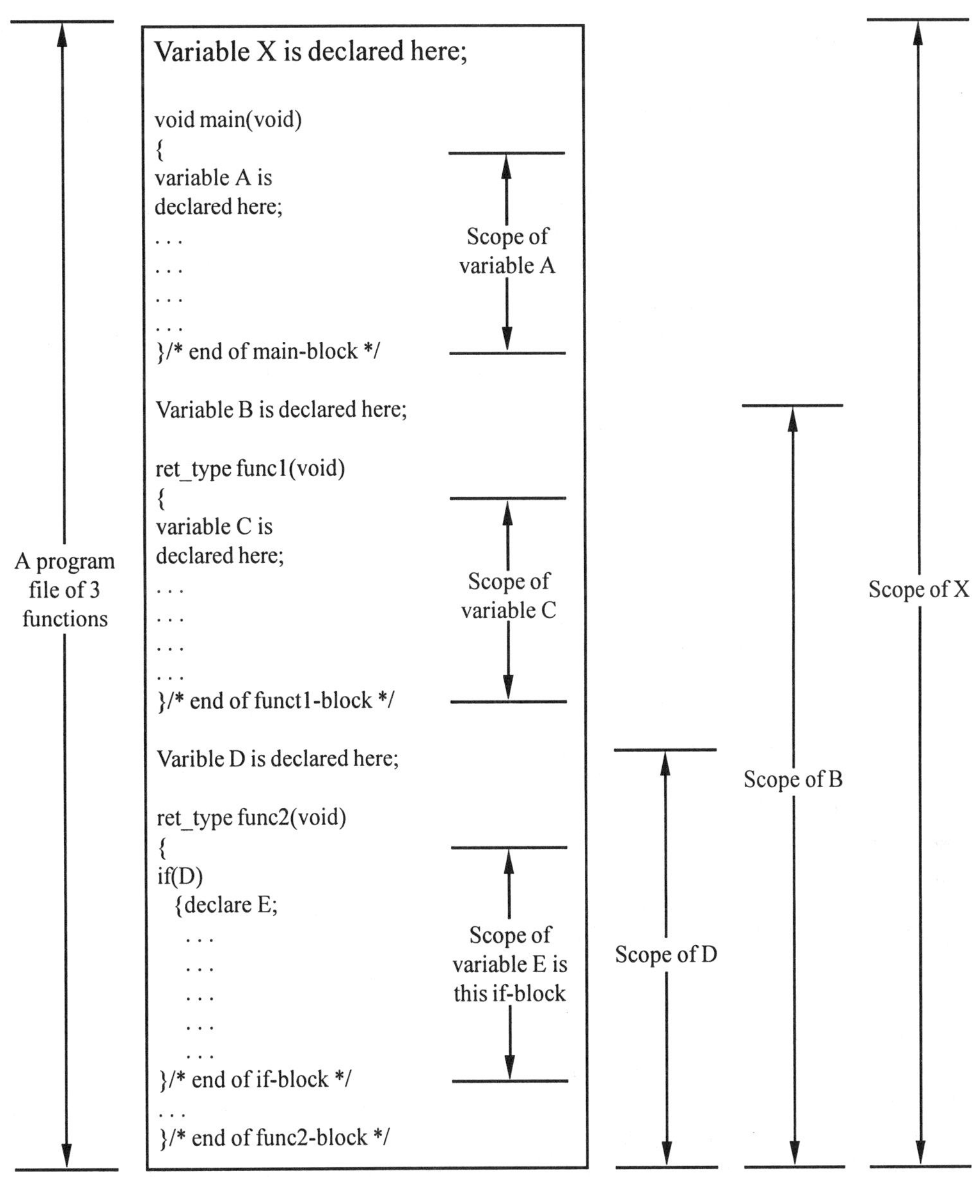


*Fig. 5.1 Variable declarations and their scopes in a file module*

If a program exists in multiple files, global variables of one file module cannot be accessed by the functions in another file module unless some special declaration (i.e., referencing) method is followed. We will discuss later how the scope of a variable can be extended to other file modules using the ***extern*** class.

The lifetime of a variable, called ***temporal scope of a variable***, is also an important availability factor. For example, a variable may exist throughout the program execution, during the function execution or during the execution of a block statement. The following sections explain how both spatial and temporal scopes of a variable can be specified during declaration.

## 5.3 What Is a Storage Class?

When a variable is declared in a program, it is normally allocated a memory element of suitable size for its existence during execution. The C-virtual machine provides three types of data storage for a running program (see ***Fig. 5.2***). They are:

- *permanent storage*
- *stack storage*
- *register storage*

The C-language machine decides memory allocation from one of these storage types, depending upon the specification of the storage type in a variable declaration. Some types are implicit in the sense that the compiler itself can decide what type of storage is required by a declaration. Other declarations explicitly specify the type of storage that they need. Basically, the storage class of a variable indicates a type of storage allocated to satisfy certain spatial and temporal scopes.

## 5.4 Storage Classes

There are four types of storage classes under which a variable can be declared:

- *External or Global*
- *Static*
- *Auto*
- *Register*

### 5.4.1 External or Global Storage Class

Any variable that is declared outside the modules (i.e., functions) of a program can be regarded as external or global. A C-compiler allocates permanent storage to all external variables, meaning the size and address of the memory area assigned to a variable and its initializing, if necessary, with a specified constant are fully decided at the time of compilation. From the time of loading a program (i.e., starting time of execution) until the end of program execution, these variables exist in the physical memory.

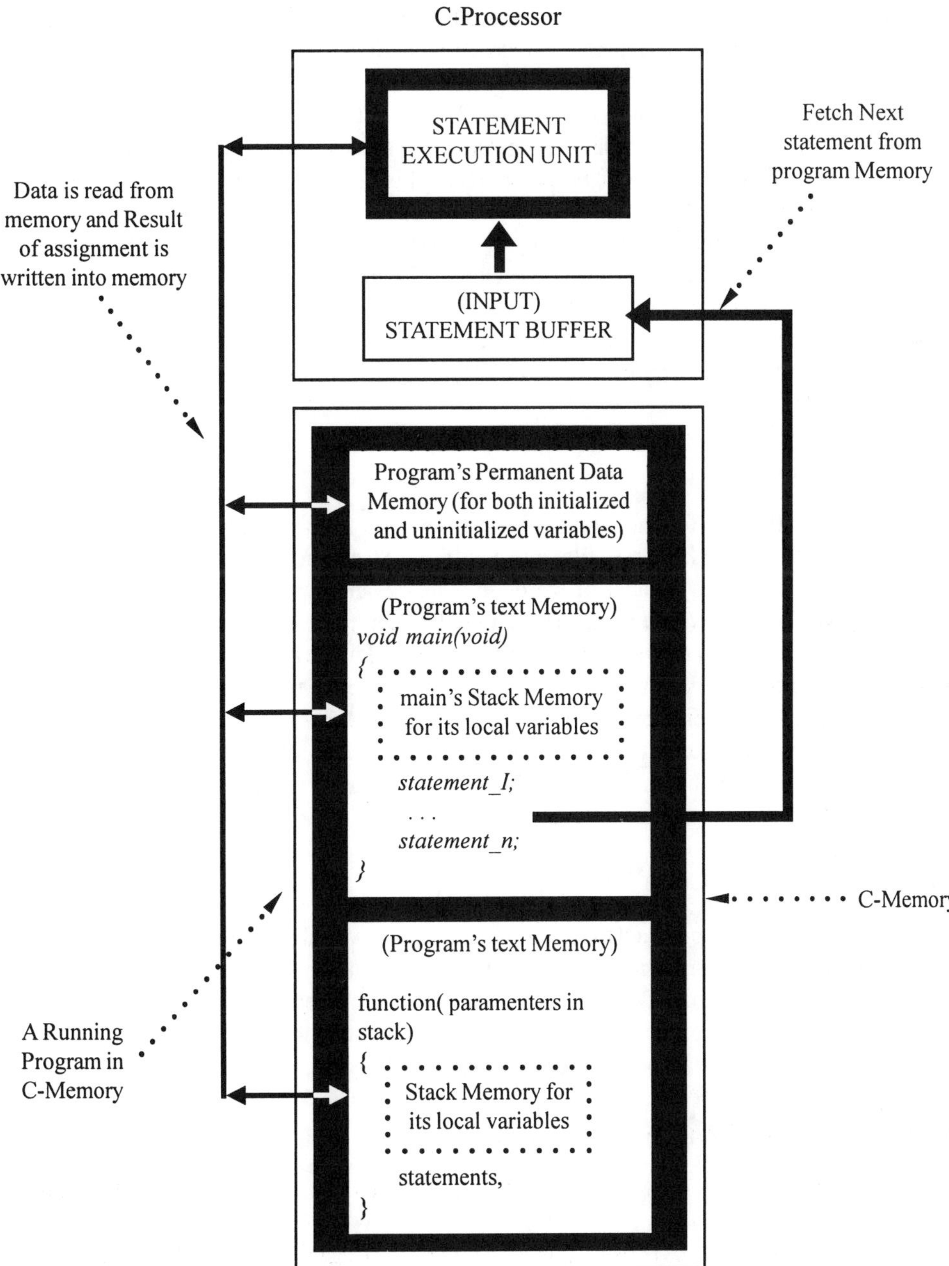


*Fig. 5.2 Memory allocation for a running program in C-virtual machine*

In general, the scope of a global variable is effective only for the functions that follow the declaration. Hence, it is normal practice to declare global variables at the beginning of a source file so that they can be accessed by all functions in that file (or file-module). There are two occasions in which the scope of a global variable may not include some functions of the same program. First, when a global variable is declared in a file such that its declaration occurs after some functions, then those functions (that precede this declaration) cannot access it. Second, large programs are usually built using multiple files (file-modules) and all global variables declared in one of these file-modules (usually in a file containing main.c). This restricts the scope to the file where the global variables are declared. When the other file-modules are compiled separately, any reference to such a global variable will present a problem to the compiler. In order to inform the compiler about the existence of the referenced global variable in some other file-module or in the latter part of the same file, a ***referential declaration*** using the keyword "***extern***" can be used.

### Example 5.1:

The program with three functional modules, as shown in ***Fig. 5.3***, calls ***readln*** to read a line from the ***stdin*** stream (or keyboard file) into a buffer of 80 characters, declared as ***buf[80]***, calls ***count_word*** to count the number of words in that line and outputs the word count (i.e., the variable, ***nword***) to the ***stdout*** stream (or terminal screen file). The input is terminated with a blank line. The ***main*** and ***count_word*** modules are stored in the ***main.c*** file and ***readln*** module is stored in the ***readln.c*** file. All global variables are defined in the ***main.c*** file. In the ***readln.c*** file, these global variables are declared using the keyword "***extern***". ***Main.c*** and ***readln.c*** files can now be separately compiled. When readln.c is compiled, all the extern declarations will indicate to the compiler that they are already defined in another file and will be resolved during the final stage of compilation, i.e., the linking phase.

## 5.4.2 Static Storage Class

The keyword "***static***" is prefixed to declarations to define variables under this class. The static type of variable is also ***permanent***, like the external or global type, except its ***scope*** is limited to a function or a file-module. When a variable (either internal or external to a function) is declared as ***static***, its memory is assigned from ***permanent storage***, and it exists throughout the program execution. A local (or internal) static variable becomes private to a function, while an external static variable becomes private to a file-module. The following example explains the qualification of a static type variable.

main.c file

```
#define SPACE     ' '
void      count_word(void)
{/* global variables are referenced here */
extern  char         buf[];
extern  int          nword;

int          j;
  nword = 0;
  for(j=0;buf[j]!= '\0';j++)
  if(j!=0 && buf[j]==SPACE)
    { nword++;  }
  nword++;
} /* End of count_word() */

/* Global variables declared here */
int          i;
char         buf[80]; /* declare 80 char buffer */
int          nword; /* declare a word counter */

void main(void)
{
  while(1)
  {
    int k;
    /*  Clear the buffer  */
    for(k=0; k<80; k++)
      buf[k] = SPACE;
    readln();
    if (i!=0)
    {
      count_word();
      printf("words: %d\n",nword);
    }
    else
      {  exit(0);  }
  } /* End of while */

} /* End of main */
```

readln.c file

```
#include <stdio.h>
/* global variables are referenced here */
extern int i;
extern char            buf[];

void      readln(void)
{
  int       ch;
  i = 0;
  while ((ch=getchar()) != '\n')
  {
    buf[i] = ch;
    i++;
  }
  buf[i] = (char)0; /* pad with Null */
}
```

Note: Since the statements are not introduced, it would be difficult to follow the codes within the functions. Just follow the descriptions given below:

(1) ***readln()*** reads characters one by one from the keyboard and accumulates in the global character buffer, ***buf[80]***, using the global integer variable, ***i***, to show the length of input line. Each line input is terminated by a new line character.

(2) ***count_word()*** goes through the buffer character by character to identify the word delimiter and keeps counting the words in the global word counter, ***nword***.

(3) ***main()*** clears the buffer before calling ***readln()***. After calling ***readln()***, it checks whether the buffer contains any line by testing the global variable, ***i***. If a line is read, then it calls ***count_word()*** and prints the number of words in that line. ***Main()*** repeats calling ***readln()*** and ***count_word()*** until there is a line received from the keyboard.

*Fig. 5.3 Use of extern storage class for Example 5.1*

In ***Fig. 5.4***, a program exists in two separate file-modules. The ***lineio.c*** file contains two functions, namely ***readln*** and ***writeln***, and has also defined the static variables (an index, ***i***, and a character buffer, ***buf***). The static declaration makes these variables invisible to functions in other files. Nevertheless, they are available as global variables (since they are defined in the beginning of the ***lineio.c*** file) for the functions in the same file. In other words, these static objects are concealed in a file, ***private*** and available only to the functions in that file. In the above example, ***main*** does not know either of the presence of these private variables or how they are used in the ***lineio.c*** file-module. It only knows the names of functions that are present in ***lineio.c*** file and how to address (i.e., call) them through ***extern*** declarations.

main.c file

```
{/* referential declarations of external
functions */
extern int          readln();
extern int          writeln();

void main(void)
{
  while(1)
  {
    if (readln() == 0)
    {
      exit(0);
    }
    else
    {
      writeln();
    }
  } /* End of while */

} /* End of main() */
```

lineio.c file

```
#include <stdio.h>
/* private global variables for this file */
static int          i;
static char         buf[128];
int       readln(void)
{
  char  ch;
  i = 0;
  while ((ch=getchar()) != '\n')
    buf[i++] = ch;
  return(i);
} /* End of readln() */

int writeln(void)
{
  int   k;
  for (k=0; k<= I; k++)
  {
    putchar(buf[k]);
  }
  putchar('\n');
} /* End of writeln() */
```

*Fig. 5.4 Use of static storage class*

In summary, a ***static*** class is useful in creating variables in the following manner:

1. *if a local variable of a function is to be permanent;*
2. *if some variables must be private to a group of functions only;*
3. *if some functions should be private to a group of functions only.*

### 5.4.3 Auto Storage Class

Unless another class is specified, any variable declared inside a function is classified as an automatic or temporary variable. The keyword "***auto***" may be used to signify explicitly the internal declarations as automatic or temporary variables. Their memory allocation is done dynamically at the time of function execution.

### Example 5.2: A program with auto variables

```
void  main(void)
  {
   int a, b;  /* a and b are implicitely created as auto variables, but will stay in the temporary
   storage until the completion of main execution. Note that main is active  throughout program
   execution  */
    . . .
  }
 void  func1(void)
  {
   auto int  i;              /* i, ch and buf are declared explicitly */
   auto char  ch,  buf[100];            /* as auto variables, but they are created in stack  storage
                                          during every invocation of func1  */
    . . .
  }

 void  func2(void)
  {
     int  i, j;  /* i and j are declared implicitly as auto variables     */
    . . .              /*  They are created in stack  during every  invocation of this function */
  }
```

Strictly speaking, it is not necessary to prefix this keyword (i.e., ***auto***) to internal declarations. Without ***auto***, all internal variables are assumed to be automatic. However, its use explicitly shows the storage class to which these variables belong, thus helping with documentation. In the above example, the internal variables of func2, i and j, also belong to the automatic class, although they were not explicitly declared as in func1.

The term ***auto*** implies that the variables declared in a function come into existence automatically when the function is entered. These internal variables are "***temporary***" because they exist only as long as the function in which they are declared, as in the execution state. In other words, the lifetime (or duration) of temporary variables is the same as the duration of the function that declares them. A function may be invoked many times during a program's execution. Every time a function is entered, the physical locations of its variables may be different.

The contents left at the end of one function call will not be available for use in the next call of the same function due to the sharing of the same temporary storage among all functions of the same program. In summary, when a function is entered for its execution, its auto variables come into existence (i.e., the memory is allocated dynamically to the internal variables) and vanish (i.e., the allocated memory is released and may be used for another function) when the executing function exits. They exist only during an instance of function execution and the values left in those variables may not be available in the next instance of the same function.

### 5.4.4 The Register Storage Class

If we analyze the hierarchy of storage types in a computer system (i.e., disk, main memory, cache memory and internal register memory), the access time of data is greatest from mass storage and will be least from an internal register. Because of the high speed nature of internal register storage, C has provided a declaration facility to allocate registers (instead of slow speed stack storage) to auto variables. The keyword "***register***" is used to prefix such declarations. However, the number of registers in a CPU is normally limited, usually varying from two to thirty-two registers. This condition restricts the usage of register class to auto variables that are used very frequently in a function. If a programmer declares more register variables than the number of registers available in a processor, some will not be given storage from registers. Registers will be assigned on a first declared, first allocated basis. Other auto variables, though declared as register class, will be assigned storage from the stack.

Also, registers are normally provided to only keep the data of integer and floating point types. This second condition means that only integer and real auto variables may be declared under this class. If a processor does not have any floating point registers, then only integer and unsigned integer variables can be effectively allocated to registers. Although pointer variables are also allowed to declare under this class, the internal representation of addresses will control the feasibility of register allocation. Most compilers know the type of registers available in the underlying hardware, and will decide whether it is feasible to fulfill the specified register class declarations, or to ignore the register class and treat them as auto declarations.

## 5.5 Storage Environment Around a Function

A program at execution state (i.e., after loading into main memory) consists of four memory segments (***Fig. 5.2*** and ***5.5***). They are as follows:

1. ***Permanent non-initialized data memory:*** This contains all global and static type variables not initialized during declaration.

> ***Note:*** *The non-initialized global and static variables may be allocated from a separate memory, sometimes called BSS memory segment. BSS, Block Started by Symbol, is a directive in the assembly language of IBM 7090. The system usually clears this memory segment before loading the variables. In other words, the variables in this memory may be initialized to zero or NULL by default*

2. ***Permanent initialized data memory:*** This contains all global and static type variables initialized during declaration.
3. ***Program text (i.e., executable portion of a program) memory***
4. ***Stack memory:*** Used as sharable temporary memory for all functions of the loaded program, this stack space is basically used to keep local variables and arguments passed to and from functions.

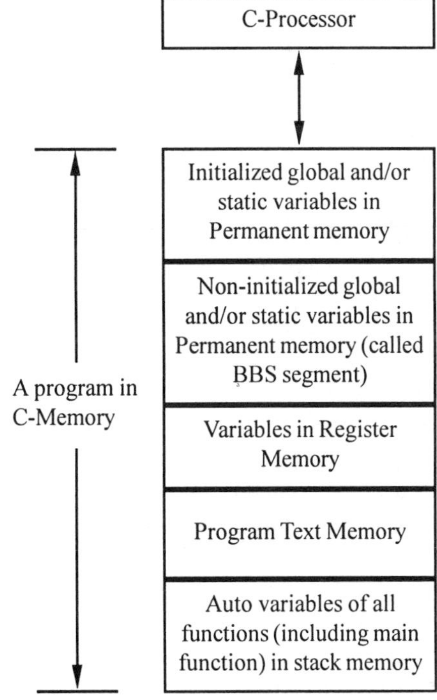


*Fig. 5.5 Storage allocation for a C-program (refer also to Fig. 5.2)*

During compilation, the ***global*** and ***static*** variables are set up in separate permanent memory images (i.e., ***initialized*** and ***uninitialized (BSS)*** images) by the compiler and loaded into the allocated physical memory before execution of a program. At the same time, a stack memory of appropriate size is provided for each program to lend space for auto variables and function call arguments. Therefore, a function (either main or a subordinate) accesses its ***global*** and ***static*** variables from ***permanent*** (and/or ***BSS***) memory, and ***local*** variables and function arguments from ***stack*** memory.

## Using the Stack for auto Storage

We will now discuss how a common stack area is used during program execution. When a program starts execution, ***main*** is invoked first. Its internal variables are created in the stack and the stack pointer is moved appropriately to show the free area of stack that can be further used if any other function is called by ***main***. During a function call, the stack pointer moves through the free stack area to accommodate the arguments being passed and any declared local variables in the called function. Meanwhile, the values passed in the call are copied into the arguments space in the stack. Function execution then commences. Once a function exits, its stack space is released by moving the stack pointer to its position maintained just before this function was called. During each subsequent function call from the same calling function, the space for the arguments and local variables will be reserved from the freed stack. When the functions are called in a flat manner, rather than nested, the local and passed parameters of each function utilize the same region of the stack. This indicates that the local variables of a function may not retain values from one call to another call to the same function. In other words, the stack is used as a dynamic memory to cater for temporary creation of variables during a function call. This explains why the local variables are called dynamic, temporary or auto variables.

Let us consider a program file with three functions, as shown in ***Fig. 5.6***. Execution starts in the ***main*** with the local or auto variables (i.e., ***I*** and ***J***) created in the stack and the stack pointer is moved to point to the top of the stack (or the beginning of free stack area). Somewhere along the execution, ***main*** calls ***fX***. When this function is entered, its internal variables (i.e., ***K*** and ***L***) are created in the remaining stack area and the stack pointer is moved again to keep track of free stack area. At the end of this function execution, the used stack area is released and the stack environment for ***main*** is restored. Now, ***main*** calls another function called ***fY***. When ***fY*** is entered, its local variables (i.e., ***M*** and ***N***) are created in the free stack in the area just released due to ***fXs*** exit. This demonstrates how the auto variables of the function ***fX*** are lost due to the reallocation of the same area to the second function.

A characteristic of a ***main*** function is that it continues executing until the completion of program execution. In other words, the execution of ***main*** is the same as program execution. The ***auto*** variables (i.e., internal variables) declared in the ***main*** function will remain in the stack throughout the program execution.

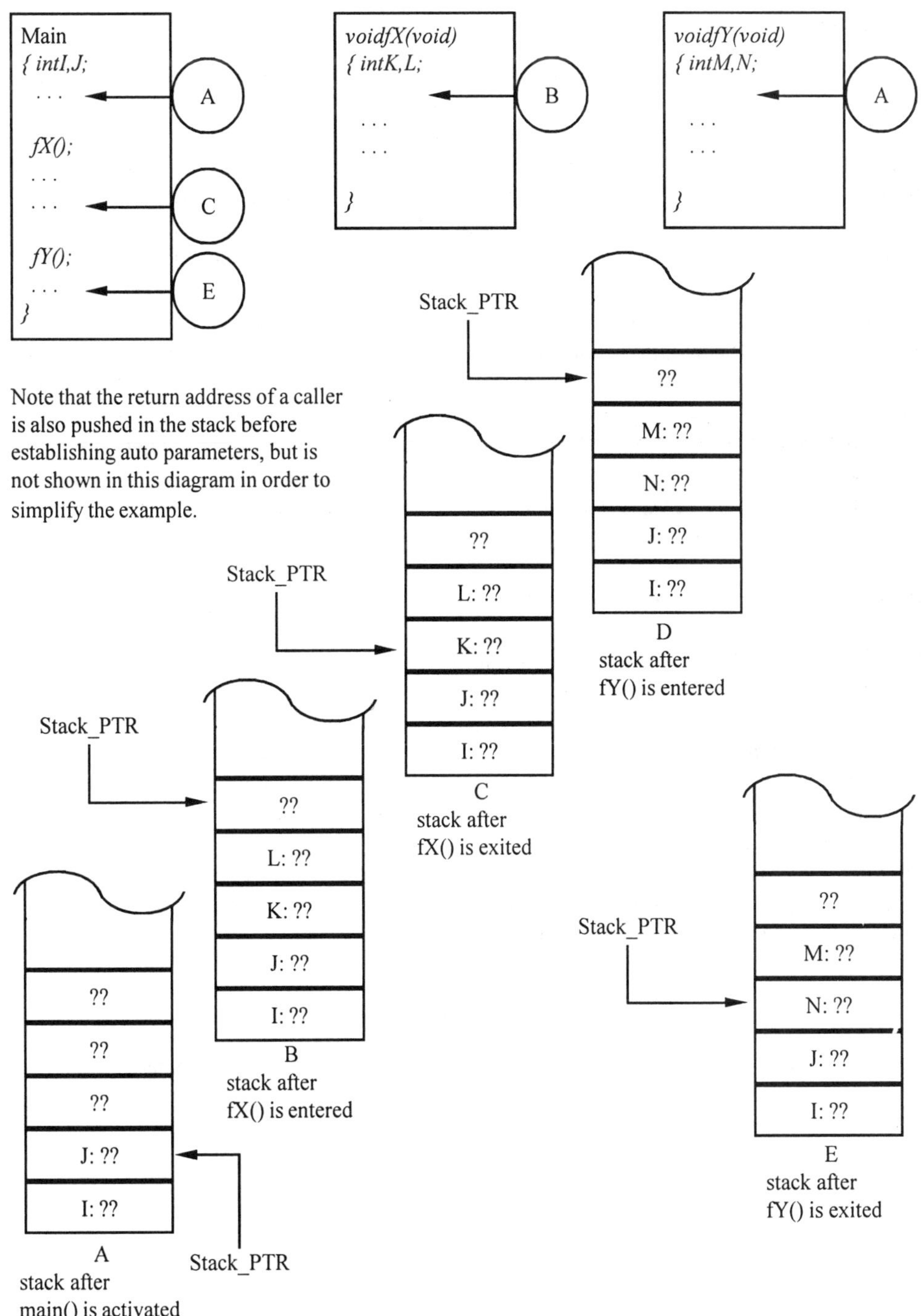


*Fig. 5.6 Auto storage class using stack*

## 5.6 Initializing Variables

A variable can be initialized at two different times:

1. *during the compilation process;*
2. *during execution.*

Any initialization explicitly shown in a declaration statement can be done by the compiler, provided that dedicated address space is used for the declared variables. Since the compiler uses dedicated address space for permanent type variables, it allows initialization for these variables. Whatever value we put in a variable's location at the time of compilation will be available during execution time. On the other hand, the compiler uses sharable address space (i.e., stack) for local variables, and this obviously does not allow initialization at compile time. However, ANSI-C allows initialization of any variable at declaration time. Let us explain now how compilers allow run-time initialization for simple (i.e., char, int or float type) variables. The following example explains how a compiler can manage to initialize local variables. A compiler translates a local declaration, such as

```
void main(void)
{
    int    k = 10;
      . . .
}
```

into

```
void main(void)
{
    int    k;
    k = 10;
      . . .
}
```

and creates machine code for the assignment statement. Every time a function is called, the initializing statements are executed to restore the initial values, which can be extended to array and composite type of variables in ANSI-C.

## 5.7 Typedef

The ***typedef*** declaration facility can be used to create new type names as synonyms for the existing types. The main advantage of this facility is that a program can maintain type names more appropriate to the data structures of an application. The format of this declaration is shown as follows:

*typedef existing_type new_type_name*

### Example 5.3:

Let us assume that we implement a program that simulates an 8-bit machine with the following CPU elements. Also, assume in our C, char creates 8-bit objects and short integer creates 16-bit objects.

- *64K memory*
- *two accumulators*
- *one 8-bit conditional code (i.e., status) register*
- *one program counter*
- *two index registers*
- *one stack pointer*

The data structure of this program can be described with abstract level type names to make the program more readable, as shown below:

```
typedef char BYTE
typedef char DATA_REGISTER
typedef unsigned short int    ADDRESS_REGISTER
/* Declare CPU elements    */
BYTE    memory[65536];        /* main memory of 64k bytes    */
DATA_REGISTER A, B;   /* Accumulators   */
DATA_REGISTER CC;     /* condition code register    */
ADDRESS_REGISTER X, Y; /* index registers     */
ADDRESS_REGISTER S;   /* stack pointer    */
```

We can also name the prototype definitions of composite data types, i.e., ***struct*** and ***union***, using ***typedef*** declaration. The use of ***typedef*** with these data types will be explained in ***Chapter 15***.

## 5.8 Dynamic Storage Type

Although it is too early to explain the concept of pointers (i.e., address type variables), it is important to note that a dynamic storage type is necessary for exploiting their full power. A pointer (or an address variable) is normally used to point to a C-defined data object (i.e., char, int, float, an array, struct or union), but a pointer can be effectively used to point to an abstract object that has a tendency to grow. For example, a linked list of structures can be structured dynamically during program execution. In such situations, the growing data structure requires the allocation of memory space dynamically. For this purpose, C allows programmers to use library functions like ***malloc***, ***realloc***, ***calloc*** and ***free*** to allocate and free storage during program execution. Using pointers and these functions, C-programs can maintain ***dynamic types of variables***. Although these variables look similar to ***auto*** variables, their duration of existence is decided by programmers. Since these functions require the knowledge of all available data structure in C, ***Chapter 16*** is dedicated to introducing the principles of creating dynamic data structures using the dynamic storage.

## 5.9 Summary

C provides a rich set of data structures that have restrictions, both spatially and temporally. This chapter introduced the way C classifies the data declarations falling into several categories such as global, static, local, external, etc., and elaborated the scope rules for the created variables under each category with the help of compile-time as well as run-time storage management. The concept of temporary storage using stack is explained to understand how functions maintain their variables, why they define them as auto variables, and how these variables are initialized. This chapter also initiated a discussion on dynamic storage management maintained by C and its scope in creating dynamic data structures.

## Exercises

5.1 Show the memory maps for the following external declarations:

```
int    i;
char  ch = 'Z';
void  main(void)
  {
    . . .
  }
float f;
char  str[] = "ABCD";
ret_type  func(void)
  {
    . . .
  }
```

5.2 Under what circumstance does the compiler require the prototype definition of a function? Explain.

5.3 What is the purpose of the ***extern*** class in declarations?

5.4 Are the following statements TRUE or FALSE?

(a) A simple local variable can be initialized.
(b) An array variable can be initialized when it is declared outside a function.
(c) A string can be initialized inside a function.
(d) The static type declaration is normally used to declare global variables.
(e) A variable declared within a block will be created in a run-time stack.

5.5 What is the meaning of the scope of a declaration?

5.6 Determine the scope of the variables in the following source program:

```
int    i;
void  main(void)
  {
    int    j;
      . . .
      if(j >10)
        {
          int    k;
            . . .
        }
  }
int    l;
void func(void)
  {
    int     m;
    static  int     n;
    int     i;
      . . .
  }
```

# 6

# Statements in C

**Chapter contents:**

*This chapter introduces various types of statements available in C. After reading this chapter, the readers will be familiar with the rich concepts of C-statements, including control and special statements, such as the ternary statement.*

**Organization:**

*6.1 Introduction*
*6.2 Simple Expression Statements*
*6.3 Control Statements*
*6.4 Compound or Block Statements*
*6.5 Miscellaneous Statements*
*6.6 Summary*
*Exercises*

## 6.1 Introduction

This chapter introduces the statement types that are provided by C. The statements can be classified broadly into two types: simple (or expression) statements and control statements. However, statements also include some additional types, such as compound and null statements. By understanding about their processing and controlling capabilities, C-programmers are able to structure their program texts very efficiently. Remember that:

- *a C-statement usually ends with a semicolon, acting as statement terminator (or delimiter);*
- *there may be more than one statement to a line, provided that each statement is delimited by a semicolon;*
- *to maintain the clarity of a program's text, C-programmers usually follow the rule of one statement per line;*
- *a statement can extend over more than one line without any restriction.*

The syntax of a C-statement is shown in ***Fig. 6.1***.

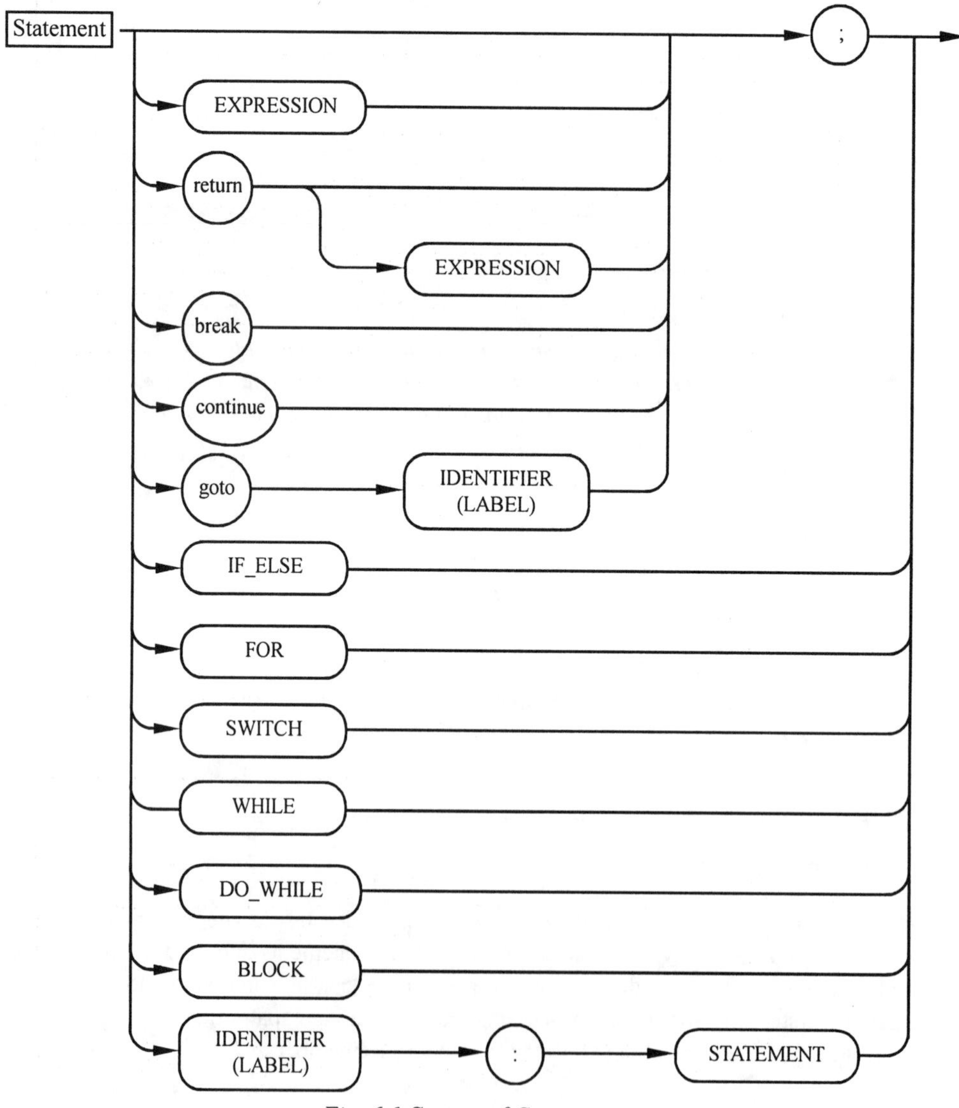


*Fig. 6.1 Syntax of C-statement*

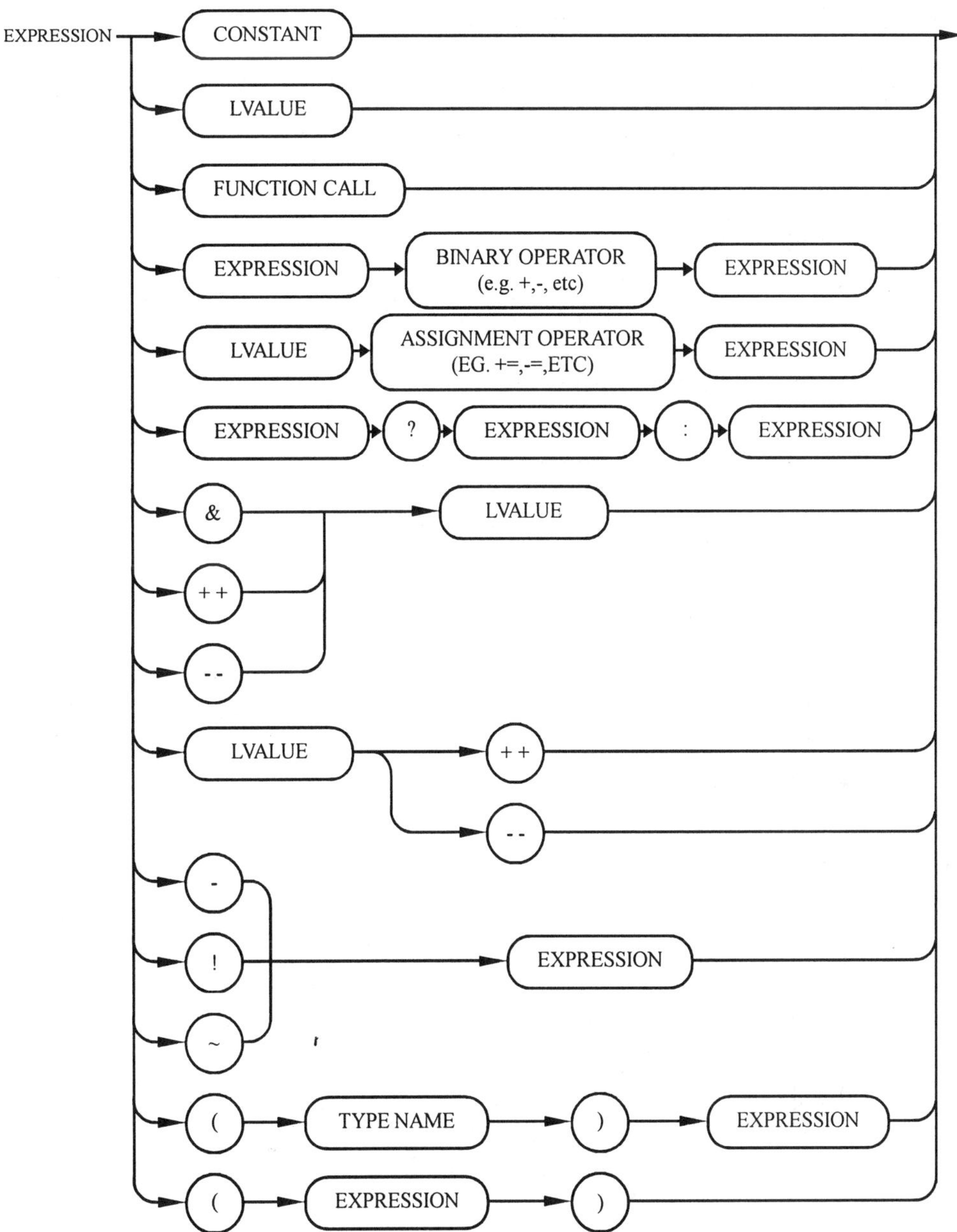


*Fig. 6.2 Syntax of expression*

## 6.2 Simple Expression Statements

Expressions are the building blocks of the C-statements that manipulate data. An expression that has completed processing, and saved its evaluated results from the C-processors buffer either explicitly or implicitly may be considered a meaningful statement. ***Fig. 6.2*** shows the syntax of C-expression.

### 6.2.1 Single Expression Statements

A single expression statement is one which contains one simple expression followed by a semi-colon. The following cases belong to this category.

**(a) Functional Expression Statement**

In this case, a statement contains a single function call expression which manipulates data elements (passed as arguments or generated implicitly) and saves the evaluated results implicitly. The syntax of a function call expression is shown in ***Fig. 6.3***. The following examples illustrate this case:

*printf("This statement is a function-call statement");*

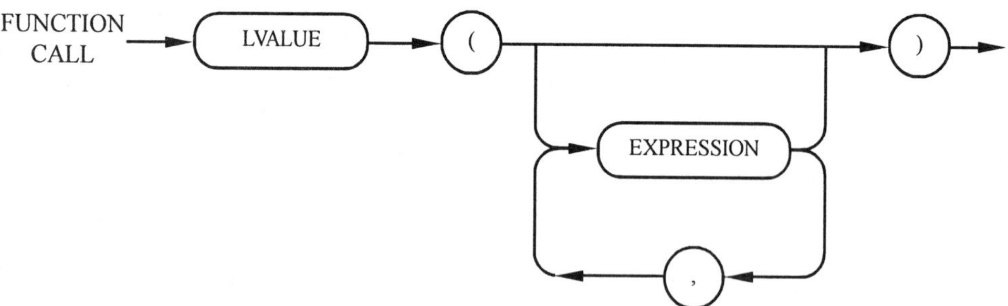


*Figure 6.3 Syntax of function call*

*puts("Print a line of Text");*

**(b) Increment/Decrement Expression Statement**

A simple variable expression with either the increment or decrement operator can form a simple statement. Assume that *i* and *j* are two declared variables in our program. Then we can write code to increment *i* and decrement *j* in simple statements, as shown below:

```
i++;        /* increment the value of i by one */
j—;         /* decrement  the value of j by one  */
```

**(c) Simple Assignment Expression Statement**
The format is:

***lvalue <assignment_operator> rvalue_expression;***
(or)
***lvalue_expression <assignment_operator> rvalue_expression;***

The following examples belong to this category:

```
i = 100;
j += 1;      /* same as j = j+1 */
k <<= 2;  /* shift bits of k left by two positions */
mem_size_of_i = sizeof(i);
float f = (float)i;
ch = getchar();
```

## 6.2.2 Multiple Expression Statements

A multiple expression statement is one in which a sequence (or group) of expressions occurs for evaluation, proceeding either from right to left or left to right. However, the result of the current expression is made available to the next step in the sequence. C provides three types of expression sequences to construct a statement of this category, namely the ***multiple assignment expression***, the ***comma expression*** and the ***ternary expression***. These types are explained below using examples.

### Case 1: Multiple assignment statement

A multiple assignment statement is an extension of the single assignment case. As we have already discussed, a single assignment statement contains two (i.e., *lvalue* and *rvalue*) expressions with one assignment operator. The evaluation is done from right to left. Evaluation starts at the rvalue expression and then proceeds to the lvalue expression before assigning the computed rvalue to lvalue. At the same time, the value of assignment expression is available in the buffer of the expression evaluation unit (recall this in our C-machine). The basic principle of multiple assignment states that this expression value (i.e., buffer contents) can be further assigned to another lvalue expression by extending the basic assignment statement.

**Format:**
***lvalue_expn1 = lvalue_expn2 = . . . = rvalue_expn;***

Example:

```
k = 0;          /* single assignment statement */
j = k = 0;    /* two assignment statement */
i = j = k = 0; /* three assignment statement */
```

### Case 2: Comma Expression Statement

A comma expression statement is one in which expressions of a given group are separated by the comma operator (','). In this case, evaluation starts from the left-most expression, proceeds sequentially through the comma-separated expressions, finally completing the statement by leaving the value of the right-most expression in the buffer.

**Format:**

***expn1, expn2, expn3, . . . , expnN;***

where the value of the whole expression is the value of the last expression, i.e., expnN.

Example:

*pi = 3.14, R = 10.0, A = pi*pow(R,2.0);*

where ***pow*** is a library function used to find out R to the power of 2.0.

Usually, a comma expression is used to put together a set of related expressions in a proper sequence, as shown in the above example. It is often used in a for-loop statement, which will be explained later.

### Case 3: Ternary expression statement

A ternary expression has three expressions: a test expression followed by a pair of target expressions. The evaluation starts from the test (or left-most) expression, the value of which is used to select one of the following two target expressions. This expression is evaluated to give the value of the ternary expression.

**Format:**

***expression_in _test ? target_expression_1 : target_expression_2;***

Example:

*(ch>='0' && ch<='9')?puts("ch:NUMERAL"):puts("ch: not NUMERAL");*

### Case 4: A statement with the combination of above expressions

A multiple expression statement can be made of a mixture of all the above mentioned types. For example:

*A =B = ( pi = 3.14, R = 10.0, pi*pow(R,2.0));*

Remember that a comma expression is evaluated from left to right, and the value of the comma expression is the value of the last (or the right_most) expression. In this case, the value of the comma expression is the value of the last expression i.e.,

*pi*pow(R,2.0)*

which is then assigned to B and A successively.

## 6.3 Control Statements

Control statements can be classified as unconditional and conditional branch statements, and loop or iterative statements. The branch type includes:

Unconditional
- *goto*
- *break*
- *return*
- *continue*

Conditional
- *if and if_else*
- *switch statement*

and the loop type includes:
- *for_loop*
- *while_loop*
- *do_while_loop*

### 6.3.1 Unconditional Branch Statements

### The goto Statement

The goto statement belongs to the unconditional type and is very rarely used in a structured program. However, a ***goto*** statement can be used to break the sequential flow of the program execution and transfer the control unconditionally to a labelled statement. The format is shown below:

```
        goto label;
        ...
label:  target statement;
```

where label is an alphanumeric symbol similar to any variable name. The compiler does not require any formal declaration of the label identifiers. A label is, in fact, acting as a symbolic address of a target statement, and a colon (':') is used as the label declarer. The presence of a label in a statement indicates that it is implicitly declared. Be aware that it is illegal to declare a label in the same functional block again.

The goto statement may be used on some special occasions such as a branch to the end of a program when an abnormal condition is detected. See the following example:

```
void main(void)
{       . . .
        Open_file;
        If (Open_file1_fails)
       {        . . .
        goto end_main;
       }
        . . .
end_main:
        printf ("file could not be open \n");
        printf ("Program Aborted \n");
}
```

Since the scope of a label is within a functional block, *a* ***goto*** *statement cannot transfer execution out of a function block.* But, at the same time, the branching is effective within a functional block from one statement block to another.

## The break Statement

A ***break*** statement is used to break out of the control of a loop or control statement being executed. It branches to the end of the control statement in which it was used – it always branches to the next statement. For example:

```
while (1)
  { ch = getchar();
    if(ch == EOF) break;  /* break loop and go to next_statement  */
       . . .
  }
next_statement;
```

## The return Statement

A return statement can be used by a function for two different reasons. First, a function can use this statement as a mechanism to return a value to its calling function. In this case, the keyword, ***return***, is followed by an rvalue expression as follows.

***return*** *expression;*

where the expression is any valid rvalue expression. For example:

```
return x;            (or)    return (x);
return x+y;          (or)    return (x+y);
return rand(x);      (or)    return (rand(x));
return 10*rand(x);   (or)    return (10*rand(x));
```

Second, even if a function does not return a value, a return statement can be used to cause a branch back to its calling function from anywhere in the function text. There are many occasions on which a function has to terminate its processing and return back to its caller. For example:

```
ret_type  func_X(void)
  {
  while (1)
    {
    read_a_command_from_terminal;
    If(it_is_exit_command) return;
    else
       process_a_command;
        . . .
    }
  }
```

However, if there is no return statement used in a function, then an automatic return happens after the execution of its last statement and no value is returned.

> ***Note:*** *This statement is meaningless in a main function because* **main** *is our starting function.*

### The continue Statement

A ***continue*** statement is used within a loop statement (i.e., for, while or do_while) statement to end an iteration. Immediately following a ***continue*** statement, the next iteration of the loop statement will start. For example:

```
while (1)
  { ch = getchar();
    if(ch == EOF) break;            /* break loop and go to next_statement */
    if(iscntrl(ch)) continue;       /* if a control character is received, ignore and go
                                       to next iteration */

    else
      { /* process the character */
          . . .
      }
  } /* End of while */
next_statement;
  . . .
```

## 6.3.2 Conditional Branch Statements

### The if_else-statement

### The syntax of IF_ELSE-statement

***if*** (expression) statement_1;
    ***else*** statement_2;

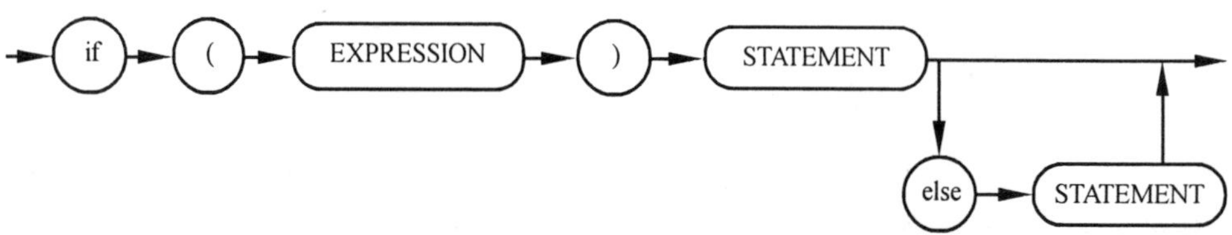


If the evaluated value of a given expression is TRUE, statement_1 is executed and control goes to the next statement ***else*** statement_2 is executed. Since a statement could be another ***if*** statement, a multiway conditional statement of any degree is possible.

The following set of ***if*** statements show multilevel and multiway conditional branching:

```
if(expression_1) statement_1;
else if (expression_2) statement_2;
 . . .
    else if (expression_n) statement_n;
else default_statement;
```

Even multiple TRUE conditions can be tested by writing a series of ***if*** clauses, as shown below:

```
if(E11) {if (E12) . . {if (E1n) statement_1; } } ... }
else . . .
```

All expressions, i.e., E11, E12, ... E1n, must be TRUE to execute statement_1. This is equivalent to:

```
if(E11 && E12 && . . . && E1n) statement_1; /*  && is logical AND  */
```

> ***Note:*** *Unlike in Pascal, the if and else constructs are treated as separate statements in C. Each if construct is delimited by a semicolon (i.e., statement delimiter) although the semantic is the same as in the if and else construct of Pascal.*

Sometimes, a null statement in an if_else statement might result in a wrong control flow, and hence, the programmers should be careful in using them. (Please see the ***Sec. 6.5.1*** for the definition of a null statement.) For example,

```
if(expression)
  statement_1;
else
  statement_2;  /* End of if(expression)  */
```

is quite different from the following construct in which an extra semicolon (i.e., a null statement) appears at the end of an else-word.

```
if(expression);  /* WRONG */
  statement_1;
else; /* WRONG */
  statement_2;  /* End of if(expression)  */
```

In the former case, if the given expression is TRUE, execute statement_1, else execute statement_2. In the latter case, if the expression is TRUE, execute statement_1 and statement_2 as if the else construct has a null statement and statement_2 does not belong to the control statement.

A general rule to avoid an error like this in a control statement is to stick to a block statement instead of a simple statement. The following example will work correctly even though a redundant null statement is present in the else construct.

```
if(expression)
  { ;  statement_1;}  /* NULL statement has no effect on the control */
else
  { ;  statement_2;}  /* NULL statement has no effect on the control */
```

## The switch-statement

A switch statement is a simplified if_else statement for achieving multiway branch depending upon the status of a given expression. Only an rvalue expression of an integer or character type can be used.

## The syntax of SWITCH-statement:

```
switch(<rvalue expression of integer or character type>)
{
  case value_1: statement_1;
          break; /* break to next_statement */
  case value_2: statement_2;
          break; /* break to next_statement */
  case value_n: statement_n;
          break; /* break to next_statement */
      ...
  default: default_statement;
}
next_statement;
```

### SWITCH-STATEMENT:

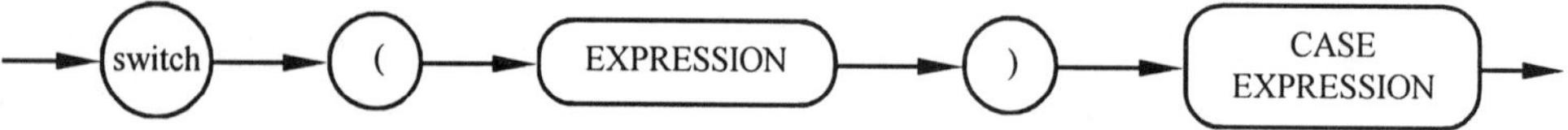


### CASE EXPRESSION:

Every time a switch-statement is executed, it checks the value of the given expression with one

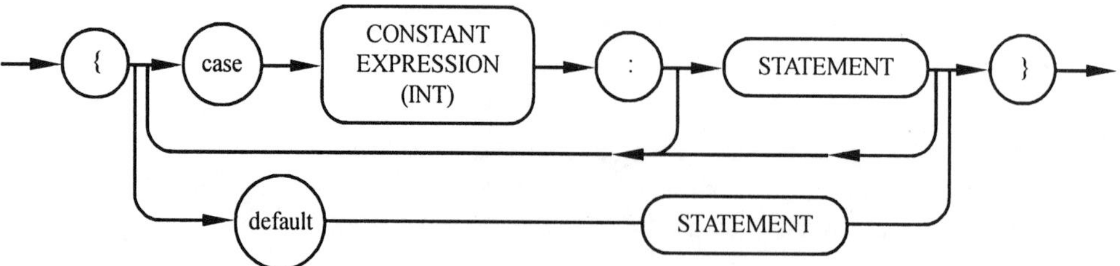


of the branch_values (i.e., cases). The corresponding case statement is executed if it finds one that matches. A "***break***" statement may be necessary as the last statement of that case to direct the execution out of the switch loop; otherwise, the execution will fall through other case statements which will be executed even though the expression being tested does not match their branch values. This is usually undesirable. When the switch-statement fails to match the value of the given expression with any of the branch values, then the default case statement will be executed. Since the default case is usually added as the last case in a switch statement, a break statement may not be necessary at the end of this case.

### 6.3.3 Loop Statements

#### The for_loop-statement

A *for_loop*-statement is useful to repeat a statement a certain number of times.

#### The syntax of the FOR-statement:

***for*** *(initializing_expression; test_expression; update_expression)*
*<statement>*

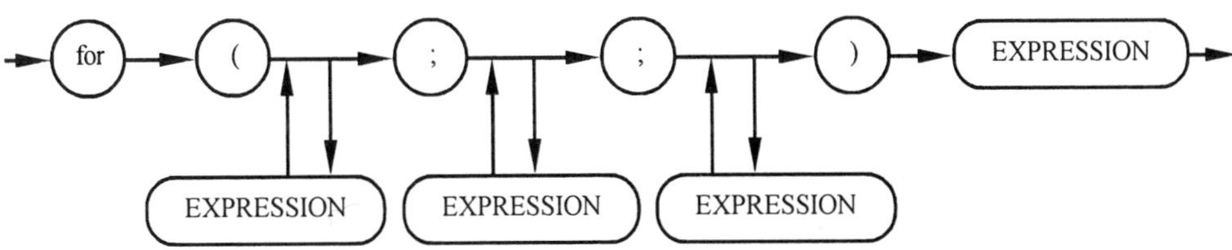


**Example 6.1:** Let us declare an array of ten integers, initialize them with the values 1 to 10, and print them on the screen.

```
#include <stdio.h>
void main(void)
{ int    i, arr[10]; /*
   for(i = 0; i < 10; i=i+1  /* (or)  i++ */  )
      arr[i] = i+1;
   printf("\n");
   for(i = 0; i < 10; i=i+1  /* (or)  i++ */  )
      printf(" %d \n", arr[i]);   /* print each value in a separate line  */
}
```

#### The while-statement

A ***while***-statement is useful to repeat a statement execution as long as a condition remains true or an event is detected. The point at which the condition being tested will change is not known in advance. The ***while***-statement tests the condition before executing the statement.

### The syntax of the WHILE-statement:

***while**(expression)* *<statement>*

### Example 6.2:

```
while((ch = getchar()) != EOF)
    { str[i] = ch;
i++; /* i.e., i = i + 1;  */
}
```

### The do_while-statement

A ***do_while***-statement is similar to the ***while***-statement, but it is executed first and then the condition is tested. In this case, the statement is executed at least once before termination.

### Syntax of the DO_WHILE-statement:

***do*** *<statement>* ***while**(expression);*

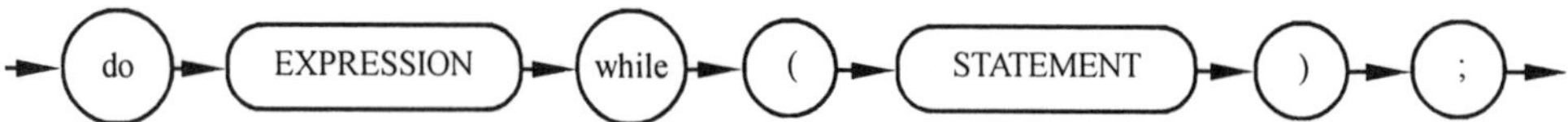


**Example 6.3:** Let us write a function that reads characters from the keyboard and puts in a string form, accumulating the characters in a buffer until an end of line character is encountered, and appending a NULL character to the returning buffer.

```
char  str[80]; /* Assume that this is declared as a global variable    */
getline()
{
   do
      {
      ch = getchar();            /* get a character from keyboard */
      if(ch == '\n')             /* is it end of line character?  */
         str[i] = '\0';          /* if true, add a NULL character to buffer   */
         else
         str[i] = ch             /* if not true, accumulate it in the buffer  */
      i++;                       /*    move index to the element in the buffer  */
      }
   while(ch != '\n');            /*    test for break condition */
}
```

## 6.4 Compound or Block Statements

A compound statement, or block statement, is basically a block which may include local declarations and a set of statements. A block is enclosed with braces, where some optional data declarations followed by a set of statements can be included. Any variable declaration within a compound statement is valid only in that block.

### The syntax of block statement:

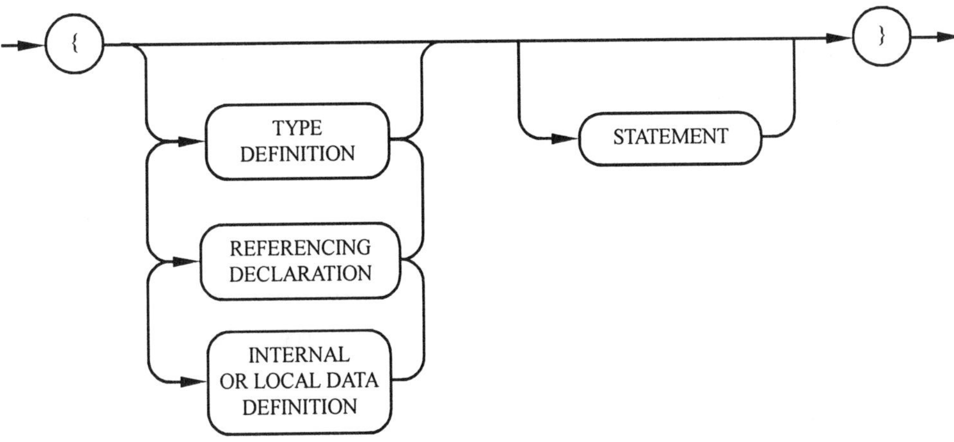

### Example 6.4:

```
{ /* A block statement */
  double pi, R; /* Note: pow receives and returns arguments of double type */
  float area;
  pi = 3.14;
  R = 10.0;
  area = pi*pow(R,2);
  printf("Radius: %f, Area: %f\n", R, area);
}
```

A compound statement appears most frequently with a branch or a loop statement in a control construct. For example:

```
if(d != 0) /* if d is NOT EQUAL to zero */
  { /* a compound statement */
    int    a; /* a can be seen by the remaining statements in this block */
    a = b+(c/d);
    printf("%d \n",a);
  }
```

A block statement is terminated by a closing brace, but not a semicolon. A semicolon is necessary to terminate only a normal or simple statement. If we add a semicolon following a block, it does no harm. This is shown in the following:

```
if(d != 0) /* if d is NOT EQUAL to zero */
  { /* a compound statement */
    int    a; /* a can be seen by the remaining statements in this block */
    a = b+(c/d);
    printf("%d \n",a);
  };
```

The extra semicolon signifies a null statement after the closing brace. In this case, the compiler ignores the null statement. The definition of a null statement can be found in the next section.

## 6.5 Miscellaneous Statements

### 6.5.1 Null Statements

A null statement can be classified as simple or compound. A simple null statement is a semicolon, while a compound null statement could be expressed by a pair of braces. Both null statements are normally used in control statements.

**Example 6.5:** A null program:

```
void main(void)
{
    ;           /* a null statement */
    ; ;         /* two null statements */;
}
```

**Example 6.6:** Let us show a situation where a NULL statement is useful. The following while-statement ignores spaces from keyboard input.

```
while((ch = getchar()) == SPACE) /* null statement */;
        (or)
while((ch = getchar()) == SPACE) {/* null compound statement */}
```

### 6.5.2 Comment Statement

A comment statement, line or field always starts with the sequence "/*" and ends with the sequence "*/".

## 6.6 Summary

This chapter formally introduces all statements available in C. The statements that are discussed here include:

- *simple expression statements, such as functions calls and assignments;*
- *conditional control statements, such as for_loop, while_loop, do_while_loop, if_else and switch statements;*
- *unconditional control statements, such as goto, continue, break and return statements;*
- *multiple expression statements, such as comma and ternary statement;*
- *block statement, NULL statement and comment statement.*

Syntax diagrams are also presented to help the readers understand the construction of the statements in a comprehensive manner.

## Exercises

6.1 How do you declare labels for goto statements?

6.2 What is the difference between a comma statement and a block statement?

6.3 Will C-compiler complain when a statement simply continues onto the next line?

6.4 What is the difference between the following constructs?

| | |
|---|---|
| while(expression) | while(expression) |
| {statement_1; | statement_1; |
| statement_2; | statement_2; |
| . . . | . . . |
| statement_n;} | statement_n; |

6.5 The for-statement is actually a special case of the while- statement, but it allows very compact coding. Rewrite the following code fragment using a while-statement.

```
int  i, j, num[20], square[20];
     for(i=0, j=0; i<20; i++, j++)
     {
          num[i] = i;
          square[i] = i*j;
     }
```

6.6 Do you find any limitation in the flexibility of the switch construct? If so, what would you suggest to improve its capability?

6.7 (a) What is the effect of the following control structure?

```
          if(x >y)
          printf("%d", x);  ;
     else
          printf("%d", y);
```

(b) Rewrite the above operation using a ternary expression statement to achieve the same result.

6.8 What is the purpose of the switch statement? (Hint: In what situation you would prefer a switch statement to an if_else statement?)

6.9 Consider the following switch control structure:

```
int    i;
. . .
i = 1;
switch(i)
{
    case 1: printf("case 1 statement is selected");
    case 2: printf("case 2 statement is selected");
    case 3: printf("case 3 statement is selected");
    default: printf("default case statement is selected");
}
```

(a) What would the output of the above statement be?

(b) What would the output be, if the statement ***'i = 1;'*** in the above program segment is replaced with ***'for(i=0; i<10; i++)'***? Explain.

# 7

# The Macro Preprocessor

**Chapter contents:**

*This chapter explains the macro features of the preprocessor. This chapter familiarizes the readers with the usage of all macro commands in C-programs.*

**Organization:**

*7.1 Introduction*
*7.2 Description of Macro Commands*
*7.3 The define Macro*
*7.4 Include Macro*
*7.5 Conditional Macros*
*7.6 Macros for Debugging*
*7.7 Miscellaneous Macros*
*7.8 Predefined Macro Names*
*7.9 The # and ## Preprocessor Operators*
*7.10 Summary*
*Exercises*

## 7.1 Introduction

The preprocessor provides a C programmer with four basic types of macro facilities. Although these facilities are not essential for running C-programs, they assist the program development phase in the following respects:

- *String substitution macros allow programmers to define constant symbols which make the source texts more readable;*
- *String substitution can also be used to define a macro function representing a small segment of frequently used statements; use of macro functions makes the source text not only readable, but also very concise;*

- *Inclusion macros allow the program development to be more dynamic in the sense that a program can grow simply by including the names of already existing source files. When modules are compiled separately, some of the common C-declarations and constant symbol definitions need not be duplicated in every module of a program. Instead, a header file containing this common information can be specified in each module with the help of an inclusion macro;*
- *The conditional macro facility helps to select text with respect to a supplied condition value. Among other things, this feature is useful for writing C-programs that are portable to systems with different versions or types of C-compilers.*

A C-compiler always accompanies its macro preprocessor. As explained in ***Chapter 2***, the first step is to resolve all the macros in the source programs before actual compilation is done for producing the target programs.

In general, the inclusion of macro preprocessor directives with source programs very effectively improves the program specification for both program development and maintenance. Specifically, such improvements make programs readable, reusable and portable.

## 7.2 Description of Macro Commands

In each of the above-mentioned cases, there could be one or more macro commands. ***Table 7.1*** lists the macro types, macro commands and the purpose of these commands. A macro command is used to construct a macro definition statement, or macro statement. A macro statement is basically one line in size. It always starts at the beginning of a line with the character '#'. In other words, a '#' in the first character of a macro statement acts as a macro identifier. If this macro identifier is missing at the beginning of a macro statement, the preprocessor will skip that line as if it were a C-statement. The command and other operand fields follow a macro identifier, or identifier field. The fields are separated by one or more white space (i.e., space or tab) character. The statement ends with a newline character.

### Format of a macro statement:

***#<command><delimiter><operand>. . .<newline>***

where the delimiter can be a white space (i.e., space or tab).

> *Note: Although a macro statement should start in column 1 of a line, some preprocessors may allow macro statements to start anywhere in a line.*

*Table 7.1 Macro types in macroprocessing*

| Macro type | macro command | Purpose |
|---|---|---|
| Text substitution | define<br>undef | To represent a string with a macro name<br>To delete a macro name from use |
| Text inclusion | include | To include texts of external files in a source programs |
| Text selection | if<br>ifdef<br>ifndef<br>else<br>elseif | To select or include a text according to the conditional parameter |
| Line numbering | line | To assign new line numbers to a segment of statements |

## 7.3 The define Macro

### 7.3.1 Parameterless Macro Definition

### The syntax of define macro:

***#define<white space>macro_identifier <white space>[object_string]***

where

- *macro_identifier is any alphanumeric string similar to a variable name;*
- *object_string is any string before a newline character; this field is optional and, hence, it may be omitted if we want to define only the existence of some symbols.*

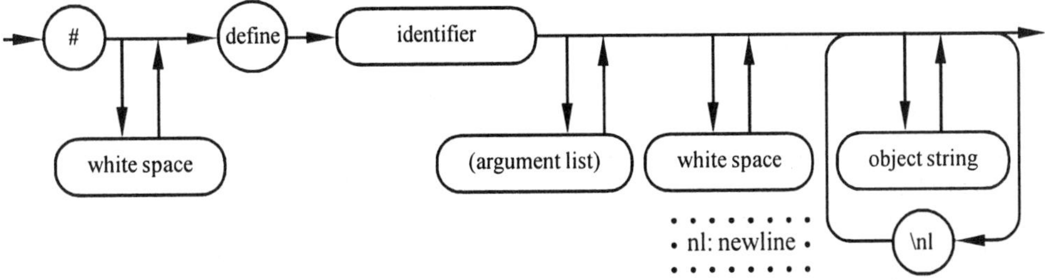

**Case 1:** A simple application of the ***define*** macro is to declare the symbolic constants which make the text more readable when we use them in our programs . For example, the following declarations show some familiar constant declarations:

```
#define MS_DOS_SYSTEM /* define the existence of the symbol */
#define TRUE    1
#define FALSE 0
#define PI      3.14
#define NEWLINE '\n'
#define TAB   '\t'
```

A command without a macro name would be treated as illegal by the preprocessor. For example:

```
#define
```

might cause an error, indicating that the macro definition requires a macro name.

### Example 7.1:

```
#define PI     3.14
void main(void)
{ float area = 0.0, R = 5.0;
      area = PI*R*R;
      printf("%f \n", area);
}
```

After preprocessing, the expanded text will be:

```
void main(void)
{ float area=0.0, R = 5.0;
      area = 3.14*R*R;
      printf("%f \n", area);
}
```

> ***Remark:*** *Can a macro be used in a string?*
>
> *C defines a string constant as a text within a pair of double quotes. Therefore, a string constant is similar to any other constants (like decimal constants). The preprocessor obviously skips any string constants that appear in a C-text. Even if a macro name appears within a string constant, it will be ignored as if it is a part of the value of that constant. This can be shown from the following* ***example****.*

## Example 7.2: DON'T USE MACROS WITHIN A STRING CONSTANT

```
#define NL   \n
#define PI     3.14
void main(void)
{ float area=0.0, R = 10.0;
    area = PI*R*R;
    printf("%f NL", area);
}
```

In the above example, the first argument to the printf() function is a control string, which is, in fact, a string constant. Since the macro name NL in the control string is transparent to the preprocessor, no substitution will be made for that macro use. After preprocessing, the expanded text will be:

```
void main(void)
{ float area=0.0, R = 10.0;
    area = 3.14*R*R;
    printf("%f NL", area);
}
```

When we compile and execute the above program, the output will be:

314.000000 NL>(Curser Position)

**Case 2:** In this case, we will discuss the macro definitions that involve expressions as object strings. For example, the following declarations define symbolic names for expressions:

```
(a) #define  SECS_PER_HR 60*60
        (or)
    #define  SECS_PER_HR 60<white space>*<white space>60
```

> *Note: Within an object string white space can occur freely.*

```
(b) #define  PUTLN    putchar('\n')
```

**Example 7.3:** Define a macro that will output a new line.

```
# define     WRITELN printf("\n")
# define     SECS_PER_HOUR    60 * 60
void main(void)
{
  WRITELN;
  printf("Number of seconds in an hour:  %d\n", SECS_PER_HOUR);
  WRITELN;
}
```

After preprocessing, the expanded text will be:

```
void main(void)
{
    printf("\n")
    printf("Number of seconds in an hour:  %d \n", 60 * 60)
    printf("\n")
}
```

**Case 3:** String substitution in nested fashion allows a macro definition to use the previously defined macro names. For example, the following are some legal declarations:

```
(a) #define N_ROW   10
    #define N_COL   10
    #define ARR_SIZE   N_ROW*N_COL

(b) #define NEWLINE    '\n'
    #define PUTLN      putchar(NEWLINE)
```

***Remark:*** *The preprocessor, after identifying a macro command, assumes the remaining text in that line to be the object string. In other words, the macro preprocessor assumes each macro definition occurs on a single line. When an object string is to be continued onto the next line, an escape sequence of a backslash character, followed by inputting a <newline> (or carriage return), can be used. Moreover, within an object string, white space can freely occur.*

### Example 7.4:

```
#define NEWLINE    '\n'
#define PUTLN     putchar(NEWLINE)
#define INPUT_MESSAGE    "Input a string that is \<newline>  less than a line"
void main(void)
{ int len;
  char str[81];
  printf("%s ", INPUT_MESSAGE);
  PUTLN;
  gets(str);
  len = 0;
  while(str[len] != '\0')
    len++;
  printf("Length of given message is  %d ",  len);
  PUTLN;
}
```

After preprocessing, the expanded output will be:

```
void main(void)
{ int len;
  char str[81];
  printf("%s \n", "Input a string that is less than a line:");
  putchar('\n');
  gets(str);
  len = 0;
  while(str[len] != '\0')
    len++;
  printf("Length of given message is  %d ", len);
  putchar('\n');
}
```

### 7.3.2 Macro Definitions with Arguments

This facility helps to construct macros like functions that can be called with arguments. The syntax of this type of definition is shown below:

***#define<white space>macro_identifier(argument_list) [white space]object_string***

In this case, the object_string may be an expression, statement or a sequence of statements that emulate a function block. However, expressions are ideal for object strings and do not produce any side effect. If we use statements for object strings, some side effects would occur, causing compilation errors. We will discuss this problem later in this section.

**Examples:**

```
#define ABS(x) (x) <0? (-x) : (x)
#define MAX(x,y)   (x)>(y)? (x) : (y)
#define MIN(x,y)   (x)>(y)? (y) : (x)
```

**Example 7.5:** Define and show the use of a macro function that will square the given argument.

```
#define SQUARE(x)    (x)*(x)
void main(void)
{ int    diameter, length, area_circle, area_square;
    length = 100;
    area_square = SQUARE(length);
    diameter = 20;
    area_circle = 3.14*SQUARE(diameter/2);
}
```

After preprocessing, the above code is transformed into:

```
void main(void)
{ int    diameter, length, area_circle, area_square;
    length = 100;
    area_square = (100)*(100);
    diameter = 20;
    area_circle = 3.14*(diameter/2)*(diameter/2);
}
```

which will not produce an ambiguous result during execution.

## Problem with argument strings

A macro call is quite different from a function call. During a function call, the parameters (even if they are expressions) are first evaluated before being passed to called functions. In the case of a macro call, which happens during preprocessing, the call token (i.e., the macro reference) is simply replaced with the object string in the definition. Before this replacement, the actual parameter expressions are simply substituted in the place of the formal parameter strings of expressions in the object string.

The actual parameter expression may consist of operators with different precedence. When these are substituted in the unparenthesized formal parameter strings, the effective object string might produce an entirely different result during evaluation. For example, let us define the SQUARE macro without parenthesis around the formal parameter strings, as shown below:

```
#define SQUARE(x)    x*x
```

The macro call, SQUARE(5+5), will be expanded by the preprocessor to:

*5+5*5+5*

which is a wrong interpretation. The actual result should be 100, but is a different value. By enclosing the formal parameter strings in the object strings, with a pair of matching parenthesis as a safe measure, this could have been avoided.

## Problem with statements in object strings

We should be careful with the object strings that contain statements. The following examples will show some implementations.

**Example 7.6:** In this example, we will implement a macro with a block statement,

```
#define PRINT(x,y)   {                         \<new line>
         printf("Bigger value: %d \n",(x));    \<new line>
         printf("Smaller value: %d \n",(y)); \<new line>
         }
```

then the macro call

```
if (i > j)
  PRINT(i,j);
else
  PRINT(j,i);
```

will be translated as

```
if (i > j)
   {
      printf("Bigger value: %d \n",(i));
      printf("Smaller value: %d \n",(j));
   } ;
else {
      printf("Bigger value: %d \n",(j));
      printf("Smaller value: %d \n",(i));
   } ;
```

In this case, a NULL statement exists redundantly at the end of the if- and else-construct as the effect of a semicolon in the macro definition. Because of the null statement after the if-construct, the else-construct is excluded from the control flow and, hence, compilation errors result.

**Example 7.7:** Now let us look at a macro implementation that avoids this side effect.

```
#define PRINT(x,y) do {                                 \<newline>
                printf("Bigger value: %d \n",(x));      \<newline>
                printf("Smaller value: %d \n",(y)); \<newline>
                }while(0)
```

where x and y are formal parameters. A macro call

```
if (i > j)
  PRINT(i,j);
else
  PRINT(j,i);
```

after preprocessing will be

```
if (i > j)
  do {
       printf("Bigger value: %d \n",(i));
       printf("Smaller value: %d \n",(j));
    }while(0);
else do {
          printf("Bigger value: %d \n",(j));
          printf("Smaller value: %d \n",(i));
          }while(0);
```

which presents an error-free source expansion.

> ***Remark:*** *When we have a statement in an object string of a macro definition, avoid the statement delimiter (i.e., the semicolon) at the end of the string.*

### 7.3.3 Undefine Macro Statement

This statement is useful to cancel the macro names that have already been defined. Once a macro is undefined, that name is no longer valid. Further occurences of that macro name will be ignored by the preprocessor.

**The syntax of undefine macro:**

**Example 7.8:**

```
#define TODAY "Monday"
void main(void)
{
  . . .
}
#undef TODAY
func1()
{
  . . .
}
```

### 7.3.4 Redefining Macros

The same define macro statement can be used to redefine a macro name that has already been defined in a file. This redefined macro value will be valid until it is redefined again in that file.

**Example 7.9:**

```
#define TODAY "Monday"
void main(void)
{
  . . .
}
#define TODAY "24th June 1991"
func1()
{
  . . .
}
```

If a macro is redefined without any change in the macro value (i.e., exactly same as the previous definition), the preprocessor will proceed quietly. However, if a redefinition changes the macro value of a standard macro that has been defined in the macro library, the preprocessor will complain. In order to avoid any such complaint, first undefine and then redefine the macro.

## 7.4 Include Macro

This statement is useful to include header files that normally keep common declarations for a multi-module program. For example, let us consider a three module program, *main.c., fun_A.c* and *fun_B.c*. Assume that the *main.c* module declares the global variables, x and y, which are accessed in every module of this program. In order to make these variables known to other functions, a header file can be prepared to contain external declaration of these variables and include the *fun_A.c* and *fun_B.c* files. When we compile these functions separately, the preprocessor contains the text of the included file before compilation starts. This action is equivalent to having included all the external declarations in each file. This technique saves not only coding time, but file space.

### Syntax diagram for include macro statement:

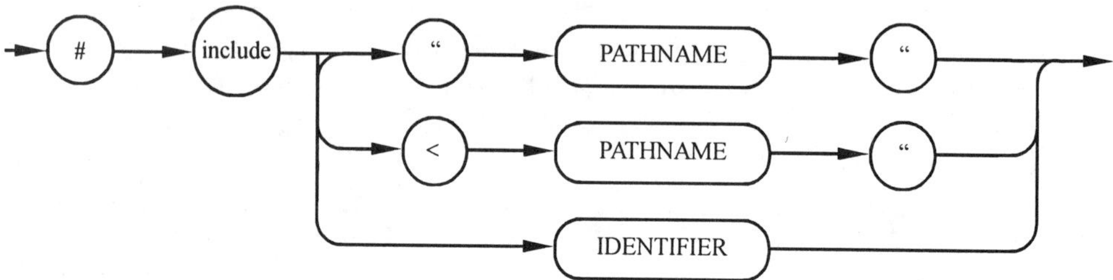


**Example 7.10:** The following program has a common header file called *common.h* where references to global variables are defined.

```
common.h file:
        extern  char  buf[];
        extern  int    buf_size;

fun_A.c file:
        #include "common.h"
        fun_A()
        {
            . . .
        }
```

```
fun_B.c file:
        #include "common.h"
        fun_B()
        {
            . . .
        }
main.c file:
        char  buf[512];
        int   buf_size;
        void  main(void)
        {
          . . .
        }
```

In this example, the include macro specifies the file name in a pair of double quotes, which is really the path name of the included file. The path name within double quotes is first searched from the current directory. If the file is not found in this search, then further searches may be carried through other search paths maintained by the system. In the above example, we have assumed that *common.h* exists in the same directory, and hence, the path of the included file is simply the name of the file. Suppose *common.h* existed in the next higher level (i.e., immediate parent) directory, then the include statements in the *fun_A.c* and *fun_B.c* modules would be written as:

```
#include    "../common.h"
```

***Note:*** *In Unix file system, one can point the locations of the current directory, a parent directory and the root directory using some special symbols. The current directory can be pointed by "." (a single dot), a parent directory by ".." (two dots) and the root directory by "/" (a slash). In the above example, the path, ../common.h, specifies that the target file (common.h) is located at the parent of the current directory. The following examples explain different path expressions to locate a file:*

| | |
|---|---|
| *common.h* | *common.h is in the current directory;* |
| *./common.h* | *common.h is in the current directory;* |
| *../ommon.h* | *common.h is in the parent of the current directory;* |
| */common.h* | *common.h is in the root directory;* |
| */usr/common.h* | *common.h is in the usr directory, located at the root directory.* |

### 7.4.1 Standard Macros and Header Files

In C, programmers commonly use standard constants and functions. If these constants and functions (provided they are small) can be defined as macros and kept in a header file, programmers may find writing code using these macros much simpler. When such a header file is available, the programmers simply have to include that file before using the defined macros from it. A single header file usable by all application programs would be quite large in size, and the inclusion of such a large macro file in a source program would make the compilation process more time consuming. Hence, the C-library comes with many small header files that are classified according to either the type of data or type of application. The following typical header files are available for C-programmers:

*Table 7.1 Standard header files*

| Header File | Purpose |
|---|---|
| assert.h | defines assert() macro |
| ctype.h | contains several macro functions for character processing |
| errorno.h | error reporting |
| float.h | defines implementation-dependent floating point value |
| limits.h | defines implementation-dependent various limits |
| locale.h | supports the setlocale() function |
| math.h | contains various prototype definitions used by math's library |
| setjmp.h | supports non-local jump |
| signal.h | defines signal values |
| stdarg.h | supports various-length argument lists |
| stddef.h | defines some commonly used constant |
| stdio.h | generally supports file I/O. It contains macro definitions for:<br>(a) data structures of ***stream*** I/O, such as ***FILE*** structure, ***EOF***, ***NULL***;<br>(b) character I/O functions, such as ***getc***(), ***putc***(), ***getchar***() and ***putchar***();<br>(c) declaration of standard stream names, such as ***stdin***, ***stdout*** and ***stderr***;<br>(d) prototype definitions of other I/O functions. |
| stdlib.h | miscellaneous declarations |
| string.h | supports the use of string functions in programs, includes the prototype definitions of all string functions, and must be included in a program that deals with string processing. |
| time.h | supports system time functions |

These standard header or macro files are stored in a standard place in the Unix's file system (i.e., in a separate include directory whose path is /usr/include). When we want to include one of these standard files, we simply put the name of the file within ***a pair of matching angle brackets***. For example:

*#include <stdio.h>*

will include stdio.h from the directory, /usr/include. If the included file is not found in this standard place, the search will simply fail.

**Example 7.11:** The following program uses the ***stream*** I/O facility to display the contents of a file.

```
#include <stdio.h>
void main(void)
{ char ch;
  FILE    *fp, *fopen();
    fp = fopen("myfile", "r");
    while((ch=getc(fp) != EOF)
      putchar(ch);
}
```

**Example 7.12:** Let us modify ***Example 7.4*** to output the number of alphabetic characters in a given string.

```
#include <stdio.h>
#include <ctype.h>
#define  INPUT_MESSAGE    "Input a string that is   \<newline>   less than 80 characters:"

  void main(void)
  { int    alpha_count, index;
    char str[81];
    printf("%s \n", INPUT_MESSAGE);
    gets(str);
    alpha_count = 0;
    index = 0;
    while(str[index] != '\0')
      {
        if(isalpha(str[index]))
          alpha_count++;
        index++;
      }
    printf("Number of alphabetic characters  in the message is  %d \n", alpha_count);
  }
```

## 7.5 Conditional Macros

This facility provides a control structure when using defined macros for varying situations such as compiling a program in different systems, introducing debugging aids during program development, avoiding any duplication of macro definitions, etc. The following examples show the use of this facility.

### Syntax diagram for Conditional macros

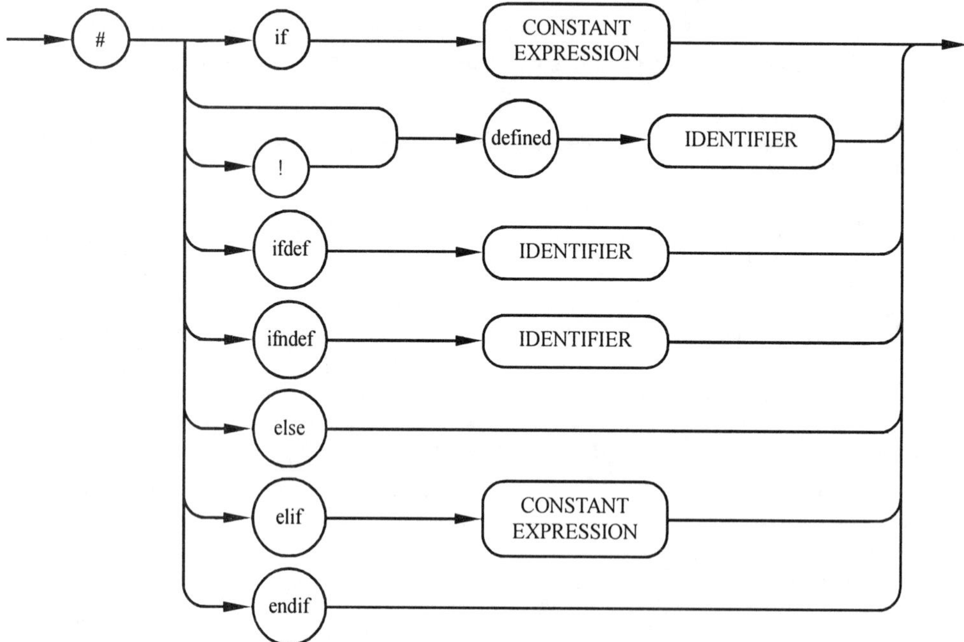


### Example 7.13:

```
#include <stdio.h>
#define DEBUG_flag
void main(void)
{
    . . .
/* This statement will only compile when DEBUG_flag is defined */
#ifdef DEBUG_flag
    printf("%d, %d, %d, . . . ", a, b, c, . . .);
#endif
    . . .
}
```

**Example 7.14:** This example shows that a macro symbol will only be defined if the preprocessor has not previously defined it.

```
#ifndef NULL
#define NULL 0
#endif
void main(void)
  {
     . . .
  }
```

## 7.6 Macros for Debugging

### 7.6.1 Line Macro

#### Purpose of Line Macro

When we compile a program, the C-compiler usually assigns line numbers to each line of the source program file. The numbering starts with 1, increasing in increments of one until the last line of that file. During compilation, if any error is detected, the compiler outputs a diagnostic message containing the name of the source file followed by a line number and the description of error. For example, a syntax error in line 10 of a program called *our_prog.c* will be reported as:

*"our_prog.c", line 10: syntax error at or near some_symbol_name*

If *our_prog.c* is a single module (i.e., with only main() function) program, then we can picture the location of the error quite easily. If this happens to be a large and multiple module program, the compiler-assigned numbering may not indicate the location of error (i.e., which line and in which function) precisely. In order to improve this situation, a programmer can use a line macro statement to start each segment (function) with a new origin and also supply a segment name (or function name). The compiler can then report error messages with the given segment name and the line in that segment. If the segment name is not supplied, then the source file name will be used in the error messages.

#### Format of line macro statement:

***#line<delimiter><line number><delimiter><segment name>***

#### Syntax diagram for line macro statement:

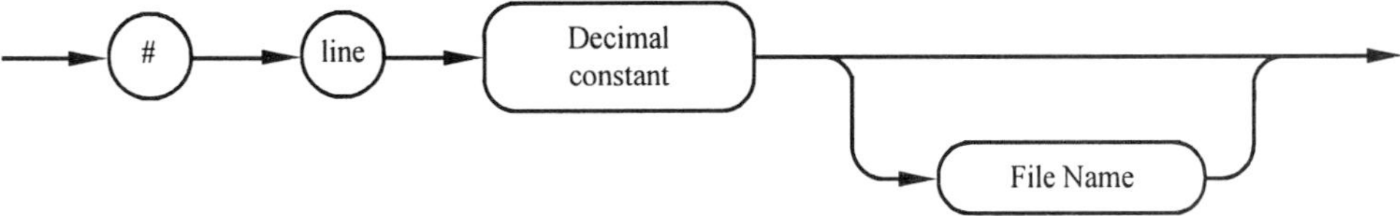

### Example 7.15:

```
                                   New Numbering
#line 1  main
#include <stdio.h>                      1
  main()                                2
{int  i;                                3
    i =100;                             4
    j = square(i);                      5
     statement_3;                       6
}                                       7

#line 1 square
square(x)                               1
int    x;                               2
{                                       3
  z =x*x;                               4
  return(z)                             5
}                                       6
```

During compilation, errors from main() and square() will be reported as:

| | |
|---|---|
| *'main', line 5:* | *j UNDEFINED* |
| *'main', line 6:* | *statement_3 UNDEFINED* |
| *'square', line 4:* | *z UNDEFINED* |
| *'square', line 4:* | *Declared assignment x is missing* |
| *'square', line 5:* | *z UNDEFINED* |

### 7.6.2 The #error Directive

The ***#error*** directive is useful for program debugging. This directive stops the program compilation and displays some implementation-dependent message. It can display any tokens included by the programmer. The format of this directive is:

*#<white space>error<white space> tokens*

### Syntax diagram for #error directive

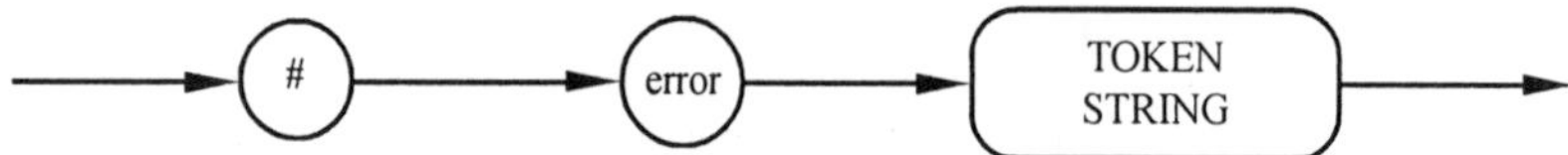

The compiler outputs the message with the other implementation-dependent items. A common display of #error is:

*Error filename line-nummessage*

where *filename* is the name of the source file, *line-num* is the line number of the error directive and *message* contains the tokens supplied by the programmer. For example:

```
#if defined (MAC) ) && defined ( IBM )
#error  "Only one computer configuration at any time."
#endif
```

and the displayed information is:

*Error main.c 13: "Only one computer configuration at any time."*

## 7.7 Miscellaneous Macros

### 7.7.1 The NULL (#) Directive

A line containing only # at the first position is called the NULL macro command. Compilers simply ignore these lines like C-comment lines.

### Syntax diagram for NULL directive

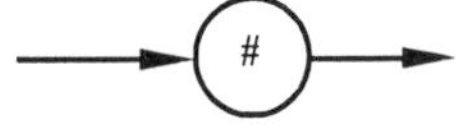


For example, NULL directives can be used to decorate an include macro, as shown below:

```
#
# include  <stdio.h>
#
```

### 7.7.2 The #pragma Directive

The ***pragma*** directive may be used:

- *to pass information to the compiler about the environment;*
- *to instruct the translator to perform some extra functions, such as optimization, diagnosing errors, etc.*

### Syntax diagram for pragma directive

As an example, let us consider a standard cross-compiler written for producing codes for the Motorola family of processors. The following directive will direct the compiler to produce the code for M68000:

```
#pragma     M68000
#include    <stdio.h>
void main(void)
{
    <declarations and statements>
}
```

## 7.8 Predefined Macro Names

ANSI-C preprocessor includes five predefined identifiers to contain the attributes related to a source file being compiled. These identifiers are:

1. ***__LINE__ :*** contains the line number of the current source line being compiled. A #line directive can reset the value of this identifier.
2. ***__FILE__:*** contains the name of the file being compiled. A line directive can change the contents from the name of the file being compiled to the name supplied as an argument.
3. ***__DATE__:*** carries the current date of a file being compiled in the form "mm dd yyyy".
4. ***__TIME__:*** carries the time of the compilation of a source file in the form "hh:mm:ss".
5. ***__STDC__:*** carries the decimal constant 1 intended to indicate that this implementation conforms to the standard.

With the exception of ***__LINE__*** and ***__FILE__***, the identifiers are constants and cannot be changed by a user. Any non-standard compiler, when coming across ***__LINE__*** and ***__FILE__***, may ignore it without any misinterpretation.

The values of some of these parameters can be displayed by the help of a program, as shown below:

```
#include <stdio.h>
void  main(void)
{
      printf("File Name:        %s \n", __FILE__);
      printf("Compiled on:   %s", __DATE__);
      printf("at time:                    %s", \n", __TIME__);
      printf("Current line:    %d\n", __LINE__);
}
```

We can also find out whether a compiler conforms to ANSI standard with the help of the following code:

```
#include <stdio.h>
void main(void)
{
#ifdef     __STDC__
              printf("This compiler conforms to the standard \n");
      #else
              printf("This compiler does not conform to the standard \n");
}
```

## 7.9 The # and ## Preprocessor Operators

ANSI-C provides two preprocessor operators: # and ##. These operators are used in define commands. The # operator converts a given operand into a string. For example:

```
#include <stdio.h>
#define   convrt(x) # x
void main(void)
{
        printf(convrt(Hello World Message));
}
```

After preprocessing, the source looks like:

```
void main(void)
{
        printf("Hello World Message");
}
```

The ## operator is used to concatenate two tokens. For example:

```
#include <stdio.h>
#define   concate(x,y)        x ## y
void main(void)
{
        printf("%d \n", concate(1000,000));
}
```

After preprocessing, the above text will look like:

```
void  main(void)
{
        printf("%d \n", 1000000);
}
```

> ***Remark:*** *These two operators may not be frequently used in our programs, except in some special situations.*

## 7.10 Summary

This chapter introduced four kinds of macros, namely string substitution, inclusion, conditional compilation and miscellaneous macros. String substitution is implemented using the ***#define*** directive. The file inclusion macro is implemented using ***#include*** directives. The conditional macro facility discussed in this chapter includes ***#if***, ***#ifdef***, ***#ifndef***, ***#else*** and ***#endif***. The line macro was discussed under miscellaneous type.

## Exercises

7.1 Identify the illegal definitions:

(a) # define
(b) #define A
(c) # define A a
(d) # define A a a
(e) # define A this is a
long text
(f) #*define A B
(g) # define S “a string
(h) # define S a string”
(i) # define A ‘B’
(j) # define A ‘B
(k) # define ‘A’ B

7.2 Show macro definitions for the following character tests and manipulations:

(a) isalpha(ch)
(b) isupper(ch)
(c) isspace(ch)
(d) tolower(ch)

7.3 Define a macro to emulate the strcpy() function.

7.4 Explain the difference between the following #include macros:

```
#include <stdio.h>
    main()
{
    . . .
    . . .
}
```

```
#include "stdio.h"
main()
{
    . . .
    . . .
}
```

7.5 Implement the following macro functions:

(a) MIN(a,b) to return the minimum value
(b) MAX(a,b) to return the maximum value
(c) ABS(a) to return the absolute value

# 8

# Integer and Real Variables

**Chapter contents:**
*This chapter introduces the structures of C-variables and explains how they are closer to machine-level data structures.*

**Organization:**


*8.1 Introduction*
*8.2 Integer Types*
*8.3 Real Type*
*8.4 Integer and Real Arrays*
*8.5 Declaration of a Buffer (Byte Array)*
*8.6 Summary*
*Exercises*


## 8.1 Introduction

Commonly used arithmetic class variables are integers and reals. When we say ***integer class***, we normally mean both the signed and unsigned set of whole numbers. Signed integer variables can hold either positive or negative whole numbers, whereas unsigned integer variables can hold only positive values. (The magnitude of a signed integer is approximately half that of an unsigned number). Variables in the ***real class*** hold values in a more realistic form (i.e., numbers with fractions). In all scientific and engineering applications, both *signed integer* and *real numbers* become significant types of data. It is not uncommon to come across the use of unsigned whole numbers in certain applications. For example, counting events, population figures, memory addresses, etc always yield values in the positive range. Since an unsigned integer is a sub-range of the ***signed integer type***, we find that programmers often use ***signed integers*** in place of the unsigned type.

This chapter explains the memory representation of both integer and real types, how they are dependent on the word length of the supporting hardware and how ANSI-C provides the portability measures by specifying minimum requirements in their ranges and precision.

## 8.2 Integer Types

### 8.2.1 Ranges of Integer Types

Unfortunately, *C* and similar languages provide data types for integer and real classes with limited value ranges due to the nature of the physical storage of these data structures in the language machines. In other words, a computer word as a unit is directly used to emulate integer or floating point (i.e., real) data structures. For example, in a 16-bit machine, one 16-bit memory word can be interpreted as a 16-bit integer word, and this 16-bit integer word can store an integer value between -32768 and +32767 assuming that the 2's complement notation is used in arithmetic processes. Similarly, a real word may be emulated in the above machine by two 16-bit memory words to cover a normal range and precision. Since the C-language is available in machines with different word lengths, the use of these two data structures in a program may raise concern. The main worry is whether application data can fit within the range of declared variables under these two classes in a given machine or C-implementation.

To help the application programmers in this respect, C provides additional integer and real types, allowing both extended and sub-range types. The ***long*** type may provide an extended (or super) range corresponding to two memory words, and the ***double*** type may extend both the range and precision of a real variable corresponding to an extended number of memory words. For example, in a 16-bit processor, C may allocate two 16-bit memory words to cover the range of a long integer between -2147483648 ( -2exp+31) and +2147483647 ((+2exp+31)-1). The range extension from normal integer to long integer is really squared times (not just doubled). A ***double*** floating point variable with twice the mantissa size doubles the precision, but with twice the size of exponent, may provide a range many times larger than a normal floating point variable. These extended ranges cover data representations in most applications, but what is the solution when the extended types are found insufficient to accommodate certain problem data? The answer is to run the C-programs in a larger word length machine or provide user defined data structures and functions to handle the necessary precision.

*C* also provides two sub-range data structures in the integer class: ***short*** (shorter than normal integer) type and very short, or character size (i.e., usually a byte size), integer type. A ***short*** integer variable may be created with one-half of the memory word to cover a smaller integer range, while a very short integer variable may be created by using the ***char*** type data structure. A ***char*** variable is usually associated with a byte of storage, and its integer value in the signed context ranges from -128 to +127. The use of these sub-range types is not always necessary, but may be significant when an application data falls in this range. The programs for this type of data must be short enough to load and run in a limited memory environment, which is quite common when designing real-time application programs, normally given limited fixed size memory.

A real-time programmer would find these sub-range types quite helpful in implementing tasks efficiently to suit the availability of memory. For example, consider a situation where a real-time C-program is to be developed for a computer with a small (e.g., 2kbytes) main memory and with no virtual memory management. In this situation, a programmer can optimize program size by selecting data structures that are suitably matched to handle the program's data.

The input data may be an 8-bit value from an analog to digital converter, and the output could be an 8-bit value from a digital to analog converter. To deal with these values, very short integer variables may be used instead of normal integer variables. The characteristics of the various integer types are shown in ***Table 8.1*** and ***Table 8.2***.

*Table 8.1 Integer types and their memory sizes*

| Integer type | | Size of memory allocated |
|---|---|---|
| Normal integer: | Bn-1 \| ...... \| B2 \| B1 \| B0 | One Computer Word (32 bits in most implementations) |
| Short integer: | Bn/2-1 \| ...... \| B1 \| B0 | Half Word (usually 16 bits) |
| Very short integer: | B7 \| ...... \| B0 | Usually a byte (8 bits) |
| long integer: | B2n-1 \| ...... \| B2 \| B1 \| B0 | Usually Two Words |

*Table 8.2 Integer types and their value ranges*

| Integer types | Value range | |
|---|---|---|
| | signed | unsigned |
| Normal integer | From -2 ^N-1 to +(2^N-1)-1 | From 0 to (2^N)-1 |
| Short integer | From -2 ^N/2-1 to +(2^N/2-1)-1 | From 0 to (2^(N/2))-1 |
| Very short integer | From -2 ^7 to +(2^7)-1 | From 0 to (2^8)-1 |
| long integer | From -2 ^N-1 to +(2^2*N-1)-1 | From 0 to (2^2*N)-1 |

### 8.2.2 Integer Constants

An integer constant is simply a whole number derived from a defined set or subset of integers. For example, 0, +20, -20, 1000, -1000000, are integer constants from the natural set varying from -∞ (minus infinity) to +∞ (plus infinity). In a programming language like C, only a subset of this natural set may be implemented, as discussed in the next section. Programmers use constants in the following programs:

**(a) Application programs**

1. to initialize integer variables, such as counters.
*Example*: To initialize an index variable in a for-loop statement:

```
For(ctr = 0; ctr < 100;  ctr = ctr + 1)
    { statements }
```

where ctr is initialized with the constant 0, compared with the counter's upper limit, 100, and incremented by another constant 1;

2. to define limits for data structures, such as array length, buffer length, line size, etc., and to set the number of iterations in loop statements. (In the above for-loop statement, ctr<100 specifies that the following statement will be repeated 100 times.);

3. to initialize or compare character variables with character constants or with simple integer values (e.g., 'A', 0x41, 61).

**(b) System programs**

1. to configure I/O controllers (or ports) by loading appropriate control words;

2. to assign (or allocate) memory addresses to some data structures of operating systems (e.g., to define interrupt vectors at fixed locations);

3. to maintain machine-level instruction-code tables in such programs as compilers, assemblers, simulators, etc.

The applications, such as (a.1) to (a.3) above, mostly use decimal constants. However, the character constants (a.4) and constants used in system programming (i.e., applications in (b)) are invariably envisaged as binary code, expressed using either hexadecimal or octal notation. In order to cover all these applications, the C-language accepts constant expressions in decimal, hexadecimal and octal form. A hexadecimal constant has the base of 16 (i.e., 2exp4), and an octal constant has the base of 8 (i.e., 2exp3). The syntax of each constant type is shown below:

**Syntax Diagram for Decimal Constant of both normal and long type:**

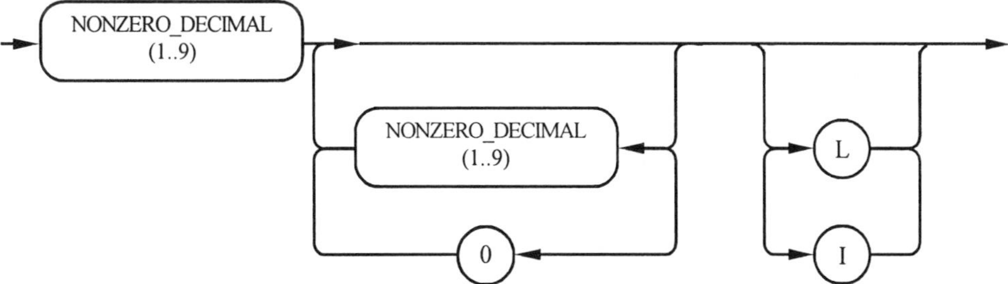


*Examples of decimal constants:* 20, 78, 299, 1000.

**Syntax Diagram for Octal Constant:**

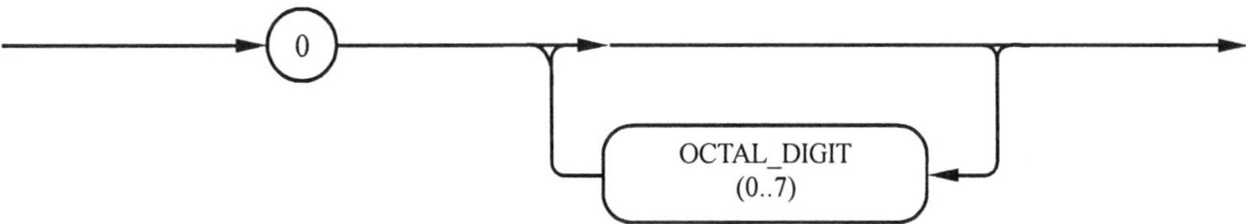


*Examples of octal constants:* 012, 0777, 05500, 0007, 0123.

**Syntax Diagram for Hexadecimal Constant:**

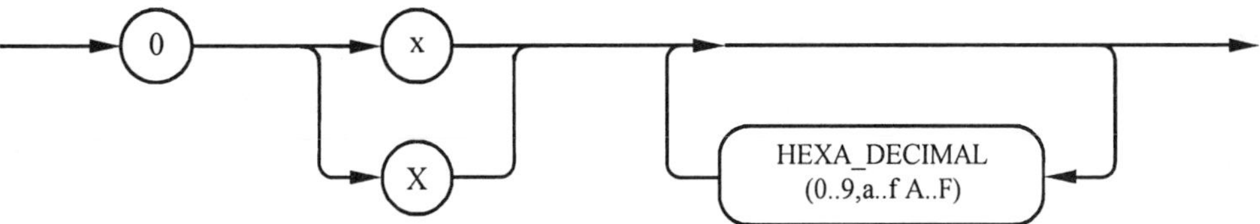


*Examples of Hexadecimal Constants:* 0x00, 0xFF, 0xAB00, 0xFFFF0, 0X7AB98.

## 8.2.3 Portability with limits.h

Since the machine architecture has direct effect on the implementation of these integral types, ANSI-C specifies the accepted range as the minimum requirement, but an implementation may provide a range which is larger than the specified one. In order to help the programmers write portable code, an implementation may define the ranges of these integral types in the header ***<limits.h>***. The ranges defined by any implementation must be at least the minimum magnitudes recommended by ANSI-C standard. The minimum requirement of ***limits.h*** is shown below:

| | | |
|---|---|---|
| CHAR_MIN | 0 | or SCHAR_MIN |
| CHAR_MAX | 255 | or SCHAR_MAX |
| SCHAR_MIN | -128 | |
| SCHAR_MAX | +127 | |
| UCHAR_MAX | 255 | |
| INT_MIN | -32767 | |
| INT_MAX | +32768 | |
| UINT_MAX | 65535 | |
| LONG_MIN | -2147483647 | |
| LONG_MAX | +2147483647 | |
| ULONG_MAX | 4294967295 | |
| SHRT_MIN | -32767 | |
| SHRT_MAX | +32768 | |
| USHRT_MAX | 65535 | |

### 8.2.4 The Meaning of Integer Variable

An integer variable is a simple data structure defined or declared to hold a whole number. This data structure is associated with memory of sufficient size (usually a computer word), to store a whole number of declared integer type, and is also associated with an identifier (or variable name) to reference that stored value. During declaration, a programmer may initialize the declared (global and local) variables with some desired integer constants. When global integer variables are not explicitly initialized, the C-compiler may initialize them with the integer zero by default. Since the local variables are created in the run-time stack, the initial values of the non-initialized local integer variables are not guaranteed.

The keywords "***int***" and "***long***" are used to declare normal and long size signed integer variables, respectively. The keywords "***short***" and "***char***" may be used to declare signed subrange integer variables. We may prefix these keywords with the keyword "***signed***" or "***unsigned***" to explicitly show that they are signed or unsigned type declarations, respectively. In general, without any prefix, the keywords "***long***," "***int***" and "***short***" will create signed integer variables by default. Although a prefixed type, like "***signed int***" (or just ***int***), looks superfluous, it may add clarity to the program as documentation. Programmers must be careful when declaring very short integer variables using the keyword "***char***." It may be necessary to explicitly declare a very short integer variable with the keyword "***signed***" or "***unsigned***" due to inconsistencies among C-compilers. ***Table 8.3*** summarizes various possibilities of integer type declarations.

*Table 8.3 Various forms of integer types*

| Integer ranges | signed types | unsigned types |
|---|---|---|
| Normal integer | int<br>signed int | unsigned<br>unsigned int |
| Short integer | short<br>short int | unsigned short<br>unsigned short |
| Very short integer | signed char | unsigned char |
| Long integer | long<br>signed long<br>signed long int | unsigned long<br>unsigned long int |

> ***Remark:*** *Without the keyword "signed," some compilers may treat the plain char_types as signed and others as unsigned. We never know what will be the implied type in a given implementation.*

The following examples show the declarations of different types of signed and unsigned integer variables:

(a) Declare ***i*** as a signed integer variable
*int i;* (or) *signed int i;*

(b) Declare ***s*** as a signed short integer variable
*short s;* (or) *signed short s;*

(c) Declare ***l*** as a long integer variable
*long l;* (or) *signed long l;*

(d) Declare ***us*** as an unsigned short integer variable
*unsigned short us;*

(e) Declare ***ul*** as an unsigned long integer variable
*unsigned long ul;*

(f) Declare ***vs*** as a signed very short integer
*signed char vs;*

(g) Declare ***uvs*** as an unsigned very short integer variable
*unsigned char uvs;*

It is also allowed to express more explicitly the sub-range and super-range types without losing any generality.

*long int l;* is same as *long l;*
*short int si;* is same as *short si;*

**Example 8.1:** Declare an integer variable, ***item***, externally and show its memory map.

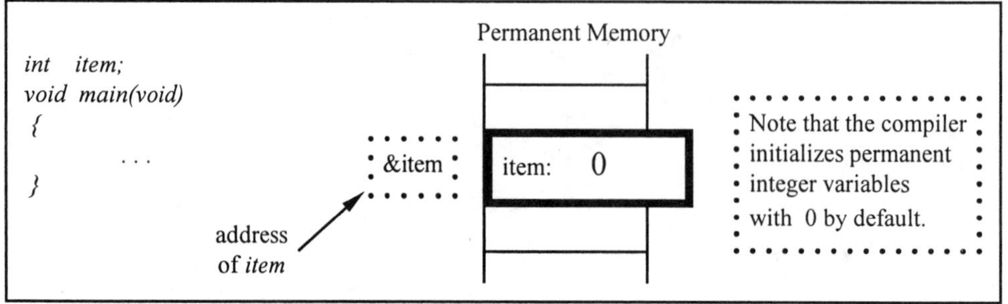


**Example 8.2:** Declare the integer variable, ***item***, with the initial value, 100.

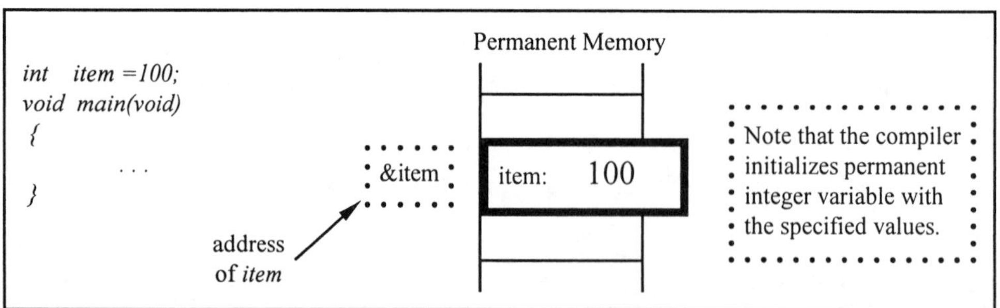


**Example 8.3:** Declare the integer variables, ***item1***, ***item2*** and ***item3***, externally, initialize ***item1*** with the constant 100, and show the memory map.

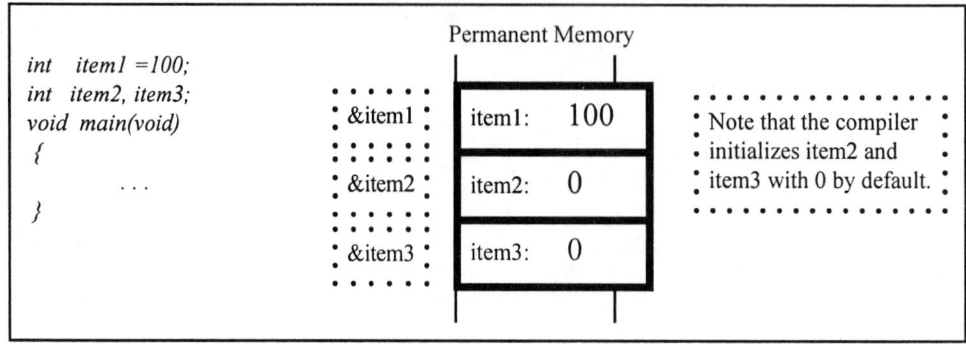

**Example 8.4:** Declare integer variables ***item1*** and ***item2*** externally and ***item3*** locally. Initialize ***item1*** with the constant 100 and show the memory map.

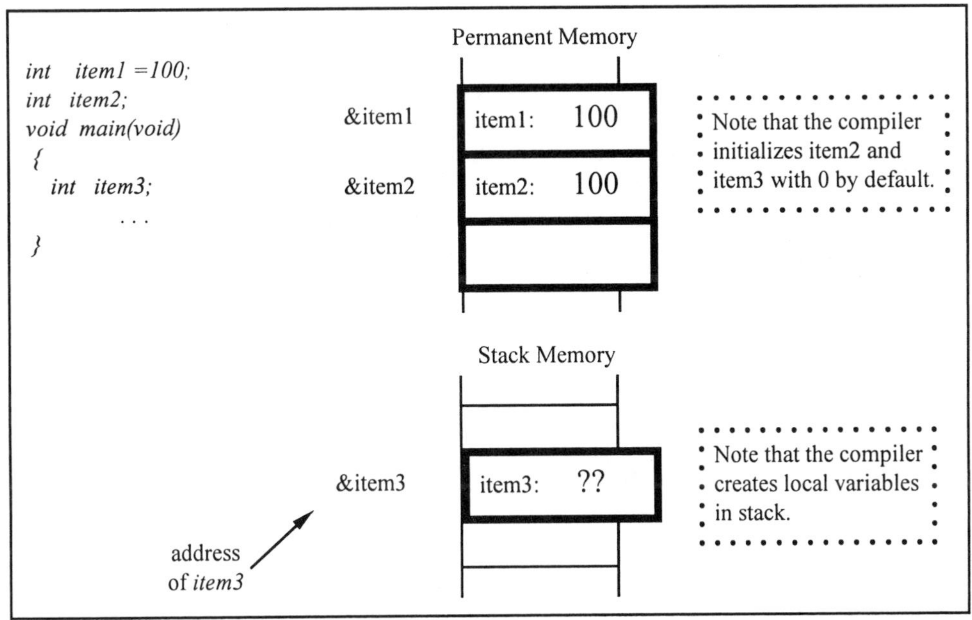


> ***Note:***
> *Meaning of discrete concept: A variable representing an application data (a data) can be satisfied using a list of values. For example, let us consider a payroll program for a small firm. Assuming that there are 100 employees in the firm, the program variable employee_identifier can maintain any value between 0 and 99. This value is usually rounded and discrete. Hence, this set of values (i.e., 0 to 99) can be classified as discrete while the associated variable is classified as discrete.*
>
> *Let us consider another example to show the use of discrete type with a different range of values. A program is designed for interrogating patients to diagnose their health status. This program may offer a set of questions and expect answers in the form of 0 (false) and 1 (true). In this case, the input values form a discrete type with two values. The associated input variable is expected to accept only one of these two values. In the first example, the discrete type contains a long list of integers and in the second example, it has only a short list of values. Both are discrete types, but each type is appropriate in a different situation. Both types are, in fact, subsets of the integer type.*
>
> *Most of the old languages provide one common discrete type, i.e., integer type, for handling all kinds of discrete data. The most popular languages like Pascal, C and Ada allow users to tailor their own discrete types to suit their application data. In this respect, ANSI-C provides enumeration type in addition to various integer types.*

## Enumeration type

In the previous section, we discussed about various integer types (i.e., *normal, unsigned, short and long*) and the declaration of variables under these types. A variable under integer type can assume any value from the integer range supported by the CPU. A compiler implemented on a 16-bit machine implicitly declares the integer values as a list starting from -32768 to 32767. Similarly, the compiler implicitly declares an appropriate lists of integer values for all other integer types. ANSI-C allows programmers to declare slightly different kind of integer types with a list of user specified values. Here, the values are expressed using symbols, helping programmers to remember the constants with less effort and, more importantly, programs can use simulatereal-life names in the data processing. The format of this declaration is as follows:

*enum tag-name {a list of symbolic values} variable-list;*
*or*
*enum tag-name {a list of symbolic values};*
*enum tag-name variable - list;*

For example, the following declaration:

*enum boolean {false, true} flag;*

declares an enumerated type under the name, *boolean*, and a variable, *flag*, of this new type. *Flag* can take either "false" or "true" as its value. The tag_name in the above declaration is optional, but it is useful for creating more variables of this declared enumerated type.

For example, we can create more variables using the name boolean as shown below:

*enum boolean flag_1;*
*enum boolean flag_2, flag_3, flag_table[10]*

Note that at 11, these boolean variables will accept either *false* or *true* as their values.

C usually assigns unsigned integer values to the list of literals or contant symbols specified in a declaration. In the above example, *false* is assigned with 0 and *true* with 1. This assignment starts from zero and goes sequentially in the unsigned integer range. Let us explain this another way:

*enum week_day {monday, tuesday, wednesday, thursday, friday, saturday, sunday};*

In this case, C assigns zero to *monday*, one to *tuesday*, two to *wednesday*, and so on. That is, the assignment starts from 0 and follows the increasing order in the unsigned range. Once assignment is made to these literals, they act as constant symbols and their assigned values cannot be changed. In a general context, programmers need not know about the internal representation of these literals because programs are going to use symbolic values in more memorable form.

In some cases, the internal values may also be significant for programmers. In those situations, assignments must be controlled by programmers themselves. In order to satisfy this requirement, C allows programmers to specify the assignment, but only with discrete values. For example, the following declaration:

*enum season_type {summer = 1, autumn, winter, spring};*

declares the season_type whose value list starts now with 1 instead of the default value, *pi*. We may state that *summer* is reassigned with a use_specified value. From this reassigned value, the compiler assigns the values in the ascending order to the remainder of the list. In the above example, *autumn* is assigned with 2, *winter* with 3 and *spring* with 4. The same principle can be applied to break the order and restart at any value. For example:

*enum some_type {A = 1, B, C = 11, D, E = 1, F, G};*

the internal assignments of the literals are as follows:

| | | |
|---|---|---|
| *A = 1* | *C = 11* | *E = 1* |
| *B = 2* | *D = 12* | *F = 3* |
| | *G = 3* | |

C allows programmers to choose the values, even from the negative range. For example:

*enum tri_state {on = 1, off = 0, inhibit = - 1};*

Since the symbols of a given list are merely integer constants, they can be used in expressions wherever an integer is used. For example:

```
  #include <stdio.h>
enum            color_of_fruit   {green, red, yellow, blue}; /* Define the type */
enum            color_of_fruit   Apple_color, banana_color; /* Declare variables*/
enum            color_of_fruit   fruit_color = green; /* Declare and initialize  */
void  main(void)
{
              . . . .
     Apple_color = red;
     Banana_color = green;
     if(fruit_color == green)
              printf("The fruit is banana  ");
     if(fruit_color == red)
              printf("The fruit is apple");
              . . . .
} /* End of main */
```

## 8.3 Real Type

The data types for handling numbers in the real class includes: "***float***" and "***double***". The type "***float***" provides a standard precision, whereas the type "***double***" doubles the precision of created objects.

### 8.3.1 Real Constants

The constants of real type normally appear as number representations having a fractional part. For example:

*0.5, 12.98, 3.14* and *.000001*

are some real constants. Sometimes, they are written in floating point form (as a combination of mantissa and exponent fields). For example:

*+0.12345exp(+6), -1.9exp(-2)* and *0.9999exp(5)*

are some real constants in floating point representation.

It is left to the programmer to choose either of the above real constant representations according to the status of the constant data. For example, a program dealing with a national budget may have to express the cost figures in terms of billions and trillions. Instead of expressing a constant as 1500000000, for example, one can easily represent it as 1.5exp(9).

### 8.3.2 Ranges of Real Types and float.h

ANSI-C provides three real types, namely ***float***, ***double*** and ***long double.*** In general, the ***double*** type may require a larger storage size than ***float***, and the size of the ***long double*** may require larger storage than ***double***. ANSI-C recommends the minimum requirements on the sizes of all these types and guarantees that

***sizeof (long double) >= sizeof ( double) >= sizeof (float)***

For example, in Turbo C, the range of values of a ***float*** number is approximately *10exp(-38)* to *10exp(+38)* in absolute value. The range of values of a ***double*** number is approximately *10exp(-308)* to *10exp(+308)* in absolute value and the range of values of a ***long double*** number is approximately *10exp(-4932)* to *10exp(+4932)* in absolute value. These ranges are satisfied by the minimum requirements specified by ANSI-C. All the minimum size requirements for real types are listed below:

| | | |
|---|---|---|
| FLT_MIN | must be no greater than | 1exp-37 |
| FLT_MAX | must yield at least | 1exp+37 |
| DBL_MIN | must be no greater than | 1exp-37 |
| DBL_MAX | must yield at least | 1exp+37 |
| LDBL_MIN | must be no greater than | 1exp-37 |
| LDBL_MAX | must yield at least | 1exp+37 |

An implementation normally maintains ***float.h*** to supply the implemented sizes of the real types. The programmers can easily verify whether an implementation conforms to the ANSI standard by checking the values given in ***float.h***.

### 8.3.3 Real Variables

A real variable, when created, is associated with a suitably sized memory location to store a real value and with a user-defined identifier to refer the value in that location. A real variable is similar to an integer variable, except that its data representation might require a different amount of memory space. For computers with smaller word length, i.e., 16 bits, two words may be allocated to a normal precision real variable and four words may be allocated for an extended precision real variable. If a computer's word length is large, i.e., 32 bits, one word may be sufficient to store the value of a real variable. In this case, an extended precision variable may be assigned two words.

The keywords ***float*** and ***double*** are used to declare normal precision and extended precision real variables, respectively. The following examples exemplify the structure of real variables.

**Example 8.5:** Declare a real variable, ***val***, externally and show the memory map.

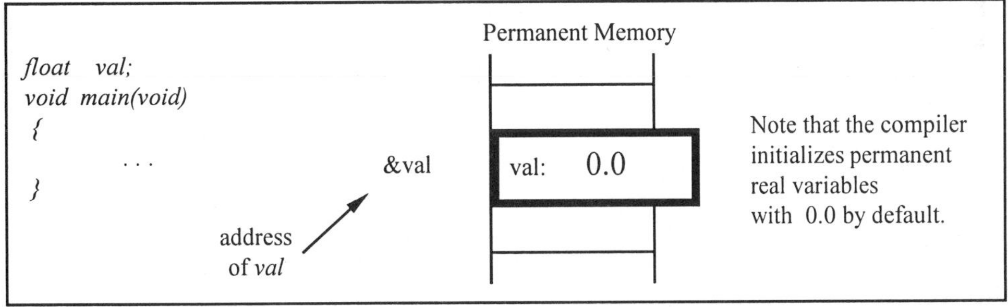

**Example 8.6:** Declare the real variable, ***val***, externally with the initial value, 100.00, and show the memory map.

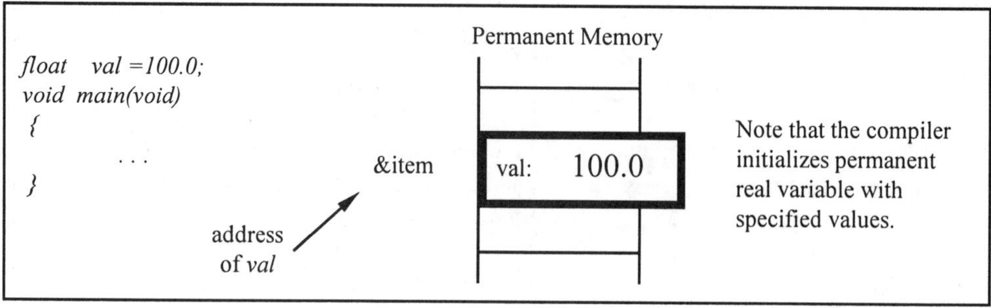
float val =100.0;
void main(void)
{
...
}
Permanent Memory
&item
val: 100.0
address of val
Note that the compiler initializes permanent real variable with specified values.

**Example 8.7:** Declare the real variables, *val1*, *val2* and *val3*, externally, initialize *val1* with 100.00, and show the memory map.

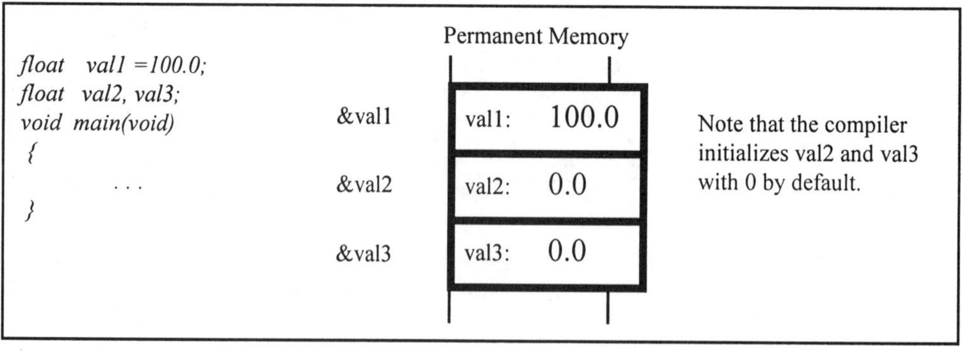
float val1 =100.0;
float val2, val3;
void main(void)
{
...
}
Permanent Memory
&val1
val1: 100.0
&val2
val2: 0.0
&val3
val3: 0.0
Note that the compiler initializes val2 and val3 with 0 by default.

**Example 8.8:** Declare the real variables *val1* and *val2* externally and *val3* locally. Initialize *val1* with the constant 100.00 and show the memory map.

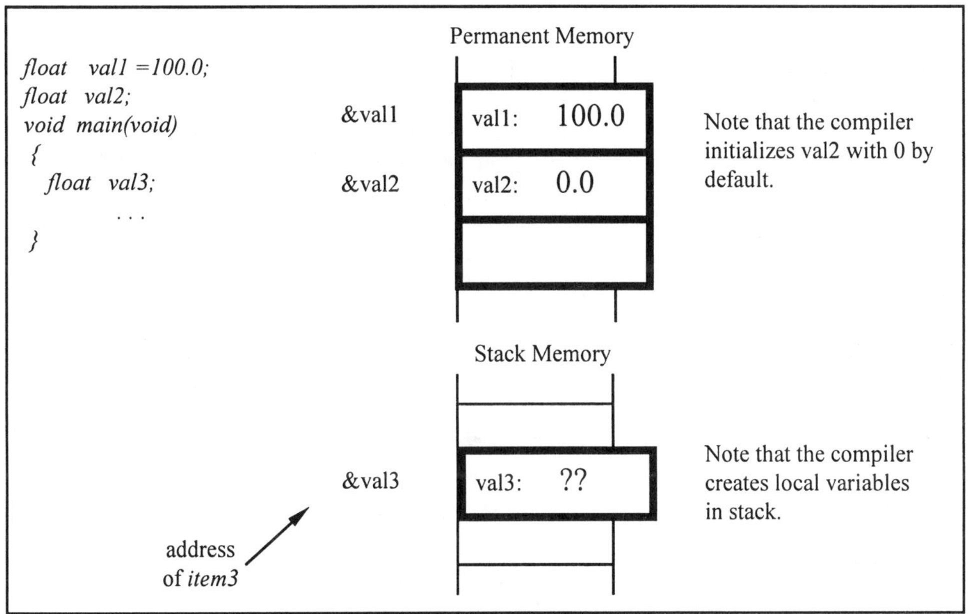


## 8.4 Integer and Real Arrays

An array in C is called aggregate. By definition an array consists of multiple elements of same type. Moreover, the items in an array are organized in a contiguous block of memory so that they can be referenced or addressed sequentially. An array declaration in C is similar to that of any other scientific language with some minor variations in the basic format. A C-array has a symbolic name followed by an index declaration. Each index is enclosed in a separate pair of square brackets. The format used to declare arrays is as follows:

1. single-dimensional array declaration:
***type_specifier array_name[size];***

```
int i[10]; /* an integer array of 10 elements i[0] to i[9] */
float f[100]; /* a real array of 100 elements f[0] to f[99] */
```

2. multidimensional array declaration:
***type_specifier array_name[size1][size2][size3] . . [sizeN];***

*int ii[10][10]; /* a 10 by 10 2-dimensional integer array */*
*float ff[20][10]; /* a 20 by 10 2-dimensional real array */*
*float fff[10][5][5]; /* a 10 by 5 by 5 3-dimensional real array */*

**Example 8.9:** Declare a one dimensional integer array of four elements externally and show its memory map.

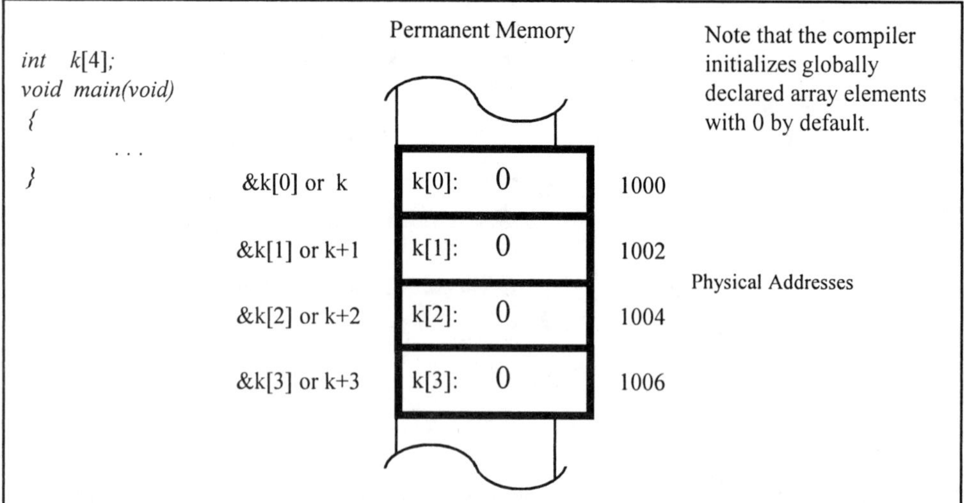


In the above example, *k[4]* is a 4-element integer array. The values of the array elements are referenced by *k[0], k[1], k[2]* and *k[3],* and their addresses are referenced by *&k[0], &k[1], &k[2]* and *&k[3]*, respectively. Since these elements are stored contiguously, we can say that the address of first element, *&k[0],* is the base address of this array. It is also true that in a single-dimensional array, the name (in this case *k*) represents the base address. In other words, the name of a single-dimensional array and the address of the first element are equivalent. In this case, *k* and *&k[0]* are equivalent. Assuming that the array *k* in the above example is allocated with memory bytes starting from the address 1000, we can say that the base address *k* and *&k[0]* are both 1000. If we assume that each integer requires 2 bytes, then each subsequent integer element's address in this array jumps by an offset of two. This is also shown in the above diagram.

***Remark:*** *Standard C does not support indexing that starts with other than zero.*

**Example 8.10:** Declare an external two dimensional integer array of 3x3 elements and show its memory map.

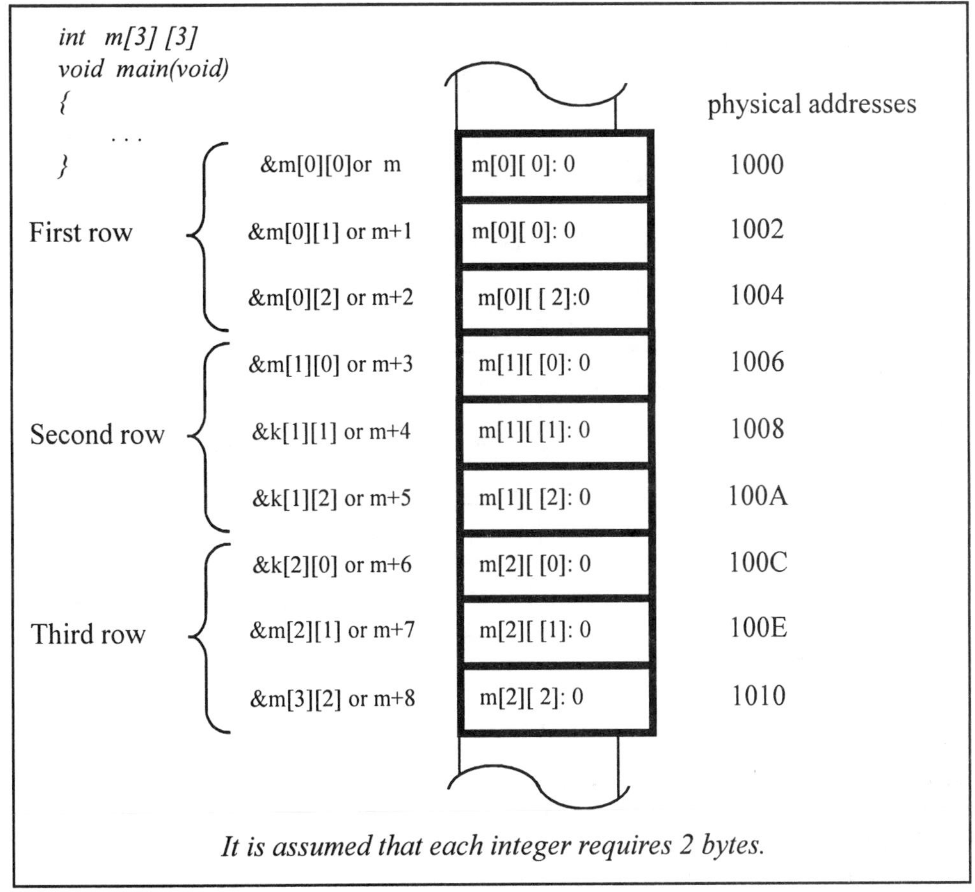


*It is assumed that each integer requires 2 bytes.*

In this example, we can consider that the 2-dimensional array contains three rows, namely ***m[0]***, ***m[1]*** and ***m[2]***, which are equivalent to the names of three linear arrays. Therefore, ***m[3][3]*** can logically be considered as three separate linear arrays, ***m[0][3]***, ***m[1][3]*** and ***m[2][3]***. Each linear array contains three elements. Thus, we can say that ***m[0]***, ***m[1]*** and ***m[2]*** are the symbolic names of these three linear arrays, respectively. These names also represent their base addresses in memory. It follows that ***m[0]*** and ***&m[0][0]*** are equivalent, representing the address of the first element in the first row or array. Similarly, ***m[1]*** or ***&m[1][0]*** is the address of the first element in the second array, and ***m[2]*** or ***&m[2][0]*** is the address of the first element in the third array.

After establishing the fact that ***m[0]***, ***m[1]*** and ***m[2]*** represent three starting addresses of rows in the declared array, we can view them as an array of addresses, i.e., ***m[3]*** or a 3-element address array. The name ***m*** refers to the base address of this 3-element array. In other words, ***m*** and ***&m[0]*** both represent the first address of this array. We can also state the following:

*m* or *&m[0]* contains the address value *m[0]* which is itself an address;
*m[0]* contains the value *m[0][0];*
(or)
The contents of the contents of *m* is *m[0][0].*

The following diagram shows the logical view of this 2-dimensional array:

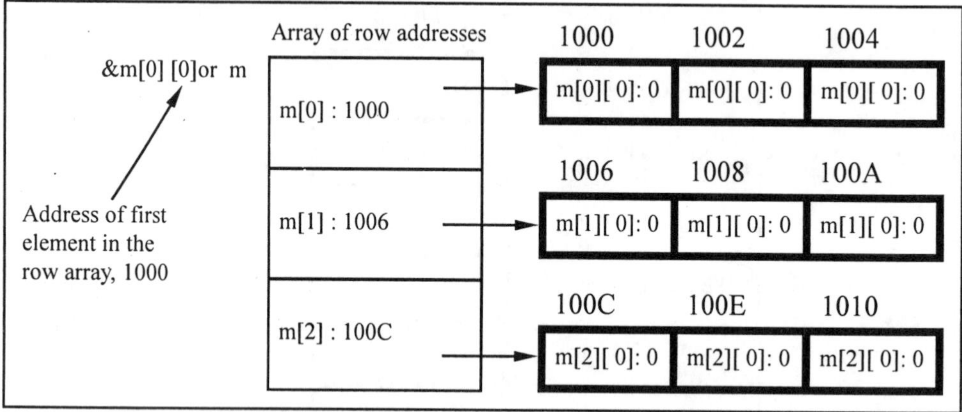


> *Remark: Although m is interpreted as a pointer to an array of row addresses, and each row address is interpreted as a pointer to an array of data elements, the actual address values of these symbolic pointers are the same because the compiler allocates a contiguous group of bytes from a linear physical memory. In the above example, the addresses of m, &m[0] and &m[0][0] are all 1000.*

## Initializing Arrays

During declaration, an array can be initialized in the same way as simple variables. The following examples show how a compiler handles initialization:

(*a*) *int* *k[3]= {10, 11, 12};* */* a 3-element array is created with initial values */*

(b) *int* *k[]= {10, 11, 12};* */* a 3-element array is created with initial values; in this case, the array dimension need not be explicitly specified; the compiler fixes the size according to the number of constant values supplied. */*

(c) *int* *m[3][3] = {10, 11, 12, 20, 21, 22, 30, 31, 32};*
*(or)*

(d)
```
int     m[3][3] = {
        {10, 11, 12},
        {20, 21, 22},
        {30, 31, 32}
            };
```

(e)
```
int     m[3][3] = {
        {10},
        { 20},
        { 30}
            };
```

In (e), the values are specified only for the first elements of each row. The compiler initializes the remaining elements to zero. Now, consider the following declaration which is ILLEGAL:

*int* *m[][] = {10, 11, 12, 20, 21, 22, 30, 31, 32};*

In this case, the compiler is not able to determine the sizes of row (i.e., first dimension) and column (i.e., second dimension). If we specify the first dimension (i.e., row size) only as in:

*int* *m[3][] = {10, 11, 12, 20, 21, 22, 30, 31, 32};*

Again, the compiler is not able to determine whether the given values belong to elements of one row or all three rows. However, the following declaration is LEGAL:

*int* *m[][3] = {10, 11, 12, 20, 21, 22, 30, 31, 32};*

In this case, the compiler is told that each row has three elements and it can proceed with its row-major initialization quite comfortably. Depending upon the number of values, the compiler creates the required number of rows. In the above case, the number of initializing values is nine and, hence, the compiler will create three rows with three elements in each row. Consider now a slightly different case:

*int* *m[][3] = {10, 11, 12, 20, 21, 22, 30, 31, 32, 40};*

In this case with ten values, the compiler creates one more row to accommodate the tenth value, initializing the remaining two elements in that row to zero. The resulting array is equivalent to

```
int    m[4][3] = {10, 11, 12, 20, 21, 22, 30, 31, 32, 40, 0, 0};
```

***Remark:*** *In the original (K&R)C, an automatic array (i.e., an array declared inside a function) cannot be initialized because of an automatic variable in stack at run time. To store the constants of an array in the stack frame, it requires the compiler to generate a lengthy code. However, (K&R)C allows the compiler to declare arrays and initialize them at the same time inside a function using static storage type.*

*On the other hand, ANSI-C allows the initialization of automatic arrays inside a function. We will ignore the size of code by the compiler to initialize automatic array, but it is important to know that whenever a function containing an initialized automatic array is entered, the array will be dynamically initialized. This may cause an overhead in the performance of a function. Imagine how much overhead would be caused by a function containing a ten thousand element's initialized automatic array called 1000 times. Hence, programmers must be careful in selecting the storage type for array declaration that require initialization, particularly when they choose ANSI-C.*

## 8.5 Declaration of a Buffer (Byte Array)

In general, all standard file storage devices (e.g., disks and tapes) are basically byte-oriented media. The data transfer with respect to these devices is normally performed in the block mode. In this mode, each read or write operation transfers a block of bytes between a program's memory and an open file. Hence, a buffer with the size of a standard block, usually a sector size, should be maintained by user programs. This buffer is merely an array of bytes (usually 512 or 1024) that should be declared as an unsigned character array. For example, the following declaration creates a buffer of 512 bytes:

```
unsigned char  buf[512];
```

## 8.6 Summary

This chapter explained the meaning of integer and real variables and how they can be declared and initialized. It explained the declaration and initialization of single and 2- dimensional arrays. It also explored the meaning of array attributes, such as name, address, element and element's address. It also discussed the meaning of discrete type and how one can declare various discrete types using enumeration type.

## Exercises

8.1 A short integer normally occupies. . .
  (a) single byte;
  (b) two bytes;
  (c) four bytes;
  (d) half the word length;
  (e) if none of the above is valid, then specify.

8.2 An integer normally occupies . . .
  (a) single byte;
  (b) two bytes;
  (c) four bytes;
  (d) depends upon the word length of a CPU;
  (e) if none of the above is valid, then specify.

8.3 Show the memory maps for the variable declarations:
  (a) signed char vsi = -10;
  (b) short si1, si2 = 100;
  (c) int ni;
  (d) long li;
  (e) unsigned ui;

8.4 Show the print statements to display the contents of the above variables.

8.5 Show the print statements to print addresses and their contents of the declared variables.

8.6 Write a program to find out the sizes of short, int and long type supported by the C-compiler in your personnel computer. (Hint: printing addresses may reveal the size.)

8.7 Write a program to find out the sizes of float and double type in your C-compiler.

8.8 What did a programmer want to declare? Show the correct declarations.
  (a) int k[0..9]
  (b) float a[10,10]
  (c) short s[-10 to +10, -10 to +10]
  (d) double float x[10,20,30]

8.9 Identify errors in the following declarations:

```
(a) int         [4] = (10 20 30 40);
(b) float       a[5] = [1.0, 2.0, 3.0, 4.0, 5.0];
(c) short       s[10] = {1,2,3,4,5,6,7,8,9,10,11};
(d) unsigned    u[3][2] = {{1,2,3},{4,5,6}};
(e) int         b[2][4] = { {0} {0} {0} {0} );
(f) long        l[3][3][3][3] = {
                    {0}
                    {0}
                    {0}
                    {0,0,0,0,0}
                };
```

8.10 Show the memory maps of the following arrays:

```
(a) int         j[5];
(b) float       a[3];
(c) long        l[2][3];
```

8.11 Can you find any error with the following local declarations?

```
(a) void main(void)
    { int  i =0;
    int  j = 10;
    int  k[3]={0,0,0};
        . . .
    }
```

```
(b) void main(void)
    { float  a = 0.0;
    float  f[4] = {1.0, 2.0, 3.0,4.0};
    float  c = 10.0;
        . . .
    }
```

# 9

# Operations on Integer and Real Variables

**Chapter contents:**

*This chapter introduces the operations that are appropriate to integer and real type variables, particularly the logical operations on unsigned integers to show C's machine language features. This chapter teaches the reader how to distinguish the integer and real types by understanding the semantics of operations.*

**Organization:**

*9.1 Introduction*
*9.2 Increment and Decrement Operations*
*9.3 Arithmetic Operations*
*9.4 Bitwise Logical Operations on Integers*
*9.5 Assignment Operation*
*9.6 Input and Output Operations*
*9.7 The sizeof Operation*
*9.8 The Cast Operation*
*9.9 Scientific Operations on Real Types*
*9.10 Summary*
*Exercises*

## 9.1 Introduction

Integers and reals are the basic computational elements (or objects) in solving numerical problems in scientific and engineering applications. C provides various sets of operations to manipulate these two types of data. Operations on simple integer and real variables can be broadly classified into the following types:

- *increment and decrement*
- *arithmetic operation*
- *logical comparisons*
- *bitwise manipulation*
- *assignment operation*
- *input and output operations*
- *size of operation*
- *cast operation*
- *scientific operations on real type*

***Table 9.1*** explains the particular operations that are applicable to integer and real variables. Arithmetic operations and some comparison operations are generally performed on signed integers. Logical operations, such as bit manipulations and some restricted arithmetic operations (only increment, decrement, addition and subtraction), are normally performed on unsigned integers.

*Table 9.1 Operations on Integers and Reals*

| **Operations** | **Integer** | **Real** |
|---|---|---|
| Increment and decrement | YES | YES |
| Arithmetic | YES | YES |
| Logical comparisons | YES | YES |
| Bitwise Manipulation | YES | NO |
| Assignment | YES | YES |
| Size of operation | YES | YES |
| Cast operation | YES | YES |

## 9.2 Increment and Decrement Operations

C provides special operators for incrementing or decrementing the value of a parameter of either integer or real type. We will see in later sessions how this operation can be applied to other types of data (e.g., pointer). The operator symbols are shown below:

++ *to increment by one*
— *to decrement by one*

For example:

*int k = 10;*
*float a = 20.0;*
*k++; /*equivalent to k = k + 1; k is incremented from 10 to 11 */*
*a—; /*equivalent to a = a - 1; a is decremented from 20 to 19 */*

These operators can be associated with variables in such a manner as to cause the increment/decrement operation to occur either before or after the evaluation of the expression in which they appear. When an increment/decrement operator is prepended to a variable, it is called pre-increment/pre-decrement. On the other hand, when the operators are appended to variables, then they are called post-increment/post-decrement operations. Some examples are shown in ***Table 9.2***.

*Table 9.2 Expression with post- and pre-increment/decrement operations*

| **int I =10, j = 10;** | | |
|---|---|---|
| **Given expression** | **Equivalent C-machine code** | **Evaluated value in C-machine's rvalue accumulator** |
| ++i + j | { i = I+1; buffer=buffer+j; } | 21 |
| ++i + j++ | { i = i+ 1; buffer=i; buffer=buffer+j; j=j+1; } | 21 |
| ++i + —j | { buffer = I; j=j-1; buffer = buffer + j; } | 20 |

Note: The buffer is an internal register of the C-machine

## 9.3. Arithmetic Operations

The standard arithmetic operations on integer and real data are

1. *addition (operator symbol: + );*
2. *subtraction (operator symbol: - );*
3. *division (operator symbol: / );*
4. *modulo division (operator symbol: % ); and*
5. *multiplication (operator symbol: * ).*

All the above operations are applicable to both integer and real types. The power operator "**" is available in other scientific languages (e.g., Fortran). In C, such an operator is not available; instead, a library function called ***pow(arg1, arg2)*** can be used. This function takes two arguments, arg1 and arg2 of double type, and returns a double value of arg1 to the power arg2. For example, ***pow(3.0, 2.0)*** returns 9.0; ***pow(2.0, -1.0)*** returns 0.5; and ***pow(-2.0, 2.0)*** returns 4.0. If programmers want to have an integer version of the power function, they can make one as shown below:

```
#include <stdio.h>
int    ipow(base, exp)
int  base, exp;
{
      int i, buffer;
      buffer = 1;
      for(i = 0; i <exp; i++)
                  { buffer = buffer*base; }
      return(buffer};
}
```

## 9.4 Bitwise Logical Operations on Integers

Usually, the bit manipulation functions, such as logical ANDing and ORing, complementing, arithmetic and logical shifting of a bit pattern, are made available at machine language level. However, the C language provides all necessary bit manipulation operations at a higher level on various integer types that may have one to one correspondence with memory elements (i.e., shifting a char variable is equivalent to shifting bits in a byte, while shifting an integer type variable is equivalent to shifting the bits in a word of memory). The bitwise operations are shown in ***Table 9.3***.

*Table 9.3 Notations for bitwise logical operations*

| Notation | Operation performed |
|---|---|
| & | bitwise AND operation |
| \| | bitwise OR operation |
| ^ | bitwise Exclusive OR (XOR) operation |
| ~ | one's complement operation |
| >> | shift right by one bit |
| >>n | shift right by n bits |
| << | shift left by one bit |
| <<n | shift left by n bits |

Remembered that most of these operations are meant to manipulate unsigned integers which represent bit patterns or bit-oriented data types. The signed integers can also be treated as bit patterns by ignoring the presence of sign bit. Shifting can be applied to both signed and unsigned integers. Shift operations on unsigned integers result in logical shifts, whereas on signed integers they could result in either logical or arithmetic shifts, depending upon the implementation. Some C implementations allow shifting on signed integer words arithmetically, which is quite useful for emulating extended multiplication and division through software means. It is not advisable to apply these operations to a real variable (or real word) because it requires a complete understanding of the internal physical representation of floating point numbers. We will see some examples of these bitwise operations on integers.

## Shift Operations

The bits of an unsigned integer can be shifted logically, either to the left or right, by a specified number of positions. The general expression formats for shift operations are as follows:

Right Shift by 1 bit position: ***lvalue_operand = rvalue_operand >> 1***
Right Shift by n bit position: ***lvalue_operand = rvalue_operand >> n***
Left Shift by 1 bit position: ***lvalue_operand = rvalue_operand << 1***
Left Shift by n bit position: ***lvalue_operand = rvalue_operand << n***

**Example 9.1** Bitwise AND operation

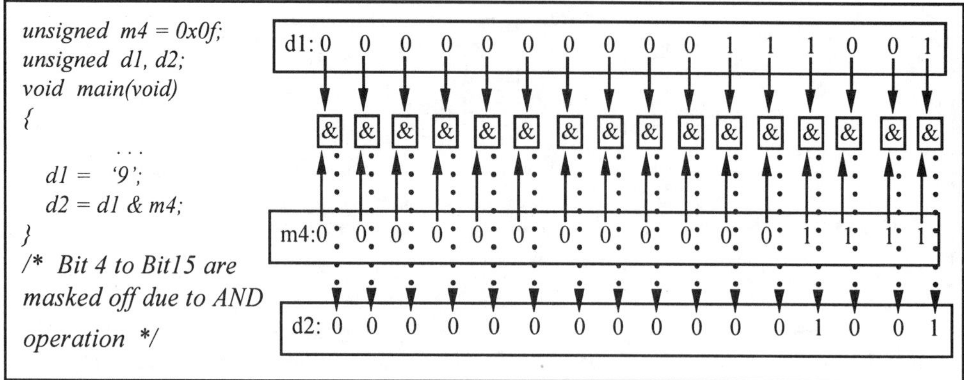
unsigned m4 = 0x0f;
unsigned d1, d2;
void main(void)
{
...
d1 = '9';
d2 = d1 & m4;
}
/* Bit 4 to Bit15 are masked off due to AND operation */
d1: 0 0 0 0 0 0 0 0 0 0 1 1 1 0 0 1
& & & & & & & & & & & & & & & &
m4: 0 0 0 0 0 0 0 0 0 0 0 0 1 1 1 1
d2: 0 0 0 0 0 0 0 0 0 0 0 0 1 0 0 1

**Example 9.2** Bitwise OR operation

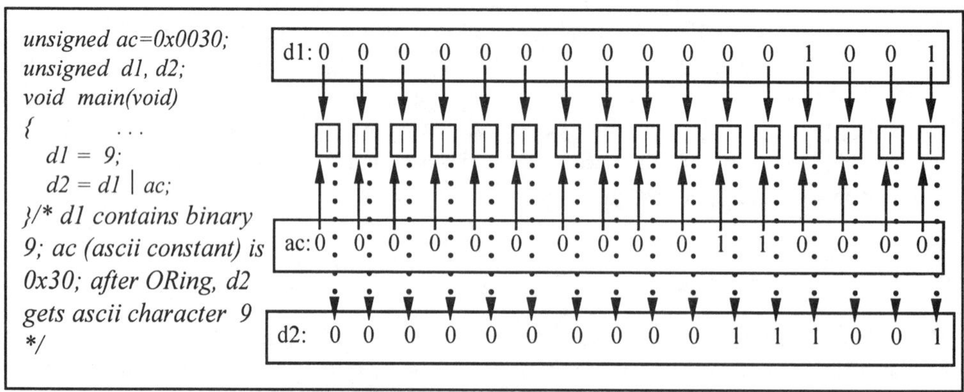
unsigned ac=0x0030;
unsigned d1, d2;
void main(void)
{ ...
d1 = 9;
d2 = d1 | ac;
}/* d1 contains binary 9; ac (ascii constant) is 0x30; after ORing, d2 gets ascii character 9 */
d1: 0 0 0 0 0 0 0 0 0 0 0 0 1 0 0 1
| | | | | | | | | | | | | | | |
ac: 0 0 0 0 0 0 0 0 0 0 1 1 0 0 0 0
d2: 0 0 0 0 0 0 0 0 0 0 1 1 1 0 0 1

**Example 9.3** Bitwise XOR operation

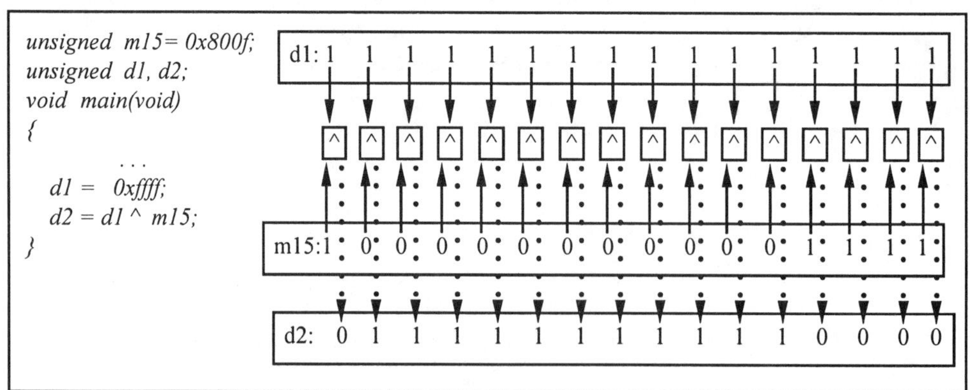
unsigned m15= 0x800f;
unsigned d1, d2;
void main(void)
{
...
d1 = 0xffff;
d2 = d1 ^ m15;
}
d1: 1 1 1 1 1 1 1 1 1 1 1 1 1 1 1 1
^ ^ ^ ^ ^ ^ ^ ^ ^ ^ ^ ^ ^ ^ ^ ^
m15: 1 0 0 0 0 0 0 0 0 0 0 0 1 1 1 1
d2: 0 1 1 1 1 1 1 1 1 1 1 1 0 0 0 0

**Example 9.4:** Bitwise 1's COMPLEMENT operation

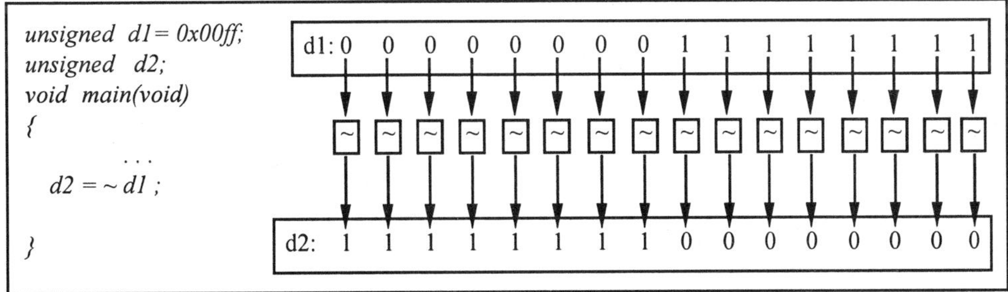


**Example 9.5:** Let ***ud*** be an unsigned integer equal to 0x00ff. Shifting an unsigned integer results in logical shift, as shown below:

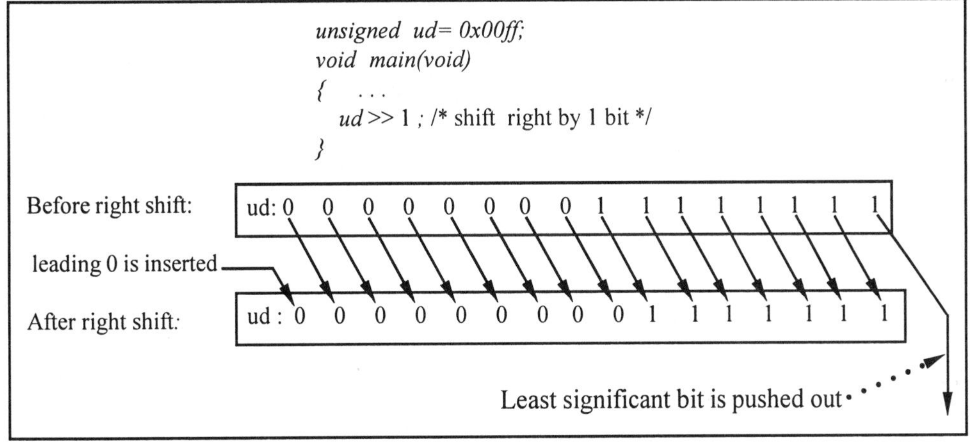


**Example 9.6:** Shifting the unsigned integer left also results in logical shift, as shown below:

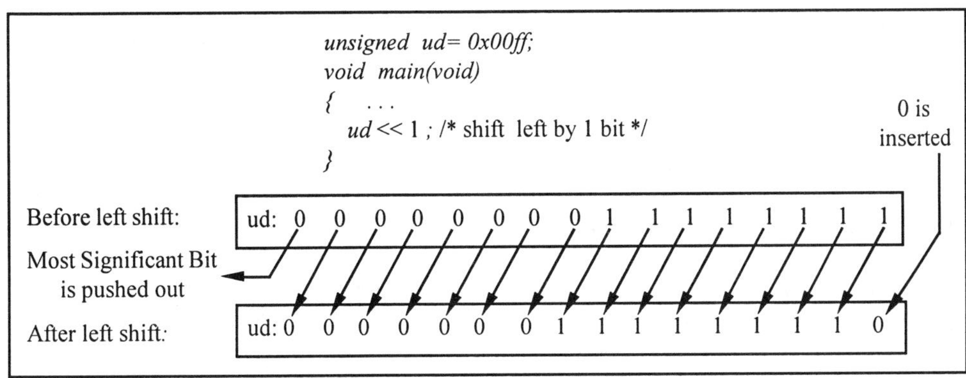

**Example 9.7:** Let ***id*** be a signed integer equal to 0x8001. Shifting a signed integer right results in an arithmetic shift, wherein the most significant bit is copied into the next significant bit in every shift to maintain the sign value. In fact, an arithmetic shift right is equivalent to dividing by 2.

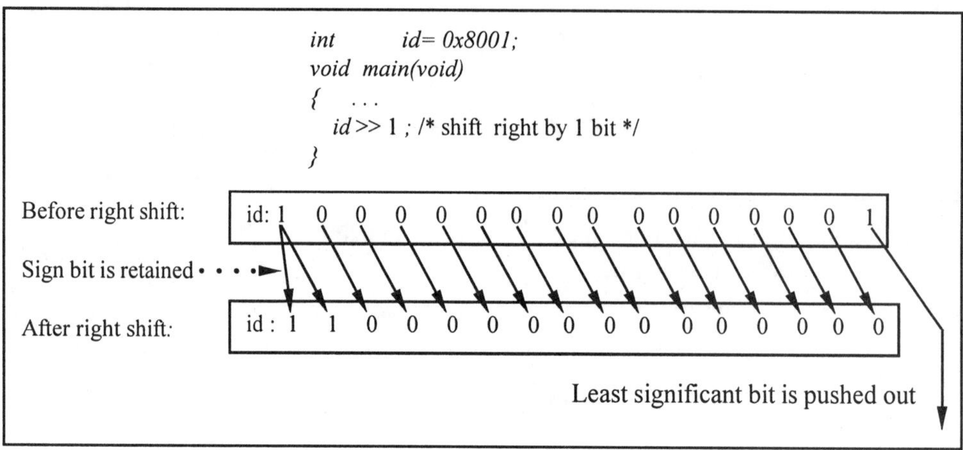


**Example 9.8:** Shifting ***id*** left by one bit position is equivalent to multiplying by 2. The most significant bit is retained and the next most significant bit is shifted out.

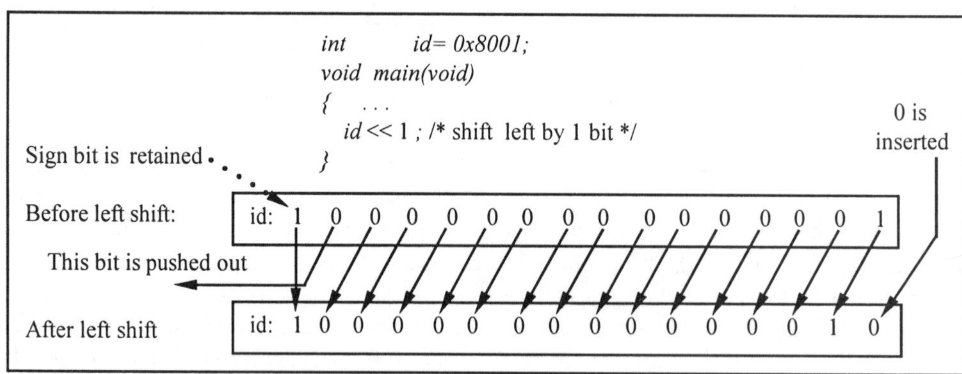


## 9.5 Assignment Operation

An assignment operation allows mixing of both integer and float types. Before assigning, the ***rvalue*** expression is evaluated to a common super type. This is used in the expression and then converted to the ***lvalue*** type during assignment. Some examples with mixed types are shown below:

(a) *int k;*
*float a;*
*k = 10.0; /* real 10.0 is converted to integer 10 before assigning */*
*a = k; /* integer value of k is converted to 10.0 before assigning */*

(b) *short s=10;*
*int k, i=100;*
*float f=1000.0;*
*k = s+i+f; /* s and i are promoted to float before evaluation */*

## 9.6 Input and Output Operations

The ***scanf*** and ***printf*** library functions can be used to input and output the variables in a formatted manner, specifically using the ***stdin*** and ***stdout*** stream, respectively. We saw in the previous chapters the use of the ***printf*** function for simple formatted output. Now we will see the use of both ***printf*** and ***scanf*** in various modes of formatting. Actually, the parameters for a ***printf*** or ***scanf*** function call include a control string followed by a list of value parameters. A ***printf*** call receives the whole parameter list as values for printing purposes, whereas a ***scanf*** call expects all the parameters in the list as reference parameters for storing the scanned values. The control string carries the format specifiers, which indicate how the value parameters will be printed or stored after scanning. For each parameter value there is a corresponding format specifier within the control string. The control string can also accommodate some optional string values in between those format specifiers. The format of ***printf*** and ***scanf*** calls are shown below:

***printf(control_string, a list of arguments, i.e., value parameters);***
***scanf(control_string, a list of arguments, i.e., address parameters);***

The control string specifies the format of arguments that are either input or output. The arguments in a ***printf*** function are purely value parameters because it is printing only values. On the other hand, the arguments in a ***scanf*** are expected to be address parameters because these functions assign the input values to the arguments.

In fact, ***scanf*** and ***printf*** are the special cases of the ***fscanf*** and ***fprintf*** functions. The difference is that the former functions, by default, deal with ***stdin*** and ***stdout***, respectively, whereas the latter require an extra argument to specify the stream address explicitly. A detailed discussion of ***fscanf*** and ***fprintf*** is given in ***Chapter 17***.

### 9.6.1 Printing Integer Values

The format specifier for printing an integer value in the form of decimal digits is either "*%wd*" or "*%wi*". The optional parameter, character *w*, specifies the field width of the printed number and may be useful to align the numbers in a column. To print integers in octal and hexadecimal form, the format specifiers are ***%wo*** and ***%wx***, respectively. Now we will study some examples of printing integer values.

**Example 9.9:** After defining *item1* as an integer variable with the initial value, 100, print the same on the screen.

**Version 1:**

```
#include <stdio.h>
int item1 = 100;
void main(void)
{
      printf("%d \n",item1);
}
```

The above program will print the value 100 on the screen and move the curser to the next line. (Remember the character '\n' in the control string is a newline character.) The screen output after execution of the above program will be:

100
% (cursor position)

**Version 2:**

```
#include <stdio.h>
int item1 = 100;
void main(void)
{
      printf("The current value of item1 is %d \n",item1);
}
```

In Version 2, the control string of the ***printf*** statement included a comment string to appear along with the *item1* value on the screen. The screen output will be:

The current value of item1 is 100
% (cursor position)

### Example 9.10:

### Version 1:

```
#include <stdio.h>
int item1 = 100, item2 = 200, item3 = 300;
void main(void)
{
     printf("%d\t%d\t%d\n", item1, item2, item3);
}
```

The above program will print all three values, *item1*, *item2* and *item3*, on a line, leaving a tab_space (indicated in the control string by \t ) in-between them. The screen output will be:

```
100     200     300
% (cursor position )
```

### Version 2:

```
#include <stdio.h>
int item1 = 100, item2 = 200, item3 = 300;
void main(void)
{
     printf("item1 is %d\titem2 is %d\titem3 is %d\n", item1, item2, item3);
}
```

The above program will print all three values, *item1*, *item2* and *item3*, along with the respective prefixed comments, as shown below:

```
item1 is 100     item2 is 200     item3 is 300
% (cursor position )
```

### Version 3:

```
#include <stdio.h>
int item1 = 100, item2 = 200, item3 = 300;
void main(void)
{
     printf("item1 is %d\n", item1);
     printf("item2 is %d\n", item2);
     printf("item3 is %d\n", item3);
}
```

Version 3 will print each item on a separate line with the descriptive information. The screen output will be:

```
item1 is 100
item2 is 200
item3 is 300
% (cursor position)
```

From the above examples, any alpha_numeric data (except format specifiers) inside the control string parameter is reproduced on the output line. The corresponding value parameter is printed in the place of a format specifier.

Using the ***%d*** specifier, the output field is correctly adjusted without printing any leading spaces. In other words, ***printf*** provides a sufficient field width for an integer value. The output will always be left-justified in the ***%d*** format.

**Example 9.11:** Show the output of various size integer values using the ***%d*** format.

```
#include <stdio.h>
void main(void)
{
  printf("%d \n", 1);
  printf("%d \n", 10);
  printf("%d \n", 100);
  printf("%d \n", 1000);
}
```

The ***%d*** format causes the output to be left justified by default, and the output of the above program will be:

```
1
10
100
1000
% (cursor position)
```

To produce a right justified output, the format specifier, ***%wd***, can be used. The following example shows the use of this format specifier.

**Example 9.12:** Set up ***printf*** statements to output the decimal constants 1, 10, 100 and 1000 on the screen in a ***right-justified*** manner within a column four digits wide.

```
#include <stdio.h>
void main(void)
{
      printf("%4d \n", 1);      /* print value 1 in a 4-digit field */
      printf("%4d \n", 10);     /* print value 10 in a 4-digit field */
      printf("%4d \n", 100);    /* print value 100 in a 4-digit field */
      printf("%4d \n", 1000);   /* print value 1000 in a 4-digit field */
}
```

The output of the above program will be:

```
∇∇∇1   (where ∇ denotes a space )
∇∇10   (right justified)
∇100
1000
%  (cursor position)
```

This format may be quite useful in commercial applications to produce a neat accounting output, as shown in the following example.

### Example 9.13:

```
#include <stdio.h>
void main(void)
{
      int  shopping, loan_repay, gas_bill, elec_bill, misc;
      int  old_balance, total_spent, new_balance;
      old_balance = 10000;
      shopping = 100;
      loan_repay= 1100;
      gas_bill = 40;
      elec_bill = 60;
      misc = 5;
      total_spent =  shopping + loan_repay + gas_bill+elec_bill + misc;
      new_balance = old_balance - total_spent;
      printf("\tBrought Forward Balance\t%5d  \n", old_balance);
      printf("\tLoan Repayment              \t \t$%4d  \n", loan_repay);
      printf("\tShopping  Expenses          \t \t$%4d  \n", shopping);
      printf("\tGas  Payment                \t \t$%4d  \n", gas_bill);
      printf("\tElectricity Payment         \t \t$%4d  \n", elec_bill);
      printf("\tOther Minor Expenses        \t \t$%4d  \n",misc);
      printf("\tTotal Expenses              \t \t$%4d  \n",total_spent);
      printf("\t Current Balance            \t$%5d  \n", new_balance);
}
```

The output of the above program will be:

```
Brought Forward Balance    $10000
Loan Repayment             $∇1100
Shopping Expenses          $∇∇100
Gas Payment                $∇∇∇40
Electricity Payment        $∇∇∇60
Other Minor Expenses       $∇∇∇∇5
Total Expenses             $∇1305
Current Balance            $∇8695
```

Integer values are stored inside memory in binary form. If we want to display those binary values, octal and hexadecimal format specifiers can be used in ***printf*** statements. We can also print an octal or hexadecimal constant as a decimal value and vice versa. The format specifiers for printing an integer in hexadecimal and octal form are ***%x*** or ***%X*** and ***%o*** or ***%O*** (using the letters o and O), respectively. The following example shows printing of various types of constants under different format specifiers.

**Example 9.14:** Print decimal, octal and hexadecimal constants on the screen.

```
#include <stdio.h>
void main(void)
{ unsigned int  uk;
    uk = 255;
    printf("%d \n", 1000);
    printf("%x \n", uk);
    printf("%d, %d, %d \n",255, 0xFF, 0377);
    printf("%o, %o, %o \n",8, 0xFF, 007);
    printf("%x, %x, %x \n",16, 0xFF, 007);
}
```

We have set up the ***printf*** statements in the above program to print integer constants in all three formats, and the screen output will be

```
1000
FF
255, 255, 255
10, 377, 7
10, FF, 7
% (cursor position)
```

Octal and hexadecimal representations can be useful to output some unsigned values, particularly binary flags, memory addresses, etc.

**Example 9.15:** Print both value and address of a variable.

```
#include <stdio.h>
int     item1; /* Assume that the compiler assigns a memory location for this variable whose
                  binary address is 1111 0000 0000 0000 */
void main(void)
{
     item1 = 100;
     printf(" The current value of item1 is %d \n", item1);
     printf(" The address of item1 is %x \n", &item1);
}
```

The output of this program will be:

```
The current value of item1 is 100
The address of item1 is F000
% (cursor position)
```

Since a memory address is normally in binary form, it is appropriate to display it in either hexadecimal or octal format. In fact, these two formats provide direct representation of a binary number. A hexadecimal digit is equivalent to four binary digits and an octal digit represents three binary digits. By grouping the digits of a pure binary number into fours or threes (starting from the least significant digit or right-most bit), we can interpret them as hexadecimal or octal digits, respectively. For example, the hexadecimal value, F000, represents the binary number 1111 0000 0000 0000. In the above program, if we had used *%o* instead of *%x* in the second ***printf*** statement, then the screen output would have been

```
The current value of item1 is 100
The address of item1 is 170000
% (cursor position)
```

**Example 9.16:** Print the contents of an integer array.

```
#include <stdio.h>
int    m[4][3] = {
                        {10, 11, 12},
                        { 20,21,},
                        { 30,},
                        {0}
            };
void  main(void)
{ int  i, j;
      for(i=0; i<4; i++)
            {
            for(j=0; j<3; j++)
                        printf("%d  ",m[i][j]);
                        printf(" \n ");
            }
}
```

After running the above program, the output will be:

10 11 12
20 21 0
30 0 0
0 0 0
% (Cursor Position)

***Table 9.4*** shows the outputs for various integer field format specifications.

*Table 9.4 Outputs for integer field format specifications*

| **int i = 999;** | | |
|---|---|---|
| **Integer Format** | **Printed Output of i (∇ represents a space)** | **Comments** |
| %d or %i | 999 | correctly justified (by default) |
| %1d or %1i | 999 | correctly justified (by default) |
| %2d or %2i | 999 | correctly justified (by default) |
| %3d or %3i | 999 | correctly justified (by default) |
| %5d or %5i | ∇∇999 | right justified |
| %-5d or %-5i | 999∇∇ | forces left justified |
| %05d or %05i | 00999 | zero padded output |

### 9.6.2 Scanning Integer Values

The ***scanf*** function with the ***%d*** or ***%wd*** format specifiers in the control string scans an integer from the keyboard file. In the second format, *w* is the width, or number of digits to be scanned from the given input.

**Examples:**

(a) For inputting an integer from the keyboard file and storing it in a variable.

```
#include <stdio.h>
int    I;
void main(void)
{
       scanf("%d", &I);
       printf("%d \n", I);
}
```

Input:

% 1000

Output:

1000

% (Prompt in the next line )

> ***Remarks:*** *The above* ***scanf*** *expects the input to be terminated by a newline (nl) before it starts scanning, ignoring leading spaces and always reading the integer until a white space occurs. (∇ represents a space)*
>
> | *Input* | *Scanned value* |
> |---|---|
> | *1000 (nl)* | *I: 1000* |
> | *∇1000 (nl)* | *I: 1000 Skips the leading space* |
> | *∇∇1000 (nl)* | *I: 1000 Skips one or more leading spaces* |
> | *∇∇1000∇(nl)* | *I: 1000 Skips one or more leading spaces and ignores the trailing specs* |

(b) For inputting a list of integers from the keyboard file and storing them in a list of variables.

```
#include <stdio.h>
int    I, J;
void main(void)
{
       scanf("%d%d ", &I, &J);
       printf("%d %d \n", I, J);
}
```

Input:

% 1000 2000

Output:

1000 2000

% (Prompt in the next line)

***Remarks:*** *The above* ***scanf*** *expects two integers, or a white space delimiter, which is necessary in a string of digit-input, even though there is no indication of a white space in-between the format specifiers of the control string. (∇ represents a space)*

| *Input* | *Scanned value* |
|---|---|
| *1000∇2000 (nl)* | *I: 1000, J: 2000* |
| *1000∇∇2000 (nl)* | *I: 1000, J: 2000* |
| *∇∇1000∇∇2000 (nl)* | *I: 1000, J: 2000* |
| *∇∇1000 (nl)2000 (nl)* | *I: 1000, J: 2000* |

(c) For inputting a list of integers with specified width from the keyboard file and storing them in a list of variables.

```
#include <stdio.h>
int     I, J;
void  main(void)
{
      scanf("%2d%3d ", &I, &J);
      printf("%d %d \n", I, J);
}
```

Input:

% 12345

Output:

12 345

% (Prompt in the next line)

***Remarks:*** *The above scanf expects two digits for I and three digits for J in an input string.*

*(i) single string input*

| *Input* | *Scanned value* | |
|---|---|---|
| *10200 (nl)* | *: 10, J: 200* | |
| *100200 (nl)* | *I: 10, J: 20* | *scanning is satisfied with first five digits* |

| *(ii) If the input has more than one string, scanning follows as shown below:* | | |
|---|---|---|
| *Input* | *Scanned value* | |
| *10∇200 (nl)* | *I: 10, J: 200* | |
| *1∇0200 (nl)* | *I: 1, J: 20* | |
| *10(nl)200 (nl)* | *I: 10, J: 200* | |
| *102∇00 (nl)* | *I: 10, J: 2* | *ignores the second string* |

### 9.6.3 Printing Real Values

The format specifiers for printing a normal and double precision real variables are ***%wf*** and ***%w.pf***, respectively. The character *f* denotes the conversion type. In this case, it is floating point. The character *w* specifies the field width in terms of the number of digits total, including the period, and *p* specifies the number of digits for precision. It should be noted that a real is always printed as double. If precision is not indicated in the format specifier with the conversion character, *f*, the value is printed with a precision of six digits by default. The conversion character, *e* or *E*, can be used to print a value in exponent form. Refer to ***Table 17.5*** for other conversion characters for printing real values.

**Example 9.17:** Declare a real variable with the initial value, 100.0, and print it on the screen in the normal real notation.

**Version 1:** Print a real value in floating point form with default precision.

```
#include <stdio.h>
float a = 100.0;
void main(void)
{
    printf("%f \n",a);
}
```

The above program will print the value, 100.0, on the screen and move the cursor to the next line. The screen output, after execution of the above program, will be:

100.000000
% (cursor position).

**Version 2:** Print the value in floating point form with 2 digit precision.

```
#include <stdio.h>
float a = 100.0;
void main(void)
{
      printf("%6.2f \n",a);
}
```

The above program will print the value, 100.0, on the screen and move the cursor to the next line. The screen output after execution of the above program will be:

100.00
% (cursor position).

Note that 6 in the format specifier indicates the total number of characters, including a period, in the output field, and 2 indicates the number of precision digits.

**Example 9.18:** Print a real value in the exponential notation.

**Version 1:**

```
#include <stdio.h>
float a = 100.0;
void main(void)
{
      printf("%e \n",a);
}
```

The above program will print the value, 100.0, on the screen and move the curser to the next line. The screen output after execution of the above program will be:

1.000000e2
% (cursor position).

***Table 9.5*** shows the outputs of a floating point number for various real field format specifications.

*Table 9.5 Real type format-conversions in a **printf** statement.*

| **float a= 600.12345678;** | | |
|---|---|---|
| **Real Format** | **Printed output of a** | **Comments** |
| %.8f | 600.12345678 | ".8" forces output with 8-digit precision |
| %12.8f | 600.12345678 | total field width is 12 with 8-digit precision |
| %14.88f | ∇∇600.12345678 | for a larger field, width output is right justified |
| %-14.8f | 600.12345678∇∇ | "-" forces output to be left justified |
| %.e | 6.001234e+02 | 6-digit precision by default |
| %.8e | 6.00123456e+02 | |
| %.15.8e | ∇6.00123456e+02 | right justified result with a leading padded space |
| %.-15.8e | 6.00123456e+02∇ | left justified result with one padded space |

### Scanf for Real Values:

Basic principle of scanning real values is similar to the scanning of an integer except that the conversion character for this case is *f*.

## 9.7 The sizeof Operation

The ***sizeof*** operation on integer and real types will be useful to find out the required memory by the created objects of these types. For example, ***sizeof(int)*** returns the size of memory (in terms of bytes) required to store an integer object. Similarly, ***sizeof(float)*** returns the size of required memory to store a real object.

The ***sizeof*** operator can also be applied directly on the created variables to determine their storage sizes. For example, if *k* is an integer variable, and *a* is a real variable, then ***sizeof k*** will return the number of bytes allocated for this variable in the memory. ***sizeof a*** will return the number of bytes that have been allocated to *a* in the main memory. Similarly, one can find out the size of storage required for an existing array. For example:

```
float a[10];
sizeof (a)    /* will return the storage required for the array, a   */
```

The size of an address parameter can also be found out:

```
int  k;
sizeof &k     /* will return the storage required for the address of k */
```

**Example 9.19:** The following program explores the sizes of short, signed int, unsigned int, long, float and double types in different systems:

```
#include <stdio.h>
void main(void)
{
  printf("size of unsigned short integer object : %d \n", sizeof(unsigned short));
  printf("size of signed short integer object : %d \n", sizeof(short));
  printf("size of unsigned integer object : %d \n", sizeof(unsigned int));
  printf("size of signed integer object : %d \n", sizeof(int));
  printf("size of unsigned long integer object : %d \n", sizeof(unsigned long));
  printf("size of signed long integer object : %d \n", sizeof(long));
  printf("size of float object : %d \n", sizeof(float));
  printf("size of double object : %d \n", sizeof(double));
}
```

If we run the above program in the SUN system, we obtain output as follows:

size of unsigned short integer object : 2
size of signed short integer object : 2
size of unsigned integer object : 4
size of signed integer object : 4
size of unsigned long integer object : 4
size of signed long integer object : 4
size of float object : 4
size of double object : 8

The same program in a 16-bit IBM-PC gives the following output:

size of unsigned short integer object : 2
size of signed short integer object : 2
size of unsigned integer object : 2
size of signed integer object : 2
size of float object : 4
size of double object : 4

### Use of the sizeof Operation

As discussed, ***sizeof*** is a unary operator which, when applied to a data type (or an existing object), returns the storage size in terms of bytes. In many situations, a program is required to find out the storage requirements of an object. For example:

1. when a program wants to create an object of a specific type dynamically, the program can request the memory manager (using the ***malloc*** function) to allocate a number of bytes for that new object. To find out the size of that object, the ***sizeof*** operation is useful; dynamic data structures, like growing strings or linked lists, are typical cases where the ***sizeof*** operator is used;

2. when a program wants to store composite data objects or arrays of integer and float types, I/O functions generally require the sizes of the objects in bytes. For instance, binary read/write functions of stream I/O (i.e., ***fread*** and ***fwrite***) require the size of the object that is being transferred as one of the parameters. In such situations, ***sizeof*** is used.

## 9.8 The Cast Operation

The ***cast*** operation is useful to convert one type to another. Since the expressions in C allow the mixing of simple variable types which are evaluated after implicitly converting the variously typed objects into a common super type, this operation may not be necessary on simple variables. Alternatively, we can use explicit ***cast*** operations in an expression that involves various types of objects. For example:

```
int i = 100, k = 9;
float a = 200.00;
      k = i + (int)a;
```

where the ***cast*** operation (*int*) on the variable a converts the real value into an integer before addition is done, as shown in ***Fig. 9.1***.

## 9.9 Scientific Operations on Real Types

In order to support scientific and engineering processing, a library of ***double precision*** mathematical functions is included as a part of the C-processing environment. Most of the functions take arguments of double type and return results of double type. The prototype definitions of these functions explain this fact, which are kept in a header file called ***math.h***. If we don't include this file along with our program, then the function used in an expression will be assumed by the compiler to be an integer instead of a double. Although this looks like a trivial mistake, the overall result may be quite different. Hence, it is necessary to include this header file so that the compiler can check if a double type variable was used to receive the returned double values.

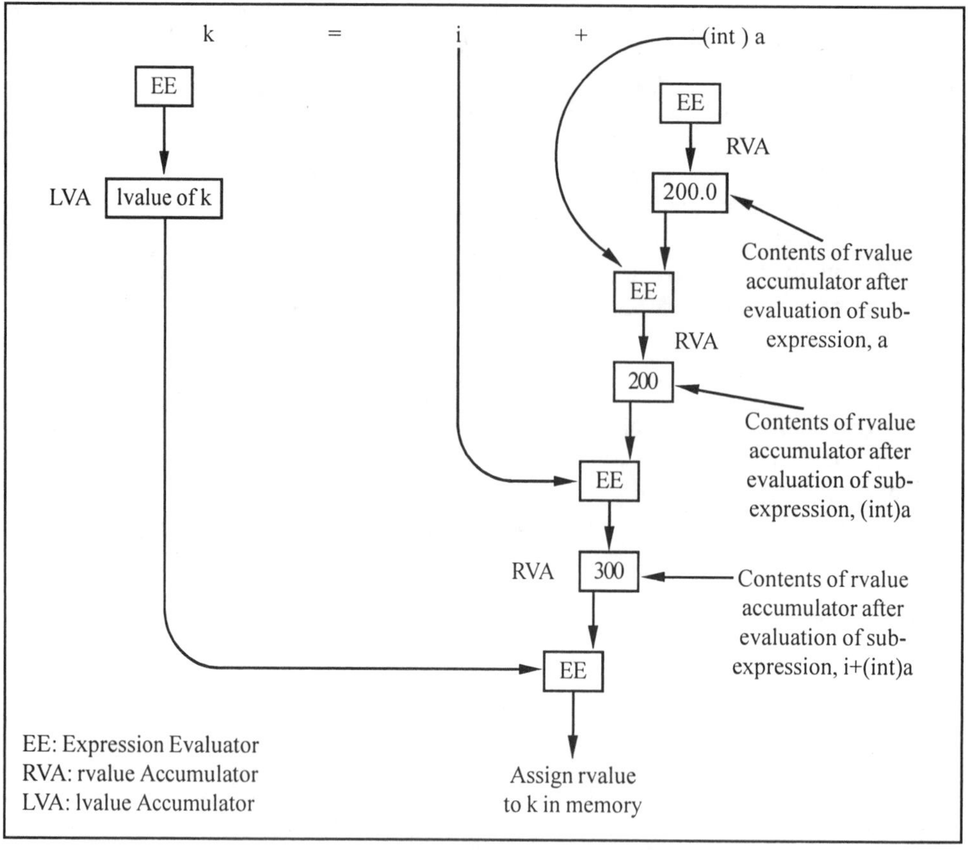


*Fig. 9.1 Evaluation of assignment expression with the **cast** operation*

This library is not an integral part of a C-processor, unlike the standard library and string functions. Therefore, the functions defined in ***math.h*** are not known to the compiler during the linking process. Hence, a programmer should inform the compiler to include the maths library functions through a suitable flag, as shown below:

*cc prog.c* ***-lm***

where the flag *lm* means to include the maths library at linking time.

This library provides the following extended precision (or double type) floating point functions:

1. exponential and logarithmic type

| | |
|---|---|
| exp(x) | Exponential value with base e |
| log(x) | Logarithmic value of x with base e |
| log10(x) | Logarithmic value of x with base 10 |

2. trigonometric type

| | |
|---|---|
| sin(x) | Sine function |
| cos(x) | Cosine function |
| tan(x) | Tangent function |

3. hyperbolic type

| | |
|---|---|
| sinh(x) | Hyperbolic sine function |
| cosh(x) | Hyperbolic cosine function |
| tan(x) | Hyperbolic tangent function |

4. power and square root type

| | |
|---|---|
| pow(x,y) | x to the power y |
| sqrt(x) | Square root of x |

5. miscellaneous type

| | |
|---|---|
| rand(x) | Random number generator |
| srand(seed) | Seeding the random number generator |

The ***parameter x*** in all functions is a ***double*** type. The functions return a ***double*** value as their result.

## 9.10 Summary

This chapter classified the type of operations that can be applied to unsigned, signed, long integers and real variables. Common operations, such as ***assignment***, ***arithmetic***, ***logical comparisons***, ***increment*** and ***decrement***, ***sizeof*** and ***casting***, are explained with respect to both integer and real types. Machine level operations, i.e., ***bitwise manipulations***, that are appropriate to unsigned types, and extended operations, i.e., scientific operations, that are appropriate to real type are also explained. Finally, the chapter explains how the ***scanf*** and ***printf*** functions are applied for inputting and outputting integers and reals.

## Exercises

9.1 Indicate correct answer:
Bitwise logical operations are normally applicable to:
(a) reals;
(b) signed and unsigned;
(c) unsigned only;
(d) characters only.

9.2 Given a set of declarations:
    int i = 48, j = 16, k = 0;
show the bit patterns of rvalue expressions after the following operations:
(a) k = i & j;
(b) {k = i | j; k = k >>4;}
(c) k = i <<5;

9.3 Show C-code that will identify whether a given integer is an odd or even.

9.4 Show the outputs of the following print statements:
***printf***("%d\t%d\t%d\n", 10, 20, 30);
***printf***("%x\t%x\t%x\n", 10, 20, 30);
***printf***("%o\t%o\t%o\n", 10, 20, 30);
***printf***("%5d\n%5d\n%5d\n", 10, 100, 1000);
***printf***("%-5d\n%-5d\n%-5d\n", 10, 100, 1000);

9.5 Show the outputs for the following print statement:
***printf***("%f\t%e %e\n", 10.0, 20.0)

9.6 Show C-code that will print the binary pattern of an unsigned integer value.

9.7 Indicate correct answer:
the ***sizeof*** operation is used to get:
(a) the range of integer type;
(b) the size of memory occupied by an array;
(c) the size of memory occupied by a data type or data object;
(d) the size of the free stack memory.

# 10

# Character and String Variables

**Chapter contents:**

*This chapter introduces the representation of character and string values as well as the declaration of character and string variables. This chapter teaches the reader how to declare these objects in their C-programs.*

**Organization:**

*10.1 Introduction*
*10.2 Character Value and Character Set*
*10.3 Character Variable*
*10.4 String Values*
*10.5 String Variables*
*10.6 Summary*
*Exercises*

## 10.1 Introduction

Text processing has become a significant part of almost any data processing application, irrespective of whether it belongs to a commercial or scientific area. In commercial applications, the text processing mostly involves reading records using a key, e.g., name of a person, ordering the records in the alphabetical order, selecting a field in a record and manipulating its value. Other general purpose tools, like word processing packages, are basically text processing programs. On the other hand, system software programs, such as interpreters, compilers and various operating system utilities, also involve extensively text processing operations. To cope with all the above mentioned applications, C-language provides a flexible, direct or indirect, text processing facility.

## 10.2 Character Value and Character Set

A character type is the atomic or basic data element used to construct a text file. At an abstract level, a text file is a sequence of alphanumeric, punctuation and white space symbols. In other words, each alphanumeric symbol in a text file is a character value. When we deal with a single character value (or a character constant) in a C-program, it is represented by an alphanumeric symbol within a pair of single quotes. For example, 'A', 'Z', 'a', 'z' and '9' are some character values, or constants. Of course, all printable characters in a character set have unique symbols that can be easily represented. The printable characters are 'A' to 'Z', 'a' to 'z', '0' to '9' as well as special characters like, '!', '@', '#', '$', '%', '&', '*'. A character set includes some control characters, such as new line, line-feed, form-feed, etc., which are non-printable, but normally used in a program to control the formatting and text processing operations. These control characters are represented by an escape sequence (***C-Notation***), as explained in ***Chapter 2***. For example, the representation of a form-feed character is '***\f***', a new line is '***\n***', a null character is '***\0***', and a tab character is '***\t***'. In general, a set of character values or constants that can be used in C programs is limited in size, depending upon the character set supported by a C-compiler.

A character value, or constant, is internally represented by a group of bits. It could be a 6, 7 or 8-bit code for each character representation. Due to the fact that the maximum number of meaningful characters required to maintain the data structure of text or file type falls within a couple of hundreds, the size of a character code need not exceed 8-bits. This implies that a byte of memory is sufficient to store a character. The compilers normally allocate a byte of storage for a character variable, irrespective of whether it supports a 6-bit, 7-bit or 8-bit character set. Under this assumption, C-programmers need not know the details of internal representation of a character as long as their programs use the standard representation (i.e., using a symbolic representation) of a character value. Nonetheless, programmers may have to use straight binary codes to represent several control characters for which there is no symbolic notation available. For example, '\004' (in octal) represents the *End Of Text* character. Hence, before using such conventions, programmers should know about the character set supported by C-language at their installations.

There are two main character sets available for implementing text data. They are ***ASCII*** (American Standards Code for Information Interchange) and EBCDIC (Extended Binary Coded Decimal Interchange Character) sets. In the former case, a character is represented internally by a 7-bit code, whereas in the latter case, a character is represented by an 8-bit code. The 8-bit (***EBCDIC***) code was originally implemented by IBM, and it is quite conceivable that IBM installations may use this character set. In fact, both character sets provide codes for the basic characters required for constructing and maintaining text files. There are some differences between the two codes. The 8-bit ***EBCDIC*** code provides 256 codes in total (i.e., 128 codes more than ***ASCII***), and even after including more control codes than in the ***ASCII*** set, there is scope for further expansion in the basic character set. On the other hand, 7-bit ASCII code can be treated as 8-bit, leaving the most significant bit unused in the character processing, but can be used as error checking (i.e., parity) bit during a character transmission. Moreover, 7-bit

ASCII is sufficient for most data processing applications and is accepted currently worldwide as a standard character set. Hence, we may assume that C implementations in almost all Unix and other similar operating systems, at present, support the ASCII character set. Although EBCDIC is not used in this text book, its character set is shown in ***Table 2*** of ***Appendix B***. This information may be useful to compare with the ASCII character codes shown in ***Table 1*** of ***Appendix B***.

> ***Remark:*** *Basically, the character type is also a discrete type. The character type for ASCII character set requires a discrete range from 0 to 127 for internal representation, whereas EBCDIC requires 0 to 255. Using enumeration type, we can show these two as follows:*
>
> ```
> enum    ASCII_type    { NUL, SOH, . . ., A, B, C, . . .
>                         a,b,c, . . . DEL}; /*  a list of 128 characters */
>
> enum    EBCDIC_type   { NUL, SOH, . . ., A, B, C, . . .
>                         a,b,c, . . . DEL}; /*  a list of 256 characters */
> ```

## 10.3 Character Variable

A character variable is a simple data structure declared to hold an ASCII character value. This data structure is associated with a memory of sufficient size, or a byte, to store a character value, and also with an identifier (or variable name) to reference that stored value. The identifier is a symbol of alphanumeric characters normally selected by programmers. The restrictions on these identifiers are the same as those for integer and real variable names. The keyword "***char***" is used to declare a character type variable. ***Example 10.1*** shows the definition of character variables outside the main function.

**Example 10.1:** Declare some external character variables and show how they are created in the main memory.

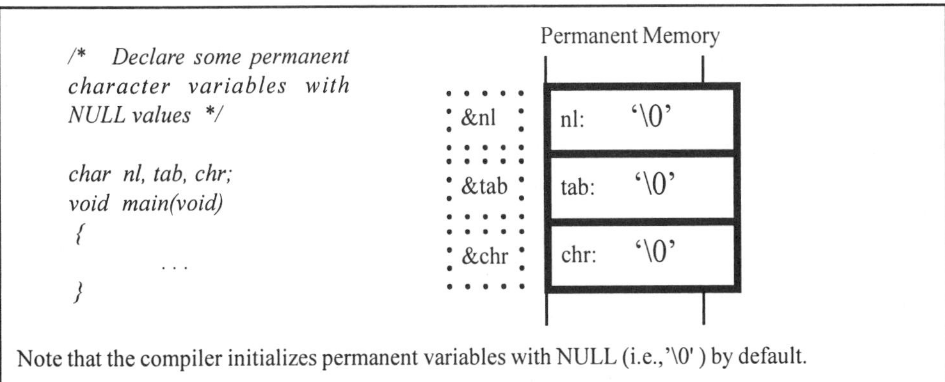
/* Declare some permanent character variables with NULL values */
char nl, tab, chr;
void main(void)
{
. . .
}
Permanent Memory
&nl
nl: '\0'
&tab
tab: '\0'
&chr
chr: '\0'

Note that the compiler initializes permanent variables with NULL (i.e.,'\0' ) by default.

A C-compiler allocates a byte of free memory from permanent storage for each externally declared variable. At the same time, the compiler initializes these externally defined variables with a NULL character.

Alternatively, a programmer can preset the values of variables explicitly during declaration, but such declarations must occur only outside a function. In other words, only external variables can be initialized during declaration, as shown in ***Example 10.2***.

**Example 10.2:** Show the declaration of some external character variables with initialization.

```
/*  Declare some permanent
character variables with some
values */
char nl = '\n';
char tab =  '\t';
char  chr = '\0';
void main(void)
{
        . . .
}
```

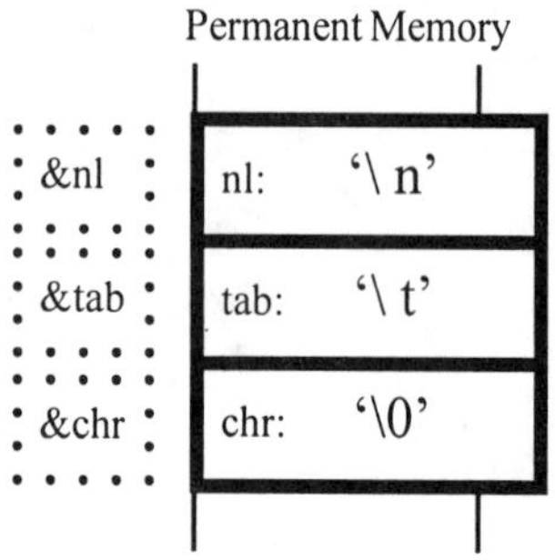

Permanent Memory

| Address | Variable | Value |
|---|---|---|
| &nl | nl: | '\ n' |
| &tab | tab: | '\ t' |
| &chr | chr: | '\0' |

When we declare the same variables inside a function, the compiler allocates storage from dynamic memory, which will not be available until a function is activated. Hence, the compiler cannot initialize the variable at compilation time. The contents of the allocated bytes will be unknown. See the following example of internal declaration.

**Example 10.3:** Declare some local character variables and show the memory map.

```
/* internal or local declaration
of character variables */

void main(void)
{
  char nl, tab,
  char  chr = 'A';
        . . .
}
```

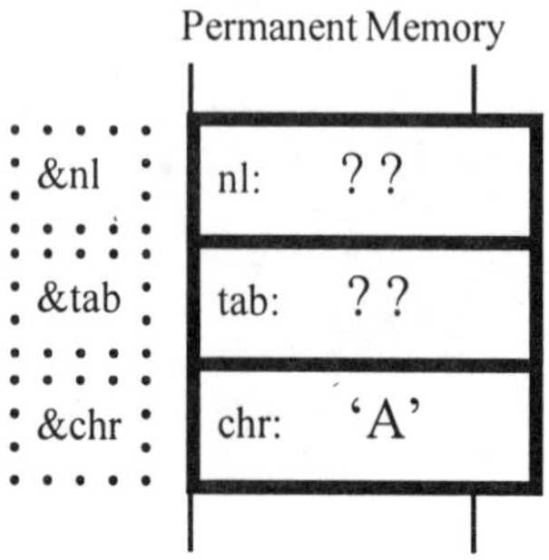

Permanent Memory

| Address | Variable | Value |
|---|---|---|
| &nl | nl: | ? ? |
| &tab | tab: | ? ? |
| &chr | chr: | 'A' |

***Remarks with respect to Example 10.2 and 10.3:***

1. *For each character variable declared, a byte of storage is allocated; &nl, &tab and &chr are the addresses of three consecutive bytes allocated to the declared character variables nl, tab and chr, respectively.*
2. *If a variable is declared outside a function, the user can explicitly initialize it with a character value; the compiler stores these values in the allocated bytes of permanent memory.*
3. *For each non-initialized character variable defined outside a function, a byte from BSS permanent segment is allocated and a default value of NULL is stored at the time of program loading.*
4. *For each non-initialized character variable defined inside a function, a byte from the run-time stack is allocated, and it will not be initialized.*

**Example 10.4:** Read a character and print its details such as numeric or alphabet.

```
#include <stdio.h>
void main(void)
{
    char ch;
ch = getchar(); <>
if((ch <= 'Z') && (ch >= 'A'))

            printf("Character belongs to uppercase alphabet \ n");
if((ch <= 'z') && (ch >= 'a'))
        printf("Character belongs to lowercase alphabet \ n");
if((ch <= '9') && (ch >= '0'))
        printf("Character belongs to numeric type \ n");
}
```

***Remarks with respect to Example 10.4:***

1. *A character variable can hold only one character value;*
2. *A character value is expressed by an ASCII or special character symbol enclosed in pair of single quotes;*
3. *A character value can be printed using the format indicator, %c.*

**Example 10.5:** Find out which character set is supported by our C-compiler.

```
#include <stdio.h>
void main(void)
{
    char nl;
    nl = '\n';
    if('A' == 65) /* (or) if('A'==0x41) */
    {
    printf("%c",nl);
    printf("ASCII Character Set");
    printf("%c",nl);
    }
    else if('A' == 193)    /* (or) if('A'==0xC1) */
    {
    printf("%c",nl);
    printf("EBCDIC Character Set");
    printf("%c",nl);
    }
}
```

## 10.4 String Values

A string value is represented by a sequence of characters enclosed within double quote characters. A string value can vary from a NULL character to multiple characters. For example:

*"" is a NULL string;*
*"Z" is a single character string;*
*"is" is a two character string;*
*"the" is a three character string;*
*"last" is a four character string;*
*"character of the English Alphabet" is a 34-character string.*

We can concatenate all the above strings into a single string form as:

*"Z is the last character of the English Alphabet"*

which is also a string. From the above examples, we infer that a string value varies in length, depending upon the amount of text within the delimiters (i.e., double quotes). It could be a no character string (i.e., NULL string), a single character string or a multiple character string. In general, a string value ranges from NULL to infinite size. For example, a large (nearly infinite size) string could be the contents of this textbook.

## 10.5 String Variables

A string variable is simply a character array. The same "***char***" keyword is used to declare string variables. Since a string value can range from no character to many characters, there is the problem of declaring a string variable of correct size. Therefore, programmers should know how that variable is to be used. By definition, a string is an array of characters terminated by an end of string character, or the NULL character (whose value is 0 in decimal, 000 in octal and 0x00 in hexadecimal). A string format in C is shown below:

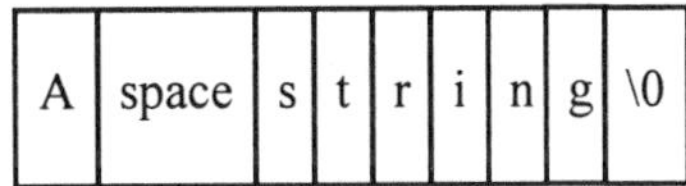


**Example 10.6:** Declare some empty string variables.

```
#include <stdio.h>
char cc[3] = "" ;               /* cc: country code */
char ac[4] = "";                /* ac: area code     */
char tn[7] = "";                /* tn: telephone number */
void main(void)
{
    ...
}
```

### 10.5.1 Initializing a String Variable

As with integer and float arrays, a string variable can be initialized when it is allocated to permanent storage, which is only possible with global and static variable definitions. Any string variable of non-static type cannot be initialized inside a function due to the dynamic storage allocation. On the other hand, static class strings can be initialized anywhere in a program. The following examples show some string declarations.

**Example 10.7:** Repeat the declaration of the string variables of ***Example 10.6*** initializing them with the appropriate string constants.

```
/* String declarations with initial values outside main */
#include <stdio.h>
char cc[3] = "91";    /* cc: country code */
char ac[4] = "052";    /* ac: area code */
char tn[7] = "471322"; /* tn: telephone number */
void main(void)
{
char temp[10];  /* This cannot be initialized */
     static char cn[] = "USA "; /* But this static variable can be initialized */
     . . .
}
```

***Figures 10.1 and 10.2*** show the memory maps for the defined variables with default and explicit initializations, respectively. Since each string is terminated by a NULL character, the declaration should allow for an extra entry in every array.

The compiler allocates contiguous storage for as many bytes as is indicated by the size in the string declarations. Each entry in a string is an array element, referenced by the name of the string with the appropriate index. In ***Example 10.7***, *cc[0], cc[1]* and *cc[2]* are the identifiers for the first, second and third element of the declared array, *cc[3]*, and their current values are '9', '1', and NULL, respectively. The addresses of bytes in which they reside are *&cc[0], &cc[1]* and *&cc[2]*.

**Example 10.8:** Write a C-program to store the string constant "C-language" in a variable called *str1* and print the contents of *str1*.

```
#include <stdio.h>
char str1[11] = "C-language";    /* (or) char  str1[]="C-language" */
void main(void)
{
     printf(" \n %s \n",str1);
}
```

**Example 10.9:** Write a C-program to store the string constants "C-language", "becomes", "very popular" in the variables *str1, str2* and *str3* and print them.

```
char str1[11] = "C-language"; /* (or) char  str1[]="C-language" */
char str2[8] = "becomes";  /* (or) char  str2[]="becomes" */
char str3[13] ="very popular" ; /* (or) char str3[]="very popular" */
void main(void)
{
     printf(" \n %s %s %s \n",str1, str2, str3);
}
```

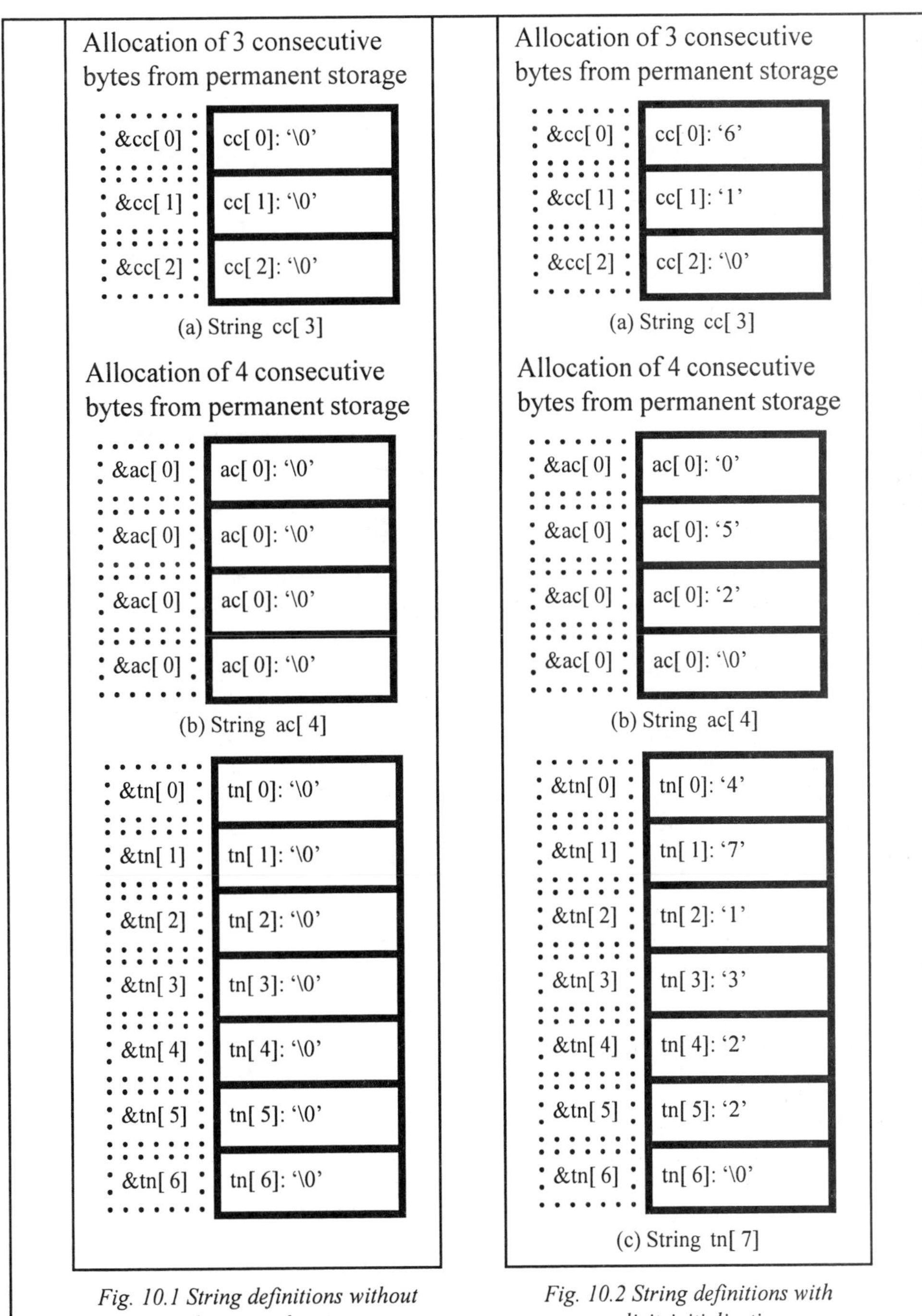


*Fig. 10.1 String definitions without explicit initialization*

*Fig. 10.2 String definitions with explicit initialization*

***Remarks with respect to Example 10.9:***

1. *In C, to assign an n-character string value the minimum size, it must be at least n+1 characters. A provision should be made for an extra character position in every string variable to store the End of String (i.e., NULL) value. On the other hand, we can declare open strings with string values, as shown in the comment fields of the above examples. For these declarations, C-compiler will allocate storage automatically.*
2. *When a string value (i.e., a character sequence within a pair of double quotes) is assigned, the compiler automatically adds a NULL ('\0') character at the end of the given string.* ***Figures 10.1 and 10.2*** *show the internal representation of created strings.*
3. *A format indicator, %s, is used to print a string value.*

In general, ANSI-C allows initialization of auto-variables. This rule even includes strings. Hence, strings can be declared and initialized with string constants. As with initializing automatic arrays, an overhead would be involved with the initialized automatic string variables. Programmers should try to avoid auto-storage for string declaration that requires initialization.

## Distinction between a string and character buffers

Both string and character buffers are arrays of character type, but a string always ends with a NULL character, whereas a buffer is meant to hold a block of characters in a raw form. A string may be meaningful text (i.e., a word, a command, a line or a sentence), and a character buffer may hold pure, encrypted or other binary character data. A buffer is a useful data structure, particularly to provide buffering between file I/O and file processing in a convenient manner. For example, I/O operations like "read data into buffer" and "write data from buffer" deal with an entire buffer. On the other hand, operations on a string are done on an array of characters, delimited by a NULL character, and cannot be applied to buffer type of data.

***Remark:*** *When a character array (or buffer) is initialized with NULL characters, it becomes a NULL string (or empty buffer). Even the NULL value of the first character is sufficient to define a NULL string, but an entire array must be cleared to have an empty buffer.*

**Example 10.10:** Show the distinction between a buffer declaration and string declaration.

```
#include <stdio.h>
char buf[80]; /* a character buffer of 80  */
char str0[10] = ""; /* a null string  */
char st1[] = "ABCD";  /* a string */
void main(void)
    {
    char  s[10];                    /*  character buffer  */
              . . .
    /* To convert a character buffer into a NULL string  */
    s[0] = '\0';                    /* either make the first element as null  */
              (or)
    for(i=0; i<10; i++)  /* or initialize entire array with null  */
              s[i] = '\0';
              . . .
    }
```

## 10.6 Summary

This chapter explained the meaning, declaration and initialization of character variables, as well as declaring non-initialized and initialized strings. The chapter also explained the meaning of a character value, character set, a string value and NULL string. Finally, it discussed the distinction between a character buffer and string.

## Exercises

10.1 Show binary codes for the following characters:
'E', '8', space, tab, newline, backspace.

10.2 Give an example in each of the following categories:
(a) non-printable character set
(b) printable character set

10.3 How is a non-printable character represented in C-text?

10.4 Show the C-notation for the following characters:
tab, newline, backspace, single quote, backslash.

10.5 Write a program to generate a section of the ASCII table showing the uppercase letters and their hexadecimal values.

10.6 Represent the following characters in octal, hexadecimal and decimal form:
A, K, Z, a, k, z, 0, 4, 9, *, space, tab

10.7 Show the memory maps of the following external declarations:

```
i. char ch = 'A';
ii. char s1[2] = "A";
iii. char s10[10] = "a word";
iv. char s5[5] = "";
v. char s7[7] = {'a', ' ', 'w','o',r','d};
```

10.8 Show the memory maps of the following local declarations:

```
void main(void)
    {
    char ch1 = 'A';
    static char s[5] = "CHAR";
        . . .
    }
```

10.9 Correct the following declarations:

```
char ch1 = 5A;
char ch2 = "A";
char s[4] = "STRING";
char str = "a string?";
char s1[19] = "a lowercase string";
char str[] = "";
```

10.10 Declare a string with the following string constant and print it on the screen.

*"The original C-language does have many defects.\nIn order
to rectify them, the ANSI standard has been proposed and
implemented.\nIn the future, most of the C-compilers will accept
only ANSI C-code".*

10.11 Assume that the following declaration reserves memory for the variable at the byte address 0x4000. Show the memory map.

```
char  str[10] = "A string.";
```

10.12 Given a program with the following string declarations:

```
char  str1[10] = "A string.";
char  str2[10] ;
void  main(void)
{char  str3[10] ;
           . . .
}
```

(a) Print the addresses of the first and last elements of each string.
(b) Using these addresses, show the memory map of this string.

# 11

# Operations on Character Variables

**Chapter contents:**
*This chapter introduces operations that can be applied on character variables. This chapter prepares the readers to be able to use the macros available in the ctype.h header file.*

**Organization:**

*11.1 Introduction*
*11.2 Expressions and Assignment Operations*
*11.3 Character I/O*
*11.4 Character Testing and Manipulation*
*11.5 Summary*
*Exercises*

## 11.1 Introduction

From the last chapter, we learned what a character constant is, what character values (i.e., ASCII or EBCDIC sets) are available in C, how a character variable can be declared and how a defined variable is represented internally in the storage. In this chapter, we study the operations that are allowed on a character variable. The operations on character variables can be classified into:

- *assignment;*
- *character I/O (These are mainly stream I/O, discussed in more detail in* ***Chapter 17****);*
- *character testing;*
- *character manipulation.*

A set of macros is available with C-compilers to perform the above operations. The macros for character I/O are made available in the stdio.h file, normally included along with any C-program. The macros for character checking and manipulation are made available in the ctype.h file.

## 11.2 Expressions and Assignment Operations

When declaring a character variable, we mean that this variable is going to be used only to hold character values. Hence, we may assign a character to a character variable, as shown below:

```
char  c = 'A';
```

Assuming that our compiler supports the ASCII character set, the 7-bit binary ASCII value for the character 'A' (65 in decimal) will be effectively assigned to the lvalue of the above assignment expression. Alternatively, if we know the ASCII value of a character, we may directly use that value to get the same result. In the following assignments, the rvalue expressions use the ASCII value of character 'A' in different notations.

```
      c = 65;      /* assign decimal value of A  */
or    c = 0x41;    /* assign hexadecimal value of A */
or    c = 0101;    /* assign octal value of A */
```

It is also possible to assign a character value to an integer type lvalue. In this case, the lower 8-bits of the integer will receive the actual character value, while the remaining upper bits of integer will be filled with zeros. For example:

```
char    c = 'A';
int     i = c;
```

is equivalent to:

```
int   i = 65;
```

On the other hand, if we assign an integer value to a character type lvalue, only the lower 8-bits of the rvalue (the integer, in this case) will be effectively assigned. For example:

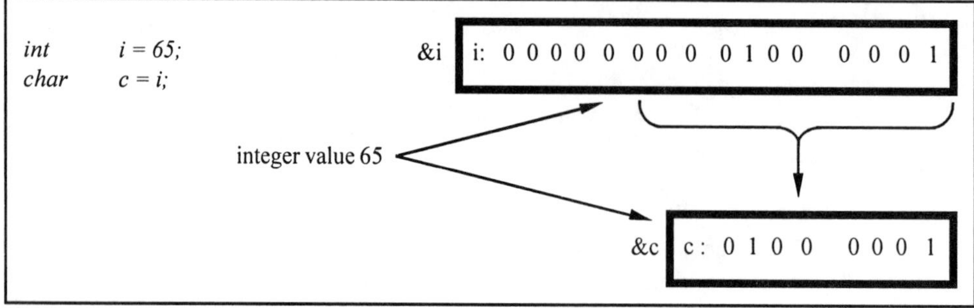

A character value is allowed in all arithmetic expressions. If we have a mixed expression of both character and integer values, as shown in ***Fig. 11.1***, the character values are promoted to integer before they are evaluated. The evaluated result is then converted into the appropriate lvalue type during the assignment operation. In this example, the evaluation of the expression, c1 + 1, will be performed by first promoting the 8-bit value of c1 to integer (the common super type in this expression) and then adding 1. Since the ***lvalue*** in this expression, i.e., c2, is an 8-bit character variable, only the lower 8-bit of the evaluated result is assigned to c2.

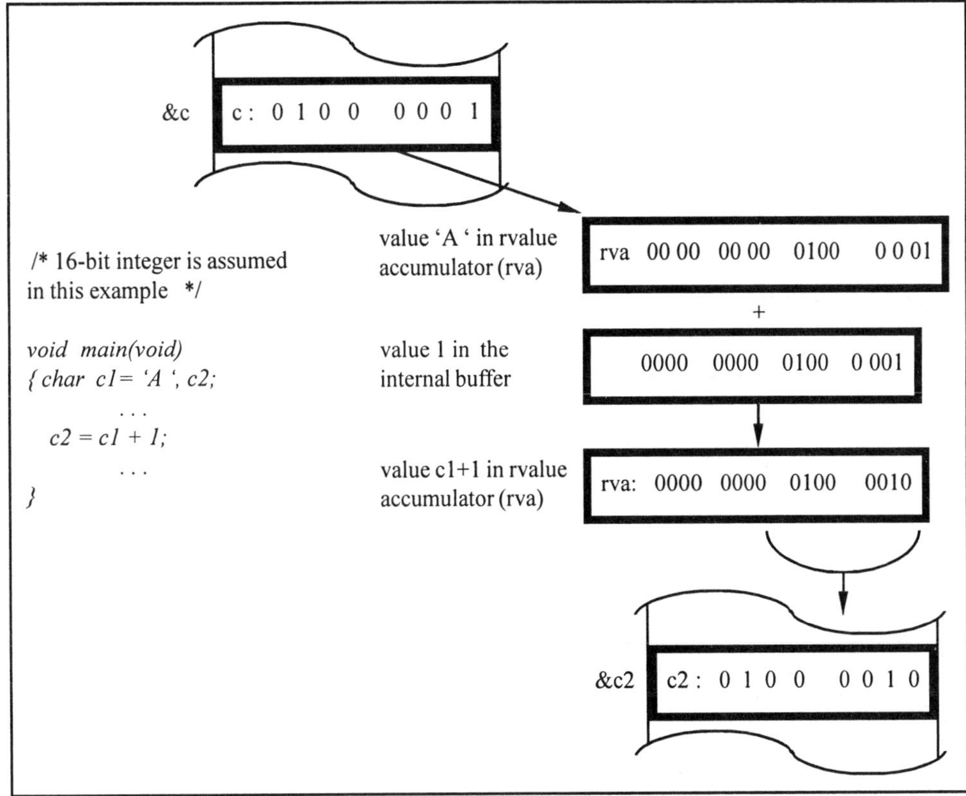


*Fig. 11.1 Expresssion with character and integer types*

We may apply such a mixed arithmetic expression to print out all twenty-six uppercase letters on the screen.

### Example 11.1:

```
void main(void)
  { char c1, c2;
    int    i;
      c1 = 'A';
      for(i=0; i<26; i++)
        {
          c2 = c1 + i;
          printf("%c ", c2);
        }
  }
```

If the ***lvalue*** in the above expression is an integer variable, however, the evaluated integer ***rvalue*** is simply assigned, as shown ***Fig. 11.2***. In this example, only the lower 8-bits of the integer type ***lvalue*** is used and the leading bits are left unused (undisturbed) after the character assignment. Clearly, then, an integer variable of either signed or unsigned type can also be used

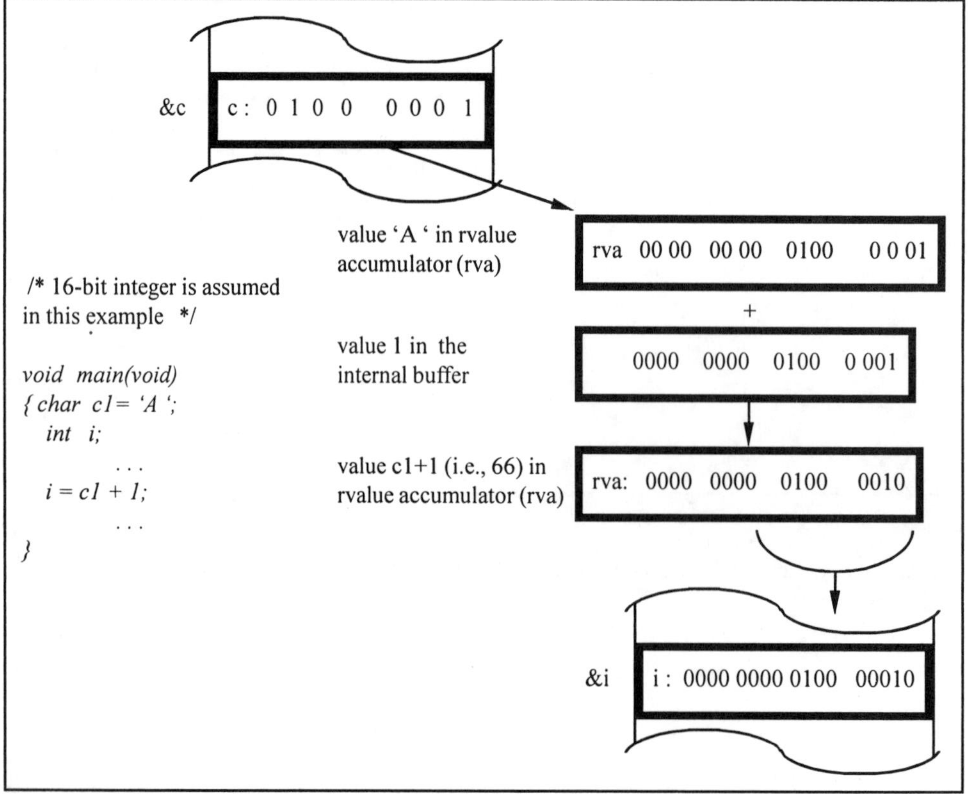


*Fig. 11.2 Assigning character value to integers*

to store character. The only drawback is that an 8-bit character value then occupies a full (i.e., 2 or 4 bytes, depending upon the word length of a computer) integer word. An integer type is sometimes used to define a character buffer for character I/O, which will be discussed in the next section.

## 11.3 Character I/O

Four functions are available for inputting and outputting characters with respect to ***stdin*** (i.e., keyboard) and ***stdout*** (i.e., screen): ***getchar*** and ***putchar*** macros and ***scanf*** and ***printf*** library functions. The macro functions are appropriate to read or write character oriented files exclusively, whereas the library functions are useful to extract character fields from a given input string or write a value in character format to an output string.

### 11.3.1 Simple Character I/O Using getchar and putchar

Both ***getchar*** and ***putchar*** are macro calls which get or put a character using standard I/O files via the streams, ***stdin*** and ***stdout***. Since ***stdio.h*** contains the definition of these macros, programs must include this file for any character I/O. For example, a program can read character by character from a keyboard file via ***stdin*** and output them to a screen file via ***stdout***, as shown below. Since a keyboard file is a variable size file, a *Control_D character* is used by the Unix system to indicate the end of this file, which, when encountered, the system transforms into an end of stream indicator (EOF or –1) and returns this to the calling program. EOF is defined as -1 in ***stdio.h***. When we read a character file using a character type buffer as shown below, a problem may exist due to some arithmetic operations involving a character value and an integer during EOF comparison.

### Example 11.2:

Read characters from the keyboard and print them on the screen file.

```
#include <stdio.h>
void  main(void)
{
 char    ch_buf;    /* CHAR TYPE MAY NOT WORK IN SIGNED MODE   */
                 (or)
 signed char ch_buf;  /* SOME IMPLEMENTATIONS MAY NOT SUPPORT EVEN THIS */
       . . .
  while((ch_buf=getchar()) != EOF) /* COMPARISON  MAY FAIL */
    {
      putchar(ch_buf);
    }
      . . .
  } /* End of main */
```

When a C-implementation does not support signed character type, the result of the EOF comparison in the above code would fail (***Fig. 11.3***).

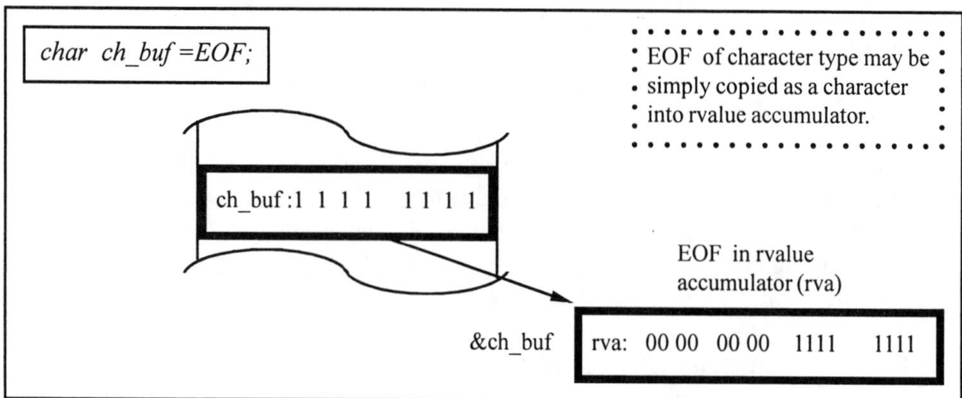
char ch_buf=EOF;
EOF of character type may be simply copied as a character into rvalue accumulator.
ch_buf :1 1 1 1 1 1 1 1
EOF in rvalue accumulator (rva)
&ch_buf
rva: 00 00 00 00 1111 1111

*Fig. 11.3 Comparison of character type EOF with the integer, -1*

In order to avoid this in a portable problem, a character buffer can always be defined as integer type. The following code will work properly.

## Example 11.3:

```
#include <stdio.h>
void main(void)
 {
  int ch_buf; /* INTEGER TYPE CHARACTER BUFFER WILL WORK */
     . . .
  while((ch_buf=getchar()) != EOF) /* COMPARISON GOES WELL */
    {
      putchar(ch_buf);
    }
     . . .
  } /* End of main */
```

***Fig. 11.4*** shows the comparison corresponding to this code. More on EOF is discussed in ***Chapter 17***.

***Remark:*** *ANSI-C supports signed character and, hence, the above problem can be removed by replacing "char ch_buf " by " signed char ch_buf. "*

### 11.3.2 Character I/O Using scanf and printf

The format specifier *%c* is used in the control string of scanf to convert a supplied character into internal (or ASCII or EBCDIC) representation. After converting, scanf stores the value in the supplied argument, an address parameter. Similarly, it is used in printf to convert a given character or integer value into a character form. The converted value is then printed as a readable character.

### Examples:

**(a) Simply read a character and print it.**

```
void main(void
{
 char    c;
   . . .
  scanf("%c", &c);     /* Expects a character to be typed in */
  printf("%c \n", c);  /* Prints the value on the screen   */
   . . .
}
```

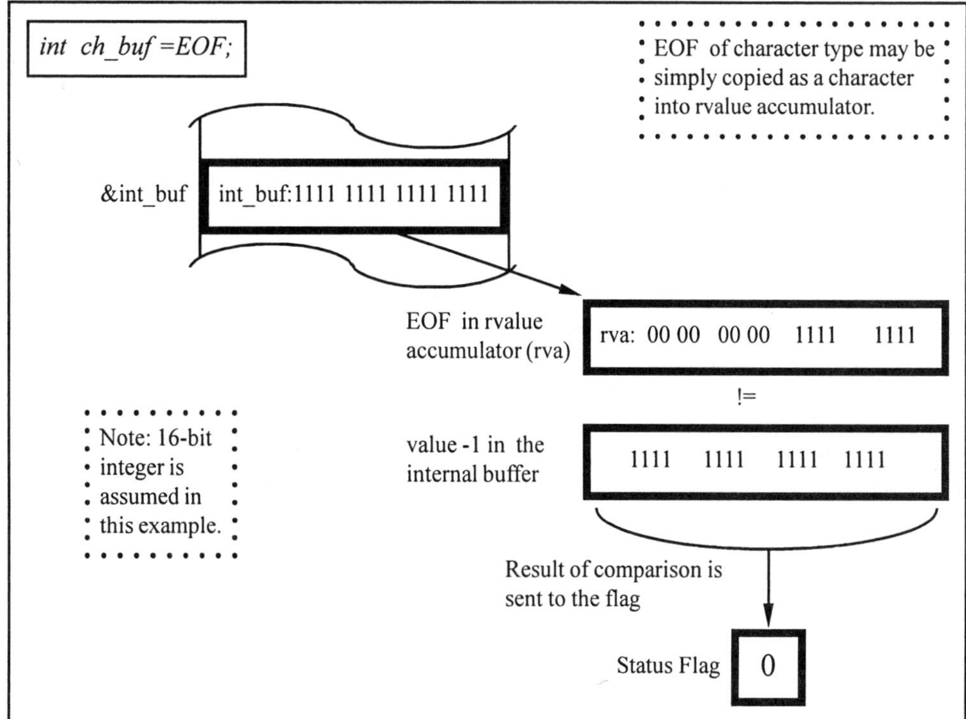


*Fig. 11.4 Comparison of integer type EOF with the integer, -1*

***Remarks:*** *The above scanf expects the input to be terminated by a newline (nl) character and always reads the first character, irrespective of whether it is a white space or non-white space character.*

| *Input* | *Scanned value* | |
|---|---|---|
| *A (nl)* | *c: 'A'* | |
| *AB (nl)* | *c: 'A'* | *ignores the second character* |
| *(nl)* | *c: ' '* | *where  denotes a white space character* |
| *A (nl)* | *c: ' '* | *ignores the second character* |
| *(nl)* | *c: '\n'* | *scans the newline character* |

**(b) To read a list of characters and print them**

```
void main(void)
{
 char    c1, c2, c3;
   . . .
  scanf("%c%c%c ", &c1, &c2, &c3); /* denotes a space */
  printf("%c%c%c\n", c1, c2, c3);
   . . .
}
```

Input:
% ABC

Output:
ABC
% (prompt in the next line)

Since there are three format specifiers in the control string of scanf, three characters are expected. Since there is no space between them, the input should also be without any space between the characters. After reading the input, it stores 'A' in the address of c1, 'B' in the address of c2 and 'C' in the address of c3.

> ***Remarks:*** *The above scanf always reads the first three characters, irrespective of whether they are white space or non-white space characters. (∇ represents a space)*
>
> | *Input* | *Scanned value* | |
> |---|---|---|
> | *ABC (nl)* | *c1: 'A', c2: 'B', c3: 'C'* | |
> | *ABCD (nl)* | *c1: 'A', c2: 'B', c3: 'C'* | *ignores 4th character* |
> | *AB∇ (nl)* | *c1: 'A', c2: 'B', c3: ' '* | |
> | *AB (nl)* | *c1: 'A', c2: 'B', c3: '\n'* | *c3 gets newline* |
> | *∇AB (nl)* | *c1: ' ', c2: 'A', c3: 'B'* | |
> | *∇∇∇(nl)* | *c1: ' ', c2: ' ', c3: ' '* | |
>
> *Similarly, the format specifiers in printf having no spaces between them makes the output without any space between them.*

### (c) To read a list of characters with spaces between them and print them

```
void main(void)
{
 char    c1, c2;
   . . .
  scanf("∇%c∇%c", &c1, &c2);  /* denotes a space */
  printf("%c∇%c \n", c1, c2);
   . . .
}
```

Input:

% ∇A∇B

Output:

A∇B

% (prompt in the next line)

> ***Remarks:*** *The above scanf looks for the non-space characters.*
>
> | *Input* | *Scanned value* | |
> |---|---|---|
> | *∇A∇B (nl)* | *c1: 'A', c2: 'B'* | |
> | *∇∇A∇B (nl)* | *c1: 'A', c2: 'B'* | *Skips one or more spaces* |
> | *∇∇A∇∇B (nl)* | *c1: 'A', c2: 'B',* | *Skips one or more spaces* |
> | *∇∇A∇∇ (nl)* | *c1: 'A', c2: '\n',* | *c2 gets newline after skipping spaces* |

## 11.4 Character Testing and Manipulation

Other operations on character values include logical comparison and bitwise manipulations like those on integer type values. For example, let us assume that the character variable **c** has an unknown character value. We can explicitly test its value to identify the type of character (i.e., alphabetic, numeric or other character) that it represents. A sample code is shown here:

```
void mai(void)
{  ...
     if( ( (c>='A') && (c <= 'Z') ) || ( (c>='a') && (c <= 'z') ))
       printf("c is ALPHABETIC");
     else
       if ( (c>='0') && (c <= '9') )
         printf("c is a NUMERIC character");
     else
         printf("c is a SPECIAL or CONTROL character");
       ...
}
```

Let us now demonstrate how a character can be manipulated explicitly. This example shows how an ASCII numeric character value is converted into its BCD (Binary Coded Decimal) value.

```
void main(void)
{int   i;
 char c = '9'; /* (or)  int     c = '9'; */
 int    ASCII_const = 0x30;
   i = c ^ ASCII_const; /* exclusive OR operation extracts the binary value of 9, which is then
                                  assigned to i  */
   ...
}
```

Although character manipulation can be carried out explicitly, as shown in the above examples, most of the character operations can be performed by using macros that are defined in the ***ctype.h*** file. We will discuss character testing and manipulation using this macro library in the following section.

### 11.4.1 Character Testing

A character value can be classified into several categories, such as alphabetic, numeric, special characters and control characters. Text processing programs must identify the type of a character that is being processed in order to take appropriate action or perform manipulation. Examples where character testing is necessary are:

- *While breaking a text into tokens, a test for a delimiter (usually a space, comma, semicolon, period or a tab character) is normally performed.*
- *When a text is searched for an end of sentence, a test on the occurrence of a period ('.') character is performed.*
- *When a line is input from a file, a program may look for a newline character.*
- *A program may be reading numerical data in the form of strings via the keyboard. Before converting this string data into binary (i.e., internal) representation, the program may have to validate whether the input contains only numeric characters.*
- *When a string is processed, a program looks for a NULL character to stop further processing.*
- *When a keyboard file is being read,* **getchar** *normally checks for an End Of File (EOF) character to terminate the input process.*

The macro functions listed in ***Table 11.1*** may be sufficient for normal text processing, but programmers can extend this facility by implementing additional macros to suit their applications.

### 11.4.2 Use of ctype.h

The ***ctype.h*** header file includes the macro definitions (listed in ***Table 11.1***) for character testing operations. Hence, we will include this file in our C-programs that use any of these macros. If we do not include this file, any macro reference in our program will be treated as a normal function, and assumed available in the C-library. During the final stage of compilation (i.e., linking), the compiler will fail to find any of the referenced macros from the standard library and, hence, the compilation will be terminated abnormally. Let us now consider a text processing example to demonstrate the use of macros in ***ctype.h***.

### Example 11.4

Let us write a program to accumulate the input from the keyboard file via ***stdin*** in a buffer of 512 characters. The input from this file may be terminated by typing a *control_D character*. The program should accept only the characters that are useful to construct a text (i.e., alphanumeric, punctuations and newline). If it detects any control character input (that may happen by mistyping), it notifies the user by outputting a bell signal.

*Table 11.1 Macros for character checking operations*

| Macro name | Description |
|---|---|
| isalnum(int ch) | Tests whether the character argument is an alphabetic or a numeric character. It returns a non-zero value if it is TRUE, otherwise returning a value of zero. |
| isalpha(int ch) | Tests whether the character argument is an alphabetic character. It returns a non-zero value if it is TRUE, otherwise returning a value of zero. |
| iscntrl(int ch) | Tests whether the character argument is a control character. It returns a non-zero value if it is TRUE, otherwise returning a value of zero. |
| isdigit(int ch) | Tests whether the character argument is a numerical character. It returns a non-zero value if it is TRUE, otherwise returning a value of zero. |
| isgraph(int ch) | Tests whether the character argument is any printing character except space. It returns a non-zero value if it is TRUE, otherwise returning a value of zero. |
| islower(int ch) | Tests whether the character argument is a lowercase letter. It returns a non-zero value if it is TRUE, otherwise returning a value of zero. |
| isprint(int ch) | Tests whether the character argument is a printable character. It returns a non-zero value if it is TRUE, otherwise returns a value of zero. |
| ispunct(int ch) | Tests whether the character argument is a printable and non-alphanumeric character. It returns a non-zero value if it is TRUE, otherwise returning a value of zero. |
| isspace(int ch) | Tests whether the character argument is a space character. It returns a non-zero value if it is TRUE, otherwise returning a value of zero. |
| isupper(int ch) | Tests whether the character argument is an uppercase letter. It returns a non-zero value if it is TRUE, otherwise returning a value of zero. |
| isxdigit(int ch) | Tests whether the character argument is an hexadecimal digit {0-9, A-Z, a-z}; it returns a non-zero value if it is TRUE, otherwise returning a value of zero. |

```
#include <stdio.h>
#include <ctype.h>
#define BELL        07  /* bell character  */
#define BUF_SIZE    512
int   c; /* safer to catch EOF (i.e., -1) properly */
char buf[BUF_SIZE];
void main(void)
{
 int text_size, i;
  text_size = 0;
  i = 0;
   while(((c = getchar()) != EOF) && (text_size < BUF_SIZE))
  /* Loop continues until control_D or buffer is full  */
  /* Note: control_D is transmitted as EOF via stdin   */
    {
    if((iscntrl(c)) && (c != '\n')) /* except newline control character  */
        putchar(BELL);
    else
      {
       buf[i++] = c; /* accumulate character in buffer and increment buffer index */
       text_size++;
      }
    }
}
```

> ***Note:*** *In Unix environment, a Control_D character from the keyboard is treated as an End Of File character. The stdin stream converts it into the* ***EOF*** *(i.e., -1) marker and returns this as the value of getchar.*

## Example 11.5:

We will include a few more testing operations on the input of the previous example, so that at the end of the keyboard input, the program will print out the text size, number of punctuations and number of alphanumeric characters in the accumulated text.

```
#include <stdio.h>
#include <ctype.h>
#define BELL       07  /* bell character   */
#define BUF_SIZE  512
int    c;
char buf[BUF_SIZE];
void main(void)
{
 int text_size, n_punct, n_alnum, i;
  n_punct = n_alnum = text_size = i = 0;
   while(((c = getchar()) != EOF) && (text_size < BUF_SIZE))
    { /* discriminate control characters except newline  */
    if((iscntrl(c)) && (c != '\n'))
      putchar(BELL);
    else
       { /* count punctuations and alphanumeric characters  */
       if(ispunct(c))  /* if c is punctuation, increment n_punct  */
        n_punct++;
       if(isalnum(c))    /* if c is alphanumeric, increment n_alnum */
        n_alnum++;
       buf[i++] = c;  /*   accumulate character in buffer and increment buffer index   */
       text_size++;
      }
    } /* End_while  */
printf("The file size is %d \n", text_size);
printf("The number of punctuation characters is %d \n", n_punct);
printf("The number of alphanumeric characters is %d \n", n_alnum);
}
```

## Example 11.6:

Expand the program in the previous example to a utility that could be used to prepare memos. The program is expected to correct the input in the following manner:

- it can signal the occurrence of a control character and ignore it;
- it can ignore redundant spaces
- it can check for an uppercase letter at the beginning of a sentence

**Step 1:** Let us first prepare, in our current working directory, a header file called ***memo.h*** to contain the following declarations required for our memo program.

```
memo.h:
        #define  TRUE        1
        #define  FALSE     0
        #define BELL          07
        #define  BUF_SIZE   512
        char  buf[BUF_SIZE];
        int     c;
        int text_size, i;
        int     spc_flag, ucase_flag;
```

**Step 2:** Now we will include the ***memo.h*** file in our coding.

```
#include <stdio.h>
#include <ctype.h>
#include "memo.h"
void  main(void)
{
 text_size = i = 0, spc_flag = ucase_flag = FALSE;
 while(((c = getchar()) != EOF) && (text_size < BUF_SIZE))
   {
    if( iscntrl(c) )
   {  if(c == '\n')
             {
             nl_flag = TRUE;
              buf[i++] = c;
         text_size++;
             }
      else
          putchar(BELL);
   }
   else  /* process space character */
      if( isspace(c) )
      {  if(spc_flag == TRUE) )  ;  /* skip extra spaces */
           else
               {
                 spc_flag = TRUE;
                   buf[i++] = c;
             text_size++;
                 }
        else      /* process  end of sentence    */
      if(c == '.')
        {
             buf[i++] = c, ucase_flag =TRUE;
             text_size++;
        }
```

```
    else
            {
            if( (islower(c) && spc_flag && ucase_flag)
                {
            c = toupper(c);
        }
        buf[i++] = c;
        text_size++, spc_flag = ucase_flag = FALSE;
            }
    }   /* End of while  */
/* At the end, display the stored text on the screen  */
  for(i=0; i<text_size; i++)
    putchar(buf[i]);
}
```

### 11.4.3 Character Manipulation

The macro function calls ***tolower(ch)*** and ***toupper(ch)*** are useful to convert uppercase into lowercase and lowercase into uppercase letters, respectively. In both functions, the character argument (i.e., ch) is changed to the required case before returning the result. These two macros (shown in ***Table 11.2***) are also defined in the ***ctype.h*** header file. Some implementations may provide these as library functions and maintain their prototype definitions in ***ctype.h***.

*Table 11.2 Macros for character manipulation operations*

| Macro name | Description |
|---|---|
| tolower (int ch) | If a given character value represents an uppercase letter, it returns the corresponding lowercase value; if the given character is already lowercase or non-alphabetic, it simply returns that character unaltered. |
| toupper (int ch) | If a given character value represents a lowercase letter, it returns the corresponding uppercase value; if the given character is already uppercase or non-alphabetic, it simply returns that character unaltered. |

**Example 11.7:**

Write a program to input text from the keyboard and output the same after changing uppercase letters into lowercase and vice versa. Special characters and numbers are unaltered.

```
#include <stdio.h>
#include <ctype.h>
void main(void)
{
 char ch;
   while((ch=getchar()) != EOF)
     {
       if(isalpha(ch))
         if(islower(ch))
             putchar(toupper(ch));
         else
           putchar(tolower(ch));
   else
    putchar(ch);
     }
}
```

## 11.5 Summary

This chapter is devoted to identifying the basic operations that can be performed on character variables. The data processing operations, such as assignment, testing, manipulation and I/O operations, are explained with respect to ASCII character data. The chapter also described the macros that are available in ***ctype.h*** for character testing and manipulation and the macros available in ***stdio.h*** (such as ***getchar*** and ***putchar***) for character stream I/O. It also showed the role ***EOF*** macro during an input from a stream.

## Exercises

11.1 Read a character from the keyboard and identify whether it is printable or non-printable character.

11.2 Read a character from the keyboard and identify whether it is a special character.

11.3 Can we input every character in the ASCII set from the keyboard?

11.4 Indicate the keys that correspond to ASCII characters given in Table 1 of Appendix B.

11.5 Write a program to change the first character of each sentence to uppercase and to introduce a space after each punctuation mark in the following string text:

> "chapter 1 gives an introduction to C-language.it also explains the general features of C-language.these features include modularity,control structure,rich library support,etc."

11.6 Add a control segment to the memo-program of ***Example 11.6*** to accept a single letter command. A list of single letter (either upper or lowercase) commands and their expected actions is as follows:

i : start inputting the text;
q : quit from memo program;
p : print the text accumulated in the buffer;
s : display the size of the text;

# 12

# Pointers and Array References

**Chapter contents:**

*The readers may have a good grounding in C, but may need to refresh knowledge of C++. For this reason, this chapter introduces an overview of C++ language before involving the design of Abstract Data Structures in C++. After reading this chapter, students will be able to read and write simple C++ programs.*

**Organization:**


*12.1 Introduction*
*12.2 Pointer Variable*
*12.3 Address Constants*
*12.4 Declaring Pointers*
*12.5 Operations on Pointers*
*12.6 Pointer Mechanism for Dynamic Data Structures*
*12.7 Summary*
*Exercises*


## 12.1 Introduction

The C-language is akin to machine language in its ability to access the CPU directly and even more powerful than any machine language in conveniently providing the pointer facility to deal with different types of address references. A pointer is basically an address value or an index to a memory location. At machine language level, programs invariably access data elements (or data objects) using addresses, either as direct or indirect memory reference operations. For indirect memory reference operations, processors often provide a separate set of index registers. For example, Motorola's M6809 has two index registers (called X and Y); PDP-11 processors have eight general purpose registers that can be used as index registers. Some processors, like the M68000 and IBM370, provide up to sixteen registers for indexing purposes. A machine language programmer will realize the importance of these index registers, particularly in processing arrays and strings at that level. A similar facility is provided in C, but it is much more versatile than the simple index registers. First, the cost of hardware limits the number of index registers in a processor. In this respect, a machine language program may find difficulty in maintaining more pointer-oriented data structures (like arrays) than the number of index registers present in the supporting processor.

A machine language pointer can point only to physical memory locations (i.e., a byte location in a byte-addressable memory.) The pointer facility in C-language removes these two limitations and acts like a powerful, high-level machine language. It allows the users to emulate pointers without any limit, and it is also possible to create pointers of various types. For example, a pointer of character type can be created to index character locations (or bytes) of a string in memory. Similarly, pointers of integer and real (or float) types can be created to point to the locations of integer and real objects, respectively, in the memory.

The direct application of pointers in C-programs is particularly useful in processing or maintaining the following data structures:

1. *aggregates or arrays.*
2. *composite data structures (struct and union).*
3. *dynamic data structures like linked lists.*

This chapter explores the meaning of a pointer variable, operations on pointers and their applications in maintaining aggregates or arrays. ***Chapter 15***, covering structures and unions, discusses more fully the application of pointers in maintaining these composite data structures.

## 12.2 Pointer Variable

A pointer variable, like any other simple variable, is associated with an allocated memory location, which contains an assigned address value, and also with an identifier to reference (or hold) the currently assigned value. A pointer variable can hold an address of its own type. For example, we can assign the address of character location to a character pointer; similarly, an integer pointer can be assigned to the address of an integer location (see ***Fig. 12.1***).

## 12.3 Address Constants

The data or value assigned to a pointer variable is simply the address of a location in memory. In a system with byte-oriented memory, it is a byte address. An address at machine level is normally a binary value, really an unsigned value. The range of address values (or allowable address constants) for a given memory is from the address of the first (byte) location (usually 0) to the address of the last (byte) location. Obviously, this depends upon physical address space of a computer. For a processor with 64kbyte main memory, the binary addresses range from 0000 0000 0000 0000 to 1111 1111 1111 1111, in hexadecimal 0x0000 to 0xFFFF. In machine level programming, a binary address within the allowable range can be directly loaded into hardware, e.g., an index register, to point to a physical location in memory. Similarly, a pointer variable in C can be initialized with an address constant that is within the range of available memory address space, but a pointer does not simply store an address as a binary number; it also includes the type of object stored in the referenced location. Hence, it is quite illegal to assign a simple binary number to a C-pointer. The complex notation used to maintain address constants is internal to C-compilers. However, C provides the cast operation which can transform a binary address to the required address type for assignment to a pointer. For example:

```
(int *)0x1000
```

represents a legal address constant of integer type that can be assigned to an integer pointer variable. The above cast expression means that the binary address 0x1000 is converted into an address of integer type.

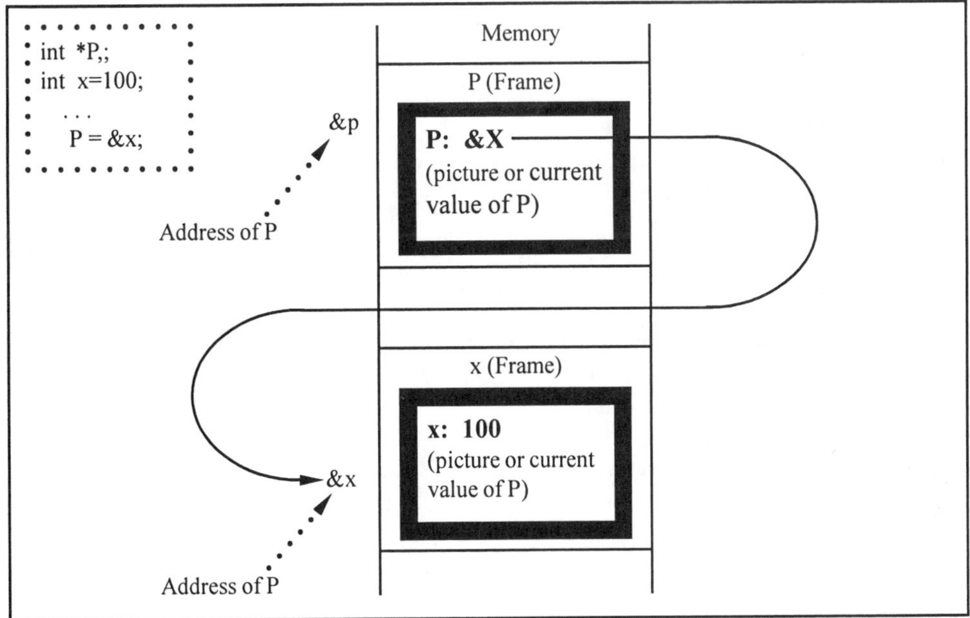


*Fig. 12.1 A pointer variable*

### 12.3.1 Meaning of a NULL Address

It is incorrect to say that an empty pointer has the value zero. In fact, zero is the address of the first (byte) location in a given memory. Properly speaking, a pointer with "NULL ADDRESS" is an empty pointer that points to nowhere in the memory. Hence, the task of creating empty pointers requires the initialization of created variables with a NULL address of appropriate type. For example, the following expressions show the explicit way of representing NULL addresses:

(char *)NULL represents the NULL address of char type;
(int *)NULL represents the NULL address of integer type;
(float *)NULL represents the NULL address of real type;

The defined value of the NULL macro in ***stdio.h*** or ***stddef.h*** is simply zero. This macro is normally used to initialize simple data variables like characters, integers and reals. At the same time, C-compilers allow us to use the same defined NULL as a NULL address. The built-in capability of C-compilers interprets the usage of this NULL macro correctly in different contexts. Hence, we may use this macro (without any explicit casting) whenever we want to initialize a pointer with a NULL address. For example:

```
char *cp  = NULL; /* A character pointer with the NULL value  is declared  */
char  ch  = NULL; /* A character variable with the NULL value  is declared  */
```

are all quite valid initializations.

## What Is a Dangling Pointer?

When a pointer is pointing to an object that is destroyed, it is either out of scope of a program or exists no more. A simple example is a non-initialized local pointer in a function. Since local variables of a function are dynamically allocated from the run-time stack, a pointer of auto type may be pointing to an object that was previously used by some other function. Effectively, a non-initialized local pointer is pointing to a dead object. Hence, programs must take care that they do not access a dangling pointer.

## The NULL Address as a delimiter

In general, any dynamic data structure, such as a file, string, linked list or pointer array, requires a unique end-mark (or a delimiter) to indicate that the processing should stop at that point. For example, file processing may terminate when presented with an EOF marker. Similarly, string processing may terminate at the occurrence of a NULL character. The same concept can be applied in maintaining the linked lists and pointer arrays. Both end with a NULL pointer, so traversing the list of elements can stop at that point. These dynamic structures with their end-markers are shown in ***Fig. 12.2***.

> ***Note:*** *A pointer array is useful when a function wants to pass a variable number of arguments to another function, which is usually achieved by storing the addresses of variables in an array and passing the address of this array to a function.*

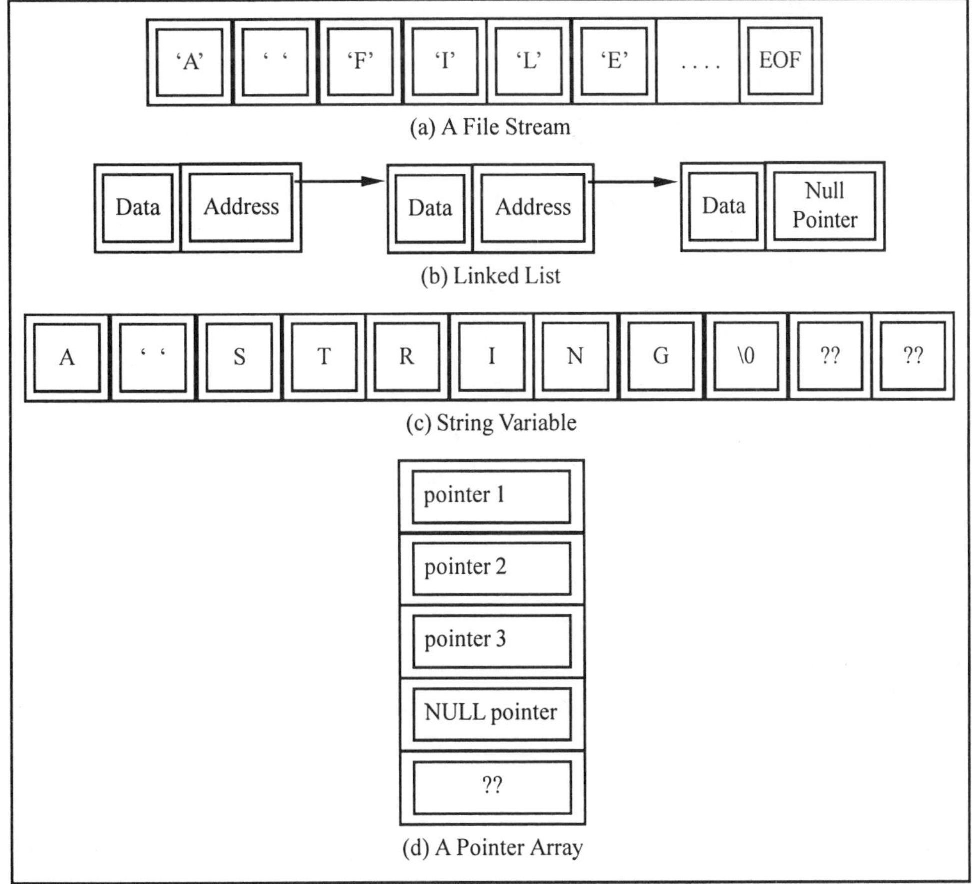


*Fig. 12.2 Various dynamic data structures with their delimiters*

## 12.4 Declaring Pointers

There is no single keyword reserved to declare pointers. Instead, an asterisk character is used along with a type keyword (i.e., char, int, etc.) to declare pointers of that type. The resulting notation for pointer type can be shown as follows:

| | |
|---|---|
| int * | to declare a pointer to integer objects |
| char * | to declare a pointer to character objects |
| float * | to declare a pointer to real objects |

Some typical pointer declarations are:

```
int      *ip1;
float    *rp1, *rp2;
char     *cp_array[10];  /* array of character pointers  */
```

Now we will show some examples of pointer declarations and their memory maps.

### Example 12.1:

Declare some pointers inside main() and show the memory map of these variables.

```
/*  Declare some pointers as local variables */
void  main(void)
{
  char  *pc; /* character pointer */
  int   *pi; /* integer pointer */
 real  *pr; /* real pointer */
        . . .
}
```

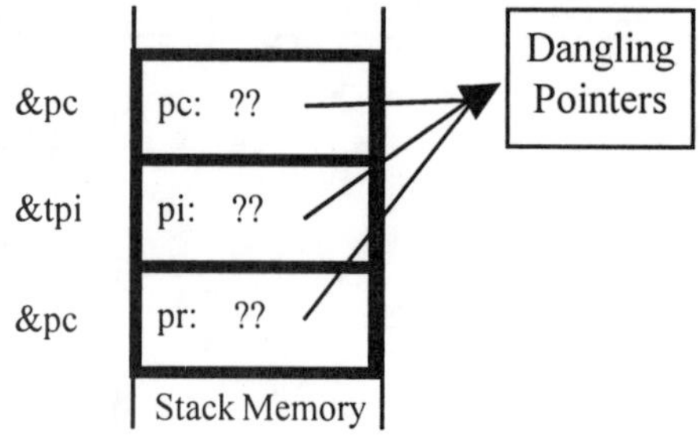

| | Stack Memory |
|---|---|
| &pc | pc: ?? |
| &tpi | pi: ?? |
| &pc | pr: ?? |

Dangling Pointers

In the above example, it is clear that the pointers are created in the memory just like normal variables. Since they are declared inside the main() function, they will be created in the run-time stack memory during execution. Hence, the compiler is not able to initialize these pointers. Since they are not initialized, they may be pointing anywhere in the memory.

On the other hand, when pointers are defined externally, the compiler creates them in permanent memory. If they are not initialized explicitly, then the C-compiler initializes them with the NULL addresses. The following examples show this.

### Example 12.2:

Declare a character pointer and an integer pointer outside the main() function and show the memory map.

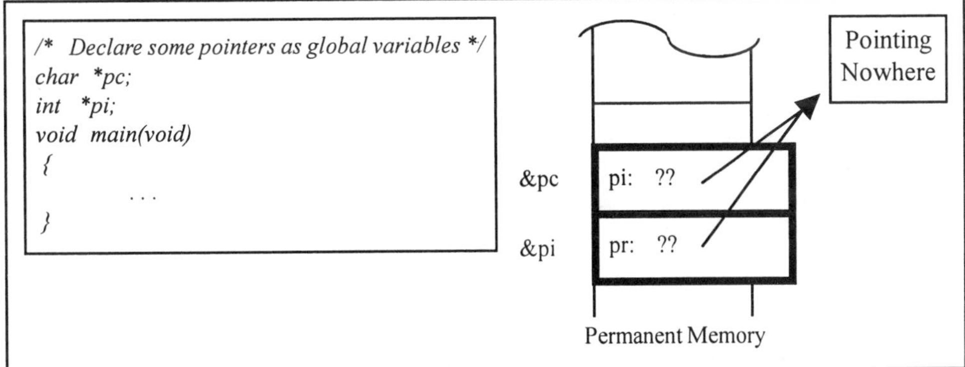
/* Declare some pointers as global variables */
char *pc;
int *pi;
void main(void)
{
. . .
}
Pointing Nowhere
&pc
pi: ??
&pi
pr: ??
Permanent Memory

### Example 12.3:

Add a string declaration to the above example and initialize the character pointer, **pc**, to point to this string. Show the effective memory map.

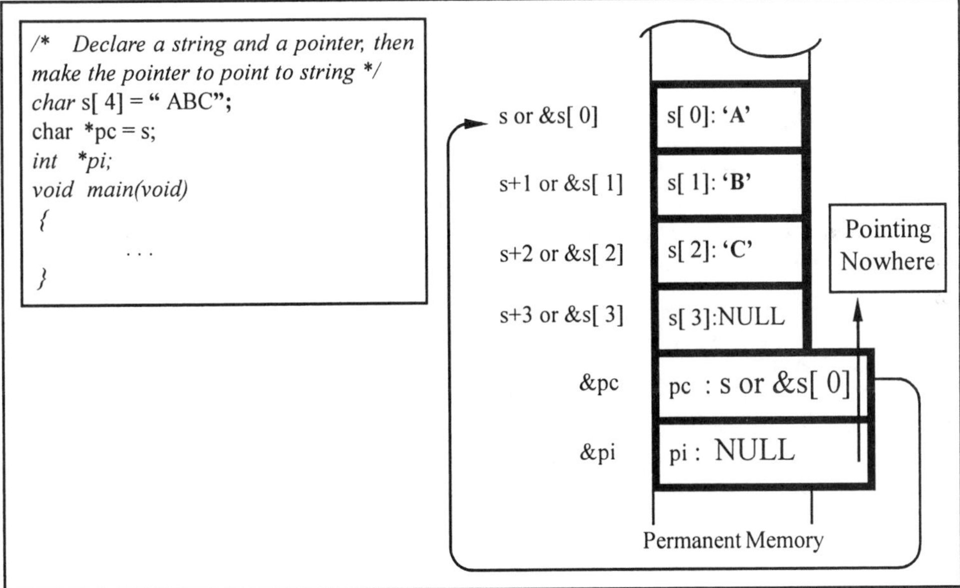
/* Declare a string and a pointer, then make the pointer to point to string */
char s[ 4] = " ABC";
char *pc = s;
int *pi;
void main(void)
{
. . .
}
s or &s[ 0]
s[ 0]: 'A'
s+1 or &s[ 1]
s[ 1]: 'B'
s+2 or &s[ 2]
s[ 2]: 'C'
s+3 or &s[ 3]
s[ 3]:NULL
Pointing Nowhere
&pc
pc : s or &s[ 0]
&pi
pi : NULL
Permanent Memory

**Effect of const on Pointer Declarations**

A pointer declaration creates a pointer variable where a program can make reference to either address value directly, or a data value pointed to by it indirectly. When we want to qualify a pointer declaration with ***const***, it is necessary to indicate whether we want to create the declared pointer as a read-only object or the data that is pointed to by this pointer as a read-only object. These cases are discussed below:

(a) To create a pointer to point to read-only data:
**const char *cp = "A Constant String";**

> ***Remark:*** *The effective value (i.e., the value that is pointed to by cp in this case) cannot be modified and is maintained as a read- only object; but at the same time, cp is itself modifiable. Hence,*
>
> **cp = 'A'; is an ILLEGAL statement and*
> *cp++; is a LEGAL statement.*

(b) To make a read-only pointer:
**char * const cp = "A String";** /* quite different from the previous one */

> ***Remark:*** *In this case, the pointer is not modifiable, but the effective value, *cp, is modifiable. Hence,*
>
> *cp++; is an ILLEGAL statement and*
> **cp = 'A'; is a LEGAL statement.*

(c) To create a read-only pointer along with read-only data:
**const char * const cp = "A Constant String";** /* quite different from the previous ones */

> ***Remark:*** *In this case, the pointer as well as the de-referenced or effective value are not modifiable. Hence,*
>
> *cp++; is an ILLEGAL statement and*
> **cp = 'A'; is also an ILLEGAL statement.*

## Meaning of Void Pointer

A ***void*** pointer, an ANSI-C invention, is a generic pointer that can point to any object. By principle, it may be understood as having the capability of pointing to an object of internal memory type whose type is anonymous or unknown (i.e., it could be byte-oriented or word-oriented). Since it is viewed as a common or generic type of pointer, any other type pointer (e.g., ***char*** pointer, ***int***, ***float*** pointer, ***struct*** or ***union*** pointer) can be cast into this type and then back to their own types without losing their values. We can find a significant use of this type with the dynamic memory allocation functions such as ***malloc()*** and ***calloc()***. These functions return a pointer to an allocated internal storage, equivalent to the requested amount of specified type. It is left to the caller to cast this allocated internal storage to its type before using the allocated space, which is discussed more in ***Chapter 16***.

Similar to any other pointer declaration, ***void*** pointer can be declared. The key word ***void*** is used as the type specifier. For example, void *vp; declares ***vp*** as a ***void*** type pointer.

A simple example shown below would explain the basic principle further. In this example, we declare two simple global variables and find out which of the two variables is kept in the higher address of the internal memory. The solution is to cast the addresses of these two variables into common type and compare them.

```
int    i;
float f;
void main(void)
 {
     . . .
  if( (void  *)&i > (void  *)&f)
    printf("i's address is bigger than f's address");
     . . .
 }
```

### 12.4.1 Defining Pointer Arrays

As with arrays of simple data types, an array of pointers of any type can be declared in a program. We have seen that a simple pointer can be used to point to an array of data objects. A pointer array contains a row of pointers, and each pointer element can point to an array of data objects. For example,

```
char *acp[4] ={ (char *)0, (char *)0, (char *)0, (char *)0};
```

declaration creates an array of four character (or string) pointers initialized with NULL addresses. Remember that these pointers don't point to any real object. Alternatively, we can declare pointers to point to some predefined strings, as shown below:

```
char *acp[4] ={ "East", "West", "North", "South"};
```

When we assign a string constant to a pointer, the compiler stores this constant in the static memory of that program segment and assigns the address of that string to the pointer. Effectively, the constant expression represents the string address. These initializations are possible only for global and static type declarations.

Similarly, an array of integer pointers can be declared and used to point to a set of rows of integer objects. For example,

```
int  *aip[4] ={ (int *)0, (int *)0, (int *)0, (int *)0}
```

creates an array of four integer pointers with NULL addresses. They can be made to point to different arrays of integer objects, as shown below:

```
int    a0[2] = {0,1}, a1[3] = {10,11,12}, a2[4] = {20,21,22,23},
    a3[5] = {30,31, 32,33,34};
aip[0]  =  a0;
aip[1]  =  a1;
aip[2]  =  a2;
aip[3]  =  a3;
```

**Example 12.4:**
Declare some strings and assign them to an array of character pointers. Show its memory map.

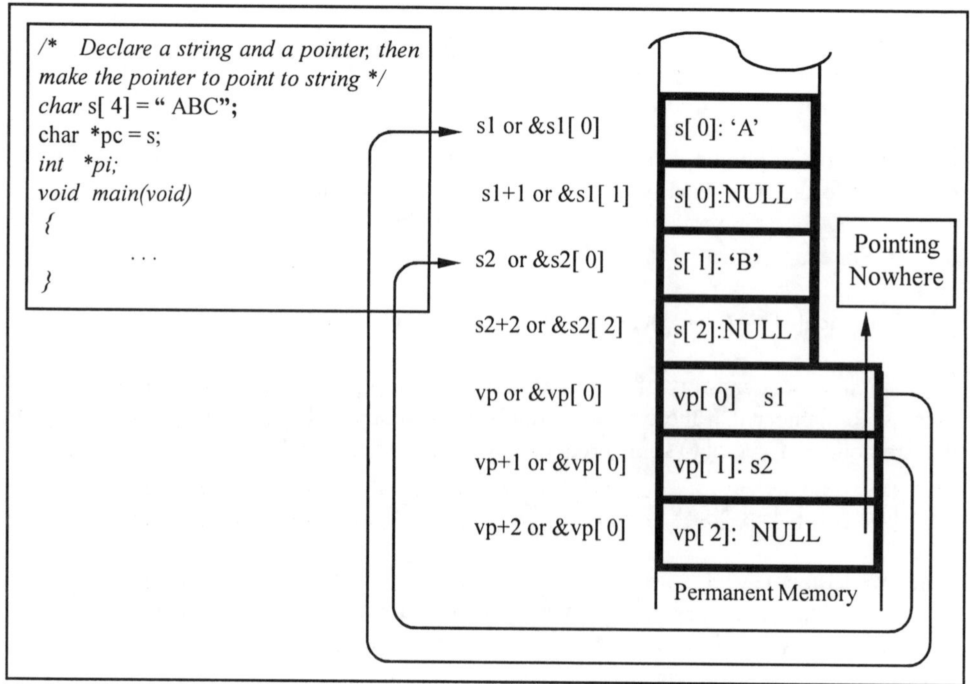

## 12.5 Operations on Pointers

All variables have one common property: they all represent some value. A normal variable represents a data value, whereas a pointer variable represents an address value. Hence, a pointer variable can be used as either an lvalue or rvalue in an assignment expression. It can be incremented or decremented; it can be used as an rvalue in arithmetic, logic and comparison expressions. It can also be used along with a prefixed indirect operator (i.e., an ***asterisk***) to reference a value parameter.

### 12.5.1 Assignment

An assignment operation with respect to a pointer changes the current value of an lvalue expression to that evaluated from an rvalue expression. It is important that the pointer expression on the right side should yield the same type value as that of the ***lvalue***.

### Example 12.5:

Declare character and integer arrays and pointers and make those pointer variables to point to their appropriate arrays.

```
/* declaring arrays and pointers /*
int arr[4] = {10, 20, 30, 40}, *pi;
char s[4] = "ABC", *pc;
void main(void)
 {
  /* assigning pointers with arrays starting addresses */
  pi = &arr[0]; /* (or)   pi = arr;  */
  pc = &s[0];     /* (or)   pc = s;    */
           . . .
           . . .
 }
```

The resulting memory map is shown in ***Fig. 12.3***. In both assignments below, the rvalue yields an address value. The rvalue in the first assignment yields an address of integer type and is assigned to the pointer of integer type while the rvalue expression in the second assignment yields an address of character type, and it is assigned to pc, also of character type.

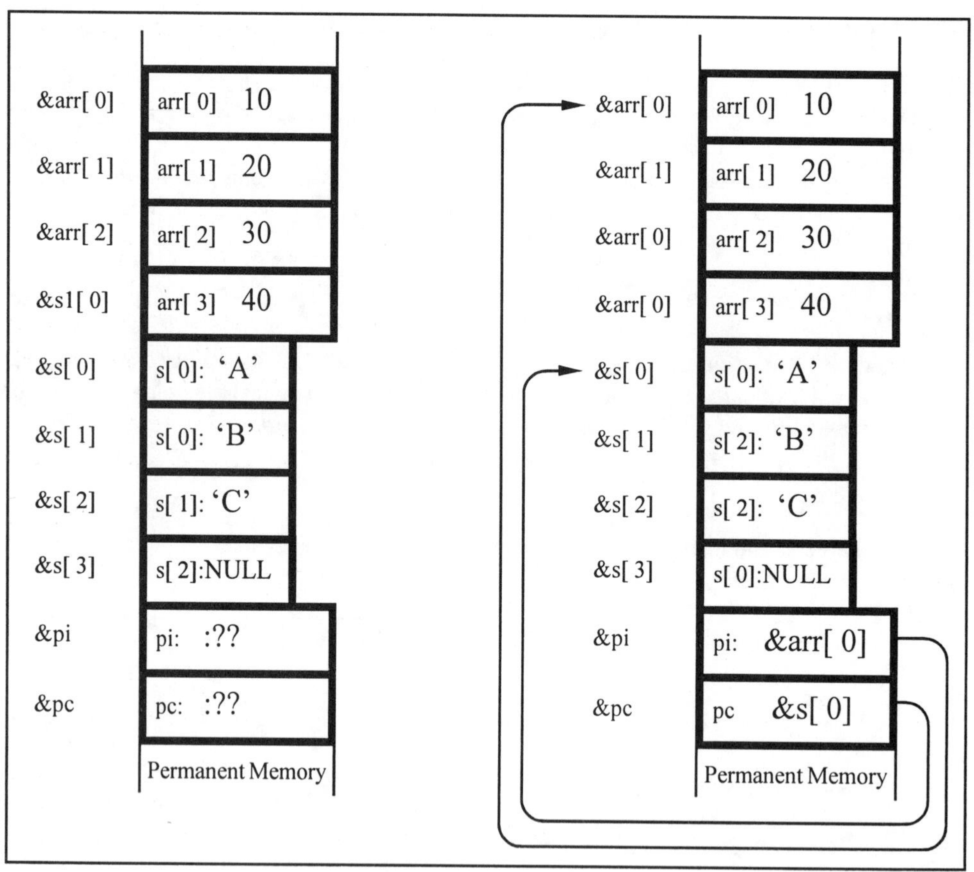


*Fig. 12.3 Memory map for arr[4] and s[4] with their pointers*

## Assignment with constant expressions

We have already discussed that the addresses of physical memory (or real address space) are in simple binary form, and those binary addresses cannot be used directly in pointer assignments. In other words, assigning a known byte address in memory directly to a C-pointer is illegal. For example, the assignment expressions:

```
    pc = 0x8000
and pi = 0x8100
```

are illegal. As we have already mentioned, address constants of simple binary type can be transformed into the required type by applying a cast operation. The following are legal assignments with constant addresses.

```
pc = (char  *)0x8000
pi = (int     *)0x8100
```

In smaller systems (such as a small stand-alone computer), the memory map of the whole system may be known to the user. In such a case, the user knows where the operating system is loaded, where the C-program will be loaded, where the remaining free memory exists, etc. Knowing all these facts, a programmer can safely assign free memory addresses to the created pointers. For example, if the memory map of a system shows that the first 2 kilobytes of main memory is kept free, then a user program can declare pointers within this area as shown below:

```
char *inbuf   = (char *)0x0000; /* input buffer starts at 0x0000  */
char *outbuf = (char *)0x0400; /* output buffer starts at 0x0400  */
void main(void)
{ /* The following is a pseudo code  */
  read data from a disk_file into inbuf;
  process data and accumulate results in outbuf;
  finally write outbuf to disk_file;
}
```

On the other hand, larger or multiuser systems usually manage virtual memory, making their exact memory maps an uncertainty. C-programs in this type of memory environment cannot deal with address constants in binary, as shown above. We normally use the constant symbols, such as array names, system defined constants like NULL, to initialize pointers.

### 12.5.2 Indirect Reference Using a Pointer

A pointer or pointer name refers to the current value in the allocated memory location. On the other hand, a pointer expression with a prefixed asterisk refers to the contents of the memory location whose address is its current value. In ***Example 12.5***, the pointer, *pc*, is an address parameter whose assigned value is *&s[0]* (i.e., the address of the first element of the array *s*), whereas **pc* means the contents of pc (or *&s[0]*) and *s[0]* (i.e., the rvalue of the first element). This is explained further in the following examples.

## Example 12.6:

Output the contents of a string.

```
#include <stdio.h>
char s[4] = "ABC";
char *pc = s;
void main(void)
{ int i;
    pc = &s[0]; /*  (or)  pc = s; pc now points to first element */
    for(i = 0; i < 4; i++) /* (or) while((*pc) != NULL) */
      {
        putchar(*pc);     /* equivalent to "putchar(s[i])  */
        pc++;           /* move the pointer to next element  */
      }
}
```

## Example 12.7:

Get a line from stdin stream (keyboard) and store it in a buffer.

```
#include <stdio.h>
#define BUF_SIZE 100
char *pc;
char buf[BUF_SIZE];
void main(void)
{ int i;
pc = buf;    /* make pc point to the start of buffer */
for(i=1; i<BUF_SIZE; i++) /* clear the buffer with NULLs */
  {
    *pc = '\0';
    pc++;
  }
/* Get characters and store them in the buffer */
pc = buf; /* make pc point to start of buffer */
while((ch=getchar()) != '\n')
  {
    *pc = ch;
    pc++;
  }
}
```

### 12.5.3 Double Indirection

If ***pc*** is a pointer to a character, then ***&pc*** is the address of the location allocated to store the pointer value ***pc***. ****(&pc)*** is same as ***pc*** and also ****(*(&pc))*** is same as ****pc*** or the character pointed to by ***pc***.

### 12.5.4 Address or Pointer Arithmetic

Arithmetic operations on addresses are essential to compute the addresses of elements in an aggregate data structure. In other words, the arithmetic operations on address parameters provide either sequential or random accesses within aggregate data structures. Arithmetic on a particular type of pointer works the same as arithmetic on integer or real data. Various pointer arithmetic operations are explained below.

#### 12.5.4.1 Increment/Decrement Operation

These operations are useful in moving a pointer along an aggregate or array data structure in a sequential manner, only requiring that a pointer variable be initialized with the starting address of an array and then incremented to move in forward direction. Similarly, we can initialize a pointer with the final address of an array and decrement it to move in a backward direction. In both cases, the movement is effectively by one element of the respective data type.

### Example 12.8:

Show the increment and decrement operations on arrays.

```
pc = &s[0]; pi = &arr[0]; /*  both point to the first elements in their respective arrays */
```

Applying increment operations:

```
pc++; pi++;  /* both pointers now point to 2nd elements */
pc++; pi++;  /* both pointers now point to 3rd elements */
pc++; pi++;  /* both pointers now point to 4th elements */
```

Similarly, pointers can be initialized to point to the end of arrays, and decremented to traverse the arrays in the opposite direction.

```
pc = &s[3]; pi = &arr[3]; /* both point to the last  elements in their respective arrays */
```

Applying decrement operations:

```
pc—; pi—; /* both pointers now point to 3rd elements */
pc—; pi—; /* both pointers now point to 2nd elements */
pc—; pi—; /* both pointers now point to 1st elements */
```

> ***Remark:*** *The above example shows that, irrespective of the number of bytes allocated to each type of element, the increment/decrement operation on a pointer moves it to next element (not to the next byte).*

### 12.5.4.2 Pointer Arithmetic in 1-Dimensional Arrays

An element of a given array can be accessed using either index notation or indirect referencing notation. For example, if we define an integer array of four elements as int k[4]; then using the index notation, we can say that k[0], k[1], k[2] and k[3] are the individual value parameters. They directly represent the respective values of the first, second, third and fourth element in the array.

If we define an integer pointer and set it to the base address of this array, then this pointer can be made to reference an element by adding an offset.

```
int    *pi;
pi = k;  /* pointer is assigned with base address */
```

Now, pi is pointing to the location of first element. The address expression, pi+1 points to the second element. The expression *(pi+1) means the contents of pi+1 and references the value (i.e., the value k[1] )in that location.

Similarly, pi+3 points to the location of the last element, and *(pi+3) references the last value parameter in that array.

Even though integers, reals and structures are created as abstract elements, they are all made up of physically addressable elements which are bytes in present-day computer architectures. An integer may be 2 bytes, a real may be 4 bytes, a structure may consume a variable number of bytes, depending upon its composition. Still, the addresses of all these elements point to byte boundaries. If we assume that the integer array, k[4], is stored in a byte-oriented memory starting from the effective address, 0x1000, then the base address, k (i.e., address of first element) is 0x1000. If each integer element requires 2 bytes, then the effective addresses k+1, k+2, and k+3 are 0x1002, 0x1004 and 0x1006, respectively (***Fig. 12.4***).

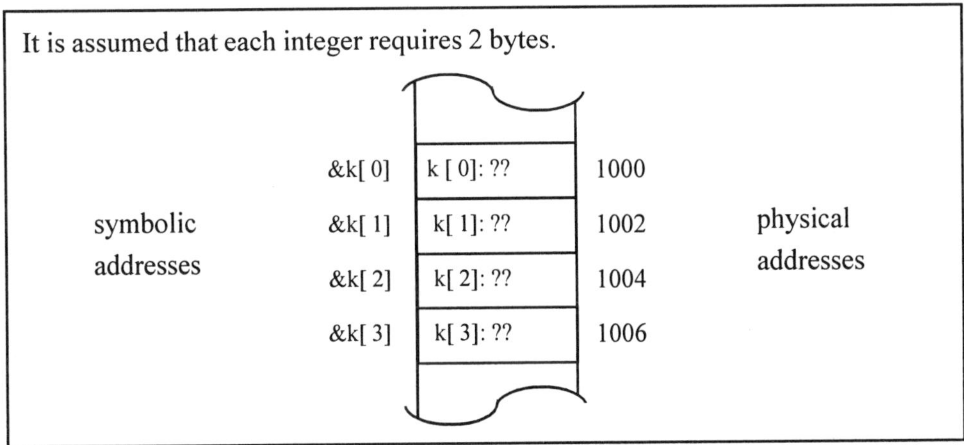


*Fig. 12.4 Address mapping for simple integer array, k[ 4]*

From the above illustration, we observe that the value of an address (or pointer expression) denotes the address value at the level of element type rather than at physical location (or byte) level. Using this concept, we can say that k+2 means the address of the third element or third integer location, and *(k+2) means the value (i.e., k[3]) in that integer location.

### 12.5.4.3 Pointer Arithmetic in 2-Dimensional Arrays

Before applying address arithmetic to multidimensional arrays, we must understand how they are stored internally. In C, a 2-dimensional array is stored ***row-wise*** (or in ***row-major*** form). That is, the elements in row 1 are stored first, then the elements in row 2, etc. are stored in contiguous locations. For example, if we define a 2-dimensional integer array with three rows and three columns as:

```
int    m[3][3];
```

assuming that its starting location (or byte address) is 0x1000, then the array is laid out in the memory, as shown in ***Fig. 12.5***.

The row names, ***m[0]*** and ***m[1]*** are constant parameters representing, the base (or start) addresses of the first and second rows. We can also say that ***m[0]*** is the address of the first element in the first row; that is ***m[0]*** and &***m[0][0]*** are same. Then ***m*** is the base address of the array of row addresses. We may interpret a 2-dimensional array as a pointer array and each pointer in that array is pointing to a row of elements.

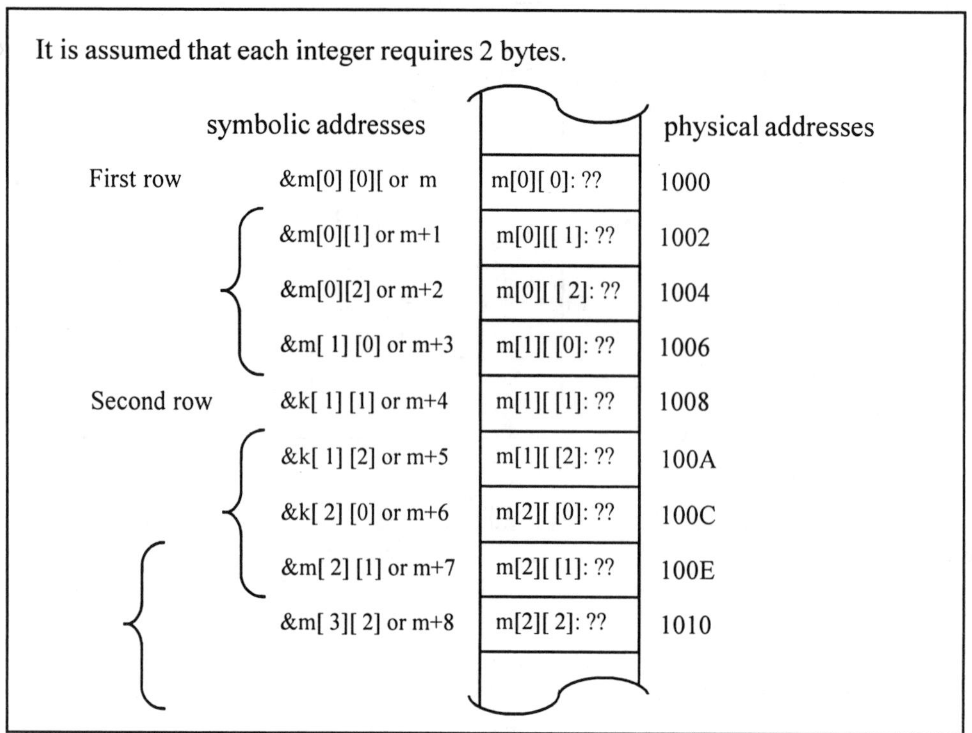


*Fig 12.5 Memory map of 2-dimensional array, m[2][ 2]*

### 12.5.4 Operations of Void Pointers

Since a void pointer points to a undefined type, many operations, such as indexing, value of (*), increment, decrement and other arithmetic operations, are unsafe on pointer variables.

## 12.6 Pointer Mechanism for Dynamic Data Structures

Pointers are quite useful for constructing dynamic data structures such as variable strings, variable or dynamic arrays and linked lists (or trees). Pointer mechanism along with the dynamic storage facility we can create data objects of the same type dynamically and link them using the pointer elements of these objects to form a linked structure. These linked data objects can be indirectly accessed and processed using the pointer operations. ***Chapter 16*** explains the use of dynamic storage management and pointers in managing these dynamic data structures.

## 12.7 Summary

This chapter discussed the meaning of pointer to normal types and pointer to ***void*** type, including their declaration formats and allowed operations. It also showed the use of pointers in processing single and 2-dimensional arrays.

## Exercises

12.1 Show the memory map for the following string type declarations:

```
char s[]=”ABC”;
char *ps = s;
```

12.2 When we increment ps (ps++), where will it be pointing now?

12.3 Show the memory map for the following integer type declarations:

```
int k[4] = {10,20,30,40};
int *pk = &k[3];
```

12.4 Consider the following pointer declarations:

```
char *pc = (char *)0x1000;
int *pi = (int *)0x1000;
float *pf = (float *)0x1000;
```

(a) To what byte address will each variable be pointing?
(b) After incrementing them, to which byte address will each variable be pointing?

12.5 What is the difference between a normal variable and pointer variable?

12.6 Consider the following declaration:

```
char *svec[4] = {“ABC”, “DEF”, “GHI”, (char *)NULL};
char  sarr[4][] = {“ABC”, “DEF”, “GHI”, “”};
```

In what ways do the above declarations differ?

12.7 Show memory maps of the following declarations:

```
int I[5], j[2];
int *n[5] = {i,j};
int **ppi = n;
```

# 13

# Advanced Concepts of C-Functions

**Chapter contents:**

*This chapter introduces the pointers to functions and explains how C-functions can be passed as arguments using their pointers.*

**Organization:**


*13.1 Introduction*
*13.2 Declaring Pointers to Functions*
*13.3 Recursion*
*13.4 Functions with Variable Number of Arguments*
*13.5 Summary*
*Exercises*


## 13.1 Introduction

In ***Chapter 1***, we overviewed the modular organization of C-programs. In ***Chapter 4***, we discussed the meaning of C-function and how to define a function in a C-program. In ***Chapter 5***, we discussed storage environment around an executing function. In addition to the concepts discussed in these chapters, this chapter introduces few advanced a concepts supported by C-functions, such as:

- *the pointer to functions;*
- *function definition with variable-length arguments;*
- *recursive functions.*

## 13.2 Declaring Pointers to Functions

We have already described that a function definition provides a kind of read-only variable which, when referred to, always computes to produce a fresh value. We have seen the memory map of a C-function (***Chapter 4***) which shows that the function definition is stored in the storage and its address is represented by the symbolic name of the function itself. Once an address is known for a function definition, it is also possible to create a pointer to hold such a function address and reference a function in an indirect manner. This concept is followed from the pointer concept applied to normal variables. The declaration format of a function pointer is as follows:

***type_specifier (*identifier)();***

where ***identifier*** is a pointer to a function, returning a value of ***type_specifier***.

## Example 13.1:

Declare a pointer to a function which returns an integer and show its memory map.

*int (*if_ptr)(); /* **if_ptr** is a pointer to a function that returns an integer value. */*

In the above declaration, the parentheses play important roles. The first pair of parentheses is necessary to indicate the identifier, *if_ptr*, is a pointer. The second pair of parentheses indicates that the identifier is a ***pointer to a function***. Without the first pair of parentheses, the declaration will be:

*int *if_ptr();*

which is interpreted as a simple function declaration that returns a pointer to integer. The parentheses bind tighter than *.

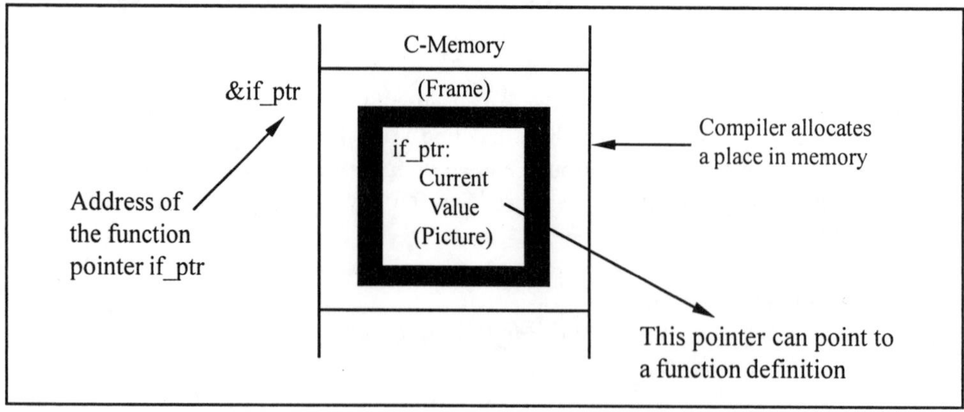


*Fig. 13.1 Memory map for a pointer to integer function (Example 13.1)*

## Example 13.2:

Declare pointers to functions returning character and real values.

```
char  (*cf_ptr)(); /* if_ptr is a pointer to a function that returns a character value. */
float (*ff_ptr)(); /* ff_ptr is a pointer to a function that returns a real value. */
```

## Assigning a function to a pointer

Once a pointer to function is declared, then that pointer can be assigned with the address of a function definition.

## Example 13.3:

Declare a function pointer and assign with the address of a function definition and show the memory map.

```
int    (*if_ptr)(); /*  if_ptr is a pointer to a function that returns an integer value. */
int    ifunc(void)
{
    . . .
  return (an_integer_value);
}
void  main(void)
{
      . . .
     if_ptr = ifunc;   /* Now if_ptr points to the ifunc's definition  */
/* or if_ptr = &ifunc;  */
      . . .
}
```

The type of the function definition and the type of function pointer must be the same for a legal assignment operation. If these two are different, then type conversion must be performed before the assignment operation. (see ***Fig. 13.2***)

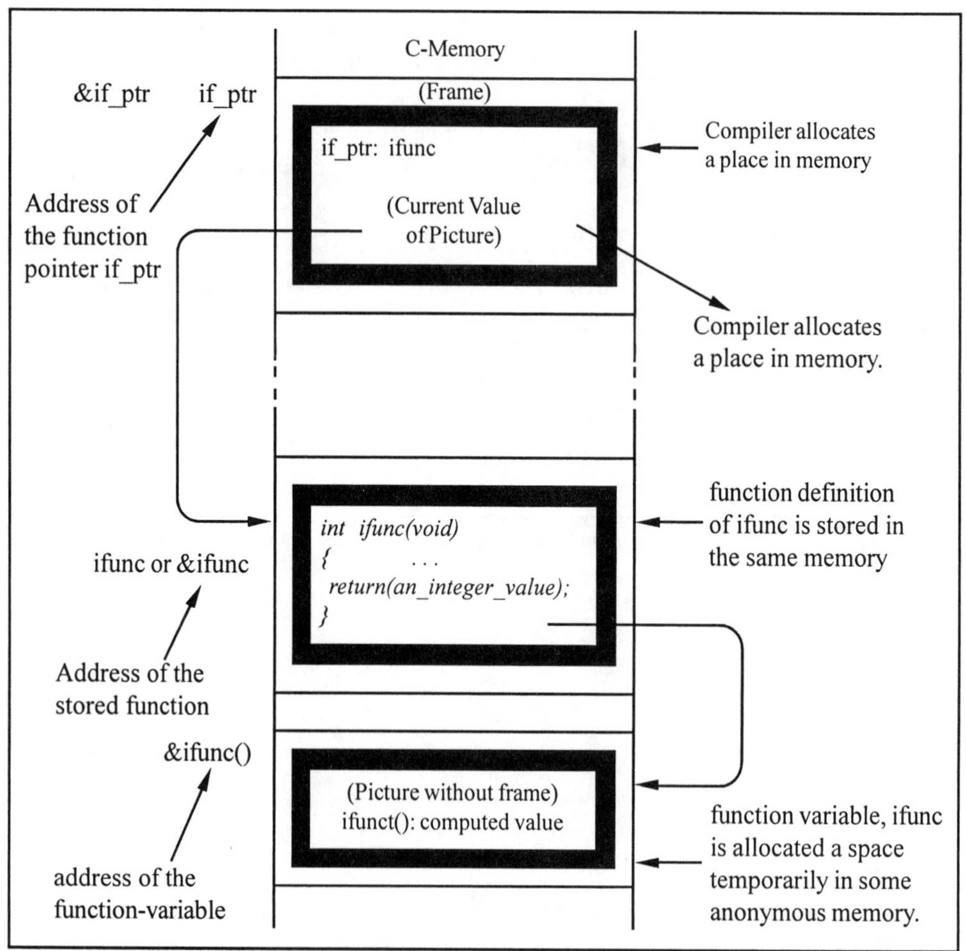


*Fig. 13.2 Memory map for Example 13.3*

## Dereferencing a function pointer

Using the dereferencing operator, i.e., *, one can call a function using its pointer. For example, if a pointer pX contains the address of a function called X, then we can issue either a direct function call:

```
X();
```

or an indirect call

```
(*pX)();
```

In the direct call, the name *X*, the starting address of the function, is used to locate the function directly, whereas in the latter *(*pX)* indicates that the target address X is to be accessed from the pointer, *pX,* to locate the function.

### Example 13.4:

Declare a pointer to function and show how it can be dereferenced.

```
void (*fX_ptr)(); /* declare fX_ptr as a pointer to a function which returns void */
void funcX(void)
{
  printf("I am funcX() \n");
} /* End of funcX() block*/

void main(void)
{
  fX_ptr = funcX; /* or fX_ptr = &funcX; */
  (*fX_ptr)(); /* This calls the function pointed to by fX_ptr i.e., funcX() */
} /* End of main block*/
```

### Function Pointer Related Declarations

The following examples show some complex declarations with respect to function pointers.

| | |
|---|---|
| *int *(*ipf_ptr)();* | *ipf_ptr is a pointer to a function that returns a pointer to an integer.* |
| *float *(*fpf_ptr)();* | *fpf_ptr is a pointer to a function that returns a pointer to a real value.* |
| *char *(*spf_ptr)();* | *spf_ptr is a pointer to a function that returns a pointer to a character or string.* |
| *char **(*psf_ptr)();* | *psf_ptr is a pointer to a function that returns a pointer to a pointer to a character value or string.* |
| *int (*if_ptr[4])();* | *if_ptr is an array of 4 pointers to function that returns integer value.* |
| *char *(*ipf_ptr[])();* | *ipf_ptr is an open array of pointers to function that returns a pointer to a character value.* |
| *char (*cpf())();* | *cpf is a function that returns a pointer to a function returning character value.* |
| *char *(*cpf())();* | *cpf is a function that returns a pointer to a function returning a pointer to a character.* |
| *char (* (*cpf()) [] )();* | *cpf is a function that returns a pointer to an array of pointers to function that returns a character value.* |

### Example 13.5:

Declare an array of pointers to function and show how they can be used.

```
void   (*fptr[2])(); /* declare an array of function pointers */
void funcX(void)
{
  printf("I am funcX() \n");
} /* End of funcX() block*/

void funcY(void)
{
  printf("I am funcY() \n");
} /* End of funcY() block*/

void  main(void)
{
  fptr[0]  = funcX;
  fptr[1]  = funcY;
  (*fptr[0])();
  (*fptr[1])();
} /* End of main() block*/
```

## 13.2.1 Passing a function to another function

Similar to passing normal data arguments, functions can also be passed as arguments to other functions with the help of the pointer to function facility.

### Example 13.6:

Show how a function address can be passed to another function.

```
void funcX(void)
{
  printf("I am funcX \n");
} /* End of funcX */

void funcY(void)
{
  printf("I am funcY \n");
} /* End of funcY */
```

```
void execute(void    (*fptr)() )
{ /* This function can call a function indirectly using
    supplied function pointer */
  (*fptr)();
}

void main(void)
{
  execute(funcX);
  execute(funcY);
} /* End of main */
```

## 13.3 Recursion

The concept of recursion is the capability of a function to call itself, wherein calling itself takes the control thread into the same code again. In this case, we say that the control thread is in the first recursive call. If the call is repeated in this phase, the control thread goes into the same code the second time and we can say that the function is called recursively second time. This can be repeated any number of times. As discussed in ***Chapter 5***, every time a call is made, the passed parameters and local variables are created in the associated stack memory, called stack frame, which provides the current environment of the called function. When each recursive call returns, the environment of the called level is brought back. In this way, C provides a suitable storage environment for implementing recursive functions. But the stack storage for a C-program may be limited and, hence, there may be a constraint in the recursion range of a program. Some simple examples are shown here to demonstrate the recursive capability of C-functions.

### Example 13.7:

Write a program to calculate the factorial of n using a recursive function and use the same to calculate the factorial of 10.

```
int factorial(int   n)
{
  if(n==1) return(1);
  else
    return(n*factorial(n-1));
} /* End of factorial block*/

void main(void)
{
  printf("%d \n", factorial(10));
} /* End of main block*/
```

### Example 13.8:

Write a program to print a string in the reverse order using a recursive function.

```
#define EOS '\0'
char str[] = "0123456789";     /* declare a global string */
char puts_rev(int i)
{
  if(str[i] == EOS) return('\n');
  else
    {
      putchar( puts_rev(str[i+1]) );
      return(str[i]);
    }
} /* End of puts_rev block*/

void main(void)
{
  puts_rev(0);
} /* End of main block*/
```

From the above example, this recursive control structure results in a concise code. This control structure is quite applicable for achieving efficient processing on some applications that involve dynamic data structures, such as linked lists and trees. More on the use of this recursive facility in solving problems using dynamic data structures is discussed in ***Chapter 16***.

## 13.4 Functions with Variable Number of Arguments

So far, we have discussed C-functions with a fixed number of arguments. This is the case in most of the languages. In C, one can define functions that can be called with any number of arguments. The typical example of this category is the ***printf*** function which is allowed to carry an unspecified number of arguments during a call. This is another unique feature of this language. The function definition and syntax diagram of a function head in this case are as follows:

***type_specifier function_name(some_parameter_declarations , . . . )***

### The syntax diagram for FUNCTION HEAD

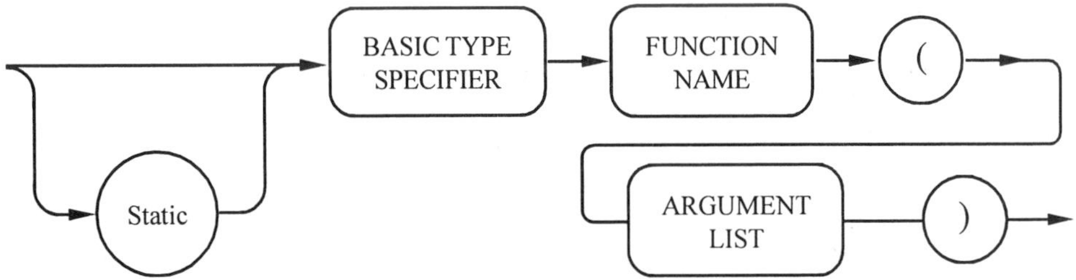


This function definition is similar to normal function definition except the declaration parameter list ends with the ellipsis notation ( , . . .). During a call to a function, this category must carry the number of arguments, which must equal or exceed the number of parameter declarations. For example, consider ***printf*** declaration and its use:

```
void printf(char   *format_string, . . .)
{ /* printf() code */
    . . .
}
void main(void)
{
  int i =10, j = 20;
  printf("%d  \n", i);
  printf("%d %d  \n", i, j);
}
```

Let us consider another simple example which sums a set of integer values.

```
int isum(int  n_arg, . . .)
{ /* isum code */
    . . .
}
void main(void)
{
  printf("%d    \n", isum(0));
  printf("%d    \n", isum(1, 10));
  printf("%d    \n", isum(2, 10, 20));
  printf("%d    \n", isum(3, 10, 20, 30));
}
```

In the above examples, the first argument is used to carry either directly or indirectly the number of arguments being passed. In the first example, the format argument of the ***printf*** call contains two integer field specifications, indicating that it expects two arguments of integer type following the format string. In the second example, the first formal parameter, ***n_arg***, is used to indicate the number of data arguments being passed in a call. Since the function ***isum*** is meant to add only integers, the designer of this function uses that fact implicitly in the function definition. What would happen if a call to ***isum*** supplies real data instead of the expected integer data (e.g., ***isum(2, 10.0, 20.0)*** )? The result will be unpredictable, depending upon the implementation.

In order to extract the passed arguments within the called function, C provides three basic functions (or macros) in a header file called ***stdarg.h***: ***va_start*** to extract the passed arguments and place them in a sequential store; **va_arg** to access the stored arguments one by one in sequence and; ***va_end*** to close the sequential store. Note that ***va_start*** can be issued after ***va_end*** to initialize the store and use it again. C has defined the sequential store type called ***va_list*** in ***stdarg.h***. The prototype definitions of these functions in ***stdarg.h*** are shown below:

*void va_start(va_list p_store, declaration of last known argument) ;*
*type_expected va_arg(va_list p_store, type_of_next_value_expected) ;*
*void va_end(va_list p_store);*

### Example 13.9:

Implement a variable argument function to add integers.

```
#include <stdarg.h>
int isum(int n_arg, . . .)
{/* isum code */
int i, sum = 0;
va_list p_store;

  va_start( p_store, n_arg); /* initialize the sequential store */
  for(i = 0; i < n_arg; i++)
     sum = sum + va_arg(p_store, int);
  va_end( p_store);      /* close the sequential store */
  return(sum);
}

void main(void)
{
  printf("%d  \n", isum(0));
  printf("%d  \n", isum(1, 10));
  printf("%d  \n", isum(2, 10, 20));
  printf("%d  \n", isum(3, 10, 20, 30));
}
```

> ***Remark:*** *Although K&R did not explicitly indicate similarities between functions and variables, we discover through our discussions that functions have much closer resemblance to variables. Function name with the function reference operator, (), represents the function variable, or the returned value that is similar to a constant variable, while the function_name itself, or "**&function_name**", represents address which corresponds with "**&variable_name**" of a variable. Similar to the indirect reference of variables using their pointers, pointers can be declared to functions and used to call them indirectly. In fact, a function definition is an abstract variable constructed with the help of system defined (or basic) data types and their related operations. A function is almost like an object which provides an abstract operation by hiding its internal details.*

## 13.5 Summary

This chapter introduced the pointers to functions, recursion in function calls and the new function definition to pass variable arguments. Pointer to function facility is found useful in passing the functions as parameters to other functions. It is also possible to maintain a table of functions and transfer it to another function. The recursive function call facility shows the scope of C in maintaining abstract data structures efficiently. Finally, the description of the new function definition shows how to implement variable argument functions. Readers can now implement their own ***printf*** and ***scanf*** functions.

## Exercises

13.1 Show the memory map for the following declaration:

```
int    (*ifunc_ptr)();
```

13.2 Show the difference between the following declarations using memory map:

```
int    (*ifunc_ptr)();
int    *ifunc();
```

13.3 Interpret the following:

(a)

```
char (*a )( ) ;
char ( (*a) ( ) );
char (*a[5] ) ( );
char ( (*a[5] ) ( ) )
char *(*a[5] ) ( );
char (*(*a[5] ) ( ) );
char **(*a[5] ) ( );
char (**(*a[5] ) ( ) );
char (*(*a) ( ) ) [ ] ;
```

(b)

```
double dfunct(int (*f1)())
{
  double d;
  int    i;
  i = *f1;
  d = (double)i;
  return d;
}
```

13.4 Can you pass a function as a parameter to another function? Explain using an example.

13.5 Implement a print function that will print only integers. The function should accept variable number of integer arguments. Assume the arguments are simple variable expressions.

13.6 Repeat the same for printing real arguments.

# 14

# Operations on String Variables

**Chapter contents:**

*This chapter introduces the standard string functions that are available in the C-library and then shows how they can be used in applications. This chapter teaches readers the semantics behind the string data structure and how to handle these structures in their programs.*

**Organization:**

*14.1 Introduction*
*14.2 The Header File, string.h*
*14.3 String Operations*
*14.4 Operations on Memory Regions (or Memory Buffers)*
*14.5 String Utility Function for Decoding System Errors*
*14.6 String Conversion Operations*
*14.7 String Composition and Decomposition*
*14.8 Summary*
*Exercises*

## 14.1 Introduction

In ***Chapter 10***, we discussed how to declare string variables and showed memory maps of initialized and non-initialized strings. We also distinguished a string variable from a character buffer: a string is a text terminated by a NULL character, whereas a buffer is viewed simply as an array of characters or bytes. The operations on a string are many and they can be classified into four main categories:

1. string input/output
   - *input string data (or line of text) from a stream;*
   - *output string data to a stream;*

2. string manipulation
   - *copying the text of one string variable into another string variable (called string copy);*
   - *joining (concatenating) the text of one string to the text of another string (called string concatenation);*

3. string checking
   - *comparing the text of one string variable with the text of another string variable (called string comparison);*
   - *searching the text of a string for the location of a specific character occurrence (called character searching);*
   - *searching the text of a string for the location of a specific substring occurrence (called string searching);*
   - *finding the length of a string text.*

4. string conversion
   - *ASCII string to integer value*
   - *ASCII string to long value*
   - *ASCII string to real value*

All these operations are performed with the help of a set of library functions that comes with C-compilers. The prototype definitions of these functions are included in a header file called ***string.h***.

Moreover, the standard introduces a number of functions similar to those for strings, but applied to a generic memory type that could be interpreted as bytes, words or even a set of bits. They are called memory-based operations and identified with the names beginning with the prefix "***mem***". These operations are implemented to receive arrays of data types other than string, and perform memory manipulation and checking by interpreting the memory as characters (or bytes). The prototype definitions of these memory functions are also included in the same ***string.h*** file. A summary of string function calls is presented in ***Table 14.1***, and a detailed explanation of these functions is given in the latter sections of this chapter.

## 14.2 The Header File, string.h

Unlike the character operations that are implemented as macro functions in ***ctype.h***, string operations are implemented as normal functions. They are kept in a C-library in compiled form, ready for linking, and those referenced will be linked with the compiled user programs during the linking stage. The purpose of the ***string.h*** file is to describe the conventions used to implement these functions – what type of arguments are required and what type of result is returned by each string function. By including this file, we enable the compiler to check if the references made to these functions in our program are syntactically correct. If we don't include this header file, then these string functions will be assumed to return integer type values by default. If we browse through ***Table 14.1***, we notice that several functions return character pointers that must be assigned to an *lvalue* of the same type. By including this header file in a C-program, a C-compiler is able to check for the type integrity of those statements that involve string operations. The following example will show the significance of ***string.h***.

*Table 14.1 Summary of prototype definitions of string functions as in string.h*

| | |
|---|---|
| char *strcpy(char *ds, const char *ss) | To copy a source string pointed to by ss into a destination string pointed to by ds. The contents of the source string are unaltered. After copying, the function returns the address of the destination string. |
| char *strncpy(char *ds, const char *ss, size_t n) | To copy n characters of a source string pointed to by ss into a destination string pointed to by ds without adding a null character after copying n characters. If a null character is copied, then the destination becomes a string, or it results in an array of characters. The contents of the source string are unaltered. After copying, the function returns the address of the destination string. |
| char *strcat(char *ds, const char *ss) | To append the source string (ss) to the destination string (ds). The function returns the address of the resulting string. |
| char *strncat(char *ds, const char *ss, size_t n) | To append the first n characters of the source string to the destination string. The function returns the address of the resulting string. |
| int strcmp(const char *s1, const char *s2) | To compare the contents of s1 and s2 lexicographically and return greater than, equal to or less than zero, if the size of s1 is greater than, equal to or less than the size of s2. |
| int strncmp(const char *s1, const char *s2, size_t n) | To compare the first n characters of s1 and s2 lexicographically and return greater than, equal to or less than zero, if the size of the first n characters of s1 is greater than, equal to or less than the size of the first n characters of s2. |
| int strcoll(const char *s1, const char *s2) | To compare the string pointed to by s1 to the string pointed to by s2, both interpreted as appropriate to the collate-sequence specified by the current locale and return greater than, equal to or less than zero depending upon the size of s1 is greater than, equal to or less than the size of s2. |

*Table 14.1 (cont.)*

| | |
|---|---|
| char *strxfrm(char *ds, const char *ss, size_t n) | To transform the string pointed to by ss and place the same in the string pointed to by ds. The transformed string can be used to compare using strcmp function. |
| char *strchr(const char *s, char ch) | To locate the first occurrence of a given character (ch) in s. The function returns the address of the first occurrence of the character or NULL pointer. |
| size_t strspn(const char *s1, const char *s2) | To find out the length of the maximal initial substring (or span) in s1 made up of characters in s2. |
| size_t strcspn(const char *s1, const char *s2) | To find out the length of the maximal initial substring (or span) in s1 is not made up of characters in s2. |
| char *strcbrk(const char *s1, const char *s2) | To locate the first occurrence of any of the characters from the string pointed to by s2 in the string pointed to by s1. The function returns the address of the location of the first occurrence. |
| char *strrchr(char *s, char ch) | To locate the last occurrence of a given character (ch) in s. The function returns the address of the location of the last occurrence of the character or NULL pointer. |
| char *strstr(char *ts, const char *ss) | To find out the occurrence of a substring (ss) in a given target string (ts). The function returns the address of the first character of the substring in the target string. |
| char *strtok(char *s, const char *dset) | To break the given string (s) into a sequence of tokens, using the delimit character set, pointed to by dset. This function requires multiple calls until the last token is extracted from s. The first call searches for a character which is not in the dset. The pointer is set to this character and the search continues until a delimit character is found and substituted by a null character. Then the call returns the pointer. Subsequent calls with the first argument as NULL pointer returns pointer to subsequent tokens. |
| size_t strlen(const char *s) | To find out the length of the given string (s). |
| char *strerror(int errnum) | To return a message corresponding to errnum; both (list of error numbers and messages) definitions depend upon the implementation. |
| void *memcpy(void *m1, const void *m2, size_t n) | To copy n units of memory region pointed by m2 into the memory region pointed by m1. After copying, the function returns address of m1. When the source and destination areas overlap, the results cannot be predicted and are implementation-dependent. |

*Table 14.1 (cont.)*

| | |
|---|---|
| void *memmove(void *m1, const void *m2, size_t n) | To copy n units of memory region pointed by m2 into the memory region pointed by m1. This function is similar to memcpy except that the memory move is guaranteed even when the source and destination areas overlap. After copying, the function returns the address of m1. |
| int memcmp(void *m1, const void *m2, size_t n) | To compare the first n units of the memory region pointed by m1 to the first n units of the memory region pointed by m2. The function returns an integer greater than, equal to or less than zero accordingly as the region pointed by m1 is greater then, equal to or less than the region pointed to by m2. |
| void *memchr(const void *m, int ch, size_t n) | To search for a character in a memory region of n units pointed to by m. The function returns the address of the first matching memory unit. |
| void *memset(void *m, int ch, size_t n) | To set or initialize the n units of the memory region pointed to by m with the value (ch) specified in the second argument. |

## Example 14.1:

The following program uses a string function (i.e., ***strchr***) to find out the position of a particular character in a given string.

```
/* THERE IS A TYPE_CONFLICT IN THIS PROGRAM     */
void main(void)
  { int    pos;
    static str[10] = "abcdef";
      . . .
    pos = strchr(str, 'e'); /* character pointer is assigned to integer */
      . . .
  }
```

This program did not include ***string.h***. The compiler simply assumes that ***strchr*** returns an integer value and could not detect any error in the assignment statement. In fact, ***strchr*** returns a character pointer which is then assigned to an integer variable. This may cause an error during program execution. To avoid this situation, we can either include the ***string.h*** file or define the function type, as shown below.

```
  #include <string.h>
     (or)
  char  *strchr(char  *s, char *ch);  /* prototype definition indicating index returns a
                                          character pointer  */
void  main(void)
  { int    pos;
   static str[10] = "abcdeg";
      . . .
   pos = strchr(str, 'e');  /*  ERROR: char_pointer is assigned to an integer  */
      . . .
  }
```

If we compile the above program, the compiler can easily detect the error due to the type mismatch in the assignment statement, which explains why prototype definition of a library function should be included in a program.

## 14.3 String Operations

### 14.3.1 I/O Operations on Strings

Externally, a string is identified by a list of characters terminated by a white space character, including a newline (nl), whereas a line is a list of characters, including some white spaces like space and tabs, but terminated by a newline character. The former may be called a word-oriented string, whereas the latter may be called line-oriented string. For example, in the following input:

*This is a list of strings (nl)*

***This***, ***is***, ***a***, ***list***, ***of*** and ***strings*** are interpreted as separate word-oriented strings. They are all delimited by some white spaces, including newline. On the other hand, the same input may be interpreted as one line-oriented string and is identified by a newline. C provides one set of library functions to deal with line-oriented string I/O or simply line I/O, and another set to deal with word-oriented string I/O. To read and write line-oriented string data with respect to standard I/O streams (i.e., ***stdin*** and ***stdout***) the ***gets*** and ***puts*** functions are used. To read and write line-oriented string data with respect to any open stream, ***fgets*** and ***fputs*** can be used. The above functions are purely for line-oriented string I/O. On the other hand, we have formatted I/O functions, such as ***scanf***, ***fscanf***, ***printf*** and ***fprintf***, that can be used to perform I/O on word-oriented string data. These functions are normally used to do I/O operations on a record of composite type in which string data may be part of the whole structure.

A detailed view of all these functions is presented in ***Chapter 17***, along with the other stream operations. We will, however, briefly go through these functions in this section.

## String I/O using gets and puts

The ***gets*** function reads a line from stdin, converts it into string format, and stores it in the supplied argument. The ***puts*** function converts a given string into a line and writes the line to *stdout*.

**Example 14.2:** Read a line-oriented string and print it.

```
#include < stdio.h>
void main(void)
{
   char    s[12];  /* define a buffer of 12 character size  */
    . . .
    gets(s);   /* Expects a line to be typed in */
    puts(s);   /* Prints the string on the screen as a line  */
     . . .
}
```

Input:
 % This is a line string.(nl)

Output:
 This is a line string.
 % (prompt in the next line)

> ***Remark:*** *The gets function reads characters into the string, s, until a newline, and appends a NULL character to make it a valid string. The puts function outputs characters from the supplied string until a NULL is found, then sends a newline character to make the output a perfect line.*
>
> | *Input:* | *Stored in s as:* |
> |---|---|
> | *This is a line string<nl>* | *This is a line string<NULL>* |

## String I/O using scanf and printf

The format specifier, ***%s***, is used in the control string of ***scanf*** to scan a word-oriented string from the ***stdin*** stream and convert it into internal string representation. After converting, ***scanf*** stores the value in the supplied argument, which should be an address parameter. Similarly, the same format specifier is used in ***printf*** to convert a string value into a printable form. The converted value is then printed on the ***stdout*** stream.

## Example 14.3: To read a word-oriented string and print it.

```
#include <stdio.h>
void main(void)
{
  char    s[12];  /* define a buffer of 12 character size */
   ...
  scanf("%s", s);      /* Expects a word to be typed in */
  printf("%s \n", s);  /* Prints the value on the screen as a word  */
   ...
}
```

Input:
% ABC(nl)

Output:
ABC
% (prompt in the next line)

***Remark:*** *The above **scanf** ignores leading white spaces, identifies a string by a white space delimiter and stores the scanned string with a NULL character.*

| *Input line* | *Scanned value in s* |
|---|---|
| *ABC (nl)* | *ABC\0 A NULL character is added as end of string* |
| *ABCDEF (nl)* | *ABC\0 Ignores the second string; ( denotes a space)* |

## Example 14.4: To read a list of word-oriented strings and print them

```
#include <stdio.h>
void main(void)
{
  char    s1[12], s2[12], s3[12];
   ...
  scanf("%s%s%s ", s1, s2, s3); /* Expects 3 words  */
  printf("%s%s%s\n", s1, s2, s3);   /* print the words with a space leaving between them;
                                        denotes a space  */
   ...
}
```

Input:

% ABC DEF GHI(nl)

Output:

ABC DEF GHI
% (prompt in the next line)

***Remarks:*** *There are three string format specifiers in the control string of* ***scanf*** *and, hence, three word-oriented strings are expected. After reading the input, it stores "ABC" in s1, "DEF" in s2 and "GHI" in s3. The following shows the scanning of the same input, but given in different ways:*

| *Input line* | *Scanned value* |
|---|---|
| *ABC DEF GHI(nl)* | *s1: ABC\0 s2: DEF\0 s3: GHI\0* |
| *ABC(nl)DEF(nl)GHI(nl)* | *s1: ABC\0 s2: DEF\0 s3: GHI\0* |
| *ABC(nl) DEF( nl) GHI(nl)* | *s1: ABC\0 s2: DEF\0 s3: GHI\0* |

## Example 14.5: To read a list of strings with width option and print them

```
#include < stdio.h>
void main(void)
{
  char    s1[12], s2[12], s3[12];
    . . .
   scanf("%2s%3s%4s ", s1, s2, s3); /* Expects 3 words of different widths */
   printf("%s\t%s\t%s\n", s1, s2, s3); /* print words with a tab leaving between them;   */

    . . .
}
```

Input:

% ABCDEFGHI(nl)

Output:

AB    CDE    FGHI
% (prompt in the next line)

### Example 14.6: To read a string after a match with a constant string

```
#include <stdio.h>
void main(void)
{
  char    s[12];
   . . .
   scanf("$%s ", s); /*   Expects a word after matching with $   */
   printf("%s\n", s);

    . . .
}
```

Input:
    % $1000.00(nl)

Output:
    1000.00
    % (prompt in the next line)

### Example 14.7: Read word-oriented strings using the scan-set option and print them

```
#include <stdio.h>
void main(void)
{
  char    s1[12], s2[12];   /* define a buffer of 12 character size */
   . . .
   scanf("%[0123456789],%s", s1, s2); /*  Expects a numerical word followed by an ASCII
                                              word */
   printf("%s \t%s\n", s1, s2);  /* Prints the words separated by a tab      */

    . . .
}
```

Input:
    % 1234ABC(nl)

Output:
    1234    ABC
    % (prompt in the next line)

> ***Remark:*** *With %s, scanf looks for a string made up of characters derived from either ASCII or EBCDIC set. With %[0123456789], scanf expects a string made up of characters finding match in this subset.*

**Example 14.8: To read a line-oriented or sentence-oriented string using complement of scan-set option**

One can specify a complement set of the given scan-set using '^'. For example:

*fscanf("%[^\n],%s", s);*

will scan any character except newline. For the input:

A line is scanned as a string(nl)

s will contain "A line is scanned as a string". In this case, a newline is acting as a delimiter, in fact, to mask other white spaces. This option is helpful to nominate even one or more new string delimiters. For example:

*fscanf("%[^.],%s", s);     scans a string until '.'*
*fscanf("%[^.;],%s", s); scans a string until '.' or ';'*
*fscanf("%[^.;\n],%s", s);  scans a string until '.' or ';' or '\n'*

**Example 14.9: To read strings with ignore ('*') option**

```
#include < stdio.h>
  void main(void)
   {
    char    s1[12], s2[12];
      . . .
      scanf("%*s%s%s ", s1, s2); /* Ignores the first string   */
      printf("%s%s\n", s1, s2);

      . . .
   }
```

Input:
   % Ignore This String(nl)

Output:
   This String
   % (prompt in the next line)

### 14.3.2 String Manipulation Operations

#### 14.3.2.1 String Copy

C offers two string copy functions. The ***strcpy*** function is used to copy the entire text of a source string variable (say s1) into a destination string variable (say s2). When this function is called, the names of these strings are supplied as parameters. The ***strncpy*** function is used to copy the first n characters of a source string into a destination string. The formats of the calling sequences of these functions are as follows:

*strcpy(char *destination_string, char *source_string)*
*strncpy(char *destination_string, char *source_string, int n_characters)*

A general requirement of these functions is that the buffer holding the destination string should be of at least as large as that of the text that is being copied.

### Example 14.10: To show memory map before and after string copy function

```
#include <stdio.h>
#include <string.h>
char *s1 = "a text";
char s2[7] = ""; /* a null string with a buffer space of 7 bytes (that can hold a text of 6
                characters plus one NULL character)  */
void main(void)
{
    . . .
    strcpy(s2,s1);
    printf("Value of s2: %s\n", s2);
    /* Since strcpy returns the address of the destination string, the above two statements
   can be coded in one statement as: printf("Value of s2: %s\n", strcpy(s2,s1));      */
    . . .
}
```

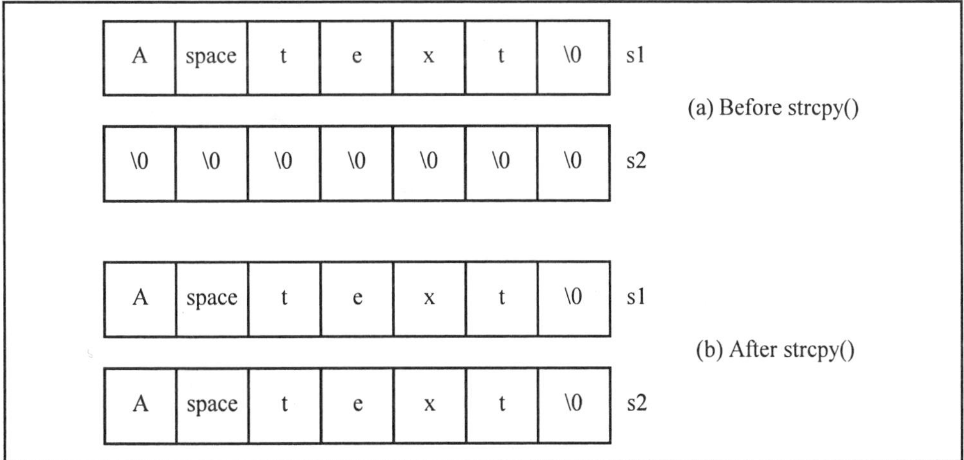


*Fig. 14.1 String values before and after strcpy (Example 14.10)*

## Example 14.11: To show the memory map before and after strncpy

```
#include <stdio.h>
#include <string.h>
char *s1 = "a text";
char s2[7] = ""; /* a null string in a buffer space of 7 bytes (that can hold a maximum of 6
                    characters plus one NULL character) */
void main(void)
{
   . . .
   strncpy(s2,s1,2);
   printf("Value of s2: %s\n", s2);
   /* Since strncpy returns the address of the destination string, the above two statements
  can be coded in one statement as: printf("Value of s2: %s\n", strncpy(s2,s1,2));   */
   . . .
}
```

## String Concatenation

As with the string copy functions, there are two functions available for joining two strings. The ***strcat*** joins the entire text of a source string to the existing text of a destination string. The resulting string is properly terminated by a NULL character. The ***strncat*** function joins the specified number of characters from a source string to the existing text of a destination string. However, the size of destination strings must be sufficient to accommodate the text extensions due to these functions. The formats of the calling sequences of these functions are as follows:

*strcat(char *destination_string, char *source_string)*
*strncat( char *destination_string, char *source_string, int n_characters)*

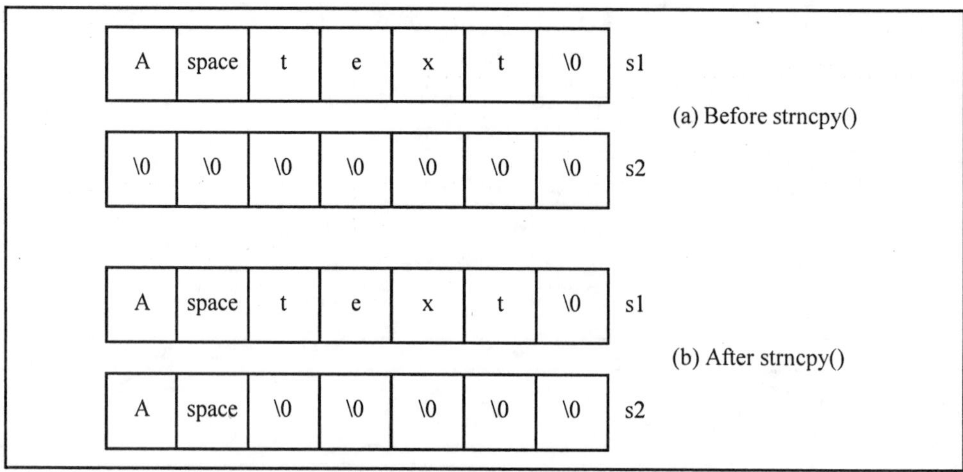


*Fig. 14.2 String values before and after strncpy (Example 14.11)*

## Example 14.12: To show memory map before and after strcat

```
#include <stdio.h>
#include <string.h>
char *s1 = "a text";
char s2[15]= "This is ";
void main(void)
{
    . . .
    strcat(s2,s1);   /* s2 has sufficient space to accommodate s1 */
    printf("Value of s2:  %s\n", s2);
    /* Since strcat returns the address of the destination string, the above two statements
    can be coded in one statement as printf("Value of s2:  %s\n", strcat(s2,s1));    */
    . . .
} /* See Figure 14.3     */
```

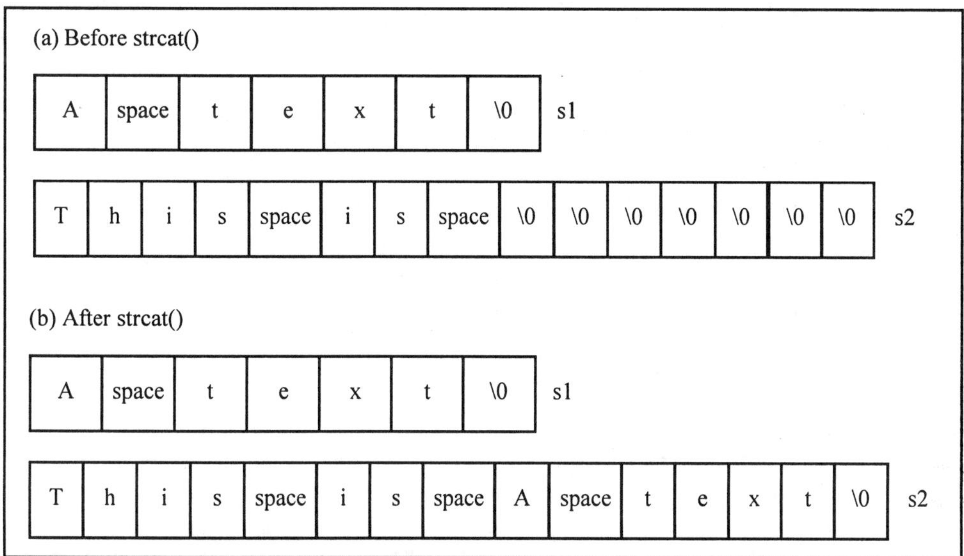


*Fig. 14.3 String values before and after strcat*

## Example 14.13: To show memory map before and after strncat

```
#include <stdio.h>
#include <string.h>
char *s1 = "a text";
char s2[15] = "This is ";
void main(void)
{
   . . .
   strncat(s2,s1,6);
   printf("Value of s2: %s\n", s2);
   /* Since strncat returns the address of the destination string, the above two statements can be
coded in one statement as: printf("Value of s2: %s\n", strncat(s2,s1,6));        */
   . . .
} /* See Figure 14.4      */
```

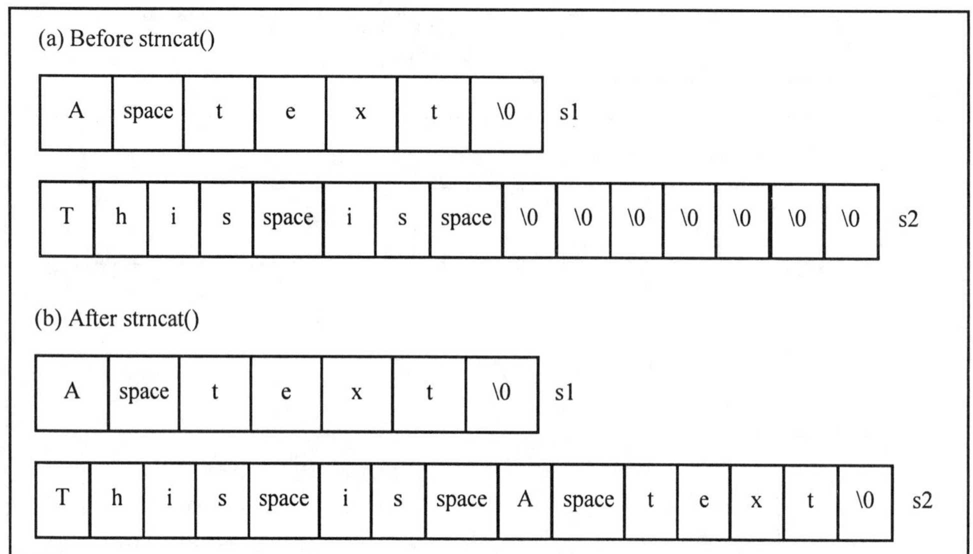


*Fig. 14.4 String values before and after strncat*

### 14.3.3 String Checking Operations

#### String Comparisons

The formats of two functions in this category are as follows:

```
int    strcmp(char *s1, char    *s2);
int    strncmp(char  *s1, char    *s2, int n);
```

The function ***strcmp(s1,s2)*** is used to compare the two given strings (s1 and s2) to determine whether they are the same or not. The function ***strncmp(s1, s2, n)*** compares the first n characters of two given strings. The result of the comparison is returned in the form of an integer value.

- *If the returned value is zero, then both s1 and s2 are same.*
- *If the returned value is negative, then s1 is lexicographically less than s2.*
- *If the returned value is positive, then s1 is lexicographically greater than s2.*

The comparison is carried out character by character from the start of the strings until the end of s1 or s2. Whenever mismatch occurs, the difference between the mismatched characters is returned as the result of the comparison.

## Example 14.14: To show the results of various comparisons

Display the results of some string comparisons.

```
#include <stdio.h>
#include <string.h>
{
char s1 = "A2", s2 = "A1";
char s3 = "A1", s4 = "B1";
char s5 = "A1", s6 = "A1";
void main(void)
{
  int     i, j, k;
    i = strcmp(s1, s2);  /* Case 1   */
    j = strcmp(s3, s4);  /* Case 2   */
    k = strcmp(s5, s6);  /* Case 3   */
    printf(" %d %d %d ", i, j, k);
    /*   OR IN ONE STATEMENT
    printf(" %d %d %d ", strcmp(s1, s2),strcmp(s3, s4), strcmp(s5, s6));      */
}
```

| Symbol value of string | | | | ASCII value of string | | | Result of comparison |
|---|---|---|---|---|---|---|---|
| s1 | A | 2 | \0 | 65 | 50 | 00 | s1 - s2 = +1 |
| s2 | A | 1 | \0 | 65 | 49 | 00 | |
| s3 | A | 1 | \0 | 65 | 49 | 00 | s3 - s4 = -256 |
| s4 | B | 1 | \0 | 66 | 50 | 00 | |
| s5 | A | 1 | \0 | 65 | 49 | 00 | s5 - s6 = 0 |
| s6 | A | 1 | \0 | 65 | 49 | 00 | |

*Fig. 14.5 Arithmetic results of comparison operation (Example 14.14)*

In case 1, the first characters are 'A' in both and they are equal, then the comparison moves to the next character. When the comparison fails, the ASCII value of '1' is subtracted from the ASCII value of '2' and the result is returned as +1. In case 2, a mismatch occurs at the comparison of the first characters and a negative is returned. In case 3, comparison continues until the end of the strings and, hence, the function simply returns zero as the result.

## Example 14.15:

Let us assume that the following program acts as a simple command line interpreter which reads strings (or lines) from the keyboard (i.e., stdin file), analyzes them to identify the given command and selects an appropriate action. The command strings for this interpreter are:

1. "wm" weather forecast of Melbourne
2. "ns" display the name of a well-known scientist
3. "pm" give me a pleasant message
4. "um" give me an unpleasant message
5. "q" quit from the interpreter

```
#include <stdio.h>
#include <string.h>
#include <ctype.h>
#define TRUE  1
#define FALSE 0
char w_mess[] =  "Mostly cloudy, no rain, gusty wind, occasional sunshine, but pleasant
                  day";
char n_mess[] = "Professor Einstien";
char p_mess[] = "World population is reducing ";
char u_mess[] = " The Greenhouse Effect will destroy this world very soon";
char cmd[3] = ""; /* declare a temporary string buffer to hold at most a  2 character
                    command */
```

```
void  main(void)
 {
  while(TRUE)
    {
      printf("Enter Your Command \n");
      gets(cmd);  /*  get a command from stdin (keyboard)  */
      if (strcmp(cmd, "wm") == NULL)
        printf("%s  \n", w_mess);
      else if (strcmp(cmd, "ns") == NULL)
          printf("%s  \n", n_mess);
        else if (strcmp(cmd, "pm") == NULL)
            printf("%s  \n", p_mess);
          else if (strcmp(cmd, "um") == NULL)
            printf("%s  \n", u_mess);
            else if (strcmp(cmd, "q") == NULL)
                exit(0);
              else printf("Illegal command; Try again \n");
    }  /* End of while Loop */
 } /* End of main */
```

## The strxfrm function

The strcmp function, by default, uses the collate sequence corresponding to ANSI-C locale. For a different locale, as specified by the setlocale function, the strings must be adjusted before they are compared using strcmp. The role of the strxfrm function is to transform a given string into an equivalent string that currently conforms to the locale set. The prototype definition is:

*size_t strxfrm(char *s1, const char *s2, size_t nchar);*

The strxfrm function transforms the string pointed to by s2, placing the converted string value in the string pointed to by s2. The transformation is effective to the specified number of characters (nchar characters) that include the terminating null character. The function returns the length of the transformed string (not counting the terminating NULL character). If nchar is specified as 0, then no conversion is performed and the resulting string in s1 is permitted to be NULL. No overlap should be allowed between s1 and s2.

## The strcoll function

The strcoll function can transform the given strings according to the status of the current locale and compare the resulting strings. The prototype definition is:

*size_t strcoll(char *s1, const char *s2, size_t nchar);*

The strcoll function compares the string pointed to by s1 with the string pointed to by s2 and returns an integer – a negative value indicating s1 is less than s2, zero indicating both s1 and s2 are the same, and a positive value indicating s1 is greater than s2. This function is the same as strcmp except that it is sensitive to locale set up.

## The strtok function

While analyzing a normal text, tokenization is an important process. For example, an editor has to tokenize a text during its search for a particular word. Another application of tokenization is the job of a lexical analyzer in a language compiler. Actually, the lexical analyzer extracts the tokens (or words) one by one from the source program text, tests whether they are allowed, and then passes it to a syntactic analyzer for further analysis. The ***strtok*** function is useful in these applications to break a given string into tokens. A sequence of calls is necessary to complete the tokenizing process on a given string. The number of calls in a sequence depends upon the number of tokens present in the string. The prototype definition is:

*size_t strtok(char *s1, const char *s2);*

The ***strtok*** function breaks the string pointed to by s1 into a sequence of tokens using a set of delimiting characters supplied in the string pointed to by s2. For example, if s2 has a space and a comma, then the function identifies a token that is delimited either by a space or a comma.

The first call is made with both s1 and s2 arguments. It is looking for the beginning of a token. If it comes across a delimiter in the beginning of the string, it returns a NULL. If it finds a character that does not belong to any of the delimiters in the given set of s2, then it interprets the character as the beginning of a token and saves its address in its own local pointer. It continues in its search until it comes across a delimiter, which once found, is replaced by a NULL character. It returns the saved address of this token to the caller. At the same time, it saves the current position of the search in the local pointer.

Each subsequent call repeats the same process to return the address of the token identified and the sequence of calls may be terminated at the time of a NULL return.

### Example 14.16: To demonstrate a use of strtok function by printing the tokens of the string: "IT is a token string."

```
#include <stdio.h>
#include <string.h>
char  *str = "This is a token string";
char  *del_str = " ."; /* the delimiters are a space and a period */
void  main(void)
{
  char  *token;
        token = strtok(str, delimit_str);
        while(token)
          {
            printf("<%s> ", token);
            token = strtok(NULL, delimit_str);
          }
}
```

The output will be:

<This> <is> <a> <token> <string>

## Character Searching

Since the command *strings "wm", "pm"* and *"um"* in the above example can be identified by the presence of 'm', we can rewrite the same program using a character-search function, i.e., ***strchr***. The ***strchr(string_argument, char_argument)*** function finds the presence of a character in the given string argument and returns the address of its location. If the search fails, then a NULL is returned. Another string function that also performs identically to ***strchr*** is ***index(string_argument, char_argument)***. ***Example 14.7*** shows the use of ***strchr***. (See ***Table 14.1*** for the prototype definitions of ***strchr*** and ***index***.)

## Example 14.17: To demonstrate the use of strchr function

```
#include <stdio.h>
#include <string.h>
#include <ctype.h>
#define TRUE   1
#define FALSE 0
char w_mess[] =  "Mostly cloudy, no rain, gusty wind, occasional sunshine, but pleasant day";
char n_mess[] = "Professor Einstein";
char p_mess[] = "World population is reducing ";
char u_mess[] = " The Greenhouse Effect will destroy this world very soon";
char cmd[3] = ""; /* declare a temporary string buffer to hold at most a 2 character command  */
```

```
void main(void)
{ int status;
   while(TRUE)
    {
      printf("Enter Your Command \n");
      gets(cmd); /* get a command from stdin (keyboard) */
      if (strchr(cmd, 'm') != NULL) /* if a command has 'm' */
          { /* then switch to one of the branches according to the first character of the given
command */
        switch(cmd[0])
         {
         case 'w': printf("%s \n", w_mess);
                break;
         case 'p': printf("%s \n", p_mess);
                break;
         case 'u': printf("%s \n", u_mess);
                break;
         default: printf("illegal command \n");
                break;
         } /* End of switch */
       } /* End of if */
      else if (strchr(cmd, 'n') != NULL)
         printf("%s \n", n_mess);
        else if (strchr(cmd, 'q') != NULL)
            exit(0);
          else printf("Illegal command; Try again \n");
    } /* End of while Loop */
} /* End of main program */
```

## Substring Searching

The ***strstr***, ***strspn*** and ***strcspn*** are some of the substring searching functions. The ***strstr*** is useful to search a substring in a given string. The format of this function is:

```
char *strstr(const char *s1, const char *s2);
```

This function finds the first occurrence of s2 in s1, and returns the base address of s2 in s1. This function can be found in the word processors where a substitution command may first find the matching existing substring and substitute it with a new substring.

The ***strspn*** function finds the maximum length of the initial substring (i.e., the span of the initial substring) in s1 made up of characters in s2. The format of this function is:

```
size_t strspn(const char *s1, const char *s2);
```

For example, a call to this function:

*strspn("88322154998","1328");*

will return the value 6, showing that the first 6 character substring in the first argument is entirely made up of the characters in the second argument.

The ***strcspn*** function is the compliment of ***strspn***. It finds of the span of subtring in the first argument, consisting entirely of characters not in the second argument. The format of this function is:

*size_t strcspn(const char *s1, const char *s2);*

For example, the following call to this function:

*strstr("88322154998","94");*

will return the value 7, showing that the substring of the first 7 characters in the first argument is exclusive of the characters making the second argument.

## Finding Length of a String

The ***strlen*** function is useful to find out the length of the text in a given string argument. This function returns an integer value as the length of the given string. (See ***Table 14.1*** for the prototype definition of this function.)

## Example 14.18:

```
#include <stdio.h>
#include <string.h>
#include <ctype.h>
char s1[] = "The length of a passenger train is 7 cars excluding the engine and guard van";
void main(void)
{unsigned i;
  i = strlen(s1);
  printf("The length of the string s1 = %d \n", i);
  /*  OR IN ONE STATEMENT
     printf("The length of the string s1 = %d \n", strlen(s1));
                                              */
}
```

> ***Remark:*** *NULL character is used only as a marker, denoting the end of textual data in a given string variable. It is meaningless to count this control character as part of the text data. Hence, the count that is returned by a strlen call is the real length of the text data in a given string.*

## 14.4 Operations on Memory Regions (or Memory Buffers)

The C-Virtual Machine has a memory of generic type (void type) and byte addressable. A memory buffer may be conceived as a memory space allocated from the C-memory to store data of any type. For example, an integer array, a real array, character array, an array of structures and an array of union type are all created by allocating sufficient buffers of generic memory. Similar to operations on strings, standard C allows operations on memory buffers. Copying one buffer into another, comparing two buffers, setting a byte or an array of bytes to a particular bit pattern or locating the address of a given bit pattern are all appropriate operations on buffer memory. Since buffer memory is generic, and there is no end of data maintained, some operations on buffers require the size of buffer memory as an argument.

### The memset function

The ***memset*** function can be used to fill up a portion of a buffer memory with a given byte value.

*void *memset(void *mbuf, int ch, size_t n);*

The ***memset*** function copies the low order byte of ***ch*** into each of the n characters of the buffer object pointed to by ***mbuf***. The function returns the address of the buffer object. It returns the address of the buffer.

### Example 14.19: Clear a memory buffer of 4 bytes and initialize the first three characters with the character $

```
#include <stdio.h>
#include <string.h>
char mbuf[4];
void main(void)
{
  int ch;
   ch = '\0';
   memset(mbuf, ch, 4); /* We made buf an empty string */
   ch = '$';
   memset(mbuf, ch, 3); /* The last character still has '\0' */
   printf("%s \n", mbuf);
}
```

## The memcpy function

The ***memcpy*** function can be used to copy a segment of source memory buffer into a destination memory buffer. When the size of memory to be copied is larger than the size of the destination buffer, or when both source and destination memory buffers overlap, the result of copying is unpredictable.

*void *memcpy(void *dmb, void *smb, size_t n);*

The ***memcpy*** function copies ***n*** characters of the object (i.e., source memory buffer), pointed to by ***smb*** into the object (i.e., destination memory buffer), pointed to by ***dmb***. If the source and destination memory buffers overlap, the characteristic of this function is not defined. Hence, this function should be avoided wherever overlapping occurs during copying. After copying, the function returns the address of the destination memory buffer.

## Example 14.20: To demonstrate the use of memset and memcpy functions

```
#include <string.h>
#include <stdio.h>
char mbuf[80], mbuf1[80], mbuf2[80];
void main(void)
{
  int ch;
   ch = '1';
   memset(mbuf, ch, 40); /* We made first half of buf contain 1s */
   ch = '2';
   memset(mbuf+40, ch, 40); /* We made second half of buf contain 2s */
   ch = '\0';
   memset(mbuf1, ch, 40); /* we made buf1 as a NULL string */
   memset(mbuf2, ch, 40); /* we made buf2 as a NULL string */
   memcpy(mbuf1, mbuf, 39); /* copy the first 39 bytes (or 1s) of buf into buf1 */
   memcpy(mbuf2, mbuf+40, 39); /* copy 39 bytes starting from buf+40 into buf2 */
   printf("%s \n", mbuf1); /* string of 39 characters of 1s will be printed */
   printf("%s \n", mbuf2); /* string of 39 characters of 2s will be printed */
}
```

### The memcmp function

The ***memcmp*** function can be used to compare a segment of one memory buffer with the same size of another memory buffer.

*void *memcmp(void *dmb, void *smb, size_t n);*

The ***memcpy*** function copies ***n*** characters of the object (i.e., source buffer), pointed to by ***smb*** into the object (i.e., destination buffer), pointed to by ***dmb***. If the source and destination memory buffers overlap, the characteristic of this function is not defined. Hence, this function should be avoided wherever overlapping occurs during copying. After copying, the function returns the address of the destination memory buffer.

### Example 14.21: To demonstrate the use of memcmp function by printing the result of a student from a result file

```
#include <string.h>
#include <stdio.h>
char result_rec[4][] ={"Tom  F",
                       "Vic  P",
                       "Mev  P",
                       "Rev  P"};
char name[4];
void main(void)
{
 name = "Tom";
 for(i=0; i<4; i++)
  if((memcmp(name, result_rec[i], 3)==0) /*find out the record that belongs to Tom*/
     {
        printf("%s \n", result_rec[i]); /* print the required record */
        break;
     }
}
```

### The memmove function

The ***memmove*** function is similar to the above function except that this allows copying even when the source and destination buffers overlap.

*void *memmove(void *dmb, void *smb, size_t n);*

The function copies the first n bytes of source memory buffer into its own local buffer, then transfers the contents of the local buffer to the destination memory buffer.

### The memchr function

The ***memchr*** function can be used to search for the occurrence of a character in a memory buffer.

*void *memchr(void *mb, char ch, size_t n);*

The function searches for the presence of the byte ch in the first n bytes of the memory buffer pointed to by mb.

### Example 14.22: To demonstrate the use of memchr function by updating the result of Tom from F to P status

```
#include <string.h>
#include <stdio.h>
char result_rec[4][] ={"Tom  F",
                       "Vic  P",
                       "Mev  P",
                       "Rev  P"};
int   rec_len = 5;
char name[4];
char ch_F, ch_P;
char *ch_pos;
void main(void)
{
 name = "Tom";
 ch_F = 'F';
 ch_P = 'P';
 for(i=0; i<4; i++)
  if((memcmp(name, result_rec[i], 3)==0) /*find the record that belongs to Tom*/
    {
      ch_pos = memchr(result_rec[i], ch_F, rec_len);
      memset(ch_pos, ch_P, 1);
      printf("%s \n", result_rec[i]); /* print the updated record */
      break;
    }
}
```

## 14.5 String Utility Function for Decoding System Errors

In the C-Virtual Machine, a list of system errors is defined in a global data structure (in the form of an array of strings) called ***sys_errlist***. The virtual machine also maintains a global integer variable, called ***errno***, to store the current error. Whenever an error happens during access of any system resources (e.g., file system), the virtual machine sets the errno to a predefined value.

It is left to the running program to detect the occurrence of any system error, decode the meaning of the error value stored in errno and take an appropriate action. The string library provides ***strerror*** to decode a system's error value.

### The strerror function

A C-program can use the ***strerror*** function to convert the integer value of ***errno*** into an error message (or string). The prototype definition, as stored in ***string.h***, is shown below:

```
char *strerror(int errnum);
```

This function uses errnum, as an ***index*** to ***sys_errlist***, to locate the error message and returns the pointer to that message.

> ***Remark:*** *The size of the sys_errlist (or total number of system errors) is available in another global variable called sys_nerr.*

### Example 14.23: To demonstrate the use of strerror function by printing all messages stored in the sys_errlist buffer

```
#include <stdio.h>
#include <string.h>
extern int sys_nerr;
void main(void)
{ int i;
  char *emess;
      for(i=0; i < sys_nerr; i++)
      {
        emess = strerror(i);
        printf(" %s \n", emess);
      }
}
```

## 14.6 String Conversion Operations

A string would normally contain text data of alphanumeric characters, plus some delimiters (such as space, newline, carriage return, etc.), and some special characters (such as underscore, hyphen, single quote, double quote, etc.). Depending upon the application of string data, its contents may be evaluated. For example, a program may require numerical data input from the keyboard file for some internal calculation. In this case, the keyboard input is a string of numerical characters (say the salary of an employee, 30000), which is a very useful notation outside a computer system. However, the internal processing of numerical values is normally carried out in the binary mode. To carry out any arithmetic operations, the numerical string data has to be converted into internal binary notation, either signed integer, unsigned integer, real (floating point) number, etc. For example, a simple adding program, shown in ***Example 14.9***, can input a sequence of numerical string data representing today's expenditure, convert them into floating point numbers, then add them together in binary mode and finally print the total expenditure. To convert numerical string data into the required internal notation, a set of string conversion functions are made available in a standard C-library (***stdlib.h***). This includes:

- *atoi(s)* *To convert a numeric string into a signed integer;*
- *atol(s)* *To convert a numeric string into a long integer;*
- *atof(s)* *To convert a numeric string into a floating point number.*

## Example 14.24: To demonstrate the use of string conversion function

See ***Table 14.2*** for more details.

```
/* A Simple Adding Machine */
#include <stdlib.h>
#define TRUE    1
#define FALSE 0
char indata[20] = "";        /* declare a string buffer to receive a string from the keyboard (stdout
stream) */
void  main(void)
  { float sum, item;
     sum = 0.0;  /* initialize the total */
     while(TRUE)
       { gets( indata);       /* get numeric data in string form */
          item = atof(indata); /* convert data from string form to real data in binary form */
          if (item == 0.0)
            {
              printf("Total Expenditure of today = $%f \n", sum);
              break;
            }
          else sum = sum + item; /* (or) sum += item;    */
       } /* End of while Loop */
   } /* End of main block */
```

*Table 14.2 Summary of string conversion functions as defined in stdlib.h*

| | |
|---|---|
| double atof(const char *ns) | To convert the initial portion of the numeric string pointed to by ns to double real type value. |
| int atoi(const char *ns) | To convert the initial portion of the numeric string pointed to by ns to signed integer type value. |
| long int atol(const char *ns) | To convert the initial portion of the numeric string pointed to by ns to long integer type value. |
| int strtod(const char *s, char *pp_endtext) | To convert the numerical text of the string pointed to by s to double type real value. The function strips off any white space in the beginning of s, then converts the numerical string into double value. Finally, it sets the pp_endtext to contain the address of the remaining text if any are found in s. The function returns zero if it didn't find any numerical string in the given string, returns HUGE_VAL or -HUGE_VAL for indicating either overflow or underflow. During an error state, it sets the global variable errno to ERANGE, indicating a range error. |
| int strtol(const char *s, char *pp_endtext, int radix) | To convert the numerical text of the string pointed to by s to signed long type integer value. The function strips off any white space in the beginning of s, then reads the numerical string based on the radix (between 2 and 36) specified, converts the same into long integer value and finally, and sets the pp_endtext to contain the address of the remaining text if any are found in s. The function returns zero if it didn't find any numerical text in the given string, returns LONG_MAX or LONG _MIN for indicating either overflow or underflow. During an error state, it sets the global variable errno to ERANGE, indicating a range error. |

*Table 14.2 (cont.)*

| | |
|---|---|
| int strtoul(const char *s, char **pp_endtext, int radix) | To convert the numerical text of the string pointed to by s to unsigned long type integer value. The function strips off any white space in the beginning of s, then reads the numerical string based on the radix (between 2 and 36) specified, converts the same into unsigned long integer value and finally, and sets the pp_endtext to contain the address of the remaining text if any are found in s. The function returns zero if it didn't find any numerical text in the given string, returns ULONG_MAX or ULONG _MIN for indicating either overflow or underflow. During an error state, it sets the global variable errno to ERANGE, indicating a range error. |

## 14.7 String Composition and Decomposition

Some applications may require the construction of a string out of a given list of data items that may include strings, integers, floating point numbers, and so on. The function ***sprintf*** serves this purpose and is similar to ***fprintf***, except that the former writes its string equivalent of the given data to a given string argument, whereas the latter writes to a stream. On the other hand, it may also be necessary to decompose a string into identifiable data items. For this purpose, the ***sscanf*** function is available, similar to ***fscanf*** function. Both ***fprintf*** and ***fscanf*** are explained in ***Chapter 17***.

### Example 14.25:

A program maintains a memory copy of the description of a data item in a string form. The program scans this string to decompose into fields, updates a field and then writes the data fields back to the string.

```
char mem_file1[] = "10 APPLES";
char s[7];
int  i;
void  main(void)
{
    sscanf(mem_file1,"%d %s", &i, s); /* read record from memory */
      i = i - 1;  /* one apple is consumed */
      printf("%d %s", i, s);
    sprintf(mem_file1,"%d %s", i, s); /* store the record back */
  }
```

## 14.8 Summary

This chapter explains the operations required for string manipulation and maintenance. These operations include string copy, string concatenation, string comparison, finding length of a string, searching a character in a string and so on. This chapter also explains other miscellaneous operations, such as converting a numeric string into a signed integer (using ***atoi*** function), converting a numeric string into a long integer (using ***atol*** function), converting a numeric string into a floating point number (using ***atof*** function), and composing and decomposing a string using ***sprintf*** and ***sscanf*** functions.

## Exercises

14.1 With the following declaration,

```
char s[10];
```

comment on the following string function calls:

(a) strcpy("ABCD", s);
(b) strcpy(s, "ABCD");
(c) strcpy(s[0], "EF");
(d) strcat("ABCD", "CD");
(e) strcat(s, "ABCD");
(f) strcat(&s[0], "EF");
(g) strcat(strcpy(s, "ABCD"), "EF");

14.2 Correct the following code segments and give your reasons.

(a)
```
{char s[5];
    if(strcpy(s, "Hello") == NULL)
      printf("strcpy() failed \n");
    else
      printf("%s \n", s);
}
```

(b)
```
{ int    i;
  char s1[] = "Hello";
  . . .
  i = strchr(s1, 'o');
}
```

(c)
```
{char s[20];;
  printf("%d \n", strlen(s));
}
```

14.3 What will the contents of s0, s1, s2 and s3 be after evaluating the given expression?

```
char s0[20];
char s1[20] = "are ";
char s2[20] = "how ";
char s3[20] = "Hello ";
        strcat(s3,strcat(s2,strcat(s1,strcpy(s0,"you"))));
```

14.4 Write a program to read the following C-text from an internal buffer and print out the number of keywords in this text.

```
void main(void)
{
   int    i, j, k;
     k = i + j;
}
```

14.5 Rewrite the above program to output each token (i.e., word) in a separate line.

14.6 Rewrite the above program to output the token identifiers using the following table.

| System-defined | | User-defined | |
|---|---|---|---|
| Symbol | Token ID | Symbol | Token ID |
| main | %1 | i | #1 |
| { | %2 | j | #2 |
| } | %3 | k | #3 |
| int | %2 | | |

# 15

# Composite Data Structures and Unions

**Chapter contents:**

*This chapter introduces the meaning of composite data structures, such as struct and union, and their use in applications. This chapter familiarizes the readers with declaring structures and unions, as well as how to address their members and pass them as parameters to functions.*

**Organization:**


*15.1 Introduction*
*15.2 Structure Declaration in C*
*15.3 Pointer to a Structure*
*15.4 Accessing Elements of a Structure*
*15.5 Union*
*15.6 Summary*
*Exercises*


## 15.1 Introduction

In general, an object in the real world always has a composite structure. For example, the structure of a house may consist of one kitchen, three bedrooms, one living room, one bathroom and one laundry, which may be put in a concise manner (or record form), as shown below:

```
structure  Small_House
    {
        kitchen_type      main_kitchen;
        room_type         bedrooms[3];
        hall_type         living_room;
        hall_type         family_room;
        bathroom_type     common_bathroom;
        room_type         laundry;
    };
```

The object (or house) description in the above example shows it is an aggregate of different items. When an object is formed from an aggregate of non-homogeneous elements, it can be referred to as a composite object, or an object with composite structure. In the above example, the keyword "***structure***" is used to describe a composite object of the real world. The label "Small_House" represents the name or tag for the body of the structure (i.e., the descriptions within braces). In other words, the above example shows a suitable convention in which we can express a type of an object. Using this definition, we can declare any number of instances of this type. For example, if we want to create house1 and house2 as instances of the above structure, we can declare as

***structure*** *Small_House house1, house2;*

The description of an object does not stop at one level; some items in a structure can be sub-structures. For example, the master bedroom in a house may itself be another structure with an aggregate of different items, such as a sleeping area, a walk-in closet and a private bathroom. In a record form, a new type of house can be described as follows:

```
structure Standard_House
    {
      kitchen_type:     main_kitchen;
      structure  master_bedroom
        {
          room_type  sleeping_room;
          bathroom_type private_bathroom;
          room_type        walkin_closet;
        }            bedroom1;
      room_type     bedrooms[2];
      hall_type       living_room;
      hall_type       family_room;
      bathroom_type common_bathroom;
      room_type     laundry;
    };
```

Following this definition, we can create 100 instances of the standard_house type by declaring:

***structure*** *Standard_House house[100];*

We can also extend our definitions to form a super-structure using the structures that are already defined. For example, we can declare a street consisting of fifty small houses, twenty standard houses and ten big houses, as shown below:

```
structure Street
    {
      structure Small_House      SML_house[50];
      structure Standard_House   STD_house[20];
      structure Big_House        BIG_house[10];
    } street_A;
```

The above definition describes street_A. Following this definition, we can create more instances using the structure name (i.e., ***structure*** Street), as shown below:

```
structure Street    neighbourhood[100];
```

Now we can use this structure to form a suburban town and, using a town, we can further define a city, and so on. This is called a ***nested structure***, describing a multilevel composite object. This process of building a composite structure forms the abstract layers. The abstraction levels use the most primitive data structures of very common type at the lowest level and reach to the most abstract type of object at the highest level. In fact, this abstraction process can be extended to realize whatever type of abstract object we wish to realize.

The structure concept that was described above can be applied to realize commonly occurring objects in the data processing domain, such as an ***employee*** in a firm, a ***customer*** in a bank, a ***student*** in an institution, a ***book*** in a library or a ***citizen*** in a country. All have their own structures. Each structure can be described as a set, or aggregate, of its attributes. Similar examples can be used to explain the concept of union data type. For example, a general purpose building is proposed in a university to accommodate many different types of events in a time-shared manner. The sharable events could be in-door sports, conferences, examinations, or convocation. In other words, one building can accommodate a union of activities. This idea can be expressed as:

```
union of {
      sport_hall_type        in_door_game_hall;
      lecture_hall_type      conference_room;
      long_hall_type         examination_hall;
      long-hall_type         public_lecture_hall;
      medium_hall_type       dinner_function_hall;
      }in_a_general_purpose_building;
```

The significant factor in choosing the overall space of the building is to select the biggest event in the given set. If the sport_hall_type requires the largest space, then this will be the space of the building which can accommodate all other smaller events. The main advantage of this common space for a union of activities is space saving. The union data type in C is based on this principle and its use in data processing may be extended more than simply for space saving.

In this chapter, we will discuss how C provides facilities to declare such composite data structures (i.e., structure and union) and to perform operations on the declared variables of these types.

## 15.2 Structure Declaration in C

A structure construct in C is similar to the structure description just discussed. Those familiar with Pascal will see the similarity between the structure declaration in C and a record declaration in Pascal. The system defined type-name "***struct***" is used to declare a structure or record of composite data elements. The syntax of this declaration is as follows:

***struct*** *optional_tag (or name)*
*{ structure_body} a_list_instance_identifiers;*

where structure_body is a sequence of variable declarations that may include other structure declarations. When we declare a structure without any instance_identifier, it simply represents a template called template declaration. The given tag represents the name of the declared template. Using template declarations, instances of structures can be declared later in a program. Hence, it is good practice to declare all required template structures at the beginning of a program and then create instances of these template types later. The compiler keeps a template declaration as a reference copy and uses it to create structures in the memory during declaration of instances of this template type.

Some examples of structure declarations, such as a student record, an employee record and a membership record of a club, are given below. In all these records, some attributes, such as address and date of birth, are composite. Hence, we will first declare the commonly used substructures as templates and then use these to declare higher level structures.

(a) *Address Template:*

```
struct   Address
{
int   house_number;
char street_name[31];
char town_name[21];
char state_name[21];
char country_name[21];
char area_code[5];
};
```

(b) *Birth Template:*

```
struct    Birth
{
 char S_sex; /* 'M': male and 'F': female */
 char day[3];
 char month[3];
 char year[5];
 char country[21];
};
```

(c) *Phone Template:*

```
struct    Phone
{
 char home_phone[12];
 char office_phone[12];
};
```

## Example 15.1:

Let us describe a student structure that can be used to construct a file of 100 students.

```
/* Template structure for a student    */
struct  Student
 {
 char    S_name[21]; /* 20 character name+NULL char */
 int     S_identifier; /* unique identifier    */
 struct  Address   S_address;
 struct  Phone     S_phone;
 struct  Birth     S_birth;
 unsigned short  S_mode; /* 0: Off campus and 1: On campus */
 unsigned short  S_year;
 char    S_major[21]; /* 20 char specialization + NULL char*/
 char    S_department[21]; /* 20 char name + NULL   char*/
 char    S_faculty[21]; /* 20 char faculty name + NULL char*/
 };
/* Create a file of 100 students in memory   */
struct  Student      stud[100];
```

## Example 15.2:

Let us now describe an employee structure to make a file of 10 employees.

```
/* Template structure for an employee    */
struct  Employee
  {
  char     E_name[21];  /* 20 character name  */
  int        E_identifier;  /*  unique identifier     */
  struct  Address     E_address;
  struct  Phone        E_phone;
  struct  Birth         E_birth;
  char     E_department[21];  /* 20 character department name  */
  char     E_designation[21];  /* 20 character department name  */
  unsigned int      Salary;
  };
/* Create a file of 10 employees in memory   */
struct  Employee    empl[10];
```

## Example 15.3:

Our third example is the description of a membership in a club. Using this template structure, create a file of 1000 members.

```
/* Template structure for a member     */
struct  Member
  {
  char     M_name[21];  /* 20 character name  */
  int        M_identifier;  /*  membership identifier */
  struct  Address     M_address;
  struct  Birth         M_birth;
  struct  Phone        M_phone;
  };
/* Create a file of 1000 members in memory   */
struct  Member      memb[1000];
```

## Structure Variable

An instance of a structure is called a structure variable. We can declare an instance of a structure in three different ways. In the first method, a structure template can be made first and, using the template name, one or more instances can be created. We have already seen some examples of this method in the previous section. In the second method, a structure description can be followed by one or more instance names. In this method, the tag or template name may not be necessary, but a tag is useful if we want to declare more instances later in our program. In the third method, we can first define a structure type using the ***typedef*** keyword, and by using the type name instances of this type can be made. All these declarations are shown below. Using a structure to keep stock of an item in a store, we can make a stock control table of 100 items.

(a) Using template declaration

```
struct  ITEM
{
    int    id;    /* unique identifier of an item  */
    int    stock;     /* current stock  */
};
struct  ITEM    item[100], temp;
```

(b) Direct declaration

```
struct
{
    int    id;    /* unique identifier of an item  */
    int    stock;       /* current stock  */
} item[100], temp;
```

(c) Using type definition facility

```
typedef struct
{
    int    id;    /* unique identifier of an item  */
    int    stock;       /* current stock  */
} ITEM_TYPE;
ITEM_TYPE  item[100], temp;
```

It is left to a programmer to choose a convenient method to declare structure instances. Each instance or variable has a name just like char, int or float type variable. In the above example, temp is the name of an instance of ITEM_TYPE created in the memory. The storage allocated is equivalent to the sum of storages occupied by the elements of this structure. In this case, temp contains two integer variables, and the total storage of this structure is the sum of two integer storage. If an integer consumes 2 bytes, then 4 bytes are allocated to temp. As with simple variables, the address of this ***composite memory*** can be derived as &temp. The memory map of the temp instance is shown in ***Fig. 15.1***.

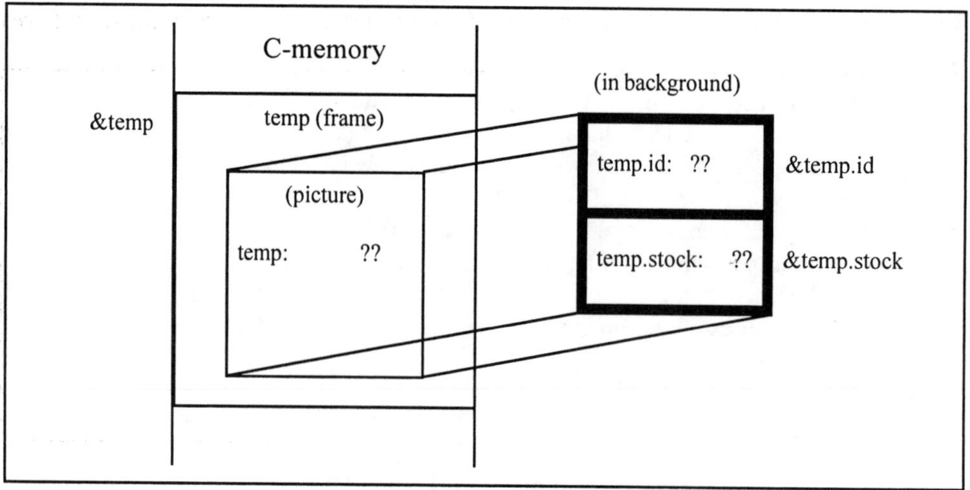


*Fig. 15.1 Memory map of temp structure*

If the created variable is an array of structures, then the required number of instances of the specified structure type are created, as mentioned, within square brackets. In the above example, the declaration of item[100] creates an array of 100 structures of ITEM_TYPE in the memory. The first item is item[0] and the last is item[99]. Similar to simple arrays, the storages for all these item elements are allocated contiguously. The address of the first item in memory is &item[0]; address of the second item is &item[1]; and the address of the last item is &item[99].

## Structure Initialization

As with the initialization of arrays and other variables, structures can also be initialized during declaration. ANSI-C even allows initialization of automatic structures (i.e., structures declared within a function). The format of the structure declaration with initialization is as follows:

```
struct  optional_tag
    {
        structure_body
    } instance_name ={ initialization_list};;
```

### Example 15.4: This example shows initialization of date and store_item structures

```
struct   date
         {
              int year;
              int month;
         int day;
         } today ={1194, 9, 20};

struct   store_item
         {
      char item_name;
      int item_stack;;
      } fruit_item ={"orange", 1000, "apple", 1000, " banana", 500, "mango", 200};
```

## Structure Declaration with const qualifier

The following example shows the effect of the ***const*** qualifier on the declared variables:

```
const struct   CURSER_LOCN
         {
         int  row;
         int  col;
         }ORIGIN={ 0, 0}; /* ORIGIN is read-only */
struct  CURSER_LOCN new_locn; /* new_locn is not read-only */
const struct  CURSER_LOCN  LAST_LOCN ={ 23, 72};  /*LAST_LOCN is read only */
```

***Remark:*** *In the above example, the members of ORIGIN are read-only, whereas the members of new_locn are normal variables which can be modified. The tag name refers to the template structure without the effect of the const qualifier.*

## Self-referential structure declaration

A self-referential structure is where one or more members refer to an element of the same structure type. If we do not take proper precaution some compilers may cause problems. Let us consider the following example to understand this declaration.

```
typedef struct
    {
        char    patient_name[20];
        char    patient_arrival_time[6];
    PATIENT_TYPE   *next;     /* ORIGIN is read-only */

        }PATIENT_TYPE;
```

In this example, the next pointer is to be declared of the PATIENT_TYPE. While declaring this variable, the type name, PATIENT_TYPE is unknown and, hence, it is illegal to declare:

```
PATIENT_TYPE   *next;
```

To overcome this problem, we can declare a tag for the declared structure and use the tag to declare any variable of self-reference type. Two ways of solving this problem are as follows:

```
typedef struct   patient_struct
    {
        char    patient_name[20];
        char    patient_arrival_time[6];
    struct   patient_struct   *next;  /* LEGAL declaration */
        }PATIENT_TYPE;
```

OR

```
typedef struct   patient_struct  PATIENT_TYPE;
typedef struct   patient_struct
    {
        char    patient_name[20];
        char    patient_arrival_time[6];
    PATIENT_TYPEt    *next;  /* LEGAL declaration */
        } PATIENT_TYPE;
```

## 15.3 Pointer to a Structure

The address of a structure variable is not the same as a byte or character type address; it is, in fact, the address of a structure type. In the above example, &temp or &item[0] are addresses of ITEM_TYPE. Using this type, we can also declare pointer variables to keep the addresses of created instances. For example,

```
ITEM_TYPE   *item_ptr;
```

creates a pointer that can be assigned with the addresses of structures of the same type. The following assignment initializes item_ptr to the address of the first item:

```
item_ptr = &item[0];
```

By incrementing the value of this pointer, we can make it traverse along the array elements. Consider the following sequence of statements:

```
item_ptr = &item[0]; /* initialize pointer to point to first element */
item_ptr++;        /* now points to item[1]  */
item_ptr = item_ptr + 98; /*now points to item[99]  */
```

It does not matter how many bytes each element occupies in the memory; arithmetic operations on the pointer treat the storage of each element as a single composite memory location.

## 15.4 Accessing Elements of a Structure

### 15.4.1 Using Structure Name

In general, an element in a structure should be addressed by using a qualifier, which can either be an instance name or a pointer to an instance. Using the name qualifier, an element in a structure is expressed as follows:

```
instance_name.element_name
```

In the above example, temp.id refers to first element inside the temp instance. Similarly, item[9] is the name of the 10th structure in the array, and item[9].id and item[9].stock refer to first and second element, respectively, in the item[9] instance.

Let us maintain, for example, a file of 100 items in a store. Our ITEM_TYPE declares only item identifier and stock fields. Now we include the name field as well to make it more meaningful. We can define the following as global variables in our program:

```
/* GLOBAL  DECLARATIONS */
#include <stdio.h>
#define N_ITEMS 100
#define TRUE   1
#define FALSE 0
typedef struct
  {
    char name[21];  /* 20 character name + NULL character */
    int   id;        /* unique identifier of an item  */
    int   stock;       /* current stock  */
  } ITEM_TYPE;
ITEM_TYPE  item[N_ITEMS];  /*  100 instances are created in memory */
int    LAST_ITEM = 0; /* shows the last added item in the array  */
```

Our first task is to initialize this file with data that is input from the ***stdin*** stream, or keyboard file. Let us assume that the function add_item() fills up the next free entry in the memory based file. The index of the entry is passed as an argument by the caller. This function returns TRUE when it has filled up a structure; or if end of input is encountered, it returns FALSE. Let us assume that the user inputs "END" for the name to terminate the input.

```
int    add_item(int  index)
{
  char  id_str[5], stock_str[10];
  printf("Input name of item: ");
  gets(item[index].name);
  if(strcmp(item[index].name, "END") == NULL)
    return(FALSE);  /*  End of input occurred; return with FALSE  */
  printf("Input the selected item_identifier: ");
  gets(id_str);
  item[index].id= atoi(id_str);
  printf("Input current stock of this item: ");
  gets(stock_str);
  item[index].stock= atoi(stock_str);
  return(TRUE);  /*  An item is filled up; return with TRUE  */
}
```

> ***Remark:*** *In the above coding, we have used the* ***atoi*** *function to convert a string of digits into an equivalent integer value.*

We will implement another function to show the contents of the stored records from our memory file. We will call this function report().

```
void  report(void)
{
  int i = 0;
  for(i=0; i<=LAST_ITEM; i++)
    {
      if(i==0) /* Print Heading  */
        printf("Item  Name    Item ID    Item Stock \n");
      printf("%s  \t %d \t %d \n",item[i].name, item[i].id, item[i].stock);
    }
}
```

Then we will implement our main() to call the above functions. Our main() function is designed to receive a single letter command to perform operations on the memory file. Let us assume that the following commands are incorporated:

A : To add items;
R : To report the details of the file;
Q : To quit from our program.

```
#include <stdio.h>
void main(void)
  { char  cmd[2];
   int i;
    do
      {
        printf("Enter Your Command \n");
        gets(cmd); /* receives a string of single character */
        switch(toupper(cmd[0]))
          {
          case 'A':  for(i=LAST_ITEM; i < N_ITEMS; i++)
                     {
                      if (add_item(i) != FALSE) break;
                      LAST_ITEM = i; /* Update LAST_ITEM */
                     }
                     break;
          case 'R':  report();
                     break;
          case 'Q':  report();
                     exit(0);
          default: printf("Illegal Command; Try Again \n");
                     break;
          } /* End of Switch */
      } while(TRUE);
  } /* End of main */
```

### 15.4.2 Using Pointer

A pointer to a structure can also be used to access an element within a structure. For example, consider the following declaration of a pointer to the item structure:

*ITEM_TYPE *p_item;*

We can make this pointer point to the first element of our memory file by the following assignment:

*p_item = &item[0];*

Using this pointer, we can access the name element by the following convention:

*p_item->name*

which is same as:

*item[0].name* or *(*p_item).name*

> ***Note:*** *In (K&R)C, it is not possible to pass a structural element as an argument to a function. This problem can be solved by passing a structure pointer to a function, which can manipulate the internal elements. This feature is a drawback in the sense that functions cannot be restricted to access the contents of a structure for reading purposes only. However, many compilers now allow passing structures (and unions) to a function just like passing the value of any other simple variable. ANSI-C incorporates this as a standard feature.*

To show the use of structure pointers, we can now write a function to extract the details of a particular item from our memory file. Call this function show(), which is:

```
void show( ITEM_TYPE  *p_item)
 {
  printf("Item Name    Item ID    Item Stock \n");
  printf("%s \t %d \t %d \n",p_item->name,p_item>id,p_item- >stock);
 }
```

We will add one more command to our main() to call the above function.

```
#include <stdio.h>
void main(void)
  { char  cmd[2];
  int    i;
    do
      {
        printf("Enter Your Command \n");
        gets(cmd);  /* receives a string of single character  */
        switch(cmd[0])
          {
          case 'A':  for(i=0; i < N_ITEMS; i++)
                  {
                  if (add_item(i) != FALSE) break;
                  LAST_ITEM = i;  /* Update LAST_ITEM  */
                  }
                  break;
          case 'R':  report();
                  break;
          case 'S':  printf("Input item number");
                  scanf("%d", &i);
                  show(&item[i]);
                  break;
          case 'Q':  exit(0);  /*  stop the program execution  */
          default: printf("Illegal Command; Try Again \n");
                  break;
          } /*End of switch */
      } while(TRUE);
  } /*End of main   */
```

### 15.4.3 I/O Operations on Structures

A significant feature of the structure type is that it acts as a record within a file. In commercial applications, programmers must be able to store or retrieve these structural components just like record I/O in other commercial languages. Although C does not provide a direct I/O facility to transfer structures with respect to files, programmers can emulate structure I/O using the binary I/O mechanism that is made available in stream I/O. The stream's binary I/O provides ***fread*** to read a block of bytes from a stream and ***fwrite*** to write a block of bytes to a stream. These two functions, in general, require

1. *the size of a block in bytes;*
2. *reference address (i.e., byte address) of the block and;*
3. *number of consecutive blocks to be transferred*

as data descriptive arguments to control the block transfer with respect to a specifed stream. Although a structure type is composite, an instance of it exists in the memory as a block of bytes. To get the size of this block, we can make use of the sizeof operation. In our example, *sizeof (ITEM_TYPE)* will give the size of the defined structure. To perform this task, we must convert the structure address into byte or character type address. To convert a structure address into a byte or character type address, a **cast** operation can be performed. In our example, the array, *item[N_ITEMS],* is stored in the memory contiguously. The *&item[0]* is the structure address of the first element and its corresponding byte address in memory can be obtained by a cast operation, as shown below:

*(char *)&item[0]*

The formats of ***fread*** and ***fwrite*** are shown below:

***int fread(char *block_address, int block_size, int n_blocks, FILE *stream);***
***int fwrite(char *block_address, int block_size, int n_blocks, FILE *stream);***

> ***Note***: *Stream is merely the file pointer of an open stream. Both functions return number of blocks transferred successfully. More on these functions is explained in* ***Chapter 17***.

The following example shows how ***fread*** and ***fwrite*** can be applied on structures.

### Example 15.5:

Show a program to write a structure-data containing an integer and a character as its members to a file called *testfile,* and read the same to print on the screen.

```
#include <stdio.h>
struct
  { int    i;
    char c;
  }temp1, temp2;      /* two instances created in memory */
char *pc; /* pc is a character type pointer  */
int    temp_size;
```

```
void  main(void)
{
  FILE  *fp, *fopen();
/*  open testfile; write temp1 structure to testfile; close testfile  */
  pc = (char  *)&temp1;  /* get byte address of temp1 structure in pc  */
  temp_size = sizeof temp1;
  fp = fopen("testfile", "w");  /* open stream for writing */
  scanf("%d %c", &temp1.i, &temp1.c);  /* set temp1 with some data  */
  fwrite(pc, temp_size, 1, fp);  /*   write temp1 as a block of bytes  */
  fclose(fp);
/*  open testfile; read a block of bytes into temp2; close testfile  */
  pc = (char  *)&temp2;  /* get byte address of temp2 structure in pc  */
  temp_size = sizeof temp2;
  fp = fopen("testfile", "r");  /* open stream for reading  */
  fread(pc, temp_size, 1, fp); /*read a block of bytes in temp2's memory*/
  printf("%d %c \n", temp2.i, temp2.c);
  fclose(fp);
}
```

Let us extend our previous example to demonstrate how ***fread*** and ***fwrite*** can be applied to maintain our item file on disk. In our example, we created a fixed size memory file of N_ITEMS. Now this restriction is removed because a disk file can grow to any extent. The global variable, LAST_ITEM is not required either. The EOF indicator can be used to control file processing. We will now rewrite the previous program so that an external file can hold the created items.

```
/* GLOBAL  DECLARATIONS */
#include <stdio.h>
#include <string.h>
#define  TRUE    1
#define  FALSE 0
typedef  struct
  {
    char  name[21];   /* 20 character name + NULL character */
    int    id;          /* unique identifier of an item  */
    int    stock;        /* current stock  */
  } ITEM_TYPE;
int     add_item(char     *fname)
  {
  ITEM_TYPE  temp;
  FILE  *fp, *fopen();
  char  id_str[5], stock_str[10];
  if((fp = fopen(fname, "w")) == NULL)
    {
    printf("File cannot open\n");
    return(FALSE);
```

```
    }
  while(TRUE) /* unconditional loop */
    {
      printf("Input name of item: ");
      gets(temp.name);
      if(strcmp(temp.name, "END") ==NULL)
        {
          fclose(fp);
          return(TRUE);
        }
      printf("Input the selected item_identifier: ");
      gets(id_str);
      temp.id= atoi(id_str);
      printf("Input current stock of this item: ");
      gets(stock_str);
      temp.stock= atoi(stock_str);
      fwrite((char  *)&temp, sizeof temp, 1, fp);
    } /* End of while  */
}

int     report() /* output the entire file on the console  */
{
  ITEM_TYPE  temp;
  int i = 0;
  FILE  *fp, *fopen();
  if((fp = fopen(fname, "r")) == NULL)
    {
    printf("File cannot open\n");
    return(FALSE);
    }
  /* Print Heading  */
  printf("Item   Name     Item ID    Item Stock \n");
  while(fread((char *)&temp, sizeof temp, 1, fp)
    {
      printf("%s  \t %d \t %d \n",temp.name,temp.id,temp.stock);
    }
  fclose(fp);
}

/* The following function searches for a record with item_name and returns a pointer to the buffer
holding the desired instance */
 ITEM_TYPE  *search(char     *item_name)
 {
  ITEM_TYPE  temp;
  int i = 0;
  FILE  *fp, *fopen();
```

```
  if((fp = fopen(fname, "w")) == NULL)
   {
   printf("File cannot open\n");
   return(NULL);
   }
  while(fread((char *)&temp, sizeof temp, 1, fp)
   {
     if(strcmp(item_name, temp.name) == NULL)
       {
         fclose(fp);
         return(&temp);
       }
   }
  return(NULL); /* item was not found; return a NULL pointer */
}

void show(struct ITEM_TYPE *p_item)
 {
  printf("Item Name    Item ID    Item Stock \n");
  printf("%s \t %d \t %d \n",p_item->name,p_item->id,p_item- >stock);
 }

void main(void)
  { char cmd[2], item_name[21];
  int i;
    do
      {
        gets(cmd); /* receives a string of single character */
        switch(cmd[0])
          {
          case 'A':          IF ( add_item() == false)exit(0);
    break;
          case 'R':            report();
    break;
          case 'S': printf("Input item name");
    gets(item_name);
    p_item = search(item_name);
    show(p_item);
    break;
          case 'Q': exit(); /* stop the program execution */
          }
      } while (TRUE);
  } /*end main */
```

### 15.4.3 Assignment Operation on Structures

ANSI-C allows us to assign one structure to another of the same type. Unlike single variable assignment, structure assignment may be time consuming. This is due to the abstract nature of structure definition. Compilers allow structures to have arbitrary sizes, depending upon the nature of application data. For example, a real-time clock structure may have three integer members representing hours, minutes and seconds. On the other hand, the structure for a student record may contain tens of entries. Assignment operations for student records will obviously be more time consuming. The syntax of the structure assignment is the same as for normal variables. An example is shown here. Using the structure definition *ITEM_TYPE* in the ***Sec. 15.4***:

```
ITEM_TYPE        a, b;
```

we can then write

```
a = b;
```

to copy the members data of *b* to the corresponding members of *a*.

## 15.5 Union

In the previous section, we saw that a structure encapsulates a group of members that may belong to different types. Each member will be allocated a separate storage and hence, all members of a structure are active at any time. C provides another similar type called ***union*** which may also contain different types of members, but when a ***union*** is declared, memory will be allocated only to its largest size member. All other members share the same memory and means only one member will be active at any time. For example:

```
union
    {
        int    i;
        char  c;
        }  int_or_char = 0;
```

represents the ***int_or_char*** union variable. The memory allocated to this will be the size of an integer. We may use this variable as an integer in one function and as a character in another function. The union variable is initialized with the integer value 0.

> ***Remark:*** *Many C-compilers, including ANSI-C, allow programs to initialize the first member of a union during declaration.*

Accessing members of a union is similar to accessing a structure member. Using the name with dot notation, any member's value can be accessed. It is used appropriately, as shown below. Assume that the above declaration has been made global in the main function.

```
void func1(void)
    {
    . . .
    int_char.i = rand();
    . . .
    printf(" %d ", int_char.i);
    . . .
    }
void func2(void)
    {
    . . .
    int_char.c =getchar();
    . . .
    printf(" %c ", int_char.c);
    . . .
    }
```

One can also declare a pointer to a union, and can access members using the pointer notation. We can use the above example to show this concept.

```
union IntCharUnion
    {
        int    i;
        char  c;
    } int_or_char;

union IntCharUnion  *pic =  &int_or_char;  /* Declare a pointer to union and initialize with
the address of the union  */
void func1(void)
    {
    . . .
    pic->i = rand();    /* member i is accessed using pointer  */
    . . .
    printf(" %d ", pic->i);  /* member i is accessed using pointer  */
    . . .
    }
```

```
void func2(void)
    {
    . . .
    pic->c =getchar();  /* member c is accessed using pointer */
    . . .
    printf(" %c ", pic->c);  /* member c is accessed using pointer */
    . . .
    }
```

***Note:*** *Those who are familiar with Fortran, can recall the usage of equivalence declaration which shows similarity in some respect to the concept of union in C. The equivalence declaration was introduced to save memory occupied by common variables – a memory can be declared usable by more than one type of variable. This idea was useful when memory shortage was a problem. The PASCAL language has similar facility with its variant records.*

## 15.6 Summary

This chapter introduces the composite type of data structures, such as structure and union. Structure is introduced with examples, showing how it is useful for implementing application data of real nature (e.g., student record, customer record). Union is shown as a data structure capable of storing multiple types of variables, but usable at any time for one of the declared variables within a union.

## Exercises

15.1 Describe structures for the following problem data descriptions:
- (a) a component in an automobile spare parts store;
- (b) a member in a social club;
- (c) an account in a savings bank.

15.2 Consider the following structure:

```
struct
    {
        char name[20];
        struct
            {
            char street_name[20];
            int     house_no;
            char city_name[20];
            } address;
        char phone[7];
    } Person;
```

(a) How will you address each member of the above structure?

(b) Assign the following values to its members:
Name of person: Carl Beaton
Address: 20 Seventh Avenue
Brighton
Phone: 568223

15.3 Show a typical application of union data type.

# 16

# Storage Management and Dynamic Data Structure

**Chapter contents:**

*This chapter introduces how C-programs can use the run-time memory (heap storage) maintained by the C-virtual machine, exploring both advantages and disadvantages of this facility. This chapter familiarizes readers with the primitives that come with the heap storage.*

**Organization:**


*16.1 Introduction*
*16.2 Dynamic Storage Management*
*16.3 Meaning of Dynamic Data Structures*
*16.4 Dynamic Arrays*
*16.5 Linked Data Structures*
*16.6 Summary*
*Exercises*


## 16.1 Introduction

While elementary data structures are useful to implement simple applications, there exists a need for abstract data structures for advanced applications. The data modeling in these advanced applications may require dynamic buffers to cope with unstructured input, dynamic queuing facilities for sharable resources and dynamic partitioning for efficient data classification and processing. Typical examples of resource management application are an operating system where a tty-buffer should expand dynamically, depending upon the length of command or data input; an I/O queue for disk resource varies in length according to the number of requests at that time and; a ready queue of processes waiting for CPU is of varying nature.

We have seen that the direct use of pointers to data structures provides a means of transferring variables between functions and efficient processing facilities, especially on abstract data structures, such as arrays and strings. The extended power of pointers, along with the dynamic storage management facility in C, allows programmers to implement advanced abstract data structures, such as dynamic arrays and linked-list data structures, that can either grow or shrink during run-time. This chapter introduces the dynamic storage management supported by C and the techniques of creating and maintaining these dynamic types of abstract data structures.

## 16.2 Dynamic Storage Management

The C-virtual machine provides a high-level storage allocation by maintaining a separate memory area called ***heap***. Programs can request a block of contiguous memory for their dynamic use and return the same for reusing at later time. In the beginning, heap starts as a single contiguous block of free memory, but after allocation has started, this divides into fragments of free and allocated memory. C maintains a list of free memory blocks, called ***free list***, and a list of allocated memory blocks called ***allocated list***. When a request arrives for a block of memory, the system searches through the free list to find a free block of required size. If it is not available, then the system slices the required size from a larger available free block for allocation by leaving at the same time a small fragment of free block with the ***free list***. After a heavy use of the heap storage, the ***free list*** might have fragments of random size that sometimes results in too many small fragments unusable for any further allocation. Hence, the system would regularly compact the ***free list*** of small blocks into a ***free list*** of large blocks which is then used for allocation.

Associated with the system's heap storage are the following basic functions:

- ***malloc*** *to allocate a block of non-initialized memory from heap;*
- ***realloc*** *to reallocate memory with different size for the already allocated memory, but at the same time, preserve the original contents;*
- ***calloc*** *to allocate an array of free blocks of equal size and clear the allocated memory;*
- ***free*** *to free the previously allocated memory.*

A detailed description of these functions is given in the following section.

### The malloc function

This function is used to allocate a non-initialized memory of specified size and return a pointer to that allocated block. This pointer belongs to the type of memory maintained by heap, which is unknown and indicated here as ***void*** type. Its prototype definition is shown below:

```
#include <stddef.h>        /* size_t is defined in this header file */
     void *malloc( size_t  size);
```

where ***size*** is simply an amount of memory units specified of ***size_t*** or ***unsigned*** type and ***malloc()*** returns a ***pointer of void type (unknown or anonymous type)*** to start the block of memory allocated, or ***NULL*** if it can't allocate.

## The realloc function

This function is used to alter the size of memory that was originally allocated by ***malloc*** or another ***realloc***. It can be called either to increase or decrease the size of memory previously allocated. The original contents of the memory are preserved, and the remaining space is non-initialized. This function also returns a pointer to the reallocated memory whose type is unknown or ***void***. The prototype definition of this function is shown below:

```
#include <stddef.h>        /* size_t is defined in this header file */
    void *realloc( void *pointer_to_allocated_block, size_t   new_size);
```

where ***pointer_to_allocated_block*** is a pointer of any type, ***new_size*** is simply the size of a recalculated amount of memory, and ***realloc()*** returns a pointer of ***void*** (unknown or anonymous) ***type*** to the reallocated block, or NULL if it can't reallocate.

## The calloc function

This function is used to allocate a required size of memory to establish an array of a known number of elements. After allocating the specified amount of memory, it fills memory with zero. Its prototype definition is shown below:

```
#include <stddef.h>        /* size_t is defined in this header file */
    void *calloc( size_t   n_element, size_t   element_size)
```

where ***n_element*** is the number of elements in an array, ***element_size*** is the amount of memory computed by the ***sizeof*** operator, and ***calloc()*** returns a ***pointer of void*** (unknown or anonymous) ***type*** to the allocated memory, or ***NULL*** if it can't allocate.

## The free function

This function is used to release a block of storage originally allocated by a ***malloc***, ***realloc*** or ***calloc*** function. Its prototype definition is shown below:

```
    void free( void   *pointer_to_allocated_block );
```

> ***Remarks:***
> *1. The prototype definitions of these memory allocation and deallocation functions are supplied in* ***stdlib.h****. Programmers should include this file in their programs that invoke any of these functions so that the compiler will be able to check whether the returned value is used consistently. Since these definitions use size_t, programmers should also include stddef.h in which size_t has been defined.*

> *2. The malloc, realloc and calloc functions return a pointer to the allocated memory from the heap storage, whose type is anonymous or not defined in the system. A heap may maintain byte-oriented, word-oriented or any other type of memory that is assumed unknown to programs. Hence, void * is used as the returned type which can be cast into any other defined type.*

## Conventions for correct usage of the heap

Although the heap storage is limited in size, C gives a complete privilege to all programs to acquire as much memory as possible without any quota restriction. Moreover, C does not demand the programs return the acquired memories, and it has no protection mechanism if programs return memories that were not acquired from the ***heap***. If a program completes execution without returning the acquired memory from the heap, the ***allocated list*** will be left with memory blocks that are neither used nor reusable. Due to many bad programs, the heap storage may end up with a large number of unreleased fragments in the ***allocated list***, which are obviously inherent drawbacks with the dynamic storage management. In order to overcome these drawbacks, the programs should strictly cooperate to request an optimum size of memory and also return only the acquired memory as soon as it is finished with it. The integrity of the heap storage can be maintained by following a strict protocol in the programs as follows:

(a) A program with a simple memory allocation:

```
void main(void)
{
    . . .
Pointer_X = (X_type) malloc(size);
    . . . /* Acquired memory is used here */
    . . . /* After this statement, dynamic memory is not needed anymore */
    free(Pointer_X);   /* Release the acquired memory
    Pointer_X = NULL; /* Relieve the pointer from holding the released memory */
    . . .
}
```

(b) A program with continual memory allocation:

```
void main(void)
{
    . . .
    Pointer_X = (X_type) malloc(size); /* First allocation */
    . . .   /* Acquired memory is used here */
    Pointer_X = (X_type)realloc(Pointer_X, new_size);
    . . .   /* Acquired memory is used here */
    Pointer_X = (X_type)realloc(Pointer_X, new_size);
    . . . /* Acquired memory is used here */
    . . . /* After this statement, dynamic memory is not needed anymore */
    free(Pointer_X); /* Release all acquired memories */
    Pointer_X = NULL; /* Relieve the pointer from holding the released memory */
    . . .
}
```

Another factor with the heap storage is its limited size. When the heap is empty or not sufficient, a call for allocation may fail. If this situation is not detected, the program may use unallocated memory, leading to memory violations. At least during debugging we may be able to check whether the allocation is done without any failure, using the ***assert*** macro. This test may be valid when a program does not hold any other allocated heap storage. A typical use of assert macro with malloc is shown below:

```
#include <stdio.h>
#include <assert.h> /* assert macro is defined in this header file */
void main(void)
{
    . . .
    Pointer_X = (X_type) malloc(size);
    assert(Pointer_X != NULL); /* if malloc fails, abort is called to kill the program */
        . . .               /* Acquired memory is used here */
}
```

## 16.3 Meaning of Dynamic Data Structures

An integer variable, a real variable, a character variable and an array are all data structures of static nature because

(a) their sizes are specified, either explicitly or implicitly, in their declarations;
(b) they are allocated during compilation with appropriate memory and;
(c) their sizes do not change during run-time.

For example, a compiler may allocate four bytes for each integer variable declared in a program. During run-time, this size cannot be altered even if the programs need larger integers to avoid any overflow situation. Similarly, an array declared with a fixed number of elements cannot be normally altered in size during run-time, implying that the static nature of these variables would impose limitations on some applications. In other words, these types of data structures can only satisfy the applications in which the nature of data is fixed and known before processing. However, there are several applications where the nature of data is more dynamic. A common example is a queue of requests for accessing a common resource. Since the number of requests in a queue varies with respect to time and cannot be predicted at run-time, a static or fixed size data structure, like an array, for maintaining a queue, would obviously tend to fail. Hence, the language systems should provide facilities to create dynamic data structures for accommodating applications with dynamic types of data.

The power of pointers, along with the dynamic storage management facility in C, allows us to realize dynamic data structures useful for many advanced applications. The dynamic data structures can be broadly classified into ***dynamic arrays*** and ***linked data structures***. The following sections explain the concepts of building these data structures.

## 16.4 Dynamic Arrays

A dynamic array usually start with some default size and grow by an increment of specified size. Programs can also return a portion of the allocated memory when they find redundant space in the arrays. Some applications of this data structure are string (or line) buffers and stacks. The following examples show the use of dynamic arrays.

### Example 16.1:

Let us write our own command line interpreter that receives Unix-like commands from the keyboard and executes the received command using the library function called ***system(command_line)***. The program has to maintain a dynamic buffer to cope with the variable length commands. An exit command is used to terminate our program.

```
#include <stdio.h>
#include <assert.h>     /* assert macro is defined in this header file */
#include <stdlib.h>
#include <stddef.h>     /* size_t is defined here */
#define INC_SIZE 16
#define TRUE 1
#define FALSE 0
char *cmd;  /* Declare a pointer to command line  */
unsigned int    I;
size_t cur_size;        /* size_t is same as unsigned integral type */
int    Exit_Flag;
void stretch_buf(void)
{ /* This function is called to reallocate more memory for cmd buffer */
```

```
    cur_size = cur_size + INC_SIZE;
    if( (cmd = (char  *)realloc(cmd, cur_size)) == NULL)
        return FALSE;
    return TRUE;
  }

  void main(void)
  { int retn_flag;
    Exit_flag = FALSE;
    do
   {
     cur_size = INC_SIZE;
      /* Start with a 16 character command buffer */
     cmd = (char  *)malloc(cur_size);
     assert(cmd != NULL);   /*  if malloc fails, call abot to kill the program  */
   i = 0;  /* Initialize index before inputting a command  */
               /* Read characters into command buffer until a newline occurs; during input,
                  if buffer is found full, call stretch_buf function to extend buffer by another
                  16 character size*/
       while ( (cmd[i++] = getchar()) != '\n')
         {
              if (i > cur_size) retn_flag = stretch_buf();
             if(retn_flag == FALSE)
                 {
                 printf("Command buffer cannot be stretched \n");
                 free(cmd);
       }
        }/* End of while  */
       /* append a NULL character to make a string  */
       cmd[—i] = '\0';  /* Replace '\n' with A NULL   */
       /* If command is Exit, then set the flag; else execute  */
       if(strcmp(cmd, "exit")
         Exit_flag = TRUE;
       else
         system(cmd);  /* Execute the Unix Command   */
       /* Before next command input return the dynamic memory  */
       free(cmd);  /* Free memories allocated so far before exit  */
     } while(Exit_flag != TRUE);
} /* End of main  */
```

Our program maintains a dynamic line buffer, called ***cmd***, which is initially allocated with a size of sixteen characters by the ***malloc()*** call in the main function. The ***do_while loop*** in the main function receives a command line in the buffer and executes the same with the help of ***system***. During command input, when the buffer reaches its end, the ***stretch_buf*** function is called to reallocate the buffer with a larger size memory. An exit command input sets *Exit_Flag* which, in turn, breaks the loop. The program shows that it always frees the allocated memory after it is used (i.e., after each command is executed).

## Example 16.2:

Let us implement a dynamic stack of integer type along with the necessary functions for its maintenance. Demonstrate the use of this stack by inputting a list of numbers and print them in reverse order.

```
#include <stdio.h>
#include <assert.h>      /* assert macro is defined in this header file */
#include <stdlib.h>
#define INC_SIZE 16
int     *stack;
unsigned int     stack_size, stack_ptr;

void    init_stack(void)
{
   stack_size = INC_SIZE;
   stack = (int *)malloc(INC_SIZE * sizeof(int) );
   assert(stack != NULL);   /* if malloc fails, call abort to kill the program */
  stack_ptr = 0;
}

void inc_stack_size(void)
{
   stack_size = stack_size + INC_SIZE;
   if( (stack =(int *)realloc(stack, stack_size * (sizeof int) ) == NULL)
     {
        perror("Memory cannot be allocated");
        free(stack);  /* Free memories allocated so far before exit */
        exit();
     }
}

void push(int item)
{
   if(stack_ptr >= stack_size)
     inc_stack();
   stack[stack_ptr++] = item;
}
```

```
int     pull(void)
{
  if(stack_ptr >= 0)
    return stack[—stack_ptr];
  else
    {
     perror("READING FROM EMPTY STACK !!!!");
      free(stack);   /* release stack memory and exit    */
      exit();
    }
}

void main(void)
{
 int int_item;

  init_stack();
  /* input 20 numbers and push them in the stack      */
  for(i=0; i < 20; i++)
    {
      scanf("%d", &int_item);
      push(int_item);
    }
  /* output the stacked values in the reverse order */
  for(i=0; i < 20; i++)
    {
      int_item = pull();
      printf("%d \n", int_item);
    }
  /* Before exiting deallocate the stack memory */
  free(stack);
} /* End of main */
```

**Remark:** The statement that initializes stack_ptr in the int_stack function may be redundant for a BSS variable, but to indicate that the stack_ptr is pointing to the next free element in the stack, this initialization statement is useful.

## 16.5 Linked Data Structures

Two types of linked data structures are common in use, namely linear linked lists and trees. A linked list is the most commonly linked structure. This data type is similar to an array consisting of elements of identical type, but can grow or shrink dynamically. This type of data structure is often used for maintaining queues, and it can also be used to emulate stacks for abstract types of data. On the other hand, the trees are used to organize data according to some classification, i.e., sorting and searching. However, we can distinguish a linked data structure from a normal array using the following differences:

- An item in an array can be either a simple or composite element. For example, we can declare an array of integers, reals, characters, structures, unions or even pointers of any specific type. On the other hand, an item in a linked data structure is always a composite data structure, usually called a node. Basically, a node is a structure containing a data part and a linking part. The data part may contain one or more data elements of different types, and the linking part contains address elements to point to other nodes in the structure. A linked data structure cannot exist without a linking part.

- Another major difference is the manner in which these items are stored and accessed. In an array, items are stored in a contiguous memory and each item can be addressed randomly using the address of the first item, whereas the nodes in a linked structure are usually stored in memory locations not necessarily contiguous, and they are all linked in a chain fashion using the address part of each node. Locating a node usually requires traversing a chain of nodes.

There are different types of linked data structures, namely ***singly linked list***, ***doubly linked list***, ***circular list*** and ***binary tree***. When the linking part contains addresses to point to both the next node and the previous node, it is called doubly linked or two-way list.

### 16.5.1 Singly Linked List

When the linking part of a node points to only the next node in the list, this structure is called singly linked list. A singly linked list starts with the first node followed by a series of nodes with forward links from one node to another node, ending with the last node pointing to a NULL node. A pointer called ***Head*** is usually associated with the list to locate the structure. The following properties characterize this list structure:

- *Nodes are linked in one direction;*
- *Address of the list is the address of the first node;*
- *Searching for a node always starts at the first node, and traverses every subsequent node in a sequential manner until the last node in the list;*
- *A pointer called **Head** is used to hold the address of the list;*
- *An optional pointer called **Tail** can be maintained to point to the end of the list, which would help to append a node quickly;*
- *The last node is pointing to a NULL node, indicating the end of the list.*

Since the linkage mode allows traversing the list in one way, it is also called ***one-way list***. ***Fig. 16.1*** shows the structure of this list type.

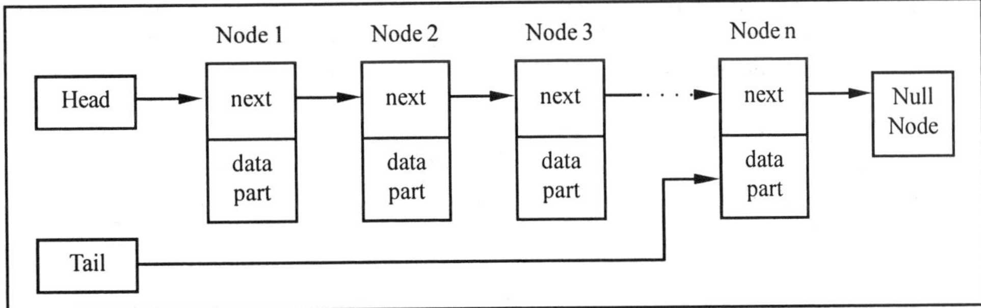


*Fig. 16.1 Singly linked list structure*

The prototype definition of a singly linked list is

```
typedef struct    node_struct
    {
        <data declarations>;
        struct  node_struct   *next;
        } TYPE_NAME;
```

## Operations on a singly linked list

The following operations are necessary in order to maintain a singly linked list.

1. *Make a new node;*
2. *Append or insert a new node;*
3. *Remove a node from the list;*
4. *Find the length of the list.*

## Steps to establish a singly linked list

1. *Define the type of a given node structure;*
2. *Declare a Head pointer to hold the address of the list of nodes of the defined type;*
3. *Implement the functions for performing the operations on the list.*

The following example demonstrates the implementation of these steps in the application of a singly linked list.

### Example 16.4:

Let us consider a busy take-out restaurant, maintaining an on-line system to serve their customers strictly according to first-come-first-serve manner. Arriving customers have to enter the following details before waiting for their services. Establish a program that uses a linked list to maintain a customer queue with the following customer structure.

*customer_name: 20 characters*
*customer_order_number: 2 digits*

### Step 1:

Let us first identify the data structures required for building a queue. From the given customer details, we can construct a data type called CUSTOMER to construct a node, as shown here:

```
typedef struct customer_struct
{
    char customer_name[21];
    int customer_order;
struct customer_struct *next;
} CUSTOMER;
```

The template structure of the CUSTOMER type is shown in ***Fig. 16.2***.

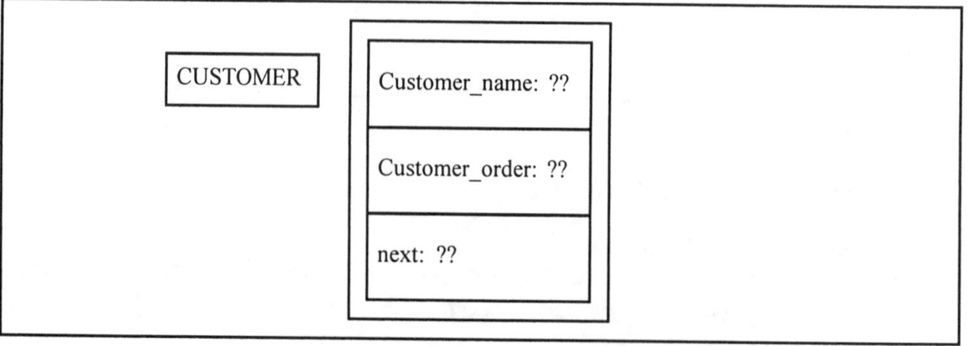


*Fig. 16.2 Template structure of CUSTOMER node*

### Step 2:

Before building a queue, we need a Head pointer to hold the queue's address. Let us declare one, as shown below:

```
CUSTOMER *Head = NULL; /* An empty queue is defined */
```

Initially the Head pointer is assigned with the value ***NULL***, indicating that there is no one waiting for service. The memory map of this empty queue is shown in ***Fig. 16.3***. Let us store these two definitions in a file called ***Customer.h***.

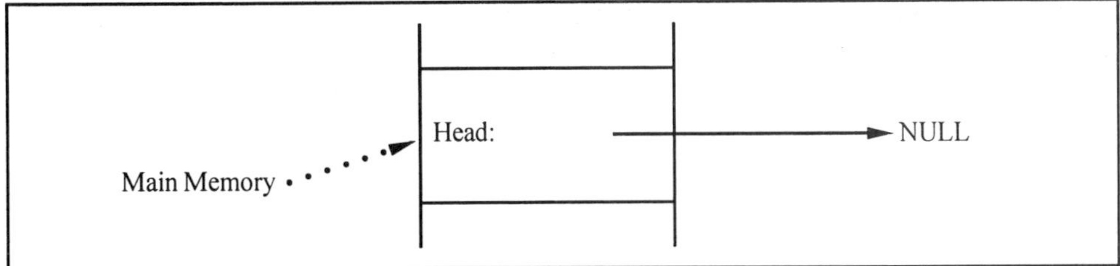


*Fig. 16.3 Memory map of the empty queue*

## Step 3:

In the steady state, arriving customers add their entries to the queue and, at the same time, after each customer is serviced, the respective node is removed from the queue. For adding a node, we have to dynamically make a new node and append it to the list. While creating a node, a memory exception may occur due to lack of space in the heap storage. Since the program cannot proceed with this state of memory, it has to stop gracefully by releasing all the memories so far allocated from heap. Hence, a housekeeping function is necessary to free the memories occupied by the list at that time. Appending a node is always done at the end of the list and, thus, it is essential to have a function to locate the end of the list. Therefore the following functions necessary for adding a CUSTOMER node to the list are:

*make_node,*
*free_all,*
*read_customer,*
*find_last_node and*
*append.*

Let us implement these functions, as shown below, and store them in a file called ***Add_node.h***.

```
CUSTOMER   *make_node(void)
{
 CUSTOMER *new_node_ptr;

  new_node_ptr = (CUSTOMER *)malloc(sizeof (CUSTOMER));
  if (new_node_ptr == NULL)
    {
     printf("No more memory in heap \n");
     free_all();    /* free all allocated memory so far, and exit    */
     exit(0);
    }
  else
    return (new_node_ptr);
} /* End of make_node() */

void free_all(void)
{
 CUSTOMER_NODE  *temp_ptr;

  while ((temp_ptr = Head) != NULL)
   {
     Head = temp_ptr->next;
     free(temp_ptr);
   }
} /* End of free_all */

void read_customer(CUSTOMER  *node)
{
  puts("Input your name and Request ID \n");
  scanf("%s %d",node->customer_name, node->customer_order);
} /* End of read_customer */

CUSTOMER   *find_last_node(CUSTOMER   *cur_ptr)
{
 CUSTOMER *last_node_ptr;
  if(cur_ptr == NULL)
    return (NULL); /* Showing empty list   */
  while(cur_ptr->next != NULL)
     cur_ptr = cur_ptr->next;
    return (cur_ptr);
} /* End of find_last_node */

void append(CUSTOMER   *new_node_ptr)
{
 CUSTOMER *last_node_ptr;
  last_node_ptr = find_last_node();
```

```
if (last_node_ptr == NULL)
  {
   Head = new_node_ptr;
   return;
  }
else
  {
   last_node_ptr->next = new_node_ptr;
   new_node_ptr->next  = NULL;
   return;
  }
} /* End of append */
```

The make_node function creates a node by getting a memory segment equivalent to the size of the CUSTOMER template from the heap memory. In this step, if malloc fails to get memory, it frees all the acquired memory and terminates the program. ***Fig. 16.4*** shows the memory map of the new, dynamically created node.

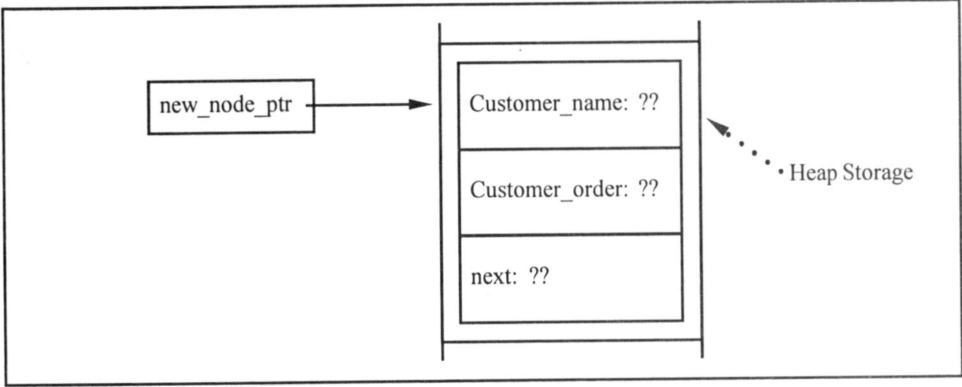


*Fig. 16.4 Memory map of the new node*

The ***read_customer*** function fills up the new node with the details of a customer read from the user. The memory map of the node after this step is shown in ***Fig. 16.5***.

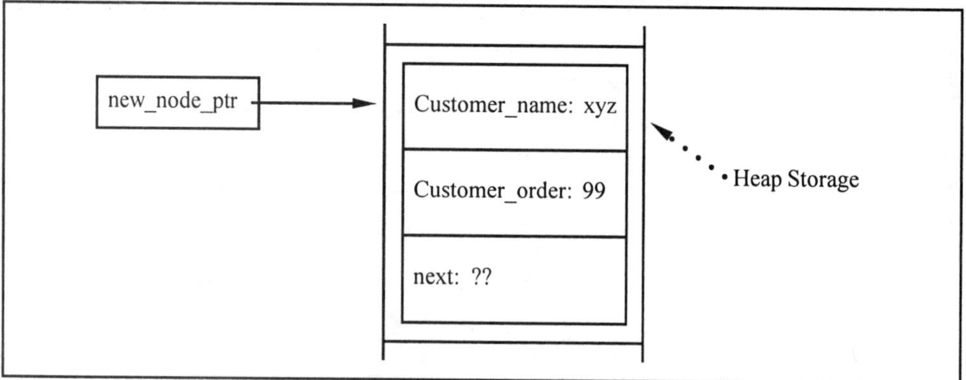


*Fig. 16.5 The new node with customer details*

The ***append*** function appends the new node to the queue pointed by Head. Since the ***Head*** pointer at this stage points to a NULL-queue, the added node forms the first as well as the last node of the queue. Since the nodes are added at the end of the existing queue, the append function has to locate the end of the queue before adding a new node. The append function uses the ***find_last_node*** function. The queue status after adding the second node is shown in ***Fig. 16.6***.

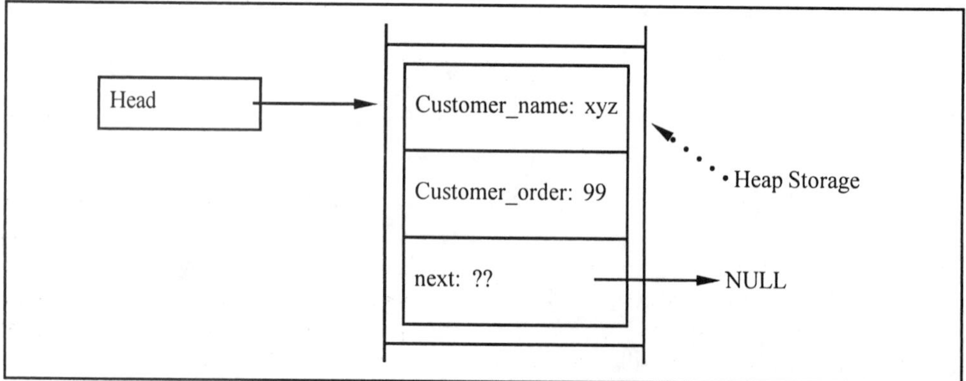


*Fig. 16.6 After appending the node to the empty queue*

After adding the second node to the queue, the memory map of the resulting linked list is shown in ***Fig. 16.7***. Even though the ***malloc*** function gets memory segments from the same heap storage, they are not contiguous. The pointers in the nodes provide the links in creating a physical queue, as shown in the figure. The last node in the queue points to the NULL node.

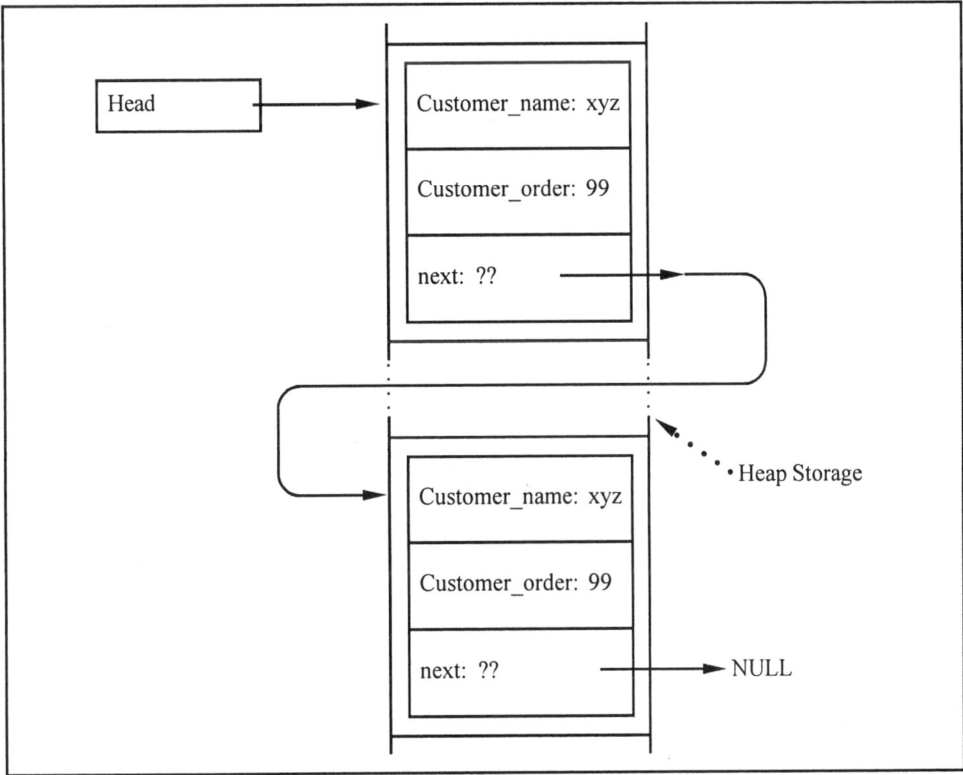


*Fig. 16.7 After appending the second node to the queue*

Another set of functions is required for dispatching the requests and removing the nodes corresponding to the serviced requests: a function to know how many more requests were pending in the queue, a function to get the details of the next request and other utility functions, like print, for all pending requests. After dispatching a request, the node must be removed from the list. This requires a function to delink a node and release the memory allocated. The server can select any of the above utility functions by inputting simple single letter commands like:

*n* : *to get the number of pending requests in the list;*
*w* : *to show the next request at the head of the queue;*
*s* : *to print all the requests in the queue;*
*q* : *to quit the program.*

To cater to this facility, a separate function to process the commands is also required. Hence, we will write the code for process_cmd, que_len, show_que, whois_next and remove_node functions and store them in the ***Dispatch.h*** file.

```
void process_cmd(char *command)
{
 switch(command[0])
  {
   case 'n': /* Find number of requests in the queue */
      printf("Number of requests in the queue:%d \n",que_len());
      break;
   case 'w': /* Show who is next in the queue */
      whois_next();
      break;
   case 's': /* Show the items in the queue */
      show_que();
      break;
   case 'q': /* Quit the program */
        QUIT_FLAG = TRUE;
        free_mem();
      break;
   default: EXIT_FLAG = TRUE;
        break;
  } /* End of switch */
} /* End of process_cmd */

unsigned int que_len(void)
{
 unsigned    length;
 CUSTOMER *temp_ptr;

  temp_ptr = Head;
  length = 0;
  while (temp_ptr != NULL)
   {
     length++;
     temp_ptr = temp_ptr->next;
   }
  return length;
} /* End of que_len */

void show_que(void)
{
 CUSTOMER *temp;
```

```
  temp = Head;
  printf("Name         Order Number " );
  while (temp != NULL)
   {
     printf("%s%d",temp->customer_name,temp->customer_order );
    temp= temp->next;
   }
} /* End of show_que */

void  whois_next(void)
{
  if(Head == NULL)
    printf("No one is waiting in the queue \n");
  else
    printf("%s  %d \n",Head->customer_name, Head- >customer_order );
} /* End of whois_next */

void  remove_node(void)
{
 CUSTOMER  *temp;

  if(Head  != NULL)
    {
      temp = Head;
      Head = temp->next;
      free(temp);
    }
} /* End of remove_node */
```

Now let us write a complete program to maintain the customer queue. This program includes the Customer.h, Add_node.h and Dispatch.h files to access the CUSTOMER definition and all utility functions.

```
#include  < stdio.h>
#include  < stddef.h>
#include  < stdlib.h>
#define  TRUE    1
#define  FALSE 0
char  cmd_line[80];
int     QUIT_FLAG;
int     EXIT_FLAG;
#include  "Customer.h"
#include  "Add_node.h"
#include  "Dispatch.h"
```

```
void main(void)
{
 CUSTOMER *new_node_ptr;
 QUIT_FLAG = FALSE;
 do
  {
   puts("$ Are you a customer? ");
   gets(cmd_line);
   if((strcmp(cmd_line, "YES") == 0)
  {
       new_node_ptr = make_node();
       read_customer(new_node_ptr);
       append(new_node_ptr);
  }
   else
  {
   EXIT_FLAG = FALSE;
   do
     {
      puts("$ "); /* Prompt for next server's command */
      gets(cmd_line);
        process_cmd(cmd_line);
     } while(EXIT_FLAG);
   }
  } while(QUIT_FLAG != TRUE);
} /* End of main */
```

The do_while loop in the main puts a prompt "$ Are you a customer?". If the reply is "***YES***", the program assumes that a customer is entering a request. In this mode, when the customer enters a request, a node is created, the customer order is written in the node and then the new node is added to the queue. If the reply to the prompt is ***not*** "***YES***", the program will assume the server is going to dispatch a request and goes into ***process_cmd*** function. Until EXIT_FLAG is set by a command other than the legal commands, ***process_cmd*** function is in the server's control.

### 16.5.2 Recursion and Linked Lists

Before discussing other types of linked structures, it is essential to consider the special nature of data representation and its effect on the processing mode. For example, freeing the whole linked list is a large problem. Since the node structures are all exactly duplicated and the processing on each node is exactly the same, this problem can be decomposed into a subproblem or subprogram of freeing a node. This subprogram, when called with the address of the first node in the list, can remove the node and then call itself by supplying the next first node of the list in a repeated manner until the whole list is removed. This type of processing is called recursion. It is a powerful, elegant and natural method of solving a large class of problems.

Let us rewrite the ***free_all*** function of ***Example 16.4*** using the recursive technique.

```
void free_all( CUSTOMER  *in_node_ptr)
{
 CUSTOMER *temp_node_ptr;

  if( (temp_node_ptr = in_node_ptr) != NULL)
    {
    in_node_ptr = temp_node_ptr->next;
     free(temp_node_ptr);    /* free one node    */
     free_all(in_node_ptr);  /* Then call itself to free next  */
    }
} /* End of free_all */
```

From the above example, we can also define recursion as a technique in which a large problem is defined in terms of itself.

### 16.5.3 Doubly Linked List

A doubly linked list, also called a ***two-way list***, is similar to a singly linked list except that it links nodes in both directions. Each node has pointers to its next node as well as its previous node in the list. ***Fig. 16.8*** shows the structure of this list type. The following properties characterize this structure:

- *Nodes are linked in both forward and backward manner, i.e., each node has one address to point to the next node and another address to point to a previous node;*
- *The last node in the list points only to its previous node and its address to the next node is NULL;*
- *Similarly, the first node points only to the second node in the list and its address to the previous node is NULL;*
- *Similar to the singly linked list, a Head pointer is maintained to hold the address of the list;*
- *Optionally, a **Tail** pointer may be maintained to append the nodes quickly;*
- *Searching for a node can be done in either way, thus it is faster than in a one-way list.*

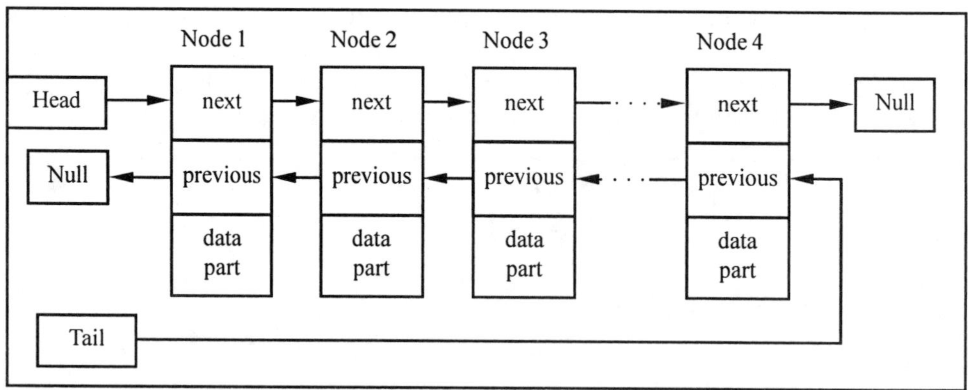


*Fig. 16.8 Schematic diagram for doubly linked list structure*

### 16.5.4 Circular List

A circular list is similar to the previous cases except that the last node of the list is made to point to the first node. The following properties characterize this structure:

- *In a one-way circular list (**Fig. 16.9**), every node points to the next node and the last node points to the first node, whereas in a two-way circular list (**Fig. 16.10**) every node points to the next as well as the previous node;*
- *The **Head** pointer can point to any node in the list. Both the doubly linked and circular lists are simply the extensions to the one-way linked lists. With the additional links in these data structures, the list operations can be implemented more efficiently.*

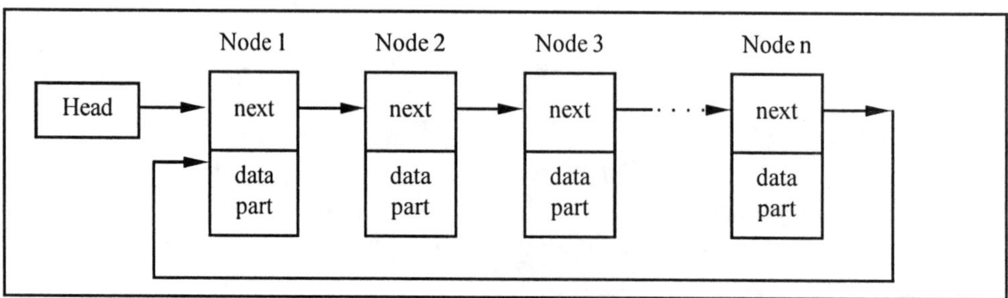


*Fig. 16.9 Schematic representation of singly linked circular list*

A circular list with links in both directions is shown in ***Fig. 16.10***. This list data structure is similar to doubly-linked list except for two additional links between the first and last nodes.

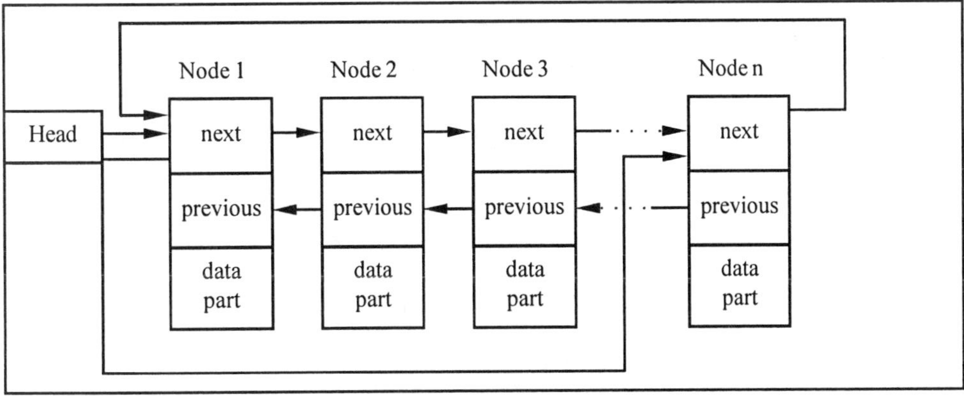


*Fig. 16.10 Schematic representation of doubly linked circular list*

### 16.5.5 Binary Tree

Another common type of linked list is the binary tree. Each node in this case has a data part and a link part, containing two links pointing to left and right child nodes, or siblings. (See ***Fig. 16.11***.)

- *Top node in the tree is called the root node;*
- *Each node may have zero, one or two child nodes;*
- *A node with no child node is called a leaf;*
- *A node with child nodes is called the internal node.*

### Operations on Binary Tree

1. *Inserting a node into a tree;*
2. *Joining two trees;*
3. *Removing a node from the tree;*
4. *Removing a subtree from its parent tree;*
5. *Traversing a tree;*
6. *Showing a subtree.*

More information on the implementation of these functions can be found in any textbook on data structures and algorithms.

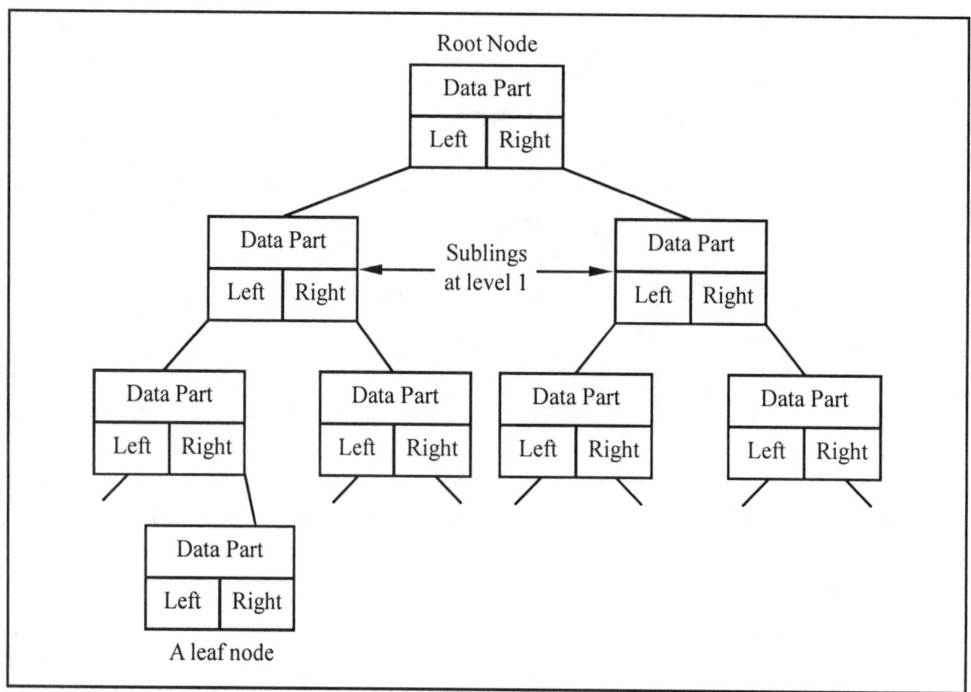


*Fig. 16.11 Schematic representation of a binary tree structure*

## 16.6 Summary

This chapter has discussed the dynamic storage management and how this facility, when combined with the pointer and structure data types, can be made more useful in realizing advanced data structures, such as dynamic arrays and linked structures. Various types of linked structures such as singly linked, doubly linked, circular list and binary tree are introduced. The study of these abstract data structures has led to the discussion of concepts like the scope of recursive processing in the linked structures.

## Exercises

16.1 Identify the correct statements from the following:

(a) malloc always allocates 1k bytes.
(b) malloc carries an argument to specify the size of memory to be allocated.
(c) malloc carries an argument to specify number of bytes to be allocated from heap memory.
(d) malloc always returns byte address.
(e) malloc returns the address of allocated memory whose type is undefined or anonymous.
(f) malloc always returns the size of memory allocated.
(g) malloc returns -1 when it fails to allocate.

16.2 Show the function call for allocating memory for the following cases:

(a) for creating a string buffer of 128 charcters;
(b) for creating an integer array of 100 elements;
(c) for creating an instance of the following structure type:

```
typedef struct
    {
    char emp_name[20];
    int  emp_id;
    char emp_sex;
    float  emp_salary;
    } EMPLOYEE;
```

16.3 Identify the correct statements from the following:

(a) realloc can be called to alter the allocated byte memory into integer memory.
(b) realloc is only used to increase the size of already allocated memory.
(c) realloc is only used to alter the size of already allocated memory.
(d) realloc returns the size of the reallocated memory.
(e) realloc returns the address of the reallocated memory whose type is not defined or anonymous.

16.4 Show the function call for doubling the size of a string originally allocated with 128 characters.

16.5 Summarize the differences between malloc, realloc and calloc.

16.6 Show the function call to create an 100 element array of EMPLOYEE type defined in the exercise 16.2.

16.7 Consider a store that maintains and services a queue of orders received in a day. Each order has the following details:

Date: 6 digits
Customer name: 20 characters
Customer ID: 4 digits
Customer Phone: 10 digits
Customer country: 10 characters
Customer State: 10 characters
Customer Town: 10 characters
Customer Street: 10 characters
Customer postcode: 4 digits
Item_ID: 2 digits
Item_name: 10 characters
Item_quantity: 4 digits

16.8 Answer the following questions with respect to constructing a singly linked list with a head pointer to maintain a queue of the arriving orders by using the above information. Assume the orders are served on a first-come-first-serve basis.

(a) Show the structure of a node in the order list.
(b) Show the structure of the head pointer.
(c) Write a function to create a new node.
(d) Write a function to find out the last node in the list.
(e) Write a function to append a node to the list.
(f) Write a function to delete a node after servicing.
(g) Write a function to find out the number of outstanding orders in the list.
(h) Write a function to print out the orders currently in the list.

# 17

# ANSI-C File System

**Chapter contents:**
*This chapter introduces an ANSI-C file system that provides a rich stream-oriented I/O environment suitable for supporting a variety of applications. Readers will become familiar with all levels of stream functions, such as character, line and binary I /O functions.*

**Organization:**

*17.1 Introduction*
*17.2 Overview of ANSI-C File System*
*17.3 Concept of Stream I /O*
*17.4 Use of stdio.h in Stream I/O*
*17.5 The stdio Streams*
*17.6 Descriptions of Stream I/O Control Functions*
*17.7 Stream Functions for Character I/O*
*17.8 String and Line I/O Operations*
*17.9 Binary I/O in Streams*
*17.10 Formatted I/O*
*17.11 Summary*
*Exercises*

## 17.1 Introduction

Originally, the C-language was designed to support two main areas: systems programming and scientific and engineering applications. The processing requirements for the scientific application involves:

- *versatile character- and string-oriented I/O operations;*
- *block I/O for transferring data in extensive manner and;*
- *file system I/O control operations.*

The processing for the engineering application involves:

- *formatted I/O for simple types of variables and;*
- *binary type of I/O operations for transferring array and composite data type variables.*

Hence, the I/O facility in standard C has been made quite rich to suit these two basic applications.

(K&R)C originally provided two basic levels of I/O facility. At low level, it accessed all I/O system calls of the Unix kernel. This system call I/O is simply called ***Unix I/O*** and it deals directly with the file system for creating, opening, reading, writing, closing, changing protection modes, and deleting, with respect to files. Hence, this I/O is also called ***direct I/O***. The system call functions in ***Unix I/O*** are primitive in the sense that they provide only block I/O which can then be used for implementing high level or application-oriented I/O functions. Hence, this I/O is also called ***basic I/O***. At high level, (K&R)C provided a set of library functions as an interface to the underlying ***basic I/O*** to support the application-oriented I/O, such as character, string, formatted and binary I/O functions, from the library that accompanies the language. Such a high-level I/O environment is called ***stream-oriented File I/O*** or simply ***stream I/O***.

While introducing the standard to C, ANSI committee adopted the stream I/O as the only file I/O. Although many C-programs in the past freely used either of the above two I/Os, the standard recommends a complete exclusion of ***Unix I/O*** in future application programs. After adding a few more functions to the existing stream I/O, it is called ***ANSI-C File System***. On the other hand, the ***POSIX*** standard committee, while considering a standard operating system interface to the languages like C, specified an Application Program Interface (API) standard based on the original Unix interface in C. When other operating systems are forced to provide a ***POSIX*** specified standard interface based on Unix interface, the ***basic I/O*** is now called ***Unix-like File I/O***. More on the ***POSIX*** standard and ***Unix-like I/O*** will be explained in ***Chapter 21***.

> ***Note:*** *Both* **Unix-like I/O** *and* **ANSI-C I/O** *support their own sets of functions to perform* **open, read, write** *and* **close** *operations on files. It is important for a C-programmer to note the distinction between these two sets of function calls. For example, when reading blocks directly, a file can be opened using the open system call, i.e.,* **open**(*file_name, access_mode*). *On the other hand, when processing a file in* **ANSI-C stream** *mode, the file can be opened using* **ANSI-C stream open** *function, i.e.,* **fopen**(*file_name, access_mode*).
>
> *In general, all stream function names start with the character 'f', whereas all system calls (or* **Unix-like I/O functions***) have their names in the normal manner. For example,* ***fopen, fread, fwrite,*** *and* ***fclose***, *are stream functions; and* **open, read, write,** *and* **close** *are* ***Unix-like I/O functions***. *The* **Unix-like I/O** *is useful for system programming applications under Unix or any other operating system environment and* **ANSI-C I/O** *is useful for portable scientific and engineering applications. A detailed discussion about this* **Unix-like I/O** *is in* ***Chapter 20***.

## 17.2 Overview of ANSI-C File System

***ANSI-C file system*** basically supports two types of files, namely:

1. text files:
   - *primitive text files*
   - *formatted text files*

2. binary or unstructured files.

A primitive text file contains a stream of characters as in a normal text document. Information can be added to these text files just like keying characters to a paper document in a typewriting machine. That means any of the characters in a given character set can be written to a text file in a sequential fashion. Instead of writing characters one by one, one can write a string of characters to text file. Similarly, instead reading character by character one may be able to read string by string. ***ANSI-C I/O*** provides one set of read/write operations at character/byte level (***fgetc*** to read a character and ***fputc*** to write a character) and one set of read/write functions at string/line level (***fgets*** to read a string and ***fputs*** to write a string). A primitive text file is simply a ***character type text file***, but in readable form. In fact, when we display the contents of a primitive text file, we can read the information as it is stored.

A ***formatted text file*** is a ***structured text file*** containing multiple type information in readable form. Each record may contain a description of an item using different types of fields. For example, a formatted employee record may contain an alphabetical string of name, a numeric string denoting employee ID, a character field denoting sex ID and a real field denoting an employee's salary. ***ANSI-C I/O*** provides a set of functions to read/write formatted records from or to an open stream (e.g., ***fscanf*** to receive formatted input data and ***fprintf*** to print formatted output data).

A ***binary file*** is used to store the binary images of data structures defined in a program and contains a sequence of binary images of any particular data structure. For example, a binary file can be created to store a sequence of integers, a sequence of real numbers, a sequence of structures or a sequence of arrays of any data type, as shown in ***Fig.*** *17.1*. ***ANSI-C I/O*** provides a set of binary I/O functions to read/write binary images (e.g., ***fread*** to read one or more binary images and ***fwrite*** to write one or more binary images) with respect to an open file.

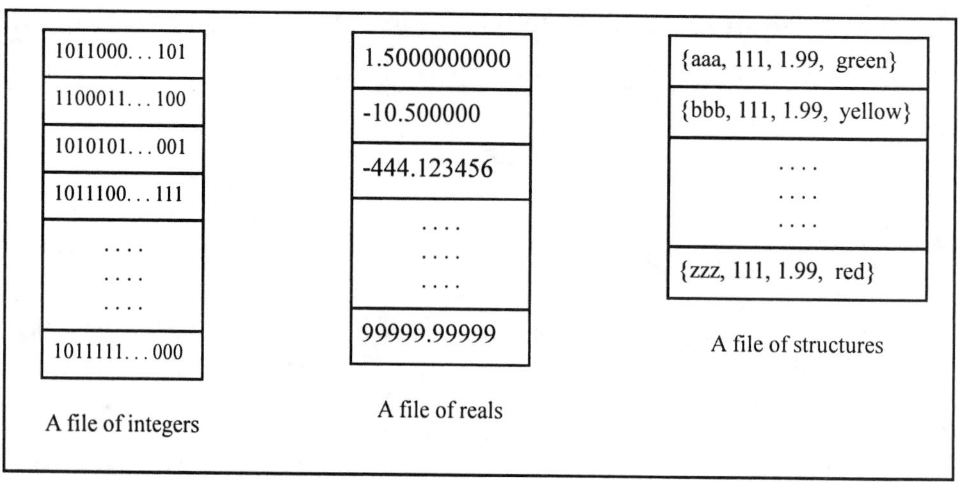


*Fig. 17.1 Binary files*

An ***ANSI-C file*** is always opened as a stream and, depending upon the mode of file processing, an appropriate set of ***ANSI-C stream functions*** can be used. The types of file processing mode that are supported by the standard are:

- *character I/O,*
- *string/line I/O,*
- *formatted I/O,*
- *binary I/O.*

*Table 17.1 Various categories of stream functions*

| Control | Character I/O | String I/O | Formatted I/O | Binary I/O | File Positioning | Error Handling |
|---|---|---|---|---|---|---|
| fopen | fgetc | fgets | fscnaf | fread | ftell | ferror |
| fclose | fputc | fputs | fprintf | fwrite | fseek | perror |
| freopen | getc | gets | scanf | | rewind | clearerr |
| fflush | putc | puts | printf | | fgetpos | feof |
| remove | getchar | | sscanf | | fsetpos | |
| rename | putchar | | sprintf | | | |
| tmpfile | ungetc | | vfprintf | | | |
| tmpnam | ungetchar | | vprintf | | | |
| setbuf | | | vsprintf | | | |
| setvbuf | | | | | | |

The structure of an ***ANSI-C*** file is merely a stream of bytes. The EOF can be determined only with the help of its size stored as an attribute in a structure associated with each file created. A read function can indicate the occurrence of EOF by generating ***EOF*** character for text files and setting a global condition variable (maintained by ***feof*** function) for binary files when it reaches the end of an ***ANSI-C file***. These mechanisms are explained in detail later in this chapter.

***Table 17.1*** shows the stream functions that are supported by standard C. ***Fig. 17.2*** shows the multilevel architecture of the I/O environment in C-Virtual Machine and reveals that the standard I/O layer is supported by the underlying Unix I/O layer.

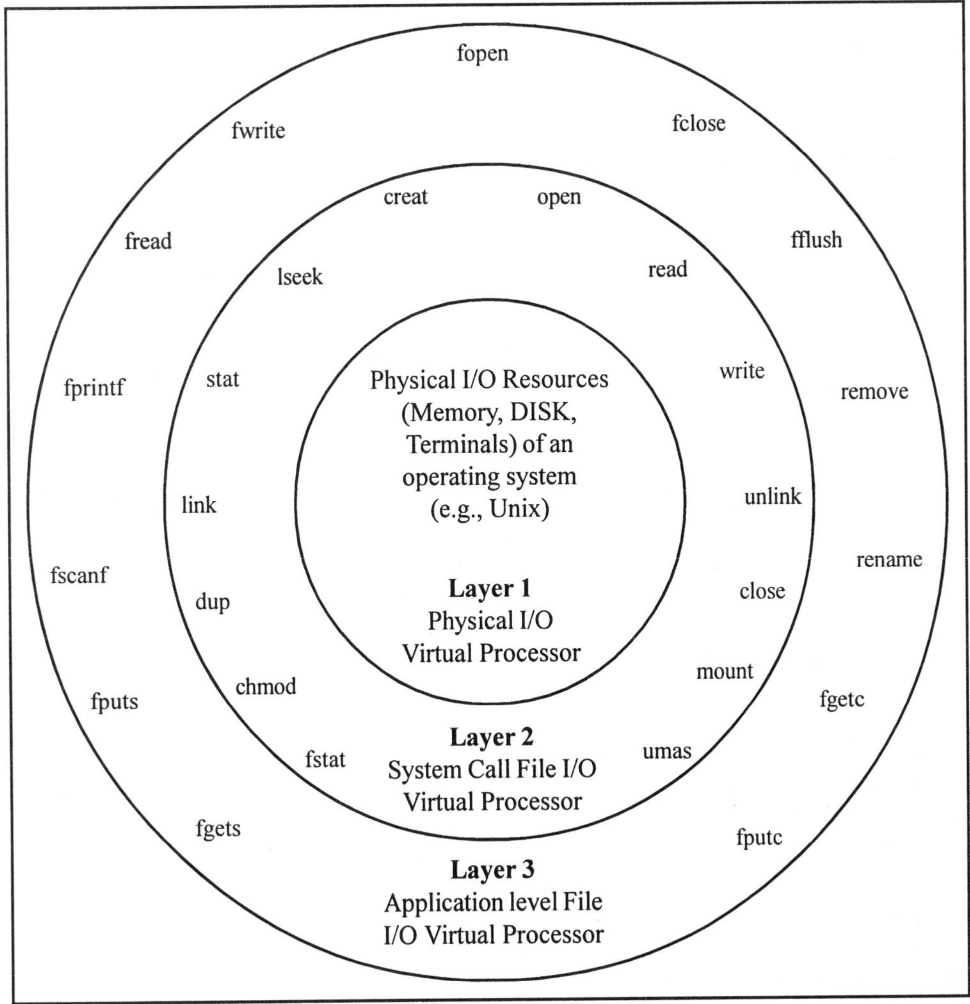


*Fig. 17.2 Multilevel (Unix-like) file system*

*Remark: After opening a file as a stream (i.e., using ANSI-C's **fopen**), the program should strictly use the stream-read and stream-write functions (i.e., ANSI-C's **fgetc, fputc, fgets, fputs,fread, fwrite,** etc). Similarly, after opening a file for **Unix-like I/O** (i.e., using the **open** system call), one should use block or direct read (i.e., **read**) and block or direct write (i.e., **write**) system calls for data transfer. It also follows that a stream must be closed by ANSI-C's **fclose,** but not by the Unix I/O's **close** system call. Similarly, a file opened for **Unix-like I/O** must be closed by the close system call, but not by the ANSI's **fclose** stream function.*

This chapter introduces:

- *the basic concept of **stream-based I/O of ANSI-C File System**;*
- *the functions available in ANSI (or stream) I/O and;*
- *their use in file processing.*

## 17.3 Concept of Stream I/O

### Meaning of Buffered (and Unbuffered) I/O

In general, an I/O transfer initiated by a program moves data between an opened file and a program's data area (i.e., user's space). The ***basic I/O*** can be used to transfer data blocks directly between a user area and a file. There is no intermediate buffer provided between these two end points. Hence, this is called ***unbuffered I/O***. Obviously this provides a fast data transfer.

On the other hand, ***buffered I/O*** can be designed so that a block of data can be read from an open file into an intermediate buffer and processed in a suitable manner required by an application (i.e., character by character or a string by string). The ***buffered I/O*** creates and maintains the intermediate buffers. The details of buffer structure (i.e., data buffer, buffer pointer, open file address or file descriptor, etc) are transparent to a user. During opening a ***stream*** (for buffered processing), fopen:

- *opens the specified file using **open** system call;*
- *creates a buffer automatically and;*
- *associates the buffer with the open file.*

After opening a ***stream (e.g., fopen)***, the ***stream-read (e.g., character-read function, such as fgetc)*** and ***stream-write (e.g., character-write function like fputc)*** operations perform data transfer with respect to this intermediate buffer instead of directly dealing with an open file. The first stream-read (a character-read, string-read or binary-read) operation automatically initiates a block-read (i.e., read system call) to fill up the associated buffer, and then the stream-read gets its requested data from this buffer. Subsequent stream-read operations get data from the buffer until it becomes empty. When a stream-read operation finds the buffer in the empty state, it will call a block-read operation to fill it up. Similarly, a program that is writing in buffered mode can accumulate data in the intermediate buffer which is then copied as a block (using a block-write system call) into open-file.

## Buffer Structure

A stream-read (e.g., fgetc) operation needs to know where the next character is available in the buffer. Similarly, a stream-write (e.g., fputc) operation should know where in the buffer it can store the next character. For this purpose, a character pointer is necessary to traverse along the buffer.

```
char *buf_ptr;  /* character pointer */
```

When a stream-read operation finds its associated buffer in the empty state, it should initiate a block-read operation to get the next block of characters from the actual file. Similarly, when a stream-write operation finds its associated buffer in the filled-up state, it initiates a block-write operation to transfer the entire contents of the buffer into the open-file. A block-read or a block-write operation is a low-level or direct I/O (i.e., a system call) operation. Read and write require the address (i.e., the file descriptor) of an open-file, starting address of the actual buffer (i.e., base address of character buffer) and number of characters (i.e., BUFSIZE) to be transferred between buffer and open file.

```
#define BUFSIZE 1024
char IOBUF[BUFSIZE];      /* actual buffer     */
int    fd;     /* saves the channel address of open file   */
char *base_adr; /* address of actual buffer   */
```

Another parameter that may be required for stream operations is a flag to indicate the access modes specified when opening a file. Hence, a flag must be associated with each open file so that every requested stream operation on that file can be checked.

```
int     access_flag;
```

For example, a user may try to write something to a file that was opened for read-only purposes. In order to avoid any illegal operation, file operations check or validate the requests using this flag. In other words, the data structure associated with each open-stream should maintain this information until the stream is closed.

Hence, a prototype of a stream buffer is maintained in stdio.h and used to create a set of stream-BUFFERS (called FILE-type structures) so that each one can be allocated for each open-stream. This segment of stdio.h is shown below:

```
#define _NFILE  20
#define BUFSIZE 1024
typedef struct
        {
         char IOBUF[BUFSIZE];
         char *buf_ptr;
         char *base_adr;
         int fd; /* file descriptor used as address of file */
         int access_flag;
        } FILE;
struct  FILE iob[_NFILE];
```

## 17.4 Use of stdio.h in Stream I/O

The ***stdio.h*** file essentially contains the information, or definitions, required for performing stream I/O operations. This information includes prototype definitions of stream buffer structure, definitions of symbolic constants, like NULL and EOF, for testing characters during character I/O, the file pointers of standard I/O streams (i.e., ***stdin***, ***stdout*** and ***stderr***) and all four basic macro functions (i.e., getc, putc, getchar and putchar) for character I/O.

***Remark:***
*1. The list of definitions in the stdio.h file may vary slightly from one implementation to another. But most of the definitions are standard ones, and we will simply assume that they are included in the stdio.h of any C-compiler.*
*2. When a program uses printf and scanf functions (which also belong to stream I/O), a user need not include stdio.h because they are already kept in the compiled state. However, for any other stream function that may use definitions from stdio.h, a user must include this file. For example, consider the following segment of a program:*

```
. . .
ch = getchar();
if (ch == EOF) exit();
. . .
```

During translation of the above code into object code, C does not know whether getchar is a macro or a library function to resolve at appropriate phase of compilation. Similarly, it wants to know whether EOF is a variable or a constant. Since these symbols are defined in ***stdio.h***, inclusion of this file will enable the compiler to resolve these symbols at compile time.

## 17.5 The stdio Streams

The terminal keyboard and screen are classified as standard input, standard output and standard error (device) files. These files are quite essential for a running program to maintain dialog with its user. Hence, the system (or ***C virtual processor***) automatically opens these files as streams for every running program. The stream addresses (i.e., file pointers) of these files are ***stdin***, ***stdout*** and ***stderr*** and user programs can simply use them to transfer data.

## 17.6 Descriptions of Stream I/O Control Functions

### 17.6.1 The fopen Function

The ***fopen*** function is used to open an existing file as a stream or to create a file and open it as a stream. The function call carries two string arguments: the first string specifies the name of a file and the second string specifies the access mode indicating the purpose for which it was opened – for reading, writing or appending purposes. The prototype definition of this function is shown below:

*FILE *fopen( char *file_name, char *access_mode);*

This function call opens the required file, associates a buffer structure with the open file and then returns a pointer to the buffer structure. Since this returned value is a pointer to the type definition of stream buffer (in ***stdio.h***) called FILE, a pointer variable (i.e., fp) of this type is required to receive the address of the stream. When an error occurs during open function, a NULL value is returned. It is very important to test this returned value before proceeding with read/write operation.

The file name can be any legal string selected during creation of a file. The access_mode information is a string of one or more characters, each specifying the mode for which an open file will react. For example, if we open a stream for reading, the stream will respond properly for a read-command. Similarly, when a stream is opened for read and write purposes, the stream will accept both read and write operations. If a stream is opened for reading only, a write request will get an error response from the open file. **Table 17.2** shows the string values of the allowed access modes.

> ***Remark:*** *When a nonexistent file is opened as a stream in either writing or appending mode, a new file is created under the supplied file name.*

*Table 17.2 **fopen's** response for various access modes*

| | | |
|---|---|---|
| **r** | To open a text file for READ ONLY | 1. if the given file exists, it is opened as a read-only stream;<br>2. file position indicator (or file cursor) is set to the beginning of the file;<br>3. if the given file does not exist, a NULL pointer is returned. |
| **w** | To open a text file for WRITE ONLY | 1. if the given file exists, it is truncated before opened as a WRITE-ONLY stream (original contents are lost);<br>2. if the given file does not exist, a new file is created and opened as a WRITE-ONLY stream;<br>3. in both cases, the file position indicator (or file cursor) is set to the beginning of the stream. |
| **a** | To open a text file for APPENDING | 1. if the given file exists, it is opened as a stream for writing;<br>2. file position indicator (or file cursor) is set to the end of the file;<br>3. if the given file does not exist, it is created before opening as a WRITE_ONLY stream; in this case, the file position indicator (file cursor) is set to the beginning of the stream. |
| **rb** | To open a binary file for READ ONLY | 1. if the given file exists, it is opened as a read-only stream;<br>2. file position indicator (or file cursor) is set to the beginning of the file;<br>3. if the given file does not exist, a NULL pointer is returned. |
| **wb** | To open a binary file for WRITE ONLY | 1. if the given file exists, it is truncated before opened as a WRITE-ONLY stream (original contents are lost);<br>2. if the given file does not exist, a new file is created and opened as a WRITE-ONLY stream;<br>3. in both cases, the file position indicator (or file cursor) is set to the beginning of the stream. |
| **ab** | To open a binary file for APPENDING | 1. if the given file exists, it is opened as a stream for writing;<br>2. file position indicator (or file cursor) is set to the end of the file;<br>3. if the given file does not exist, it is created before opening as a WRITE_ONLY stream; in this case, the file position indicator (file cursor) is set to the beginning of the stream. |
| **r+** | To open a text file for READ and WRITE | 1. if the given file exists, it is opened as a stream for both reading and writing;<br>2. file position indicator (or file cursor) is set to the beginning of the file;<br>3. if the given file does not exist, a NULL pointer is returned. |
| **w+** | To open a text file for WRITE and READ | 1. if the given file exists, it is truncated before opened as a stream for both writing and reading (original contents are lost);<br>2. if the given file does not exist, a new file is created and opened as a WRITE-ONLY stream;<br>3. in both cases, the file position indicator (or file cursor) is set to the beginning of the stream. |

*Table 17.2 (cont.)*

| | | |
|---|---|---|
| **a+** | To open a text file for APPENDING (writing at the end) and READING | 1. if the given file exists, it is opened as a stream for writing at the end (appending) and reading;<br>2. file position indicator (or file cursor) is set to the end of the file;<br>3. if the given file does not exist, it is created before opening as a stream for writing and reading; in this case, the file position indicator (file cursor) is set to the beginning of the stream. |
| **rb+** | To open a binary file for READ and WRITE | 1. if the given file exists, it is opened as a stream for both reading and writing;<br>2. file position indicator (or file cursor) is set to the beginning of the file;<br>3. if the given file does not exist, a NULL pointer is returned. |
| **wb+** | To open a binary file for WRITE and READ | 1. if the given file exists, it is truncated before opened as a stream for both writing and reading (original contents are lost);<br>2. if the given file does not exist, a new file is created and then open as a WRITE-ONLY stream;<br>3. in both cases, the file position indicator (or file cursor) is set to the beginning of the stream. |
| **ab+** | To open a binary file for APPENDING (writing at the end) and READING | 1. if the given file exists, it is opened as a stream for writing at the end (appending) and reading;<br>2. file position indicator (or file cursor) is set to the end of the file;<br>3. if the given file does not exist, it is created before opening as a stream for writing and reading; in this case, the file position indicator (file cursor) is set to the beginning of the stream. |

## Example 17.1:

Show a formal procedure to open a file as stream. Assume that the file already exists and named "file1". Open this file for reading.

```
#include <stdio.h>
void main(void)
{
  /* Convention to open a stream   */
  FILE     *fopen();  /* prototype definition of fopen function to inform compiler that it returns a
pointer to FILE type*/
   FILE      *fp1;   /* declare a variable to get the address of the buffer or the FILE structure
associated with open-stream  */
   fp1 = fopen("file1", "r"); /* open "file1" as a stream for reading and get the address of stream
*/
   if(fp1 == NULL)     /* check whether file is opened successfully   */
     {
       printf("%s cannot open \n", "file1");
       exit(0);
     }
```

```
    else
      {
        /* use fp1 to perform I/O with respect the open file via buffer); */
          . . .
      }
      . . .
} /* End of main */
```

In the above example, fopen opens file1, creates a buffer structure of FILE type, associates the buffer with the open file and returns a pointer to this buffer structure as the stream address. The returned value in fp1 can then be used as a reference address in stream-read operations and is tested to find out the success of the stream-open (i.e., fopen). When fopen fails, it returns a NULL pointer value.

A program can open as many streams as it needs provided that buffer space is not exhausted. Due to the limitation of systems resources, a restriction is generally imposed on the number of files or streams that can be kept open by a user program at any time. The number of files allowed for each program (or process) may be limited by maintaining an optimum size array of FILE structures (or buffers). The _NFILE macro in ***stdio.h*** will indicate the number of buffers available for a user. When we include this file along with our program, this restriction is automatically imposed. Whenever we open a stream, a free element of the buffer structure array is allocated, and its pointer is returned. In general, the fopen function always checks whether the number of files that are currently open has reached the limit (i.e., _NFILE) before opening a file. For example, a system may set _NFILE as 20 to allow each running program (or process) open 20 streams simultaneously.

> ***Remark:*** *Since each program or process is provided with three standard streams (stdin, stdout and stderr) that are already opened, the maximum number of disk files that can be opened as streams will be (_NFILE - 3).*

## 17.6.2 The fclose Function

The ***fclose(fp)*** function is used to formally close a stream and carries the file pointer of the opened file (i.e., stream) as its argument. While closing a stream, ***fclose*** flushes the buffer and disassociates it from the open file to indicate that a file is closed. The function returns an integer value indicating the status of the close operation. The prototype definition of this function is shown below:

```
int    fclose(FILE *file_pointer);
```

If ***fclose*** is successful, the value 0 is returned, or else -1 or EOF is returned.

## Example 17.2:

Show formal procedure for closing a stream.

```
#include <stdio.h>
void main(void)
{
  int    cl_status;
  FILE *fp1;
  FILE *fopen();
  fp1  = fopen("file1", "r") /*open the file "file1" for reading  */
  if(fp1 == NULL)
    {
      printf("%s cannot open \n", "file1");
      exit(0);
    }
    else
      {
        /* use fp1 to read from stream*/
          . . .
      }
    . . .
  /* Convention to close a stream  */
  cl_status = fclose(fp1);  /* close the stream, fp1   */
  if(cl_status != 0)
    {
      printf("%s cannot close \n", "file1s stream");
      exit(0);
    }
    . . .
}
```

In the above paragraph, it was mentioned that one of the functions of ***fclose*** is to flush the associated buffer before closing a file. This happens only for those files that have been opened as output streams. After opening a file as an output stream (i.e., for writing purpose), a program may send data to the open file. In this process, the data is first accumulated in the buffer, and then, if the buffer is filled up, its contents are automatically transferred to the actual file. It is possible that when a program has completed its last send operation, the buffer may not be full and requires someone to perform the transfer of incomplete buffer to the open file. This is accomplished by an fclose call. An ***fclose*** call performs the following functions:

- *checks whether a file is open for writing purpose, and if so, flushes the buffer;*
- *closes the open file using the close system call;*
- *releases the stream buffer so it can be used by another fopen call.*

### Closing files by the exit function call

It is not always necessary to close the open streams using the explicit fclose function call. When a program executes an ***exit*** function call, fclose is performed for each opened stream, and then the ***_exit*** system call is executed to immediately stop the program execution. Even when a program simply falls through the last statement without closing the open streams, an exit will be executed implicitly to close all open streams, suggesting that user programs need not explicitly close the open streams. However, users may close the streams that are no longer required. For example, assume that our program has opened files and completed all writing to those files. While the program execution proceeds without closing the streams, it may be terminated either by a signal from our terminal or from some other process. In this case, the buffers of unclosed streams may be lost.

> ***Remark:*** *When streams are opened either for appending or writing purpose, make sure that they are closed as soon as the last writing is over.*

## 17.6.3 The fflush Function

The ***fflush*** function saves the contents of a stream buffer after the last write operation. In this case, a program need not issue an ***fclose*** to flush the buffer. After ***fflush***, the program can continue safely. The prototype definition of this function is:

```
int  fflush( FILE   *file_pointer);
```

where the argument ***file_pointer*** is the address of the stream that is opened for writing or appending. The function returns 0 if successful and -1 if unsuccessful. It is similar to ***fclose*** except that stream is still in the open state after flushing its buffer.

### A Note about file-cursor

The term "***file-cursor***" means a byte pointer to an open file. This pointer moves along an open file while a reading or writing process proceeds. In other words, it indicates the current position (in an an open file) at which the next read/write should take place. This file-cursor is a long integer maintained by the channel created by the ***open*** system call. (More about the channel data structure and the file cursor is dealt with in ***Chapter 21***.) An ***fopen*** call for reading opens a stream and sets the cursor to the beginning of the associated file. On the other hand, a ***fopen*** call for appending sets the cursor to the end of that file. It is also possible to move a file cursor to anywhere within an open file using a separate function called ***fseek***, discussed in the following section.

> ***Remark:*** *We should be able to distinguish the pointers: file pointer, buffer pointer and file cursor. A file pointer is the address of the allocated stream buffer that is associated with a file on opening a stream belonging to the address of FILE type. A buffer pointer is an integer maintained within a buffer structure of a stream to indicate the character (or byte) position at which the next stream-read or stream-write should proceed. When the buffer pointer reaches the end of the buffer, then the buffer should be either filled or emptied, depending upon whether a stream-read or stream-write is being done. A file-cursor is similar to a buffer pointer, but it moves along the actual open file. A user program does not need to know anything about a buffer pointer, but knowing the position of the file-cursor may be quite useful for a program for emulating random access. A program can find out the current position of the file-cursor with the help of the ftell function.*

### 17.6.4 The fseek Function

The ***fseek*** function is used to move the ***file-cursor*** to a desired position in a file. It carries three arguments to specify a cursor position. The first argument is the file pointer, the second and third arguments are offset and reference origin, respectively. The prototype definition of this function is shown below:

*int fseek(FILE *file_pointer, long offset, int reference_origin);*

where the second argument ***offset*** is a ***long signed integer*** and the third argument ***reference_origin*** is a simple ***integer***. The value of ***reference_origin*** indicates which origin is effective in determining the target position of the file-cursor. The following table shows the values of this argument and their meanings:

| Reference_origin value | Meaning |
|---|---|
| 0 | Beginning of file |
| 1 | Current cursor position of file |
| 2 | End of file |

An ***fseek*** call moves the cursor to point to a character (byte) position in an open file by using the following formula:

*cursor position = reference_origin + offset*

***Returned Value: fseek*** returns an integer value: 0 after a successful seek operation, or non-zero after an unsuccessful seek operation.

### Example 17.3:

After opening a file for reading, move the cursor to the end of the open file.

```
#include <stdio.h>
void main(void)
 { FILE *fp1;
   FILE *fopen();
 if((fp1 = fopen("file1", "r"))== NULL)
   { /* stream-open failed  */
     printf("%s cannot open \n", "file1");
     exit(0);
   }
   else /* file1 is open and its cursor is at the beginning by default */
   { int     sk_status;
     sk_status = fseek(fp1, 0L, 2);  /* move the cursor to the end of file  */
     if(sk_status == 0) /*  check for successful seek operation */
     . . .
   }
 }
```

*Note: 0L in the above fseek statement is the long constant representation of zero.*

### Example 17.4:

After opening a file for reading, move the cursor to the 100th character (or byte) position of the open file.

```
#include <stdio.h>
void main(void)
 { FILE *fp1;
   FILE *fopen();
 if((fp1 = fopen("file1", "r"))== NULL)
   { /* stream-open failed  */
     printf("%s cannot open \n", "file1");
     exit(0);
   }
 else              /* file1 is open and cursor is at the beginning by default */
   {
     fseek(fp1, 99L, 0);  /* move cursor to point to 100th character in the open file  */
     . . .
   }
 }
```

*Note: 99L in the above fseek statement is the long constant representation of 99.*

### Example 17.5:

After opening a file for reading, move the cursor back 10 bytes from the end of the open file.

```
#include <stdio.h>
void main(void)
{ FILE *fp1;
  FILE *fopen();
if((fp1 = fopen("file1", "r"))== NULL)
  { /* stream-open failed */
    printf("%s cannot open \n", "file1");
    exit(0);
  }
else /* file1 is open and cursor is at the beginning by default */
  {
  fseek(fp1, -10L, 2); /*  move the cursor back 10 bytes from the end of file */
    . . .
  }
}
```

## 17.6.5 The ftell Function

The ***ftell*** function call is used to find out the current file-cursor position of the open file. The prototype definition of this function is shown below:

***long ftell( FILE *file_pointer);***

The call returns a long integer value as the offset from the beginning of the open file.

### Example 17.6:

After opening a file for reading, find out the length of the file using an ftell call.

```
#include <stdio.h>
void main(void)
{ FILE *fp1, *fopen();
  long ftell(),  long file_pos;
  if((fp1 = fopen("file1", "r")) == NULL)
    { /* fopen() is unsuccessful */
      printf("Cannot open file1 \n");
      exit();
    }
```

```
    else /* file1 is opened successfully and the cursor is at the beginning by default */
    {
      if(fseek(fp1, 0L, 2) == 0) /*  move the cursor to the end of file  */
      {
        file_pos = ftell(fp);
        printf("Length of file1 is %d \n", file_pos);
      }
      . . .
    }
  . . .
}
```

## The fgetpos function

The ***fgetpos*** function call is used to record the current value of the file position indicator (file cursor) for the open stream. The type of the file position indicator (called fpos_t and defined in stdio.h) is an unsigned one to cover the largest size of an ANSI file. The prototype definition of this function is shown below:

```
#include <stdio.h>
int fgetpos( FILE *stream, fpos_t *pos);
```

The call stores the current value of the file position indicator in the object pointed to by ***pos***. The stored value can be used to reset the indicator to its original position using the complementary function called ***fsetpos***. A call to ***fgetpos*** returns zero for successful operation and nonzero when an error occurs. An error is indicated in the global variable ***errno*** by storing an implementation defined value.

## The fsetpos function

The ***fsetpos*** function call is used to restore the file position indicator (file cursor) to its original position. It is assumed that the original value of the indicator for the stream has been saved previously by a ***fgetpos*** call. The prototype definition of this function is shown below:

```
#include <stdio.h>
int fsetpos( FILE *stream, const fpos_t *pos);
```

The call stores the value of the object pointed to by ***pos*** in the file position indicator of the stream. It also sets/resets the end of file indicator if necessary. A ***fsetpos*** call returns zero for successful operation and nonzero when an error occurs. An error is indicated in the global variable ***errno*** by storing an implementation defined value.

### The rewind function

The ***rewind*** function call is used to reset the file position indicator (file cursor) for the open stream to the beginning of the file. The prototype definition of this function is shown below:

```
#include <stdio.h>
void rewind( FILE *stream);
```

One can also use the random access function, ***fseek***, to set the file position indicator to the beginning of the open file. The difference is that ***rewind*** is simpler for this function.

**Example 17.7:** Count number of 'A's and 'Z's in a file.

```
#include <stdio.h>
void main(void)
{
  FILE *fp;
     fp = fopen('myfile.txt', 'r');
     while(!feof)
           { if (getc(fp) == 'A')
                A_ctr++;
           }
     rewind(fp);
     while(!feof)
           { if (getc(fp) == 'Z')
                Z_ctr++;
           }
}
```

## 17.6.6 Miscellaneous Functions

### The rename function

The ***rename*** function call is used to change the existing file name to a new name. The prototype definition of this function is shown below:

```
#include <stdio.h>
int rename( char *old_fname, char *new_fname);
```

The ***rename*** function call generates a file name unique and distinct from any other file name in the current directory. It returns zero on successful operation, or a nonzero value to indicate that an error occurred.

**Example 17.8:** Rename a given file.

```
#include <stdio.h>
void main(void)
{
    if (rename('assign1.c', 'assign2.c') != 0)
      printf(' The file cannot be renamed \n');
    else
      printf(' The file name is changed \n');
}
```

## The tmpfile function

The ***tmpfile*** function call is used to create a temporary file. The prototype definition of this function is shown below:

```
#include <stdio.h>
FILE *tmpfile(void);
```

The ***tmpfile*** call creates a temporary file and automatically opens the same as a stream for updating purposes. It returns the file pointer of the open stream on successful operation, or returns a NULL pointer. The files that are created by this call will be automatically removed when the files are closed or at program termination.

## The tmpnam function

The ***tmpnam*** function call is used to generate a valid file name unique and distinct from the file names in the current directory. Programmers mainly use these names for creating new (and temporary) files. Both these parameters are defined in ***stdio.h***. The prototype definition of this function is shown below:

```
#include <stdio.h>
char *tmpnam(char *tfname);
```

The call stores the generated name in the string object pointed to by ***tfname*** and returns the pointer to that object. When the argument is a NULL pointer, the generated file name is stored in an internal string object and returns its pointer. There are two limitations that should be considered before using this function. First, a program can create maximum of ***TMP_MAX*** names. Second, the string argument used to bring the generated name should be at least ***L_tmpnam*** characters. The standard specifies the value of ***TMP_MAX*** should be at least 25. That is, a program can create at least twenty-five temporary files. The value of ***L_tmpname*** may be specified by an implementation.

### The remove function

The ***remove*** function call is used to erase an existing file from the current directory. The prototype definition of this function is defined in stdio.h, as shown below:

*int remove( char *fname);*

The ***remove*** function call returns zero on successful operation, or a nonzero value to indicate that it is not able to remove the file.

**Example 17.9:** Remove a file from the current directory.

```
#include <stdio.h>
void main(void)
{
    if (remove( 'old_file.dat') != 0)
        printf(' The file cannot be removed \n');
}
```

## 17.7 Stream Functions for Character I/O

### 17.7.1 Character I/O Using getc, putc and ungetc

#### 17.7.1.1 The getc Macro (or fgetc Function)

The ***getc*** macro is used to read a character from a stream. This call carries the file pointer of the stream as its argument and returns the next character from the buffer. The function returns a character in the form of an integer value. The prototype definition of this macro function is shown below:

*int getc( FILE *file_pointer);*

For example, a typical call to read a character from the keyboard is:

```
{
    int    ch;
           . . .
    ch = getc(stdin);  /* the keyboard file that is already open as stream whose file
                          pointer is stdin  */
}
```

> ***Remark:*** *When getc finds a character, it returns a character value, but when the cursor reaches the end of the open file, it returns -1 as the EOF marker. In order to catch this negative value properly, an integer parameter may be more appropriate, which is further discussed in Section 17.3.3. The library functions, fgetc and fputc, are equivalent to getc and putc macros except for some difference in performance.*

## Example 17.10:

Input a key (i.e., a character) from the keyboard file and find the number of occurrences of this character in a text file called file1.

```
#include <stdio.h>
void main(void)
{ FILE *fp1, *fopen();
  int     count;
  char  key_ch, file_ch;
    if((fp1 = fopen("file1", "r")) == NULL)
    {
       printf("Cannot open file1 \n");
       exit();
    }
  else /* file1 is open and the cursor is at the beginning by default */
    {
       key_ch = getc(stdin); /* get a key character from the stdin stream*/
       count = 0;
       while( (file_ch = getc(fp1)) != EOF)
         {
           if (file_ch == key_ch)
             count++;
         }
       printf("Number of occurrences of '%c' is %d \n", key_ch, count);
    }
}
```

### 17.7.1.2 The putc Macro (or fputc Function)

The ***putc*** macro is used to write a character to an open stream. It takes two arguments to perform this task: the character and the file pointer of the open stream. The prototype definition of this macro function is shown below:

```
int    putc( int  character_value,    FILE  *file_pointer);
```

It returns the character value if successful, or returns EOF (i.e., -1) if unsuccessful.

### 17.7.1.3 The ungetc Macro

The ***ungetc*** macro pushes a character back into the input stream. Its definition is:

int ungetc(int character_value, FILE *file_pointer)

## Example 17.11:

Display the contents of a disk file called *chapter1.txt* and the number of characters displayed, on the screen file.

```
#include <stdio.h>
void main(void)
{ int ich, count=0;
  FILE    *fp_chap1, *fopen();
  fp_chap1 = fopen("chapter1.txt", "r");
  if (fp_chap1 == NULL)
    {
      printf("Cannot open chapter1.txt \n");
      exit();
    }
   while((ich=getc(fp_chap1) != EOF))
    { putc(ich,stdout);
     count++;
    }
   printf("Number of characters displayed is %d \n", count);
}
```

## Example 17.12:

Write a program to copy the characters from file1 to file2.

```
#include <stdio.h>
void main(void)
{ FILE *fp1, *fp2;
  FILE *fopen(); /* prototype definition to indicate that fopen returns a pointer to
                    FILE structure */
  int  ch;
   if((fp1 = fopen("file1", "r")) == NULL) /* open file1 as a stream */
   {
     printf("Cannot open file1 \n");
     exit(0);
   }
   if((fp2 = fopen("file2", "w")) == NULL)  /* open file2 as a stream */
   {
     printf("Cannot open file2 \n");
     exit(0);
   }
```

```
    while((ch = getc(fp1)) != EOF) /* read a character from fp1-stream */
          putc(ch, fp2);     /* and copy it to fp2-stream if it is not EOF */
    if(fclose(fp1) == -1)
    printf("Cannot close fp1-stream (file1) \n");
    if(fclose(fp2) == -1)
    printf("Cannot close fp2-stream (file2) \n");
}
```

The C-virtual machine has already opened the terminal screen file as two separate streams called stdout and stderr. The stderr stream is used for sending error messages, whereas stdout is for normal output from a program. ***Example 17.8*** shows how the same macro is used to output messages to the terminal. ***Examples 17.9*** and ***17.10*** show how the macros getc and putc are used to copy files.

## Example 17.13:

Write a program to copy the characters from file1 to stdout stream.

```
#include <stdio.h>
void main(void)
{ FILE *fp1;
  FILE *fopen();
  int  ch;
   if((fp1 = fopen("file1", "r")) == NULL) /* open file1 as a stream */
   {
     printf("file1 cannot open \n");
     exit(0);
   }
   while((ch = getc(fp1)) != EOF)   /* read a character from fp1-stream */
         putc(ch, stdout);          /* and copy it to stdout until EOF */
   if(fclose(fp1) == -1)
   printf("Cannot close fp1-stream (file1) \n");
}
```

### 17.7.2 Character I/O Using getchar, putchar and ungetchar

As mentioned in ***Table 17.2***, the ***getchar*** and ***putchar*** macros are specifically used for character I/O of the stdin and stdout streams respectively. A minor advantage of these two macros is that we don't need to specify the stream addresses (i.e., file pointers, stdin and stdout) in these calls. In fact, the standard I/O coding is simplified further. Actually, getchar and getc(stdin) are exactly same. Similarly, putchar(c) and putc(c, stdout) are the same. Hence, as an example, we can use either:

***putc('A', stdout)*** or ***putchar('A');***

both will display the character 'A' on the terminal screen.

### Example 17.14:

Read characters from stdin and write them to stdout using getchar and putchar macros.

```
#include <stdio.h>
void main(void)
{ char   ch;
  while((ch = getchar()) != EOF)  /*get a character from stdin */
    {
      putchar(ch);  /* display the character on the screen   */
    }
  /* when control_D is input, program exits here  */
}
```

### Example 17.15:

Write a program to count the characters in a line input from the keyboard. Assume that the line is terminated by a newline character.

```
#include  <stdio.h>
void main(void)
{ int count = 0; /*  Note: a simple local variable can be initialized    */
    while(getchar() != '\n') count++;
 printf("The line length is %d \n", count);
}
```

### Example 17.16:

Show the C-code when a line is terminated by either a newline character or EOF.

```
#include  <stdio.h>
void main(void)
{ int count = 0, ich;
   while(((ich =getchar()) != '\n') && (ich != EOF)) count++;
    printf("The line length is %d \n", count);
}
```

### 17.7.3 What Is EOF?

A disk file in the Unix file system can be assumed to contain a series of data bytes. That is, every byte (including the last byte of a file) is considered a data byte. Since there is no special byte used to indicate the end of file, a stream-read operation (i.e., ***getc*** macro or ***fgetc*** function) adopts an indirect mechanism to indicate that the reading process has encountered the end of file. The stream-read returns a character when it finds the next character available in the open file and returns -1 as End Of File (***EOF***) indicator when there is no next character available in the open file.

> ***Remark:*** *The keyboard of a terminal is also treated as a file, but it is a virtual file without any stored data. It is assumed that it is a dynamic file with a capability of supplying a variable amount of data. Hence, the keyboard file is assumed to maintain an end of file character, which is Control_D. In this case, stream-read is looking for Control_D character from the keyboard to generate the End Of File flag (-1) and return it to the calling program.*

## Significance of returned value of getc or getchar

***getc*** returns an 8-bit character when data is available and an integer value, -1 as ***EOF***, when the stream-reading process reaches the end of the open file. The returned value is really a union of character and integer. For this reason, ***getc*** always returns an integer which can carry either a character or integer value. Hence, it is more appropriate to assign the returned value to an integer variable so that the ***EOF*** value can also be received and then tested at a later time to detect the ***EOF*** condition. On the other hand, if we assign the returned integer value to a character variable, the lvalue will receive a lower (8-bit) rvalue. When -1 is received, the lower 8-bit value will represent the unsigned value of 255 and testing this value for the end of file condition will present a problem. Even if we define a character variable as:

```
signed char ch;
```

some compilers may always create unsigned character variables. If we conduct a test for EOF condition as shown in the following example, it may fail.

```
#define TRUE    1
    . . .
char ch;
    while(TRUE)
    {
    ch = getc(fp);
    if (ch== EOF) break;  /* This test may miss end of file condition  */
        else { process the character in ch;}
    }
```

## Integer variable to receive returned value of getc or getchar

It is always safe to use an integer to receive the returned value of ***getc*** or ***getchar***. This integer can be used at a later time to test for the ***EOF*** condition. The following code shows this case.

```
#define  TRUE     1
     . . .
int  k;
     while(TRUE)
     {
     k = getc(fp);
     if (k== EOF) break;  /* test will be successful when end of file occurs  */
          else { process character in k;}
     }
```

> ***Remark:*** *In order to make sure that the test catches the end of file condition, irrespective of which compiler compiles our program, we will always use an integer variable as a character buffer. The following codes will be valid for all compilers:*
>
> ```
> #include <stdio.h>
> void  main(void)
> {int ich;
>    . . .
>    ich = getchar();  /*gets a character from the keyboard file */
>    if (ich ==EOF) /* test for end of file condition   */
>                /* (EOF is defined as -1 in stdio.h)   */
>      exit();        /* if end of file is true, then stop program   */
>    else
>      /* process the character   */
>    . . .
> }
> ```

However, the problem described above can be overcome by testing the value of ***getc*** (or ***getchar***) expression directly instead of storing it and then testing it in a separate expression. This is shown below:

```
#include <stdio.h>
#define TRUE   1
void main(void)
{ char   ch;
  while(TRUE)
  {
  if ((ch = getc(fp)) == EOF)) break;  /*  test will catch end of file condition  */
  else
    {
      /* process the character in ch;  */
        . . .
    }
  }
```

or

```
#include <stdio.h>
 void main(void)
{ char   ch;
    . . .
   while((ch=getchar()) != EOF)
    {
      /* process the character in ch;  */
        . . .
    }
    . . .
}
```

In the above coding, the evaluated value of *ch = getc(fp)* is still available in the expression buffer. When -1 is returned, the buffer accumulates this value which can then be used for a valid EOF comparison test. In this case a character variable does not cause any harm. In the above example, the expression in the while statement is evaluated as follows:

- *getchar returns character value in C-processor's buffer; this value is a normal integer;*
- *then the buffer value is assigned to ch; only lower 8-bits of this buffer is assigned to ch;*
- *the value of this assignment expression is still available as full integer value in the buffer, and is used in the next subexpression, i.e., comparison test with EOF (-1).*

This provides a valid integer test which would eventually catch the end of file condition.

## 17.8 String and Line I/O Operations

There are four string I/O functions available in the standard I/O library: ***gets*** and ***puts*** for specifically line I/O with respect to the standard input and output files (or the ***stdin*** and ***stdout*** streams), and ***fgets*** and ***fputs*** for string I/O with respect to any file. They are also called line I/ O functions.

### 17.8.1 String I/O Functions (fgets and fputs)

The string I/O functions read or write strings with respect to a text file which may be either a disk file or a terminal file that is opened as a stream. In these functions, a newline character is treated the same as all other characters as a part of the string.

### The fgets function

The prototype definition of the ***fgets*** function is shown below.

```
char *fgets( char  *str, int n, FILE *fp);
```

The purpose of this function is to read a string of n-1 characters from a stream whose file pointer is fp, and store the extracted data, along with a ***NULL*** character in the given string argument (str). Reading continues until either the n-1th character, a newline or ***EOF*** occurs. If n-1 characters are read without any newline or ***EOF***, then a ***NULL*** ('\0') character is appended as the nth character. If a newline occurs during reading, then it is also stored in the string and then a ***NULL*** character is appended to make a legal string. When ***EOF*** is read, it is stored as a newline and then a ***NULL*** character is appended. ***fgets*** treats the entire contents of an open stream as one long string and is used to read segment by segment for processing. Hence, a newline character is also treated as a normal character.

The returned value shows whether the operation is successful or not. If a call is successful, it returns a pointer to the string argument, otherwise it returns a ***NULL*** value. If we want to read a string from the keyboard file, we can use the following function call:

```
{
    char *pstr;
      . . .
    pstr = fgets(char *str, int n, stdin);
}
```

Since the keyboard file is already open as a standard input stream, and its file pointer is ***stdin***, the above call will read a string, including a newline character, from the keyboard device. When we input ***EOF*** (***Control_D***) from the keyboard file, ***fgets*** will return a NULL pointer, indicating the end of the ***stdin*** stream or keyboard file.

### The fputs function

The *fputs* function is used to write a string of characters to a stream whose file pointer is *fp*. We know that a string is delimited by a *NULL* character, and hence, the writing operation continues until a *NULL* marker is encountered. Remember that *fputs* is meant to write the exact contents of a string to a open stream; it does not add any additional characters (i.e., a newline character) at the end of string output. On the other hand, there is a separate *puts* function for the *stdout* stream which outputs a newline character following every string to make a line output. This is explained in the following section. The prototype definition of the *fputs* function is shown below:

```
int    fputs(char *s, FILE *fp);
```

The function returns a positive integer (i.e., number of characters written) showing the normal status of the operation. When it returns EOF (i.e., -1), it indicates that the operation has failed. This error may be due to a stream being closed.

## 17.8.2 The line I/O (i.e., gets and puts) functions

The terminal files (or *stdio* streams) are used to maintain an interactive dialog between a running program and the user. In this mode, the keyboard input, as well as screen output, are normally in the form of lines. For example, a command line interpreter outputs a prompt line and receives a command line. To facilitate this requirement, *gets* and *puts* have been implemented.

### The gets function

The *gets* function is used to extract a string from a line of data input via stdin and store it in the string, **s**. This function reads character by character from the keyboard file (via *stdin* stream) into the string argument until it encounters a newline character. When it reads the newline character, it replaces this character with a NULL character in the given string. The prototype definition of this function is shown below:

```
char  *gets( char *s );
```

This function returns the address of the string, s. When it comes across an end of file character from the keyboard (i.e., Control_D), it returns a NULL pointer.

### The puts function

The *puts* function is treated as a line output function for the *stdout* stream rather than a simple string output function, as the case with fputs (str,stdout). After outputting the string contents,

***puts*** always puts in a newline character. This function outputs the NULL-terminated text from the given string (***s***) to the ***stdout*** stream. When it comes across the ***NULL*** character, it outputs a newline character to mark output as a line on the screen. The prototype definition of the ***puts*** function is shown below:

```
int    puts(char  *s);
```

The function normally returns a positive integer, showing the number of characters written. When it fails, it returns EOF (-1).

## 17.9 Binary I/O in Streams

So far we have seen character and string I/O in streams. These I/O operations are quite useful for maintaining and processing files of character and string data structures. However, many of our applications, particularly the commercial ones, use composite data structures (structures and unions) as fundamental elements of a file. Some programs may accumulate arrays of data in a file for later processing. These programs may be required to store or retrieve such data objects (either composite data elements or arrays) in binary form to or from a file. For this purpose, stream I/O provides the ***fwrite*** and ***fread*** functions. The ***fwrite*** function can write one or more data objects to a file through an open stream. Similarly, the ***fread*** function can read one or more data objects from an open stream. The prototype definitions of these two functions are shown below:

```
int  fread( char   *buffer, int   block_size, int   n_blk, FILE  *fp);
int  fwrite( char   *buffer, int  block_size, int  n_blk, FILE  *fp);
```

where ***buffer*** may contain data of some integral number of records or blocks; ***block_size*** is the number of bytes (or characters) per record or block; ***n_blk*** is the number of blocks or records to be read or written and; ***fp*** is the file pointer of an open stream.

Both functions normally return an integer showing how many blocks or records have been successfully read or written. If an error occurs, both return zero and set the error indicator for stream.

**Example 17.17:**
Write the contents of an integer array to a disk file.

```
#include <stdio.h>
int  k[6] = {0, 1, 2, 3, 4, 5};
void main(void)
  { FILE *fp, *fopen();
   int i, n_blk;
   /* Now store the array k in a file called afile */
     if((fp = fopen("file1", "w")) == NULL) /* open file1 as a stream */
     {
       printf("file1 cannot open \n");
       exit(0);
     }
    n_blk = fwrite((char *)k, 6*(sizeof(int)), 1, fp);
    printf("%d Number of blocks stored : %d \n", n_blk);
    if(fclose(fp) == -1)
      printf("file1 cannot close \n");
  }
```

In the above example, k is a 6-element integer array. Since ***sizeof(int)*** supplies the number of bytes required to store an integer element, the size of the whole array is calculated as

*6 * (sizeof(int))*

bytes. The name k is a pointer to the first integer element. The starting byte address of this contiguous array memory can be obtained by the following cast operation which converts an integer address into a byte address:

*(char *)k*

In the ***fwrite*** function call, the first parameter (char *)k is the byte address of k, the second parameter 6 * (***sizeof(int)***) is the size of the block of memory, the third parameter, 1, indicates that we are to write a single block and the fourth parameter is the stream address.

## Example 17.18:

Read the contents of the file created in the above example into another integer array and print the same on the screen file.

```
#include <stdio.h>
void main(void)
  { FILE *fp, *fopen();
   int  m[6];
   int i, n_blk;
   /* Read file1 back into array m */
     if((fp = fopen("file1", "r")) == NULL) /* open file1 as a stream */
     {
       printf("file1 cannot open \n");
       exit();
     }
    n_blk = fread((char *)m, 6*(sizeof(int)), 1, fp);
    printf("%d Number of blocks stored : %d \n", n_blk);
    if(fclose(fp) == -1)
      printf("file1 cannot close \n");
    /* Now print the array contents */
    for(i = 0; i < 6; i++)
      printf(" %d ", m[i]);
    printf(" \n");
  }
```

### Example 17.19:

Write the contents of a 2-dimensional array of real type to a disk file.

```
#include<stdio.h>
float a[3][2] = {00, 01, 10, 11, 20, 21};
void main(void)
{ FILE *fp, *fopen();
  int n_blk, i;
  if ((fp = fopen("file2", "w")) == NULL)
    {
      printf("file2 cannot open ");
      exit();
    }
   n_blk = fwrite((char **)a, 2*(sizeof(float)), 3, fp);
   printf("No. of blocks written: %d \n",n_blk);
   if(fclose(fp) == -1)
     printf("file2 cannot close \n");
}
```

In the above example, ***a*** is a 2-dimensional real array. It contains three rows and two columns. Hence, it contains totally 3*2 (6) real elements. Since each real element consumes ***sizeof(float)*** bytes, the whole array is stored in a contiguous memory of

*6 * (sizeof(float))*

bytes. The program writes this whole memory as three blocks and each block is of row size. Hence, each row (block) size is

*2*(sizeof(float))*

The names ***a[0]***, ***a[1]*** and ***a[2]*** are pointers to first, second and third rows, and the name ***a*** is the pointer to array of row addresses. Hence, the starting byte address of this array in memory can be obtained by the following cast operation which converts an address of address to real element into byte address:

*(char **)a*

In the ***fwrite*** function call, the first parameter (char **)***a*** is the byte address of ***a***, the second parameter 2*(***sizeof(float)***) is the size of the block of memory, the third parameter, 3, is to write three blocks and the fourth parameter is the stream address.

## Example 17.20:

Read the contents of ***file2*** into another real array and print the same on screen file.

```
#include<stdio.h>
float b[3][2];
void main(void)
{ FILE *fp, *fopen();
  int n_blk, i, j;
  float b[3][2];
  if ((fp = fopen("file2", "r")) == NULL)
    {
     printf("file2 cannot open ");
     exit();
    }
  n_blk = fread((char **)b, 2*(sizeof(float)), 3, fp);
  printf("No. of blocks read: %d \n",n_blk);
  for(i=0; i < 3; i++)
    for(j=0; j < 2; j++)
      printf(" %d, ",b[i][j]);
  printf(" \n ");
}
```

## Use of feof during binary input

Usually, when a file is open for input, the EOF indicator that is part of the FILE structure is set to false (or the zero value). When the reading process reaches the physical end of the file, then the end of file indicator is set to true (or a non-negative value). The end of file indicator value can be obtained by using ***feof*** function. The prototype definition of this function is defined in stdio.h as:

*int feof( FILE *stream);*

During reading, fread returns number of blocks read from the open file. If the returned value is less than the number of blocks attempted during a fread call, either the EOF might have reached or an I/O error could have occurred. In order to verify whether the EOF condition occurred, one can use the feof function.

**Example 17.21:** Write a program that uses feof during input from an integer binary file. Assume that the binary file contains an unknown number of integers.

```
#include <stdio.h>
void main(void)
{ FILE *fp;
  int item, not_eof;
     fp = fopen('int_file', 'rb');
     not_eof = 1;
     do
       {
      if (fread(&item, sizeof item, 1, fp) == 1)
          {/* process the item */
            printf ( ' %d \n', item);
          }
      else
          { /* check whether end of file or an error has occurred */
           if (feof(fp) == 0) /* end of file is not reached */
           {
             printf(' Read Error occurred. \n');
             exit();
           }
           else
             not_eof = 0
          }
      }while(not_eof)

}
```

One can also use the feof function to control the binary reading, as shown in the following example.

**Example 17.22:** Write a program that uses feof to control the binary reading. Assume that the binary file contains an unknown number of integers.

```
#include <stdio.h>
void main(void)
{ FILE *fp;
  int item;
    fp = fopen('int_file', 'rb');
    while(!feof(fp) )
     {
    if (fread(&item, sizeof item, 1, fp) == 1)
        {/* process the item */
          printf ( ' %d \n', item);
        }
    else
        { /* an I/O error has occurred */
             printf(' Read Error occurred. \n');
             exit();
        }
    }; /* End of while loop */
}
```

## Use of ferror in binary I/O

Whenever an error occurs during a stream I/O operation, the file error indicator that is a part of the FILE structure is set to true (or non-zero value). The value of the file error indicator can be obtained by using the feof function. The prototype definition of this function is defined in stdio.h as:

***int ferror( FILE *stream);***

During reading, fread returns the number of blocks read from the open file. If the returned value is less than the number of blocks attempted during a fread call, either the end of file might have been reached or an I/O error occurred. In order to verify whether the EOF condition occurred, one can use the feof function.

## Use of ferror in text I/O

After opening a text file for reading, getc may be used to read characters until EOF is returned. The getc function returns EOF in two situations:

1. *when the file position indicator of the opened file reaches the physical end of the file, it returns EOF to indicate that there is no more character to read;*
2. *when an I/O error occurs, then it also returns EOF.*

In order to verify at what condition getc has returned an EOF, the ferror function can be used. This is explained in the following example.

**Example 17.23:** Write a program that uses ferror to control the text reading. Assume that a text file called ch_file exists.

```
#include <stdio.h>
void main(void)
{ FILE *fp;
  int ch;
     fp = fopen('ch_file', 'r');
     while((ch = getc(fp)) != EOF)
       {
       /* process the item */
         printf( ' %c \n', ch);
       }
     if(ferror(fp) != 0)
       { /* an I/O error has occurred */
       printf(' Read Error occurred. \n');
       exit();
       }
}
```

## clearerr

The ***clearerr*** function is useful to clear the file error and EOF indicators of a specified sream. The prototype definition of the function as stored in ***stdio.h*** is:

*void clearerr(* stream);*

**Example 17.24:** Write a program that uses clearerr to control the text reading. Assume that a text file called ch_file exists that is displayed on the screen file.

```
#include <stdio.h>
void main(void)
{ FILE *fp;
  int ch;
    fp = fopen('ch_file', 'r');
    while((!feof)
      {
        ch = getc(fp);
        if (ferror(fp))
          {
          clearerr(fp); /* clear the file error indicator */
          printf( ' A file error occurred \n');
          }
        else
          putchar(ch);
      }/* End of while */
}
```

## 17.10 Formatted I/O

We have looked at character and string I/Os with respect to streams. These functions are useful only for text processing, but most of the data processing applications read mixed data either from the console terminal or from a data file. Such inputs would normally include different types of data in one line. Similarly, different types of data from memory can be formatted in a line of output to the terminal or to another file. These I/O are basically accomplished by ***fscanf*** and ***fprintf***.

### 17.10.1 The fscanf Function

The ***fscanf*** reads a text file to extract the values for the given arguments using the given format specification. The format of this function call is shown below:

```
int    fscanf( FILE *file_pointer, char *control_string, arg_list);
```

where ***file_pointer*** is the stream address, ***control_string*** specifies the format information, and ***arg_list*** (i.e argument list) carries the addresses of variables (or reference parameters). The ***fscanf*** function normally returns an integer value showing the number of inputs successfully done (or number of values successfully extracted, converted and stored in arguments). If a matching error exists between an input and control string, zero is returned. For example, assume that an ***fscanf*** call expects 10 values; but receives only 5. In this case, it returns 5, indicating that it received 5 values. On the other hand if input ends before first conversion or first matching failure, EOF is returned. ***Table 17.3*** shows the various format specifiers for this function.

*Table 17.3: Format Specifiers and flags for fscanf (or scanf) function*

| Format Specifier | Input Data Type expected |
|---|---|
| d | Decimal Integer (eg. 9999) |
| i | An Integer (a decimal, an octal or an hexadecimal; (eg. 16 or 020 or 0x10) |
| o | Octal Integer (eg. 077 or simply 77); this conversion interprets the given input as an octal whether a leading zero is supplied or not. |
| x | Hexadecimal Integer (eg. 0xffff or simply ffff); this conversion interprets the given input as an hexadecimal whether a leading 0x is supplied or not. |
| u | Unsigned Decimal Integer (eg. 1024). |
| c | Just a Character (ie. external representation of a character that need not be within a pair of single quotes; eg. A); a white space character is also treated as a significant value. |
| s | An array of Characters delimited by a white space (ie. external representation of a string; it need not be within a pair of double quotes; eg. TEXT ). |
| e, f, g | Optionally a signed Real number with optional decimal point, or with optional exponent. |
| l, L | When l or L flag precedes d, i, or o, the conversion leads to long integer type. |
| h | When this flag precedes d, i, o, or h, the conversion leads to short integer type. |
| l | When this flag precedes f, e, or g, the conversion leads to double type. |
| L | When this flag precedes f, e, or g, the conversion leads to long double type. |

### Example 17.25:

Write a program to scan an integer from the stdin stream and print the same on the screen file.

```
#include <stdio.h>
void main(void)
     { int k;
fscanf(stdin,"%d", &k);
     printf("k = %d \n", k);
}
```

When we run this program, it waits for the input from stdin. The following input will be scanned and printed.

Keyboard input:
36<new_line>

Screen output:
k = 36
%(cursor position)

> ***Remark:*** *So far we have seen that scanf requires the address of k to store the scanned value in that location. If k was sent instead of &k, we simply pass the value, which is of no use for storing purpose.*

**Example 17.26:** Write a program to scan four integers from the stdin stream and print them on the screen file.

```
#include <stdio.h>
void main(void)
{ int a[4], i, scan_status;
   scan_status = fscanf(stdin, "%d,%d,%d,%d", &a[0],&a[1],&a[2],&a[3]);
          /*  or  */
 /* scan_status = fscanf(stdin, "%d,%d,%d,%d", a,a+1,a+2,a+3);    */
   printf("Number of scanned data items = %d", scan_status);
   for(i = 0; i < scan_status; i++)
     printf("%d; ",a[i]);
   printf( \n");
}
```

When we run this program, it waits for the input from stdin. In this case, the format specifies that four integer inputs, delimited by commas, are expected from the keyboard file. This is shown below:

Keyboard input:

    10,20,30,40<new_line>

Screen output:

    Number of scanned data items = 4
    10; 20; 30;40;
  %(cursor position)

The *fscanf* function normally ignores all white spaces (space, tab, newline, etc) and scans the text only for the values. That means, when the above program is run, the four input values can be supplied with freely intermixed white spaces.

## Scanning procedure for integers and reals

While scanning the contents of a stream, the *fscanf* function follows the rules given below:

- It ignores the leading white spaces (space, tab and newline) while scanning for numerical strings.
- If more than one data item is scanned, *fscanf* looks for the delimiter that is specified in the control string before it extracts the next value.

  "%d,%d " : indicates that a comma must follow after inputting the first value.

- In the multiple input case, if a delimiter is missing or the next character does not match the current format, scanning will not proceed further. **fscan** will return the number of data items read successfully.
- If the delimiter is not specified, then white **space** is assumed as a delimiter.

  "%f%f " : no delimiter is specified; *fscanf* expects a white space by default.

## The scanf function

The *scanf* function is the special case of *fscanf* in that it always receives the input from the terminal's keyboard file. Its format is shown below:

***int scanf(char *control_string, pointers to arguments);***

For example, *scanf("%d", &i);* will read a numerical string from the keyboard and convert it to integer(i.e., binary) and then store it in the location &i.

The same formatted input using ***fscanf*** is:

*fscanf(stdin, "%d", &i);* which reads a numerical string from the ***stdin*** stream (i.e., keyboard), converts it to integer (i.e., binary) and stores it in the location &i.

### 17.10.2 The fprintf Function

We have already shown many examples that use ***printf*** to display the formatted output on the terminal's screen file. Actually ***fprintf*** is the general purpose function for outputting formatted information to an addressed stream, whereas **printf** by default writes to the ***stdout*** stream. The arguments to a ***fprintf*** call are similar to ***fscanf***: the first argument is stream address, the second argument is a control string to specify the formats and then an argument list. In the case of ***fscanf***, the argument list is a list of address parameters to store the scanned values, whereas in ***fprintf*** it is a list of purely value parameters for printing. The formats of the ***fprintf*** and ***printf*** functions are shown below:

*void fprintf(FILE *stream, char *control_string, argument_list);*
*void printf(char *control_string, argument_list);*

***Table 17.4*** shows the conversion characters used in the format specifiers along with the description of the corresponding outputs. Since the basic principle in using ***fprintf*** is the same as ***printf***, and the usage of ***printf*** has been demonstrated quite extensively in the previous chapters, it is sufficient to show just one or two appropriate examples for ***fprinf***. Both ***fprintf*** and ***printf*** return number of characters transmitted after successful operation and return negative value when an error occurs.

*Table 17.4: Format specifiers and flags for fprintf (or printf) function*

| Format Specifier | Output Data Type |
|---|---|
| d,i | Signed Decimal output |
| o | Unsigned Octal output with a leading |
| x | Unsigned Hexadecimal output with a leading 0x (eg. 0xffff) |
| X | Unsigned Hexadecimal output with a leading 0X (eg. 0XFFFF) |
| u | Unsigned Decimal output |
| c | Character is printed. |
| s | The supplied string argument is output in a readable text form. |

*Table 17.5 (cont.)*

| | |
|---|---|
| f | The supplied real argument is output with 6-digit precision by default. Eg. printf("%f \n", 100.0) prints 100.000000. |
| e, E | The supplied real argument is output in scientific notation with 6-digit precision by default.<br>eg. printf("%e \n", 100.0) prints 1.000000e+002<br>printf("%E \n", 100.0) prints 1.000000E+002. |
| g, G | The supplied real argument is output in either f or e, whichever is shorter. |
| h | When h precedes d, i, o, h, or u, the integer argument is short integer or unsigned short integer type. |
| l | When l precedes d, i, o, h, or u, the integer argument is long integer or unsigned long integer type. |
| L | When L precedes f, e, g, or u, the real argument is long double type. |
| - | When this flag is used the output is left justified.<br>eg. printf("%5d ", 100) prints right justified result as ,,100, whereas printf("%-5d ", 100) prints left justified as 100,,. |
| + | When this flag is used in the specification the output always begin with +.<br>eg. Printf("%+d ", 100) prints the result as +100 |
| Space | When a space flag is used in the specification, a leading space is printed along with the output. |
| # | When this flag is used, output is made more legible.<br>1. This flag when used with o produces output to begin with 0.<br>Eg. printf("%#o ", 100) prints 0144<br>2. This flag when used with x (or X) produces output to begin with 0x (or 0X). Eg. printf("%#x ", 100) prints 0x64<br>3. This flag when used with f, e, g or G produces output always with decimal.<br>Eg. printf("%#g ", 100) prints 100 (without any decimal), whereas<br>printf("%#g ", 100) prints 100.000 (with decimal). |

**Example 17.27:**

Create a student file to store the results of 100 students. Assume that each input line from terminal consists of the following fields: student name (20 characters), followed by three numerical strings representing marks of three courses fields delimited by a space. Let us write a function, ***make***, to read data from the terminal, compute totals and result status, and then write all this data to a student file.

```
#include <stdio.h>
char st_name[21], result;
int mark1, mark2, mark3;
int total;
void make(void)
 {FILE *fopen(), *fp;
  if((fp=fopen("st_file", "w") == NULL)
    {
      printf("st_file cannot open ");
      exit();
    }
  for(i=0; i<100; i++) /* store results of 100 students */
    {
      scanf("%s %d %d %d ", st_name, &mark1, &mark2, &mark3);
        total = mark1+mark2+mark3;
        if(mark1 >=50 && mark2 >=50 && mark3 >= 50)
        result = 'P';
      else
        result = 'F';
      fprintf(fp ,"%s, %d %d %d %d %c", st_name, mark1, mark2, mark3, total, result);
    }
}
```

## Example 17.28:

Write another function called ***report*** to read each record from the student file and write to the terminal.

```
report()
 {FILE *fopen(), *fp;
  char st_name[21], result;
  int mark1, mark2, mark3;
  int total;
  if((fp=fopen("st_file", "r") == NULL)  /*open st_file to read only */
    {
      printf("st_file cannot open ");
      exit();
    }
   for(i=0; i<100; i++) /* store results of 100 students */
     {
        fscanf(fp ,"%s %d %d %d %d %c",st_name, &mark1,&mark2,&mark3,&total, &result);
        printf( "%s, %d %d %d %d %c",st_name,mark1,mark2,mark3,total,result);
     }
}
```

## The vprintf, vfprintf and vsprintf functions

These functions are similar to printf, fprintf and sprintf except that they can process a variable number of arguments in a different manner. These functions accept the arguments through a pointer stack of arguments instead of a list of arguments along with the call. The prototype definitions of these functions as stored in ***stdio.h*** are:

```
int vprintf(const char *format, va_list *arg_ptr)
int vfprintf(FILE *stream, const char *format, va_list *arg_ptr)
int vsprintf(const char *format, va_list *arg_ptr)
```

where the type ***va_list*** is defined in the ***stdarg.h*** file, the string format carries the type specifiers along with some text, and the pointer ***arg_ptr*** points to a stack of the arguments that should be printed. In order to set up and maintain this argument stack, the functions ***va_list*** and ***va_end***, defined in ***stdarg.h***, are required. Please recall the introduction of these functions in ***Chapter 13***. The following example shows the use of this kind of printing function.

**Example 17.29:** Write a common print function using ***vprintf***.

```
#include <stdio.h>
#include <stdarg.h>
void main(void)
{char *s = 'Hello World';
 cprint('%s \n', s);
 cprint('%d apples  \n', 10);
 cprint('%d apples %d oranges and %d bananas \n', 10, 20, 30);
 cprint('%c %f \n', 10.00);
}

void cprint(char *format, . . .)
{ va_arg args;

     va_start(args, format); /* set up the argument stack */
      vprintf(format, args);  /* print the arguments */
}
```

## The perror function

The ***perror*** function can be used for printing errors that are generated due to some illegal use of or malfunction of a system resource. This function gets the error value from the global variable, ***errno***, and prints the corresponding error message. This function also uses the system's global variable ***sys_errlist[]*** which maintains the diagnostic messages corresponding to the system call error numbers that are listed in the system.

In standard C, the File I/O functions only deal with the system resources. These functions may access the system resources directly or indirectly via operating systems functions. Hence, ***perror*** is useful during I/O programming to determine the cause of error within the system. When this function is called, it accesses ***errno*** to get the error code (an integer), uses this code as index to the diagnostic array (***sys_errlist[]***) to get the corresponding error message and then prints it on the ***stdout*** stream. The prototype of this function as stored in ***stdio.h*** is shown below:

```
void perror( const char *user_message);
```

where ***user_message*** is a string (or a character pointer) which is usually the function name. When this function is called, it will print the ***user_message*** first, append a colon, then print the diagnostic message in ***sys_errlist[]*** corresponding to the value of ***errno*** and output a newline. A C-program is shown below with file I/O and the usage of ***perror***.

```
#include <stdio.h>
void main(void)
    {FILE    fp;
        . . .
    fp = fopen(a list of arguments);
    if (fp == NULL)
        {
            perror("Error at fopen call");
            exit();
        }
    else
        {
        . . .
        }
    }
```

***Remark:*** *Since perror uses the global variables, errno and sys_errlist[], it includes in its code the following prototype declarations:*

```
extern int errno;
extern char sys_errlist[];
```

*Hence, we don't need to declare those variables in our programs that call peeror.*

## 17.11 Summary

This chapter explains the concept of character stream I/O and how it is built on top of the system call I/O. It shows the significance of the macros in stdio.h for configuring the stream I/O. It has presented all input and output functions with respect to character I/O, string I/O, binary I/O and formatted I/O.

## Exercises

17.1 Indicate which of the following statements is correct:

(i) An ANSI-file is
- (a) a sequence of binary numbers or integers.
- (b) a sequence of records.
- (c) a sequence of 7-bit ASCII characters.
- (d) a sequence of bytes.

(ii) The ANSI-File system treats the keyboard as
- (a) a file of 26 alphabetical characters, 10 numerical characters and a set of special and control characters.
- (b) a dynamic input file of unlimited size capable of supplying ASCII characters in a sequential manner.
- (c) a read-only file of fixed size.
- (d) an input file to key in graphics.

(iii) A stream is
- (a) a file that is open for reading/writing data in record format;
- (b) a file that is open for reading/writing data in block (i.e., disk sector) size.
- (c) a file that is open for reading/writing data in a sequence of bytes (or characters).
- (d) a file that is open for reading/writing the whole file at a time.

(iv) Stream I/O reads/writes characters
- (a) directly from/to the disk file.
- (b) from/to a buffer of block or sector size.
- (c) from/to a buffer of single character.

(v) A file pointer is
- (a) an integer that is used as index to the current character position in the stream,
- (b) a character pointer to the buffered data.
- (c) a pointer to a structure called FILE which describes the intermediate buffer.

(vi) The stdin and stdout are
- (a) simply synonyms for standard input (i.e., terminals keyboard) and standard output (i.e., terminals screen).
- (b) simple integer values (0 and 1) used as stream addresses of keyboard and screen files, respectively.
- (c) file pointers for standard input and standard output files that are already kept open for a C-programmer.

(vii) fopen is
  (a) a system call to open a disk file.
  (b) a C-function simply to open a file.
  (c) a C-function to open a file and associates a buffer structure called FILE to enable stream operations.

17.2 The stdio.h header file must be included in every program that performs stream I/O because
  (a) stdio.h contains macro definition for NULL and EOF.
  (b) stdio.h contains macro functions for character manipulations.
  (c) stdio.h contains macro functions for character and string manipulations.
  (d) stdio.h contains macro definition for FILE (i.e., buffer structure) definition and other macros, such as getc, putc, getchar, putchar, NULL, EOF.

17.3 What is EOF in the ANSI-File system?

17.4 Why are ***getc***, ***putc***, ***getchar*** and ***putchar*** implemented as macros instead of regular functions?

# 18

# Signal and Time Management

**Chapter contents:**

*This chapter introduces the signal facility, to manage some abnormal conditions of the execution environment, and the time management facility to implement time-related application programs.*

**Organization:**

*18.1 Introduction*
*18.2 Signal Management*
*18.3 Time Management in Standard C*
*18.4 Summary*
*Exercises*

## 18.1 Introduction

The two types of events useful for the C-programs are asynchronous type, generated at any time during a program execution, and synchronous event, generated by systems basic interval clock. The asynchronous events, or ***signals***, are generated by supporting and application environments to inform the running program about the occurrence of some exceptional conditions. The standard C provides some mechanisms to handle the signals gracefully to achieve the predictable behavior of C-programs. Synchronous events are useful for maintaining several application-oriented timers. The standard C provides a set of library functions to access all these timers.

## 18.2 Signal Management

### 18.2.1 Types of signals

Basically, signals are generated by several sources within the C-Virtual Machine, such as CPU-hardware due to some abnormal conditions, running the program to handle some abnormal data conditions, and keyboard interrupts initiated by users to interact with their running programs. There are at least six types of signals defined by ANSI standard that can be handled by C-

Programs. These signals are given symbolic names, although they are identified internally as integers. The definitions of these signals, their symbolic names and their equivalent integer values, are included in the ***signal.h*** header file and are shown in ***Table 18.1***.

*Table 18.1 Signal types supported by ANSI-C*

| signal type | Event description | Core dump |
|---|---|---|
| SIGABRT | Abnormal termination, such as the abort function. | yes |
| SIGFPE | Erroneous floating point operation, such as arithmetic overflow. | yes |
| SIGILL | Illegal instruction is found in the object program. | yes |
| SIGINT | Interactive signal sent from the keyboard (usually ctrl-c key, DEL key or an implementation defined key). | no |
| SIGSEGV | Segmentation violation due to illegal memory access. | yes |
| SIGTERM | Termination request sent to the program. | yes |

### 18.2.2 Signal Processing

Signal processing is similar to interrupt handling at the hardware level. When a signal occurs, a running program is stopped and a signal processing routine is called. For most signal types, signal processing is set to the default action of terminating and/or producing a core dump of the interrupted process. Alternatively, programs can invoke a user specified routine for catching a type of signal. A signal interrupt will stop the running program and transfer the control to the corresponding user specified routine. After processing a signal, the routine will return the control back to the stopped program, allowing it to continue.

### 18.2.3 Signal Control Functions

There are two signal-based functions available in the standard C-library to control signals: the ***signal*** function, helping to nominate appropriate action in the event of occurring a signal, and the ***raise*** function, to raise or generate a signal by a running program.

#### The signal function

The ***signal*** function call can be used to specify a user routine to be associated with a signal type. It defines a function, ***action_function***, to be called if the specified signal is received by the running program. The prototype definition of this call as defined in ***signal.h*** is:

***void*** (*signal( ***int*** signal_type, ***void*** (*action_function)(int) ) ) (int)

where ***signal_type*** is a signal number (or signal name that is defined in the ***signal.h*** file); ***action_function*** is the address of the user defined signal processing function or one of the system defined symbols, such as ***SIG_DFL*** to use the system defined (or default) function for the specified signal_type or ***SIG_IGN*** to define no action (or ignoring the action), for the specified signal_type and; ***signal()*** returns a pointer to a function which is the previous value of the action_function.

***Error Flag:*** If the call has failed, it returns SIG_ERR (defined in signal.h) and sets errno. The error may be due to one of the following reasons:

- illegal signal type
- the address argument of signal processing function (i.e., action_function) points to an invalid address.

## Use of SIG_DFL and SIG_IGN

As mentioned earlier, a program can set up its own signal catching routines that are appropriate to an application environment. If necessary, the program can reset a signal so that it can be caught by its original or default function. In some situations, a program may want to continue (until the completion of some ***critical section*** or the whole program) without any signal interruption. For example, the transactions updating their database, once started, should be allowed to proceed without any interruption. If a transaction program is interrupted during writing to its database, the information stored may be forced to be inconsistent. In such a situation, the signals from the controlling terminal must be suppressed. In this case, a kernel must be instructed to ignore the specified signals. To provide these facilities, there are two system-defined signal processing functions available, identified by ***SIG_DFL*** and ***SIG_IGN*** codes. (These codes too are defined in ***signal.h***.) User programs can pass ***SIG_DFL*** or ***SIG_IGN*** to the kernel via signal(), as shown in the following example.

```
#include <stdio.h>
#include <signal.h>
void main(void)
 {    ...
    ...
   signal(SIG_INT, SIG_IGN );    /* after this call, an interrupt signal generated by the
                                      interrupt (ctrl-c or DEL) key will be ignored; */
   signal(SIG_QUIT, SIG_IGN);   /* after this call, a quit signal generated by the FS
                                      or ctrl-\ key will be ignored; */

    ...
    ...                  /* perform some critical operation  */
    ...
   signal(SIG_INT, SIG_DFL);     /* after this call, an interrupt signal generated by the
                                                       DEL key will terminate the job;
*/
   signal(SIG_QUIT, SIG_DFL);  /* after this call, a quit signal by the FS key will
                                                       terminate the job and save the
core image  */
    ...                      /*  perform the remaining non-critical operations     */
}
```

## Example 18.1:

Write a program that employs its own signal processing routine for a SIGINT signal.

```
#include <signal.h>
void myroutine(int);
int count;
void main(void)
{
  count = 0;
  signal(SIGINT, myroutine); /* set up the signal catching routine */
  while(1);
}

void myroutine(int sig_type)
{
   system ("date"); /* system() executes the date command at program level;
                      see remark-2 below on this function */
   signal(SIGALRM, myroutine); /* set the trap again because it is reset after every
                                  trap */
   if(++count < 100) return; /* control is returned to the place where signal
                                interrupt occurred */
   else
      exit(sig_type);
}
```

***Remarks:***

*1. After associating the **myroutine** routine with the interrupt signal type, the program goes into a while loop. When an interrupt signal arrives from the keyboard, the control goes to the **myroutine**. When this routine returns, the control goes back to the while loop to continue from where the signal interruption occurred.*

*2. The **system** function may be available in an implementation to execute a shell command at the program level. It requires only one string argument as the command to be executed. The prototype definition is shown below:*

```
int    system( const char    *command);
```

*The function returns the exit status of command process. The prototype definition of this function is given in the **stdlib.h** file.*

### The raise function

The ***raise*** function is useful to generate any of the defined signals within the running program. Particularly, this can be a useful mechanism in catching the program-detected exceptional conditions, such as when a device does not respond or a value received from a device is out of range. The format of the call is:

*int raise(int sig);*

When the operation is successful, the function call returns zero, or returns a non-zero value.

### Communication with the system

Library functions, such as ***abort***, ***exit*** and ***atexit***, are useful to communicate with the supporting environment for either abnormal or normal termination.

### The abort function

The ***abort*** call terminates a running program when an abnormal condition arises and raises the ***SIGABRT*** signal which, when caught, will cause the execution of a nominated routine without any return. Otherwise, it will cause the termination of the program which called this function. The format of this function call as defined in stdlib.h is:

*void abort(void);*

Before terminating the program, output streams may be flushed and temporary files may be closed.

### The atexit function

The ***atexit*** function call can be used to register a function so that it can be executed during the normal exit of a program. The format of the call as defined in ***stdlib.h*** is:

*int atexit(void (*func)(void) );*

When the call is successful, zero is returned, or a non-zero value is returned. A program can register up to thirty-two functions to be called during exit.

## The exit function

The ***exit call*** is a software event from the program that communicates with the system for terminating purposes. Before the system gets the control from the exiting program, all the open output files are flushed and closed, and all temporary files are closed, all the registered functions are called. The format of the call as defined in ***stdlib.h*** is:

```
void exit(int status);
```

## setjmp and longjmp facility

ANSI-C adopted a ***non-local goto*** statement which allows a program function to transfer control to a statement in another function. The ***longjmp*** call is designed to perform this type of branch within a C-program, which is useful for a signal processing routine to jump to the start of the interrupted program segment. Another application of this facility is to facilitate ***exception handling*** in C-programs. In order to accomplish this non-local jump, the **setjmp** call is used to mark a jump-point in a program. A ***setjmp*** call needs a ***jmp_buf*** type buffer to store the context of a target location (i.e., a state vector of that location comprising of current values of all CPU-registers) so that a ***longjmp*** call can use this context information to rewind the state of the program to its original context of that location. The ***jmp_buf*** type is defined in the ***setjmp.h*** header file. ***Chapter 20*** explains more about this facility. The prototype definitions of these two functions are as follows:

```
#include <setjmp.h>
int setjmp(jmp_buf recovery_state);
void longjmp(jmp_buf recovery_state, int status);
```

The ***setjmp()*** call marks the jump location by saving the current state of the running program (the current context of the program) in the *recovery_state* buffer argument. It returns *zero* when the call is successful. For example, the main of a program can mark a jump point as

```
#include <setjmp.h>
jmp_buf recovery_state;
void main(void)
{
    ...
  int status = setjmp(recovery_state);/* mark the recovery state */
  /* recovery_state points here */
    ...
}
```

longjmp returns here

The ***longjmp()*** call causes a non-local jump by changing the current context to the state saved in the *recovery_state* buffer. It returns control to the point after the ***setjmp()*** call and before assignment. Although the ***longjmp()*** call does not return any value, it emulates the return of ***setjmp*** by storing the second argument (*status*) in the "***rvalue accumulator***" of the CVM. The returned value is assigned to the local variable, as shown in the figure above.

## Exception Handling in C

Exception handling in a limited manner can be implemented using setjmp and longjmp facility. Any function in a C-program expects the occurrence of some abnormal state, sets a return point using the setjmp call and the subsequent code can check for any abnormal situation. When an abnormal situation is detected by the code, it can reset the program state to the start of the function. It can either retry or abort the program, depending upon the application. The following example shows the use of setjmp and longjmp calls.

```
#include <stdio.h>
#include <setjmp.h>    /* setjmp structure type is defined in this header file */
jmpbuf ret_state;
void main(void)
{
    int num, deno, exception;
    exception = setjmp(ret_state); /* store current state in the ret_state buffer */
            if (exception = -1)
    {/* service the exception */
            printf("Numeric Error occurred, Program aborted \n");
            exit(1);
    }
    scanf("%d %d ", &num, &deno);
            result =division _fn(num, deno); /* if division unsuccessful, control goes to
main */
    printf("The result is %d \n", result); /* else print the result */
} /* End of main */

int division_fn(int num, int deno)
{
int error;
    if(deno == 0)
            error =-1, longjmp(ret_state, error);/* rewind to the state saved in ret_state */
    else
            return (num/deno);
}
```

The program sets the recovery point by calling the setjmp function. The ***setjmp*** returns zero after its successful operation. Then the main receives arguments from the user and calls the division function. Before it performs the operation, it validates the denominator. If the denominator happens to be zero, the division will lead to overflow. In order to avoid this, the function raises an exception by calling longjmp. The ***longjmp*** function in turn jumps to the exception handler code in the main function.

## 18.3 Time Management in Standard C

Both system and application programming disciplines require time and date functions to perform several time-dependent tasks. For example, a job management program requires some useful time and date functions for performing periodic duties, such as daily archival, collection of heap storage fragments and running batch jobs. Similarly, programs in the data processing applications, such as monthly salary processing, inventory control, and maintaining a bulletin board for broadcasting regular messages, require time-related functions for performing their regular tasks. In real-time applications, schedulers require real-time clock functions to synchronize the tasks with the specified conditions of the physical processes. Real-time systems may also need watchdog timers to maintain the fault tolerant feature.

The ***Standard C*** provides a set of time and date management functions to satisfy the timing needs of all the above applications. These functions deal with elapsed and calendar times. The ***time.h*** file contains the prototype definitions of these functions and some data types, including a structure to hold the broken-down time. ***Table 18.2*** lists all these definitions.

*Table 18.2 Contents of time.h*

```
CLK_TCK         /* defined as number of clock ticks per second */
clock_t         /* a discrete type (int or long) that is implementation dependent */
time_t          /* implementation dependent type */
struct tm
{
int tm_sec;     /* seconds after minute, 0..59 */
int tm_min;     /* minutes after hour, 0..59 */
int tm_hour;    /* hours after midnight, 0..23 */
int tm_mday;    /* day of the month, 1..31 */
int tm_mon;     /* month since January, 0..11 */
int tm_year;    /* year since 1900 */
int tm_wday;    /* day since Sunday, 0..6 */
int tm_yday;    /* day of a year since 1st of January, 0..365 */
int tm_isdst;   /* daylight saving time flag:
                if zero, daylight saving is not in effect,
                if positive, daylight saving is in effect,
                if negative, this information is not available. */
};
```

```
/* prototype definitions of functions */
clock_t   clock(void);                              /* gets number of clock ticks since the
                                                       program started */
time_t    time(time_t *timer);                      /* gets the current calendar time */
char      *ctime(const time_t *timer);              /* convert calendar time into text format */
double    difftime(time_t t1, time-t t2);           /* difference between calendar times in
                                                       seconds*/
char      *asctime(const struct tm  *timeptr);      /* convert broken-down time into text */
time_t    mktime(struct  tm   *tmptr);              /* convert broken-down time into calendar time */
struct tm *localtime(const time_t  *timer);         /* convert calendar time into local time */
struct tm *gmtime(const time_t  *timer);            /* convert calendar time into Universal
                                                       Coordinated time (UCT) */
size_t strftime(char *s, size_t size, const char *format, const struct tm *timptr)
                                                    /* format locale specific time */
```

## The clock function

The ***clock*** function is useful for timing the execution steps within a program. For example, the clock function can be used to determine the execution times of real-time tasks so that an appropriate real-time task scheduler can be designed to meet the tasks' deadlines. Other applications of this function include evaluation of software overheads in operating systems, efficiency of algorithms, etc.

The ***clock*** function returns the value of an incremental clock that is associated with a running program. When a program starts its execution, the clock also starts to increment from zero. At the end of a program, the clock's value represents the execution time of the program. If we want to measure the timing of a program step (a statement, a group of statements, or a function call), we have to use the ***clock()*** calls before and after the step and find out the difference for getting the relative timing of that step. The prototype definition of the clock function as given in ***time.h*** is:

*clock_t      clock(void);*

where ***clock_t*** is the type of the returned value. Since the clock is counting the number of ticks, the returned value is generally a discrete value. Depending upon the size of the clock, an appropriate discrete type (***int*** or ***long***) is assigned to ***clock_t***. It is mainly left to the implementation.

Another attribute of this clock is the time interval between two consecutive ticks. This is called *tick interval* and varies from one implementation to another. The standard C specifies a tick interval as one microsecond. However, one may use the standard attribute called ***CLK_TCK***, defined as number of ticks per second in ***time.h***. This attribute can be used to convert the *relative* time unit into the *absolute* time unit. For example, if a ***clock()*** call returns 2,500 000 and the CLK_TCK is defined as 1,000 000, then the actual time elapsed since the program started is (2,500 000/1,000 000), or 2.5 seconds.

## Example 18.2:

Find out the time taken by a for_loop. Show the results in both relative and absolute time units.

```
#include <stdio.h>
#include <time.h>
void main(void)
{
  clock_t tick_count1, tick_count2, for_loop_ticks;
  double ForLoopTime;
  int i;
    tick_count1= clock();
    for(i=0; i<10000; i++) /* null statement */;
    tick_count2 = clock();
        for_loop_ticks = tick_count2 - tick_count2;
   printf("Relative Time taken for 10000 loops is %d clock ticks \n", ForLoopTime);
   ForLoopTime=(double)((time2 -time1)/CLK_TCK);       /* in seconds */
   printf("Time taken for 10000 loops is %f seconds \n", ForLoopTime);
}
```

## Example 18.3:

Find out the time taken by a sort algorithm. Bubble sort on an array of 10 elements is selected for this timing. Show the results in both relative and absolute time units.

```
#include <stdio.h>
#include <time.h>
void main(void)
{
  clock_t tick_count1, tick_count2, bubble_sort_ticks;
  double ticks_elapsed;
  int arr[10] = {5, 20, 15, 90, 70,10, 25, 30, 40,50};
        tick_count1= clock();
        simple_bubble_sort(arr, len);
        tick_count2 = clock();
              ticks_elapsed = tick_count2 - tick_count2;
        printf("Relative Time by bubble sort algorithm is %d clock ticks \n",ticks_elapsed);
       sort_Time=(double)((tick_count2 - tick_count1)/CLK_TCK);    /* in seconds */
        printf("Absolute ime by bubble sort algorithm is %f seconds \n", sort_time);
} /* End of main */

void simple_bubble_sort(int iarr[], int len)
{
       int i, j, temp;
        for(i = 1; i < len-1; i++)
```

```
        for(j = 1; j < len-1; j++)
        {
                if (iarr[j] > iarr[j+1]
                {
                 temp = iarr[j];
                iarr[j] = iarr[j+1];
                iarr[j+1] = temp;
        } /* End of simple_bubble_sort */
```

## The time function

The ***time*** function call returns a calendar time (current system date and time) in an implementation specified format (i.e., ***time_t*** type). A filter is necessary to convert this calendar time into a readable string output. For example, the ***localtime*** function breaks this time_t type information into various levels of real-time, such as seconds, minutes, hours, and days, and stores it in a structure form. We will see the use of this localtime function later. The ***time*** function returns (time_t)(-1) when time is not available. The prototype definition of this call as in ***time.h*** is:

```
time_t          time(time_t  *timer);
```

### The ctime function

The ***ctime*** function is used to convert the calendar time of the type ***time_t*** into the local time in a readable string format, actually performing the work of ***localtime*** and ***asctime*** functions explained later in this chapter. The prototype definition of this call as in ***time.h*** is:

```
char   *ctime(const time_t  *timer);
```

**Example 18.4:**
Display the current local time.

```
#include  <stdio.h>
#include  <time.h>
void  main(void)
{
  time_t  t;
  int  i;
  char *s;
   t = time(NULL);
   s = ctime(&t);                 /* convert calendar time into printable string format */
   printf("Current local time and date: %s  \n", s);
}
```

The output of the above program is:

*Current local time and date: Fri Mar 16 15:19:58 1999*

### The difftime Function

The prototype definition of this function as described in time.h is

*double difftime(time_t this_time, time-t previous_time);*

This function call returns the difference between two calendar times (i.e., this_time and previous_time) in seconds.

## Example 18.5:

Write a program that shows the use of the ***difftime*** function to idle for ten seconds.

```
#include <time.h>
#include <stdio.h>
void main(void)
{
  time_t start_time, stop_time;
  int i;
  char *s;
   printf("I am going to sleep now \n");
   start_time = time(NULL);
   while( difftime(time(NULL) - start_time) != 10) /* null statement */ ;
   printf("I woke up after ten seconds \n");
}
```

### The mktime function

The mktime function converts a given broken-down time into calendar time of encoded type time_t. This function is useful to reset the system's timer. If we want to initialize the timer, the value of the time_t type must be supplied via the initializing function. The programmer expresses the local time as broken-down time in a tm structure and converts this local time into a value for time_t using mktime. The returned value of mktime can be used to initialize the system's timer. ***mktime*** can also be used for a known date (e.g., 4th August 1990) where one can find out the name of the day. The following example explains this case. The prototype definition of the ***mktime*** call as in ***time.h*** is:

*time_t mktime(struct tm *tmptr);*

## Example 18.6:

Find out the name of the day on the first day of year 2000.

```
#include <time.h>
#include <stdio.h>
char day_name[][] = {"Monday", "Tuesday", "Wednesday", "Thursday",
              "Friday", "Saturday", "Sunday"};
void main(void)
{
 struct tm br_down;
    br_down.tm_sec = 1;
    br_down.tm_min = 0;
    br_down.tm_hour = 0;
    br_down.tm_mday = 1;
    br_down.tm_mon = 0;
    br_down.tm_year = 2000 - 1900;
    if(mktime(&br_down) == -1)
     printf("Cannot convert into broken-down format \n");
    printf("The day is: %s \n", day_name[br_down.tm_wday]);
}
```

## The asctime function

The ***asctime*** function is useful to convert the broken-down time into a readable text format. This function is used in conjunction with the localtime and gmtime functions to display times in a readable format. The prototype definition of this call as in **time.h** is:

```
char  *asctime(const struct tm  *timeptr);
```

**Example 18.7:**
Given a broken-down time as:

year: 1996
month: 10
day of the month: 15
weekday: 0
hour: 14
minutes 55
seconds: 58

display the time in a readable format.

```
#include <time.h>
#include <stdio.h>
void main(void)
{
 char *s;
 struct tm br_down;
     br_down.tm_sec = 58;
     br_down.tm_min = 55;
     br_down.tm_hour = 14;
     br_down.tm_mday = 15;
     br_down.tm_mon = 10;
     br_down.tm_year = 1996 - 1900;
     /* call mktime to fill up tm_wday and tm_yday */
     if((s = asctime(br_down)) == NULL)
            printf("Cannot convert into broken-down format \n");
     printf("The day is: %s \n", s);
}
```

The above program will display the time as:

Sun Sep 15 14:55:58 1996

### The localtime function

The ***localtime*** function converts the calendar time (returned by time function) into local time of broken-down format. It receives a pointer to the calendar time of ***time_t*** type and returns a pointer to a structure of ***tm*** structure type. The prototype definition, as in ***time.h***, is shown below:

*struct tm *localtime(const time_t *timer);*

## Example 18.8:

Show the use of localtime by displaying the current local time.

```
#include <time.h>
#include <stdio.h>
void main(void)
{
 struct tm *br_down_ltime;
 time_t cal_time;
   cal_time = time(NULL); /* get the current calendar time from system clock */
   br_down_ltime = localtime(&cal_time);
   printf("The current local time: %s \n", asctime(br_down_ltime));
}
```

## The gmtime function

The ***gmtime*** function is similar to localtime except that it returns Greenwich time. The function receives a pointer to the calendar time and returns a pointer to a structure of tm structure type containing the broken-down Greenwich time. The prototype definition, as in ***time.h***, is:

*struct tm  *gmtime(const time_t  *timer);*

## Example 18.9:

Show the use of ***gmtime*** by displaying the current Greenwich time.

```
#include <time.h>
#include <stdio.h>
void main(void)
{
 struct tm  *br_down_gwtime;
 time_t  cal_time;
   cal_time = time(NULL); /* get the current calendar time from system clock */
   br_down_gwtime = gmtime(&cal_time);
   printf("The current local time: %s \n", asctime(br_down_gwtime));
}
```

## The strftime function

The ***strftime*** function is used to output the current time in a locale specific format supplied as an argument along with a call. The prototype definition, as in ***time.h***, is

*size_t strftime(char *ds, size_t size, const char *format, const struct tm *timptr)*

where *ds* is the destination string in which the current time is built, according to the supplied format. The *size* argument indicates the size of the destination string, *ds*. A pointer to the structure (*timptr*) that has the current time is passed as the source argument. The *format* string contains the conversion description using the following conversion specifiers:

| | |
|---|---|
| %a: | the locale's abbreviated name for the day of the week |
| %A: | the locale's full name for the day of the week |
| %b: | the locale's abbreviated name for the month |
| %B: | the locale's full name for the month |
| %c: | the locale's default representation for the date and time |
| %d: | the day of the month as an integer (01 to 31). |
| %H: | the hour as an integer (00 to 23). |
| %I: | the hour as an integer (01 to 12). |
| %J: | the day of the year as an integer (001 to 366). |

%m: the month as an integer (01 to 12).
%M: the minute as an integer (00 to 59).
%p: the locale's way of indicating morning (A.M.) or afternoon (P.M.).
%S: the second as an integer (00 to 59).
%U: the week of the year as an integer (00 to 53); regard Sunday as the first day of the week.
%w: the day of the week as an integer (0 to 6); regard Sunday as the first day of the week
%W: the day of the week as an integer (0 to 6); regard Monday as the first day of the week
%x: the locale's default representation of the date.
%X: the locale's default representation of the time.
%y: the year within the century (00 to 99).
%Y: the full year, including century.
%Z: the name of the locale's time zone.

## 18.4 Summary

This chapter explained the features of ANSI-C that are useful for a program to react with the environment. Signals can be used for writing fault tolerant programs and controlling a running program. The time functions are useful for accounting resource utilization and to support real-time applications.

## Exercises

18.1 Explain the meaning of a signal.

18.2 What are the sources of signals? Explain.

18.3 What are the types of signals supported by ANSI-C? Explain.

18.4 What is the difference between an interrupt and a signal?

18.5 Does every signal delivery result in core dumping? Why or why not?

18.6 What is the use of the CLK_TCK macro in time.h?

18.7 Design a more efficient bubble sort algorithm and compare it with the time taken by the algorithm shown in ***Example 18.3***.

18.8 What is the time unit associated with the *time_t* type?

18.9 What is the time unit associated with the *clock_t* type?

18.10 What is the role of the *mktime* function? Explain.

18.11 Why is the clock_t interval smaller than the time_t interval?

# 19

# Standard Unix-Kernel Interface

**Chapter contents:**

*This chapter introduces the facility in C that accesses Unix functions. Some basic concepts, such as the meaning of operating system kernel, the meaning of system call, and the POSIX standard for Unix interface, are also explored in this chapter. This chapter familiarizes readers with the architecture of the standard Unix interface available in the C-virtual machine.*

**Organization:**


*19.1 Introduction*
*19.2 The Meaning of Operating System Kernel*
*19.3 Unix Kernel*
*19.4 Error Handling with System Calls*
*19.5 What Is Systems Programming?*
*19.6 C as a System Programming Language*
*19.7 Why Standard for Operating System Interface?*
*19.8 What Is POSIX Standard?*
*19.9 System Identification*
*19.10 Summary*
*Exercises*


## 19.1 Introduction

Unlike other languages, C has the privilege of accessing the Unix operating system functions at user level because almost all functions of the Unix kernel are implemented in C. This clearly indicates that C provides a mechanism to interface with the Unix kernel and, thus, becomes a perfect tool for maintaining Unix. Several attractive features suitable for supporting operating system make C the obvious choice for all other applications related to system programming. In 1980s and 1990s the use of C, largely under Unix platform, has been demonstrated in the following system programming aspects:

- *Adding more services to the Unix kernel (e.g., new system calls for accounting the usage of resources, accessing networked resources, supporting real-time processing, etc);*
- *Developing more software resources (e.g., new languages, software tools, etc.);*
- *Adding higher level functions to suit different applications (e.g., to emulate random access files, indexed files, etc.).*

After introducing the ANSI-standard, C has restricted its support for the Unix interface because of the portability issue. However, the standard has been extended with the ***POSIX*** specifications by the recommendation of the ***IEEE committee*** so C may provide Unix-like interface as an optional service. This extended standard C allows programmers to write programs with system's flavor that are completely of portable nature; system programs implemented under ***POSIX*** compliant Unix can be ported to any other ***POSIX*** compliant operating system and vice versa.

This chapter explains the meaning of ***Unix kernel*** and summarizes the list of standards, as in ***POSIX***-specified ***Application Program Interface*** (***API***). ***Unix System*** functions that can be directly accessed via standard C. At the end of this chapter, the reasons for recommending ***POSIX*** standard is discussed. Since the study of system calls requires a thorough knowledge of the Unix kernel, it is difficult to cover such a comprehensive review in a few chapters spared for this purpose. However, the following chapters try to introduce the Unix system interface and keep the readers at application level as much as possible.

## 19.2 The Meaning of Operating System Kernel

A bare machine is a processor (or CPU) along with the interconnected I/O devices and is clearly visible to a programmer via a set of machine instructions of the CPU. At this level, programmers write their programs using machine level language and perform resource management, such as allocating space in memory and disk, and system operations, such as loading and running, manually. In other words, the overall control of the executing environment is very primitive.

Alternatively, we can use a set of system administrative functions that automatically manage the resources and perform user requested operations in an efficient manner. For example, some functions may be provided to create and maintain directories and files; some functions may be provided to create processes for carrying out the execution of user-requested programs; some functions may be scheduling processes that allocate resources like CPU and disk; and some functions may be provided for accounting the usage of resources and so on. These functions maintain the systems data structures, such as tables for active programs (also called process tables), tables for created files, tables for opened files and opened devices, buffers to control data input and output, and so on. These resource management functions, in general, act as the library of system functions. When this systems library is added on top of a raw machine, this combination represents a versatile virtual machine called a ***kernel***, or a ***system call machine***. The resource management function calls (i.e., simply ***system calls***) act as the language of a kernel machine. In general, the size of a kernel machine depends upon the number of system calls which, in turn, depends upon factors such as the amount of resources available, how they are maintained and what types of services are being provided by an operating system kernel. A system call has the following format:

***int*** *system_call__name( a list of arguments with respect to resource)*

The call takes a set of arguments and returns an integer showing whether the operation is successful or not. The number of arguments varies from one resource to another.

We can also interpret this virtual machine as a set of logical components (or abstract level functions), each of which is constructed by adding a layer of software data structure over a systems primitive data structure or physical resource. A system call function, with the help of appropriate library functions, can effectively access the addressed physical resource by accessing the overlaying data structure. The term "***Application Program Interface*** (***API***)" as suggested by the POSIX standard, is basically the same as the term "***System Call Interface***" (as used in ***Unix*** terminology).

## 19.3 Unix Kernel

The Unix operating system's basic philosophy is to provide an efficient and very versatile programmers' workbench. Under this criteria, Unix design provides the following characteristics:

- *Hierarchical File System;*
- *Unlimited growth of file system;*
- *Logical file system management (both files and devices are maintained in the same way);*
- *File Protection at different levels;*
- *Hierarchical Process Management;*
- *Signal facility for controlling processes and;*
- *Interprocess Communication for concurrent processing.*

To cater to these and many other extended requirement specifications, Unix provides many types of system calls. ***Table 19.1*** shows most of the system calls available in a normal Unix system.

*Table 19.1 List of POSIX-complaint Unix system calls (or API functions)*

Process related System calls:

| System call | Description |
|---|---|
| **(i) Process Management:** | |
| fork | To create a new process; |
| exec** | To execute a new program in a (created) process (** : There are six exec system calls altogether.); |
| wait | To wait until a child process completes its execution; |
| waitpid | To wait until a specified process has terminated; |
| exit | To stop process from execution; |
| brk | To increase/decrease the data segment size of a process. |
| **(ii) Process Environment:** | |
| getpid | To get the process identifier of the calling process; |
| getppid | To get the process identifier of the parent of the calling process; |
| getuid | To get the real user identifier of the calling process; |
| geteuid | To get the effective user identifier of the calling process; |
| getgid | To get the real group identifier of the calling process; |
| getegid | To get the effective group identifier of the calling process; |
| getgroups | To get the supplementary group identifiers of the calling process. |
| **(iii) Accessing User Name:** | |
| getlogin | To get the name associated by the login activity with the control terminal; |
| cuserid | To get the name associated with the effective user identifier of the calling process. |
| **(iv) Identifying Process Group:** | |
| getpgrp | To get the process group identifier of the calling process; |
| setpgrp | To set process group identifier for job control. |
| setsid | |
| **(v) System Identification:** | |
| uname | To get various details (name, release, version, etc) of the current operating system |
| **(vi) Access of Process Times:** | |
| time | To get the system time in seconds; |
| times | To get user and system times of the current process and terminated child process. |
| **(vii) Environment Access:** | |
| getenv | To get the value of a specified environment variable. |

*Table 19.1 (cont.)*

| | |
|---|---|
| (viii) Terminal Identification: | |
| ctermid | To generate terminal path name which can be used by a process refer to the current controlling terminal; |
| ttyname | To determine terminal device name; |
| isatty | To determine whether the file descriptor associated with a terminal is valid or not; |
| sysconf | To enquire about the configurable system variables. |
| Process Control by signal handling: | |
| kill | To send a signal to other processes; |
| sigaction | To specify the action to be associated with a signal type; |
| sigprocmask | To change the calling process' s signal mask; |
| sigpending | To store the set of signals that are blocked from delivery and pending for the calling process; |
| sigsuspend | To replace the calling process's signal mask with the given set of signals; |
| alarm | To set an alarm signal to call the calling process after a specified time; |
| pause | To suspend the calling process until a signal arrives; |
| sleep | To allow the calling process to sleep for a specified time; |
| sigemptyset | To exclude all defined signals from the set; |
| sigfillset | To include all defined signals in the set; |
| sigaddset | To add a specified signal to the signal set; |
| sigdelset | To delete a specified signal from the signal set; |
| sigismember | To test a specified signal whether it belongs to the set. |
| File Management: | |
| (i) Directory control operations: | |
| mkdir | To create a new directory; |
| opendir | To open a directory; |
| readdir | To read an entry from the open directory; |
| rewinddir | To position the directory pointer to the start of the open directory; |
| closedir | To close the open directory; |
| chdir | To change the current working directory to the specified directory; |
| rmdir | To remove a specified directory; |
| getcwd | To get the absolute path name of the current working directory. |
| (ii) Control on a closed file: | |
| creat | To create a file; |
| open | To open a file for direct and block I/O; |
| link | To link a file to a new name in the same file system; |
| unlink | To remove a directory entry of a file; |
| rename | To change the name of a file. |

*Table 19.1 (cont.)*

| | |
|---|---|
| (iii) Special file control: | |
| pipe | To create a pipe for interprocess communication; |
| mkfifo | To make a fifo special file under the specified path name; |
| mknod | To create a special file, such as a directory or a device file; |
| mount | To mount a new file system on a directory; |
| unmount | To detach a mounted file system from a parent file system. |
| (iv) File I/O: | |
| read | To read a block of data directly from a file; |
| write | To write a block of data directly to a file. |
| (v) Control on an open-file: | |
| dup | To give an alternate descriptor for the same open file; |
| dup2 | To give an alternate descriptor of user choice; |
| fcntl | To provide a control over an open file; |
| close | To close a file by releasing a file descriptor; |
| lseek | To move the file position indicator (file cursor) to a specified position. |
| (vi) File Characteristics: | |
| stat | To get information about a specified file; |
| fstat | To get information about an open file; |
| access | To get the file access permissions of a specified file; |
| utime | To set the access and modification times of the named file. |
| (vii) Change File Protection: | |
| umask | To set the user's default file creation mask; |
| chmod | To set protection on a file; |
| chown | To change the owner of a file. |
| (viii) Configuration Limits: | |
| pathconf | To know the current value of a configuration limit associated with a specified file; |
| fpathconf | To know the current value of a configuration limit associated with an open file. |
| Access to system databases: | |
| getgrgid | To access the group database using group id; |
| getgrnam | To access the group database using group name. |

Since the Unix kernel functions are implemented in C, they may be treated by a C-program in the same manner as a normal function that comes with the standard C-library. In other words, there is no apparent difference between a call to a C-library function and a call to a kernel function. In fact, these system calls provide an interface between a C-user and the Unix kernel, as shown in ***Fig. 19.1***.

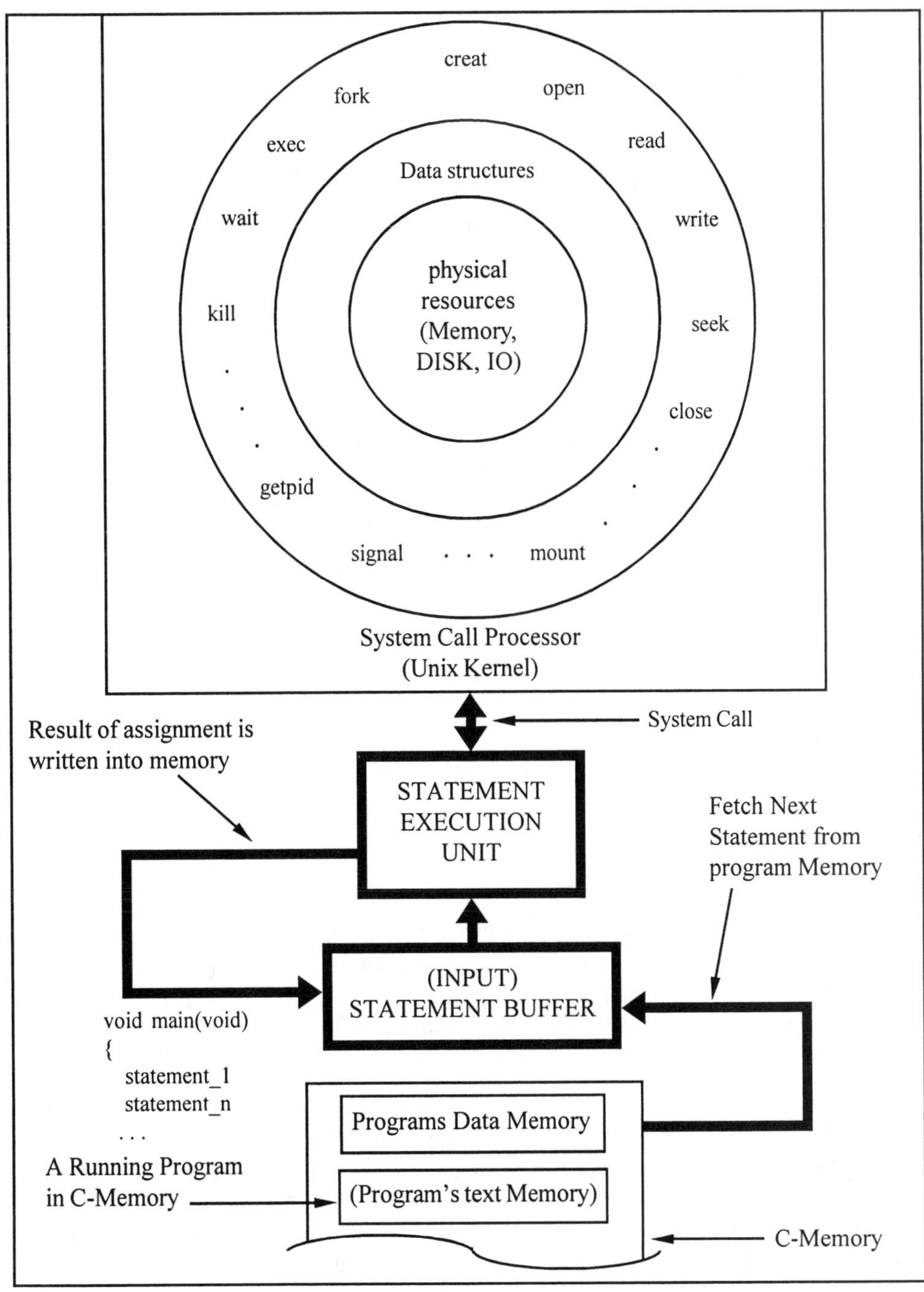


*Fig. 19.1 C-virtual machine with Unix kernel interface*

## 19.4 Error Handling with System Calls

A normal C-compiler does not check a system call expression in a C-program to determine whether the number and type of arguments are correct. As mentioned earlier, system call functions deal with internal resources. If a system call with an error were allowed to proceed, then the accessed resource might be corrupted. Hence, for a system call to be successful, it must go through a validation phase at execution time in order to maintain the integrity of systems resources. In general, the validation checks during execution will include:

- *whether a user is the owner of the accessed resource*
- *whether a call accesses the correct resource*
- *whether a call accesses an existing resource*
- *whether a call carries legal arguments*

Unix's system call interface is implemented using a standard that requires a system call to return a legal (positive integer) value or an error value (-1). The returned negative value indicates that the call has failed and, at the same time, a code indicating the reason for failure is saved as an integer in a Unix kernel's global variable called ***errno***. The calling program can then access this variable and print the error number in the case of a malfunction during a system call. The following convention explains how this global variable can be accessed:

```
#include <stdio.h>
#include <unistd.h>
extern int   errno;
void  main(void)
  {
    . . .
    if (a_sys_call() == -1)
      printf(" Error in sys_call(): %d", errno);
    . . .
  }
```

Simply printing the error number as shown above will not explain the cause of error. One way to find out the meaning of the printed error number is to refer to ***intro(2)*** of the Unix System Manual which lists all error numbers and their symbolic names along with diagnostic messages in brief form.

### Use of errno.h

The ***errno.h*** header file contains the macros to define symbolic names for the numerical error codes. These symbolic names, or macro names, are easier to use during an analysis of error condition caused by a system call in our programs. For example, let us say that the error number 5 is defined as ***EIO*** (error due to physical device failure during file I/O system calls) in the ***errno.h*** file. A program using file I/O can check for this error condition using this macro name as follows:

```
#include <stdio.h>
#include <errno.h>
extern  int    errno;
void  main(void)
  {
      . . .
     return_value = An_IO_sys_call();
     if(return_value == -1)
         {
    if(errno == EIO) /* if phsical I/O error    */
    { /* it could be a transient error and try again     */
        for(i=0; i<10; i++)
              if(An_IO_sys_call() != -1) break;
    printf("Program aborted due to I/O breakdown");
    exit();
         }
       }
      else
        if(errno == . . . ) /* if it is another type of error */
         {/* take appropriate fault tolerance action or abort */
                 . . .
         }
       }
         . . .
  }
```

## 19.5 What Is Systems Programming?

The program components of an operating system can be classified into four categories:

1. *Nucleus or internal functions (process scheduler, device drivers, interrupt handlers, etc.) and System Calls of a kernel virtual machine (i.e., resource managemen' functions);*
2. *User interface program for obtaining the services of operating system (e.g., shell in Unix);*
3. *Application-oriented library functions (e.g., stream I/O);*
4. *Service programs (i.e., software tools, such as assemblers, language compilers, lcaders, editors, macroprocessors, application packages, and simulators/emulators).*

The process of developing and maintaining such programs is called systems programming. A distinct characteristic of systems programming lies in accessing and manipulating the data structures of the kernel to improve the usability of the system resources in a secured manner. In general, the systems programming requires a thorough understanding of the underlying hardware, the kernel's data structures and the kernel's control structure.

Systems programming with respect to a kernel virtual machine involves:

1. *adding or modifying process schedulers, device drivers, memory management functions, etc., that are part of the operating system's nucleus;*
2. *maintaining and modifying the existing system calls to continually improve the power and efficiency of the virtual machine;*
3. *adding system calls related to new resources (e.g., system calls to support networking).*

## 19.6 C as a System Programming Language

Since the Unix kernel is implemented in C, only C-programmers can maintain the whole kernel. C has the privilege to access any kernel function and, hence, it can be used to implement new system calls with the help of the existing system calls.

System programming with respect to the user interface involves providing a user friendly interactive language. Since C has a complete interface with the Unix kernel, it is the ideal language to implement any type of shell program for a Unix operating system.

The system calls access the operating system resources directly and, hence, their use is still of a somewhat primitive nature. However, application programs require functions at a higher level than the system call level. For example, a text processing program can use I/O system calls to read or write with respect to a file. These functions handle I/O in terms of blocks rather than in a more appropriate form, such as character, string and record. In fact, the text processing programs read/or write using characters or strings. Use of I/O system calls in such programs requires additional code to convert blocks of data to and from character or string form. In order to avoid such a situation, abstract level I/O functions, such as stream I/O library functions, can be developed using the system calls and maintained as an application library. This makes application programming less tedious. The task of providing a layer of functions over the system call layer is a part of system programming and C, with several application libraries, proves itself to be a system programming language.

Systems programming with respect to service programs involves developing new tools. Since C has all the necessary features, such as memory addressing using pointers, bit manipulation facilities, stream I/O, and block I/O, it adequately provides for the coding of service programs or software tools.

## 19.7 Why Standard for Operating System Interface?

Although C was originally supported by Unix operating systems, due to its system programming features, it became a part of almost every other operating system for application development. Depending upon the services provided by the host operating systems, C has changed its interface with the system. Since C has become a standard language, it is necessary to demand other operating systems to also provide Unix-like interface so that the system programs can be ported not only among Unix systems, but also among different types of operating systems.

There are several factors associated with the structure of an underlying operating system that cause a variation in the system interface with C and, eventually, steer the C source code differently under different operating systems. Some of those factors are explained below.

### (a) Various Unix Systems

C has been used for system programming purposes under Unix systems, and it has become a common practice to move system programs developed under one Unix to another Unix system. Since C has shown some significant differences on different Unix operating systems due to continual upgrades in the Unix kernel, porting the system programs has become problematic. For example, C-interface with System - V kernel is different from the interface with the BSD-Unix kernel. Moreover, the C-interfaces with the Unix from the same vendors seem to vary from version to version. This situation warrants a standard Unix interface.

### (b) Different File Systems

The useful service of maintaining files is offered by an operating system. When a system is designed, the file system takes its own structure depending upon the requirements of the application environment. Hence, operating systems are invariably different in providing file system services. For example, some of the application requirements, such as file name conventions, types of files supported by the systems, file security mechanisms, and directory structure that may be different.

### (c) Mode of Program Execution

Factors, such as job model and process model, may be different among the systems. Systems vary in forking processes, providing interprocess communication, controlling processes, etc. and, hence, the format of the system calls supporting these functions varies from one system to another.

### (d) Application-Oriented Services

In general, operating systems tend to provide services depending upon the type of applications for which the systems are designed. For example, Unix comes with a set of library functions appropriate for system programming.

### (e) Hardware-Sensitive functions

Certain system programs, like a timer function, might have been designed to maintain a timing precision based on the characteristics of the underlying hardware. Hence, the programs that use such hardware-specific functions may need modifications.

> ***Note:*** *Similar to the evolution of several versions of C, Unix clones started functioning in many sites. Each Unix clone might have introduced new features which in turn would have influenctial in modifying some of the basic Unix functions or adding some new system functions. Particularly, system programs (i.e., programs that depend upon the system functions) written in one Unix environment cannot be run in another Unix environment unless the Unix calls are modified to suit the latter.*

## 19.8 What Is POSIX Standard?

In order to support both efficiency and the portability of applications in general (and system programming in particular) across all operating systems, the ***IEEE 1003.1*** working group proposed a standard operating system interface for computer enviroments called ***IEEE Std 1003.1-1988***. In fact, several other related standards (operating systems, utilities, languages and user interface) have been proposed for open system enviroment, and all these standards are called ***POSIX Standards***, or ***Portable Operating System Interface for Computer Environments***.

***POSIX.1*** refers to the standard for the operating systems interface with the languages like C. While proposing this standard, the committee recognized the Unix-interface with C as a typical model and adopted a subset of this interface as the standard system interface. Since ***POSIX.1*** is derived from Unix interface, almost all Unix systems, with minor modification, can become a part of this standard. On the other hand, non-Unix operating systems may require a major modification to become compliant with ***POSIX.1***. In fact, any other operating system that complies with this standard may look like Unix for an application programmer. This is the reason why this standard is sometimes called Unix-like interface standard.

The ***POSIX.1*** standard for systems interface provides the *standard terminology*, *standard headers*, *standard system services* and *definitions of functional interface* to access those services, including C-language specific services as specified by ***ANSI-standard***. The standard, however, helps only to construct *portable programs* at source language level, and does not guarantee that the object code will execute under different conforming implementations even if the hardware is identical. The remaining chapters introduce the Unix programming in C, often using the ***POSIX*** standard convention.

Other extended standards are ***POSIX.1b*** and ***POSIX.1c***. ***POSIX.1b*** specifies the standard ***API*** for real-time operating systems. ***POSIX.1c*** specifies the standard ***API*** for the multithreaded programming.

> ***Note:*** *Other de facto standards are System V Interface Definition (SVID) and X/OPEN. The SVID is the standard maintained by AT&T for the application program interface of Unix System V. X/OPEN represents a consortium of computer vendors, mostly from Europe, specifying the definition for a common software interface for operating systems, languages and their interfaces. This standard is based on the current developments of the ANSI-C, POSIX.1 and POSIX.2 standards.*

This book discusses only ***POSIX.1***, ***POSIX.1c*** and ***Unix-specific*** application interfaces. Even though ***ANSI-standard*** and ***POSIX*** standard overlap in several features the programmers must know to which standard their programs comply. One way to confirm whether their programs comply with ***POSIX*** is by inserting the following define statement in the beginning of their programs.

*#define _POSIX_SOURCE*

If the compiler compiles without any complaint with this macro, then we can assume that these programs comply with the standard.

### 19.8.1 Use of unistd.h

The ***unistd.h*** header plays its role to contain the prototype definitions of all POSIX compliant API (Application Program Interface) functions. In addition, it defines the symbolic constants and structures referenced in POSIX conforming programs. These constants include the integer arguments to functions like ***access***, ***lseek***, ***sysconf***, ***pathconf*** and ***fpathconf***. The header also includes compile-time as well as execution-time symbolic constants for portability specifications. These definitions can be found in ***Appendix E***.

## 19.9 System Identification

Sometimes it is necessary to identify the system details such as name of the operating system, version, node in which it is running and the processor details. Such information can be useful for system programmers while adding utilities or any other system software developed in other systems. The standard recommends the following system call derived from ***System V Unix system***.

### The uname function

The ***uname*** call is used to get the details of the supporting operating system. The details returned by this call may include system name, operating system release, release of version and processor architecture. The format of this call is:

*int uname(struct utsname *name);*

where the ***utsname template*** is defined in the ***<sys/utsname.h>*** header file. The members of the ***utsname*** structure are:

| | |
|---|---|
| *sysname* | Name of this implementation of the system |
| *nodename* | Name of this node within an implementation-specified communications network |
| *release* | Current release level of this implementation |
| *version* | Current version level of this release |
| *machine* | Name of the hardware type the system is running on. |

The function returns a zero upon successful completion and returns a non-zero value when it fails.

## 19.10 Summary

This chapter introduced the principle of system interface and the requirement of ***POSIX*** standard for adding this feature to C-language. A list of system calls specified by the standard is also presented as a useful guide.

## Exercises

19.1 What is the difference between a system call and a normal library function? Give some examples for each case.

19.2 Would you regard C as a systems programming language for any system or only with respect to Unix? Give reasons to support your claim.

19.3 Which of the following belongs to systems programming?

(a) writing a real-time clock function;
(b) writing a program that computes prime numbers;
(c) writing a program that tells you disk quota
(d) writing a game package
(e) writing a cross-assembler
(f) writing a compiler
(g) writing a processor scheduler

19.4 Write a C-function which will do the same as perror.

# 20

# Process Management Using System Calls

**Chapter contents:**

*This chapter introduces system calls used to create and maintain processes in C-programs. It also explores the process synchronization using signals and process communication using pipes in Unix style. This chapter prepares the readers to be able to write concurrent programs in C.*

**Organization:**

*20.1 Introduction*
*20.2 Process Concept*
*20.3 Process Model in Unix*
*20.4 Description of Process Management System Calls*
*20.5 Signaling System Calls*
*20.6 Summary*
*Exercises*

## 20.1 Introduction

Process management system calls are available to create new processes, execute programs using the created processes, create interprocess communication channels for use by the created processes in exchanging information, allow one process to control other processes via signaling, etc. These system calls allow us to write C-programs that can perform a job in a multitasking or concurrent mode and can be run in a Unix kernel supported by either uniprocessor or multiprocessor hardware. This implies that the C-language can be used as a concurrent programming language with any modification in single processor, but with some modifications, particularly in the interprocess communication facility, to support applications in multiprocessor. To exploit the concurrent facility of C, it is essential to understand the process model supported by the Unix kernel. This chapter briefly introduces the process model of Unix and the way in which the system calls help C-programs manage concurrent processes in this process model.

## 20.2 Process Concept

A process is basically an execution thread that can be used to execute in an address space which is constituted from the data, text and stack segment of a given program. A process always starts at the beginning of the given text segment and terminates at the occurrence of an exit command in the text. When a process is assigned a specific address space, it becomes a useful task. When a process or task proceeds without any interaction, it is called an independent, or simple, process. In this case, the data manipulation is done entirely by a single process.

> ***Note:*** *Although there is a distinction between the terms, process and task, in normal context the term process is used to mean both. In concurrent programming, they carry distinct meaning – a process is simply an execution thread and a task is the execution of a specified job by a process.*

When many independent processes, usually occurring in a multiprogramming environment, compete for accessing common resources (such as terminal, line printer or any non-sharable resources), particularly in a multiprogramming environment, they have to cooperate or synchronize to use them properly. Due to this nature, these processes are called competing or cooperating processes.

On the other hand, a group of processes can be assigned a task in such a way that each process can manipulate a section of the task's data or the common data concurrently. In this mode, processes have to synchronize (interact with each other) using some form of communication to produce the global results in a consistent manner. The processes that are used to perform a common task are called concurrent or interactive processes.

The process concept is a major aspect of any operating system design, involving process creation, process maintenance and process termination with the use of kernel functions (or system calls).

## 20.3 Process Model in Unix

The context of a process consists of three phases:

- *process execution on the user data structure that represents an application and is manipulated by its own functions.*
- *process execution on the system's data structures that represent the resources (files, devices, etc.) maintained by the supporting OS-kernel and are accessed by system calls;*
- *kernel's execution to control the process' states (or to schedule the process), depending upon the resources requirement and their availability.*

In other words, both the user process and the kernel are involved in maintaining the context of a process. When a process manipulates its own data structure, it executes in the user mode; when it accesses system's resources using system calls, it executes in the system mode; when a process does not get the requested resources, it stays in a waiting mode. ***Fig. 20.1*** shows the process execution in these two modes and it is called the in-process model.

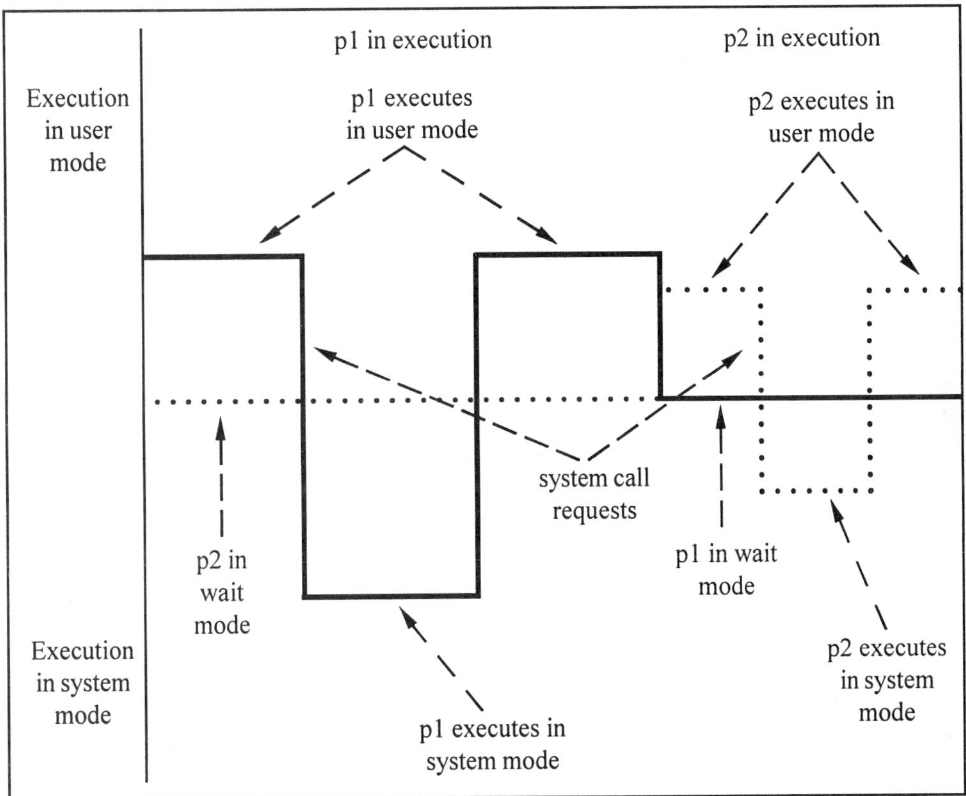


*Fig. 20.1 Process execution in Unix (in-process model)*

> ***Note:*** *The process model, in which a process is represented by a single thread of execution, and the same thread is used to continue in the system mode, is called the in-process model. On the other hand, a user process can be a separate thread (called client) which then can request the system's thread (called server) to access any resources. This is called the out-of-process model.*

### 20.3.1 Control Structure of Unix Process Model

In Unix, every process is accompanied by two data structures, ***process structure*** and ***user structure*** (or ***user area***), to control the process execution. (See ***Fig. 20.2.***) First, the existence of a process is represented by process structure, showing the current status of a process. This structure contains the necessary information about a process that is required by the Unix kernel

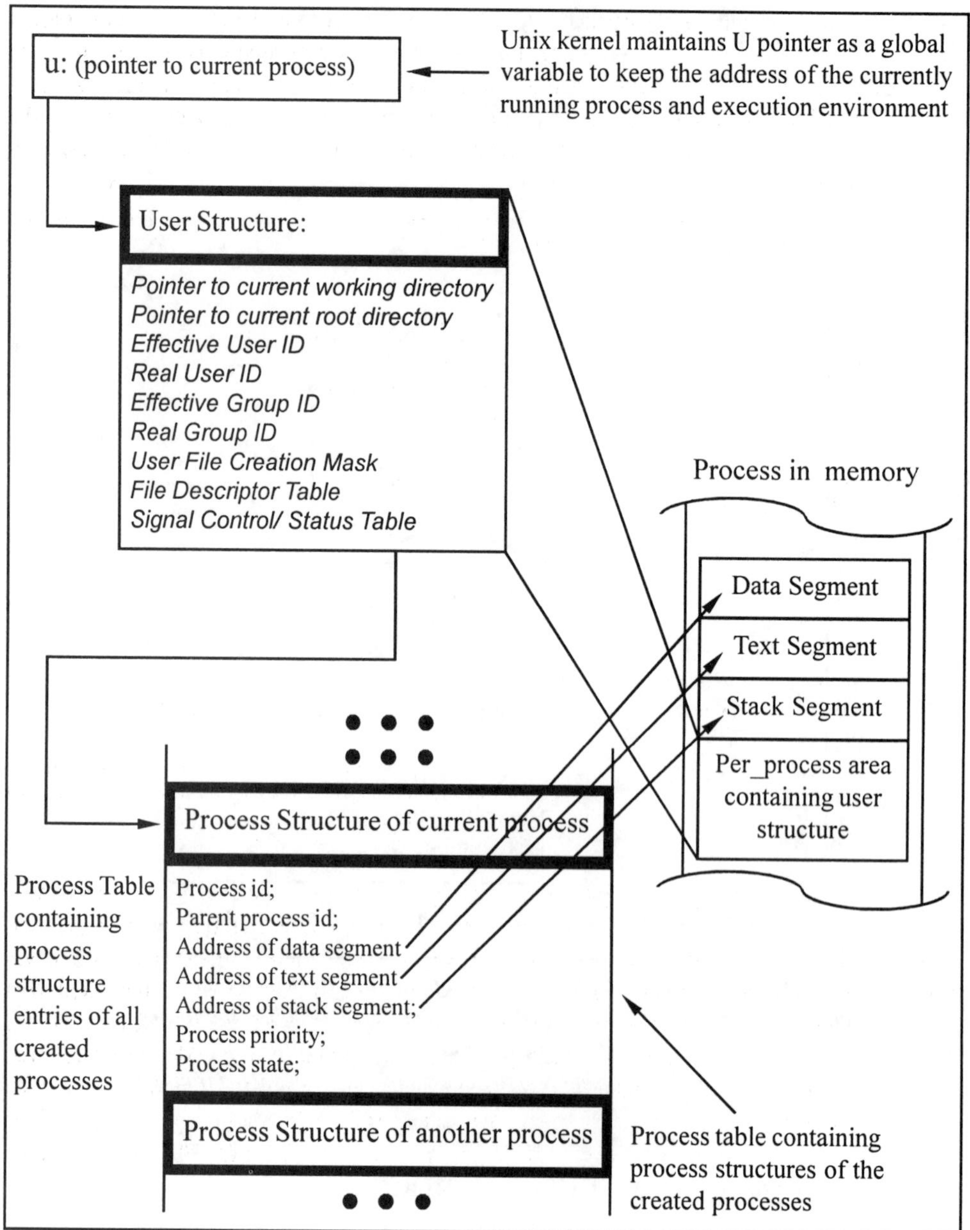


*Fig. 20.2 Control structure of process model in Unix*

for controlling or scheduling purposes. The entries in the process structure include process identifier, parent's identifier, process state, address of the loaded program in memory and many other details, as shown in ***Fig. 20.3***. A table of process structures is called the ***process table***. Initially, the table entries (i.e., process structures) are empty. For each process created in the system, an entry is used to keep the process details. When a process terminates, its corresponding entry is cleared.

```
/ * The structure of an entry in the process table */
struct    P_struct
{
          pid_t      p_pid;              / * process identifier */
          pid_t      p_ppid;             / * parent process identifier */
          gid_t      p_pgid;             / * process group identifier */
          uid_t      p_uid;              / * user id of process */
          char       p_stat;             / * process state */
          int        p_pri;              / * process priority */
          int        p_cpu;              / * cpu-time consumed */
          int        p_time;             / * resident time of process */
          int        p_tty;              / * process */
          int        p_sig;              / * waiting signal of process */
          int        *p_addr;            / * the address of process */
          int        p_stvec[ NREG];     / * state vector of process */
          sigset_t p_sigmask;            /* unwanted signals */
          sigset_t p_sigpending          /* pending signals when they were blocked */
};
struct  P_struct    proc_table[ 100];  / * table for 100 processes */
```

*Fig. 20.3 Prototype version of process structure in Unix*

Second, the user structure is maintained for each process to keep the execution environment that is created for the process. This structure contains such details as effective and real user and group identifiers, a pointer to its current working directory, a pointer to its current root directory, a table of pointers to open-files, a signal table showing how this process would respond to each recognized signal in the system, a file creation mask that is used as a default file protection code by the file creation system call, entries to keep the arguments, returned values and error codes of system calls, etc. The entries in this structure reflect the execution environment associated with a user. The user structure which is created for the user's login shell (or the initial process for a user) is inherited by every created process for that user. ***Fig. 20.4*** shows a prototype of this structure.

```
/ * The user execution environment structure */
struct                                  user
{
        int      u_uid;                 /* effective user  identifier */
        int      u_gid;                 /* effective group identifier */
        int      u_ruid;                /* real user identifier */
        int      u_rgid;                / * real group identifier */
        char     *u_cdir;               /* pointer to current working directory */
        int      *u_croot;              / * pointer to current root directory */
        int      u_signal[NSIG ]        / * signal status table */
        int      u_ofile[NFILE];        /* file descriptor table pointing to open file channels */
        int      u_arg[NARG];           /* arguments to current system call */
        int      u_error;               /* system call's returned error value is saved here*/
        int      *u_buf;                /* pointer to user buffer during read/ write calls */
        int      u_count;               /* bytes remaining for read/ write */
        int      u_offset;              /*  file cursor during read/ write */
        int      u_utime;               /* execution time for this process in user mode */
        int      u_stime;               /* execution time for this process in system mode */
        int      u_cutime;              /* execution time for children in user mode */
        int      u_cstime;              /* execution time for children in system mode */
        int      u_cmask;               /* file creation mask */
        int      *u_procp;              /* pointer to process structure */
      int     u_stvec[ NREG];           / *  CONTEXT of process */
};
```

*Fig. 20.4 Prototype version of the user structure in Unix*

### 20.3.2 The Communication Environment around a Unix Process

When a process is created, the system opens three basic streams, ***stdin***, **stdout** and ***stderr***, for basic communication with respect to the process' control terminal. In addition, it knows its current working directory for performing file I/O. This is shown in ***Fig. 20.5***.

### 20.3.3 The Shell Environment around a Unix Process

The login shell (i.e., the initial process of a terminal or user) maintains a description of the environment in the form of a table of pointers to strings. This table is called the ***environment pointer*** or vector table. Each string represents an environmental variable name and its current value in the following format:

*<variable_name> = <current_value>*

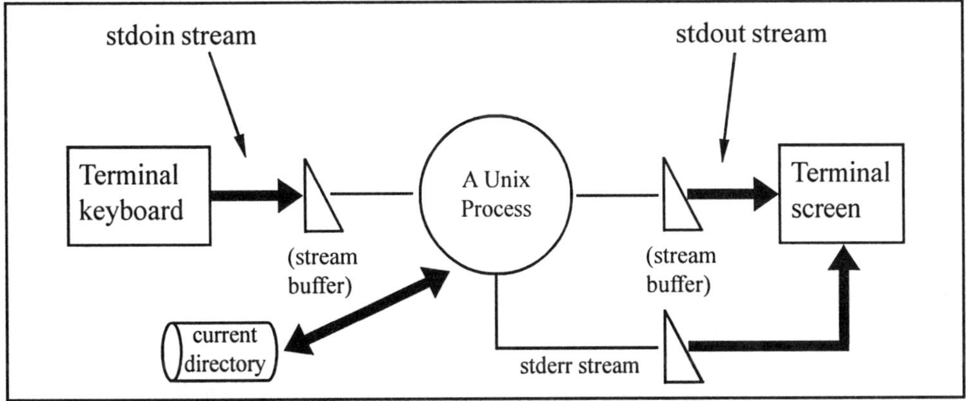


*Fig. 20.5 Communication environment around a Unix process*

For example,

TERM=VT100
USER=nsk
LOGNAME=nsk
HOME=/u/staff/nsk
PWD=/u/staff/nsk/project
PATH=. : /bin : /usr/local/bin

are some typical environmental data maintained by the table. Uses of this table include:

- *First, the shell process uses the path information in this table to locate the binary file matching a given command; for example, when a shell receives the following command,*

  *$cc prog.c*

  *shell will use each path in the PATH variable in the same specified sequence until it finds the location of the* **cc**-*binary file.*

> ***Remark:*** *The shell does not directly use this table, but it creates a child process and calls the exec system call, along with command arguments, in order to execute a command program. This exec system call, in fact, uses the environment table inherited from its shell parent to locate the command program. How the shell executes a command is explained in the next chapter.*

- *Second, shell commands or command programs use this table to display the current value of an environment variable. For example, the shell command **%pwd** will scan the environment table to get the value of the shell variable, PWD, and display its value on the screen, for example /u/staff/nsk/project.*

- *Third, a software tool such as the **vi**-editor may use this table to identify the terminal type (controlled by the shell environment) by looking at the **TERM** variable in order to map the control functions onto the appropriate character set.*

## Access to the Shell Environment Table

A global variable called ***environ*** is maintained by the Unix kernel, and it can be used by a process to access its own shell environment table. Using an ***extern*** declaration, a process can get access to it, as shown in ***Fig. 20.6***.

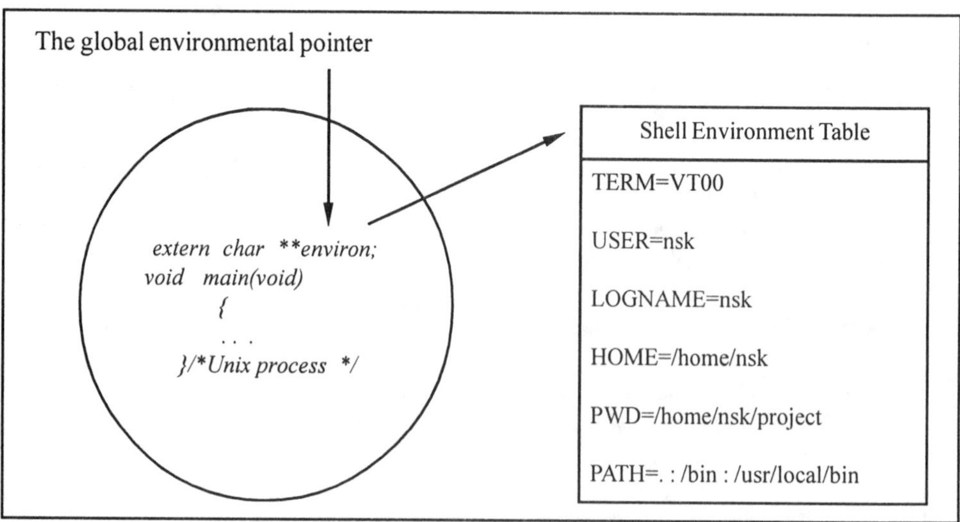


*Fig. 20.6 Shell environment around Unix process*

## Example 20.1:

Write a program to display the current working directory of the shell.

```
#include <stdio.h>
#include <unistd>
#include <string.h>
```

```
void main(void)
  {
    extern char **environ; /* make the externally defined pointer available to this program*/
    char **temp;      /* make a temporary pointer to move along the table  */
      temp = environ;
      while(*temp != NULL)
        {
          if(strncmp(*temp, "PWD", 3) == 0)
            {
              puts(*temp);
              exit(0);
            } /* End of if   */
        temp++;
        } /* End of while loop  */
  } /* End of main */
```

### Example 20.2:

We will display the contents of the environment table with the help of the environ pointer.

```
#include <stdio.h>
#include <unistd.h>
void main(void)
  {
    extern char **environ; /* declare a pointer to the environment table */
    char **temp;      /* make a temporary pointer to move along the table  */
      temp = environ;
      while(*temp ) /* same as: while(*temp != NULL) */
        {
          puts(*temp++);
        } /* End of while loop  */
  } /* End of main */
```

## The getlogin System Call

The **getlogin** call can be used to get the login name associated with the login activity of the controlling terminal. The format of this call is:

```
#include <unistd.h>
char *getlogin();
```

The call returns either a NULL terminated string upon successful completion or a NULL pointer when the login name cannot be found.

### 20.3.4 Creation of Processes

In Unix, only a process can create another process. Assuming there is a process existing, it can create any number of processes, which are simply duplications of the former. The process that creates processes is called parent process and the created processes are called children. Each child can, in turn, create more processes, or grandchildren. This process of creation can continue until a required tree of processes is achieved. In general, Unix allows a user process to create a hierarchy of processes, as shown in ***Fig. 20.7a.*** Processes use the ***fork*** system call to create a new process.

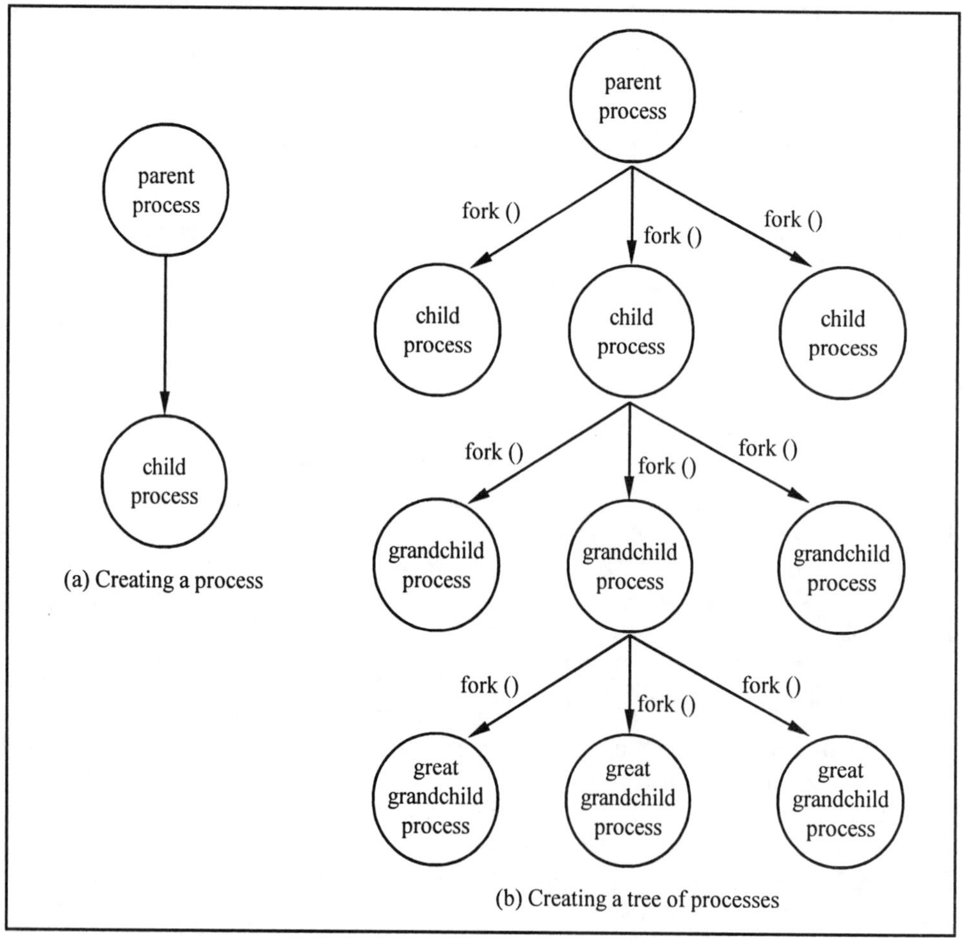


*Fig. 20.7a Signal communication between processes*

### 20.3.5 Inheritance of resources

Children inherit the entire execution environment from the parent (See ***Fig. 20.7b***). That is, an exact copy of the parent's user structure is given to every created child. This inherited information includes the parent's resources, such as ***stdin***, ***stdout*** and ***stderr*** streams, and any open disk files, current working directory, current root directory, file creation mask, etc. (see ***Fig. 20.8***). In general, children get the resources that were owned by the parent at the time of their creation.

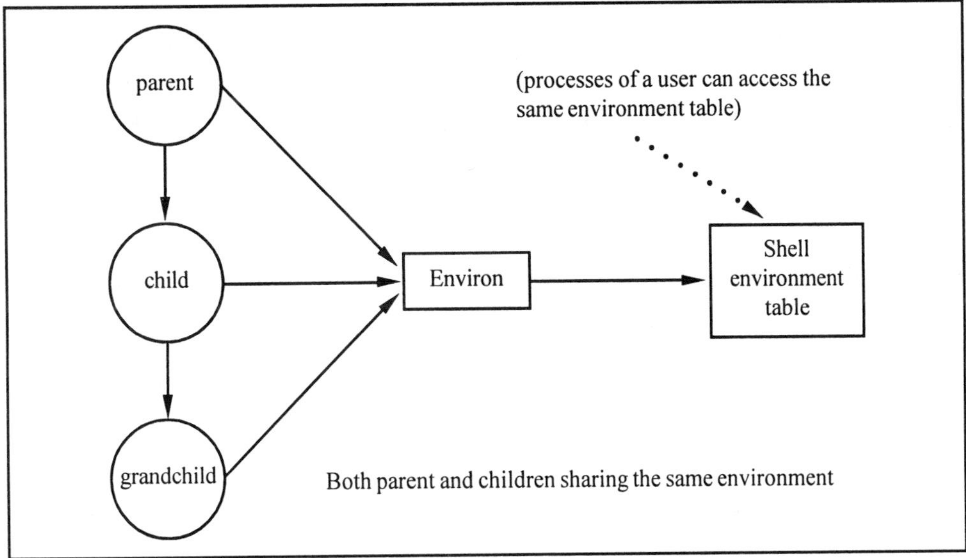


*Fig. 20.7b Both parent and children sharing the same environment*

> ***Remark:*** *If a parent creates a resource after creating a child, that new resource will not be inherited by that child.*

### 20.3.6 Creation of Process Groups

A process group is a tree or a subtree of processes whose leader is the root process of that tree. During creation of a tree of processes, the starting process becomes the group leader and the created processes become part of its group. At the same time, a leaf process can also nominate itself as a new group leader and then create its own process group. All the processes of a group have the same group identifier inherited from their group leader. The purpose of creating a process group is to execute the tasks or subtasks of a job concurrently so that a job can be done in less time. When many process groups are in progress, it is convenient to exercise control over each group using group identifiers.

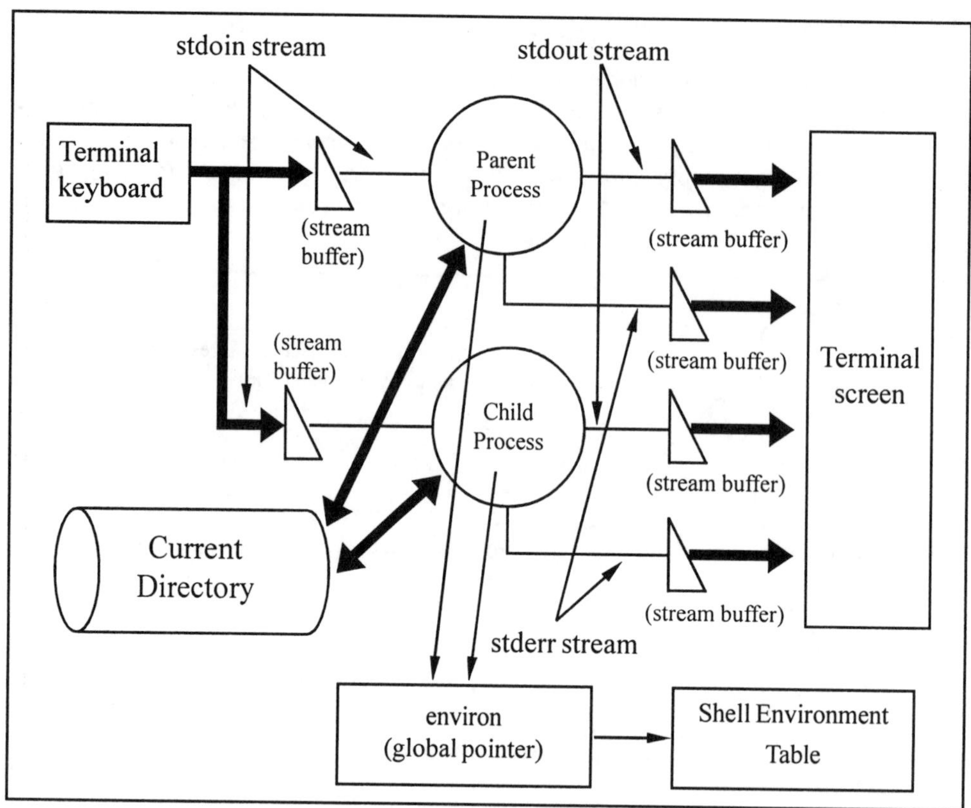


*Fig. 20.8 Child inherits parent's resources*

**Example 20.3:** "Kernel Process Group of Unix"

While Unix is booted, the kernel process group can be established to support either uniprogramming or multiprogramming process control environments. In either case, the ***kernel*** process is the first process that comes into existence automatically when the system is booted, making it the ***root*** process of the whole system. The ***process id*** and ***process group id*** of this kernel process are both 0 (i.e., zero). In establishing a multiprogramming environment, the ***kernel*** process then creates the ***init*** process with ***process id*** of 1 and ***group id***, 0, inherited from the parent process 0, showing that process 1 is part of process group 0. The ***init*** process (i.e., process 1) is created to create and manage the terminal processes for active terminals in the system. (See ***Fig. 20.9***.)

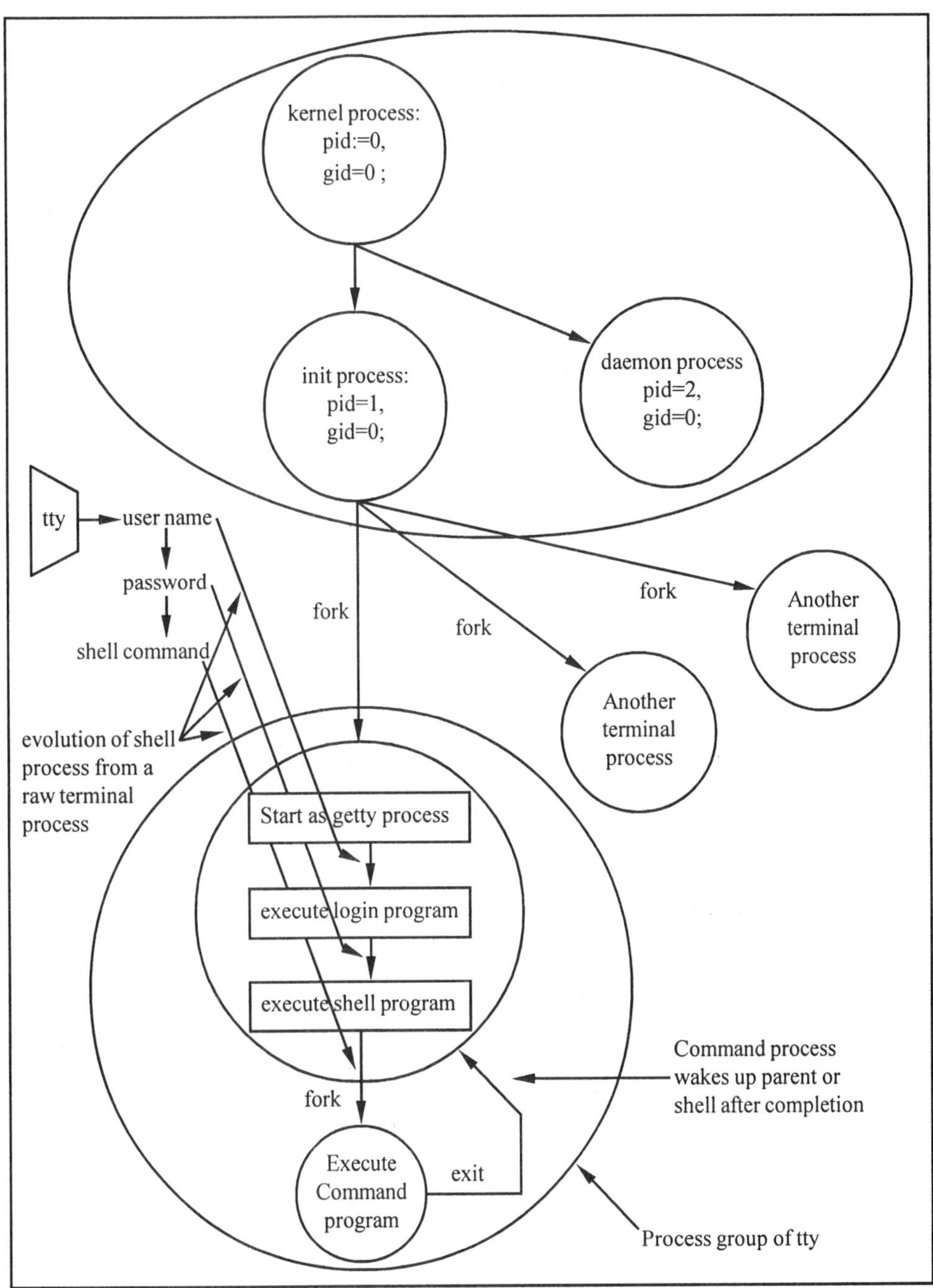


*Fig. 20 9 Kernel and terminal process groups in Unix*

At the time of creation each terminal process belongs to process group 0 and is made to execute a ***terminal line-conditioning*** program called ***getty***. Once each terminal process (now called a ***getty process***) establishes communication with the associated terminal, it displays a login message and waits for a user to input a user name. When a user starts a dialogue, the ***getty process*** receives the user name and leaves the task of validating the users password to another program called ***login***. The same terminal process is now called a ***login process***. The ***login process***, after validating the users password, calls a command line program, the ***login shell***, to run in the same process. The same terminal process is now called a ***shell process***. Each ***shell process*** now establishes a new process group (using an appropriate system call) and becomes ready to process the user commands.

**Example 20.4:** "Terminal Process Group"

A shell process is the initiating process by which each terminal maintains the user session. While interpreting a simple command, a shell creates an execution thread (i.e., a new process) and then assigns the requested program to this thread. Both the shell and new processes proceed independently in separate execution threads. The shell normally waits until the created command process completes its execution.

### 20.3.7 Control of Processes

In Unix, processes can be controlled with the help of software signaling mechanisms. A user can send a signal to a process or process group, or one process can send a signal to another process to redirect process execution. For example, a parent process can send a signal to terminate a child or a process group. (See ***Figures 20.10 and 20.11***.)

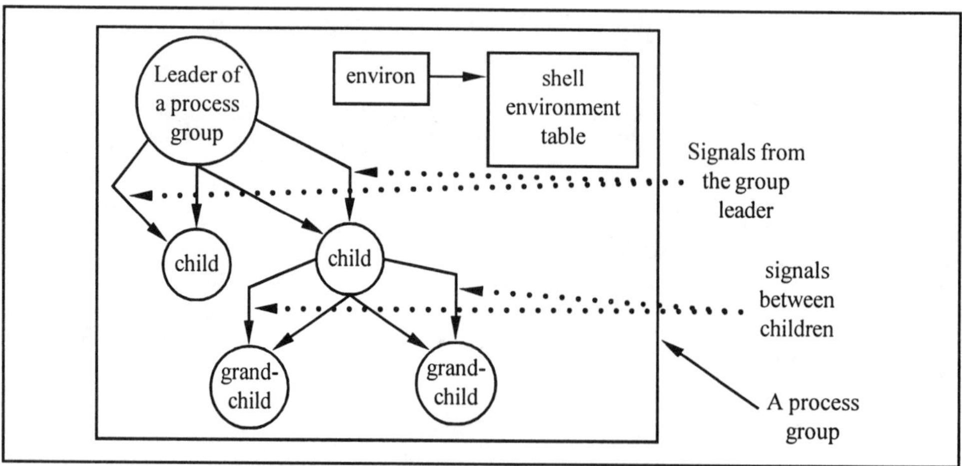


*Fig. 20.10 Signal communication between processes*

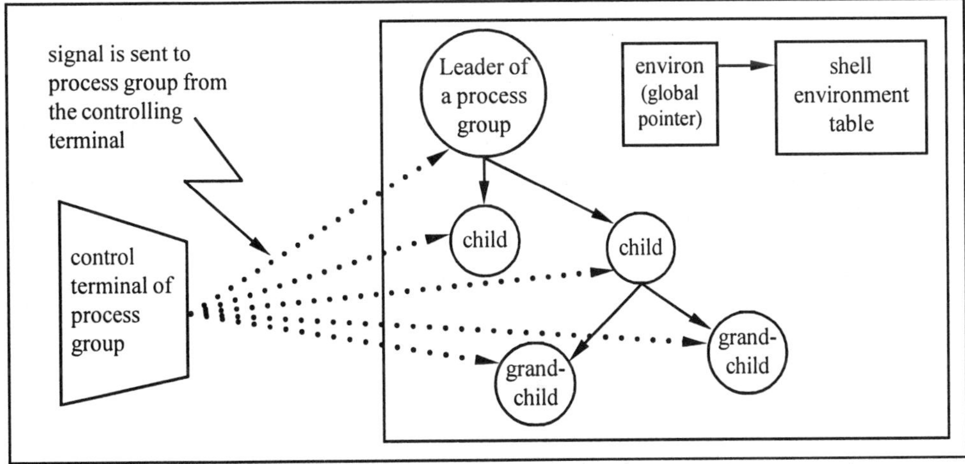


*Fig. 20.11 Signal communication between terminal and its process group*

## 20.3.8 Interprocess Communication within Process Group

When a process group executes a job cooperatively, processes can transfer data using a *pipe* mechanism. A group leader can create a set of pipes which are then inherited by its processes for transferring data between them. Each pair of processes can then share a *pipe* and this allows the use of the pipeline type of concurrent processings for a given set of input data. For example, ***Fig. 20.12*** shows how a shell process organizes processes and their communication using pipes for a pipeline command like:

*ls | mc | more*

where the ***ls*** command is to list the contents of current directory, ***mc*** is to convert the output of ***ls*** into multicolumn format and ***more*** is to show the output of ***mc*** one page at a time on the screen. The vertical stroke character ('|') is used to denote a *pipe* at the command level.

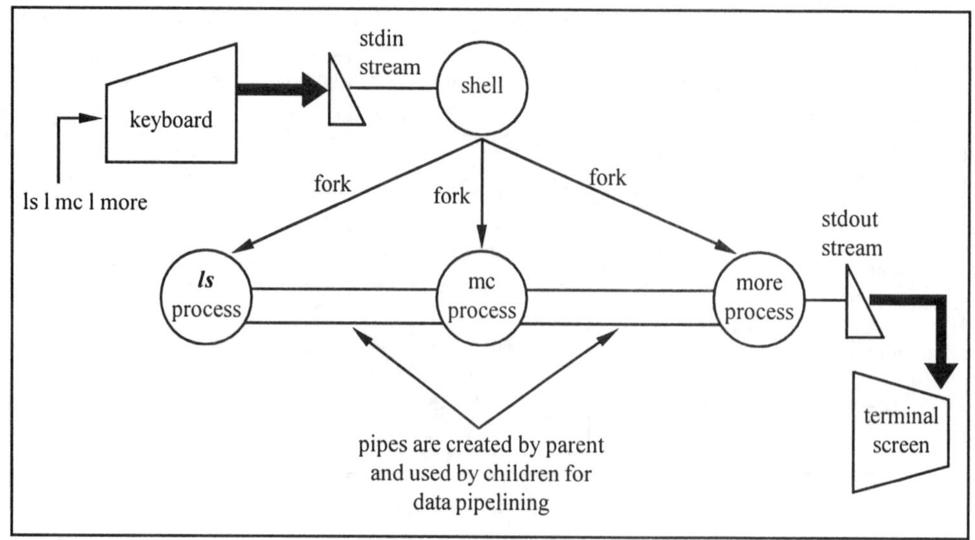


*Fig. 20.12 Pipes for communication*

## 20.4 Description of Process Management System Calls

### 20.4.1 The fork System Call

The ***fork*** call splits the calling process into two. That is, a process which executes a ***fork*** call is called the parent process and a process that is created by a ***fork*** call is called the child process. Since a ***fork*** call duplicates the memory image of the parent program, both parent and child proceed to execute the remaining text of the same program, but independently. The prototype definition of the ***fork*** system call is:

```
#include <sys/types.h>     /* pid_t is defined in this header  */
    pid_t  fork( void );
```

***fork*** returns a process identifier for the created child process; if the returned value is -1, an error occurred during the fork operation.

***Error Flag:*** The returned value, -1, indicates that the fork call has failed due to one of the following reasons:

- *the user cannot create any more process (or the number of processes created will exceed the limit);*
- *the number of processes created in the whole system will exceed the limit (or there is no free entry available in the process table);*

Following a ***fork*** call, both parent and child exist and both receive a returned value from this function. The parent receives the process identifier (PID) of the created child, whereas the child process receives simply a NULL or zero value. If the returned value happens to be a negative value, then the parent can assume that its ***fork*** call has failed to create a process. When a ***fork*** operation is successful, the returned values can be used to control the execution of both processes. That is, each process, after identifying whether it is a parent or child, can select the appropriate portion of the remaining text. The following code segment shows a method of using a ***fork*** call.

```
/* Program Name:  fork.c   */
 #include <stdio.h>
 #include <sys/types.h>   /* pid_t is defined in this header   */
 #include <unistd.h>
void  main(void)
  {
   pid_t  child_id;
     If((child_id = fork()) == -1)
       { perror(" During fork() ");
         exit(0);
       }
     if(child_id ==0)  /* processes select their texts  */
       { /* child executes here  */
         child_text();
         exit(0)
       }
     else
       { /* parent executes here */
         parent_text();
         exit(0);
       }
  }
```

## Example 20.5:

Write a C-program to create a child process and allow the parent to display "I am the parent" and the child to display "I am the child" on the screen. Call this program ***conc_prog1.c***.

```
/* Program Name:   conc_prog1.c */
 #include <stdio.h>
 #include <sys/types.h>  /* pid_t is defined in this header   */
 #include <unistd.h>
void main(void)
  {
   pid_t  child_id;
    if((child_id = fork()) == -1)
      {
      perror("During fork() ");
      exit();
      }
    if(child_id ==0)
      { printf("  I AM THE CHILD PROCESS \n");
        exit(0);
      }
    else
      { printf("  I AM THE PARENT PROCESS   \n");
        exit(0);
      }
  }
```

***Remarks:***

1. *After forking, it is necessary to test whether a process is created successfully; if fork fails, terminate the executing program.*

2. *A fork expression must be used carefully in a loop statement; if forking continues inside a loop without a control, an heap of processes will be populated and system resources, like memory, will be exhausted.*

```
for(i=0; i < 10; i++)
     fork();
```

   *would create an unexpected process tree.*

3. *Since both parent and child proceed asynchronously (i.e., which will be scheduled first may not be known), outputs may be in any order. If we execute the above program a few times, the outputs may be as shown below:*

   *At first run:* *I AM THE CHILD PROCESS*<br>*I AM THE PARENT PROCESS*<br>*At second run:* *I AM THE PARENT PROCESS*<br>*I AM THE CHILD PROCESS*

### 20.4.2 The getpid and getppid System Calls

The ***getpid*** and ***getppid*** system calls can be used by a current process to get its own unique process identifier and its parent's process identifier, respectively. The prototype definitions of these system calls are

(a) *#include <sys/types.h>   /* pid_t is defined in this header */*
*pid_t   getpid( void );*

The ***getpid*** system call returns the process identifier of the caller process; if the returned value is -1, an error occurred.

(b) *#include <sys/types.h>   /* pid_t is defined in this header */*
*pid_t   getppid( void );*

The ***getppid*** system call returns the process identifier of the caller process' parent; if the returned value is -1, an error occurred during the open operation.

> ***Error Flag:*** The returned value, -1, indicates that the getppid call has failed because the parent process does not exist.

### Example 20.6:

Write a C-program to create one child process and one grandchild process, and code their texts to print their identification messages. Call this program ***conc_prog2.c***.

```
/* Program Name:   conc_prog2.c */
#include <stdio.h>
#include <sys/types.h>      /* pid_t is defined in this header   */
#include <unistd.h>
pid_t    my_pid;
pid_t    my_parent_pid;
pid_t  child_id;
void  main(void)
  {
    if((child_id = fork()) == -1)
      {
        perror("ERROR at fork() child");
        exit(0)
      }
    if(child_id !=0)
      { /* parent executes here */
        my_pid = getpid();
        printf("  I am the PARENT; \n");
```

```
        printf(" My process ID is: %d \n", my_pid);
        exit(0);
    }
  else
    { /* child executes here and it creates its own child */
      pid_t    grand_child_id;
      if((grand_child_id = fork()) == -1)
        {
          perror("ERROR at fork() grandchild");
          exit(0)
        }
      if(grand_child_id !=0)
      { /* child continues here */
          my_pid = getpid();
          printf(" I am the CHILD;  \n");
          printf(" My process ID is: %d \n", my_pid);
          my_parent_pid = getppid();
          printf(" My parent's process ID is: %d \n", my_parent_pid);
          exit(0);
      }
      else
        { /* grandchild executes here */
          printf(" I am the grandchild;     \n");
          my_pid = getpid();
          printf(" My process ID is: %d \n", my_pid);
          my_parent_pid = getppid();
          printf(" My parent's process ID is: %d \n", my_parent_pid);
          exit(0);
        }
} /* End of main program */
```

***Remarks:***

1. *When the above program is executed, three processes come into existence, as shown below, that share the same program text;*

2. *As mentioned earlier, the processes are running asynchronously, and their output sequence cannot be predicted.*

### 20.4.3 Process Synchronization Using wait

A parent, after creating a child, may proceed concurrently or wait by leaving its child to perform the assigned task, depending upon the processing environment that is appropriate for these concurrent processes. For example, when we give a command to the Unix shell, shell creates a child process and runs the command program in the created process. Since both processes are allowed to share the terminal, shell (i.e., parent in this case) can wait, leaving the command process to use the terminal freely. It should be noted that a waiting process can only be woken up by an ***exit*** call of one of its created children, meaning only a parent is allowed to issue a ***wait*** call.

A ***wait*** call can also be used to identify the exiting child as well as determine the termination status of the child. The prototype definition of the ***wait*** call is:

```
#include <sys/wait.h> /* macros to test returned argument are defined in this header */
#include <sys/types.h>    /* pid_t is defined in this header   */
pid_t wait(int *p_status);
```

where

**p_status** must be an integer pointer; it brings back information about how a child terminates. When the call is completed, the integer word of this argument contains, in its lower two bytes, the following information :

1. Upon an abnormal termination due to a signal, the value in the lowest byte indicates a signal identifier that terminated the child; at the same time, the second lowest byte is returned with the zero value.

2. Upon normal termination, the lowest byte contains zero and the next lowest byte brings the value (the status of process termination) that was passed as an argument via the **exit(status)** call. (See **section 20.4.5**.) This value may show where a child exits. For example, a simple **exit** (with the status code zero, i.e., **exit(0)**) in a child's text shows, by convention, that it terminates normally. For any abnormal exit, a programmer can use different codes that can be interpreted by the parent process.

**wait** returns an integer indicating the process identifier of the exiting child. If the returned value is -1, an error occurred.

**Error Flag:** The returned value, -1, indicates that the wait call has failed due to one of the following reasons:

- a process waits without a child;
- the pointer argument points to an illegal address.

## Example 20.7:

Rewrite the program shown in ***Example 20.5*** to ensure that the child's message appears on the screen first.

```
/* Program Name:   conc_prog3.c */
#include <stdio.h>
#include <sys/types.h>   /* pid_t is defined in this header   */
#include <sys/wait.h>    /* macros to test returned argument defined in this header   */
#include <unistd.h>
void main(void)
  { int ch_exit_status;
  pid_t child_id;
    if((child_id = fork()) == -1);
      {
        perror("During fork() ");
        exit(0);
      }
    if(child_id ==0)
      { printf("  I AM THE CHILD PROCESS \n");
        exit(0);  /*   the child exits and wakes its waiting parent */
      }
    else
      { wait(&ch_exit_status);  /* the parent is waiting until the child exits */
        printf("  I AM THE PARENT PROCESS   \n");
        exit(0);
      }
  }
```

The output of the above program will be:

*I AM THE CHILD PROCESS*
*I AM THE PARENT PROCESS*

## Example 20.8:

Use the ***sleep*** system call to order the outputs of processes.

```
/* Program Name:   con_prog4.c */
#include <stdio.h>
#include <sys/types.h>    /* pid_t is defined in this header   */
#include <sys/wait.h>     /* macros to test returned argument defined in this header   */
#include <unistd.h>
void main(void)
  { int status;
   pid_t  exit_ch;
   pid_t  child_id;
    if((child_id = fork()) == -1)
      {
      perror("During fork() ");
      exit();
      }
    if(child_id ==0)
      {
        sleep(5); /*  wait until parents first message  */
       printf("  I AM THE CHILD PROCESS  \n");
        exit(0); /* child exits normally & wakes its parent */
      }
    else
      { /* parent is ready to wait until child exits */
        printf(" I AM THE PARENT WAITING FOR CHILD PROCESS  \n");
         if((exit_ch = wait(&status)) == -1)
         {
           perror("During wait() ");
           exit();
         }
        printf("I AM THE PARENT NOW EXITING    \n");
         exit(0);
      }
  }
```

*Note: In the above program, the output of the child process is delayed by five seconds, using the* ***sleep(5)*** *call, with the assumption that the parent would output its first message within this interval.*

### The waitpid System Call

The ***waitpid*** call is similar to wait except that it can wait for a specific process. The format of this call is:

```
#include <sys/types.h>     /* pid_t is defined in this header */
#include <sys/wait.h>      /* macros to test returned argument defined in this header */
pid_t waitpid(pid_t pid, int *status, int options);
```

This call behaves differently for various values of pid, as shown below:

- *If pid is equal to -1, the calling process will wait for any child process to terminate and send the status.*
- *If pid is greater than zero, the calling process will be waiting for a child with its ID the same as pid.*
- *If pid is equal to zero, the calling process will be waiting for the status of any child whose process group is the same as the process ID of the calling process.*
- *If the pid is less than -1, the calling process will be waiting for the status of any child whose process group ID is the same as pid.*

This function's behavior is also controlled by a number of bit-mapped options. The options argument can be constructed by bitwise inclusive OR of the following flags that are defined in the ***sys/wait.h*** header file:

***WNOHANG*** The waitpid call returns immediately, even the status of a specified child is not available immediately.

***WUNTRACED*** The waitpid call can return the status of both stopped and terminated processes.

The ***sys/wait.h*** also has macros to test the status value returned by a wait or waitpid call. The included macros are listed in ***Table 20.1***.

## 20.4.4 General Rules for Waiting

1. *When a parent creates a child process, it is almost always preferable to put the parent in* ***wait*** *state so that child can freely use the resources. This is a type of synchronized use of a common resource.*

2. *A* ***wait*** *expression cannot be used to wait for a specific child process. It waits, in general, for one of the created child process to exit. When more than one child process exists, a parent has to issue one* ***wait*** *call for each process.*

*Table 20.1 Macros defined in* **sys/wait.h** *for testing the returned value (i.e., status argument)*

| Macro name | Description |
|---|---|
| WIFEXITED(status_value) | Evaluates to non-zero value when the child process terminated normally. |
| WEXITSTATUS(status_value) | The macro value as non-zero, the value evaluates to the low order of 8-bits of the status returned by _exit function. |
| WIFSIGNALED(status_value) | The macro value as non-zero indicates that the child was terminated by a signal that was not caught by the child. |
| WTERMSIG(status_value) | The macro value as non-zero represents the signal number that caused the termination of the child process. |
| WIFSTOPPED(status_value) | The macro value as non-zero indicates that the child has stopped. |
| WSTOPSIG(status_value) | The macro value as non-zero represents the signal number that caused the child process to stop |

## Example 20.9:

The following program shows a parent that creates four child processes and wait four times before it exits.

```
/* Program: test_wait.c */
#include <stdio.h>
#include <sys/types.h>   /* pid_t is defined in this header   */
#include <sys/wait.h>    /* macros to test returned argument defined in this header   */
#include <unistd.h>
pid_t  child_id[4],  exit_ch;
void  main(void)
{
  . . .
  for(i =0; i <4; i++)
    {
    if((child_id[i] = fork()) == -1)
      {
       perror("During fork() ");
        . . .   /* terminate created processes, if any, before exit */
       exit();
      }
```

```
if(child_id[i] ==0)
  {
   printf(" I AM THE CHILD PROCESS [PID:%d] \n", getpid());
   exit(0); /* a child exits normally and wakes its parent */
  }
else
  { /* the parent is ready to wait until all children exit */
   for(i =0; i <4; i++)
     {
       if((exit_ch = wait(&status)) == -1)
         {
         perror("During wait() ");
         exit();
         }
       printf( "Child with PID: %d terminated  \n", exit_ch );
     }
   printf("PARENT terminates now \n");
   exit(0);
  }
 } /* End of fork */
{ /* End of main */
```

## 20.4.5 The _exit System Call

The ***_exit*** system call can be used to terminate a process at any point in the program that is in execution. It is an optional call, and if it is not used, the process will exit at the last statement of the text. An advantage of ***_exit*** is that when a child process detects any abnormal condition, it can exit and send an appropriate code to its parent. The prototype definition of the ***_exit*** system call is:

```
#include <stdlib.h>   /* macros for status_code are defined in this header */
void  _exit( int  status_code);
```

where ***status_code*** is an integer argument to indicate the status of process termination, and ***_exit*** never returns and hence no value is expected.

The argument, ***status_code***, can be either an unsigned integer or unsigned character. By convention a zero (or no value) argument means a normal termination of a child process. For example,

```
#include <stdlib.h> /* EXIT_SUCCESS is defined in this header */
_exit(EXIT_SUCCESS)
```

means normal termination. A user can use other values in an ***_exit*** call to denote different error conditions that may occur in a process. Only a parent and its children have knowledge of the values used by this code. For example, *_exit(1)* may mean that a child couldn't open a file, *_exit(2)* may mean that it couldn't write to an open file, etc. In general, the macro ***EXIT_FAILURE*** can be used as the argument of exit for a non-zero value indicating some error condition. Basically, it provides a means of interprocess communication between a parent and its children.

> ***Remark: EXIT_SUCCESS*** *and* ***EXIT_FAILURE*** *are defined in* ***stdlib.h.***

A parent receives the exit code of a child by means of a ***wait(&status)*** system call. An *_exit* call can transmit its status code successfully only when its parent has called ***wait*** with a legal status argument. As already mentioned, the transmitted exit's status code is received in the second lowest byte of the argument in a parent's ***wait*** call. It helps a parent process to understand the completion status of a child's given task.

> ***Remark****: The exit function of ANSI-C is a wrapper function over _exit system call.*

### 20.4.6 The setpgid System Call

The ***setpgid*** system call is used by a process to nominate itself as a process group leader. Any process created by this leader becomes a part of this group. Maintaining a process group is particularly useful in applying control over the processes, which is discussed in the following section. The prototype definition of this system call is:

```
#include <unistd.h>
int     setpgid( void );
```

where ***setpgid*** returns an identifier for a new process group led by the caller; if the returned value is -1, an error occurred during this operation.

## 20.5 Signaling System Calls

A process can be controlled either from a controlling terminal or from another process, or in response to any abnormal condition via a ***software interrupt*** called a ***signal***. For example, a user can interrupt a running process by hitting the DEL key (or Control-C key, depending upon which one is configured as the interrupt key). This action sends an interrupting signal (whose symbolic name is SIGINT) to stop the running process. By default, this signal will terminate the running process. Similarly, a quit (SIGQUIT) can be generated from the Control-\ key to terminate a running process with a core dump for later analysis. Disconnecting a line (switching off a terminal or hanging up a phone) will send a hang up (SIGHUP) signal to indicate some defined action (by default terminate action) on the processes that were created via that communication line.

Sometimes a process can generate a signal to terminate itself. For example, the ***abort*** function call in a program generates a signal to terminate the caller abnormally. Signals are also generated by a process to terminate its related processes. A parent process, after waiting for a certain interval, can send a kill signal to its children, for instance.

Another source of signals is the ***hardware exception***, such as ***memory*** (or ***segment***) ***violation***, execution of an ***illegal instruction***, and ***divide by zero***. The operating system kernel can also generate signals to indicate that some abnormal software conditions occurred. For example, kernel generates a signal when it finds that a process writes to a ***pipe*** and, at the same time, there is no reader process (or reader processes are terminated).

### 20.5.1 Signal Types

A list of signals that can control a process is defined in the include file called ***/usr/include/signal.h***. ***Table 20.2*** shows the description of commonly available signals.

*Table 20.2a Signals supported by POSIX*

| Symbolic Constant | Default Action | Description |
|---|---|---|
| SIGABRT | Abnormal termination of the process | Abnormal termination signal caused by the abort function. (Included in the C-standard.) |
| SIGALRM | Abnormal termination of the process | Generated by alarm clock. |
| SIGFPE | Abnormal termination of the process | Generated by the kernel at the occurrence of a floating point overflow. (Included in the C-standard.) |
| SIGHUP | Abnormal termination of the process | Generated by hanging up phone. |
| SIGILL | Abnormal termination of the process | Generated by the kernel when CPU executes an illegal instruction. (Included in the C-standard.) |
| SIGINT | Abnormal termination of the process | Generated by hitting DEL or Break key to get the attention of the process. (Included in the C-standard.) |
| SIGKILL | Abnormal termination of the process | Generated by a user process to terminate a process without any delay. This signal may not be ignored or caught. |
| SIGPIPE | Abnormal termination of the process | Generated by a broken pipe which has no process to read. |

*Table 20.2a (cont.)*

| | | |
|---|---|---|
| SIGQUIT | Abnormal termination of the process | Generated by FS or Control-\ key. |
| SIGSEGV | Abnormal termination of the process | Generated by memory protection violation due to illegal access of a location. (Included in the C-standard.) |
| SIGTERM | Abnormal termination of the process | Generated to terminate a process gracefully. (Included in the C-standard.) |
| SIGUSR1 | Abnormal termination of the process | Reserved as application-defined signal 1. |
| SIGUSR2 | Abnormal termination of the process | Reserved as application-defined signal 2. |

*Table 20.2b Job control signals defined by POSIX*

| **Symbolic Constant** | **Default Action** | **Description** |
|---|---|---|
| SIGCHLD | Abnormal termination of the process. | Generated when a child process is terminated or stopped. |
| SIGCONT | Continue the process if it is currently stopped, else ignore the signal. | Signal is sent to make the stopped process continue. |
| SIGSTOP | Stop the process. | Stop signal not from terminal. This signal may not be ignored or caught. |
| SIGTSTP | Stop the process. | Stop signal from terminal. |
| SIGTTIN | Stop the process. | Generated when a member of a background process group attempts to read from control terminal. |
| SIGTTOU | Stop the process. | Generated when a member of a background process group attempts to write to control terminal. |

### 20.5.2 Signal Sets and Signal Mask

The concept of signal sets is introduced in the later Unix systems to improve the reliability of signal handling. A signal set is merely a bitmap corresponding to the signal types defined in a system. The size of this bitmap depends upon the number of signal types. A ***bitmap*** variable can be declared by the ***sigset_t*** type (defined in the ***signal.h*** header). The ***bitmap*** variables are used to define a signal set, either for the purpose of masking signals or for maintaining the pending signals. For example, ***sigset_t*** variable and its ***bitmap*** are shown below and in ***Fig. 20.13***:

```
#include <signal.h>
sigset_t ss;
```

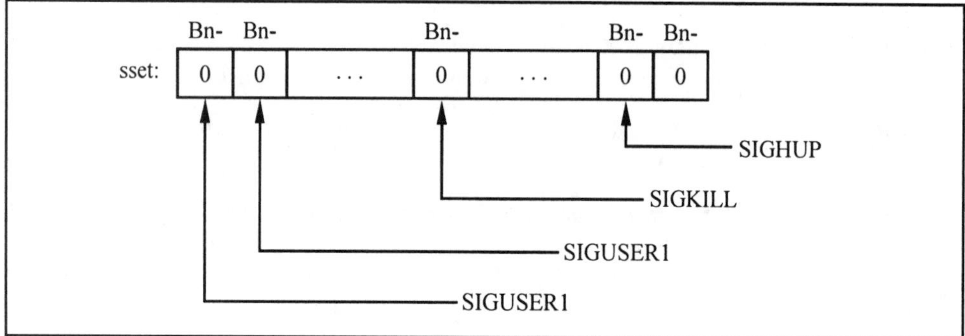


*Fig. 20.13 Bitmap of ss variable*

The ***signal mask*** attribute of a process is also a ***sigset_t*** type variable. It may be part of either the ***process structure*** or ***u-structure*** of a process. It is meant to contain a ***bitmap*** of the signal types that should be blocked during the execution of the corresponding process. When a process is created, this mask is inherited from its parent. Usually, the shell process gets its ***signal mask*** with the ***default bitmap*** from the system's init process. One possible value of the default bitmap may not block any signal at all. The standard Unix provides a set of system calls to alter or overwrite the entire ***bitmap***.

```
#include <signal.h>
int sigemptyset(sigset_t *ss);
int sigfillset(sigset_t *ss);
int sigaddset(sigset_t *ss, int signal_type);
int sigdelset(sigset_t *ss, int signal_type);
int sigismember(const sigset_t *ss, int signal_type);
```

The ***sigemptyset*** system call is used to return an effective empty mask set via the *ss* argument. When we store such an empty mask set in the signal mask of a process, all the signals will be allowed to interrupt the process. The call returns 0 after successful operation and -1 when an error occurs.

The complementary function to ***sigemptyset*** is ***sigfillset***. The ***sigfillset*** system call is used to return an effective mask set via the argument to include all signal types. When we store this set in the mask set of a process, no signal will be able to arrive to the running process. This call also returns 0 after successful completion and -1 when an error occurs.

The ***sigaddset*** system call can be used to add a signal type, specified in the second argument to the set in the ***ss*** argument. Complement to the ***sigaddset*** function, the ***sigdelset*** system call can be used to delete the specified signal type from the set in the *ss* argument.

## The sigprocmask System Call

The ***sigprocmask*** call is useful either to examine the current setting of the signal mask or change the setting of the signal mask of the calling process. The format of the call, as defined in signal.h, is:

```
#include <signal.h>        /* sigset_t is defined in this header   */
int sigprocmask(int setmode, sigset_t *newset, sigset_t *oldset);
```

This function changes the mask setting of the calling process by combining the ***oldset*** with the ***newset*** according to the manner specified in the ***setmode*** field. The values of ***setmode*** and the resulting set combinations are shown below:

| Value of the setmode argument | Description |
|---|---|
| SIG_BLOCK | The resulting set in the mask of the calling process is the union of the current set pointed to by oldset and the set pointed to by newset; |
| SIG_UNBLOCK | The resulting set in the mask of the calling process has excluded the signals specified in the newset from the signal set of the oldset. This is obtained by the intersection of the current set pointed to by oldset and the complement of the set pointed to by newset. |
| SIG_SETMASK | The resulting signal set in the mask of the calling process is the signal set pointed to by the newset. |

All the above values are defined in ***signal.h***. At the successful completion, the call returns zero, else it returns -1 and sets ***errno*** appropriately. The possible error could be due to an illegal value leading to the EINVAL value of ***errno***.

**Example 20.10:** We will show the code to set the signal mask of a process to block the SIGINT and SIGTERM signals.

```
#include <stdio.h>
#include  <unistd.h>
#include  <signal.h>          /* kill system call is defined        */
 void main(void)
{
 sigset_t ss;
   sigemptyset(&ss);            /* reset the ss */
   sigaddset(&ss, SIGINT);   /* add the interrupt signal type to be masked */
   sigaddset(&ss, SIGTERM);/* add the termination signal type to be masked */
   sigprocmask(SIG_SETMASK, ss, 0); /* store the bitmap of ss into signal mask field of
                                            the process */
}
```

The siprocmask system call can also be used to receive the existing signal mask of a calling process. For example, the following call returns the value of the signal mask of the calling process:

```
      . . .
   sigset_t dummy_set, current_set;
   sigemptyset(&dumy_set);
   sigprocmask(SIG_BLOCK, &dummy_set, &current_set);
      . . .
```

After the successful return of the ***sigprocmask*** call, the ***current_set*** argument will contain the current value of the signal mask of the calling process.

## The sigismember System Call

The ***sigismember*** call is useful to test whether a given signsl type is set in a given signal set. This system call is quite useful to find out whether a particular signal type is blocked in the current signal mask of a calling process. The format of the call, as defined in ***signal.h***, is:

```
#include <signal.h>       /* sigset_t is defined in this header   */
int sigismember(const sigset  *signal_set, int sig_type);
```

The ***sigismember*** returns 1 if the specified ***sig_type*** is set in the ***signal_set***, 0 if the specified ***sig_type*** is not set in the ***signal_set*** and -1 if the call fails to perform the test.

**Example 20.11:** We will show the code to set the signal mask of a process to block the SIGINT and SIGTERM signals.

```
#include <stdio.h>
#include  <unistd.h>
#include  <signal.h>         /*  kill system call is defined        */
 void  main(void)
{
 sigset_t  dummy_set, current_set;
 int  ret_value;

    sigemptyset(&dumy_set);
    sigprocmask(SIG_BLOCK, &dummy_set, &current_set);
    if((ret_value = sigismember(&signal_set, SIGTERM)) == 1)
      printf("SIGTERM is blocked \n);
   else
         if(ret_value== 0)
          printf("SIGTERM is not blocked \n");
      else
             if(ret_value == -1)
                perror("sigismember failed");
} /* End of the main program  */
```

### 20.5.3 Signal Handling at System Level

We have already seen the signal handling in the standard C which is, in fact, based on the signal processing at system level. In Standard C, the ***signal*** function is used to nominate a user implemented handler for a specific signal type. System supports a similar, but more versatile, function called ***sigaction***. There are several other signal-related system calls that should be made available if any system complies with POSIX.1 standard. All those functions are summarized in the following sections.

#### The sigaction System Call

The ***sigaction*** call is useful to examine the action currently associated with a specified signal type or change the action by associating a new signal service routine with a specified signal type. The call conveys the description of the new action handler as well as the screening of signals from this handler via an argument structure of ***sigaction*** type shown below:

```
struct sigaction
    {
     void     (*sa_handler)(int sig_type);
     sigset_t  sa_mask;
     int      sa_flags;
    };
```

The format of the sigaction call, as defined in signal.h, is:

```
#include <signal.h> /* struct sigaction is defined in this header */
int sigaction( int sig_type, struct sigaction *newaction, struct sigaction *oldaction);
```

When the ***newaction*** argument is not NULL, it carries the details of new action handler and associated conditions, such as the signal set to be masked. When the ***oldaction*** argument is not NULL, it brings back the existing action details. It should be noted that the SIGKILL and SIGSTOP signals cannot be masked. The data type, ***struct sigaction***, is defined in the ***signal.h*** header file.

During a ***sigaction*** call, the new signal handler is passed via the ***sa_handler*** field. If the ***newaction*** argument is not NULL, the ***sa_mask*** is interpreted as a set of signals that should be blocked when the handler specified in ***newaction*** is running. When the new handler is called, the ***sig_type*** is automatically passed to the handler. The ***sa_flags*** can be used to alter the behaviors of the specified signal. The standard specifies the SA_NOCLDSTOP flag either to allow the generation of the SIGCHLD signal or not when a child process stops. This flag constant is also defined in ***signal.h***.

The installed signal handler will be effective until one of the ***sigaction*** calls installs another handler. If a ***sigaction*** call fails, the old action handler will continue to be effective. At the end of a successful operation, the call returns zero, or returns -1 and sets the ***errno*** appropriately. The possible error could be due to illegal value of the ***sig_type*** parameter leading to the EINVAL value of ***errno***. The following pseudo code shows the role of sigaction call in defining a user-defined signal handler.

```
#include <stdio.h>
#include <unistd.h>
#include <signal.h>

void user_sig_handler(sig_type)
{
    ... /* action as defined by user */
    printf("The signal type, %d is successfully caught and processed \n", sig_type);
}
```

```
void main(void)
 {
   struct sigaction   newaction, oldaction;
      newaction.sa_handler = user_sig_handler;
      sigemptyset(&newaction.sa_mask); /* no signal is masked */
            . . .
```

## 20.5.4 Use of SIG_DFL and SIG_IGN

As mentioned earlier, a program can set up its own signal catching routines that are appropriate to an application environment. If necessary, the program can reset a signal so it can be caught by its original or ***default function***. In some situations, a process may want to continue, until its completion or until a critical section is over, without any signal interruption. For example, a background program, once started, should be allowed to proceed without any interruption. In such a situation, the signals from the controlling terminal must be suppressed and a kernel must be instructed to ignore the specified signals. To provide these facilities, there are two system-defined signal processing functions available, and they are identified by ***SIG_DFL*** and ***SIG_IGN*** codes. (These codes are defined in ***signal.h***.) User programs can pass ***SIG_DFL*** or ***SIG_IGN*** via the ***sa_handler*** field of a ***sigaction*** call to the kernel, as shown in the following example.

```
#include <stdio.h>
#include <unistd.h>
#include <signal.h>
void main(void)
 {
   struct sigaction   newaction, oldaction;

      newaction.sa_handler = SIG_IGN;
      sigemptyset(&newaction.sa_mask); /* no additional signal is masked      */
            . . .
       sigaction(SIGINT, &newaction, &oldaction ); /* after this call, the signal generated
                                                  by the DEL key will be ignored; */
      sigaction(SIGQUIT, &newaction, &oldaction); /* after this call, the signal generated
                                           by the FS key will also be ignored; */
            . . .
            . . . /* perform some critical operation during which */
            . . .       /* interrupt and quit signals are ignored            */

      newaction.sa_handler = SIG_DFL;
      sigaction(SIGINT, &newaction, &oldaction); /* after this call, any signal generated
                                           by the DEL key will terminate the job; */
      sigaction(SIGQUIT, &newaction, &oldaction); /* after this call, any signal generated
      by the FS key will terminate the job and save the core image*/
            . . .       /* perform the remaining non-critical operations     */
}
```

### The sigpending System Call

The ***sigpending*** call is useful to examine the pending signals that are blocked for the calling process. The format of the call, as defined in signal.h, is:

```
#include <signal.h> /* sigset_t is defined in this header */
int sigpending(sigset_t *pending_set);
```

The call records the pending signal mask of the process in the space that is pointed to by *pending_set*. At the successful completion, the call returns zero, or returns -1 and errno will be set with an appropriate error value.

### The sigsuspend System Call

The ***sigsuspend*** call is useful in replacing the calling process' signal mask with the given set of signal mask and suspend the process until the delivery of a signal whose action is either to execute an action handler or terminate the process. After occurring the signal and executing the associated action handler, the original signal mask of the process is restored. The format of the call as defined in signal.h is:

```
#include <signal.h> /* sigset_t is defined in this header */
int sigsuspend(sigset_t *temp_mask);
```

The temporary mask set pointed to by *temp_mask* replaces the original mask set of the process and suspends the process. Since the calling process is suspended indefinitely, it always returns -1 with EINTR (error due to interrupted system call) in ***errno***.

### 20.5.5 The kill System Call

The ***kill*** call is used by a process to send any of the defined signals to another process or to a process group. The name "***kill***" suggests a rather narrow interpretation of the duties expected/ performed by this system call, although a common use is to "kill" processes. The prototype definition of this system call is:

```
#include <sys/types.h>/* pid_t type is defined in this header */
#include <signal.h> /* symbolic constants of signal types defined in this header */
    int kill(pid_t pid, int signal_type);
```

where

**pid** is the address of a process to which a signal is sent;

**signal_type** is a signal_number (or signal symbolic name that is defined in the **signal.h** file), denoting the type of signal to be transmitted;

**kill** returns zero after successful transmission of the given signal type; if the returned value is -1, an error occurred during the open operation.

**Error Flag:** The returned value, -1, indicates that the kill call has failed due to one of the following reasons:

- *the given signal_type is not a valid signal;*
- *the sending process has no privilege to pass a signal to the addressed process;*
- *the addressed process does not exist in the system.*

**Example 20.12:** Let us write a program to receive a process ID from the terminal and terminate the corresponding process without any failure.

```
#include <stdio.h>
#include <sys/types.h>      /* pid_t is defined in this header */
#include <unistd.h>
#include <signal.h>         /* kill system call is defined     */
  void main(void)
{
  int kill_status;
  pid_t unwanted_process;

  scanf("%d", &unwanted_process);
     kill_status = kill(unwanted_process, SIGKILL);
  if(kill_status == -1)
        perror("kill call failed");
  else
        printf("PID: %d does not exist anymore \n", unwanted_process);
  }
```

In the above example, the scanf function receives the process identifier from the user and uses the ***kill*** system call to terminate the corresponding process. The ***kill*** system call sends the SIGKILL signal to terminate the ***unwanted_process*** positively. The SIGKILL can never be ignored, meaning the receiving process of SIGKILL cannot ignore.

**Case 1:** If pid >0, the signal is sent to a process whose process identifier is the same as pid.

### Example 20.13:

Let us write a program in which a parent terminates its child.

```
#include <stdio.h>
#include <sys/types.h>
#include <unistd.h>
#include <signal.h>
void main(void)
{pid_t     child_id;

    child_id = fork();
    if (child_id ==0)
      {/* child process */
          printf("I am the child and I will be waiting until I am killed \n");
        pause();       /* simply waits  */
      }
    else
      { /* parent process */
      printf("I am the child and I will be waiting until I am killed \n");
          /* parent may perform some task and then  */
          if( kill(child_id, SIGKILL) == -1)
            perror("kill system call failed");
      }
} /* End of main */
```

***Remark:***
*(a) A process can send a signal to itself;*
*e.g., kill(getpid(), SIGKILL)*
*where getpid system call gets the callers process identifier.*
*(b) A process can send a signal to its parent;*
*e.g., kill(getppid(), SIGKILL)*
*where getppid system call gets the callers parents process identifier.*

**Case 2:** If pid = 0, the calling process wants to send a signal of given type to all processes in its group, including the sender.

### Example 20.14:

Let us show a program that controls a process group.

```
#include <stdio.h>
#include <sys/types.h>
#include <unistd.h>
#include <signal.h>
void main(void)
{
 pid_t child_1 = fork();
  if (child_1 ==0)
   {/* child process */
    setpgid(); /* the child becomes a leader of a new group */
    for(i = 0; i <4; i++)
    if (fork() == 0)
      { /* text of grand children */
     printf("I am a child waiting until killed \n"); /* child does some task and */
        pause(); /* simply waits */
      }
    sleep(10);    /* the child waits for 10 seconds and the whole group */
    kill(0, SIGKILL); /* sends kill-signal to all processes of its group, including itself */
   }
  else /* parent */
   {/* parent creates a group of child processes */
    for(i = 0; i <2; i++)
    if (fork() == 0)
      { /* text of grandchildren */
        pause(); /* simply waits */
      }
    sleep(10);    /* parent waits for 10 seconds and then */
     kill(0, SIGKILL); /* sends kill-signal to its own group*/
   }
}/* End of main */
```

**Case 3:** ***If pid = -1***, but the effective user identifier of sender is not super-user and a signal will be sent to all processes whose real user identifier is the same as that of sender.

**Case 4:** ***If pid = -1***, but the effective user_id of sender is super-user, signal will be sent to all processes in the system except some vital system processes. This facility is used by system programmers (with super-user capability) during systems shut down period.

***Remarks:***
*1. When a program is running, its process descriptor contains several pieces of information, including a real user identifier and an effective user identifier. The real user identifier indicates the identifier of the user who invoked the program. The effective user identifier will indicate which privilege domain is effective during the execution. In normal circumstances, when a program is executed, its effective user identifier is the same as the real identifier of the user who invokes that program. It does not matter whether a program belongs to the invoker or some other user. In other words, a program can be executed as long as its execution privilege is given to the invoker. An extension to this privilege is to execute a program by the invoker in the program owners privilege_domain. The provision for changing the user privilege_domain is another feature of the Unix kernel, wherein this feature one user can get the power of exercising privileges of another user domain. For example, assume that user_A has a program that will terminate all background jobs. At the same time, this user has allowed execution rights to some user, user_B, and set the program's special flag, called SET_USER_FLAG, to indicate that this program will execute in the owner's privilege_domain. Using this facility, user_B can run this program and terminate user_A's background processes.*

*2. Since this chapter and the following chapters present only the basic concepts of system programming in C, readers cannot expect a detailed description of Unix.*

**Case 5:** If pid < 0, but not –1, the calling process sends a signal of the given type to a process group whose process group identifier is the absolute value of pid. For example,

```
kill(-100, SIGKILL);
```

will terminate all processes of a group whose group identifier is 100.

We can also modify ***Example 20.11*** such that instead of the child's call to its own group, kill(0, SIGKILL), the parent's code can include a call to send a signal to its child's group first,

```
kill(-child_1, SIGKILL);
```

and then it can send signal to its own group

```
kill(0, SIGKILL);
```

### Example 20.15:

This example shows that parent process can kill the child process' group.

```
#include <stdio.h>
#include <sys/types.h>
#include <unistd.h>
#include <signal.h>
void main(void)
{
  pid_t child_1;

  child_1 = fork();
  if (child_1 ==0)
    {/* child process */
      setpgid(); /* the child becomes a leader of a new group whose id is the same as the child's
process id */
     for(i = 0; i <4; i++)
     if (fork() == 0)
       { /* text of grand children */
         pause(); /* simply waits */
       }
     pause(); /* child- 1's group leader also waits */
    }
  else /* parent */
    {/* the parent creates a group of child processes */
     for(i = 0; i <2; i++)
     if (fork() == 0)
       { /* text of grand children */
         pause(); /* simply waits */
       }
     group_1 = -child_1;
     kill(group_1, SIGKILL); /* the parent sends kill signals to child_1's group*/
     kill(0, SIGKILL); /* parent sends kill signals to its own group that includes itself */
    }
} /* End of main */
```

## The alarm System Call

The ***alarm*** call can be used to schedule signal to interrupt the calling process at a specific time. The format of this call, as defined in signal.h, is:

```
#include <signal.h>
unsigned int alarm(unsigned int time_in_seconds);
```

The SIGALRM will be generated by the system and sent to the calling process after the interval of ***time_in_seconds***. It should be noted that the alarm requests are not stacked and only one SIGALRM signal will be scheduled to occur. If the ***time_in_seconds*** is zero, then any previous alarm request is cancelled. In this case, the returned value would indicate the amount of time remaining before the SIGALRM signal is scheduled to occur. The returned zero value indicates that there was no alarm request made previously.

The ***alarm*** is always successful and, hence, is not designed to bring back any error flag.

## Process Suspension Calls

When a process wants to wait for an event to occur, it can suspend itself either for a specified time interval or indefinitely. For example, a child process, after completing its task, can suspend itself until its parent terminates. Sometimes, a process can periodically monitor an external device by executing a loop in which it can suspend for a specified period after attending the device.

## The pause System Call

The ***pause*** system call is useful for suspending a calling process indefinitely from execution. The format of this call is:

*int pause(void);*

The calling process will be in the suspended state until a signal is received. If the signal action is meant to terminate the process, the call will not return. If the signal causes the execution of a signal-catching routine, the ***pause*** call will return to the calling process.

Since the ***pause*** call is meant to cause the calling process to be suspened indefinitely there is no return value for successful operation. It can return -1 when it fails to put the process in suspension.

## The sleep System Call

The ***sleep*** system call is useful for suspending a process for a specified time of interval. The format of this call is:

*int sleep(int time_in_seconds);*

The call causes the calling process to be suspended for an interval of ***time_in_seconds*** from the execution. The process can be waked up either by an arrival of a signal before the specified time interval or by the timer event after the expiry of the specified time interval.

### Example 20.16:

Let us write a program in which a child process waits for five seconds before exiting. In this program we use the ***sleep*** system call to order the outputs of processes.

```
/* Program Name:   sleep_sync.c  */
#include  <stdio.h>
#include  <sys/types.h>  /* sigset_t is defined in this header      */
#include  <signal.h>
#include <unistd.h>

void  main(void)
  { int status;
   pid_t  exit_ch,  child_id;

    if((child_id = fork()) == -1)
      {
      perror("During fork()");
      exit();
      }
    if(child_id ==0)
      {
        sleep(5);  /*  wait until parents first message  */
       printf("  I AM THE CHILD PROCESS  \n");
        exit(0);  /* child exits normally & wakes its parent */
      }
    else
      { /* parent is ready to wait until child exits */
        printf(" I AM THE PARENT WAITING FOR CHILD PROCESS  \n");
        if((exit_ch = wait(&status)) == -1)
        {
          perror("During wait()");
          exit();
        }
        printf("I AM THE PARENT NOW EXITING    \n");
        exit(0);
      }
  }
```

### Example 20.17:

Write a program that displays the real time of a day every 60 seconds, 100 times.

```
#include <stdio.h>
#include <unistd.h>
#include <signal.h>
int  count;
void display(sig_type)   /* pototype  definition */
struct sigaction   newaction, oldaction;
void  main(void)
{
   newaction.sa_handler = display;
   sigemptyset(&newaction.sa_mask); /* no additional signal is masked   */
      . . .
   count = 0;
   sigaction(SIGINT, &newaction, &oldaction );  /* after this call, the signal generated
                                        by the DEL key will be ignored; */
  alarm(60);
  while(1);      /* alarm signal occurs during this indefinite loop; then display is called  */
}

void  display(sig_type)
{
  alarm(60);
  system ("date");/*   system executes the date command at program level; see remark-
              below on this function  */
   sigaction(SIGALRM, &newaction, &oldaction ); /* after this call, the signal generated
                                        by the DEL key will be ignored; */

  if(++count < 100) return;  /* control is returned to the place where signal interrupt occurred  */
  exit(0);
}
```

After associating the display routine with the alarm signal and starting the alarm, the program goes into a while loop. When an alarm signal arrives at the set interval, the control goes to the display routine. When this routine returns, the control goes back to the while loop to continue from where the signal interruption occurred. Before returning to while loop in the calling code the ***sigaction*** is again called to install the signal handler again.

The system function may be available in an implementation to execute a shell command at the program level. It requires only one string argument that is the command to be executed. The prototype definition is shown below:

```
int     system( const  char    *command);
```

The function returns the exit status of command process.

## Revisit to the setjmp and longjmp facility

The signal processing is almost the same as interrupt processing at hardware level. That is, when a signal interrupts a running program, the context of the program (i.e., a state vector of that location comprising of current values of all CPU-registers) is saved before the program thread jumps to the associated signal processing routine. The signal processing routine after attending the signal jumps (or ***longjumps***) back to continue from the point where the program was interrupted. A difference between the interrupt processing and signal processing is that the longjump occurs in the former case between system level program and a user program, whereas the longjump in the latter case occurs within a program between functions. This feature, supported by standard C, provides a pair of library calls, namely ***setjmp*** and ***longjmp***. The ***setjmp*** call is used to mark a jump-point in the currently running program thread. A ***setjmp*** call needs a ***jmp_buf*** type buffer to save the ***context of a target location***. A ***longjmp*** call can use this saved ***context information*** to jump to the execution point to allow the interrupted thread to continue. The prototype definitions of setjmp and longjmp, as well as the definition of ***jmp_buf*** type, can be found in the ***setjmp.h*** header file. The following example shows the use of this facility.

### Example 20.18:

Write a monitor program that tests typing speed.

```
#include <stdio.h>
#include <unistd.h>
#include <signal.h>
#include <setjmp.h>        /* jmp_buf type is defined in this header file  */
jmp_buf    returnpt;       /* declare buffer to store the context of return location */
int    flag, count;
struct sigaction   newaction, oldaction;
void   (*starttest)(),(*endtest)(),  (*endprg)();   /* prototype definitions    */
void  menu();
void  main(void)
{
   setjmp(returnpt);
   menu();
   printf("\t Press  ctrl-c  to start test\n");
   newaction.sa_handler = starttest;
   sigemptyset(&newaction.sa_mask); /* no signal is masked      */
   sigaction(SIGINT, &newaction, &oldaction );  /* after this call, the signal generated
                                        by the ctrl-c key will call starttest */
   newaction.sa_handler = endtest;
   sigemptyset(&newaction.sa_mask); /* no signal is masked      */
```

```
  sigaction(SIGSTOP, &newaction, &oldaction );  /* after this call, the signal generated
                                    by the ctrl-z key will call starttest */
  newaction.sa_handler = endprg;
  sigemptyset(&newaction.sa_mask); /* no signal is masked    */
  sigaction(SIGQUIT, &newaction, &oldaction );  /* after this call, the signal generated
                                    by the ctrl- \ key will call endprog*/
  while(1);
} /* End of main */

void  starttest(void)
{
  int   char;
  count = 0;
     newaction.sa_handler = endtest;
     sigemptyset(&newaction.sa_mask); /* no signal is masked     */
     sigaction(SIGALRM, &newaction, &oldaction );  /* after this call, the signal gener-
ated
                                    by the ctrl-z key will call starttest */
      printf("\n\n...TIMER starts at end of message....\n");
      system ("stty cbreak");
      alarm(60);
      flag = 1;
     while (flag)
       {
         char = getc(stdin);
         count++;
       }
   } /* End of starttest*/

  void  endtest(void)
  {
     newaction.sa_handler = starttest;
     sigemptyset(&newaction.sa_mask); /* no signal is masked     */
     sigaction(SIGINT, &newaction, &oldaction );  /* after this call, the signal generated
                                    by the ctrl-c key will call starttest */
     system ("stty -cbreak");
      printf("\n\n..You have a rating of %d chars per min \n\n",count);
     printf("\t ctrl-c  to restart test\n");
     count = 0;
     flag = 0;
     longjmp(returnpt, 0);
```

```
  } /* End of endtest */

void endprg(void)
{
  printf ("\n\t END-OF-Typing Skill Test PROGRAM \n");
  printf ("\n\t GOOD BYE \n");
  exit(0);
} /* End of endprg */

void menu(void)
{
  printf("** Typing Skill Test ***\n");
  printf("\n PRESS: ctrl-c to start the test \n");
  printf("\t ctrl-z to end test\n");
  printf("\t ctrl-\ to quit program\n");
} /* End of menu */
```

In the above program, the main function first defines the signals with new signal handlers. The SIGINT (ctrl-c key) is used to start or restart the typing skill test. The SIGINT calls ***starttest*** to start the test, but before starting, the ***starttest*** function defines SIGALRM to call ***endtest*** function. The function then starts the alarm and goes into while loop to count the keyed input. At the end of the alarm interval, SIGALRM wakes up the ***endtest*** function which again prepares for restarting the test. While proceeding with the test the user can stop any time by sending SIGSTOP (i.e., pressing ctrl-z key). To end the session, the user can press ctrl-\ (or generate the SIGQUIT signal that calls the ***endprg*** function). Once a signal is processed, it goes back to the original definition. The program has to use the ***sigaction*** call to bind the signal with the required handler again.

### 20.5.6 Process Synchronization

### The pipe System Call

A ***pipe*** is a bi-directional channel that can be opened by a parent and inherited by child processes for the purpose of interprocess communication. A ***pipe*** can also be viewed as a file that is created in the main memory for both reading and writing. A major difference between a normal file and this special file is that an open call to a ***pipe*** returns two separate file descriptors, one for read-end and one for write-end. By using the write-end file descriptor, a process can write a block of data to a ***pipe*** and, similarly, by using the read-end file descriptor, another process can read the contents. A ***pipe*** is always created with a fixed size, usually with 512, 1024, 2048 or 4096 bytes. The PIPE_BUF in ***limits.h*** defines the size of the file associated with a pipe in a system.

To open a ***pipe***, a program can use the ***pipe*** system call. Once a ***pipe*** is opened, the same ***read*** and ***write*** system calls used for normal files can be used. The prototype definition of a ***pipe*** call is shown below:

```
#include <unistd.h>
     int fd[2];
          . . .
int    pipe( int  *fd);
```

where ***fd*** is the address of a two element array of integer type to get a pair of file descriptors. The first element of the passed array, ***fd[0]***, always receives the file descriptor for read-end and the second element, ***fd[1]***, receives the file descriptor for write-end. When a ***pipe*** call creates a *pipe* successfully, it returns ***0***, or it returns an error value, ***-1***, to the calling program. (See ***Fig. 20.14***.)

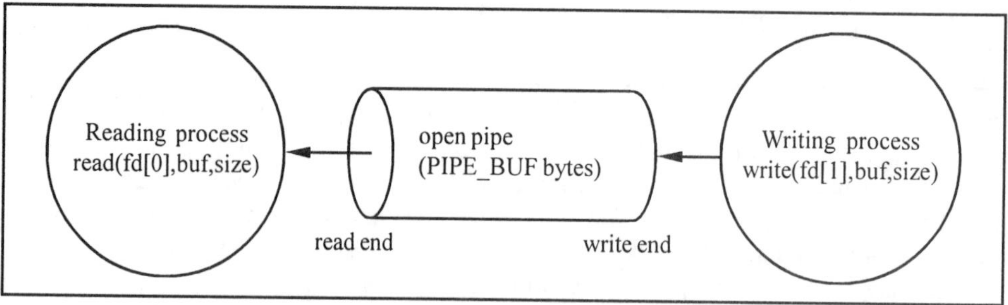


*Fig. 20.14 Pipe for communication*

Unlike a regular file, a ***pipe*** is a fixed size file whose size is defined in the ***limits.h*** header. This minimum value is called _POSIX_PIPE_BUF. The usual minimum value is 512 bytes. This value suggests that any process that has opened a ***pipe*** for writing can write in a call the amount of information into the pipe without waiting. Certain restrictions exist with respect to pipes:

1. *When a process tries to write more bytes than the size of the pipe size, then the process is blocked until a reader process empties the filled up pipe. The remaining data is written into the pipe.*

2. *More than one process can write to the same pipe simultaneously. When the data size of each process is less than or equal to _POSIX_PIPE_BUF (minimum size of standard pipe), or PIPE_BUF of the implementation, the data will arrive at the other end first-in-first-out basis. However, when the data size exceeds the size of the pipe (i.e., PIPE_BUF), processes may have to wait to write their remaining chunks. Since the writing processes are put in a race condition, their subsequent writings may not be in*

*order. Hence, the reader at the other end will receive mixed data, suggesting programmers have to use a proper mutual exclusion to allow multiple writings without any mixing.*

3. *When a process writes to a pipe whose read end is closed, the SIGPIPE signal is generated to indicate that there is no one to read. At the same time, the call records the EPIPE error in* ***errno****.*

4. *When a process tries to read an empty pipe whose write end is closed, then the value 0 is returned to indicate the EOF.*

5. *There must be at least two processes to communicate via a pipe. One simple situation is that both parent and child can communicate via a pipe. It is suggested that when one (say parent) process wants to use the write end, it closes the read end. Similarly when another (say child) process wants to use the read end, it can close the write end. These steps save file descriptors and, more importantly, whether a process is waiting at each end. See the sample code below for this convention.*

```
/* Consider a situation where parent is the reader and the child is the writer  */
#include  <stdio.h>
#include  <unistd.h>
#include  <limits.h>  /*  _POSIX_PIPE_BUF is defined in this header  */
#include  <string.h>
#define  BUFSIZE  _POSIX_PIPE_BUF
int  fd[2];
void main(void)
{int  fd[2];
char buf[BUFSIZE]; /* BUFSIZE  is 512 bytes */
  pipe(fd);      /* open a pipe  */
  if (fork() == 0)
    {/* child process works here  */
      close(fd[0]);  /*  child closes the read end of the pipe  */
      strcat(buf, "Child's message:HelloWorld");
        write(fd[1], buf, BUFSIZE); /*  child uses read end of the pipe  */
      exit(0);
    }
  else
        { /* parent process works here  */
         close(fd[1]);  /* parent closes the write end  */
         read(fd[0], buf, BUFSIZE);  /* parent uses only read end of the pipe  */
        printf("parent received the child's message: %s \n");
        exit(0);
      }
 } /* END OF PROGRAM  */
```

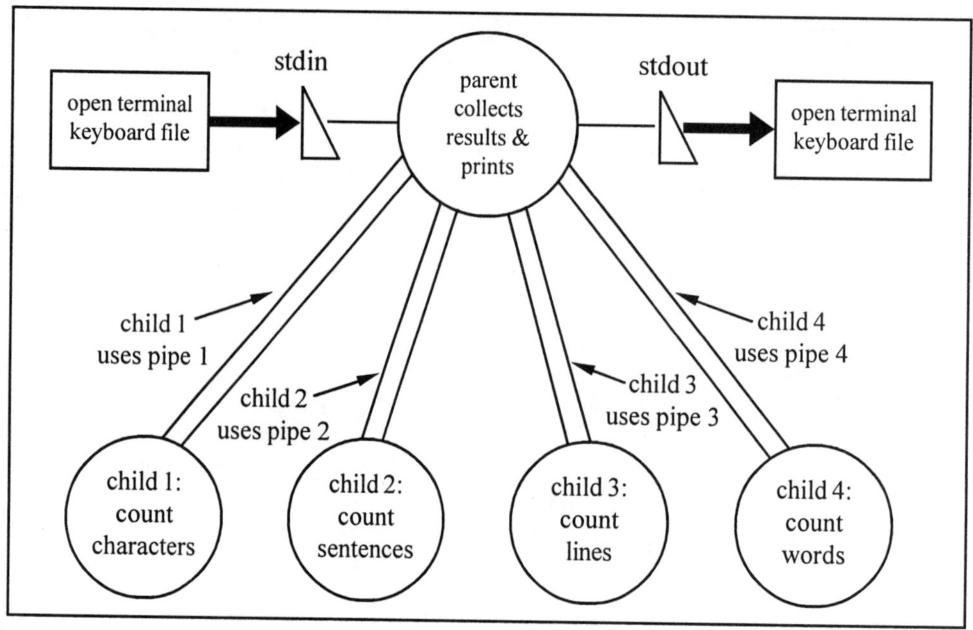


*Fig. 20.15 Concurrent word-count program*

## Example 20.19:

Write a concurrent word-count program (as shown in ***Fig. 20.15***) to count characters, words, sentences and lines in a given file.

```
/* wc.c program */
# include <stdio.h>
#include <sys/types.h> /* pid_t is defined in this header */
#include <sys/wait.h> /* macros for returned values are defined in this header */
#include <unistd.h>
void main(void)
{
 FILE *ifp, *fopen();
 char c;
 pid_t pid1, pid2, pid3, pid4;
 int wctr, lctr, sctr, cctr, status;
 int pipe1[2], pipe2[2], pipe3[2], pipe4[2], n;
 char filepath1[] = "/home/nsk/file1.txt";
 char filepath2[] = "/home/nsk/file2.txt";
 char filepath3[] = "/home/nsk/file3.txt";
 char filepath4[] = "/home/nsk/file4.txt";
 /* parent opens pipes to communicate with children */
```

```
    pipe(pipe1);
    pipe(pipe2);
    pipe(pipe3);
    pipe(pipe4);
  /* parent forks first child      */
if ((pid1 = fork()) == 0)
    { /* child 1 */
      close(pipe1[0]), close(pipe2[0]), close(pipe2[1]), close(pipe3[0]), close(pipe3[1]),
     close(pipe4[0]), close(pipe4[1]); /* dispose all unwanted file descriptors  */
      ifp = fopen (filepath1, "r");
      while ((c = getc (ifp)) != EOF )
           cctr++;
      printf("chars%d",cctr);
      write(pipe1[1], &cctr, sizeof cctr);
      exit(0);
    } /* end child 1 */
  /* parent continues in forking  */
    if ( ( pid2 = fork() ) == 0)
        { /* child 2 */
          close(pipe1[0]), close(pipe1[1]), close(pipe2[0]), close(pipe3[0]), close(pipe3[1]),
          close(pipe4[0]), close(pipe4[1]); /* dispose all unwanted file descriptors  */
          ifp = fopen(filepath2, "r");
          while (( c = getc (ifp)) != EOF )
               if ( c == '.')
                 sctr++;
          printf("sentences%d",sctr);
          write(pipe2[1], &sctr, sizeof sctr);
          exit(0);
        } /* end child 2 */
  /* parent continues in forking  */
    if (( pid3 = fork() ) == 0)
      { /* child 3 */
        close(pipe1[0]), close(pipe1[1]), close(pipe2[0]), close(pipe2[1]), close(pipe3[0]),
        close(pipe4[0]), close(pipe4[1]); /* dispose all unwanted file descriptors  */

        ifp = fopen(filepath3, "r");
        while (( c = getc (ifp)) != EOF )
          if ( c == '\n')
            lctr++;
    printf("lines%d",lctr);
        write(pipe3[1], &lctr, sizeof lctr);
        exit(1);
      } /* end child 3 */
  /* parent continues in forking  */
      if (( pid4 = fork () ) == 0)
        { /* child 4 */
```

```
        close(pipe1[0]), close(pipe1[1]), close(pipe2[0]), close(pipe2[1]), close(pipe3[0]),
        close(pipe3[1]), close(pipe4[0]); /* dispose all unwanted file descriptors */

      ifp = fopen(filepath4, "r");
      wctr=0;
         while ((c = getc (ifp)) != EOF )
            if ( c == ' '|| c=='\n' || c == '.' || c == ',')
              wctr++;
      printf("words%d", wctr);
      write(pipe4[1], &wctr, sizeof wctr);
         exit(1);
      } /* end child 4 */

   { /*parent now waits for each child and reads their pipes */
    int i;
     close(pipe1[1]), close(pipe2[1]), close(pipe3[1]), close(pipe4[1]); /* dispose all
                                               unwanted file descriptors */

    for(i=0; i<4; i++)
    {
        n = wait(&status);
    if(n == pid1)
      { read(pipe1[0], &cctr, sizeof cctr);
           printf("\n TOTAL CHARACTERS IN file1.txt: %d\n", cctr);
      }
    else
      if(n == pid2)
      { read(pipe2[0], &sctr, sizeof sctr);
             printf("\n TOTAL SENTENCE IN file2.txt: %d\n", sctr);
      }
      else
        if(n == pid3)
          { read(pipe3[0], &lctr, sizeof lctr);
                 printf("\n TOTAL LINE IN file3.txt: %d\n", lctr);
          }
        else
          if(n == pid4)
            { read(pipe4[0], &wctr, sizeof wctr);
                  printf("\n TOTAL WORD IN file4.txt: %d\n", wctr);
            }
      }/* End of parents waiting */
   exit(0);
   }/* End of parents code */
}/* End of main */
```

## Process Times

POSIX acknowledges the ***time*** function of ANSI-C and, in addition, provides the times function, mainly to extract the process times of a user program. The process times include how long a user process executes in processing on its own data structure and the kernel data structures or system resources. These times may be used in charging the users or controlling the usage of the resources in a multiuser environment.

## The time System Call

This function is useful to get the elapsed time in seconds since the Epoch (considered to be the beginning of recorded history, 00:00:00, 1st January 1970). This function is adopted by POSIX from C-standard. The format of this call is:

```
#include    <sys/types.h> /* time_t is defined in this header  */
#include    <time.h>
time_t   time(time_t  *p_tloc);
```

The call returns the current time and stores the same in the location pointed to by *p_tloc*. If the function call fails, it *returns (time_t)-1.*

## The times System Call

This function may be used to get various types of times related to the CPU-resource usage by processes. The function sends a structure of type ***tms*** to get all those details. The format of this call is:

```
#include  <sys/times.h>    /*  clock_t and tms structure defined in this header  */
clock_t  times(struct  tms  buffer);
```

The buffer brings the following times:

- *time spent by a process in user context;*
- *time spent by a process in system context;*
- *time spent by terminated child processes in user context;*
- *time spent by terminated child processes in system context.*

The actual ***tms*** structure is implemented in the ***sys/times.h*** as:

```
struct   tms
    {
        clock_t  tms_utime;   /* user CPU time */
        clock_t  tms_stime;   /* system CPU time    */
        clock_t  tms_cutime;  /* user CPU time of terminated children*/
        clock_t  tms_cstime;  /* system CPU time of terminated children   */
    }
```

After successful completion, the function returns the clock ticks accumulated in a relative timer register since the beginning of an era defined by an implementation. This era might be the last booting of the system. The return value in this situation may show the elapsed time since the system has started. It can also be used indirectly to measure the execution times of programs or program segment. For example, we may want to measure the time consumed by a function, say a sort routine. We can insert the ***times()*** calls before and after the function under test, and then the time consumed by the function can be calculated as the difference between the two returned values.

```
#include <sys/times.h>
void main(void)
{ int  array[1000] = {100, 20, 50, . . . . };
          . . .
     clock_t time_before_sort = times(NULL);
     sort(array, 10000);
     clock_t  time_after_sort = times(NULL);
     time_taken_by_sort = time_after_sort - time_before_sort;
          . . .
}
```

The clock ticks returned by the function may be converted into real-time units with the help of the CLK_TCK macro defined by ANSI-C standard in the ***time.h*** header file. The programs that comply with POSIX standard may use the ***sysconf*** function to get this value indirectly. The format of this function is:

```
#include  <unistd.h>
long  sysconf(int  macro_name);
```

Several macro_names (or symbolic constants), including the limits imposed by POSIX standard, are defined in the ***unistd.h*** file. One of the symbolic constants is _SC_CLK_TCK, which can be sent as the parameter to return the real-time equivalent of the clock ticks (i.e., number of clock ticks per second). Note that the name _SC_CLK_TCK indicates that it is an argument to the ***sysconf***(_SC_) call to get the implementation defined CLK_TCK parameter. A call to get CLK_TCK is:

*long tickspersec = sysconf( _SC_CLK_TCK );*

### Example 20.20:

Let us write a program to find out the CLK_TCK (clocks per second) defined in an implementation.

```
#include <stdio.h>
#include <unistd.h>
void main(void)
{
  long clock_ticks_per_second;
    clocks_ticks_per_second = sysconf(_SC_CLK_TCK);
    printf("clocks per second in this implementation is: %d \n", clocks_ticks_per_second);
}
```

### Example 20.21:

Let us now write a program to print out the process times by using the ***times*** system call.

```
#include <stdio.h>
#include <unistd.h>
#include <times.h>
int factorial(int N)
{
  int I, J;
      if(N == 0)
         return(1);
    I = N-1;
    J = fact(I);
    return (N*J);
} /* End of factorial */

void main(void)
{
  struct tms tmsbuf1, tmsbuf2;
  long CTPS;
  int N = 100, F;
  clock_t clock_ticks_before, clock_ticks_after;
      clocks_ticks_per_second = sysconf(_SC_CLK_TCK);
      clock_ticks_before = times(&tmsbuf1);
```

```
        F = factorial(N);
        clock_ticks_after = times(&tmsbuf2);
        func_time_in_ticks = clock_ticks_after - clock_ticks_before;
        func_time_in_sec = func_time_in_ticks/CTPS;
        printf("clocks per second in this implementation: %d \n", CTPS);
        printf("Clock Ticks spent in factorial: %d \n", func_time _in _ticks);
        printf("Time spent in factorial: %d seconds \n", func_time _in _sec);
        printf("user time by factorial: %d \n",
                (tmsbuf1.tms_utime - tmsbuf2.tms_utime)/CTPS);
        printf("system time by factorial: %d \n",
                (tmsbuf1.tms_utime-tmsbuf2.tms_utime)/CTPS);
}
```

## 20.6 Summary

This chapter introduced the process concept and the process management functions, such as ***fork***, ***wait***, ***exit***, ***getpid***, ***getppid***, ***signal***, ***kill***, and ***pipe***, supported by Unix. It also explains how C-programs can be written for creating concurrent processes and managing them with appropriate interprocess communication at user level.

## Exercises

20.1 When a program becomes a process, what details of that program are stored in a process table entry?

20.2 What is the shell environment? Show the typical contents of a shell environment table.

20.3 How do we set up a shell environment table? Does it have any limitations in accumulating data? Explain.

20.4 Write a program called ***whatisterm*** to display the terminal type supported by the shell environment.

20.5 Write a program called ***whatishome*** to display your home directory.

20.6 Write a program called ***whoami*** to display your user name.

20.7 Describe the fork system call using an example.

20.8 Draw the process tree for the following forking loop:

```
for(i=0; i<3; i++)
    fork();
```

20.9 A program has three functions and creates a separate process to execute each function. Show the C-code.

20.10 What is a process? Explain briefly the process model supported by Unix.

20.11 How is a system call error handled? (Explain the mechanism provided by the Unix kernel.)

20.12 When a process is forked, what resources are inherited from its parent? What discipline should be followed by these concurrent processes while using their resources?

20.13 What is the significance of the wait system call?

20.14 What is the purpose of the _exit system call?

20.15 Define the term ***"process group"***. How is a process group created; and for what purpose?

20.16 What is a signal? How is it processed?

20.17 Explain the characteristics of signals that are generated from a terminal.

20.18 What is the use of kill system call? How is this system call different from the kill command?

20.19 What is the use of the ***sigaction*** system call? How does this call differ from ***signal*** library call supported by ANSI-C?

20.20 What is a pipe? How is it used for interprocess communication?

# 21

# Unix File I/O

**Chapter contents:**

*This chapter introduces the file system supported by Unix and the interface available in C, preparing the readers to be able to handle file I/O in their C-programs.*

**Organization:**


*21.1 Introduction*
*21.2 Concept of Direct (or Basic) I/O*
*21.3 How Is a File Maintained in Unix?*
*21.4 File Protection and File Creation Mask*
*21.5 Directories*
*21.6 System Calls for Regular Files*
*21.7 Inode-Related System Calls*
*21.8 FIFO (Named Pipe) File*
*21.9 Device Files*
*21.10 Configuration Information of File System*
*21.11 The sync System Call*
*21.12 Summary*
*Exercises*


## 21.1 Introduction

As mentioned in ***Chapter 19***, a set of system call functions, called Basic Unix I/O, is made available at the Unix kernel level for file management. These functions are extensively used for fast file processing because of the direct nature of their I/O. They are also called Direct Unix I/O functions. After the introduction of POSIX standard for the portable operating system interface, Unix's system call interface has almost become the base of the standard. As explained in ***Chapter 17***, this Unix-like interface is also a standard Application Program Interface. In general, C-programmers, after learning about ***ANSI-File I/O*** (which is slow due to buffering), should also be aware of this ***Basic Unix-like I/O*** so they will also be able to implement portable system programs.

The file types supported by a Unix system conforming to POSIX.1 standard include regular file, directory file, FIFO file, and device file. System calls of the Standard Unix file system were listed in ***Chapter 19***. This chapter introduces these system calls in a detailed manner.

## 21.2 Concept of Direct (or Basic) I/O

The I/O system calls provide the basic mechanism for file handling in the Unix system. Even the ANSI-I/O (i.e., stream I/O) functions indirectly use these system calls to perform all stream functions. That is, ***fopen*** calls the ***open*** system call; ***getc*** indirectly calls the ***read*** system call; ***putc*** indirectly calls the ***write*** system call; and ***fclose*** indirectly calls the ***close*** system call. The difference lies with the introduction of intermediate buffering in the stream I/O to control the data flow at different abstract levels, such as character, string, and formatted data.

The basic feature of direct I/O is the transfer of data between an open file and a program directly without any intermediate buffering, which is why direct I/O is called low-level I/O and stream I/O is called high-level I/O. Due to the speed efficiency of direct I/O, some operating systems utilities (or service programs) prefer it for file processing. For example, the ***cp*** utility (i.e., file-copy program in Unix) can be better implemented using basic or direct I/O rather than using low speed stream functions. The following pseudo code is sufficient to show the use of system calls in the ***cp*** program.

```
/* file-copy program */
void  main(void)
    {char user_buff[sector_size];
     open (source_file for direct_IO);
     open (destination_file for direct_IO);
    repeat
     {
       read (a block of sector size from source_file into user_buf);
       write (user_buf of sector size to destination_file);
     } until end of source file;
    close (source_file);
    close (destination_file);
  }
```

Similarly, the data transfer programs, such as ***sendfile***, ***getfile***, and ***sendmail***, in a computer network can do their tasks faster if they use ***direct I/O*** system calls for reading and writing data with respect to disk files.

Direct I/O can handle the data in blocks that are the same size as disk sectors or tracks., which is why the direct I/O is also called block I/O. The usual size of a block will be multiples of 512 bytes (512, 1024, 2048, 4096, etc.). These sizes are the typical sector/block sizes of disk/magnetic tape devices. This does not mean that we cannot use direct I/O to read/write data chunks of other sizes. We can even read/write chunks of a single byte or an arbitrary number of bytes, but it will be less efficient (theoretically) to read/write small chunks of data rather than a block at a time from a block device (e.g., disk ).

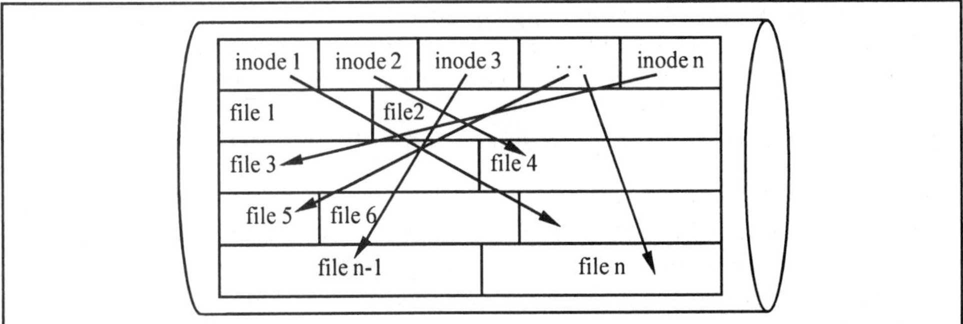


*Fig. 21.1 Schematic diagram showing files and their inodes in the Unix file system*

## 21.3 How Is a File Maintained in Unix?

Even though a POSIX conforming file system can be implemented in a different manner than the Unix file system, it is interesting to know how files are maintained in Unix. A file in Unix is a stream of bytes usually stored on a block device like disk or magnetic tape. When a file is created, it possesses a set of attributes like the size of the file, starting address of the file in disk, owner of the file, date of creation, etc. These permanent attributes of a file are maintained in a data structure (or simply a file record) called an ***inode***. For each file created in the system, an ***inode*** or a file record is also created to keep the details of the created file. An ***inode*** is permanent and exists until the corresponding file is removed from the system. (See ***Fig. 21.1***) In other words, when we delete a file, its ***inode*** is removed and the file space in the disk is recovered. An ***inode*** contains the following details about a created file:

- *owner identifier, i.e., user id*
- *file type (i.e., regular file, directory file or special file)*
- *file size (in bytes)*
- *number of links for this file*
- *time of file creation*
- *time of last file access*
- *time of last file modification*
- *list of access rights (i.e., read, write and execution permissions)*
- *physical address of file on the disk*

Normally, the ***inodes*** of all created files are kept in a separate area of a disk volume. Whenever we open a file, its corresponding inode is brought into main memory, and this active inode is kept there until the open file is closed. The active inodes are mainly used to locate the beginning of an open file on the disk, and to verify that the every I/O request comes from a valid user and obeys the specified access permission criteria.

### 21.3.1 Control Channel (or Access Path)

When a program opens a file using an ***open*** system call, a control channel is created between the program and the file. After creating a channel, ***open*** returns the address of this channel (or logical address of the open file) called the ***file descriptor*** value. This control channel is created to maintain information, such as:

- *the access mode specified in the open call*
- *a file cursor showing exactly where the next read/write should commence,*
- *a byte or character count.*

To perform an I/O operation, both permanent attributes, such as file location, file owner, and file access rights, stored in inode as well as some dynamic variables, such as access mode specified in an open call, and current position of I/O, must be considered. What an ***open*** call does is create a control channel that contains both static and dynamic variables required to control I/O to and from an open file. In other words, a control channel can be viewed as a single logical table containing all attributes necessary for read/write operations on an open file. Actually, an open control channel contains an ***open_file table***, including the dynamic variables and the ***inode*** associated with the open file. The address of the open file table is stored in an entry of the ***file descriptor table***. The index of that entry is returned as the address of open control channel (or simply the logical address) of the open file.

### 21.3.2 Open_File Table

When we perform either read or write operations, it is important to maintain the processing status of an active file. Such status information includes:

1. A file cursor (or byte offset)

> ***Remark:*** *Processing a file may involve more than one read or write operation. After reading or writing a certain number of characters, file curser should indicate that the processing (i.e.,read/write) has been done on the file up to this point, and the next read/write operation should continue from the marked point in that file, similar to a bookmark.*

2. The inode address

> ***Remark:*** *The actual location and other attributes of a file are kept in an inode. Hence, this inode information is necessary to validate each read or write call and access the required data from the file device.*

3. The access mode

> ***Remark:*** *The purpose for which a file has been opened, such as reading or writing, must also be recorded so that every read/write request can be checked for an illegal access. For example, a file may be opened for reading, but a* ***write*** *call may be issued by mistake. The* ***write*** *call would check the access mode recorded in the open file table before it performs writing. In this case, determining the access to be read only,* ***write*** *would fail to complete its task.*

The operating system provides a structure called an open file table for each open file in order to keep the abovementioned information. The system maintains a pool of these tables from which an ***open*** call can have one allocated to form a control channel associated to a particular file. Once the file is closed, this table is returned to the pool. In summary, the ***read*** and ***write*** system calls consult this table before proceeding with their actual operation.

### 21.3.3 File Descriptor

Basically, an ***open*** call copies the inode of the specified file from disk into memory, acquires an open file table, and then fills up all the entries of this table, including the address of inode. The ***open*** call stores the address of the open file table in another table called the ***file descriptor table*** and returns the index into the table as the address of the created open control channel. This returned file descriptor value, a simple integer, can then be used in ***read*** and ***write*** calls so they can locate the open file table and inode table to perform their tasks.

The ***file descriptor table*** is part of the ***user structure*** of a process created for each running program. Before a process is started, the operating system opens the three standard I/O files (keyboard as standard input, screen as standard output and again screen as standard error), and makes the corresponding channel addresses available in the first three entries of the ***file descriptor table***. Hence, a process can readily use these file descriptor values for read/write operations with respect to standard I/O files.

> ***Remark:*** *When a child process starts, its file descriptor table (i.e., a part of user structure) is a copy of its parent and, consequently, all the open files of the parent are available to the child process. In Unix, the shell process acts as the parent of our command processes and normally keeps the standard I/O files open for its communication. When a command process is created (or when a user process begins), the inherited file descriptor table is empty except for the first three entries (0, 1 and 2). Each time a file is opened by a running program, the next free entry in the file descriptor table is filled up with the address of the created control channel (or the address of the associated open file table). Since the usual size of the file descriptor table is 20 (which may vary from one Unix implementation to another), a process' I/O processing can span over twenty open files, including three standard I/O files.*

In summary, an ***open*** call sets up a file access path or control channel by linking a file descriptor table entry, an open file table and an inode table. Then it returns the file descriptor table index as the logical address of the open file. This logical address is used by ***read*** and ***write***, as well as by other file control system calls (e.g., ***close***, ***lseek***, ***fstat***, etc.), that perform their tasks on an open file. All these system calls are explained in the following section.

## 21.4 File Protection and File Creation Mask

The Unix File system divides the file permission into three levels: ***user***, ***group*** and ***others***. At the same time, it allows three different operations on files: ***read***, ***write*** and ***execute***. When a file is created, the user specified access permissions are recorded at the same time. That is, a file's permission can give any combination of privileges at three levels. For example, the user can have read, write and execute, then the group and others can have read and execute permission. Depending upon the type of file (***regular***, ***directory***, ***FIFO***, etc.), users can appropriately set the permission mode so that the files are protected from any illegal use.

The users can set the permissions at the creation of a file or reset the permissions after creating a file. The normal practice is to create files with a default permission mode and then reset their permissions more appropriately according to their particular applications. For example, a course directory is created first with a default permission mode and then its permission mode can be changed to "read, write and execute for the user and the group of instructors" and "read and execute for others or student community." (See ***Table 21.1*** for various permission modes.)

Unix system gives a facility that allows each user to have a ***file creation mask (cmask)*** to define a default ***permission mode*** and provides the ***umask*** system call to modify the same from time to time. Whenever we create a ***regular file*** using the ***creat*** (or ***open***) system call, a ***directory file***, using the ***mkdir*** system call and a ***FIFO file*** using the ***mkfifo*** system call, ***cmask*** is used to modify the permission mode. We will see later in this chapter how this mask affects the permission mode of the created files in these system calls.

### 21.4.1 The umask System Call

The ***umask*** system call is useful to change the value of the ***cmask*** defined in the ***user structure*** of a process. The new mask will be effective during the execution of a process which issues this call. This mask is also effective to the forked processes due to inheritance of the user structure. The prototype definition of this system call is:

```
#include <sys/types.h>
#include <sys/stat.h>
mode_t   umask(mode_t  cmask);
```

where

***cmask*** is the new value of the permissions to be denied during file creations in the calling process;

***umask*** sets the ***file creation mask*** with the supplied ***cmask*** value and returns the old value of the ***file creation mask***.

*Table 21.1 Permission mode used in the file creation system calls*

<table>
<tr><td colspan="4">Three basic operations: Read (R), Write (W) and eXecute (X);<br>Three types of users: Owner (USR), Group (GRP) and Others (OTH); | is OR-operator</td></tr>
<tr><td>Access Rights in Binary</td><td>Rights in octal</td><td>Access symbolic constants (defined in sys/stat.h)</td><td>Description</td></tr>
<tr><td>owner group others<br>b8b7b6 b5b4b3 b2b1b0</td><td></td><td></td><td></td></tr>
<tr><td>100 000 000</td><td>0400</td><td>S_IRUSR</td><td>owner (user) can read</td></tr>
<tr><td>010 000 000</td><td>0200</td><td>S_IWUSR</td><td>owner can write</td></tr>
<tr><td>001 000 000</td><td>0100</td><td>S_IXUSR</td><td>owner can execute</td></tr>
<tr><td>000 100 000</td><td>0040</td><td>S_IRGRP</td><td>group can read</td></tr>
<tr><td>000 010 000</td><td>0020</td><td>S_IWGRP</td><td>group can write</td></tr>
<tr><td>000 001 000</td><td>0010</td><td>S_IXGRP</td><td>group can execute</td></tr>
<tr><td>000 000 100</td><td>0004</td><td>S_IROTH</td><td>others can read</td></tr>
<tr><td>000 000 010</td><td>0002</td><td>S_IWOTH</td><td>others can write</td></tr>
<tr><td>000 000 001</td><td>0001</td><td>S_IXOTH</td><td>others can execute</td></tr>
<tr><td>111 000 000</td><td>0001</td><td>S_IRWXU</td><td>owner can read, write and execute</td></tr>
<tr><td>000 111 000</td><td>0001</td><td>S_IRWXG</td><td>group can read, write and execute</td></tr>
<tr><td>000 000 111</td><td>0001</td><td>S_IRWXO</td><td>others can read, write and execute</td></tr>
<tr><td>100 100 100</td><td>0444</td><td>S_IRUSR |<br>S_IRGRP |<br>S_IROTH</td><td>owner, group others can read</td></tr>
<tr><td>010 010 010</td><td>0222</td><td>S_IWUSR |<br>S_IWGRP |<br>S_IWOTH</td><td>owner, group and others can write</td></tr>
<tr><td>001 001 001</td><td>0111</td><td>S_IXUSR |<br>S_IXGRP |<br>S_IXOTH</td><td>owner, group and others can execute</td></tr>
<tr><td>110 000 000</td><td>0600</td><td>S_IRUSR|S_IWUSR</td><td>owner and others can read & execute</td></tr>
<tr><td>101 000 000</td><td>0500</td><td>S_IRUSR|S_IXUSR</td><td>owner and group can read & write</td></tr>
<tr><td>011 000 000</td><td>0300</td><td>S_IWUSR|S_IXUSR</td><td>owner, group and others can read, write & execute</td></tr>
</table>

**Examples:** Use of symbolic constants defined in sys/stat.h in umask system call.

*umask(S_IRWXU);* */* cmask is assigned with read, write and execute permissions only for the ownerof the process that issues this call */*
*umask(S_IRWXU | S_IRGRP | S_IXGRP);* */* cmask is assigned with read, write and execute permissions for owner, and read and execute to group. No permission is given to others */*
*umask(S_IRWXU | S_IRWXG | S_IROTH | S_IXOTH);* */* cmask is assigned with read, write and execute permissions for owner and group, then read and execute to others. */*

> ***Remark:*** *File-making system calls (i.e., creat, open, mkdir and mkfifo) receive permission mode as one of the arguments which is then modified by the value of the file creation mask (defined in the user structure of every process as u_cmask). The file creation mask bits indicate what permissions are to be denied. These calls modify the given permission, simply to make sure that the permission mode of the created file complies within the default permission mode specified indirectly in the file creation mask. The calls use the following formula to modify the given permission mode* ***(perm_mode)****:*
>
> ***modified_permission = perm_mode & ~u_cmask***
>
> *The system usually sets the value of u_cmask as 0022 for all users; this value can be changed by a user process with the help of the umask system call, explained later in this chapter.*

## Example 21.1:

Let us write a program to display the current value of the user creation mask.

```
#define <sys/types.h>  /* mode_t is defined in this header  */
#define <sys/stat.h>          /* symbolic constants for various permissions defined here  */
#define <stdio.h>
void main(void)
{ mode_t   cur_fcmask;
  mode_t     temp_mask = S_IWGRP|S_IWOTH /*  temp_mask is assigned with  0022  */
     cur_fcmask = umask(temp_mask);   /* get the original value of file creation mask */
     printf(" The current file creation mask is %d \n", cur_fcmask);
     umask(cur_fcmask );  /* restore the original value in user structure   */
}
```

## 21.5 Directories

Applications generally use file system quite extensively. Even in single user systems like PC at present, one can witness the growing number of files due to both software suppliers and users. Unless these files are organized in a partitioned manner, users will simply be spending their time locating their files. Hence, the concept of the directory came into the picture. For example, a directory can be created to contain the indices of all header files; another directory can be created to contain the files of a particular user.

A directory is merely a special file holding the indices of files that belong to a particular category. A directory is used as a symbol table containing a set of entries, each of which in turn may contain the symbolic name of a file, its location details, protection details, owner details, etc.

### 21.5.1 Directory Management

Similar to normal files, the directory special file is managed with the help of a set of functions. These directory management functions include creating, removing, opening, reading, rewinding, and closing a directory.

### 21.5.2 Directory System in Unix

The directory system in the Unix file system is basically designed to support the multiple users in time-shared manner. Hence, it should provide a separate directory called home directory, for each user and, under the home directories, users can organize files in subdirectories. The resulting structure under Unix is in a tree form. The directory tree starts with a ***root*** directory at the top. All subdirectories or tree branches start from the root directory. The name of the root is simply /. The leaves of the tree are Unix files. The tree allows one directory to link to another directory as in an acyclic graph. The ***Fig 21.2*** shows a typical organization of the Unix directory system.

### 21.5.3 Directory Structure

In the original Unix system, the structure of a directory is very simple. Each directory is a sequence of fixed size records, and each record contains a name field of 14 characters and a file, or inode number field, of two bytes. The directory reading is done in these systems using the traditional file-oriented functions, such as open, read, write and close system calls. In order to introduce portability of system programs, The POSIX.1 standard has recommended somewhat higher level functions that can be emulated to interface with the underlying file-oriented functions of any type. In fact, the internal structure of directories and the basic operations are implementation defined. A directory, according to the POSIX.1 standard, is also a sequence of entries, but each directory entry can be of variable length, depending upon the length of the file name in that entry. A ***file name*** of up to ***256 characters*** is allowed in the standard. Each directory entry describes the location of a file in the file storage medium in some manner. The format of a directory entry is explained in a data structure called **dirent**.

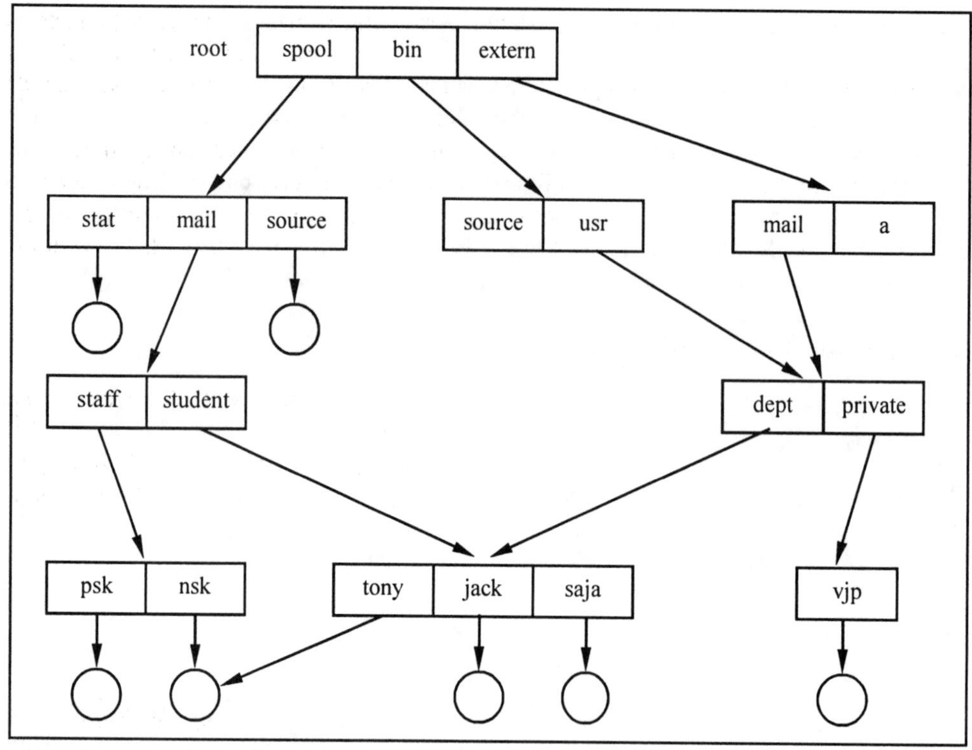


*Fig 21.2 Acyclic directory structure*

## The dirent.h Header

The definitions of the ***DIR*** type and the ***dirent structure*** are made available in the ***dirent.h*** header file. The DIR similar to FILE type, introduced in the ANSI-stream, can be used to create a buffered I/O for reading or writing directory entries.

## The mkdir System Call

The ***mkdir*** call can be used to create a new directory with the specified permission mode. The format of the call is:

```
#include <sys/types.h>          /* mode_t is defined here */
#include <sys/stat.h>           /* symbolic constants are defined here */
int mkdir(const char *pathname, mode_t perm_mode);
```

This call creates a new directory under the supplied path name with the given access permission mode and returns a zero value. If the call fails, then -1 is returned. The effective permission mode is derived by exclusive-oring the file mode creation mask with the given permission mode (i.e., *perm_mode*). During error return, an error code is stored in ***errno***.

Upon the successful completion, the ***mkdir*** call marks for the updates of the time fields (i.e., time of last access, time of last modification and time of last file status change), and also marks for the update of times in the parent directory. The owner ID and group ID are set appropriately. Since mode_t is defined in the types.h, the latter must be included with the source file.

## The opendir System Call

The ***opendir*** call opens the named directory as a stream and returns a *pointer* to DIR structure. This is similar to opening a normal file as an ANSI-C stream and obtaining a pointer to FILE structure. Once a directory stream is opened, the directory entries can be read with the help of the directory pointer. The directory pointer can also be used to rewind and close the directory. The format of the ***opendir*** system call is:

```
#include <sys/types.h>
#include <dirent,h>
DIR *opendir(const char *pathname);
```

The call creates a stream structure that is an instance of DIR, opens the named directory file, fills up the stream structure with the details of the opened directory file (such as file descriptor and current position of the stream), and returns a pointer to the stream structure. This call sets the stream position to the first directory entry.

## The readdir System Call

The ***readdir*** call reads a directory entry from the current location of the stream. The format of this call is:

```
#include <sys/types.h>
#include <dirent.h>
struct dirent *readdir(DIR *dirp);
```

The call copies the contents of the directory entry at the current location into an instance of the dirent structure and returns a pointer to that structure. It returns ***NULL*** when the end of directory is encountered or an error occurred. To find out whether any error has occurred, the global variable ***errno*** can be checked. Before any ***readdir*** operation, this variable can be set to zero and after the operation, it should be checked whether any read error occurred. It should be noted that the end of directory does not set ***errno***.

## The rewinddir System Call

The **rewinddir** system call can be used to move the pointer to the beginning of the stream or to the first directory entry. The format of this call is:

```
#include <sys/types.h>
#include <dirent.h>
void rewinddir(DIR *dirp);
```

## The closedir System Call

The ***closedir*** call is used to close an opened directory. The format of this call is:

```
#include <sys/types.h>
#include <dirent.h>
int closedir(DIR *dirp);
```

**Example 21.2:** We will now write a program that uses some of the abovementioned system calls to print the list of files in the directory called */home/nsk/WWW*. We want to demonstrate the use of *opendir*, *readdir* and *closedir* through this example.

```
/*****************************************************************/
/* This program will list the names of all files in a directory */
/*****************************************************************/
#include <stdio.h>
#include <sys/types.h>
#include <unistd.h>
#include <dirent.h>

void main(void)
{
  DIR *dptr;
  struct dirent *dentry;
  char pathname[] = "/home/nsk/WWW"; /* initialize pathname with directory path */
    dptr = opendir(pathname); /* get the directory pointer */
    if(dptr == NULL)      /* check whether the directory exists */
      perror("directory does not exist");
    else          /* if it exists, then print the file names */
      while ((dentry = readdir(dptr)) != NULL)
      printf("%s \n", dentry->d_name);
    closedir(dptr);/* it is safe to close the directory as soon as directory is processed */
}
```

The above program opens the directory whose path is supplied via the string variable, ***pathname***. After opening the directory, the returned directory pointer is stored in ***dptr***. Then the program goes into a loop to read the directory entries one by one and print the name field, ***d_name***, on the screen, which is a field in the ***dirent*** structure as defined in the ***dirent.h*** header. The successive calls to read the directory moves ***dptr*** sequentially along the entries towards the end. Once ***readdir*** hits the end of the directory, it returns NULL, indicating that there is no more entry to read. The while-loop stops at this instance and the next statement closes the directory. The program outputs the list as shown below:

```
.
..
scc271
scc281
scc388
scc622
nsk_dir
index.html
271.tar
scc271.tar
```

**Example 21.3:** We will now write a program that shows the list of files in the directory called ***/home/nsk/WWW*** in reverse order. We want to demonstrate the use of the ***rewinddir*** call through this example.

```
/********************************************************************/
/*     This program prints the list in the reverse order:             */
/*          - first counts number of files in the directory           */
/*          - uses this number to repeat traversing through the open directory   */
/*          - in each iteration, it prints the last entry and the iteration size is   */
/*            reduced by one                                           */
/********************************************************************/
#include <stdio.h>
# include <sys/types.h>
#include <unistd.h>
#include <dirent.h>

void main(void)
{
 DIR      *dptr;
 struct dirent *dentry;
 char pathname[] = "/home/nsk/WWW";
 int nfiles, last;
```

```
    nfiles = 0;
    dptr = opendir(pathname);  /*  get the directory pointer */
    if(dptr == NULL)  /* check whether the directory exists  */
       perror("directory does not exist");
    else               /* if it exists, then count the file */
      while ((dentry = readdir(dptr)) != NULL)
      {
                              nfiles++;
      }

    last = nfiles;
    for(int j=0; j < nfiles; j++)      /*  traverses the directory nfiles times */
     {
       rewinddir(dptr);                               /* rewind before next iteration  */
      for(int k=0; k<last; k++)                  /* move the pointer to last entry */
        {
         dentry = readdir(dptr);
        }
      printf("%s \n", dentry->d_name); /* print the last entry of this iteration */
     last—;                         /* last shrinks one by one              */
    }
    closedir(dptr);/* it is safe to close the directory as soon as directory is processed */
}
```

The first segment of the above program first finds out total number of files, ***nfiles***, in the given directory. In this segment, reading the directory entries one by one is done until no more entry can be read. The ***readdir*** call brings NULL when it reaches the end of the directory. The resulting count of the number of readings in ***nfiles*** indicates the number of files in that directory. We can print the file names in reverse order by printing ***nfiles***-th first, then ***nfiles***-1 and so on until 1st entry. After each pass, ***rewinddir*** call is issued to bring back the pointer to the beginning. That is where ***rewinddir*** call is useful. The program outputs the list, as shown below:

```
scc271.tar
271.tar
index.html
nsk_dir
scc622
scc388
scc281
scc271
..
.
```

### The rmdir System Call

The ***rmdir*** call can be used to delete a named directory from the system. The named directory will be deleted only if it is empty. If the named directory is either root directory or being used as the current working directory by a process, the outcome of this call is unpredictable and implementation dependent. The format of this call is:

```
#include <unistd.h>
    int rmdir(const char *pathname);
```

The call returns a zero after a successful completion and returns -1 when it fails. During error return, an error code is stored in errno. The most common errors are:

- *search permission is denied (EACCESS);*
- *the named directory is being used (EBUSY);*
- *the named directory is not empty (ENOTEMPTY or EEXIST);*
- *the length of the path argument is too long (ENAMETOOLONG);*
- *the named entry is non-existent (ENOENT).*

During successful completion the ***link count*** in the inode is decremented and if the ***link count*** becomes zero and no process has the directory open, the space occupied by the directory will be freed and non-existent.

### The chdir System Call

The ***chdir*** call can be used to change the current working directory. The format of this call is:

```
#include <unistd.h>
int chdir(const char *pathname);
```

This call causes the named directory to become the current working directory. When the operation is successful, it returns zero; otherwise, it returns -1. When the operation is not successful, the current working directory is kept as it was.

### The getcwd System Call

The ***getcwd*** system call can be used to get the path of the current working directory. The format of this call is:

```
#include <unistd.h>
#include <sys/types.h>
    char *getcwd(char *buf, size_t size);
```

This call stores the path of the current working directory in the buf argument and returns a pointer to the path data. When the returned value is a ***NULL*** pointer, then the operation is not successful.

## 21.6 System Calls for Regular Files

### The creat System Call

The creat system call is generally used to create a new file after which it keeps the created file in open state automatically for appending purpose. The prototype definition of this system call is shown below:

```
#include <sys/types.h>
#include <sys/stat.h>
int creat(const char *pathname, mode_t perm_mode);
```

where

***pathname*** is a string argument (either string variable or string constant) containing the path name; for example, */home/nsk/newfile* gives the path of the newfile's location, i.e., the path goes through the root directory ('/') and 'nsk' directory before locating newfile.

***perm_mode*** is a 9-bit integer value specifying the access rights of the owner, the owner's group and other users. The most significant 3-bits specify read, write and execute status of the owner, the next 3-bits refer to the owner's group and the last 3-bits to others. (See ***Table 21.1*** for a description of the different modes.)

> ***Remark:*** *When the created file already exists, then the given protection_mode value is ignored and its original mode is retained, but the file will be truncated.*

***creat*** returns the index of the file descriptor table entry that contains the address of the open file table. This index is an integer value that can be used as the logical address of the open file. If the returned value is -1, an error occurred during the create operation.

***Error Flag:*** The returned value, -1, indicates that the create call has failed due to one of the following reasons:

- *the location, or the directory in which the new file is to be created, is not searchable (i.e., the given pathname is illegal);*
- *the pathname exists, but it is a directory;*
- *the pathname exists, but does not allow writing;*
- *the target directory does not allow writing;*
- *there is no more disk space available;*
- *the pathname is a sharable file which is currently executed;*
- *the pathname variable points to an invalid memory address or NULL;*
- *the current program or process has already opened too many files (i.e., the open-file quota, which is usually 20, for a process has been reached).*

## Example 21.4:

Create a file called "***newfile***" with the protection mode described as follows:

(a) Read and write permission for the owner;
(b) Read permission for the owners group;
(c) Read permission for others.

```
/* Program: Create_file.c */
#include <sstdio.h>
#include <unistdt.h>
#include <sys/types.h>
#include <sys/stat.h>
void main(void)
{ int fd;
  int perm_mode;
  perm_mode = S_IRUSR|S_IWUSR|S_IRGRP|S_IROTH; /* perm_mode = 0644; */
  if( (fd = creat("newfile", prot_mode) ) == -1)
    { /* if the call fails */
      perror("newfile");
      exit(0);
    }
  . . .
}
```

When creating a file, the ***creat*** function allocates an empty ***inode*** table (or file record) and fills up its entries with relevant details. It allocates an open file table and an entry in the file descriptor table to construct an access path or control channel. The allocated open file table is filled with the address of the inode of the open file, the initial value of the file offset, i.e., 0, and the access (read or write) flags. The address of this table is entered into the allocated file descriptor table entry. Finally, ***creat*** returns the index of the file descriptor table entry as an identifier of the access path through which read and write can be performed.

## The open System Call

The ***open*** call requests the operating system to open a file directly. In response to this call, the system opens a file by setting up an access path and returns the file descriptor.

An open system call is used either to open an already existing file or to create a new file. In the former case, the call requires two arguments, namely, the name of the file and flags to indicate the types of access mode. In the latter case, a call requires three arguments: the first two are the same as before and the third one is set_flag to indicate the access rights of the created file. The prototype definitions of open system call are shown below:

**Case 1**: A simple ***open*** call

```
#include <sys/types>
#include <fcntl.h>   /* access mode macro constants are defined in this header */
    int  open( const char *pathname, int   access_mode_flag)
```

where

***pathname*** is a string argument (either string variable or string constant) containing the path name;

***access_mode_flag*** is an integer value. ***Table 21.2*** shows the integer values for various access modes.

***open*** returns a file descriptor as the logical address of the open file (or the address of the open channel for this file); if the returned value is -1, an error occurred during the open operation.

***Error Flag:*** The returned value, -1, indicates that the open call has failed due to one of the following reasons:

- the location (or the directory in which a file is to be opened) is not searchable (i.e., the given path name is illegal);
- the *pathname* exists, but it is a directory;
- the *pathname* exists, but the access mode does not match with the file's access rights;
- the *pathname* is a sharable file which is currently executed;
- the *pathname* variable points to an invalid memory address or NULL.
- the current program or process has already opened too many files (i.e., the open-file quota, which is usually 20, for a process has been reached);

*Table 21.2 Access mode flags for open system call, as defined in* ***fcntl.h***

| Access mode in macro form | Description |
|---|---|
| O_CREAT | Create a file if it does not exist. |
| O_EXCL | Exclusive use of flag. |
| O_NOCTTY | Don't assign a controlling terminal. |
| O_TRUNC | Truncate flag. |
| O_APPEND | Open for appending |
| O_NONBLOCK | Open for direct mode. |
| O_RDONLY | Open for reading only. |
| O_RDWR | Open for both reading and writing. |
| O_WRONLY | Open for writing only. |

**Case 2:** The ***open*** call with create option

```
#include <sys/types.h>
#include< sys/ fcntl.h>
int open(char *pathname, int access_mode_flags, mode_t perm_mode)
```

where the type of third parameter indicates the access control status of the created file for various user types. (See **creat** and **Table 21.1**)

### Example 21.5:

Open "file1" as an input file and "file2" as an output file.

```
/* Program:   opn_files.c */
#include <stdio.h>
#include <sys/types.h>
#include <fcntl.h>
void main(void)
{ int fd1, fd2;  /* declare file descriptor variables  */
  int perm_mode = S_IRUSR|S_IWUSR|S_IRGRP|S_IROTH; /* perm_mode = 0644;  */
  if( (fd1 = open ("/home/nsk/file1", O_RDONLY) ) == -1) /* open file1 for read-only */
    {
      perror("During open() at file1");
      exit(0)
    }
  . . .
  perm_mode = S_IRUSR|S_IWUSR|S_IRGRP|S_IROTH; /* perm_mode = 0644;  */
  if( (fd2 = open ("/home/nsk/file2", O_WRONLY, perm_mode) ) == -1) /* create and open
                              file2 for writing only */
```

```
        {
          perror("During open() at file2");
          exit(0)
        }
      . . .
    }
```

***Remark:*** *When the same file is opened more than once, the open calls return different file descriptors. All these file descriptors point to the same control channel.*

## The read System Call

The ***read*** system call can read a block of bytes from an open file into a user specified buffer. Usually this call takes the logical address of an open file (i.e., the file descriptor), the buffer address and the amount of data to be read as parameters. Its prototype definition is shown below:

```
#include <sys/types.h>        /* size_t and ssize_t are defined in this header */
#include <unistd.h>
ssize_t  read( int fd,  void *buffer_address,  size_t  nbytes);
```

where

***fd*** is the logical address of open file (or the address of open channel for this file);

***buffer_address*** is the address of user defined buffer;

***nbytes*** is the number of bytes to be transferred from the current position of file; note that the ***size_t*** is equivalent to *unsigned int.*

***read*** returns the number of bytes successfully transferred; if the returned value is zero, then the end of file has been reached; if the returned value is -1, an error occurred during the read operation. The returned type, ***ssize_t***, is equivalent to *signed int.*

***Error Flag:*** The returned value, -1, indicates that the ***read*** call has failed due to one of the following reasons:

- the file is not open or the file descriptor does not identify an open control channel;
- the access mode for which the file is opened does not allow reading;
- buffer address is illegal.

## The write System Call

The ***write*** system call can write a block of bytes from a user specified buffer to a specified file. Similar to the ***read*** system call, ***write*** also carries three parameters: the file descriptor, the address of the buffer, acting as a source, and the number of bytes to be transferred. Its prototype definition is shown below:

```
#include <sys/types.h>        /* size_t and ssize_t are defined in this header */
#include <unistd.h>
ssize_t write( int fd, void *buffer_address, size_t nbytes);
```

where

**fd** is the logical address of the open file (or the address of the open channel for this file);

**buffer_address** is the address of the user defined buffer;

**nbytes** is the number of bytes to be transferred from the current position of file; the type, ***size_t***, is equivalent to *unsigned int*.

**write** returns the number of bytes successfully transferred; if the returned value is -1, an error occurred during the write operation. The returned type, ***ssize_t***, is equivalent to *signed int*.

***Error Flag:*** The returned value, -1, indicates that the ***write*** call has failed due to one of the following reasons:

- the file is not open or the file descriptor does not identify an open control channel;
- the access mode for which the file is opened does not allow writing;
- the buffer address is illegal.

## The lseek System Call

The ***lseek*** system call is used to move the file cursor to a desired position in an open file. It carries three arguments to reposition the file cursor. The first argument is the file descriptor, and the second and third arguments are displacement and reference origin, respectively. The prototype definition is shown below:

```
#include <sys/types.h>         /* off_t is defined in this header */
#include <unistd.h> /* synbols for reference_origin are defined in this header */
off_t lseek(int fd, off_t displacement, int reference_origin);
```

where

***fd*** is the logical address of the open file (or the address of the open channel for this file);

***displacement*** is the offset value by which the file cursor is to be positioned with respect to the selected origin; this argument is of long integer type to accomodate the movement of the file cursor in any size file. The ***off_t*** type is equivalent to *long int*.

> ***Remark:*** *The name "lseek" denotes a long seek.*

***reference_origin*** indicates which origin is effective to determine the target position of the file cursor. ***Table 21.3*** shows the values of this argument and their meanings.

***lseek*** returns a long integer value showing the current position of the file cursor with respect to the beginning of the file; if it returns -1, an error occurred during the seek operation;

***Error Flag:*** The returned value, -1, indicates that the ***write*** call has failed due to one of the following reasons:

- the file is not open or the file descriptor does not identify an open control channel;
- the value of reference_origin is illegal (other than 0, 1 and 2);
- the new file cursor position is negative or displacement is out of the file boundary. (See the following remark.)

*Table 21.3 Values of reference_origin as defined* ***unistd.h***

| **Reference_origin (symbolic form)** | **Reference_origin (integer)** | **Description** |
|---|---|---|
| SEEK_SET | 0 | set offset with respect to beginning of file |
| SEEK_CUR | 1 | set offset with respect to current position of file |
| SEEK_END | 2 | set offset with respect to end of file |

> ***Remark:*** *An* ***lseek*** *call moves the file cursor to a character/byte position in an open file using the following formula:*
>
> ***file cursor position = reference_origin + displacement***
>
> *where displacement is a signed integer. The range of new cursor position should always be positive.*

## Example 21.6:

After opening a file for reading, move file cursor to the end of the file.

```
/* Program: mv_cursor.c */
#include <stdio.h>
#include <sys/types.h>   /* system_defined types are in this header */
#include <fcntl.h>   /* access mode symbols are defined in this header */
#include <unistd.h> /* synbols for reference_origin are defined in this header */
void main(void)
{ int fd; /* declare a file descriptor variable */
  off_t   cursor_pos;
   if( (fd1 = open ("/home/nsk/file1", O_RDONLY) ) == -1) /* open file1 for read-only */
                  /* and the file cursor is set at the beginning by default */
   { /* if open call fails */
     perror("During open() at file1");
     exit(0);
   }
  if( (cursor_pos = lseek(fd, 0L, SEEK_END) ) == -1) /* set cursor at the last byte */
   { /* if lseek call fails */
     perror("During lseek() in file1");
     exit(0);
   }
  printf("Current position of the file cursor: %d \n", cursor_pos);
  close(fd);
}
```

> ***Remark:*** *A long constant in an expression is a string of digits followed by the letter 'L' (or 'l'). In the above example, 0L is the long constant zero.*

### Example 21.7:

After opening a file for reading, position the file cursor at the 100th byte from the beginning of the file.

```
/* Program: mv_cursor.c */
#include <stdio.h>
#include <sys/types.h>   /* system_defined types are in this header */
#include <fcntl.h>       /* access mode symbols are defined in this header */
#include <unistd.h> /* synbols for reference_origin are defined in this header */
void main(void)
{ int fd;  /* declare a file descriptor variable */
  off_t   cursor_pos; /* long cursor_pos; */
   if( (fd = open("/home/nsk/file1", O_RDONLY) ) == -1) /* file1 is opened, and the file
                            cursor is set at the beginning by default */
    { /* if open call failed */
      perror("During open() at file1");
      exit(0);
    }
  if( (cursor_pos = lseek(fd, 99L, SEEK_SET) ) == -1) /* set cursor at 100th byte */
    { /* if lseek call fails */
       perror("During lseek() in file1");
      exit(0);
    }
  printf("Current position of the file cursor: %d \n", cursor_pos);
   close(fd);
}
```

### Example 21.8:

After opening a file for reading purpose, move the curser back to 10 positions from the end of the open file.

```
/* Program: mv_cursor.c */
#include <stdio.h>
#include <sys/types.h>   /* system_defined types are in this header */
#include <fcntl.h>       /* access mode symbols are defined in this header */
#include <unistd.h> /* synbols for reference_origin are defined in this header */
void main(void)
{ int fd;                  /* declare a file descriptor variable */
 off_t   cursor_pos;  /* long cursor_pos; */

   if( (fd = open("/home/nsk/file1", SEEK_SET) ) == -1) /* file1 is opened, and the file
                               cursor is set at the beginning by default */
    { /* if open call fails */
      perror("During open() at file1");
```

```
        exit(0);
    }
    if( (cursor_pos = lseek(fd, -10L, SEEK_END) ) == -1)  /* set cursor at last-10 */
     { /* if lseek call fails   */
        perror("During lseek() in file1");
        exit(0);
     }
    printf("Current position of the file cursor: %d \n", cursor_pos);
  close(fd);
}
```

## The dup System Call

When a file is opened, a control channel is created and the address of that channel is stored in the next available entry of the file descriptor table. The index of this entry is returned as the logical address of that open file. The ***dup*** system call duplicates the file descriptor or logical address for the same open channel of a file. In other words, a ***dup*** call with a specified file descriptor value can create another entry in the file descriptor table pointing to the same control channel and return the index of this new entry. The old and new file descriptors are both effectively acting as logical address to the same open file. The prototype definition of this call is:

```
#include <unistd.h>
int    dup( int  existing_file_descriptor);
```

where

| | |
|---|---|
| ***existing_file_descriptor*** | is the channel address of an already open file; |
| ***dup*** | returns a new file descriptor for the same open channel; if the returned value is -1, an error occurred during the ***dup*** operation; |

***Error Flag:*** The returned value, -1, indicates that the ***dup*** call has failed due to one of the following reasons:

- an illegal existing_file_descriptor;
- a free entry in the file descriptor table is not available.

This system call allows manipulation of the file descriptors. This technique can be applied to redirect the standard streams from their default terminal files to specified files. This is discussed in more detail in ***Chapter 22***.

We have seen that the dup system call returns another file descriptor for the same open file channel. The drawback with this system call is that it can allocate only the smallest unused numerical value as the duplicated file descriptor. However, the ***dup2*** system call can allocate a specified number as the duplicated file descriptor for an open file channel. When the specified number is already allocated to another open file channel, the call closes the file channel and allocates as the duplicate file descriptor to the requested open file channel. The format of this call is:

```
#include <unistd.h>
    int dup2(int existing_file_descriptor, int new_file_descriptor);
```

For example,

```
int another_fd = dup2(old_fd, 5);
```

will return 5 as the duplicated file descriptor to the open file whose existing file descriptor is ***old_fd***.

## File Control System Calls

### The fcntl System Call

The ***fcntl*** call can perform various functions on an open file. It is almost a general purpose function on an open file and one can perform even the functions performed by other system calls on an open file. For example, ***fcntl*** can perform the function of dup2.

```
int new_fd = dup2(fd, required_fd);
```

can be performed

```
int new_fd = fcntl(fd, F_DUPFD, required_fd);
```

Other functions of this system call include ***file locking*** and ***access of open_file table flags***. The general format of the call is:

```
#include <sys/types.h>
#include <unistd.h>
#include <fcntl.h>
int fcntl(int fd, int command, <command dependent argument>);
```

The various commands and their symbolic values, as defined in ***fcntl.h***, are presented below:

| **Symbolic value of command** | **Description** |
|---|---|
| F_DUPFD | Duplicate file descriptor. |
| F_GETFD | Get file descriptor flags. |
| F_GETLK | Get record locking information. |
| F_SETFD | Set file descriptor flags. |
| F_GETFL | Get file status flags. |
| F_SETFL | Set file status flags. |
| F_SETLK | Set record locking information. |
| F_SETLKW | Set record locking information; wait if blocked. |

## 21.7 Inode-Related System Calls

### The link System Call

The ***link*** call links the existing inode of a file to a new entry in a directory. When we create a file, the ***creat*** system call creates an inode and its inode number is entered in the directory entry along with the given name of the file. To indicate that there is a link, the links field in the inode table is stored as 1. Whenever we use the ***link*** system call to make another entry for the same file, either in the same directory or in a different directory, then the links field of that files inode is incremented. A ***link*** call cannot be used to make an entry for a file that exists in a different file system. This facility allows the same file to be shared by more than one user in the same file system. The prototype definition of this call is:

```
#include <unistd.h>
int    link(const char *existing_pathname, const char *alias_pathname);
```

where

***existing_pathname*** is a string argument containing the path name of an existing file;

***alias_pathname*** is a string parameter containing the path name of the alias file;

***link*** returns value 0 for a successful link operation; if the returned value is -1, an error occurred during the link operation;

***Error Flag:*** The returned value, -1, indicates that the ***link*** call has failed due to one of the following reasons:

- the location of the target directory in *existing_pathname* is not searchable (i.e., the given path name in the first argument is illegal);
- the location of the target directory in *alias_pathname* is not searchable (i.e., the given path name in the second argument is illegal);
- *existing_pathname* does not exist in the target directory of the first argument (or in the source directory);
- *alias_pathname* already exists in the target directory of the second argument (or in the destination directory);
- the destination directory does not have write permission;
- variable argument (either *existing_pathname* or *alias_pathname*) is pointing to an invalid memory address or NULL.

## The unlink System Call

The ***unlink*** call is useful to remove a link between a file entry in a given directory and the file's inode. This is the only system call available to remove a file from a file system. When a file is created, the links field of its inode shows the link count as 1. A ***unlink*** call removes the file name entry from a directory and, at the same time, decrements the link count of the links field of the corresponding inode. When this count becomes zero, this inode is removed from the file system. If the link count of a file's inode is N, then the corresponding file can be removed only after Nth unlink call. The prototype definition of this call is:

```
#include <unistd.h>
int     unlink(const char *pathname);
```

where

***pathname*** is a string argument containing the path name of the existing file;

***unlink*** returns value 0 for successful operation; if the returned value is -1, an error occurred during the unlink operation;

***Error Flag:*** The returned value, -1, indicates that the ***unlink*** call has failed due to one of the following reasons:

- the location of the target directory in the given path is not searchable (i.e., the given path name in the argument is illegal);
- *pathname* does not exist in the target directory;
- the target directory, in which *pathname* exists, does not have write permission (See the following note.);
- the *pathname* variable points to an invalid memory address or NULL.

> ***Note:*** *Each entry in a directory contains the pathname and inode number. An inode number is always a short integer value other than 0. If any entry in a directory file contains 0 in the inode field, it is regarded as unlinked or empty entry. Unless write permission is given, unlink cannot write 0 in the inode number field of the given entry.*

## The access System Call

The ***access*** call is useful to determine whether a specified access type is available for a user. For example, we can enquire whether we have been given write permission for a file that belongs to another user. If ***access*** returns a favourable reply, then this user can proceed with that file processing. In some other situation, we may test whether we have been given write permission in a directory so that we can create a link, copy a file, rename a file or even remove (or unlink) a file. Hence, an ***access*** call is a useful mechanism to determine if any processing can be done on a file or directory. The prototype definition of this call is:

```
#include <unistd.h>  /* symbolic constants for various permissions defined here */
int     access( const char  *pathname,  int   access_mode_in_test);
```

where

***pathname*** is a string argument containing the path name of the existing file;

***access_mode_in_test*** is an integer (usually OCTAL) indicating the type of access that is being tested. The unistd.h header defines a set of symbolic constants listed below (***Table 21.4***) to enquire the access status of the file.

*Table 21.4 Values of access_mode_in_test as defined in* ***unistd.h***

| access_mode_in_test | Description |
|---|---|
| R_OK | to test **read** access permission of the file |
| W_OK | to test **write** access permission of the file |
| X_OK | to test **execute** permission of the file |
| F_OK | to test the **existence** of the file specified in the path |

***access*** returns 0 when the specified access is allowed for the file; if the returned value is -1, an error occurred during the link operation.

- the location of the target directory in the given path is not searchable (i.e., the given *pathname* in the first argument is illegal);
- the target directory does not allow to read its contents;
- *pathname* does not exist in the target directory;
- *pathname* points to an invalid memory address or NULL.

The ***access*** system call searches the ***inode*** of the given file to find out whether the specified access permission is allowed by a user who issues this command. The function will identify the user level (i.e., as owner, group or other) and then test ***access_mode_in_test*** with respect to the corresponding access mode stored in the in the st_mode field of the inode.

## The chmod System Call

The ***chmod*** system call is useful to change the access mode of a file or directory. The access mode that is stored in the inode of a file contains three levels (i.e., user, group and others) of protection codes. Using this system call, the owner of a file can change the access privilege at any of these levels. The prototype definition of this system call is

```
    #include <sys/types.h>          /* mode_t is defined here  */
    #include <sys/stat.h>           /* symbolic constants for various permissions defined here
*/
    #include <unistd.h>
    int  chmod(const char *pathname, mode_t perm_mode);
```

where

***pathname*** is a string argument denoting the name of a file, including the pathname component;

***perm_mode*** is an integer (usually a 4-digit OCTAL value) indicating the type of access that is to be set. Except the most significant digit, each of the following octal digits denotes read, write and execute access for a type of user. The most significant digit is used to accommodate the set_user_id and set_group_id flags, the next digit relates to the owner, the next digit to the group and the least significant digit to others. This integer code is same as the one used in a ***creat*** system call. (See ***Table 21.1***.)

For example,

04000 or S_ISUID To set set_user_id flag on execution;
02000 or S_ISGID To set set_group_id flag on execution;
00700 or S_IRWXU read, write and execute permission for the owner;
00070 or S_IRWXG read, write and execute permission for the group;
00007 or S_IRWXO read, write and execute permission for others;
00777 or S_IRWXU | S_IRWXG | S_IRWXO read, write and execute permission for all.
*< any other combination of the permissions>*

***chmod*** returns 0 when the mode is changed successfully; if the returned value is -1, an error occurred during the ***chmod*** operation; when an error occured, the original value of the protection mode is unchanged.

***Error Flag:*** The returned value, -1, indicates that the ***chmod*** call has failed due to one of the following reasons:

- The location of the target directory in the given path is not searchable (i.e., the given *pathname* in the first argument is illegal);
- *pathname* does not exist in the target directory;
- The target directory does not allow to write;
- *pathname* points to an invalid memory address or NULL.

> ***Remark:*** *The permission mode of a file can be changed only by the owner or a super user who owns the whole system.*

## The chown System Call

The ***chown*** call is useful to change the owner or group ID of a file (or directory). The owner and group IDs that are stored in the inode of a file are effectively changed along with the time at which the change occurred. The prototype definition of this system call is:

```
#include <sys/types.h>        /* uid_ and gid_t types are defined here */
#include <unistd.h> /* _POSIX_CHOWN_RESTRICTED defined here */
int   chown( const char *pathname, uid_t new_owner_id, gid_t new_group_id);
```

where

**pathname** is a string argument denoting the name of a file, including the pathname component;

**new_owner_id** is an integer denoting the identifier of a user to whom the ownership of the specified file is to be transferred.

**new_group_id** is an integer denoting the identifier of a group user to whom the ownership of the specified file is to be transferred.

**chown** returns 0 when the specified ownerships are stored in the inode of a given file; if the returned value is - 1, an error occurred during the **chown** operation; when an error occured, the previous values of the owner and group identifiers in the inode are unchanged. If the _POSIX_CHOWN_RESTRICTED is in effect, the users can change only the group_ids to which the owner of the process belongs to.

***Error Flag:*** The returned value, -1, indicates that the ***chown*** call has failed due to one of the following reasons:

- the location of the target directory in the given path is not searchable (i.e., the given *pathname* in the first argument is illegal);
- *pathname* does not exist in the target directory;
- the target directory does not allow to write;
- *pathname* points to an invalid memory address or NULL.

> ***Remark:*** *The ownership of a file can be changed only by an owner or a super user. After changing the ownership, the old owner cannot reverse the process because the file now belongs to another owner.*

## The stat and fstat System Calls

We know that an inode record describes the permanent attributes of a created file. To extract the details stored in an inode record, the ***stat*** or ***fstat*** system call is useful. The prototype definitions of these calls are shown below:

```
#include <sys/types.h>          /* various types used in stat structure are defined here */
#include <sys/stat.h> /* stat structure is defined here      */
#include  <unistd.h>
int    stat( const  char  *pathname,    struct stat   status_buf);
int    fstat( const int  fd,    struct stat   status_buf);
```

Two system calls are available. The ***stat*** system call is applied to an unopened file, whereas ***fstat*** is applied to an open file.

where

**pathname** is a string variable containing the path or pathname as a string constant;

**fd** is the file descriptor of open file;

**status_buf** is an instance of the prototype structure, called ***stat***, which is already defined in the ***stat.h*** header;

**stat** returns 0 when the ***stat*** call is successful; if the returned value is -1, an error occurred during the ***stat*** operation.

***Error Flag:*** The returned value, -1, indicates that the ***stat*** call has failed due to one of the following reasons:

- the location of the target directory in the given path is not searchable (i.e., the given path name in the first argument is illegal);
- *pathname* does not exist in the target directory;
- the target directory does not allow to read;
- the *pathname* variable points to an invalid memory address or NULL.

In the above format, the argument ***status_buf*** is a variable of the prototype structure ***stat***. The ***stat*** system call simply copies the details of the given file's inode into ***status_buf*** which can then be inspected by the users. This structure contains the attributes corresponding to the inode items that can be inspected by a common user. This prototype structure is shown below:

```
struct stat
    {
      dev_t  st_dev;    /* device of inode  */
      ino_t  st_ino;    /* inode number  */
      short  st_mode; /* mode bits for file type & protection type      */
      short  st_nlink;  /* number of links to this file  */
      short  st_uid;    /* user id in integer form  */
      short  st_gid;    /* group id in integer form*/
      dev_t  st_rdev;   /* for special files */
      off_t  st_size;   /* file size in characters  */
      time_t st_atime;  /* time of last file access  */
      time_t st_mtime;  /* time of last modification  */
      time_t st_ctime;  /* time of file creation     */
    }
```

*Remark: As already mentioned, the stat type is defined in the stat.h header file. Some of the type definitions (like dev_t, ino_t, etc) used in the stat structure are defined in another file called types.h. When we use **stat** or **fstat** system call in our programs, we should include both stat.h and types.h. The header files, including these two that are used in system programming, are located in a separate directory called "sys" within the /usr/include directory. Hence, the correct path of these two files is /usr/include/sys and they can be included in our programs with the following convention:*

```
#include <sys/types.h>
#include <sys/stat.h>
```

### Example 21.9:

Assume that a file called "***ourfile***" exists in our directory. Show the attributes of this file.

```
/* Program:   stat_test2.c   */
#include <stdio.h>
#include <unistd.h>
#include <sys/types.h>
#include <sys/stat.h>
void main(void)
{
   struct stat status_rec;
   if(stat("/home/nsk/ourfile", &status_rec) == -1)  /* call stat with a complete path */
     {
       perror("During stat() at ourfile");
       exit(0);
     }
   printf("Size of ourfile:   %d \n",  status_rec.st_size);
   printf("UID of ourfile: %d \n",  status_rec.st_uid);
   printf("GID of ourfile: %d \n",  status_rec.st_gid);
   printf("Number of links to ourfile: %d \n",  status_rec.st_link);
   printf("Size of ourfile:   %d \n",  status_rec.st_size);
   printf("Time of last access of ourfile:   %d \n",  status_rec.st_atime);
   printf( "Time of last modification of ourfile: %d \n", status_rec.st_mtime);
}
```

## 21.8 FIFO (Named Pipe) File

A FIFO is a fixed size file used for communication. It is created by the ***mkfifo*** system call with a ***pathname***. After creating a FIFO file, an entry is created in the target directory. It is quite similar to a ***regular*** file except for its size and removing the written information after reading. In ***Chapter 20***, we introduced the ***unnamed pipe***. An unnamed pipe is usually created by a parent process before the inherited processes can use the same for communication. The function of FIFO is similar to unnamed pipes, but it has the name attribute. Hence, it is also called named pipe. Unlike the unnamed pipes, a FIFO can be used by unrelated processes to communicate with each other. That is, one process can create a FIFO and open it for writing and a process of another group can open the same pipe to read information. It is also possible that more than one process can open either for reading, writing or for both reading and writing. These processes need not be the children of the same parent. When more than one process performs read or write on the same FIFO file, a proper mutual exclusion procedure must be adopted to avoid any corruption on the data handled through this FIFO. The system calls such as ***read***, ***write***, ***close***, ***stat*** and ***unlink*** used for regular files can also be used for FIFO files.

## The mkfifo System Call

The ***mkfifo*** call creates a new FIFO special file and makes an entry in the target directory specified in the call. The format of the call is:

```
#include <sys/types.h>          /* mode_t type is defined here       */
#include <sys/stat.h> /* symbolic constants for various permissions defined here  */
int  mkfifo(const char  *pathname, mode_t  perm_mode);
```

The permission bits of the created file are initialized from the specified mode argument. While setting the permission bits, the mode is modified by the process' file creation mask (***umask***). The ***perm_mode*** *(or **permission**) bits* can be expressed using the symbolic constants defined in the ***sys/stat.h*** header. Also, the ***mode_t*** type is defined in ***sys/types.h***. Hence, these two files must be included whenever this special file is created. The call returns zero after successful completion and -1 otherwise. The ***errno*** flag will be set to indicate an error during error return.

We can open a created FIFO file either normally or with the O_NONBLOCK flag. In the former case, the process that issued the open call for reading is blocked until another process opens the same file for writing. Similarly, the process that opens for writing will be blocked until another process opens the same for reading. In the latter case, when there is no process in the other end, the process that opens in this end is not blocked and returned with -1. At the same time, the ***errno*** is set to EAGAIN. The non-blocked process is free to check the FIFO again after doing some useful work.

> ***Note:*** *Original Unix interface provided **mknod** system call to make special files like directory and FIFO files. Since the POSIX standard introduced separate calls, such as **mkdir** and **mkfifo**, **mknod** is available only to create device files. Unix programmers should also note that the standard has omitted the **mount** and **umount** system calls from the interface.*

**Example 21.10:** We will show a program to create a FIFO file and communicate between two processes.

```
/*********************************************************************/
/* This program opens a fifo for communication                      */
/*********************************************************************/
#include <stdio.h>
#include <sys/types.h>
#include <sys/stat.h>
#include <unistd.h>
#include <fcntl.h>
#include <errno.h>
#include <limits.h>
#define BUFLEN _POSIX_PIPE_BUF
void main(void)
{
 int fd_in, fd_out;
 char fifo_name[] = "/home/nsk/ddd/c_dir/TEST_DIR/myfifo";
 char inbuf[BUFLEN], outbuf[BUFLEN];
 int i;
   for(i=0; i<BUFLEN; i++) /* clear the buffer with null */
     {
      inbuf[i]='\0';
      outbuf[i]='\0';
     }
   mkfifo(fifo_name, S_IRWXU | S_IRWXG | S_IRWXO);
     if(fork() != 0)
        { /* parent process */
        fd_out = open(fifo_name, O_RDONLY | O_NONBLOCK);
        if (fd_out == -1)
          perror("fifo cannot open");
         sleep(5);
        if(read(fd_out, outbuf, BUFLEN-1)<0)
         {
          perror("Read error");
          exit(0);
         }
        printf("parent received the message: %s \n", outbuf);
        exit(0);
       }/* End of parent */
```

```
else
    { /* child process */
    if ((fd_in = open(fifo_name, O_WRONLY | O_NONBLOCK) == -1)
        perror("fifo cannot open");
    puts("input a message <<< ");
    scanf("%s", inbuf); /* get a message from the user */
    printf("child sends this message: %s \n", inbuf);
    write(fd_in, inbuf, BUFLEN-1);
    exit(0);
    }/* End of parent */
}/* End of main program */
```

In the above program, the parent process creates a FIFO file, called myfifo, in the target directory specified in the pathname and creates child by using a fork call. Then the parent wants to wait (by sleeping) for 5 seconds before it can look for any message in the myfifo pipe. Meanwhile, the child process prepares a message (from the keyboard file) and writes the same into the fifo and it exits. Eventually, the parent gets the message and writes to the terminal. The output of the program is shown below:

```
% a.out
input a message:
Hello World
child sends this message: Hello World
parent receives the message: Hello World
```

## 21.9 Device Files

A device file in Unix is basically a wrapper file structure around a physical device, such as terminal, printer, modem, disk drive, magnetic tape drive or any other byte-stream-oriented block device. Similar to regular files, a device file is also represented as a directory entry and an ***inode***, meaning we can open a device file and read or write the information just like a regular file. There are two types of physical devices: character special and block special types. Some device files may be read only, write only, or read and write, depending upon the physical characteristics. Similar to regular files, a device file is also created with appropriate permission mode. That is, the ***inode*** of a device file has most of the information common with the inodes of regular files. The ***st_mode*** of a file indicates the type of file. All device files in ***Standard Unix*** are created in the "***/dev***" directory. A device file can be created in the system using ***mknod*** system call. The format of ***mknod*** call is shown below:

```
#include <sys/types.h>          /* mode_t is defined in this header */
#include <sys/stat.h> /* constants of permissions and device type are defined here */
#include <unistd.h>
int mknod(const char *pathname, mode_t perm_mode, int dev_addr);
```

where

***pathname*** carries the location of the target directory where the device files are to be created.

***perm_mode*** carries the read, write and execution permissions of owner, group and others. It also carries the type of decice created.

***dev_addr*** carries the major and minor device numbers. The lowest byte of *dev_addr* represents the *minor device number* and the next byte represents the *major device number.*

The ***mknod*** call returns 0 after successful operation and -1 when it fails to create a device file. In Standard Unix, only the super user is allowed to make device files. Once a device is created in the system, a user may have permission to open for read or write information. Similar to regular files, a device file can also be removed from the system by using the ***unlink*** system call. The ***stat*** system call can be used to find out the characteristics of device files. Users must be careful in using the ***lseek*** system call on device files. It may work well with disk or tape device files, but not with terminal files.

For example, let us create a character device with major and minor device numbers of 5 and 15, respectively.

```
mknod("/dev/tty15, S_IFCHR | S_IRWXU | S_IRWXG | S_IRWXO, (5<<8) | 15);
mknod("/dev/dk03, S_IFBLK | S_IRWXU | S_IRWXG | S_IRWXO, (3<<8) | 4);
```

In the first example, S_IFCHR in the mode field indicates that a character device file is created. The second example creates a block device by specifying S_IFBLK flag in the mode field. The mode field in both examples show that both device files are created with all permissions to all users. That is, anyone can open these files for reading or writing. The major device number identifies the ***driver*** type (or device type) and minor device number identifies the actual physical device. There is a separate driver program for each type of device. For example, the terminal type is associated with a driver in raw mode. Similarly, there is a driver for disk, a driver for magnetic tape, etc.

## 21.10 Configuration Information of File System

### The pathconf and fpathconf System Calls

Both the ***pathconf*** and ***fpathconf*** are useful to get the limits of various parameters (or variables) around a file or directory. The configurable parameters specified by ***POSIX.1*** and the symbolic constants (or name values) that must be sent as an argument to enquire as to their limits are shown in the following table:

| Parameter name | Name value defined in ***unistd.h*** | Description |
|---|---|---|
| LINK_MAX | _PC_LINK_MAX | To enquire about the maximum number of links that can be made to an inode. |
| MAX_CANON | _PC_MAX_CANNON | To enquire about the maximum length of a formatted input line. |
| MAX_INPUT | _PC_MAX_INPUT | To enquire about the maximum length of an input line. |
| NAME_MAX | _PC_NAME_MAX | To enquire about the maximum length of a file name. |
| PATH_MAX | _PC_PATH_MAX | To enquire about the maximum length of a relative path name, starting with this directory. |
| PIPE_BUF | _PC_PIPE_BUF | To enquire the size of the pipe buffer |
| POSIX_CHOWN_RESTRICTED | PC_CHOWN_RESTRICTED | To enquire whether the chown system call is restricted on this file. If the path name or fd refers to a directory, the test is applied to all files in that directory. |
| _POSIX_NO_TRUNC | _PC_NO_TRUNC | To create a file with a name longer than the maximum in the directory without any error |
| _POSIX_VDISABLE | _PCVDISABLE | Disabling special character processing for terminals |

The format of these calls are:

```
#include <unistd.h> /* symbolic constants for param_id are defined here */
long pathconf(const char *pathname, int param_id);
long fpathconf(int fd, int param_id);
```

The first call requires *pathname* of an unopened file, whereas the second call requires the file descriptor of an open file. The ***param_id*** argument is one of the name values explained above. These values are defined in ***unistd.h***.

## 21.11 The sync System Call

Unix supports the ***delayed write*** mode in which the modified blocks that have to be written to disk are transferred to buffers that are then queued for later writing. It is the duty of the kernel to initiate write operation at some later time. Usually when the kernel is left with no other buffer, it starts flushing the buffers as much as possible. In addition to demand-based buffer flushing, a periodical flushing is also supported by the kernel. Moreover, during the shut down period, we may have to force the kernel to flush all the pending buffers out to disk so that no data is lost after shutting down the system. In order to help these two situations, the kernel is provided with the ***sync*** system call. The format of this call is shown below:

```
#include <unistd.h>
void sync(void);
```

When the system is running normally, a timer interrupt at regular intervals (of 20 to 30 seconds) issues the sync call to initiate flushing the buffers waiting for writing. During shutting down, the operator issues the sync call at shell command level at least three times to make sure all the buffer contents are saved promptly.

## 21.12 Summary

This chapter explains the basic concept of the Standard Unix file system and the system call interface to access the file system. The working principle of this system call I/O, including:

- *how different types of files are maintained internally;*
- *how a control channel is organized for an open file;*
- *how this channel is used during reading and writing;*
- *how this channel is closed*

are discussed in detail. The ***inode*** structure used to store the attributes of a created file, and the use of ***stat*** system call in accessing the file attributes are discussed as well.

The chapter discussed three categories of system calls, i.e., ***file access calls***, ***file protection calls*** and ***miscellaneous calls***, that can be used by programs in creating and maintaining the files. The file access type system calls, such as ***creat***, ***mkdir***, ***mkfifo***, ***mknod***, ***open***, ***read***, ***write***, ***close***, and ***unlink***, can be used to perform normal file-oriented functions. File protection system calls, i.e., ***umask***, ***chmod*** and ***chown***, can be used to set appropriate levels of protection for each created file. Under the miscellaneous type, ***lseek***, ***link***, ***stat***, and ***dup*** system calls are discussed.

## Exercises

21.1 What is file creation mask? Set this flag with the read, write and execute permission to owner, read and execute permission to group and none to others.

21.2 Write a program to count number of files in a directory.

21.3 Write a program to list entries in the given directory, excluding the dot and double dot entries.

21.4 Write a program to list the directory files in a given directory.

21.5 What is the effect of the following system calls: (Assume that user creation mask is 0022)

a. creat("newfile", 0644); /* newfile did not exist before */
b. creat("oldfile", 0644); /* oldfile already exists */

21.6 What is the effect of the following system calls: (Assume that user creation mask is 0022)

a. open("newfile", 0); /* newfile does not exist */
b. open("oldfile", 0); /* oldfile already exists */

21.7 Write C-code to open a file for appending purpose. (Hint: you may have to use more than one system call.)

21.8 What values are returned for the following cases:

a. open("nofile", 2) when "nofile" does not exist in the system;

b.
```
char c;
int i;
i = read(0, &c, 1); /*read one byte from the keyboard file whose file_descriptor is 0 */
```

c.
```
/* assume "file1" is in our directory and its size is 1000 characters */
int fd, i;
long l;
char buf[10];
/* the following segment is executed      */
fd = open("file1", 1);
l = lseek(fd, 100L, 0);
l = lseek(fd, 50L, 1);
l = lseek(fd, 0L, 2);
i = write(fd, "A 21 character record", 10);
l = lseek(fd, 0L, 0);
i = read(fd, buf, 10);
```

21.9 When we open a file, the inode of that file is brought to main memory. Why?

21.10 When we close a file, the inode is copied back onto disk. Why?

21.11 What is an open file table? Why is it necessary for an active file?

21.12 What is a file descriptor? Why is it necessary? Where is it kept in the system?

21.13 What are the differences between stream binary I/O functions and block (or direct) I/O system calls? Which one would you prefer for implementing simple file processing?

21.14 Which factor limits the number of open files per process?

21.15 Which system call is used for deleting a file from the file system? Explain using an example.

21.16 Can you use the ***stat*** system call to display your directory? If yes, then write the code to display all the files with their protection codes, dates and owners in your home directory.

# 22

# Program Call Interface

**Chapter contents:**

*This chapter introduces the program-to-program interface provided in C, which is particularly useful to provide a facilty for transferring arguments from a command line to the called program. This chapter teaches the readers how to write command line programs.*

**Organization:**

*22.1 Introduction*
*22.2 The execve Function*
*22.3 Derived exec** Functions*
*22.4 Argument Retrieval and Processing by a Called Program*
*22.5 Unix Command Programs*
*22.6 How shell Executes Command Programs*
*22.7 Environment Around a Command Process*
*22.8 Structure of a shell Command*
*22.9 Summary*
*Exercises*

## 22.1 Introduction

The function call mechanism is a standard feature in any programming language. During a function call, the execution thread passes through a called function and comes back to continue in the calling function. In addition, C provides a unique feature that allows a program to call another program. In this mechanism, the execution thread goes to a called program, but never comes back to the calling program. In other words, a program call is used to overlay the calling program with a called program and execute the entire text of that new program in the same process. Similar to argument passing in a function call, a program can also pass a set of arguments via a program call. Although the function and program calls look similar, the program-to-program communication is more involved and is done with the help of the operating systems kernel.

To facilitate the program-to-program call facility, the ***execve*** system call is provided in the Unix kernel. An ***execve*** call, along with a ***fork*** system call, provides a powerful mechanism to create a new process and execute another C-program in that created process. In fact, the Unix shell (i.e., command line interpreter of Unix) uses these system calls to execute requested command programs. This chapter explains how the program-to-program interface is achieved in C-programs and how this technique is applied in systems programming, particularly in writing command utility programs.

## 22.2 The execve Function

The ***execve*** call is the basic system call supported by the Unix kernel for executing (or calling) a program. Since the handling of arguments by this system call is at a somewhat conceptual level, five other functions are made available at the user level in the system. Each one of the derived ***exec**** functions basically differs in the handling of argument passing. In fact, these five functions internally call ***execve*** to achieve the actual program call. The prototype definition of the ***execve*** system call is:

```
#include <unistd.h>
int execve( char *path_of_program_file, char **argument_vector_table, char
    *environment_vector_table[]);
```

where

***path_of_program_file*** is a string argument that indicates the name and location of the called command program;

***argument_vector_table*** is an array of pointers pointing to argument strings; these arguments are used by the called program to perform a task; if a called program does not require any argument, then a table of NULL pointers can be passed;

***environment_vector_table*** is also a table of string pointers pointing to a set of processes' environment parameters; a default environment exists for processes under each user; if a new environment is required for a called program, then the appropriate environment, in the form of a table, can be passed by a calling program; these parameters convey to a called program such environmental details as the name of the current directory, terminal type, path specification (that should be used in the called program for accessing the specified program file), etc.

> ***Remark:*** *A calling program can overlay the default shell environment with a new environment by sending an appropriate table to a called program.*

## 22.3 Derived exec** Functions

### 22.3.1 The execl Function

The prototype definition of this function call is:

> *#include <unistd.h>*
> ***int** execl( **char** *path_of_program_file, **char** *just_program_name, **char** *arg2, . . .
> . ., **char** *argN, (**char** *)NULL );*

where

***path_of_program_file*** is a string argument that indicates the name and location of the called command program;

***just_program_name*** is also a string argument telling the process or called program what its name is (useful when a called program ends with an abnormal state and wants to print an error message along with its name.);

***arg2. . argN*** is a list of string arguments that are used by a called command program for performing its task; when a program does not require any argument, then the program call need not carry any of these arguments.

**NULL** is necessary to indicate the end of the argument list in an execl call; it is simply a null character pointer expressed as (char *)0.

> ***Remark**: The name execl means to execute (i.e., call) a program by passing a detailed list of arguments supplied along with the call.*

In general, command utility programs in Unix (such as ***echo***, ***cd***, ***cp***, ***mv***, ***more***, ***ls***, ***cat***, etc.) are designed to receive arguments via a program call and perform their functions accordingly. The number of arguments expected by a command program depends upon its task. For example, the ***cd*** (change working directory) command program expects only two arguments, its (binary file) name and a directory name; the copy command program, ***cp***, requires three arguments, its name, a source file and a destination file. When a C-program calls one of these command programs, it has to pass appropriate arguments.

## Example 22.1:

Let us now show the use of execl by writing a test program, test_execl.c, to call the **echo** command program whose path is /bin.

```
/* Program test_execl.c */
#include <stdio.h>
#include <unistd.h>
void main(void)
{
        if((execl("/bin/echo", "echo", "Hello World", (char *)0) == -1)
          {
            perror("test_execl.c");
            exit(0);
          }
        /* else control never returned here; */
}
```

During execution, a process starts with this program, and then the ***execl*** call overlays in the same process with the ***echo*** program. When echo comes into execution, it displays on the screen with the message "***Hello World.***"

### 22.3.2 The execlp Function

The prototype definition of this function call is:

```
#include <unistd.h>
int execlp( char *program_file_name, char *just_program_name, char *arg2, . . . ,
     char *argN, (char *)NULL);
```

This function and the previous one differ only in the first argument. This function requires only the name of the called program as a string, and it will locate the program in the file system with the help of the path environment of the running process.

> ***Remark:*** *The letter 'p' in the name execlp indicates that this function will resolve the path of a called program*

## Example 22.2:

Let us show the use of ***execlp*** to call the same ***echo*** command program. In this case, instead of a complete path description of the program file, simply the name of the program file is enough as the first parameter. ***execlp*** will correctly locate this binary file and execute it.

```
/* Program: test_execlp.c */
#include <stdio.h>
#include <unistd.h>
void main(void)
{
  if((execlp("echo", "echo", "Hello World", (char *)0) == -1)
    {
      perror("test_execlp.c");
      exit(0);
    }
  /* else control never returned here; */
}
```

### 22.3.3 The execle Function

The ***execle*** function is similar to execve except that the arguments that are required by the called program are listed in the function call. The prototype definition of this function call is:

```
#include <unistd.h>
int execle( char *program_file_name, char *just_program_name, char *arg2, . . . ,
    char *argN, (char *)NULL, char *environment_vector _table[]);
```

### 22.3.4 The execv Function

The prototype definition of this function call is:

```
#include <unistd.h>
int execv(char *path_of_program_file, char *argument_vector_table[]);
```

where the first argument is a string indicating the location of a called program in the file system and the second parameter is the address of a table containing the pointers to string arguments. The ***execl*** and this function are similar, but differ in the manner of passing arguments to the called program. In this function, all program arguments are put in table form and the address of this table is passed instead of a complete list of string arguments. The first pointer in the argument vector table points to the name of the called program, and the following pointers point to other string arguments expected by the program. The last entry in the argument vector table is filled with a NULL pointer to indicate the end of the argument list.

> ***Remark:*** *The letter 'v' in the name execv indicates that this function carries a list of arguments via an argument vector (i.e., pointer) table.*

### Example 22.3:

Let us show the use of ***execv*** to call the same ***echo*** command program. In this case, all the arguments expected by ***echo*** are sent via a table.

```
/* Program: test_execv.c */
#include <stdio.h>
#include <unistd.h>
char *argv[3];
char *prog_name = "echo";
char *message = "Hello World";
void main(void)
{
  argv[0] = prog_name;
  argv[1] = message;
  argv[2] = (char *)0; /* (or) NULL */
  if((execv("/bin/echo",argv)) == -1)
    {
      perror("test_execv.c");
      exit(0);
    }
  /* else control never returned here; */
}
```

### 22.3.5 The execvp Function

The prototype definition of this function call is:

```
#include <unistd.h>
int execvp(char *program_name, char *argument_vector_table[]);
```

This function and the previous one differ only in the first argument. This function requires only the name of the called program as a string, and it will then locate the program in the file system with the help of the path environment of the running process. Other arguments are passed via an argument vector table, as in the previous case.

> ***Remark:*** *The letter 'p' in the name execvp indicates that this function will resolve the path of a called program.*

## Example 22.4:

Let us show the use of ***execvp*** in calling the same ***echo*** program. In this case, all the arguments expected by ***echo*** are sent via a table.

```
/* Program: test_execvp.c */
#include <stdio.h>
#include <unistd.h>
char *argv[3];
char *prog_name = "echo";
char *message = "Hello World";
void main(void)
{
  argv[0] = prog_name;
  argv[1] = message;
  argv[2] = (char *)0; /* (or) NULL */
  if((execvp(prog_name, argv)) == -1)
 /* or if((execvp(argv[0], argv)) == -1) */
    {
      perror("test_execvp.c");
      exit(0);
    }
  /* else control never returned here; */
}
```

***General Remarks:***

1. *All exec** calls expect only string arguments;*

2. *The first argument must be the file name of a called program;*

3. *The arguments to a called program are a list of string parameters ending with a NULL pointer. The first argument of this list is, conventionally, the name of a called program;*

4. *execl, execle and execlp are useful program calls when the number of arguments is known. The same call cannot be used with a different number of arguments. On the other hand, execv and execvp are dynamic and can be used as a general calling mechanism. The same exec expression can be repetitively used to call the same or different programs with different numbers of arguments using a dynamic argument vector table. This facility is useful to design a command line interpreter which may use the same exec call expression for every command line request. This is explained later in this chapter;*

5. *These system calls may fail due to one of the following reasons:*
   * *program file does not exist in the given path;*
   * *program file located in a path does not have execution permission to the user of the calling program*

## Execution Privileges of Program Files

We have seen the different types of exec** functions that can be used to execute any specified program by the calling process. These functions are basically allowed to locate a program anywhere in the file system and execute the same, meaning a user process can execute a program which may belong to another user in the same file system. This aspect helps sharing programs and cuts down the overhead in the process of program development. However, this sharing of program execution will not produce the desirable results at some situations. In a common situation, a program is designed to use the resources that belong to the owner of a calling process. When the program belonging to one user is executed by some other user process, it will not create any problem to its owner. For example, compilers are of this nature. Although they belong to the super-user of the system, when processes execute them, they process on the source files and the output files of their owners. This is quite safer.

In some other situations, a program may maintain the private resources of its owner. In order to do this, the processes of other users can be avoided completely by denying permission to execute those programs. This is achieved by creating (using the ***creat*** system call) a program file with the appropriate permission or setting up the permission status on a created file with the help of the ***chmod*** system call. An interesting situation occurs when the private resources of a user must be accessible, but in a controlled manner, by the processes of other users. For example, to change password, a user has to access the password file strictly maintained by the super-user. In this situation, there are two problems to be solved: first, the password file should be protected from reading or writing by any user in the system except the super-user and, second, this file must be allowed to access by a user process. In order to solve these problems, the system has provided the ***set_user_id*** and ***set_group_id*** permission flags, which can be set to program files by a owner similar to setting other (i.e., *read, write* and *execute*) permissions.

The ***set_user_id*** flag permission to a program, when executed by a process, gives the privilege of the owner. Hence, users can allow other user processes to execute certain programs that access their private resources in a controlled manner. The ***passwd*** program of the super-user is an example of this case. If we get into the ***/etc*** directory, we would notice the presence of ***set_user_id*** flag in the entry of passwd program. When a user process executes this program for changing the password, it gets the privilege of the super-user to access the password file.

In order to achieve this solution, system maintains two sets of ***user ids*** in the data structures (i.e., user structure and process structure) of a process. The ***real_user_id*** is the true user identifier which is first created in the password file and then copied into data structures of a process. Until a user is enrolled in the system, it remains the same. The other type, called the ***effective_user_id***, is maintained to effectively access the resources of a user. Before every resource is accessed, its owner id is checked with the ***effective_user_id*** of the process. If they are the same, then the process can proceed, else it may stop due to access violation. Usually, the ***effective_user_id*** of a process is set to the value of ***real_user_id***, showing that the process has the owner's privilege in executing a program. The value of this id in a process can be moved from the original ***real_user_id*** to some other ***real_user_id*** with the setting of ***set_user_id*** (or ***set_group_id***) of a program that is being executed.

## System Call functions to access Real and Effective User Ids

Kernel provides the ***getuid***, ***getgid***, ***geteuid*** and ***getegid*** system calls to examine the values of the ***real_user_id*** and ***effective_user_id*** fields stored in the user structure of a process. Although these functions don't seem to be essential, in some instances a process working at a different user privilege can get and save the real and effective uids, and be able to use them for switching between its own mode (i.e., real uid) and the different user mode (i.e., saved effective user mode), and thus be able to access resources in both. The definitions of these system calls are as follows:

```
#include <sys/types.h> /* uid_t and gid_t types are defined in this header */
uid_t getuid(void);
uid_t geteuid(void);
gid_t getgid(void);
gid_t getegid(void);
```

**Example 22.5:** Let us write a program that will display the contents of real and effective user ids.

```
#include <stdio.h>
#include <unistd.h>
#include <sys/types.h>
void main(void)
{ uid_t     real_uid, effective_uid;
  gid_t     real_gid, effective_gid;
    real_uid = getuid();
    effective_uid= geteuid();
    printf(" Real User ID is %d \n", real_uid);
    printf(" Effective User ID is %d \n",effective_uid);
    real_gid = getgid();
    effective_gid = getegid();
    printf(" Real Group ID is %d \n", real_gid);
    printf(" Effective Group ID is %d \n",effective_gid);
}
```

Kernel also provides system calls to alter the values of *real* and *effective user* (*group*) *id* fields of both user and process structure of a process. They are:

```
#include <sys/types.h>          /* uid_t is defined in this header */
int  setuid(uid_t  uid);
int  setgid(gid_t  uid);
```

But the effect on the resulting changes depends upon the type of user who issues one of these system calls. When a super-user process issues ***setuid(uid)*** (or ***setgid(uid)***), *real_uer_id* (or *real_group_id*) and *effective_user_id* (or *effective_group_id*) in both user structure and process structure will be changed to the supplied value, ***uid***. The ***uid*** value supplied by the super-user can be any user id. This facility is used by the super-user process while setting up shell processes for the active terminals. On the other hand, if a call is generated from a normal user process, then the *effective_user_id* (or *effective_group_id*) field of user structure is only changed to the supplied ***uid***. In this case, the uid value can be the process' own, or *real_user_id* (or *real_group_id*), or the saved *effective_user_id*, which may be a different user's *real_user_id* (or *real_group_id*).

> ***Note:*** *Although each created process is accompanied with a process structure for scheduling purpose and a user structure for maintaining execution environment, the real and effective user ids are maintained in both structures for the following reason.. When a process goes to sleep, the user structure is also swapped out, along with the data, text and stack segments. Process structures of sleeping processes are always kept in the memory for the kernel to schedule them at later time. For example, when a signal arrives from a user terminal to its sleeping processes, kernel can then identify all those processes with the help of user ids in the process table and pass the signal to all those processes.*

## 22.4 Argument Retrieval and Processing by a Called Program

In every C-program the main function acts not only as the starting function during execution, but also provides an interface to receive arguments from a program call. If a C-program does not require any argument, its main function is declared simply as:

```
/* A main with no formal arguments  */
void  main(void)
  {
     . . .
  }
```

On the other hand, when a C-program is designed to receive some arguments from another program, then its main function must contain a declaration of two formal arguments. One is an argument count indicating how many arguments are passed and the other is a table of pointers to receive argument strings. A main function with formal argument declarations is shown below:

```
/* A main with declaration of formal arguments   */
void main(int argc, char *argv[])
/*  int     argc: number of arguments passed    */
/* char  *argv[]:  a table of pointers for string arguments supplied along with the command  */
  {
    . . .
  }
```

Now let us demonstrate, using some simple examples, how a program can be implemented to receive and process the arguments that are passed by another program.

### Example 22.6:

Similar to the systems ***echo*** command program, let us implement our own echo program. We shall call this utility program "***our_echo***". For example, when we execute this program with the command,

***our_echo C-Programming,***

the program will print the text (i.e., the second) argument on the screen once:

***C-Programming***

We should note that our_echo expects only two arguments: program name and the message to be displayed. The argument count should be checked to make sure that the program receives the correct number of arguments. The main function of the our_echo program is shown below:

```
/* Version 1: simple echo program */
#include <stdio.h>
#include <unistd.h>
void main(int argc, char *argv[])
{
 if(argc != 2)
   printf("Program expects two arguments \n");
 else
   printf("%s \n", argv[1]);
}
```

Now we understand why the argument count is useful for a command program. The above program prints a prompt message if the command does not have any message argument to echo. Instead of a general prompt, it is more appropriate to give a prompt that shows the name of the command input by the user and a helpful message showing how to use that command. The second version includes this option.

```
/* Version 2: our_echo program with proper command-line error handling */
#include <stdio.h>
#include <unistd.h>
void main(int argc, char *argv[])
{
  if(argc == 1 )
    {
      printf("Error: message_argument is missing\n");
      printf("Usage: %s message_argument\n", argv[0]);
      exit();
  if(argc > 2 )
    {
      printf("Error: Too many arguments\n");
      printf("Usage: %s message_argument\n", argv[0]);
      exit();
    }
  else
     printf("%s \n", argv[1]);
}
```

When we call the above program without a message argument, such as % ***our_echo***, the echo program will prompt on the screen:

***Error: message_argument is missing***
***Usage: our_echo message_argument***

The above prompt displays the command line format for this command to make the error message more informative, which explains why the command name is also passed as one of the arguments to a command program. (Programs can assume that the first string argument contains the command program's name; in the above example, a printf statement prints an error message along with the command name, arg[0].)

### Example 22.7:

Let us extend the our_echo program of Example 1 and 2 to the multiple echo program. This program echoes as many times as requested via the second argument of a given echo command. For example, the command % ***our_echo 3 C-Programming*** will echo on the screen three times:

***C-Programming***
***C-Programming***
***C-Programming***

```
/* Multiple echo program */
#include <stdio.h>
#include <unistd.h>
#include <ctype.h>
void main(int argc, char *argv[])
{
 if(argc < 3 )
  {
   printf("Error: Missing Arguments \n");
   printf("Usage: %s numeric_argument message_argument\n", argv[0]);
   exit(0);
  }
 if(argc > 3 )
  {
   printf("Error: Too many arguments\n");
   printf("Usage: %s numeric_argument message_argument\n", argv[0]);
    exit(0);
  }
 if(!isdigit(*argv[1])) /* if the second argument is not an integer    */
  {
    printf("Error: Second argument must be a numeric_argument ");
  printf("Usage: %snumeric_argument message_argument\n", argv[0]);
     exit(0);
  }
 else
    { int   i, n;  /* i and n are temporary variables in this block */
     n = atoi(argv[1]); /* convert ascii number string into an integer  */
     for(i = 0; i < n; i++)
          printf("%s \n", argv[2]);
  }
}
```

## 22.5 Unix Command Programs

Every command program in Unix is implemented in the same fashion, as explained in the above example. All command programs (in binary form) are kept in the systems binary (/bin) directory. In general, command programs, such as ***more***, ***ls***, ***cat***, etc in Unix, are designed to receive arguments from a user and perform their functions accordingly. Actually, a user command (or command line) presented via the terminal activates the corresponding command program with the help of the shell interpreter. The basic role of the shell interpreter is to read arguments from a command line and pass these arguments, using an exec** call, to the requested command program. The function of the shell interpreter is discussed in more detail in the following sections.

## 22.6 How shell Executes Command Programs

In this section, we will discuss some conceptual details of the shell interpreter of the Unix system. A command line interpreter (CLI) is designed to provide an interface between users and the Unix kernel. Its basic function is to receive a command line from a user and start the specified command program. When the CLI receives a command line, it always interprets the first word of a command line as the name of the requested command program and the remaining words as parameters for that program. After collecting the arguments, the CLI has to employ a separate process to execute the requested command program. The reason for this is that if the CLI itself directly executes a command program, the exec** call will not return the control and, eventually, the CLI will die at the end of command execution. In order to avoid this, the CLI forks a process and allows the new process to execute or call the requested command program. The CLI process can wait until its child completes a command execution and then attend the terminal to receive another command. Remember that after forking, a child inherits the I/O environment as well as the current state of the data structures, including the argument table prepared by the parent process. The basic function of the shell is shown as a flowchart in ***Fig. 22.1***.

When the shell interpreter receives a command line, each argument is scanned and stored in a separate string. The addresses of these argument strings are stored in a table called argv. Shell forks a new process and allows this new process to execute the requested command program. A pseudo code for the basic function of a shell corresponding to the flowchart is shown below:

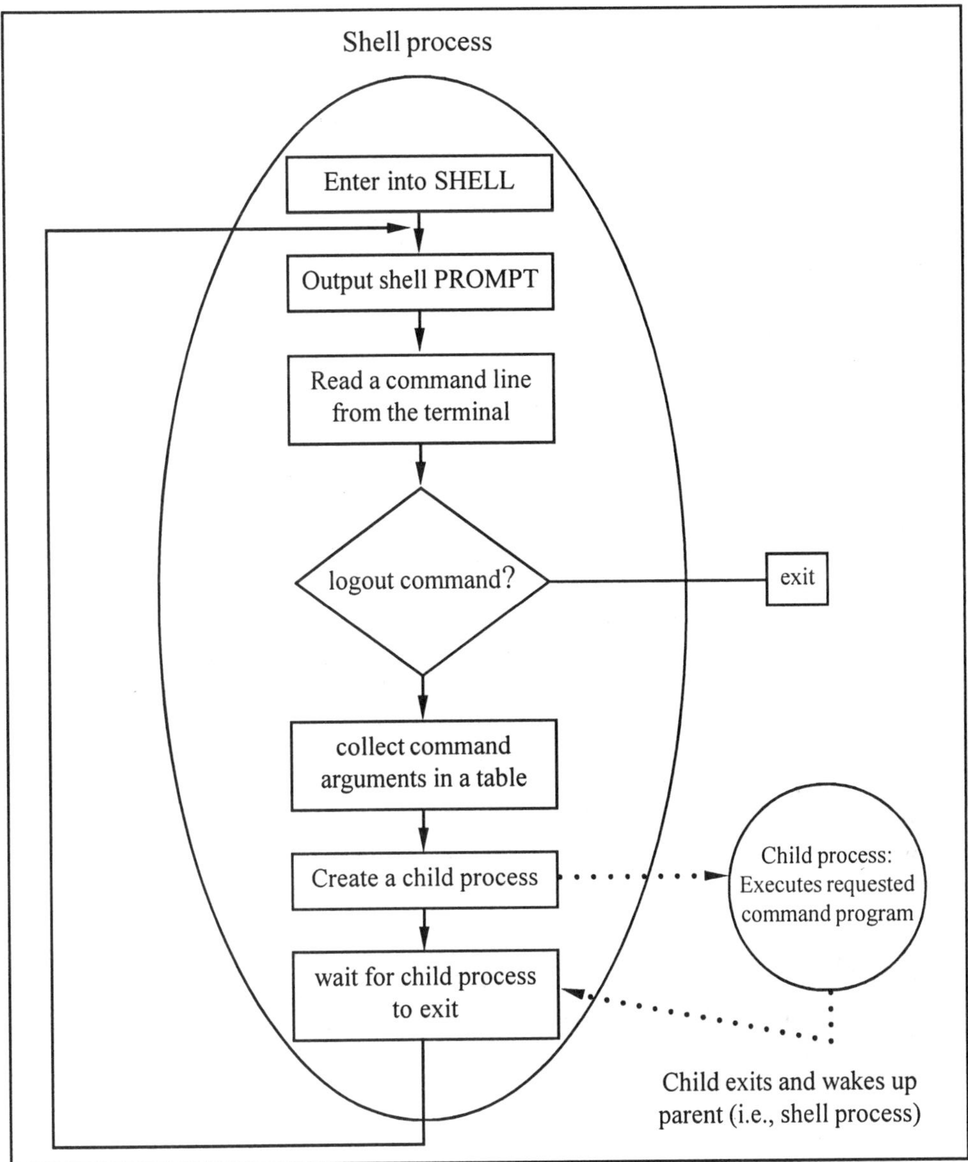


*Fig. 22.1 Basic functions of shell program*

```
/* shell program */
#include <stdio.h>
#include <unistd.h>
#include <sys/types.h>
void main(void)
  { char *argv[some_maximum_size]; /* argument table declaration */
  Repeat
  {
    Read_a_commandline;
    Put_arguments_in_argv_table; /* say, argv[] is the table */
    if(fork() ==0)
      {/* child process */
        execvp(argv[0], argv )
          /* if the exec call fails, control comes back here; else this process exits in the command
program */
        exit(0);
      }
    /* parent (i.e., shell) continues */
    /* parent waits until child finishes the given task */
    wait();
  } /* end of repeat loop */
```

The ***execvp*** call in the child process inherits all the information of the parent at the time of the fork and will use the inherited argv[] table in setting up a program call for the requested command program. (***Fig.*** *22.2* shows the argument tables prepared by a shell after receiving command lines of different ***rm*** commands.) ***Fig.*** *22.3* shows the role of the shell interpreter in a somewhat detailed form.

## 22.7 Environment Around a Command Process

A command program or process has three open streams, ***stdin***, ***stdout*** and ***stderr***, that are inherited from its parent process (i.e., shell). By default, these streams are directed to terminal files; ***stdin*** is attached to the ***keyboard*** file, ***stdout*** to the ***screen*** file and ***stderr*** to the ***screen*** file. In general, most of the command programs are designed to receive their formal input data via ***stdin***, send their formal output data via ***stdout*** and output any error via ***stderr***. (A ***stream*** is only a type of path or channel attached to a open file. The same ***stream*** can be redirected to any

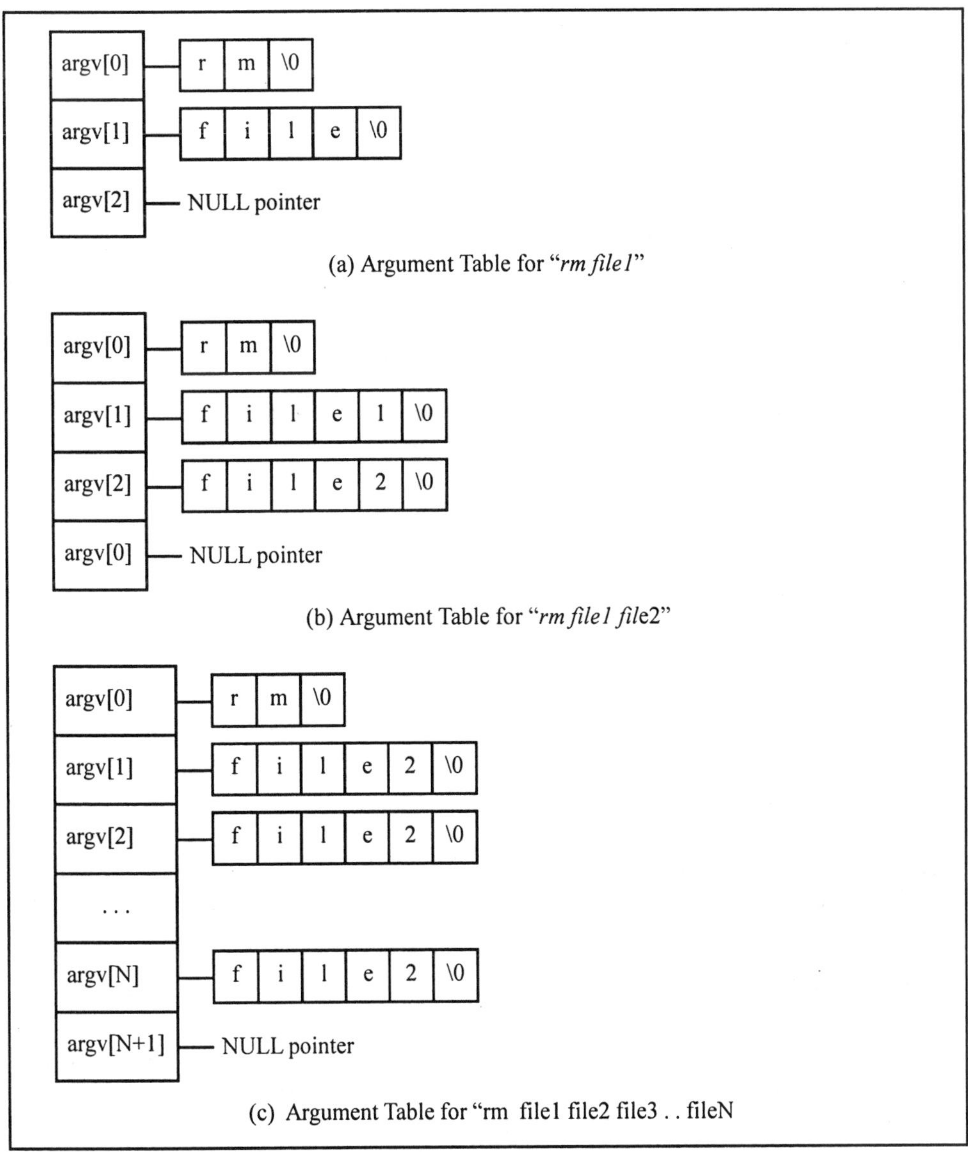


*Fig. 22.2 Argument vector tables and argument count for "rm" commands*

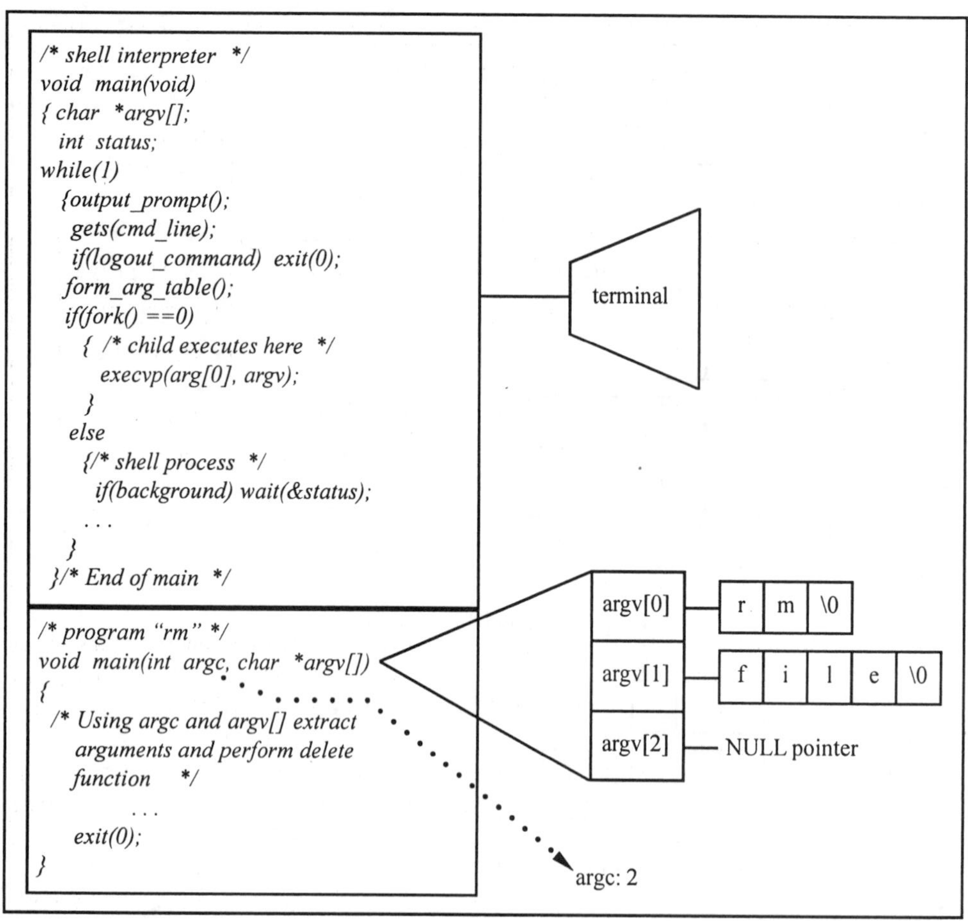


*Fig. 22.3 Role of shell during a command processing*

other open file with the help of some system calls. This is discussed later in this chapter.) The default status of the standard streams for a command program is shown in ***Fig. 22.4***. For example, a simple ***cat*** command (without any formal argument) will read the ***keyboard*** file via the ***stdin*** stream and display on the ***screen*** file via the ***stdout*** stream.

A command program is also supplied with a table of argument strings and an argument count needed for command processing. In addition, it can access its environment table via a global pointer, ***environp***. The contents of the environment table contain a set of string pairs explaining the resource environments such as terminal type, allowed path names, etc. around the running process.

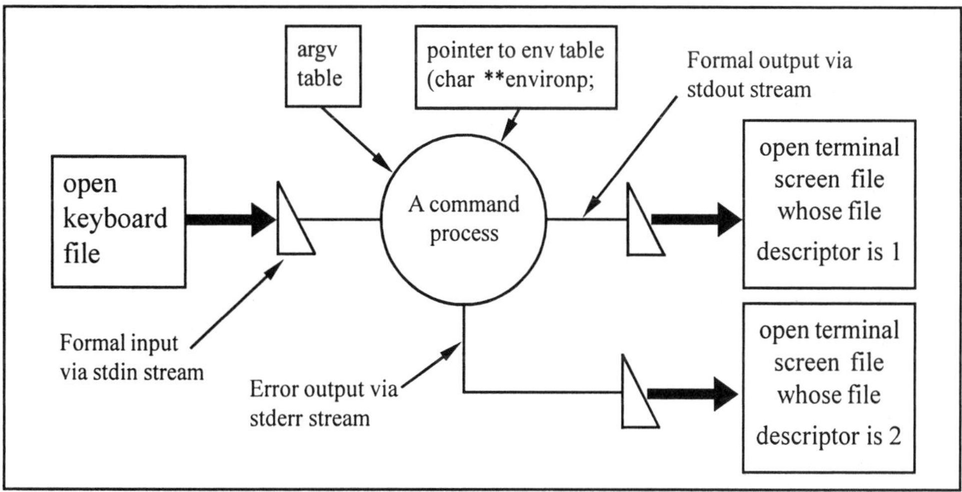


*Fig. 22.4 Environment of command program*

## 22.8 Structure of a shell Command

A user command specifies the command name as the first word and a number of arguments in the following words. The command name specifies the name of the utility (or binary program) that is to be run, and the accompanying arguments may be some optional flags and some expected formal operands for the named utility. Such programs are designed with multiple optional functions and, depending upon the optional flags that follow the command name, an appropriate set of functions will be performed. On the other hand, a formal argument may be a data object, such as a file, user name, or process identifier. When an expected file object is not supplied, the command program assumes that it can use one of the appropriate standard I/O files (i.e., keyboard or screen file). Various types of command programs are explained below.

### Types of Command Lines

The shell command lines can, in general, be classified into four categories as shown below:

1. Normal commands (to execute commands in foreground without any redirection)
2. Background commands
3. Commands with redirection of I/O from default files to specified files
4. Concurrent commands (with piped data between them)

## Case 1: Normal Commands

Some utilities are quite simple, and they may not require any formal arguments. The command lines for these programs are simply the command names. For example, some Unix commands in this category are as follows:

| | |
|---|---|
| *date* | to display the time of day on the terminal screen |
| *clear* | to clear the terminal screen |
| *pwd* | to know the present (current) working directory |
| *lpq* | to show the line printer queue |

Commands in the second category always require a fixed number of formal arguments; some utilities may expect one formal argument, some may expect two, and others may expect a greater, but fixed, number. For example,

| | |
|---|---|
| ***cd*** *work* | where "***cd***" is the name of command program and "work" is a formal argument, or directory name; the effect of this command line is to change the current directory to the directory called ***work***; usually, this command requires one formal argument and if it is omitted, the program substitutes a default directory name; |
| ***mv*** *work project* | change current file (or directory) name from "work" to "project"; the string "***mv***" is the program_name argument, "work" is the first formal argument and "project" is the second formal argument; all together there are three arguments in this command line. |
| ***cp*** *file1 file2* | copy the contents of source file, "file1", into the destination file, "file2"; the string, "***cp***", is the program name argument, and the strings, "file1" and "file2," are two operand arguments; all together there are three arguments in this command line. |

The third category of command programs may accept a variable number of optional arguments. For example, the ***rm*** command is meant to remove (or delete) one or more specified files. The following examples show some ***rm*** commands with varying numbers of arguments:

| | |
|---|---|
| ***rm*** *file1* | *To delete or remove "file1"* |
| ***rm*** *file1 file2* | *To delete "file1" and "file2" at the same time* |
| ***rm*** *file1 file 2 . . filen* | *To delete many files at the same time* |

### Case 2: Background Commands

A background command is specified by appending the character '**&**' at the end of a command line. For example, the following commands are to be executed in the background mode:

***cp** file1 file2&* (cp process copying in the background mode)
***lpr** f1 f2 f3 f4&* (printing proceeds in the background mode)

Background mode means that the created command process is left alone to do its job. The shell process, instead of waiting for the command process, simply proceeds with its foreground task of attending the terminal for further commands. The basic flowchart that includes this feature is shown in ***Fig. 22.5***.

### Case 3: Commands with Redirection of I/O

In the normal interactive mode, users expect some command programs to derive inputs from the default input (i.e., keyboard) file and direct outputs to the default output (i.e., screen) file. The following commands belong to this type:

*date* date output is sent to screen file via ***stdout*** stream
*cat* cat input is read from the default keyboard file via ***stdin*** stream and output goes to the default screen file via ***stdout*** stream;
*mail* mail reads the input from the keyboard and sends it to a specified user spool file.

In many instances, users may prefer to save these outputs in disk files for later use, which is equivalent to saying that users may like to redirect the default outputs to disk files instead of the screen file. Similarly, users may prefer command programs to read input from a disk file instead of the keyboard file. To provide this redirection service, the shell allows command lines with a redirection specification using the symbols, '>' and '<'. The basic principle behind this redirection can be shown by the following examples:

*date > time_file* date output is now sent to time_file via ***stdout*** stream
*cat file1* cat input is read from the given file, file1, and output goes to the default screen file via ***stdout*** stream;
*cat file1 > file2* cat input is read from the given file, file1, and output goes to file2 via ***stdout*** stream;
*mail nsk* mail input is read from the default keyboard file via ***stdin*** stream and output goes to the addressed user, nsk;
*mail nsk<mail_txt* mail input is read from the given file, mail_txt, and output goes to the addressed user, nsk;

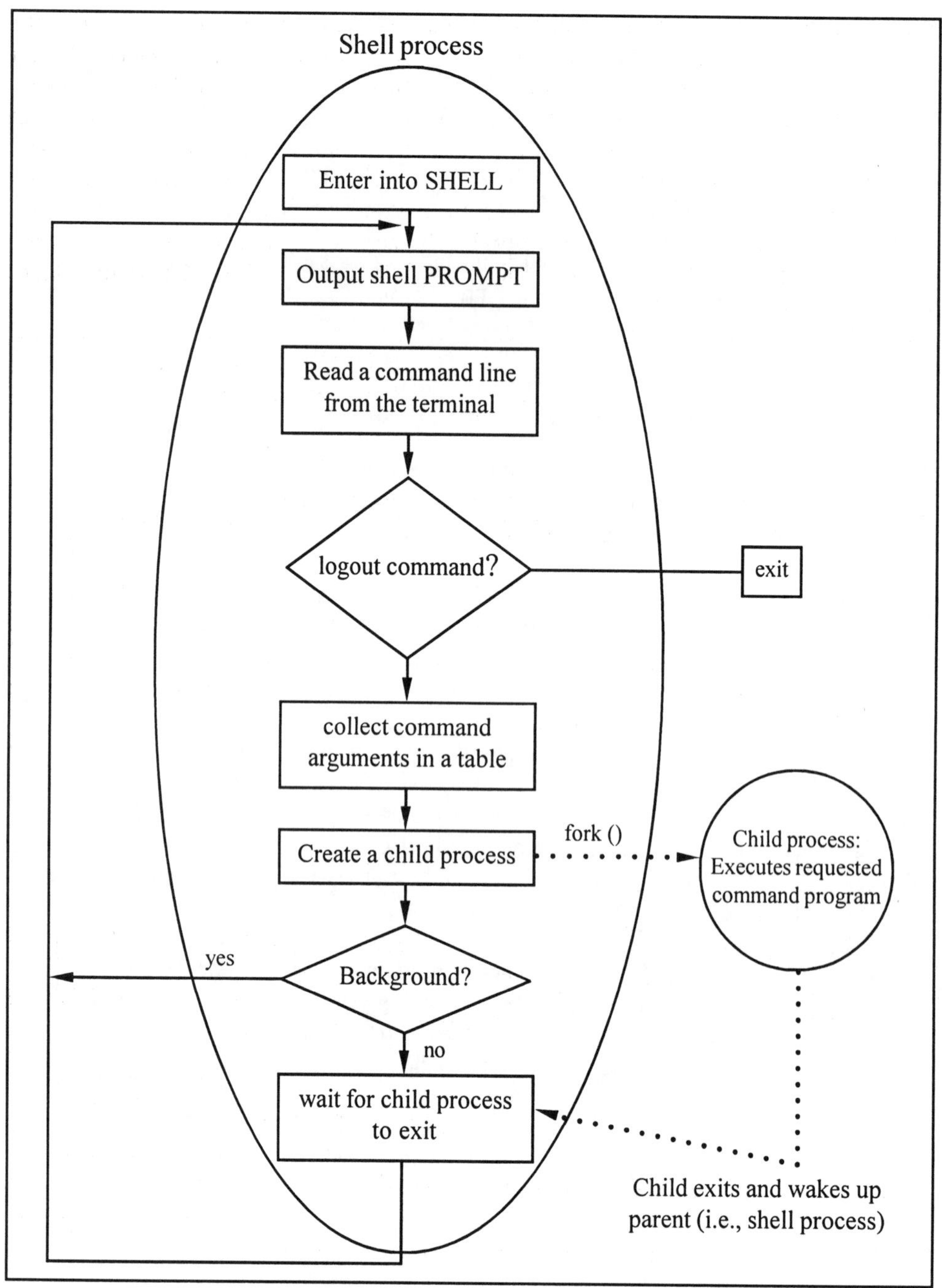


*Fig. 22.5 Basic function of shell program with background option*

This is called I/O redirection at the shell command level and is handled by shell, not by the invoked command program. When shell finds redirection information in a command line, it substitutes the appropriate default file with the file name that follows the redirection symbol. Now the standard streams will be directing the I/O with respect to these substituted files. With this modified I/O environment, shell forks a process and then calls the requested command program with the other arguments. The redirection of streams to specified files by the shell action is quite transparent to command programs. With redirected streams, even though a command program reads or writes with respect to the standard streams, it does not know what open files are attached to those streams. This is shown in ***Fig. 22.6***. The technique of redirection is discussed in the next section.

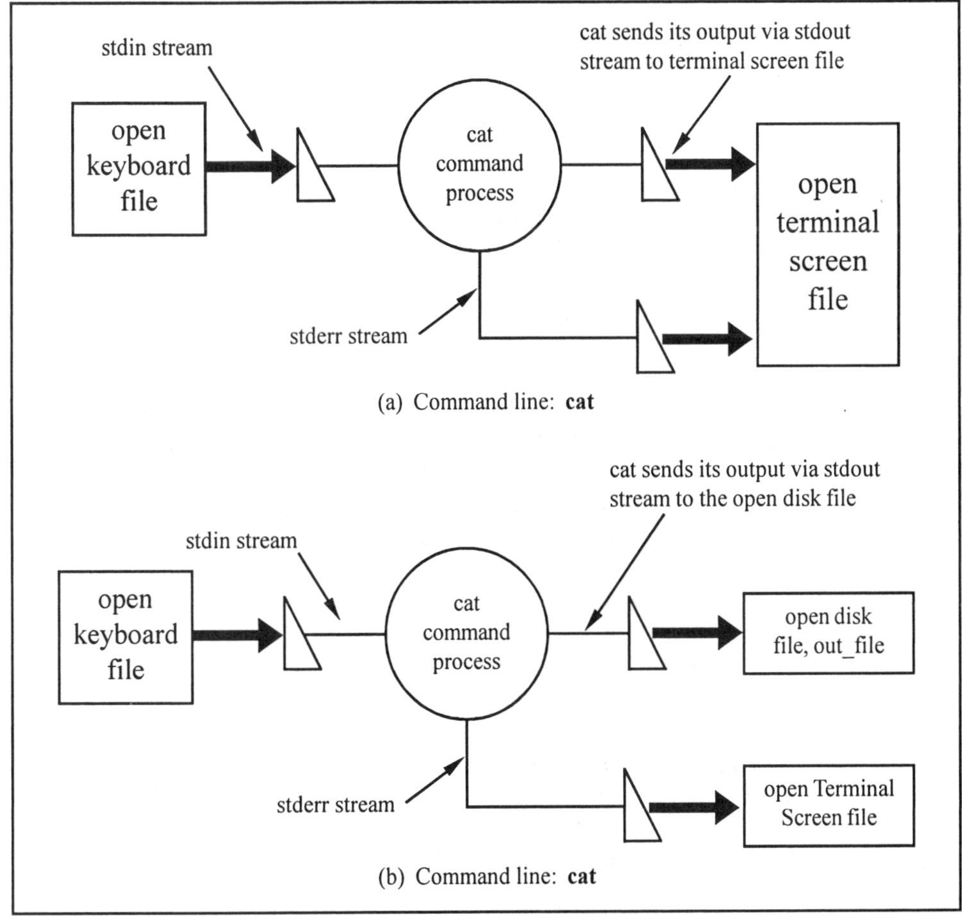


*Fig. 22.6 IO redirection for cat command*

### Handling file redirection by shell

When shell receives a command with a file redirection, it allows a command process to close the appropriate file descriptor of a stdio file and open the specified file to get the same file descriptor. In this way the required file descriptor entry of the associated stdio stream is made available for another file. For example, a ***cat*** command with redirection is

*cat >out_file*

When shell receives this command, it organizes the output redirection before forking and allowing new process execute ***cat*** program. The shell steps are as follows:

1. *Shell receives **cat** command and checks for redirection;*

2. *Shell collects the arguments of **cat** command in a table;*

3. *Shell forks a process which inherits the standard I/O environment of shell; after forking, shell may wait until child completes its execution;*

4. *For output redirection, the child process closes the file descriptor 1 so that this logical or channel address (or the corresponding entry in the file descriptor table) is made available;*

5. *When the child opens **out_file**, a control channel is created; and its address is stored in the first available entry of the file descriptor table, entry 1, and becomes the logical address of the **out_file**. Since the **stdout** stream is always associated with this file descriptor entry, i.e., 1, the control channel of **out_file** now becomes the redirected path. The new I/O environment around the child process is now as follows (Fig. 22.6(b)):*
   *stdin is attached to **keyboard**,*
   *stdout to **out_file** and*
   *stderr to **screen**.*

6. *Child process then calls or executes the requested (in the above example, **cat**) program, which then reads text from the keyboard file via **stdin** and writes the same to **out_file** via **stdout**;*

7. *At the end of command processing, the child wakes up the waiting parent (i.e., shell).*

The equivalent shell program is shown below in pseudo form:

```
#include   <fcntl.h>
/* fcntl.h defines RDONLY, WRONLY, etc */
void main(void)  /* shell's main  */
{
 char *argv[n];
 repeat
  {
   get_(cat)_command;
   collect_command_arguments_in_argv_table;
    {
     if(fork() == 0);    /* create a process  */
       { /* child executes command program   */
        if(command has output redirection only)
         {
          close(1);  /* release file descriptor 1 from screen file */
          open("out_file", WRONLY); /* out_file gets 1 as its fd */
         }
        execvp(command_name, argv);
        . . .
       }
   wait(); /* parent waits   */
     . . .
  } /* End of repeat loop   */
}/*  End of shell main  */
```

## Case 3: Concurrent Commands with Piping

Shell also allows a command line to specify that more than one command program can be run concurrently and data can be passed from one program to another program using piping mechanism.

## Use of dup for piping data between processes

A pipeline command specifies that more than one command program are to be executed and the output of one program should act as the input of another program. For example, in the following pipeline command

*ls | more*

> ***Note:** The vertical stroke character | is used to represent the pipe symbol*

Both ls and more command programs are to be executed concurrently and the output of the ***ls*** program is sent as input to the ***more*** program via a connected pipe. When shell receives such a pipeline command, the following manipulation on file descriptors is done:

- *shell reads the pipe command (i.e., ls | more);*
- *it opens a pipe and gets two new file descriptors, say pp_fd[0] and pp_fd[1]; where pp_fd[0] is file descriptor for read end and the other one for write end of the pipe;*
- *it collects the arguments of first command (i.e., ls command);*
- *forks a new process;*
- *child closes the file descriptor 1 so that it can be used as file descriptor of the write end of the pipe;*
- *it dups the write end of the pipe, i.e., pp_fd[1], so that file descriptor 1 is available as a duplicate file descriptor of the write end of the pipe; it closes the redundant pp_fd[1];*

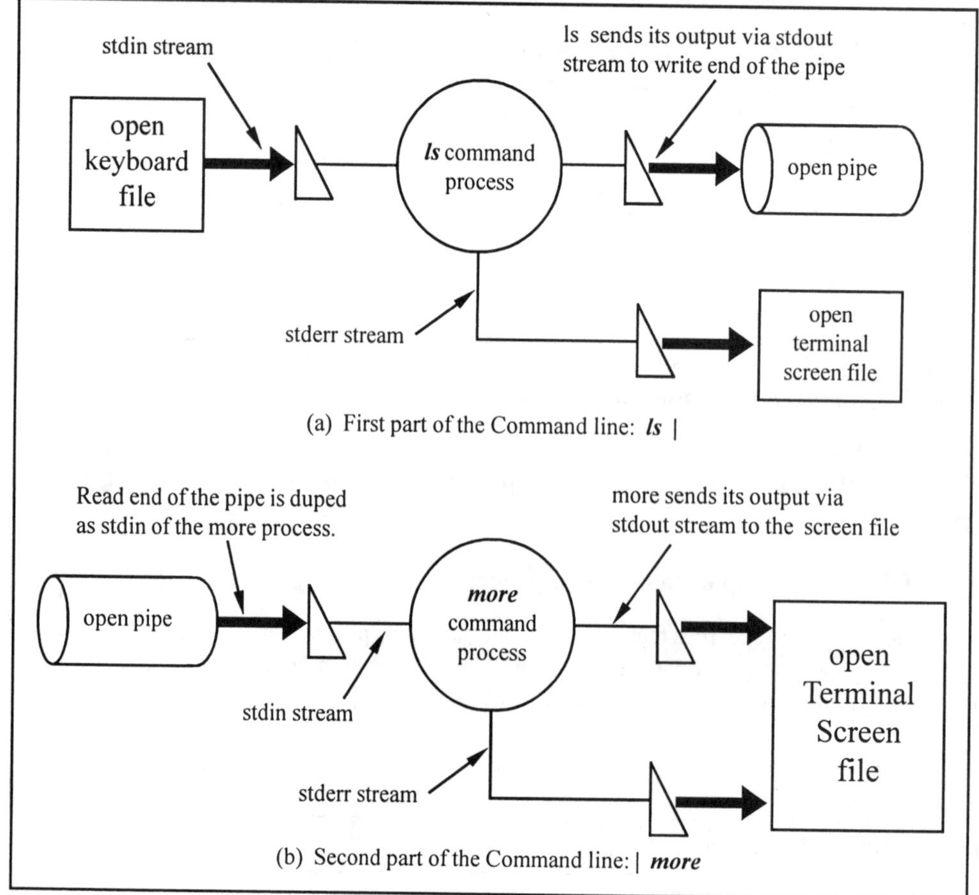


*Fig. 22.7 IO environments of* **ls** | **more** *command*

- *with this new I/O environment, child executes* ***ls;***
- *parent or shell collects arguments of more command;*
- *it forks another process and goes into wait state;*
- *child closes the file descriptor 0 so that it can be used as file descriptor of the read end of the pipe;*
- *it dups the read end of the pipe, i.e., pp_fd[0], so that file descriptor 0 is available as a duplicate file descriptor of the read end of the pipe; it then closes the redundant pp_fd[0];*
- *with this new I/O environment, child executes* ***more;*** (See ***Fig. 22.7***)

The equivalent shell program is shown below in pseudo form:

```
void main(void)  /* shell's main  */
{
 int   pp_fd[2];
  repeat
  {
   get_(ls l more)_command;
   if(command_needs_piping)
    {
     collect_ls_arguments_in_argv_table;
     pipe(pp_fd);     /* make a pipe */
     if(fork() == 0);     /* creates a process */
      { /* child executes command program    */
        close(1);      /* release file descriptor 1 from screen file*/
        dup(pp_fd[1]);    /* get file descriptor 1 as a duplicate file descriptor of the write end of
                              pipe */
        close(pp_fd[1]);  /* get rid of the redundant file descriptor of the write end */
        close(pp_fd[0]);
        execvp("ls", argv of ls);
        . . .
      }
     collect_more_arguments_in_argv_table;
     if(fork() == 0)     /* creates a process */
      {
      /* organize redirection for the read end of pipe   */
      close(0);  /* release file descriptor 0  */
      dup(pp_fd[0]);    /* get file descriptor 0 as a duplicate file descriptor of the read end of the
pipe */
      close(pp_fd[0]);     /* get rid of the redundant file descriptor of the write end */
       close(pp_fd[1]);
      /* child executes command program    */
       execvp("more", argv of more);
       . . .
      }
```

```
      close(pp_fd[1]);
      close(pp_fd[0]);
    wait(); /* parent waits for ls process   */
    wait(); /* parent waits for more process */
      . . .
    } /* End of repeat loop  */
  }/*  End of shell- main  */
```

**Example 22.8:** Let us write a simple command line interpreter that executes a given command with or without the background option. We will call this program myshell.

```
/************************************************************ ***/
/*                Program: myshell.c                            */
/************************************************************ ***/
#include <stdio.h>
#include <unistd.h>
#include <string.h>
#include <ctype.h>
#define QUITMSG     "logout"
#define CMD_SIZE   80
#define MAX_ARGS   10
char *arg_table[MAX_ARGS], cmd_line[CMD_SIZE];
int bkgrd_sw;
/***************************************************************/
/* gets the next command and also checks for the background flag;  */
/* returns 1 for valid command input, 0 otherwise                   */
/***************************************************************/
int get_cmd(void)
{
   int i;

   for( i = 0; (cmd_line[i] = getchar()) != '\n'; i++ );
   cmd_line[i] = NULL;
   if ( !i )   return(0);
   /* skip trailing spaces */
   while( isspace(cmd_line[i-1]) )   i--;
   if( cmd_line[i-1] == '&' )
      {
      bkgrd_sw++;   i--;
      }
   cmd_line[i] = NULL;
   return(1);
}
```

```
/*****************************************************************/
/* breaks the command line into substrings separated by nulls and      */
/* creates a table of pointers to point to each substring              */
/*****************************************************************/
int get_args(void)
{
   int arg_num = 0;
   char *chr = cmd_line;

   while( isspace(*chr) ) chr++;
   arg_table[arg_num++] = chr;
   while( *chr != NULL )
      {
      if( *chr == ' ')
         {
         *chr++ = NULL;
         while( isspace(*chr) ) chr++;
         arg_table[arg_num++] = chr;
         }
      chr++;
      }
   arg_table[arg_num] = NULL;
   return(arg_num);
}

/*****************************************************************/
/* execute the command either in foreground or background              */
/*****************************************************************/
void  execute_cmd(void)
{
   int child, status;

   if ( (child = fork()) == 0)
      {
      execvp(arg_table[0],arg_table);
      printf("\nNo such process found....\n");
      exit(0);
      }
   if (!bkgrd_sw)
      wait(&status);
}
```

```
/******************************************************************/
/* main function of myshell.c                                     */
/******************************************************************/
void main(void)
{
   int cmd_cnt = 1;

   while(1)
      {
      bkgrd_sw = 0;
   /*    output a prompt along with command count */
      printf("\n#%-3d mysh*> ",cmd_cnt);
      if (get_cmd())
         {
         if ( strcmp(cmd_line,QUITMSG) == 0 )
            break;
         else if( get_args() )
            {
            execute_cmd();
            cmd_cnt++;
            }
         else
            printf("Command Syntax Error\n");
         }
      else
         printf("Command Syntax Error\n");
      /* remove a zombie process if one exists */
      waitpid(0,NULL,WNOHANG);
      } /* END while(1) */
   printf("\nQUIT! Exit.... %-d Commands Performed.\n\n",cmd_cnt);
} /* End of main */
```

## 22.9 Summary

This chapter introduced a special set of system calls, i.e., ***exec*** calls, to facilitate executing a different program in a running process. This exec call facility is used by shell programs to run a user command in a separate process. The chapter also discusses other issues related to command processing, such as handling commands with redirected I/O and pipeline commands. A simple shell program is shown to demonstrate the significant use of the ***exec*** call facility in system programming.

## Exercises

22.1 What are the differences between a normal function call and an exec** system call?

22.2 When an exec** call fails, what action can be taken to find the error?

22.3 Why is the argument count always passed when a program is called with arguments?

22.4 Why is the first argument to a program always the name of that program?

22.5 Show the argument count and argument vector table for the following commands:
(a) who
(b) pc test.p
(c) cc -o exer.o exer.c
(d) grep malloc *.c

22.6 Write a command program to rename a program. Assume that the command format is:
rename old_file_name new_file_name.

22.7 How does shell execute a Unix command?

22.8 Why should a shell interpreter always execute a command in a separate process?

22.9 Briefly explain how shell interprets the file redirection of the following command before execution:
ls > save.ls

22.10 Show the argument count and argument vector table passed to the command programs of the following commands:
(a) who > save.who
(b) mysort < mydata > myresult

22.11 How does a shell interpreter organize command executions for the following commands:
(a) ls | more
(b) prog1 | prog2 | prog3

22.12 Show the arguments count and argument vector table for the following command:
mysort < mydata | mc > myresult

22.13 What is the effect of the following command?
mysort < mydata | mc > myresult &

# 23

# Programming with Threads

**Chapter contents:**

*This chapter introduces the concept of thread and the POSIX interface facility provided in C for multithreaded programming. This chapter also explains the meaning of concurrent programming and its role in developing real-time systems, as well as the synchronization problems involved with concurrent programming and the necessary POSIX-supported mechanisms to avoid such problems*

**Organization:**

*23.1 Introduction*
*23.2 Meaning of Concurrent Programming*
*23.3 Concept of Thread*
*23.4 The pthread.h Header*
*23.5 Thread Creation and Termination*
*23.6 Synchronization Mechanisms for Thread Concurrency*
*23.7 Miscellaneous Functions*
*23.8 Summary*
*Exercises*

## 23.1 Introduction

Since most of our applications show the presence of simultaneity, a new type of program notation is necessary to create processes to carry out these simultaneous actions. In general, a concurrent program is one that enables a computer system to do more than one activity simultaneously. These processes perform the indicated actions of a program to effectively solve a single problem. When a process is created to perform an action of a program called activity, it is sometimes called a subtask. In a concurrent program, we may say either multiple processes or multiple subtasks are in progress at the same time. Hence, a concurrent program is also called a multiprocess or multitask program. The simultaneity characteristic makes program expression more complex, and even a trivial error can make a concurrent program behave in an irreproducible, erratic manner, making‘ program testing impossible.

This chapter briefly introduces the concept of concurrent programming and the POSIX complied thread-based concurrent programming facility is available in C's Application Program Interface.

## 23.2 Meaning of Concurrent Programming

Concurrent programming is a notation in which a program is written to express potential parallelism so, when it is executed in a multiprocessing unit, it runs fast. This abstraction deals with simultaneity in expression and some correctness formalism. Both speed efficiency and correctness formalism are important aspects of this abstraction. In this respect, the concurrent programming notation provides appropriate control mechanisms to protect resources, make processes cooperate and avoid deadlock situation, and produce correct results. The programming notation should include:

- *expression of precedence relations among the processes working for a common goal;*
- *expression of synchronization between concurrent processes;*
- *expression of mutual exclusion during the access of a common resource.*

Hence, the concurrent programming environment should support with a powerful software engineering tool (or concurrent language) to specify the process descriptions of a concurrent program and an operating system, creating the specified processes and managing them during program execution. The following sections show how C and the supporting operating system provide a thread-based concurrent programming environment.

> *Note: Concurrent programming is used to cope with an environment in which many things need attentions at the same time. This characteristic makes concurrent programming more suitable to control real-time environment.*

## 23.3 Concept of Thread

We previously studied the concept of process in Unix's context. In Unix, only a process can create another process, and the processes in a created group are independent and have their own set of resources. That is, a Unix process having its own state vector, data segment, text segment and stack segment can be classified as ***heavyweight process (HWP)***. Because of the heavyweight nature of processes, Unix supports concurrent processing or multitasking using pipeline mode. In pipeline mode, Unix processes are restricted to communicate and synchronize via inherited pipe descriptors (***Fig. 23.1***). Usually, the kernel schedules all heavyweight processes.

A ***lightweight process (LWP)***, on the other hand, shares the data segment along with the other members of its family, but has its own text, stack and state vector. Similar to HWP, the scheduling on LWP is done by the kernel at operating system level, and the overhead due to the presence of context switching is still significant. Hence, the efficiency of multitasking programs with LWPs is still questionable.

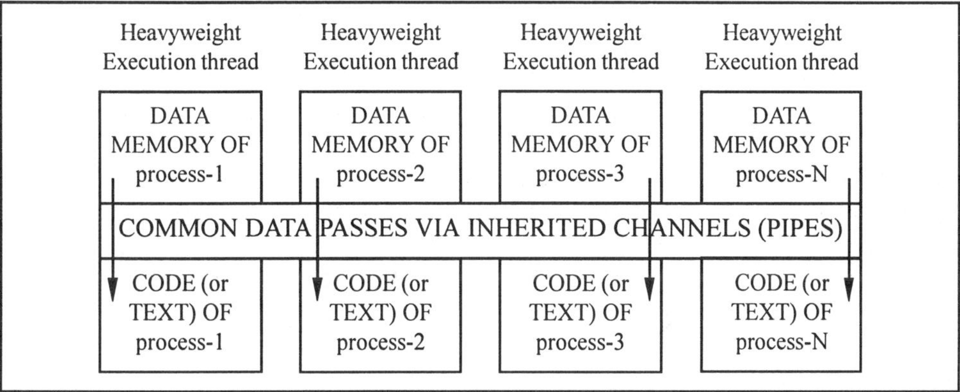


*Fig. 23.1 Concurrent programming model in Unix*

Particularly, the emerging new system architectures based on window technology depend upon programming efficiency for their high performance. Hence, systems are extended to support processes lighter than ***LWP***, called ***threads***. Threads are lighter because they share both data and text segments and can be scheduled at the level of user program by switching only register contents (***Fig. 23.2***). There is no need to save a complete context, implying that multithreading can be more efficient.

A multithread program starts with a single thread and then creates child threads to split the given job. At the end of their execution, they can wait or join before the job completes.

A thread goes through several states in its lifetime. When it is being created, it may go through the ***chrysalis*** state due to resource limitation. Once it comes into existence, it goes to ready state. When it reaches the head of the ready state, it goes into RUN state. During running, a thread may go to ***blocked*** state, while waiting for critical sections, or to ***wait*** state for an event. When a thread completes its execution, it goes to terminated state. ***Fig. 23.3*** shows the state transition diagram of ***POSIX***-threads.

The threads can be scheduled at two levels, i.e., either at system level or user level. Usually, the processes are scheduled by a system level or kernel-scheduler and threads are scheduled at user level by a library function. When the system level scheduler dispatches a process, it calls the user level scheduler to dispatch the threads.

When a thread issues any of the kernel-level system calls, the system-level (or process-level) scheduler is invoked to effect the calling process. For example, when a thread issues a ***sleep*** call, the whole process (including all other threads) goes to sleep. Similarly, when a thread calls issues an ***exit*** system call, all threads of that process will be terminated. Only a parent thread may issue exit call after its child threads have joined with itself. Hence, programmers must be careful in handling system calls within threads.

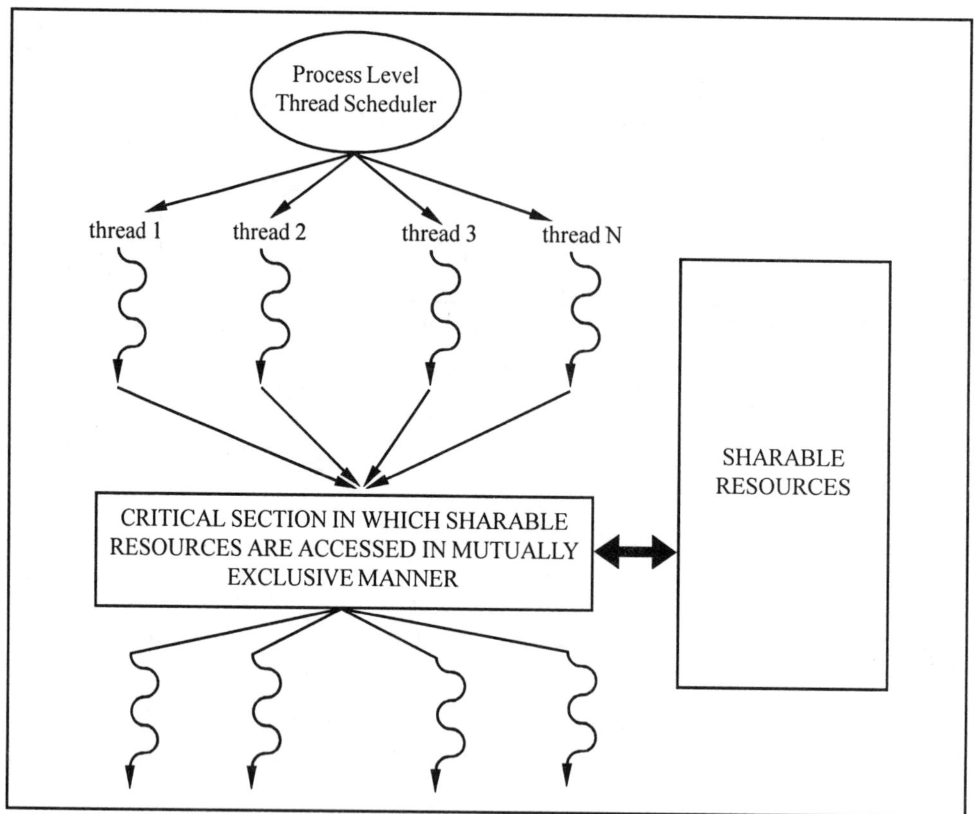


*Fig. 23.2 Multithreaded program execution model*

## 23.4 The pthread.h Header

The ***pthread.h*** header contains several prototype definitions of library functions and type definitions related to multithread programming.

## 23.5 Thread Creation and Termination

Before creating a thread, thread Ids are defined using the ***pthread_t*** type, defined in the ***pthread.h*** header. One should include this header in a multithread program. A list of basic primitives provided to create and terminate threads is shown in ***Table 23.1***.

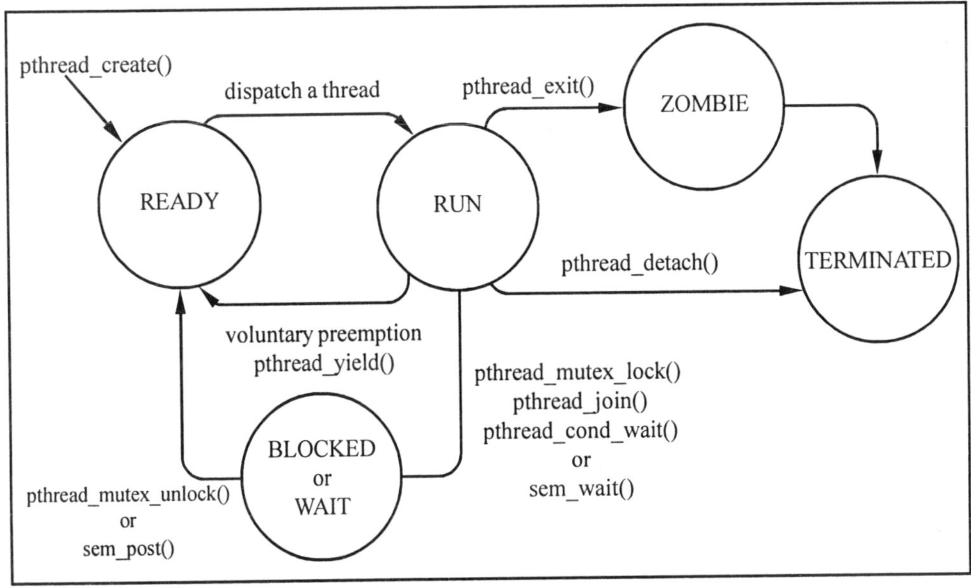


*Fig. 23.3 State Diagram showing the life of a pthread*

## The pthread_create function

The pthread_create function is used to create a new thread to share the task. The new thread starts its execution at the address of the text supplied along with this function call. The prototype definition of this function is:

```
int pthread_create( pthread_t *tid_ptr, const pthread_attr_t *attr_ptr,
                    void *(*func_ptr)(void *), void *argptr);
```

*Table 23.1 List of functions for thread creation and termination*

| Name of the thread-related function | Description |
|---|---|
| *pthread_create* | Creates a child thread. |
| *pthread_self* | A thread gets its own thread identifier. |
| *pthread_exit* | Calling thread exits from execution and merges with its parent thread. |
| *pthread_detach* | A detached thread exits from execution. |
| *pthread_join* | Parent thread waits for a child thread to exit. |

The call requires four arguments: ***tid_ptr*** to receive indirectly the identifier of the new thread; ***attr_ptr*** can be used to set the created thread with some properties; ***func_ptr*** denotes the address of a function that should be executed by the created thread and; ***arg_ptr*** is the argument passed to the function. For example:

```
pthread_t   ch_thr;
message_type  mesg;
    . . .
pthread_create(&ch_thr, pthread_attr_default,  (void *) &ch_func, (void  *) mesg);
```

During this call, a thread is created and allowed to execute the text whose address is ***ch_func*** with the message argument *mesg*. The ***ch_thr*** returns the identifier of the new thread. When the call is successful, 0 is returned; otherwise, -1 is returned.

## The pthread_join function

The ***pthread_join*** function can be used by a parent thread to wait for the termination of a specific child thread or any one of the created threads. The prototype definition of this function is:

```
int pthread_join(pthread_t tid, void  **ret_status_ptr);
```

The call requires two arguments: ***tid*** specifies the identifier of an exiting thread for which the caller is waiting, and ***ret_status_ptr*** to receive indirectly the return status of the exiting thread. When the first argument is supplied, then the calling thread waits for the termination of the specified thread.

For example, the pthread in the following code waits for the child thread ***ch_thr***:

```
thread_t   ch_thr;
message_type  mesg;
status int *thr_status;
    . . .
pthread_create(&ch_thr, pthread_attr_default,  (void *) &ch_func, (void  *) mesg);
pthread_join(ch_thr, (void **)&thr_status);/* waits for the termination of ch_thr  */
    . . .
```

On the other hand, the ***pthread_join*** in the following code shows that the parent waits for any one of the child threads:

```
thread_t   ch_thr1, ch_thr2, ch_thr3;
message_type  mesg;
status int *thr_status;
      . . .
pthread_create(&ch_thr1, pthread_attr_default,  (void *) &ch_func, (void  *) mesg);
pthread_create(&ch_thr2, pthread_attr_default,  (void *) &ch_func, (void  *) mesg);
pthread_create(&ch_thr3, pthread_attr_default,  (void *) &ch_func, (void  *) mesg);
pthread_join(0, (void **)&thr_status); /* waits for the termination of a child thread */
      . . .
```

In the above case, if the parent wants to wait for the termination of all three child threads, it can have three ***pthread_join*** calls or, alternatively, a loop statement with ***pthread_join*** call. The following code shows this:

```
thread_t   ch_thr1, ch_thr2, ch_thr3;
message_type  mesg;
status int *thr_status;
      . . .
pthread_create(&ch_thr1, pthread_attr_default,  (void *) &ch_func, (void  *) mesg);
pthread_create(&ch_thr2, pthread_attr_default,  (void *) &ch_func, (void  *) mesg);
pthread_create(&ch_thr3, pthread_attr_default,  (void *) &ch_func, (void  *) mesg);
pthread_join(0, (void **)&thr_status); /* waits for the child that exits first */
pthread_join(0, (void **) &thr_status); /* waits for the child that exits next */
pthread_join(0, (void **)&thr_status); /* waits for the child that exits last */
      . . .
```

(or)

```
thread_t   ch_thr1, ch_thr2, ch_thr3;
message_type  mesg;
status int *thr_status;
      . . .
pthread_create(&ch_thr1, pthread_attr_default,  (void *) &ch_func, (void  *) mesg);
pthread_create(&ch_thr2, pthread_attr_default,  (void *) &ch_func, (void  *) mesg);
pthread_create(&ch_thr3, pthread_attr_default,  (void *) &ch_func, (void  *) mesg);
while(!pthread_join(0, (void **)&thr_status)); /* waits all children */
      . . .
```

### The pthread_exit function

The ***pthread_exit*** function can be used by a child thread to exit (or merge with its waiting parent thread). At the same time, the child can pass its terminating status to its waiting parent. The prototype definition of this function is:

```
int pthread_exit( void *status_ptr);
```

The call requires one argument: status_ptr to carry indirectly the return status. For example:

```
#include <pthread.h>
pthread_t   ch_thr;
message_type  mesg;
void main(void)
{
  status int  *p_thr_status;
      . . .
pthread_create(&ch_thr, pthread_attr_default,  (void *) &ch_func, (void  *) mesg);
pthread_join(ch_thr,(void **) &p_thr_status); /* waits for the termination of ch_thr  */
      . . .
}

void *ch_func(void *mesg)
{
  status exit_status = 0;
      . . .
          pthread_exit((void *)&extit_status);  /* ch_thr  exits and merges with its parent
*/
}
```

### Example 23.1:

Write a concurrent program to work with two threads. The child thread, after outputting a greeting message, joins back to its parent thread.

```
#include <stdio.h>
#include <pthread.h>

void *ch_func(void *mesg)
{
 char  *str;
      str =(char *) mesg;
         printf("%s " , str);
         printf("\n");
}

void  main (void)
{
 pthread_t  ch_thr;/* declare a variable to get thread ID  */
 char  *mesg = "Hello World \n";
       pthread_create(&ch_thr, pthread_attr_default, (void *) &ch_func, (void  *), NULL);
       printf("I am the parent thread \n");
          printf("I am going to wait for child termination. \n");
       pthread_join(child_thread, &status);
       printf("Child thread joined the parent thread \n");
       exit;
}
```

## The pthread_detach function

The ***pthread_detach*** function can be used to exit by a thread that does not have any thread to wait and receive its exit status. The prototype definition of this function is:

*int pthread_detach( void *status_ptr);*

The argument in this case is simply NULL.

## The pthread_self function

The ***pthread_self*** function can be used by a thread to get its own thread ID. The prototype definition of this function is:

*int pthread_self( void);*

## Example 23.2:

Write a concurrent program to work with two threads. The threads, after outputting their thread Ids, terminate after joining together.

```
#include <stdio.h>
#include <pthread.h>
void *ch_func(void *mesg)
{
 int my_tid; /* declare a variable to get thread ID */
     my_tid = (int)pthread_sef();
     printf("I am the child thread and my tid is: %d \n", my_tid);
     pthread_exit(status);
}
void main (void)
{ status int p_thr_status;
 pthread_t ch_thr;
 int my_tid; /* declare a variable to get thread ID */
 char *mesg = "Hello World \n";
     pthread_create(&ch_thr, pthread_attr_default, (void *) &ch_func, (void *), NULL);
     my_tid = (int)pthread_self();
     printf("I am the parent thread and my tid is: %d \n", my_tid);
       printf("I am going to wait for child termination. \n");
     pthread_join(ch_thr, (void **) &p_thr_status); /* wait for child to exit */
     printf("Child thread joined the parent thread \n");
     exit;
}
```

## Thread Attributes

A thread is characterized by a set of attributes, including stack size, stack address, detach state (i.e., whether a thread can be joined or not), contention scope at program level or system level, and scheduling parameters. The attributes are normally specified during thread creation. When the user does not specify the attributes explicitly, the system will set them to their default values. The system can be told about this by passing the ***pthread_attr_default*** via the attribute argument in the ***pthread_create*** call.

The attributes can be queried and set to new parameter values with the appropriate functions. For example, the stack size can be queried or reset by ***pthread_attr_getstacksize*** and ***pthread_attr_setstacksize***, respectively. Similarly, ***pthread_attr_getstackaddr*** and ***pthread_attr_setstackaddr*** can be used to get the current address and to set to new address, respectively.

## 23.6 Synchronization Mechanisms for Thread Concurrency

### 23.6.1 Problems in Concurrent Programming

Since the simultaneous execution of a job allows multiple threads to deal with a common set of resources, there are many problems that may arise during execution time, such as with a common non-sharable resource, a ***critical resource***. For example, a public telephone is a non-sharable resource, and only one person can use it at any time. When more than one person tries to access such a resource at the same time, a conflict may arise to lead towards a unpleasant situation, such as fighting to get the handset, breaking the cable or damaging the booth. In this situation, the people cannot use the resource meaningfully, nor can the resources can be maintained in a consistent state. The problem due to concurrent access to a critical resource is called the ***critical section*** problem. In order to avoid this situation, a discipline may be imposed such that a non-sharable resource can be used strictly by only one person at a time. This ***mutual exclusion technique*** allows a user to use the accessed resource in an ***atomic*** manner. That is, after one user uses a resource completely, another user is allowed to access it.

Another problem exists when persons doing a joint task refuse to cooperate during their actions. For example, if a person assigned with the payment activity fails to wait for another person to draw money, the result of payment may fail. This is called the ***non-synchronization*** problem.

The third problem may arise due to missing events and is called ***deadlock***. For example, if the person who started banking suddenly met with an accident and dies before completing his or her task, then the other co-persons will be left in the wait state forever.

All the above problems can exist in any concurrent processing system and can be effectively used to characterize a concurrent system. The following measures are, in general, essential to design any concurrent system.

### Safety measures

- *mutual exclusion (i.e., no more than one process is allowed to access the common resources)*
- *synchronization among the concurrent tasks so that a cooperative task would produce correct result*

### Liveliness maintenance

- *deadlock prevention*

### What Is a Critical Section?

- *When a resource is available for simultaneous use by more than one thread, it is classified as a critical resource.*
- *A critical resource must be protected from any conflict by mutual exclusion principle, i.e., allowing only one thread at any time to use a critical resource; the code that manipulates a common and non-sharable resource is called critical section.*
- *When a critical resource is protected with a mutual exclusion mechanism, it is then called protected critical section.*
- *When a thread is in a mutually excluded region, that process is in its critical section.*

## 23.6.2 Mutual Exclusion by Locks

The mutual exclusion (***mutex***) lock is a simple mechanism by which the racing problem during concurrent access to sharable resources can be avoided. A program can declare ***mutex locks*** and logically associate with the declared sharable resources. A thread, before accessing a common resource, should lock the respective ***mutex lock*** and, after using the resource, it should release the lock so that other threads can also access the same resource. When the threads find that a resource is locked, they are all blocked until the resource is available. (See the state diagram in ***Fig.*** *23.3*.) When the resource is released, one of the blocked threads is allowed to lock the resource for its use.

A ***mutex lock*** can be declared using the ***pthread_mutex_t*** type defined in ***pthread.h***. (Don't forget to include this file in thread programs.) For example, the following statement creates two locks, lock1 and lock2.

```
pthread_mutex_t lock1, lock2;
```

Once the locks are created, they can be initialized with appropriate attributes and then used in protecting the resources. After their use, they can be disposed or reused. ***Table 23.2*** shows a list of functions available to maintain the mutex locks.

The locks, lock1 and lock2, created in the previous example, can be initialized with default attributes, as shown below:

```
pthread_mutex_init(&lock1, 0);
pthread_mutex_init(&lock2, 0);
```

*Table 23.2 List of mutex functions*

| *Name of the mutex function* | *Description* |
|---|---|
| *pthread_mutex_init(pthread_mutex_t *p_lock, pthread_mutexattr_t *p_attr);* | *Initializes the lock with the specified attributes.* |
| *pthread_mutex_lock(pthread_mutex_t *p_lock);* | *When the addressed lock is in unlocked state, the calling thread sets the lock to locked state and enters into critical section. When the lock is found already in locked state, the thread is blocked.* |
| *pthread_mutex_unlock(pthread_mutex_t *p_lock);* | *The calling thread sets the lock to unlocked state and goes out of the critical section.* |
| *pthread_mutex_trylock(pthread_mutex_t *p_lock);* | *This function is similar to pthread_mutex_lock, except that it is treated as a spin lock. That is, the calling thread keeps checking the lock until it finds the lock released.* |
| *pthread_mutex_destroy(pthread_mutex_t *p_lock);* | *Dispose the lock.* |

## Example 23.3:

Let us simulate a clock using two threads; one is updating the time and the other is displaying the time. Because both are concurrently executing, they are competing to access the clock variables. We will show how the mutext_lock can be used to mutually exclude the threads in accessing the clock..

```
#include <stdio.h>
#include <pthread.h>
int hours=0, minutes=0, seconds=0;
pthread_mutex_t  timer_lock;

void update(void *)
{ int  status;
   while(1)
      {
      for(k=1; k<100000; k++);   /* assume this loop elapses for a second */
      pthread_mutex_lock(&timer_lock);  /* lock the timer and get into critical section */
      seconds = seconds+1;
```

```
        if(seconds ==60
            minutes = minutes+1;  /* lock the timer critical section */
        if(minutes == 60)
            hours = hours+1;  /* lock the timer critical section */
        if(hours== 24)
            hours = 0;  /* lock the timer critical section */
        pthread_mutex_unlock(&timer_lock);  /* unlock the timer critical section */
     }
}

void display(void *)
{ int  status;
    while(1)
      {
      pthread_mutex_lock(&timer_lock);  /* lock the timer and display time*/
      printf("%d: %d :%d \n", hours, minutes, seconds);
      pthread_mutex_unlock(&timer_lock);  /* unlock the timer critical section */
      }
}

void  main (void)
{
 pthread_t  u_thr, d_thr;       /* variables to hold thread IDs  */
     pthread_mutex_init(&timer_lock,1 ,0); /* initialize timer_lock */
     pthread_create(&u_thr, pthread_attr_default, (void *) &update, (void  *), NULL);
     pthread_create(&d_thr, pthread_attr_default, (void *) &display, (void  *), NULL);
     pthread_join(0, &status); /* wait for the first terminating thread  */
     pthread_join(0, &status); /* wait for the first terminating thread  */
     printf("Children joined the parent thread \n");
     exit;  /* Program exits via parent thread  */
}
```

The main function initializes the timer_lock before creating the threads. Each thread loops infinitely and the parent thread will wait forever because of the nature of the real-time clock program. In each iteration, the update thread elapses one second, then locks the critical section (i.e., timer) before updating the critical variables. It unlocks the critical section so the other thread can use the critical section. Similarly, the display thread locks the critical section before reading the variables. After displaying the critical variables, it unlocks the timer_lock so that the critical section can be used by the update thread.

### 23.6.3 Condition Variable for Thread Synchronization

We saw the use of mutex locks in solving critical section or racing problem while sharing the common resources. In this section, we will study the use of condition variables to achieve coordination among the concurrent threads during a cooperative task. In fact, using condition variable is a more natural means of synchronizing the activities of cooperating threads. POSIX.1c introduced a set of condition-related primitives to support concurrent programming. ***Table 23.3*** lists of those primitives.

*Table 23.3 List of condition-related functions*

| *Name of the condition-related function* | *Description* |
|---|---|
| *int pthread_cond_init(pthread_cond_t *cp, pthread_condattr_t *argp);* | *Initializes the condition variable with a set of attributes. If the attribute argument is null, then the system uses default properties.* |
| *int pthread_cond_wait(pthread_cond_t cp, pthread_mutex_t *mutex_p, struct timespec *tp);* | *Calling thread checks the condition specified. If not favorable condition, it unlocks the mutex lock and waits on the condition.* |
| *int pthread_cond_timedwait(pthread_cond_t cp, pthread_mutex_t *mutex_p);* | *Calling thread checks the condition specified. If not favorable condition, it unlocks the mutex lock and waits on the condition until the specified time elapses.* |
| *int pthread_cond_signal(pthread_cond_t *cp);* | *Calling thread notifies a waiting thread that the specified condition is satisfied and allows the waiting thread to proceed now.* |
| *int pthread_cond_broadcast(pthread_cond_t *cp);* | *Calling thread notifies the waiting threads that the specified condition is satisfied and allows all those threads to proceed now.* |
| *int pthread_cond_destroy(pthread_cond_t *cp);* | *To dispose a condition variable.* |

A program can declare condition variables using the ***pthread_cond_t*** data type. For example, *pthread_cond_t c1, c2;* creates two condition variables called c1 and c2. In general, a condition variable must be initialized before it is used. The ***pthread_cond_init*** function can be used to initialize a condition variable. For example, the above variables are initialized as shown below:

```
pthread_cond_init(&c1,0); /* initialize c1 with default properties*/
pthread_cond_init(&c2,0); /* initialize c2 with default properties */
```

## Example 23.4:

Write a concurrent program to perform a task with two threads. The first thread reads message from keyboard and puts message in a buffer and the second thread reads the message from the buffer and writes to screen. Show the use of condition variable in maintaining the consistency of the output.

The coordination between the treads is achieved with the help of two semaphores. The reader thread waits until the buffer is empty and then fills up the buffer. Similarly, the writer waits until the buffer is full and then it empties the buffer.

```
#include <stdio.h>
#include <string.h>
#include <pthread.h>
char buffer[80];
pthread_cond_t bempty, bfull;

void produce(void *)
{ int status;
  char str[80];
    while(1)
      {
      gets(str);
      strcpy(buffer, str);
      pthread_cond_signal(&bfull);  /* wake up the thread waiting on this semaphore */
      pthread_cond_wait(&bempty, NULL); /* wait until buffer becomes empty */
      }
    pthread_exit(&status);
}

void consume(void *)
{ int status;
  char str[80];
    while(1)
      {
      pthread_cond_wait(&bfull, NULL); /* wait until buffer becomes full */
      strcpy( str, buffer);
      pthread_cond_signal (&bempty) /* wake up the thread waiting on this semaphore */
      puts(str);
      }
    pthread_exit(&status);
}

void main (void)
{
 pthread_t p_thr, c_thr;      /* variables to hold thread IDs */
```

```
    pthread_cond_init(&bempty,1 ,0); /* initialize bempty  */
    pthread_cond_init(&bfull,0); /* initialize bempty  */

    pthread_create(&p_thr, pthread_attr_default, (void *) &produce, (void  *), NULL);
    pthread_create(&c_thr, pthread_attr_default, (void *) &consume, (void  *), NULL);

    pthread_join(0, &status); /* wait for the first terminating thread  */
    pthread_join(0, &status); /* wait for the first terminating thread  */
    printf("Children joined the parent thread \n");

    pthread_cond_destroy(&bempty);
    pthread_cond_destroy(&bfull);

    exit;  /* Program exits via parent thread  */
}
```

The main function creates two condition variables for synchronization. Then it creates two threads, one to execute the producer function and the other to execute the consumer function. It waits for the termination of the threads through two ***pthread_join*** function calls and terminates itself using the exit system call.

Both producer and consumer threads are shown as looping threads. Initially, the consumer is blocked on ***bfull*** condition and the producer, after filling up the buffer, signals the consumer via ***bfull*** condition. It is ready to wait on ***bempty*** condition before it repeats its cycle. The consumer then consumes the buffer and signals the producer. It then waits on ***bfull*** condition again. Both threads synchronize using handshaking protocol with the help of two condition variables.

## 23.6.4 Semaphore for Thread Synchronization

POSIX.1b introduced a set of functions to create semaphore objects and them in thread synchronization. We saw that a ***mutex lock*** is useful for protecting critical and a condition variable is suitable for thread synchronization. The semaphore is an abstract type that can be used as a ***mutex lock*** to protect critical sections, as well as handshake protocol mechanism for thread synchronization. It is implemented as an integer lock. It can be initialized, incremented or decremented by appropriate functions. For each sharable resource, a separate semaphore can be declared as a protecting mechanism. A concurrent thread tests a semaphore to access the corresponding resource. When the value of a semaphore is positive, its value is decremented and the testing thread is allowed to access the resource. When the semaphore value is negative, it shows that the corresponding resource is used by another thread and, thus, the testing thread is blocked. The thread that releases a resource increments the semaphore value. When the semaphore value becomes more than zero, a blocked thread is woken up. ***Table 23.4*** shows the list of semaphore functions available under POSIX standard.

The ***semaphore.h*** header file contains all protype and type definitions required for semaphore usage.

*Table 23.4 List of semaphore functions*

| *Name of the semaphore-related function* | *Description* |
|---|---|
| *int sem_open* | *Opens a semaphore similar to a file with all access control properties.* |
| *int sem_init(sema_t *sp, int ival, int type, void *argp);* | *Initializes the semaphore with an initial value (integer). If the addressed semaphore does not exist, a semaphore is created.* |
| *Sem_getvalue* | *Returns the current value of semaphore.* |
| *Sem_close* | *Closes a semaphore data structure that was open by sem_open.* |
| *Sem_wait* | *Decrements the semaphore by one and if the value is already zero, the calling thread is blocked.* |
| *Sem_trywait(sema_t * sp);* | *The same as sem_wait, except that the calling thread is not blocked.* |
| *Sem_post(sema_t * sp);* | *Increments semaphore value by 1.* |
| *Sem_destroy(sema_t * sp);* | *Removes a semaphore that was created by sem_init.* |
| *Sem_unlink* | *Deletes semaphore.* |

**Example 23.5:**

Write a concurrent program to perform a task with two threads. The first thread reads message from the keyboard and puts it in a buffer, and the second thread takes the message from the buffer and writes to the screen. Show the use of semaphore in maintaining the consistency of the output.

Here the coordination between the treads is achieved with the help of two semaphores. The producer thread waits until the buffer is empty and then fills it up. Similarly, the consumer waits until the buffer is full and then it empties the buffer (see ***Fig. 23.4***).

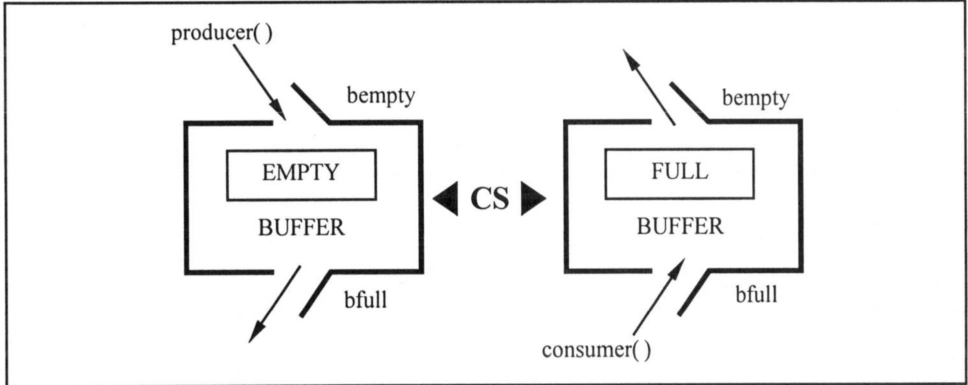


*Fig. 23.4 Use of semaphore in coordination*

```
#include <stdio.h>
#include <string.h>
#include <pthread.h>
#include <semaphore.h>
char  buffer[80];
sema_t  bempty, bfull;
void produce(void *)
{ status  int  status = 0;
  char  str[80];
    while(1)
      {
      gets(str);
      sem_wait(&bempty); /*  wait on this semaphore until buffer becomes empty*/
      strcpy(buffer, str);
      sem_post(&bfull) /* wake up the thread waiting on this semaphore  */
      }
    pthread_exit((void *)&status);
}

void consume(void *)
{ status int  status = 0;
  char  str[80];
    while(1)
      {
      sem_wait(&bfull); /* wait for the buffer to become full*/
      strcpy( str, buffer);
      sem_post(&bempty) /* wake up the thread waiting on this semaphore  */
      puts(str);
      }
```

```
   pthread_exit((void *)&status);
}

void main (void)
{ status int thr_status = 0;
 pthread_t p_thr, c_thr;        /* variables to hold thread IDs */

     sem_init(&bempty,1,USYNC_THREAD,0); /* create bempty semaphore with 1 */
     sem_init(&bfull,0,USYNC_THREAD,0); /* create bfull semaphore with 0 value */

      pthread_create(&p_thr, pthread_attr_default, (void *) &produce, (void *), NULL);
      pthread_create(&c_thr, pthread_attr_default, (void *) &consume, (void *), NULL);

     sem_destroy(&bempty);
     sem_destroy(&bfull);

     pthread_join(0, (void **)&thr_status); /* wait for the first terminating thread */
     printf("First thread joined with the exit status = %d\n", *thr_status);
     pthread_join(0, &thr_status); /* wait for the second terminating thread */
     printf("First thread joined with the exit status = %d\n", *thr_status);
     exit; /* Program exits via parent thread */
}
```

The main function creates two semaphores to emulate like condition variables. The ***bempty*** is initialized to reflect the empty state of the buffer. The producer is allowed, in the beginning, to start filling the buffer. The ***bfull*** is initialized such that the consumer is blocked to start with. Main also creates two threads; one to execute the producer function and the other to execute the consumer function. It waits for the termination of the threads through ***pthread_join*** function calls. Finally, it terminates itself using the exit system call.

Both producer and consumer threads are shown as looping threads. Initially, the consumer is blocked on bfull semaphore, and the producer gets through the bempty semaphore successfully to produce the item and wake up the consumer. Because the buffer is full, the producer is now ready to wait on the bempty, until the consumer wakes it, after emptying the buffer. In this way, both threads synchronize in coordinating their subtasks.

## 23.7 Miscellaneous Functions

### The sched_yield function

This function is used by a thread to voluntarily preempt itself and give up the remaining execution time to other threads of the same priority. The syntax of the function call is:

*int sched_yield(void);*

### The pthread_sigmask function

This function is used to set the signal mask of the calling thread. The syntax of the function call is:

*int pthread_sigmask(int mode, sigset_t *p_signal_set, sigset_t *old_signal_set);*

### The pthread_kill function

This function is used by a thread to send a signal to another thread. The syntax of the function call is:

*int pthread_kill(pthread_t thread_id, int signal_number);*

## 23.8 Summary

This chapter presented the POSIX interface and conventions for writing concurrent programs using threads. The readers can now distinguish threads from normal processes and understand the execution environment required for multithreaded programming.

## Exercises

23.1 What is concurrent programming?

23.2 What are the concurrency problems? Explain using examples.

23.3 Distinguish lightweight process (LWP) from heavyweight (HWP) process.

23.4 How do you classify a Unix process? Support your answer with an example.

23.5 What is the difference between an LWP and a thread?

23.6 Why is multitasking with threads more efficient than with heavyweight processes?

23.7 What is the purpose of getting the thread ID during pthread_create?

23.8 What is the difference between exit and pthread_exit?

23.9 What is the role of pthread_join? How does it achieve synchronization between threads?

23.10 Will the child thread print its message in the following code? Why or why not?

```
#include <stdio.h>
#include <pthread.h>
void main (void)
{
 pthread_t ch_thr;/* declare a variable to get thread ID */
   pthread_create(&ch_thr, pthread_attr_default, (void *) &ch_func, (void *), NULL);
  exit;
}

    void *ch_func(void *mesg)
    {
    char *str;
          str =(char *) mesg;
          printf("%s " , str);
          printf("\n");
    }
```

23.11 What is the difference between the mutex_lock mechanism and condition variable?

23.12 What is the difference between condition variable and semaphore variable?

23.13 What is the meaning of a semaphore with an initial value of three?

23.14 Match the following:

| | |
|---|---|
| (a) sem_trywait | 1. increment semaphore value |
| (b) pthread_join | 2. semaphore test with blocking |
| (c) exit | 3. writing application programs made easy |
| (d) sem_wait | 4. the whole program termination |
| (e) pthread_exit | 5. semaphore test with non-blocking |
| (f) sem_post | 6. parent thread waits for the termination of child thread |

# Appendix A

## Glossary

### A.1 Keywords in C

**Keywords of data types:**

| | | | | | |
|---|---|---|---|---|---|
| char | double | enum | float | int | long |
| short | signed | struct | union | unsigned | void |

**Keywords of storage classes:**

| | | | | | |
|---|---|---|---|---|---|
| auto | const | extern | register | static | volatile |

**Keywords of statements:**

| | | | | |
|---|---|---|---|---|
| break | case | continue | default | do |
| else | for | goto | if | return |
| switch | while | | | |

**Miscellaneous Keywords:**

| | |
|---|---|
| sizeof | typedef |

**C-defined Symbols**

| | | | |
|---|---|---|---|
| __OK | _ONE_ | __TWO__ | __DONE__ |
| | | | |
| EOF | EDOM | ERANGE | errno |
| FILE | NULL | | |
| clock_t | ptrdiff_t | | |
| size_t | time_t | | |
| wchar_t | | | |
| stdin | stdout | stderr | |

***Note: sizeof*** operation returns ***unsigned*** type which is type_defined as ***size_t***.

## A.2 Types of Operators in C

### Binary Operators

<table>
<tr><th>Operator Type</th><th>Operator Notation</th><th>Meaning of Operator</th></tr>
<tr><td>Arithmetic Operators</td><td>+<br>-<br>*<br>/<br>%</td><td>Addition<br>Subtraction<br>Multiplication<br>Division<br>Modulo Division</td></tr>
<tr><td>Comparison Operators<br>Equality and Relational<br>Operators</td><td>==<br>!=<br>><br>>=<br><<br><=</td><td>Equal<br>Not Equal<br>Greater<br>Greator or Equal<br>Lesser<br>Lesser or Equal</td></tr>
<tr><td>Logical Comparison<br>Operators</td><td>||<br>&&</td><td>Logical OR<br>Logical AND</td></tr>
<tr><td>Bitwise Operators</td><td>|<br>&<br>^<br>~<br>>><br><<</td><td>Bitwise Logical OR<br>Bitwise Logical AND<br>Bitwise Logical Exclusive OR<br>Bitwise Logical Negation<br>Bitwise Shift Right<br>Bitwise Shift Left</td></tr>
<tr><td>Assignment Operators</td><td>=</td><td>Simple Assignment</td></tr>
<tr><td>Composite Assignment</td><td>+=<br>-=<br>*=<br>/=<br>%=<br>|=<br>&=<br>^=<br>~=<br>>>=<br><<=</td><td></td></tr>
<tr><td>Miscellaneous Operator</td><td>,</td><td>Comma Operator</td></tr>
</table>

## Unary Operators

| Operator Type | Operator Notation | Meaning of Operator |
|---|---|---|
| Assignment Operators | ++<br>--<br>- | Increment<br>Decrement<br>Negation |
| Bitwise Logical Operator | ~ | Bitwise Complement |
| Miscellaneous Operators | *<br><br><br>&<br>sizeof<br>(object_type) | Indirect reference operator used address operands; it is interpreted "**contents of**"<br>Address Reference<br>Size of Operator<br>Cast Operator |

# Appendix B

## Character Sets

### B.1 ASCII Character Set

| ASCII Value | | | Character | ASCII Value | | | Character | ASCII Value | | | Character |
|---|---|---|---|---|---|---|---|---|---|---|---|
| hex | oct | dec | | hex | oct | dec | | hex | oct | dec | |
| 00 | 00 | 00 | NUL | 12 | 22 | 18 | (control-R) DC2 | 24 | 44 | 36 | $ |
| 01 | 01 | 01 | (control-A) SOH | 13 | 23 | 19 | (control-S) DC3 | 25 | 45 | 37 | % |
| 02 | 02 | 02 | (control-B) STX | 14 | 24 | 20 | (control-T) DC4 | 26 | 46 | 38 | & |
| 03 | 03 | 03 | (control-C) ETX | 15 | 25 | 21 | (control-U) NAK | 27 | 47 | 39 | ‘ (single quote) |
| 04 | 04 | 04 | (control-D) EOT | 16 | 26 | 22 | (control-V) SYN | 28 | 50 | 40 | ( |
| 05 | 05 | 05 | (control-E) ENQ | 17 | 27 | 23 | (control-W) ETB | 29 | 51 | 41 | ) |
| 06 | 06 | 06 | (control-F) ACK | 18 | 30 | 24 | (control-X) CAN | 2A | 52 | 42 | * |
| 07 | 07 | 07 | (control-G) BEL | 19 | 31 | 25 | (control-Y) EM | 2B | 53 | 43 | + |
| 08 | 10 | 08 | (control-H) BS | 1A | 32 | 26 | (control-Z) SUB | 2C | 54 | 44 | , (comma) |
| 09 | 11 | 09 | (control-I) HT | 1B | 33 | 27 | ESC | 2D | 55 | 45 | - (hyphen) |
| 0A | 12 | 10 | (control-J) LF | 1C | 34 | 28 | FS | 2E | 56 | 46 | . (period) |
| 0B | 13 | 11 | (control-K) VT | 1D | 35 | 29 | GS | 2F | 57 | 47 | / |
| 0C | 14 | 12 | (control-L) FF | 1E | 36 | 30 | RS | 30 | 60 | 48 | 0 |
| 0D | 15 | 13 | (control-M) CR | 1F | 37 | 31 | US | 31 | 61 | 49 | 1 |
| 0E | 16 | 14 | (control-N) SO | 20 | 40 | 32 | space | 32 | 62 | 50 | 2 |
| 0F | 17 | 15 | (control-O) SI | 21 | 41 | 33 | ! | 33 | 63 | 51 | 3 |
| 10 | 20 | 16 | (control-P) DLE | 22 | 42 | 34 | “ | 34 | 64 | 52 | 4 |
| 11 | 21 | 17 | (control-Q) DC1 | 23 | 43 | 35 | # | 35 | 65 | 53 | 5 |

**B.1 ASCII Character Set (Cont.)**

| ASCII Value | | | Character | ASCII Value | | | Character | ASCII Value | | | Character |
|---|---|---|---|---|---|---|---|---|---|---|---|
| hex | oct | dec | | hex | oct | dec | | hex | oct | dec | |
| 36 | 66 | 54 | 6 | F | 117 | 79 | O | 68 | 150 | 104 | h |
| 37 | 67 | 55 | 7 | 50 | 120 | 80 | P | 69 | 151 | 105 | i |
| 38 | 70 | 56 | 8 | 51 | 121 | 81 | Q | 6A | 152 | 106 | j |
| 39 | 71 | 57 | 9 | 52 | 122 | 82 | R | 6B | 153 | 107 | k |
| 3A | 72 | 58 | : | 53 | 123 | 83 | S | 6C | 154 | 108 | l |
| 3B | 73 | 59 | ; | 54 | 124 | 84 | T | 6D | 155 | 109 | m |
| 3C | 74 | 60 | < | 55 | 125 | 85 | U | 6E | 156 | 110 | n |
| 3D | 75 | 61 | = | 56 | 126 | 86 | V | 6F | 157 | 111 | o |
| 3E | 76 | 62 | > | 57 | 127 | 87 | W | 70 | 160 | 112 | p |
| 3F | 77 | 63 | ? | 58 | 130 | 88 | X | 71 | 161 | 113 | q |
| 40 | 100 | 64 | @ | 59 | 131 | 89 | Y | 72 | 162 | 114 | r |
| 41 | 101 | 65 | A | 5A | 132 | 90 | Z | 73 | 163 | 115 | s |
| 42 | 102 | 66 | B | 5B | 133 | 91 | [ | 74 | 164 | 116 | t |
| 43 | 103 | 67 | C | 5C | 134 | 92 | \ | 75 | 165 | 117 | u |
| 44 | 104 | 68 | D | 5D | 135 | 93 | ] | 76 | 166 | 118 | v |
| 45 | 105 | 69 | E | 5E | 136 | 94 | ^ | 77 | 167 | 119 | w |
| 46 | 106 | 70 | F | 5F | 137 | 95 | _ (underscore) | 78 | 170 | 120 | x |
| 47 | 107 | 71 | G | 60 | 140 | 96 | ‘ (accent) | 79 | 171 | 121 | y |
| 48 | 110 | 72 | H | 61 | 141 | 97 | a | 7A | 172 | 122 | z |
| 49 | 111 | 73 | I | 62 | 142 | 98 | b | 7B | 173 | 123 | { |
| 4A | 112 | 74 | J | 63 | 143 | 99 | c | 7C | 174 | 124 | \| |
| 4B | 113 | 75 | K | 64 | 144 | 100 | d | 7D | 175 | 125 | } |
| 4C | 114 | 76 | L | 65 | 145 | 101 | e | 7E | 176 | 126 | ~ (tilde) |
| 4D | 115 | 77 | M | 66 | 146 | 102 | f | 7F | 177 | 127 | DEL |
| 4E | 116 | 78 | N | 67 | 147 | 103 | g | | | | |

## B.2 EBCDIC Character Set

| EBCDIC Value | | | Character | EBCDIC Value | | | Character | EBCDIC Value | | | Character |
|---|---|---|---|---|---|---|---|---|---|---|---|
| hex | oct | dec | | hex | oct | dec | | hex | oct | dec | |
| 00 | 00 | 00 | NUL | 17 | 27 | 23 | POC | 2E | 56 | 46 | ACK |
| 01 | 01 | 01 | SOH | 18 | 30 | 24 | CAN | 2F | 57 | 47 | BEL |
| 02 | 02 | 02 | STX | 19 | 31 | 25 | EM | 30 | 60 | 48 | |
| 03 | 03 | 03 | ETX | 1A | 32 | 26 | UBS | 31 | 61 | 49 | |
| 04 | 04 | 04 | SEL | 1B | 33 | 27 | CU1 | 32 | 62 | 50 | SYN |
| 05 | 05 | 05 | HT | 1C | 34 | 28 | IFS | 33 | 63 | 51 | IR |
| 06 | 06 | 06 | RNL | 1D | 35 | 29 | IGS | 34 | 64 | 52 | PP |
| 07 | 07 | 07 | DEL | 1E | 36 | 30 | IRS | 35 | 65 | 53 | TRN |
| 08 | 10 | 08 | GE | 1F | 37 | 31 | IUS/ITB | 36 | 66 | 54 | NBS |
| 09 | 11 | 09 | SPS | 20 | 40 | 32 | DS | 37 | 67 | 55 | EOT |
| 0A | 12 | 10 | RPT | 21 | 41 | 33 | SOS | 38 | 70 | 56 | SBS |
| 0B | 13 | 11 | VT | 22 | 42 | 34 | FS | 39 | 71 | 57 | IT |
| 0C | 14 | 12 | FF | 23 | 43 | 35 | WUS | 3A | 72 | 58 | RFF |
| 0D | 15 | 13 | CR | 24 | 44 | 36 | BYP/INP | 3B | 73 | 59 | CU3 |
| 0E | 16 | 14 | SO | 25 | 45 | 37 | LF | 3C | 74 | 60 | DC4 |
| 0F | 17 | 15 | SI | 26 | 46 | 38 | ETB | 3D | 75 | 61 | NAK |
| 10 | 20 | 16 | DLE | 27 | 47 | 39 | ESC | 3E | 76 | 62 | |
| 11 | 21 | 17 | DC1 | 28 | 50 | 40 | SA | 3F | 77 | 63 | SUB |
| 12 | 22 | 18 | DC2 | 29 | 51 | 41 | SFE | 40 | 100 | 64 | SP |
| 13 | 23 | 19 | DC3 | 2A | 52 | 42 | SM/SW | 41 | 101 | 65 | RSP |
| 14 | 24 | 20 | RES/ENP | 2B | 53 | 43 | CSP | 42 | 102 | 66 | |
| 15 | 25 | 21 | NL | 2C | 54 | 44 | MFA | 43 | 103 | 67 | |
| 16 | 26 | 22 | BS | 2D | 55 | 45 | ENQ | 44 | 104 | 68 | |

**B.2 EBCDIC Character Set (Cont.)**

| EBCDIC Value | | | Character | EBCDIC Value | | | Character | EBCDIC Value | | | Character |
|---|---|---|---|---|---|---|---|---|---|---|---|
| hex | oct | dec | | hex | oct | dec | | hex | oct | dec | |
| 45 | 105 | 69 | | 5C | 134 | 92 | * (asterisk) | 73 | 163 | 115 | |
| 46 | 106 | 70 | | 5D | 135 | 93 | ) | 74 | 164 | 116 | |
| 47 | 107 | 71 | | 5E | 136 | 94 | ; | 75 | 165 | 117 | |
| 48 | 110 | 72 | | 5F | 137 | 95 | | 76 | 166 | 118 | |
| 49 | 111 | 73 | | 60 | 140 | 96 | - (hyphen) | 77 | 167 | 119 | |
| 4A | 112 | 74 | c | 61 | 141 | 97 | / | 78 | 170 | 120 | |
| 4B | 113 | 75 | . (period) | 62 | 142 | 98 | | 79 | 171 | 121 | ‘ (accent) |
| 4C | 114 | 76 | < | 63 | 143 | 99 | | 7A | 172 | 122 | : (colon) |
| 4D | 115 | 77 | ( | 64 | 144 | 100 | | 7B | 173 | 123 | # |
| 4E | 116 | 78 | + | 65 | 145 | 101 | | 7C | 174 | 124 | @ |
| 4F | 117 | 79 | \| | 66 | 146 | 102 | | 7D | 175 | 125 | ‘ (single quote) |
| 50 | 120 | 80 | & | 67 | 147 | 103 | | 7E | 176 | 126 | = |
| 51 | 121 | 81 | | 68 | 150 | 104 | | 7F | 177 | 127 | “ |
| 52 | 122 | 82 | | 69 | 151 | 105 | | 80 | 200 | 128 | |
| 53 | 123 | 83 | | 6A | 152 | 106 | \| | 81 | 201 | 129 | a |
| 54 | 124 | 84 | | 6B | 153 | 107 | , (comma) | 82 | 202 | 130 | b |
| 55 | 125 | 85 | | 6C | 154 | 108 | % | 83 | 203 | 131 | c |
| 56 | 126 | 86 | | 6D | 155 | 109 | _ (underscore) | 84 | 204 | 132 | d |
| 57 | 127 | 87 | | 6E | 156 | 110 | > | 85 | 205 | 133 | e |
| 58 | 130 | 88 | | 6F | 157 | 111 | ? | 86 | 206 | 134 | f |
| 59 | 131 | 89 | | 70 | 160 | 112 | | 87 | 207 | 135 | g |
| 5A | 132 | 90 | ! | 71 | 161 | 113 | | 88 | 210 | 136 | h |
| 5B | 133 | 91 | $ | 72 | 162 | 114 | | 89 | 211 | 137 | i |

**B.2 EBCDIC Character Set (Cont.)**

| EBCDIC Value | | | Character | EBCDIC Value | | | Character | EBCDIC Value | | | Character |
|---|---|---|---|---|---|---|---|---|---|---|---|
| hex | oct | dec | | hex | oct | dec | | hex | oct | dec | |
| 8A | 212 | 138 | | A2 | 242 | 162 | s | BA | 272 | 186 | |
| 8B | 213 | 139 | | A3 | 243 | 163 | t | BB | 273 | 187 | |
| 8C | 214 | 140 | | A4 | 244 | 164 | u | BC | 274 | 188 | |
| 8D | 215 | 141 | | A5 | 245 | 165 | v | BD | 275 | 189 | |
| 8E | 216 | 142 | | A6 | 246 | 166 | w | BE | 276 | 190 | |
| 8F | 217 | 143 | | A7 | 247 | 167 | x | BF | 277 | 191 | |
| 90 | 220 | 144 | | A8 | 250 | 168 | y | C0 | 300 | 192 | { |
| 91 | 221 | 145 | j | A9 | 251 | 169 | z | C1 | 301 | 193 | A |
| 92 | 222 | 146 | k | AA | 252 | 170 | | C2 | 302 | 194 | B |
| 93 | 223 | 147 | l | AB | 253 | 171 | | C3 | 303 | 195 | C |
| 94 | 224 | 148 | m | AC | 254 | 172 | | C4 | 304 | 196 | D |
| 95 | 225 | 149 | n | AD | 255 | 173 | | C5 | 305 | 197 | E |
| 96 | 226 | 150 | o | AE | 256 | 174 | | C6 | 306 | 198 | F |
| 97 | 227 | 151 | p | AF | 256 | 175 | | C7 | 307 | 199 | G |
| 98 | 230 | 152 | q | B0 | 260 | 176 | | C8 | 310 | 200 | H |
| 99 | 231 | 153 | r | B1 | 261 | 177 | | C9 | 311 | 201 | I |
| 9A | 232 | 154 | | B2 | 262 | 178 | | CA | 312 | 202 | SHY |
| 9B | 233 | 155 | | B3 | 263 | 179 | | CB | 313 | 203 | |
| 9C | 234 | 156 | | B4 | 264 | 180 | | CC | 314 | 204 | ⑀ |
| 9D | 235 | 157 | | B5 | 265 | 181 | | CD | 315 | 205 | |
| 9E | 236 | 158 | | B6 | 266 | 182 | | CE | 316 | 206 | ⑁ |
| 9F | 237 | 159 | | B7 | 267 | 183 | | CF | 317 | 207 | |
| A0 | 240 | 160 | | B8 | 270 | 184 | | D0 | 320 | 208 | } |
| A1 | 241 | 161 | ~ (tilde) | B9 | 271 | 185 | | D1 | 321 | 209 | J |

**B.2 EBCDIC Character Set (Cont.)**

| EBCDIC Value | | | Character | EBCDIC Value | | | Character | EBCDIC Value | | | Character |
|---|---|---|---|---|---|---|---|---|---|---|---|
| hex | oct | dec | | hex | oct | dec | | hex | oct | dec | |
| D2 | 322 | 210 | K | E2 | 342 | 226 | S | F2 | 362 | 242 | 2 |
| D3 | 323 | 211 | L | E3 | 343 | 227 | T | F3 | 363 | 243 | 3 |
| D4 | 324 | 212 | M | E4 | 344 | 228 | U | F4 | 364 | 244 | 4 |
| D5 | 325 | 213 | N | E5 | 345 | 229 | V | F5 | 365 | 245 | 5 |
| D6 | 326 | 214 | O | E6 | 346 | 230 | W | F6 | 366 | 246 | 6 |
| D7 | 327 | 215 | P | E7 | 347 | 231 | X | F7 | 367 | 247 | 7 |
| D8 | 330 | 216 | Q | E8 | 350 | 232 | Y | F8 | 360 | 248 | 8 |
| D9 | 331 | 217 | R | E9 | 351 | 233 | Z | F9 | 371 | 249 | 9 |
| DA | 332 | 218 | | EA | 352 | 234 | | FA | 372 | 250 | \| |
| DB | 333 | 219 | | EB | 353 | 235 | | FB | 373 | 251 | |
| DC | 334 | 220 | | EC | 354 | 236 | ┤ | FC | 374 | 252 | |
| DD | 335 | 221 | | ED | 355 | 237 | | FD | 375 | 253 | |
| DE | 336 | 222 | | EE | 356 | 238 | | FE | 376 | 254 | |
| DF | 337 | 223 | | EF | 357 | 239 | | FF | 377 | 255 | EO |
| E0 | 340 | 224 | \ | F0 | 360 | 240 | 0 | | | | |
| E1 | 341 | 225 | NSP | F1 | 361 | 241 | 1 | | | | |

| | |
|---|---|
| BEL | Bell |
| BS | Back Space |
| BYP/INP | Bypass/Inhibit Presentation |
| CAN | Cancel |
| CR | Carriage Return |
| CSP | Control Significance Prefix |
| CU1 | Customer U se 1 |
| CU3 | Customer Use 3 |
| DC1 | Device Control 1 |
| DC2 | Device Control 2 |
| DC3 | Device Control 3 |
| DC4 | Device Control 4 |
| DEL | Delete |
| DLE | Data Line Escape |
| DS | Digit Select |
| EM | End of Medium |
| ENQ | Enquiry |
| EO | Eight Ones |
| EOT | End of Transmission |
| ESC | Escape |
| ETB | End of Transmission Block |
| ETX | End of Text |
| FF | Form Feed |
| GE | Graphic Escape |
| HT | Horizontal Tab |
| IFS | Interchange File Separator |
| IGS | Interchange Group Separator |
| IR | Index Return |
| IRS | Interchange Record Separator |
| IT | Indent Tab |
| ITB | Interchange Transmission Block |
| IUS | Interchange Unit Separator |
| LF | Line Feed |
| MFA | Modify Field Attribute |
| NAK | Negative Acknowledge |
| NBS | Numerical Back Space |
| NL | New Line |
| NSP | Numeric Space |
| NUL | Null |
| POC | Program-Operator Communication |
| PP | Presentation Position |
| RES/ENP | Restore/Enable Presentation |

| | |
|---|---|
| RNL | Required New Line |
| RPT | Repeat |
| RSP | Required Space |
| SA | Set Attribute |
| SBS | Substitute |
| SEL | Select |
| SHY | Syllable Hyphen |
| SI | Shift In |
| SO | Shift Out |
| SOH | Start of Heading |
| SP | Space |
| STX | Start of Text |
| SUB | Substitute |
| SYN | Synchronous Idle |
| TRN | Transparent |
| UBS | Unit Back Space |
| VT | Vertical Tab |
| WUS | Word Underscore |

# Appendix C

## ANSI-C Standard Libraries and Their Header Files

### C.1 Standard Headers

| | | | | |
|---|---|---|---|---|
| <assert.h> | <ctype.h> | <errno.h> | <float.h> | <limits.h> |
| <locale.h> | <math.h> | <setjmp.h> | <string.h> | <stdarg.h> |
| <stddef.h> | <stdio.h> | <stdlib.h> | <string.h> | <time.h> |

### C.2 Definitions in the Standard Header Files

#### C.2.1 assert.h

This file contains diagnostic-related definitions.

```
NDEBUG
void assert(int expression);
```

#### C.2.2 ctype.h (Character handling macro definitions)

```
int isalnum(int ch);
int isalpha(int ch);
int iscntrl(int ch);
int isdigit(int ch);
int isgraph(int ch);
int islower(int, ch);
int isprint(int ch);
int ispunct(int, ch);
int isspace(int ch);
int isupper(int ch);
int isxdigit(int ch);
int tolower(int ch);
int toupper(int ch);
```

### C.2.3 **errno.h** (Error-related definitions)

EDOM
ERANGE
errno

### C.2.4 **stddef.h** (Some common definitions)

NULL
offsetof
ptrdiff_t
size_t
wchar_t

### C.2.5 **locale.h**

LC_ALL
LC_COLLATE
LC_CTYPE
LC_MONETARY
LC_NUMERIC
C_TIME
NULL
struct lconv
char *setlocale(int category, const cahr *locale);
struct lconv *localeconv(void);

### C.2.6 **math.h** (Definitions of maths functions and related constants)

**Constants**
HUGE_VAL

**Functions**

***(a) logarithmic type***

double log(double x); Logarithmic value of x with base e
double log10(double x); Logarithmic value of x with base 10

***(b) trigonometric type***

double sin(double x);
double cos(double x);
double tan(double x);
double asin(double x);
double acos(double x);
double atan(double x);
double atan2(double y, double x);

(c) ***hyperbolic type***

```
double sinh(double x);
double cosh(double x);
double tanh(double x);
```

(d) ***exponential and square root type***

```
double exp(double x);
double frexp(double value, int *exp);
double ldexp(double value, int exp);
double pow(double x, double y);       /* x to the power y */
double sqrt(double x);
```

(e) ***miscellaneous type***

```
double ceil(double x);
double fabe(double x);
double floor(double x);
double modf(double value, double *iptr);
double fmod(double x, double y);
```

### C.2.7 **setjmp.h** (Definitions related to nonlocal jumps)

```
jmp_buf
int setjmp(jmp_buf env);
void longjmp(jmp_buf env, int val);
```

### C.2.8 **signal.h** (Signal-related definitions)

### C.2.9 **stdarg.h** (Definitions related to variable arguments)

```
va_list
void va_start(va_list ap, paramn);
type va_arg(va_list ap, type);
void va_end(va_list ap);
```

### C.2.10 **stddef.h** (Includes types and macros)

Types:

| | |
|---|---|
| ptrdiff_t | Signed integral type resulting out of pointer subtraction |
| size_t | Unsigned integral type resulting from sizeof operator |
| wchar_t | An integral type whose range of values represent all members of the largest character set specified in the supported locales. |

Macros:

NULL

offsetof(type, member_designator) Expanded into a constant expression of size_t representing an offset in bytes to the structure member (member_designator) from the beginning of its structure.

### C.2.11 **stdio.h** (Supports ANSI-C stream I/O)

(a) Type definitions

| Type name | Description |
|---|---|
| FILE | It is an object (of structure) type to contain all the essential information required to maintain an open stream. The information of this object includes file position indicator, buffer pointer, error indicator, end of file indicator, etc. |
| fpos_t | It is an anonymous (a kind of unsigned) type used to record or remember previous position in an open stream. |
| size_t | It is an anonymous (a kind of unsigned) type applicable to indicate the size of memory allocated to a C-object. |

(b) Macro definitions

| | | |
|---|---|---|
| BUFSIZ | | |
| EOF | | |
| FOPEN_MAX | | |
| FILENAME_MAX | | |
| _IOFBF | | |
| _IOLBF | | |
| _IONBF | | |
| L_tmpnam | This parameter specifies the maximum length of a temporary file name created by tmpnam function. | tmpnam |
| NULL | | |
| SEEK_CUR | | |
| SEEK_END | | |
| SEEK_SET | | |
| TMP_MAX | This parameter specifies the maximum number of temporary file names that a user program can generate. | tmpnam |
| stderr | | |
| stdin | | |
| stdout | | |

(c) prototype definitions

```
int remove(const char *filename);
int rename(const char *oldname, const char *newname);
FILE *tmpfile(void);
char *tmpnam(char *s);
int fclose(FILE *file_pointer);
int fflush(FILE *file_pointer);
FILE *fopen(const char *filename, const char *mode);
FILE *freopen(const char *filename, const char *mode, FILE *file_pointer);
void setbuf((FILE *file_pointer, char *buf);
void setvbuf((FILE *file_pointer, char *buf, int mode, size_t size);
int fprintf(FILE *file_pointer, const char *format, . . .);
int fscanf(FILE *file_pointer, const char *format, . . .);
int printf(const char *format, . . .);
int scanf(const char *format, . . .);
int sprintf(char *s, const char *format, . . .);
int sscanf(const char *s, const char *format, . . .);
int vfprintf(FILE *file_pointer, const char *format, vs_list arg);
int vprintf(const char *format, vs_list arg);
int vsprintf(char *s, const char *format, vs_list arg);
```

```
int fgetc(FILE *file_pointer);
char *fgets(char *filename, FILE *file_pointer);
int fputc(int ch, FILE *file_pointer);
int fputs(const char *filename, FILE *file_pointer);
int getc(FILE *file_pointer);
int getchar(void);
char *gets(char *s);
int putc(int ch, FILE *file_pointer);
int putchar(int ch);
int puts(const char *s);
int ungetc(int ch, FILE *file_pointer);
size_t fread(void *ptr, size_t size, size_t nmemb, FILE *file_pointer);
size_t fwrite(const void *ptr, size_t size, size_t nmemb, FILE *file_pointer);
int fgetpos(FILE *file_pointer, fpos_t *pos);
int fseek(FILE *file_pointer, long int offset, int whence);
int fsetpos(FILE *file_pointer, const fpos_t *pos);
long int ftell(FILE *file_pointer);
void rewind(FILE *file_pointer);
void clearerr(FILE *file_pointer);
int feof(FILE *file_pointer);
int ferror(FILE *file_pointer);
void perror(const char *s);
```

### C.2.12 **stdlib** (General utility library functions)

```
double atof(const char *real_str);
long int atol(const char *numerical_str);
double strtod(const char *real_str, char **endptr);
long int strtol(const char *numerical_str, char **endptr, int base);
long int strtoul(const char *numerical_str, char **endptr, int base);
int rand(void);
void srand(unsigned int seed);
void *calloc(size_t new_mem, size_t mem_size);
void free(void *mem_ptr);
void *malloc(size_t mem_size);
void *realloc(void *mem_ptr, size_t size);
void abort(void);
int atexit(void (*exit_time_function) (void) );
void exit(int exit_status);
char *getenv(const char *name);
int system(const char *a_command_string);
```

## C.2.13 string.h

*(a)* ***string-related data types***
NULL
size_t

*(b)* ***string-related functions***
char *strcpy(char *ds, const char *ss)
char *strncpy(char *ds, const char *ss, size_t n)
char *strcat(char *ds, const char *ss)
char *strncat(char *ds, const char *ss, size_t n)
int strcmp(const char *s1, const char *s2)
int strncmp(const char *s1, const char *s2, size_t n)
int strcoll(const char *s1, const char *s2)
char *strxfrm(char *ds, const char *ss, size_t n)
char *strchr(const char *s, char ch)
size_t strspn(const char *s1, const char *s2)
size_t strcspn(const char *s1, const char *s2)
char *strcbrk(const char *s1, const char *s2)
char *strrchr(char *s, char ch)
char *strstr(char *ts, const char *ss)
char *strtok(char *s, const char *dset)
size_t strlen(const char *s)
char *strerror(int errnum)
void *memcpy(void *m1, const void *m2, size_t n)
void *memmove(void *m1, const void *m2, size_t n)
int memcmp(void *m1, const void *m2, size_t n)
void *memchr(const void *m, int ch, size_t n)
void *memset(void *m, int ch, size_t n)

## C.2.14 time.h (Date- and time-related constants, types and functions)

*(a)* ***time-related constants and data types***
CLOCKS_PER_SEC
NULL
clock_t
time_t
size_t
struct tm

*(b)* ***time-related functions***

```
clock_t clock(void);
double difftime(time_t time1, time_t time0);
time_t mktime(struct tm *timeptr);
time_t time(time_t *timer);
char *asctime (const struct tm *timeptr);
char *ctime (const time_t *timer);
struct tm *gmtime(const time_t *timer);
struct tm *localtime(const time_t *timer);
size_t strftime(char *s, size_t maxsize, const char *format, const struct tm *timeptr);
```

# Appendix D

## Implementation Limits in ANSI-C: Header Files

### D.1 limits.h (Limits of integral types)

| | | | |
|---|---|---|---|
| MB_LEN_MAX | 1 | (Maximum number of bytes in a multibyte character for any supported locale) | |
| CHAR_BIT | 8 | | |
| CHAR_MIN | 0 | or | SCHAR_MIN |
| CHAR_MAX | 255 | or | SCHAR_MAX |
| SCHAR_MIN | -128 | | |
| SCHAR_MAX | +127 | | |
| UCHAR_MAX | 255 | | |
| INT_MIN | -32767 | | |
| INT_MAX | +32768 | | |
| UINT_MAX | 65535 | | |
| LONG_MIN | -2147483647 | | |
| LONG_MAX | +2147483647 | | |
| ULONG_MAX | 4294967295 | | |
| SHRT_MIN | -32767 | | |
| SHRT_MAX | +32768 | | |
| USHRT_MAX | 65535 | | |

## D.2 float.h (Limits of real values)

*Number of decimal digits*

| | |
|---|---|
| FLOAT_DIG | 2 |
| DBL_DIG | 10 |
| LDBL_DIG | 10 |

*Radix of exponent representation*

| | |
|---|---|
| FLT_RADIX | 2 |

*Maximum normalized positive floating-point number*

| | | |
|---|---|---|
| FLT_MAX | must yield at least | 1exp+37 |
| DBL_MAX | must yield at least | 1exp+37 |
| LDBL_MAX | must yield at least | 1exp+37 |

*Difference between 1 and the least value greater than 1*

| | | |
|---|---|---|
| FLT_EPISILON | must be no greater than | 1exp-5 |
| DBL_EPISILON | must be no greater than | 1exp-9 |
| LDBL_EPISILON | must be no greater than | 1exp-9 |

*Minimum normalized positive floating-point number*

| | | |
|---|---|---|
| FLT_MIN | must be no greater than | 1exp-37 |
| DBL_MIN | must be no greater than | 1exp-37 |
| LDBL_MIN | must be no greater than | 1exp-37 |

# Appendix E

## POSIX Unix Interface: Standard Calls and Related Headers

### E.1 POSIX.1 Standard Headers

| | | | | |
|---|---|---|---|---|
| <dirent.h> | <fcntl.h> | <grp.h> | <pwd.h> | <setjmp.h> |
| <signal.h> | <stdio.h.h> | <sys/stat.h> | <sys/times.h> | <sys/utsname.h> |
| <sys/wait.h> | <termios.h> | <time.h> | <utime.h> | |

### E.2 Definitions in the Standard Headers

#### E.2.1 dirent.h (Diagnostic-related definitions)

This header defines a structure and a defined type that can be used for the management of directories.

(a) The structure dirent has an element of char type called d_name.
(b) The type DIR definition represents a directory stream which is an ordered sequence of directory entries.

#### E.2.2 fcntl.h (Character handling macro definitions)

This header contains the definition of the symbolic values of the command argument of the fcntl() call. It also defines various flags that are used in fcntl and open system calls. The following is the list of such definitions.

(a) Symbolic value of command argument:

| | |
|---|---|
| F_DUPFD | Duplicate file descriptor. |
| F_GETFD | Get file descriptor flags. |
| F_GETLK | Get record locking information. |
| F_SETFD | Set file descriptor flags. |
| F_GETFL | Get file status flags. |
| F_SETFL | Set file status flags. |
| F_SETLK | Set record locking information. |
| F_SETLKW | Set record locking information; wait if blocked. |

(b) File descriptor flag:

FD_CLOEXEC Close the file descriptor upon the execution of an exec system call.

(c) Lock-type values for record locking:

| | |
|---|---|
| F_RDLCK | Shared lock for reading. |
| F_UNLCK | Unlock. |
| F_WRLCK | Exclusive lock for writing. |

(d) oflag values for open system call:

| | |
|---|---|
| O_CREAT | Create a file if it does not exist. |
| O_EXCL | Exclusive use of flag. |
| O_NOCTTY | Don't assign a controlling terminal. |
| O_TRUNC | Truncate flag. |

(e) File status flags used in open and fcntl system calls:

O_APPEND
O_NONBLOCK

(f) File access modes used in open and fcntl system calls:

| | |
|---|---|
| O_RDONLY | Open for reading only. |
| O_RDWR | Open for both reading and writing. |
| O_WRONLY | Open for writing only. |

(g) Mask for use with file access modes:

O_ACCMODE Mask for file access modes.

### E.2.3 grp.h

This header contains the definition of a structure called ***group*** to access the group database. A prototype of this structure is shown below:

```
#include <types.h>
struct group
{
 char   *gr_name;  /* The name of the group    */
 gid_t  gr_gid;    /* The numerical identifier */
 char   **gr_mem;  /* A NULL-terminated vector of pointers
                to the individual member names          */
}
```

Functions that use this header: ***getgrgid***, ***getgrnam***

## E.2.4 pwd.h

This header contains the definition of a structure called ***passwd*** to access the user database. A prototype of this structure is shown below:

```
#include <types.h>
struct  passwd
{
  char   *pw_name;  /*   user's login name   */
  uid_t   pw_uid;    /*  user identifier   */
  gid_t   pw_gid;    /*  group identifier */
  char   *pw_dir;    /*  initial working directory */
  char   *pw_shell;  /*  initial shell             */
}
```

Functions that use this header: ***getpwuid***, ***getpwnam***

## E.2.5 setjmp.h (Definitions related to nonlocal jumps)

This header contains a structure called ***sigjmp_buf*** to mark the execution environment which can then be used for branching.
Functions that use this header: ***sigsetjmp***, ***siglongjmp***

## E.2.6 signal.h

The header includes the definitions for symbolic values of valid signal types, data types and default signal handlers.

*(a) symbolic constants*

*(i) symbolic values of signal types*

| Symbolic Constant | Default Action | Description |
|---|---|---|
| SIGABRT | Abnormal termination of the process | Abnormal termination signal caused by the abort function. (Included in the C-standard.) |
| SIGALRM | Abnormal termination of the process | Generated by alarm clock. |
| SIGFPE | Abnormal termination of the process | Generated by the kernel at the occurrence of a floating point overflow. (Included in the C-standard.) |
| SIGHUP | Abnormal termination of the process | Generated by hanging up phone. |
| SIGILL | Abnormal termination of the process | Generated by the kernel when CPU executes an illegal in struction. (Included in the C-standard.) |
| SIGINT | Abnormal termination of the process | Generated by hitting DEL or Break key to get the attention of the process. (Included in the C-standard.) |
| SIGKILL | Abnormal termination of the process | Generated by a user process to terminate a process without any delay. This signal may not be ignored or caught. |
| SIGPIPE | Abnormal termination of the process | Generated by a broken pipe which has no process to read. |
| SIGQUIT | Abnormal termination of the process | Generated by FS or Control-\key. |
| SIGSEGV | Abnormal termination of the process | Generated by memory protection violation due to illegal access of a location. (Included in the C-standard.) |
| SIGTERM | Abnormal termination of the process | Generated to terminate a process gracefully. (Included in the C-standard.) |
| SIGUSR1 | Abnormal termination of the process | Reserved as application-defined signal 1. |
| SIGUSR2 | Abnormal termination of the process | Reserved as application-defined signal 2. |

Job Control Signals defined by POSIX

| Symbolic Constant | Default Action | Description |
|---|---|---|
| SIGCHLD | Abnormal termination of the process. | Generated when a child process is terminated or stopped. |
| SIGCONT | Continue the process if it is currently stopped, else ignore the signal. | Signal is sent to make the stopped process continue. |
| SIGSTOP | Stop the process. | Stop signal not from terminal. This signal may not be ignored or caught. |
| SIGTSTP | Stop the process. | Stop signal from terminal. |
| SIGTTIN | Stop the process. | Generated when a member of a background process group attempts to read from control terminal. |
| SIGTTOU | Stop the process. | Generated when a member of a background process group attempts to write to control terminal. |

(ii) Symbolic values used in the ***sigprocmask()*** call for the "***how***" argument:

| | |
|---|---|
| SIG_BLOCK | The resulting set is union of the current set pointed to by oldset and the set pointed to by newset; |
| SIG_UNBLOCK | The resulting set is the intersection of the current set pointed to by oldset and the complement of the set pointed to by newset. |
| SIG_SETMASK | The resulting set is the signal set pointed to by the newset. |

***(b) data types***

***(i) structure argument to sighandler function:***

```
struct sigaction
    {
     void      (*sa_handler)();
     sigset_t  sa_mask;
     int       sa_flags;
    };
```

***(ii) signal set type:***

sigset_t

### E.2.7 sys/stat.h

This header contains the definitions that are useful to find out the characteristics of a file. These definitions are as follows:

***(a) the stat structure***

This definition is used by stat and fstat system calls. This definition requires the inclusion of sys/types.h containing the type definitions that are used here.

```
#include <sys/types>
struct stat
{
 mode_t st_mode;      /* file mode */
 ino_t  st_ino;       /* file serial or inode number */
 dev_t  st_dev;       /* ID of device containing this file */
 nlink_t st_st_nlink; /* Number of links for this file */
 uid_t  st_uid;       /* User ID of the owner of this file */
 gid_t  st_gid;       /* Group ID of the owner of this file */
 off_t  st_size;      /* Size of this file in bytes; this parameter
                         is specified only for normal files */
 time_t st_atime;     /* Time of last access of data, e.g. read() */
 time_t st_mtime;     /* Time of last data modification, e.g. write() */
 time_t st_ctime;     /* Time of last status change, e.g. chmod() */
};
```

***(b) test macros for file types***

| | |
|---|---|
| S_ISDIR(m) | Test macro for directory file. |
| S_ISCHR(m) | Test macro for character special file. |
| S_ISBLK(m) | Test macro for block special file. |
| S_ISREG(m) | Test macro for regular file. |
| S_ISFIFO(m) | Test macro for named pipe or fifo file. |

*(c) definitions of symbolic values for file mode bits*

| | |
|---|---|
| S_IRUSR | Read permission bit for owner class. |
| S_IWUSR | Write permission bit for owner class. |
| S_IXUSR | Search or Execute permission bit for owner class. |
| S_IRWXU | Read, Write, Search (for a directory) or execute (for other files) permissions mask for the owner class of a file. |
| | |
| S_IRGRP | Read permission bit for group class. |
| S_IWGRP | Write permission bit for group class. |
| S_IXGRP | Search or Execute permission bit for group class. |
| S_IRWXG | Read, Write, Search (for a directory) or execute (for other files) permissions mask for the group class of a file. |
| | |
| S_IROTH | Read permission bit for others. |
| S_IWOTH | Write permission bit for others. |
| S_IXOTH | Search or Execute permission bit for others. |
| S_IRWXO | Read, Write, Search (for a directory) or execute (for other files) permissions mask for all other users. |
| S_ISUID | Set user ID on execution of the file. |
| S_ISGID | Set group ID on execution of the file. |

### E.2.8 stdarg.h

***Definitions related to variable arguments***:
va_list

### E.2.9 stdio.h (Supports ANSI-C stream I/O)

This header defines also some definitions used in the Unix interface.
***L_cuserid***, a constant definition used by ***cuserid()*** call for its argument length.

### E.2.10 termios.h

This header contains the definition of a structure called termios and the symbolic values of the flags that are members of the structure describing the characteristics of a control terminal.

### E.2.11 sys/types.h

This header defines ***primitive system data types*** that can be used in arithmetic expressions. The names of these definitions end with "_t".

| Type name | Description |
|---|---|
| dev_t | device number type |
| gid_t | group ID type |
| ino_t | inode ID type |
| mode_t | file type and file permission type |
| nlink_t | link count type |
| off_t | size of file type |
| pid_t | process ID type |
| time_t | time unit (in seconds) of arithmetic type<br>(also defined in time.h of standard C-library) |
| uid_t | user ID type |

### E.2.12 sys/wait.h

This header contains symbolic values used for the ***options*** argument in a waitpid() call and a set of macros to interpret the ***stat_val*** (value of the status location) argument of ***wait()*** and ***waitpid()*** calls.

(a) Symbolic values:

WNOHANG The waitpid function shall not suspend the execution of calling process if status of one of the processes specified by pid is not immediately available.

WUNTRACED
Interpreter The staus of any of the processes specified by pid that did not return status after stopping shall be reported to the requesting process.

(b) Macro definitions:

| | |
|---|---|
| WIFEXITED(stat_val) | Evaluates whether a child process terminated normally. Returns a non-zero value if it is true. |
| WEXITSTATUS(stat_val) | If the value of WIFEXITED() macro call is true, this macro evaluates using the last 8-bits of status whether a child process has terminated using an explicit exit() (or _exit()) call or returned from main. Returns a non-zero value if it is true. |
| WIFSIGNALED(stat_val) | Evaluates whether a child process has terminated due to the receipt of a signal that was not caught. Returns a non-zero value if it is true. |
| WTERMSIG(stat_val) | If the value of WIFSIGNALED is true, this macro evaluates to the signal type that caused the child process' termination. Returns a non-zero value if it is true. |
| WIFSTOPPED(stat_val) | Evaluates whether a child process has stooped. Returns a non-zero value if it is true. |
| WSTOPSIG(stat_val) | If the value of WIFSTOPPED() is true, this macro evaluates to the signal type that caused the process to stop. Returns a non-zero value if it is true. |

### E.2.13 time.h

This header defines date and time related constants, types and functions.

***(a) time-related constants and data types***

CLOCKS_PER_SEC
NULL
clock_t
time_t
size_t
struct tm

***(b) time-related functions***

clock_t clock(void);
double difftime(time_t time1, time_t time0);
time_t mktime(struct tm *timeptr);
time_t time(time_t *timer);
char *asctime (const struct tm *timeptr);
char *ctime (const time_t *timer);
struct tm *gmtime(const time_t *timer);
struct tm *localtime(const time_t *timer);
size_t strftime(char *s, size_t maxsize, const char *format, const struct tm *timeptr);

### E.2.14 sys/times.h

The definitions include:

(a) ***clock_t*** is defined as an arithmetic type.

(b) struct ***tms***

```
{
 clock_t tms_utime   /* User CPU time  */
 clock_t tms_stime   /* System CPU time  */
 clock_t tms_cutime  /* User CPU time of terminated child processes */
 clock_t tms_cstime  /* System CPU time of terminated child processes */
}
```

### E.2.15 unistd.h

The following definitions can be found in unistd.h:

***(a) symbolic constants for the access function***

| Constant | Description |
|---|---|
| R_OK | Test for read permission |
| W_OK | Test for write permission |
| X_OK | Test for execute or search permission |
| F_OK | Test for existence of file |

***(b) symbolic constants for the lseek function***

| Constant | Description |
|---|---|
| SEEK_SET | set file offset to offset. |
| SEEK_CUR | Set file offset to current plus offset |
| SEEK_END | Set file offset to EOF plus offset |

***(c) compile-time symbolic constants***

_POSIX_JOB_CONTROL
_POSIX_SAVED_IDS
_POSIX_VERSION

*(d) configuration information limitation used for pathconf and fpathconf*

| Name value defined in unistd.h | Description |
|---|---|
| _PC_LINK_MAX | To enquire about the maximum number of links that can be made to an inode. |
| _PC_MAX_CANNON | To enquire about the maximum length of a formatted input line. |
| _PC_MAX_INPUT | To enquire about the maximum length of an input line. |
| _PC_NAME_MAX | To enquire about the maximum length of a file name. |
| _PC_PATH_MAX | To enquire about the maximum length of a relative path name starting with this directory. |
| _PC_PIPE_BUF | To enquire the size of the pipe buffer |
| _PC_CHOWN_RESTRICTED | To enquire whether the chown system call is restricted on this file. If the path name or fd refers to a directory, the test is applied to all files in that directory. |
| _PC_NO_TRUNC | To create a file with a name longer than the maximum in the directory without any error |
| _PC_VDISABLE | Disabling special character processing for terminals |

### E.2.16 utime.h

This header defines a structure called utimbuf which is used by utime() call.

```
<sys/types.h>
struct utimbuf
        {
          time_t   actime       /*  Access time
          time_t   modtime     /*  Modification time*/
        }
```

# Appendix F

## Bibliography


**Bach, M. J.,** The Design of the Unix Operating System, Prentice-Hall Publication,1986.

**Banahan, M.,** The C Book: Featuring the draft ANSI C Standard, Addison-Wesley Publication,1988.

**Ben-Ari J,** Principles of Concurrent Programming, Prentice-Hall International, Inc. Englewood Cliffs, NJ. (USA), 1982.

**Berry, J. T.,** Advanced C Programming, Prentice-Hall Publication, New York, 1986.

**Bourne, S. R.,** "Unix Time-Sharing System: The Unix Shell," Bell Sys. Tech. Journal, 57(6), 1978.

**Bourne, S. R.,** The Unix System V Environment, Addison-Wesley Publication,1987.

**Chan T.,** UNIX System Programming Using C++, Prentice-Hall PTR Publication, New Jersey, 1997.

**Crowley C.,** Operating Systems (Chapter 6), Irwin Publication, US, 1997.

**Eisenberg, M. A. And McGuire, M. R.,** Further Comments on Dijkstra's Concurrent Programming Control Problem, CACM, Vol. 15, No. 11, Nov 1972, page 999.

**Fielder, D.,** "The Unix Tutorial, Part 1: An Introduction to Features and Facilities," Byte, August, 1983, pp. 186-210.

**Hansen, Brinch P.**, The Programming Language Concurrent Pascal, IEEE Trans. On Software Engineering, SE-1, 2, June 1975, pp. 199 - 207.

**Haviland, K. and Ben Salama,** Unix System Programming, Addison-Wesley Publication,1987.

**Jaeschke, R.,** Portability and the C Language, Hayden Books, Indiana, 1989.

**Johnson, S. C. and Kernighan, B. W.,** "The C Language and Models for Systems Programming," Byte, August, 1983, pp. 46-60.

**Joyce, J.,** "A C Language Primer: Constructs and Conventions," Byte, August, 1983, pp. 64-78.

**Kernighan, B. W. and Rob Pike,** The UNIX Programming Environment, Prentice-Hall Publication,1984.

**Kernighan, B. W. and Ritchie,** The C Programming Language, Prentice-Hall Publication, Engelwood Cliffs, New Jersey, 1978.

**Lebey, G.,** Porting Unix Software, O'Reilly & Associates, Inc, CA., August, 1995.

**Lewine, Donald A.,** POSIX Programmer's Guide, O'Reilly & Associates, Inc, CA., August, 1991.

**Mark William Company,** ANSI C: A Lexical Guide, Prentice-Hall Publication, Engelwood Cliffs, New Jersey, 1988.

**Miller, L. and Alex Quilici,** C Programming Language: An Applied Perspective, John Wiley & Sons, NewYork, 1987.

**Miller, P.J.,** The Standard C Library, Prentice-Hall, NJ., 1992.

**Plaugher, B.,** Programming with Pthreads, O'Reilly $ Associates, Inc, CA, 1996.

**Schildt, H.,** The Annotated ANSI C Standard / American National Standard for Programming Languages-C / ANSI/ISO 9899-1990, Published by Osborne McGraw-Hill, Berkeley, Ca., USA, 1990, ISBN 0-07-881952-0.

**Sobell, M. G.,** Unix System V: A practical Guide, The Benjamin/ Cummings Publishing Company, Inc., 1995.**Schildt, H., C** : The Complete Reference, Published by Osborne McGraw-Hill, Berkeley, Ca., USA, Second Edition, ISBN 0-07-881538-X.

**Stevens W. R.,** Advanced Programming in the Unix Environment, Addison-Wesley Publishing Company, Reading, 1992.

**Thomas, R., Lawrence R. Rogers and Jean L. Yates,** Advanced Programmer's Guide to UNIX System V, Osborne McGraw-Hill Publication,1986.

**Wagner, T. and Don Towsley**, Getting Started With POSIX Threads, Department of Computer

**Walmer, L. R. and Mary R. Thompson,** A Programmer's Guide to the MACH User Environment, Department of Computer Science, Carnegie Mellon University, Pittsburgh, PA 15213,1989.

**X/Open Company, Ltd.,** X/Open Portability Guide, Prentice Hall, New Jersey, August, 1988.

# Index

\n, 40
/, 523
&, 100
_exit(), 482
_NFILE, 386
_POSSIX_PIPE_BUF, 504
_SC_CLK_TCK, 510
#, 173, 175
##, 175
#error, 172
#pragma, 173
.c, 27
.o, 27

**A**
a.out, 27, 28
abort(), 427
Abstract data structure, 118, 349, 350
access(), 543
Access mode, 518, 533
Access path, 518
alarm(), 497
AND (operator), 13
ANSI-C, 1, 2, 15, 16, 73, 98, 107, 130, 181, 183, 188, 190, 191, 194, 198, 246, 332, 338, 442, 453
ANSI-C File System, 377
ANSI-file I/O, 515
ANSI-stream, 376, 524
API (Application Program Interface), 16, 442, 443
API functions, 444
Arguments
  to functions, 109
 Call by value
  to functions, 109
Arrays
  Automatic, 198
  Byte, 198
  Dynamic, 354
  Integer, 193
  Real, 193
asctime(), 433, 435
ASCII, 39, 228, 242, 247, 250, 423
ASCII Character set, 617
assert, 51, 353
assert.h, *(See* Header files)
Associativity, 81
atexit(), 427
atof(), 319, 320
atoi(), 319, 320
atol(), 319, 320

**B**
Basic 1/0, (*See* I/O)
BCD, 250
Binary 1/0, (*See* I/O)
Binary tree, 358, 371
Block 1/0, (*See* I/O)
Block structure, 9
BSS, 126, 127
Buffer structure, 381

**C**
C-memory, 75
 -processor, 75
 -program model, 19
 -Virtual machine, 16, 18, 53, 74, 314, 379, 398, 447
Call by reference, 109
Call by value, 109
calloc(), 350, 351
cast (*See* Operator)
cc command, 27, 28
Character
 Array, 236
 Buffer, 236
 Control D, 251
 EOF, 245, 246, 251, 253
 manipulation, 250, 256
 Non-white space, 249
 NULL, 64, 262
 signed, 246
 stream I/O, 50
 Testing, 250
 Value, 228
 Variable, 229
 White space, 36, 249
chdir(), 529
chown(), 545
clearerr(), 411
CLI, 572
CLK_TCK, 431
clock(), 431
clock_t, 431, 509
closedir(), 526
cmask, 520, 521
Command programs, 572
Command process, 574
Commenting in C, 36
Compiler, 26
Compiling, 26
Composite memory, 331
Concurrent programming, 592
Condition variable, 605
const, 265, 333
Constants
 Address, 260
 ASCII, 250
 decimal, 12, 183
 hexadecimal, 12, 183
 integer, 181
 octal, 12, 183
 real, 190
Constant variables, 70
creat(), 520, 530, 531
ctime(), 433
ctype.h (*See* Header files)

**D**
Data objects
 declaring, 43
 naming, 43
Data types
 Char, 67, 184
 Const, 70
 Double, 67
 Enum, 69, 188
 Float, 67
 Int, 67, 184
 Long, 70, 184
 Short, 70, 184
 Struct, 68, 328
 Union, 69
 Volatile, 70
Dangling pointer (*See* Pointer)
Delimiter, 135, 145
 Double quote, 232
 NULL address, 262
difftime(), 434
DIR type, 524

Direct I/O, 376, 516
Directory
  Root, 523
  Unix, 523
dirent, 523, 524
dirent.h (*See* Header files)
do statement, 34, 148
double, 67
double indirection, 273
dup(), 539, 583
dup2(), 540
Dynamic
  Data structure, 276, 353
  Storage allocation, 350
  Storage, 132

**E**

EBCDIC, 39, 228, 242, 247
EBCDIC Character set, 619
Effective_group_id, 568
Effective_user_id, 566, 567
EIO, 448
End of file (EOF) (*See* Character)
environp, 576
EOF, 35, 379, 382, 399, 400, 401, 403
ERANGE, 321
errno, 317, 318, 420, 448, 525
errno.h (*See* Header files)
Escape sequence, 160
Exception handling, 428, 429
execl(), 561
execle(), 563
execlp(),562
execv(), 563
execve(), 560
execvp(), 564, 574
exit(), 388, 428
EXIT_FAILURE, 483
EXIT_SUCCESS, 482, 483

Expressions
  arithmetic, 80
  assignment, 82, 87, 270
  cast, 91
  comma, 90
  constant, 270
  equality, and relational, 88
  logical comparison, 89
  mixed, 92
  multiple assignment, 87
  simple, 80
  sizeof, 91
  ternary, 89
  void , 93
Expression status flag, 88
Extern (*See* Storage class)

**F**

FALSE, 336
fclose(), 386
fcntl(), 540
feof, 379, 409
ferror(), 410
fflush(), 388
fgetc(), 377, 380, 381
fgetpos(), 392
fgets(), 377, 403
File
  ANSI-C, 378, 379
  binary, 377
  device, 516, 551
  directory, 516, 520
  FIFO, 516, 520, 548
  keyboard, 576
  regular, 516, 520
  screen, 576
  text, 377
File creation mask, 520
File-cursor, 388, 518

File descriptor, 518, 519
File descriptor table, 518, 519
File operation
  Execute, 520
  Read, 520
  Write, 520
File pointer, 383, 386, 389
FILE Stream Buffer type, 382,383,385, 386, 389
fopen(), 383
for statement, 33, 147
fork(), 472
fpathconf(), 553
fprintf(), 321, 377, 416
fputc (), 377, 380, 381
fputs(), 377, 403, 404
fread(), 340, 341, 377, 405
free(), 350, 351
Free list, 350
Free-standing environment, 16
fscanf(), 321, 377, 412
fseek (), 388, 389, 393
fsetpos(), 392
fstat(), 546
ftell(), 391
Function
  arguments, 286
  definition, 98, 103
  dynamic variable, 102
  header, 3
  interface, 108
  main, 4
  pointer (assigning), 281
  pointer (declaration), 279
  pointer (dereferencing), 282
  prototype definition, 106
  read-only variable, 101
  recursion, 285
  variable, 99
  void, 108
fwrite(), 340, 341, 377, 405

**G**

getc(), 395
getchar(), 245, 398
getcwd(), 529
getegid(), 567
geteuid(), 567
getgid(), 567
getlogin(), 465
getpid(), 475
getppid(), 475
gets(), 297, 404
getuid(), 567
getty, 470
gid_t, 545
gmtime(), 437

**H**

Header files, 35
  assert.h, 53
  ctype.h, 11, 250, 251, 256
  dirent.h, 524
  errno.h, 448
  fcntl.h, 532, 533
  float.h, 190
  limits.h, 183, 503, 504
  math.h, 168, 224
  pthread.h, 594, 602
  semaphore.h, 607
  setjmp.h, 501
  stddef.h, 262, 351
  stdio.h, 11, 245, 262, 382, 386, 420
  stdlib.h, 11, 319, 351
  signal.h, 424, 425, 486, 487
  stat.h, 530

string.h, 11,107, 292
time.h, 430, 431
times.h, 509
types.h, 472, 509
unistd.h, 453
wait.h, 477, 481
Heap, 350, 352
Hosted environment, 16
Host operating system, 7

**I**

IBM370, 260
Identifier, 63
if-else (*See* Statements)
if statement (*See* Statements)
Incremental compilation, 31
index(), 311
Index register, 14
Indirect reference, 271
Information hiding, 8
Inode, 517
Int (*See* Variable types)
Integer
Arithmetic, 202
Bitwise logical, 202
Increment/decrement, 202
Input/output, 209
Shift, 205
I/O
ANSI-C, 376, 377
ANSI-I/O, 516
Binary, 378, 405
Basic, 376, 380, 516
Buffered, 380
Character, 378, 395
Conventions, 48
Direct, 376, 516
Formatted, 378, 412
library, 11
Line, 404
Stream, 376
String, 378
Text, 411
Unbuffered, 380
Unix-, 376
Unix-like, 376, 515
isalnum(), 252
isalpha(), 252
iscntrl(), 252
isdigit(), 252
isgraph(), 252
islower(), 252
ISO, 1
isprint(), 252
ispunct(), 252
isspace(), 252
isupper(), 252
isxdigit(), 252

**J**

jmp_buf, 428

**K**

(K&R)C, 2, 15, 103, 105, 338, 376
Kernighan, 2
kill(), 492

**L**

Line I/O, 11, 403
Line macro, 8
link(), 541
Linked data structure, 354, 357
Linked list, 357
circular, 358, 370
doubly, 358, 369
singly, 358, 359
Linking, 26
lm-flag, 224

localtime(), 433, 436
Logical operators, 13
longjmp(), 428, 429, 501
lseek(), 535, 552
lvalue, 83, 107, 112, 243, 244
lvalue expression, 64

**M**
M6809, 259
M68000, 259
Macro call, 162
Macro commands, 156
 define, 157
 endif, 170
 if, 170
 ifdef, 170
 ifndef, 170
 include, 166
 line, 171
 undef, 164
main(), 34
malloc(), 350, 355, 364
memchr(), 295, 317
memcmp(), 295, 316
memcpy(), 294, 315
memmove(), 295, 316
memset(), 295, 314
Memory map, 100
mkdir(), 520, 524
mkfifo(), 520, 548, 549
mknod(), 551
mktime(), 434
mode_t, 520, 524, 549
Mutual exclusion, 602

**N**
Nested structure, 327
Node, 358
Non-empty set, 89
Non-white space (*See* Character)
NULL
 address or pointer, 261, 262, 360, 361
 block, 3
 character, 230, 232, 403
 constant, 271
 definition, 35
 directive, 173
 node, 358
 queue, 364
 statement, 145, 151
 string, 232, 236
 value, 126, 350, 361, 525

**O**
off_t, 536
One-way list, 358
open(), 519, 520, 532
opendir(), 525
Open_file table, 518
Operating system interface, 450
Operation
 decrement, 273
 increment, 273
Operator precedence, 73, 81
Operators
 assignment, 13, 79
 binary, 79
 bit-wise, 13, 79
 cast, 94, 223 (*See also* Expression)
 comma, 79, 94
 composite, 79
 equality, 13, 79
 indirect, 269
 logical, 13, 79
 relational, 79
 shift, 13, 79
 sizeof, 94, 190, 221, 222, 406
 ternary, 79

unary, 78

**P**
pathconf(), 553
pause(), 498
PDP-11, 259
Permission mode, 520
perror(), 419
pid_t, 472
pipe(), 503
Pipeline command, 583
Pointer
  arithmetic, 273, 274, 275
  arrays, 267
  dangling, 262
  function, 280-283
  NULL, 386
  variable, 260
  void, 266, 267, 276
Portability, 15, 181
POSIX, 16, 376, 442, 452, 484, 510, 516, 517, 523, 553, 607
pow(), 140, 141
Pragma directive, 173
Predefined macros
  __DATE__, 174
  __FILE__, 174
  __LINE__, 174
  __STDC__, 174
  __TIME__, 174
Preprocessor operators, 175
printf(), 37, 245, 297, 416
Process
  Concept, 458
  Creation, 466
  Group, 467
  Heavyweight, 592
  Lightweight, 592
  Login, 470
  Shell, 470
  Model, 458
  Structure, 461
Program
  single function, 3
  multiple function, 3
pthread.h (*See* Header files)
pthread_cond_broadcast (), 605
pthread_cond_destroy (), 605
pthread_cond_init (), 605
pthread_cond_signal (), 605
pthread_cond_t, 605
pthread_cond_timedwait (), 605
pthread_cond_wait(), 605
pthread_create(), 595
pthread_detach(), 595
pthread_exit(), 595
pthread_join(), 596
pthread_kill(), 596
pthread_mutex_destroy(), 603
pthread_mutex_init(), 602, 603
pthread_mutex_lock(), 603
pthread_mutex_t, 602
pthread_mutex_trylock(), 603
pthread_mutex_unlock(), 603
pthread_self(), 595
pthread_sigmask(), 611
pthread_t, 596
putc(), 395, 396
putchar(), 245, 398
puts(), 49, 297, 404

**Q**
Qualifier
  const, 65, 70, 112
  long, 70
  short, 70

signed, 70
unsigned, 70
volatile, 65, 70, 71

**R**

raise(), 427
read(), 519, 534
readdir(), 525
real_group_id, 568
real_user_id, 566, 567
realloc(), 350, 351
Real
Printing, 219
Scanning, 221
Scientific operation, 223
Recursion, 368
Referential declaration, 122
Registers, 14, 118
Register storage (*See* Storage class)
remove(), 395
rename(), 393
Ritchie, 2
rmdir(), 529
Return statement (*See* Statements)
rewind(), 393
rewinddir(), 526
rvalue, 83, 109, 244
rvalue accumulator, 429
rvalue expression, 64

**S**

scanf(), 245, 247, 297, 415
sched_yield(), 610
Scope of variable, 118
Spatial, 118
Temporal, 118
SEEK_CUR, 536
SEEK_END, 536
SEEK_SET, 536
sem_close(), 608
sem_destroy(), 608
sem_getvalue(), 608
sem_open(), 608
sem_post(), 608
sem_unlink(), 608
sem_wait(), 608
semicompiled file, 27
setgid(), 568
set_group_id, 566
setjmp, 428, 429, 501
setjmp.h (*See* Header files)
setpgid(), 483
setuid(), 568
set_user_id, 566
Shell, 462, 464 , 470
Shell interpreter, 572
Shell command
Background, 579
Command lines, 577
Redirection, 579, 582
SIGABRT, 424, 427, 484
sigaction(), 489
SIGALRM, 484, 498, 503
SIGCHLD, 485
SIGCONT, 485
SIG_DFL, 425, 491
sigemptyset(),486
sigfillset(), 486
SIGFPE, 424, 484
SIGHUP, 483, 484
SIG_IGN, 425, 491
SIGILL, 424, 484
SIGINT, 424, 483, 484, 503
SIGKILL, 484, 493
sigismember(), 488
signal(), 424, 425
signal.h (*See* Header files)
Signal mask, 485

Signal sets, 485
signal types, 424, 484
sigpending(), 492
SIGPIPE, 484, 505
sigprocmask(), 487
SIGQUIT, 483, 485, 503
SIGSEGV, 424, 485
sigset_t, 486
SIGSTOP, 485, 503
sigsuspend(), 492
SIGTERM, 424, 485
SIGTSTP, 485
SIGTTIN, 485
SIGTTOU, 485
SIGUSR1, 485
SIGUSR2, 485
sizeof (*See* Operators)
size_t, 350, 351, 437
sleep(), 478, 498
Software interrupt, 483
Source program, 26
sprintf(), 321
sscanf(), 321
Stack
  run-time, 14
  auto storage, 128
Standard header files, 168
stat(), 546, 552
stat.h (*See* Header files)
Statements
  Block, 33, 149
  Break, 142
  Comment, 151
  Continue, 144
  do while, 34, 148
  for_loop, 33, 147
  goto, 141
  if-else, 33, 144
  NULL, 145, 151
  return, 2, 8, 143
  switch, 33, 146
  while, 34, 147
stderr, 382, 383
stdin, 245, 382, 383
stdio.h (*See* Header files)
stdout, 245, 382, 383
Storage type
  dynamic (heap), 350
  global, 127
  permanent, 120, 122
  stack, 120
  temporary, 125
Storage class
  auto, 125
  extern,120
  register, 120, 126
  static, 122, 124
Stream 1/O
Stream
  Stderr, 19
  stdin, 245
  stdout, 245
String
  comparison, 306
  concatenation, 303
  conversion, 318
  NULL, 232
  searching, 312
  value, 232
strcat(), 293, 303
strcbrk(), 294
strchr(), 294, 311
strcmp(), 293, 306
strcoll(), 293, 309
strcpy(), 293, 302
strcspn(), 294, 313

strerror(), 294, 318
strftime(), 437
string.h (*See* Header files)
strlen(), 294
strncat(), 293, 303
strncpy(), 293, 302
strncrnp(), 293, 306
strrchr(), 294
strspn(), 294, 312, 313
strstr(), 294, 312, 313
strtod(), 320
strtok(), 294, 310
strtol(), 320
strtoul(), 321
struct, 328
Structure
  assignment operation, 344
  declaration, 328
  elements, 335
  I/O operation, 339
  pointer, 334
  self-referential, 333
  variable, 331
strxfrm(), 294, 309
Subroutine, 108
sync(), 554
sysconf(), 510
sys_errlist[], 317, 318, 420
sys_nerr, 318
system(), 354, 426, 500
System call, 442
System call interface, 443
System programming, 16, 449
SYSTEM V, 452, 453

**T**
Threads, 592
  POSIX-, 593
time(), 433, 509
time.h (*See* Header files)
Time management, 430
times(), 509
times.h (*See* Header files)
time_t, 433
tm, 436, 437
tmpfile(), 394
tmpname(), 394
tms, 509, 510
tolower(), 256
toupper(), 256
tree, 358
TRUE, 336
Two-way list, 369
Type
  Abstract, 102
  Conversion, 93
  FILE, 389
  Unsigned, 350
typedef, 131, 331

**U**
uid_t, 545
ULONG_MAX, 321
ULONG_MIN, 321
umask, 520, 521
uname(), 453
union, 327
unlink(), 542, 552
unistd.h (*See* Header files)
Unix, 451
Unix-like interface, 451
Unix kernel, 442
Unix system calls, 444
User structure, 519, 520
utsname, 453